Applications Development in Microsoft® Access 2000

Dirk Baldwin
David Paradice

Thomson Learning™

ONE MAIN STREET, CAMBRIDGE, MA 02142

Australia • Canada • Denmark • Japan • Mexico • New Zealand • Philippines
Puerto Rico • Singapore • South Africa • Spain • United Kingdom • United States

Applications Development in Microsoft Access 2000 is published by Course Technology.

Associate Publisher:	Kristen Duerr
Senior Product Manager:	Jennifer Muroff
Production Editor:	Jennifer Goguen
Developmental Editor:	Jill Batistick
Associate Product Manager:	Tricia Coia
Editorial Assistant:	Elizabeth Wessen
Composition House:	GEX Publishing Services
Text Designer:	GEX Publishing Services
Cover Designer:	Efrat Reis
Associate Marketing Manager:	Meagan Walsh

Disclaimer

Course Technology reserves the right to revise this publication and make changes from time to time in its content with out notice. The Web addresses in this book are subject to change from time to time as necessary without notice.

For more information, contact Course Technology, One Main Street, Cambridge, MA 02142;
or find us on the World Wide Web at www.course.com.

For permission to use material from this text or product, contact us by
- Web: www.thomsonrights.com
- Phone: 1-800-730-2214
- Fax: 1-800-730-2215

ISBN 0-7600-7108-X

Printed in Canada
2 3 4 5 WC 03 02 01 00

Brief Contents

TABLE OF CONTENTS

Preface

THE INTENDED AUDIENCE

This book is intended for students who have completed an introductory course in Microsoft Access and an introductory course in database design. In many cases, these two prerequisites may be satisfied in a single course. Ideally, students will have also completed an introductory programming course and a course in systems analysis and design. The programming exercises in this book use Visual Basic for Applications. While the particular programming language covered in the introductory course is not important, Visual Basic, C, or some similar procedural language probably prepares the student for the exercises in this book better than COBOL or Java.

This book can be used in a database design course or in a capstone project development course. It can be used in any course emphasizing event-driven application development, database application development, object-based application development, or any combination of these topics.

THE APPROACH

Creating database application is a multifaceted activity. This book focuses primarily on the programming facet. In order to develop database applications in Microsoft Access, students must have a solid understanding of the programming constructs used by Access/Visual Basic for Applications (VBA), and they must be able to apply these constructs within the Access/VBA development environment. To accomplish this goal, each chapter begins with a general discussion of the construct that is the focus of the chapter. Then, syntax and examples are introduced to illustrate how the constructs are used in Microsoft Access.

The examples used in the book come from two applications: the MU-DSci application and the Swim Lessons application. The MU-DSci application is a finished system that tracks prospects, graduate students' performance, and alumni at a university. The code for this system is listed throughout the book so that the students can analyze it in detail.

Students develop the second application as they read the chapters of the book. In addition to illustrating the necessary code, step-by-step instructions are provided for implementing and testing the application's features.

Most students will want to study the code from both applications. While advanced students may not need to actually type the code for the Swim Lessons application, they should study the code. Less advanced students will benefit from typing the code and using the debugging feature (introduced in Chapter 4) to understand in detail how the system works.

In addition to programming constructs, features of a quality application are woven throughout the chapters of the book. These features include techniques for protecting data integrity, the organization of an object-based application, and naming conventions. The space limitations of the book do not permit coverage of all facets of developing a database application, however. Users of the book will still need to consult other sources for vital concepts such as user requirements, project management, and in-depth table design issues.

OVERVIEW OF THIS BOOK

This book begins with a review of database concepts. We cover in a very small amount of space the topics that fill an entire semester in an introductory database design class. Clearly, this coverage is no substitute for the in-depth coverage of database design issues covered in a semester-long class. However, the material should provide an adequate review for students who have successfully mastered this material in such a class. We also review topics that would be mastered in a course that covers Microsoft Access at an introductory level. This material is intended to refresh a student's existing knowledge and is (again) not intended to substitute for an actual class on the topic.

Chapter Four introduces Visual Basic for Applications (VBA) and other programming-oriented concepts such as command bars and menus. Chapter Five covers objects and properties and Chapter Six covers events and event processing. These concepts are presented in the context of Microsoft's ADO data model, which underlies all the examples in this book. Understanding the contents of these three chapters is critical to successful assimilation of the topics in the rest of the text. Building custom applications in Access requires utilizing VBA to manipulate object properties in response to events.

Chapter Seven goes into greater coverage of modules; Chapter Eight explores object-based programming in greater detail. Modules are the fundamental containers for the custom VBA code written to implement an Access application. Object-based programming requires an understanding of manipulating property values and executing pre-defined methods associated with objects. This chapter addresses both of these topics, among others.

Chapter Nine covers coding and debugging issues that arise in the development of an Access application. Access provides extensive facilities for troubleshooting an application that is not executing as expected. We discuss preferred programming styles and cover many of the debugging features provided in Access.

Since many Access applications will be shared in a network environment, Chapter Ten covers issues that arise when multiple users access a database concurrently. Although Access provides many features to automatically control the problems that can occur when concurrent data access is possible, there are ways to build additional protection into an application using VBA. This chapter presents those approaches.

Chapter Eleven presents the design and development of Help files. Users expect Help files that are useful. Microsoft provides tools to create online Help facilities that look as professional as the ones developed at Microsoft. We show students how to create custom online documentation in this chapter.

In Chapter Twelve we explore data access pages in more detail. These are new in Access and provide a means for making data available via the Internet. Additionally, we illustrate the use of Active Server Page (ASP) technology interfaced with an Access database in this chapter.

Chapter Thirteen presents issues related to securing an Access application. We illustrate the use of user and group accounts, passwords, workgroup files, and .mde files.

FEATURES

This book contains several features found in all of the books published by Course Technology. They are designed to enhance the learning process. These features are:

- ◆ **Chapter Objectives** Each chapter in this book begins with a list of the important concepts to be mastered within the chapter. This list provides you with a quick reference to the contents of the chapter and is a useful study aid.

- ◆ **Illustrations and Tables** Illustrations help you visualize common components and relationships. Tables list conceptual items and examples in a visual and readable format.

- ◆ **Step-by-Step Methodology** This unique Course Technology methodology keeps students on track. They enter program code, click buttons, or press keys always within the context of a running scenario in the book.

- ◆ **Tips** Chapters contain Tips designed to provide you with practical advice and proven strategies related to the concept being discussed.

- ◆ **Chapter Summaries** Each chapter's text is followed by a summary of chapter concepts. These summaries provide a helpful way to recap and revisit the ideas covered in each chapter.

- ◆ **Review Questions** End-of-chapter assessment begins with a set of approximately 20 review questions that reinforce the main ideas introduced in each chapter. These questions ensure that you have mastered the concepts and have understood the information you have learned.

- ◆ **Hands-on Projects** Although it is important to understand the concepts behind topics, no amount of theory can improve on experience. To this end, along with conceptual explanations, this book provides five Projects at the end of each chapter. These projects are designed to help you apply what you have learned to business situations much like those you can expect to encounter in a technical support position. They give you the opportunity to construct an application in a controlled environment.

CT TEACHING TOOLS

All the teaching tools for this text are found in the Instructor's Resource Kit, which is available from the Course Technology Web site (www.course.com) and on CD-ROM.

- **Instructor's Manual** The Instructor's Manual has been written by the authors and has been quality assurance tested. It is available on CD-ROM and through the Course Technology Faculty Online Companion on the World Wide Web at www.course.com. The Instructor's Manual contains the following items:

  - Answers to all the review questions and solutions to all the programming exercises in the book.

  - Teaching notes to help introduce and clarify the material presented in the chapters.

  - Technical Notes that include troubleshooting tips.

- **Course Test Manager Version 1.2 Engine and Test Bank** Course Test Manager (CTM) is a cutting-edge Windows-based testing software program, developed exclusively for Course Technology, that helps instructors design and administer examinations and practice tests. This full-featured program allows instructors to randomly generate practice tests that provide immediate on-screen feedback and detailed study guides for incorrectly answered questions. Instructors can also use CTM to create printed and online tests over the network. Tests on any or all chapters of this textbook can be created, previewed, and administered entirely over a local area network. CTM can grade the tests automatically at the computer and can generate statistical information on individual as well as group performance. A CTM test bank has been written to accompany this text and is included on the CD-ROM. The test bank includes multiple-choice, true/false, short answer, and essay questions.

- **Solution Files** Solution files contain possible solutions to all the problems students are asked to create or modify in the chapters. (Due to the nature of software development, student solutions might differ from these solutions and still be correct.)

- **Data Files** Data files, containing all data that readers will use for the chapters and exercises in this textbook, are provided through the Course Technology Web site at www.course.com as well as on the Instructor's Resource Kit CD-ROM.

- **PowerPoint Presentations** PowerPoint slides are available for each chapter. These are included as a teaching aid for classroom presentation, to make available to students on the network for chapter review, or to be printed for classroom distribution.

ACKNOWLEDGMENTS

My deepest appreciation goes to the many reviewers and Course Technology employees who worked to make this book possible. Special mention, however, must be made of Jill Batistick and Jennifer Muroff, who worked incredibly hard refining our efforts into the book you have before you. If any errors are found in this book, you can be sure that neither of these persons is responsible for them.

Special thanks go to friends who always provided support when I needed it: particularly Pandora, Jill and the Ally group, Bob D., Professor Fuz, the Christmas Eve travelers, Kenda, Attie, Shady, and especially the red-haired girl in Tennessee.

Finally, a very special "thank you" to the woman who will swim with dolphins one day, for her encouragement, support, and so much more.

David Paradice

I would like to thank everyone involved with the development and production of this book. In particular, special appreciation goes to the reviewers Kathie Doole, Asheville-Buncombe Technical Community College, Pat Coulter, Pennsylvania College of Technology; Timothy Fullam, University of Alaska, Southeast; Hu Bonar, New York City Technical College; Dolores Fisher, Gateway Technical College; Brajendra Panda, University of North Dakota; and Michael Doherty, Ivy Technical State College. The reviewers provided valuable comments that were used to enhance descriptions and clarify the examples that are used throughout the chapters. I would also like to thank the technical editor, Vernon Rupp, for working through the examples and making sure that the descriptions were technically accurate and clear. Special thanks go to Jill Batistick and Jennifer Muroff. Jill worked long hours helping us to refine the book. I appreciated her wit and "author advocacy" approach to editing the book. Jennifer had the difficult task of managing the various schedules and activities that are necessary to complete the book.

I could not write this book without the patience, understanding, and love of my wife, Graciela. For me, writing a book requires many hours. Thank you, Graciela, for your understanding and encouragement throughout the process. I also thank my children, Gisela, Peter, and Marcus. I am blessed with the best children in the world (largely due to the best wife in the world). I apologize for some lost weekends and evenings. Their patience and love amaze me. I am also blessed with the best Mom and Dad in the world. I thank them for their understanding when the book took time away from visiting.

Finally, I would like to thank my students at UW-Parkside. I appreciate their understanding. I apologize for passing back homework and projects a little later than usual.

Dirk Baldwin

READ THIS BEFORE YOU BEGIN

Carefully read this section for technological and instructional information that you need to successfully complete this book and its components.

Computing Environment of the Authors and Testers

Dirk Baldwin and David Paradice wrote this book based on Access 2000 in the Microsoft Office 2000 suite. The authors installed the software from CDs on a network running Microsoft NT Server. The client machines ran Windows 95, Windows 98, and Windows NT. Testers involved with this book ran the software on non-networked computers running Windows 95 and Windows 98.

Your Computer

Access 2000 runs best on computers with fast processors and a lot of memory. For computers running Windows 98, processor speeds exceeding 400 MHz and at least 64 MB of RAM are preferred, and a color monitor is assumed.

Your Computing Environment

To execute Internet-related technologies such as Active Server Pages, you will want a server running Microsofts IIS (Internet Information Server) with the latest service packs installed. You will also need FrontPage extensions installed on the server. Visit www.microsoft.com for more information on these topics.

Databases

The database that is built throughout this book provides students with practice implementing concepts that they encounter within the text. When all the chapters are complete, the student will have constructed a complex database application. Because each chapter's database builds on the database from the previous chapter, the chapters must be completed in order. Each instructor has solution files that exemplify the condition that the database should be in at the end of each chapter.

The five hands-on projects at the end of each chapter provide students with practice implementing some of the topics covered in that chapter. When all the exercises in all the chapters are completed, the student will have constructed five databases that illustrate many of the important topics that were covered in the textbook. Because each hands-on project's database builds on the respective hands-on project database from the previous chapter, the projects must be completed sequentially. Each instructor has solution files that exemplify the condition that the databases should be in at the end of each chapter.

1

TOUR OF ACCESS

In this chapter you will:

♦ Start and exit Microsoft Access

♦ Open and run an Access application

♦ Identify the major elements of the Access programming environment

♦ Explore the menus and the Object Bar associated with the Database window

♦ Explore the Design view and other views of forms, pages, reports, tables, queries, macros, and modules

♦ Define key Access concepts such as events, procedures, methods, modules, and properties

♦ Invoke Access Help

♦ Learn the different ways in which Access databases can be incorporated into applications

This book assumes that you have already been exposed to Microsoft Access and are comfortable with the process of creating and using tables, queries, forms, macros, and reports. To refresh your skills, this chapter and the next two will reacquaint you with the objects that are used to develop Microsoft Access applications. As you work through these chapters and the remainder of this book, you will examine an application developed for a fictitious university. This application—called MU-DSci—facilitates the admitting, advising, and tracking of graduate students in the Decision Sciences department at Metropolitan University. You will also enhance a second application—called Swim Lessons—that supports the decision-making processes associated with running a school that provides swimming lessons to students.

INTRODUCTION TO THE MU-DSci APPLICATION

A **database management system (DBMS)** is a vital component of an organization's software collection. From the perspective of an end user, a DBMS simplifies the storage, retrieval, and updating of data. Access is a DBMS. Examples of data stored by a DBMS might include hotel and airline reservations, inventory, employee records, customer lists, budgets, and sales transactions. A DBMS supports the day-to-day operations of a business (for example, making reservations and recording sales) and provides important information needed for decision making.

But data are only one part of the story. Decision makers need some mechanism for manipulating data. An application program that works with a database is one such mechanism. For example, the Decision Sciences department at Metropolitan University manipulates application information so as to evaluate a candidate's application to the graduate program. The Swim Lessons application, which Chapter 2 will introduce in detail, manipulates data about student registrations and payments so as to inform the swimming instructors about their class members.

In a sense, a DBMS is analogous to a file clerk in that both simplify the storage, retrieval, and updating of data. Imagine storing applicant, student, graduate, and course information in a file cabinet in the Decision Sciences department. This information must be stored in such a way as to make its retrieval as efficient as possible. For example, applicant information could be sorted by the applicant's last name and cross references could be created to locate an applicant by his or her major. When the file clerk is inefficient, end users must retrieve and update the applicant data themselves; in addition, they must understand the file and indexing scheme and spend time searching for the data. When the file clerk is efficient, he or she retrieves or updates the applicant data based on an end user's request, and the end user does not spend valuable time trying to locate and store data. You can think of a well-designed DBMS as a very efficient file clerk.

Preparing MU-DSci for Use in Access

The MU-DSci application works with two files. The first, **MU-DSci.mdb**, contains the code that displays and manipulates the data. The second, **Data.mdb**, stores the data in tables. Developers usually place the tables containing the data in one database file and the forms, queries, and modules in another database file. This practice allows developers to modify forms and other objects without interrupting the user's access to the data in the tables.

The core function of any database application consists of data storage and retrieval. In Access, data storage is based on the relational database model, which organizes data into one or more tables. A **table** is the fundamental structure of a **relational database management system (RDBMS)**; it stores data in **records** (rows) and **fields** (columns). A field in the table contains a specific item of information, such as a last name. Records in the table contain all information related to one entry. In our university example, this information might include a name, an address, and other pieces of information about a particular student.

> **TIP** In relational database terminology, a table is also called a *relation*, and a column is called an *attribute*. In some older books, a row might also be called a *tuple*.

By default, the Database window is the first window displayed in an Access application. The startup procedure of an application, however, might hide the Database window or change the menus and toolbars associated with it. Thus, when you are updating or working with an application, you will typically override the startup procedure. In addition, when you are developing an application, to make normal menu items available you should hold down the Shift key while the application opens.

To open the MU-DSci database while overriding the startup procedure:

1. Start Access, if necessary. In the first window that appears, verify that the **Open an existing file** option button is selected, verify that the **More Files...** choice is highlighted in the scroll box, and then click **OK**.

2. In the Open window, navigate to the location of **MU-DSci.mdb**, select it, and then press the **Shift** key while clicking the **Open** button.

Before you can execute MU-DSci for the first time, its linked tables must be refreshed. **Refreshing** linked tables is required whenever you move an Access application to a different directory, as you did when you copied it from the Student Disk. Although most end users will never need to refresh links to tables and many Access applications contain routines that automatically refresh linked tables, as an Access developer, you will be expected to refresh linked tables manually. To refresh the links, you must have overridden the normal startup activities when opening MU-DSci.mdb, as you did in the previous steps.

To refresh linked tables:

1. Click the **Tools** on the menu bar, point to **Database Utilities**, and then click **Linked Table Manager**. The Linked Table Manager window appears, as shown in Figure 1-1. The path names in the dialog box depend on the location of the database the last time the links were refreshed.

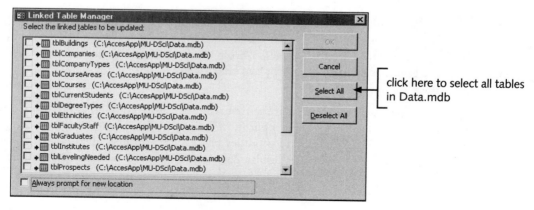

Figure 1-1   The Linked Table Manager

2. In the Linked Table Manager window, click the **Select All** button to select all tables, check the **Always Prompt for New Location** check box, and then click the **OK** button.

3. If Access prompts you for a new table location, use the **Look In** drop-down list box to locate **Data.mdb**, click **Open**, and then click the **OK** button in the subsequent window.

4. Click the **Close** button to close the Linked Table Manager and then click the **Tables** object type in the Database window Object Box. Your screen should match Figure 1-2.

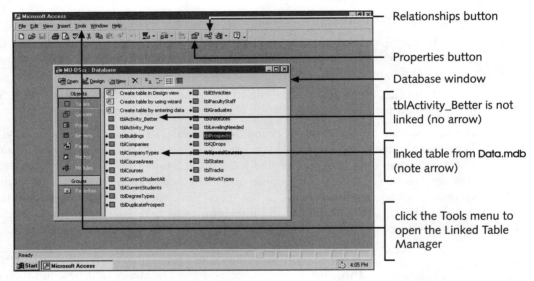

Figure 1-2   MU-DSci database window

5. Close the database.

If a Switchboard window with a Prospect button, a Current Student button, and other components appears on your screen, you probably did not hold down the Shift key while you clicked the OK button. Close the database window and reopen it while exactly following the previous two sets of steps.

By default, the Database window is the first window displayed in an application. It organizes the objects used in the MU-DSci application. The tables listed in the Database window store data, and the queries, macros, and modules process data located in storage and control the application. The forms and pages display data, and the reports provide data output.

Exploring the MU-DSci Application as an End User

The first window of an application displays information about that application. In general, windows that display information on the monitor are called **forms**. An opening form often contains **command buttons** that, when clicked, display other forms. Forms that open other forms are called **switchboards**. In MU-DSci, all forms have names that begin with the "frm" prefix. Most Access applications adhere to the same naming convention.

The MU-DSci system is designed to retrieve and update student, class, and faculty information. You are now ready to use the MU-DSci database and see what it can do.

To open the MU-DSci switchboard:

1. Click the **Open** button on the toolbar, and then use the Open window to locate and select **MU-DSci.mdb**.

2. Click the **Open** button. The Decision Sciences Department Graduate Students Database switchboard appears on your screen, as shown in Figure 1-3.

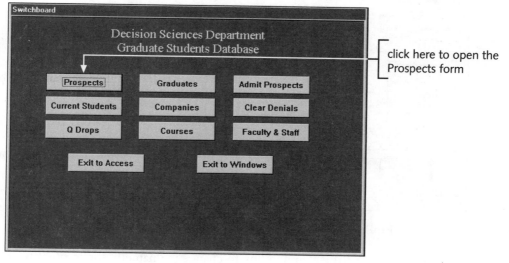

Figure 1-3   MU-DSci switchboard

This first form of the MU-DSci application displays the full name of the department and the application—Decision Sciences Department Graduate Students Database. When you click the buttons on the Decision Sciences Department Graduate Students Database switchboard, other forms in the MU-DSci application will appear on your screen.

Metropolitan University refers to applicants to the Decision Sciences department as "prospects." MU-DSci allows a user to add new prospects to the database, find information about a particular prospect, and update a prospect's status to "admitted" or "denied."

To browse the prospect information:

1. Click the **Prospects** button. The Prospects form appears on the screen, as shown in Figure 1-4. This form contains both data and command buttons. In addition, the menu at the top of the screen is designed to support the Prospect data. The data displays in text boxes and combo boxes. To update text box data, you simply place the cursor in the text box and begin typing. A combo box is an input object that lets you either type an entry or select a value from a list.

2. Click the **Application** tab to display the prospect's qualifications. The portion of the form that shows the transcript information for the student appears on the screen.

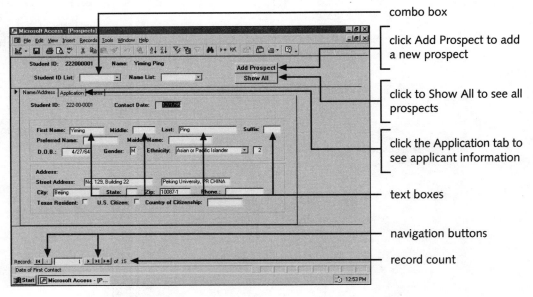

Figure 1-4   frmProspects form

3. Use the **Institute** combo box to change the name of the institution attended by the currently displayed student. Access saves changes to the database as you make them. You can change the Institute for the student, as well as any other data in the MU-DSci database, because the database is merely a copy that you are using to evaluate for the application that your team will eventually develop.

4. Click the **Status** tab. The prospect's admission status appears on the screen. The section of the form labeled *Admit Decision* is an option group. In an option group, only one option button may be clicked at any time.

5. Click the **list arrow** on the Name List combo box at the top of the screen, and then click **James Davis**. The Prospects form now displays the information for the selected student. The Record indicator at the bottom of the screen indicates that only one prospect meets the criteria (that is, has the selected prospect's name and Student ID).

6. Click the **Show All** button to display all prospects. The Record count at the bottom of the screen shows at least 15 students. The navigation buttons at the bottom of the screen allow you to move through the prospect-related records.

7. Click the **navigation buttons** to move through the prospects.

8. Click the **Close** button to close the Prospects form.

The Current Students form is similar to the Prospects form except that most of the buttons appear in a toolbar. Next, you will browse the Current Students information. In our scenario, a leveling course is a prerequisite for the Decision Sciences graduate program and a Q Drop occurs when a student drops a certain type of course. A graduate student is allowed only two Q Drops. To view this type of information, you can open the Current Students form by clicking the Current Students button on the switchboard.

To browse the Current Students data:

1. Click the **Current Students** button on the switchboard. The form appears on your screen, as shown in Figure 1-5.

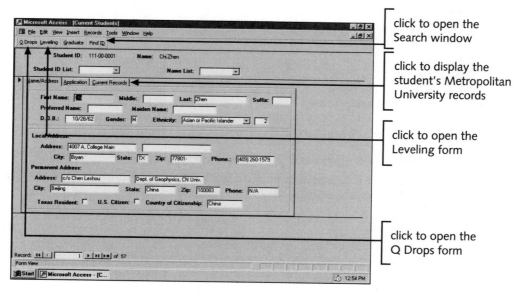

Figure 1-5   frmCurrentStudents form

2. Click the **Find ID** button in the toolbar located above the Current Students form.

3. Use the Student ID drop-down list in the Search Window to locate and select the name **Sharath Sheedy**. The ID number 111000010 appears in the Student ID drop-down list.

4. Close the **Search Window**, and then click the **Current Records** tab. The form displays information about Sharath Sheedy's records at Metropolitan University. The window also shows that the student has zero Q Drops.

5. Click the **Leveling** button, and then scroll through the form shown in Figure 1-6. The form indicates that eight leveling courses are needed.

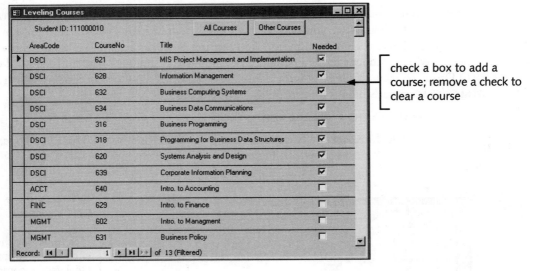

check a box to add a course; remove a check to clear a course

Figure 1-6   frmLeveling form

6. Click any **check box** that contains a check mark. The check mark disappears.

7. Close the **Leveling** form. Notice that the Leveling text box changed from 8 to 7.

8. Close the **Current Students** form, exit the application, and click **OK** to any backup reminder dialog box that appears.

If you click the Exit to Access button, you will close the MU-DSci database. If you click the Exit to Windows button, you will close the MU-DSci database *and* quit Access.

Now that you've previewed the application, it's time to think about how you can improve it. As you go through the subsequent sections on application development and further explore MU-DSci, keep the following questions in mind:

- What features of the MU-DSci application are helpful to you as a user?

- What features could be improved?

- What additional features should be added to the application as it is developed?

TOURING THE ACCESS DEVELOPMENT ENVIRONMENT

In addition to being a DBMS, Access offers a user interface and programming tools for developing complete applications. The forms, menus, toolbars, and other objects of MU-DSci and the actions performed by MU-DSci (for example, searching for data) were created by a developer who was working within the Access environment. The Access programming environment incorporates Visual Basic and resembles the environments provided by other programming languages (for example, PowerBuilder).

Although Access uses a relatively modern approach to developing applications, it is useful to organize its features around the traditional business framework that required input, output, storage, and processing of data. For example, a payroll system uses time cards as input, stores employee payroll records, determines gross and net pay (that is, processes the information), and outputs a paycheck. A student system at a university must accept new student data as input, store the student data, calculate grade-point ratios, and print out transcripts.

EXPLORING THE DATABASE WINDOW

Many objects in an Access application facilitate the previously mentioned real-world operations. The Database window organizes the objects used in the application into seven sections that, in general, correspond to the input, output, storage, and processing framework, as shown in Figure 1-7.

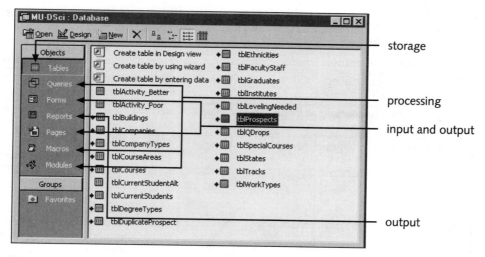

Figure 1-7   Input, process, output, and storage objects

The tables specify how to store data, and the queries indicate how to process data located in storage. The forms and pages build an interface for the input and output of data, the reports design printouts for data output, and the macros and modules hold the code that processes data and controls the application. Thus the Database window is a central area that gathers the objects making up an Access application. The Object Bar on the left side of the window allows you to see different types of objects.

The menu used in conjunction with the Database window also contains several useful commands. Menus are context-sensitive. When the Database window is active, the menu and toolbar options available help manage the database itself. When a form is active, however, different menu and toolbar options become available. Table 1-1 summarizes some of the commands available for working with the Database window.

Table 1-1   Commands in the database menu

Menu	Submenu	Command	Description
File		Get External Data	Imports objects from other applications. Links tables from other databases.
File		Database Properties	Opens the Properties window, which displays attributes (for example, modified date) of the application as a whole.
Edit			Allows Access forms and reports to be manipulated using the Cut, Copy, Paste, Delete, and Rename operations, just as in any other Windows programs.
View		Properties	Opens the Properties window for the item selected in the Database window.
View	Toolbars	Customize	Supports the development of custom menus and toolbars.
Insert			Creates a new object (table, query, form, report, macro, module, or class module). Performs the same operation as the New button in the Database window.
Tools	Database Utilities	Repair Database	Fixes database corruption problems.
Tools	Database Utilities	Compact Database	Defragments the database and reduces the application's file size.
Tools	Database Utilities	Linked Table Manager	Refreshes and reestablishes the link to linked tables.
Tools	Database Utilities	Switchboard Manager	Supports the creation of a form that contains buttons that open other forms.
Tools	Add-Ins	Add-In Manager	Retrieves custom or third-party programs that support the development of Access applications.
Tools		Startup	Opens the Startup window, which allows the specification of a simple startup procedure.
Tools	Security		Supports passwords and user and group permissions for an application.
Tools		Options	Opens the Options dialog box, which allows for the specification of default characteristics of the application.

The File, Edit, and Insert menus contain many of the same commands employed in other Windows-based programs. The Tools menu includes several commands that support the development of Access applications. In particular, within the Database Utilities submenu, Repair Database tells Access to fix a corrupt application. (A corrupt application is one that works incorrectly or that does not work at all. Corruption can result from a power failure that occurs in the middle of an application's execution, a bad sector on a disk, or an error in the Access program.) Compact Database, also located in the Database Utilities submenu, reduces the database size.

The Startup window, shown in Figure 1-8, is used to specify a default application menu, a form that should open when the application starts, the status of the Database window (hidden or visible), the icon associated with the application, and the wording of the application's title bar. In addition, the Startup window also allows you to hide the status bar from the user.

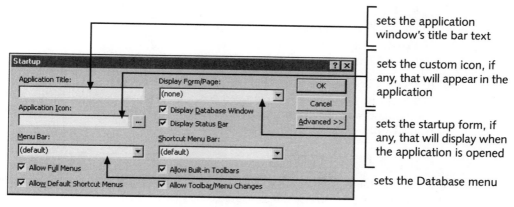

Figure 1-8   Startup window

The Options window—just like the Options window found in other Windows programs—allows you to set several default characteristics for your application.

Exploring and Using the MU-DSci Database Window

Running the MU-DSci application earlier helped you get a feel for using a database. To help construct the application, you will also need to be familiar with its development environment.

To explore the Database window and the Database menu of MU-DSci:

1. If necessary, open **MU-DSci.mdb** (hereafter called MU-DSci) while overriding the startup procedure.

2. Click the **Tables** object type in the Database window Object Bar, if necessary, to view the names of the tables used in the application, and then click the other object types in the Database window Object Bar to view the names of the queries, forms, pages, reports, macros, and modules used in the application.

3. Click **File** on the menu bar, and then click **Database Properties**. The MU-DSci Properties window opens.

4. Click each **tab** in the Properties window. The General tab contains the same information that is displayed when you right-click the name of a file in the Windows Explorer and then click Properties on the shortcut menu. The only difference is that the Attributes settings are read-only when these properties are viewed in Microsoft Access. The Summary tab includes information that you enter so as to help the user identify a database both from within Microsoft Access and from other programs such as the Windows Find Files program. The Statistics tab indicates the date and time when the active database was created and the last date and time when it was modified, accessed, and printed. The Contents tab lists the names of the objects contained in your database. The Custom tab specifies any custom properties you have entered that become properties of the UserDefined Document object in the Documents collection.

5. Click the **Cancel** button to close the MU-DSci Properties window, click the **Forms** object type in the Database window Object Bar, if necessary, and then select **frmProspects** from the forms in the Database window.

6. Click **View** on the menu bar, and then click **Properties**. The frmProspects Properties window opens. You can add a description or hide the form in the Database window. All other settings in the frmProspects Properties window are read-only.

 If Properties is not an option on the View menu, you may not have overridden the normal startup activities when you opened MU-DSci. Click File, click Exit to quit Access, and then repeat the previous steps.

7. Click the **Cancel** button to close the frmProspects Properties window.

Now that you have a feel for the Database window and its menu, you are ready to change the startup settings of MU-DSci to ensure that your application uses the Access default menu.

To change MU-DSci's default menu:

1. Click the **Tools** menu, and then click **Startup**. The Startup window appears.

2. Click the **list arrow** of the Menu Bar list box in the Startup window, and then select **(default)** in the list box, if necessary.

3. Click the **OK** button.

When you originally installed and ran the MU-DSci application, you noticed that the switchboard did not contain a Close button. If you wanted to include a Close button so that you could easily return to the Database window, you would not change the original switchboard. Instead, you would make a copy of frmSwitchboard and then modify the copy. Then, if you made a mistake, you could always return to the original and start over.

To make a copy of frmSwitchboard:

1. Click the **Forms** object type in the Database window Object Bar, if necessary, to list the forms.

2. Click **frmSwitchboard**.

3. Click **Edit** on the menu bar, and then click **Copy**. A copy of frmSwitchboard is placed on the Windows Clipboard.

4. Click **Edit**, and then click **Paste**. The Paste As window opens.

5. Type the name **frmSwitchboardCopy** in the Form Name text box, and then click the **OK** button to close the Paste As window and return to the Database window. The new form, frmSwitchboardCopy, appears in the listing of forms.

Access organizes data into one or more tables. To list these tables in the Database window, you click the Tables object type in the Database window Object Bar.

EXPLORING TABLES

Tables can be displayed in two views. First, the contents of a table may be displayed in **Datasheet view**, which represents a standard way to view the rows in a table. In this view, fields in the table represent attributes that describe the item being represented. For example, the tblProspects table shown in Figure 1-9 contains a row for each student; each row includes a student ID number, name, and address, and other fields. The Prospects table contains the information that was displayed in the frmProspects form that you saw previously.

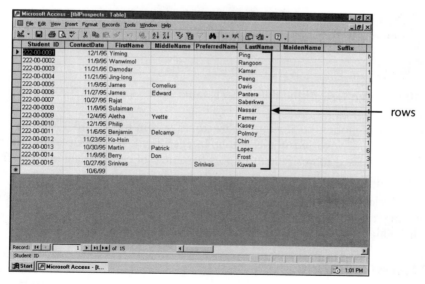

Figure 1-9   Datasheet view of the tblProspects table

You can use the Open button in the Database window to display the selected table in Datasheet view. The menu associated with this view enables you to retrieve, insert, edit, delete, and sort data.

To create a table, you can click the New button in the Database window when tables are listed in the window. Alternatively, you can double-click the "Create table in Design view" list entry, the "Create table by using wizard" list entry, or the "Create table by entering data" list entry. All table names in the MU-DSci application have the prefix "tbl." "Tbl" is a widely used prefix for Access table names. Another widely used prefix is "tdf" (tabledef).

You also can view a table in Design view. A selected table is shown in **Design view** when you click the Design button in the Database window. The menu associated with a table's Design view also allows you to modify the table's structure, as shown in Figure 1-10.

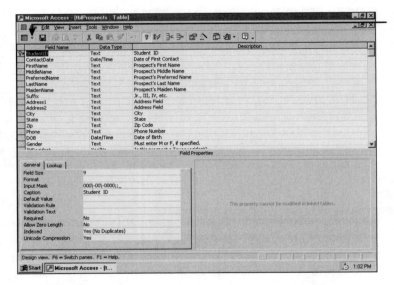

Figure 1-10   Design view of the tblProspects table

The Field Name identifies the attribute to be stored within the record. The Data Type indicates the kind of data involved (for example, Integer, Text). Field Properties contain other information that is used to verify and support the entry of correct data into the fields. The Description column provides a place for you to describe the attribute.

To define the relationships among tables in a database, you use the Relationships window. Arrows linking tables in the Relationships window indicate that the value of one field matches the value of another field that is located in a different table.

The Jet Database Engine

The **Jet database engine** is the component of Access that is responsible for storing and retrieving data. It maintains the tables, queries, and relationships. Data are communicated back and forth between the Jet database engine and the Access application. This book uses *application* to refer to the entire database system, including forms, pages, and reports. In contrast, *database* refers to the objects (tables, queries, relationships) managed by the Jet database engine.

An Access application does not require the Jet database engine. In fact, Access can communicate with other DBMSs (for example, Oracle, Sybase, SQL Server) through Open Data Base Connectivity (ODBC) drivers. **ODBC** is a standard communications protocol that allows an application to retrieve and store information in different DBMSs, as shown in Figure 1-11.

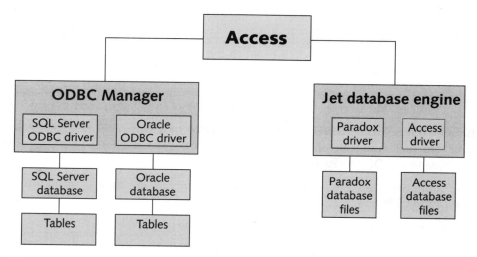

Figure 1-11   Relationships among Access, the ODBC drivers, and the Jet database engine

Most DBMSs supply their own ODBC-compliant drivers. If such a driver is available to Access, Access can store data in and retrieve data from the DBMS. In addition, other applications that obtain an Access driver (for example, Visual Basic, PowerBuilder) can use the Jet database engine.

Exploring tblProspects

Several of the MU-DSci forms display the contents of the tblProspects table. You can explore the relationship among the Datasheet view, Design view, and Relationships window by looking at the tblProspects table.

To display and explore the Datasheet view of the tblProspects table:

1. Click the **Tables** object type in the Database window Object Bar, click **tblProspects**, and then click the **Open** button. The Datasheet view displays. The date at the bottom of the ContactDate column reflects the system date setting on your computer.

2. Click **Edit** on the menu bar. The Edit menu for the table's Datasheet view contains commands to select, cut, copy, delete, and find records. This menu also includes a Go To submenu that moves the cursor to a specified record.

3. Point to **Insert** on the menu bar, and then observe the choices available on the Insert menu.

4. Point to **Records** on the menu bar, observe the choices available on the Records menu, and then click somewhere on the screen away from the Records menu to close this menu.

5. Display the various **ToolTips** by placing the cursor over each toolbar button and pausing for a moment.

6. Click the **View** drop-down list arrow, and then click **Design View**. You can use the View flyout to switch between the Datasheet view and the Design view. A message box informs you that the tblProspects table is linked and that some properties cannot be modified.

7. Click **Yes** to open the table in Design view. The Design view displays.

Because the tblProspects table was created in **Data.mdb**, many of the characteristics of the table structure cannot be changed in **MU-DSci.mdb**. Nevertheless, you can view the table's structure in **MU-DSci.mdb**.

The commands associated with the Design view menus and toolbar manipulate the structure of the table rather than the table's data.

To explore the Design view of the tblProspects table:

1. Explore the menus associated with the table's Design view, noting the various available options.

2. Move the cursor over the **Insert Rows** button on the toolbar. Observe the **ToolTip**. The Insert Rows button adds a field to the table.

3. Move the cursor over the **Delete Rows** button on the toolbar. The Delete Rows button removes a field from the table.

4. Click the **View** button on the toolbar to return to the Datasheet view. If Access prompts you to save changes, answer **No**.

5. Close the **tblProspects** table.

To reveal the relationships among tables in MU-DSci, you click the Relationships button found in many of the toolbars.

To explore the Relationships within the MU-DSci application:

1. Click the **Relationships** button on the toolbar. The Relationships window opens. Observe the relationships among the tables in the application. You can use the Relationships window to view, define, and modify relationships between tables.

TIP If the Add Table window appears, close the window and click the Show All Relationships button in the toolbar. Click the Save button to save this layout.

2. Close the **Relationships** window.

Although tables store data, an Access application still needs queries, macros, or modules to process the information.

EXPLORING QUERIES

Queries are statements that retrieve or update data in the database tables. Queries that retrieve data, called **select queries**, can select particular rows and fields from a table, combine data from multiple tables, and perform calculations that summarize a table's data. Like tables, the data retrieved with a select query can be displayed in forms and reports.

You can list queries in the Database window by clicking the Query type icon in the Object Bar of the Database window. In Access, you can also create action queries. **Action queries** insert, delete, or update data in the database. To create a query, you can click the New button in the Database window when queries are listed in the window. Alternatively, you can double-click the "Create query in Design view" list entry or the "Create query by using wizard" list entry, both of which appear in this window. All query names in the MU–DSci application have the prefix "qry." "Qry" is a widely used general prefix for Access query names.

Several windows support the development of a query. The Datasheet view of a query is similar to the Datasheet view of a table. This view displays the information that satisfies the query's specification. The Design view of a query specifies the columns and rows that should be retrieved, as shown in Figure 1-12. The upper portion of Design view displays the tables and queries used to provide data. The columns of the Design view grid indicate the fields in the table that should be tested or displayed, and the Criteria row specifies a condition to test.

Queries created in Design view are automatically transformed into the Structured Query Language (SQL). **SQL** is the standard query language supported by relational databases. The **SQL view** of a query displays the SQL statement that implements the query. It is useful when you need to develop advanced queries or create SQL code to copy and paste into a module.

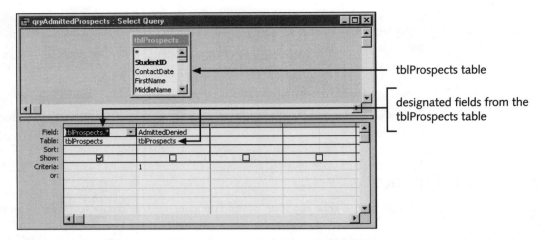

tblProspects table

designated fields from the
tblProspects table

Figure 1-12   Design view of the qryAdmittedProspects select query

Finally, the Query property sheet provides additional information to Access. For example, it indicates how many records to retrieve and whether each retrieved record should be unique. To display this property sheet, you right-click while the cursor is located in the gray area of the query design view where tables used in the query are displayed. Select Properties from the pop-up menu to view the Query property sheet.

Exploring MU-DSci Queries

The qryAdmittedProspects query retrieves those students from the tblProspects table who have been admitted to Metropolitan University.

To display windows associated with the qryAdmittedProspects query:

1. Click the **Queries** object type in the Database window Object Bar, click **qryAdmittedProspects** in the Queries list in the Database window, and then click the **Open** button. The Datasheet view of the query appears. Only two records in the tblProspects table of the MU-DSci application meet the criteria in the qryAdmittedProspects query.

2. Click the **View** button in the Query Datasheet toolbar. The qryAdmittedProspects query is displayed in Design view.

3. Click the **Properties** button in the Query Design toolbar. The Query Properties sheet appears.

TIP
If the Field List Properties sheet opened, you probably clicked in the tblProspects table at the top of the query's Design view before you clicked the Properties button. Close the Field List Properties sheet, click anywhere in the Design view other than in the tblProspects table, and repeat the previous steps.

4. Click the **tblProspects** table. The Query Properties sheet changes to the Field List Properties sheet.

5. Close the Field List Properties sheet.

6. Click the **View** drop-down list arrow, and then click **SQL View**. The qryAdmittedProspects: Select Query window opens. This window contains the SQL statement corresponding to the qryAdmittedProspects query.

> If the Datasheet view appears, you probably clicked the Datasheet View button rather than the View drop-down list arrow. Use the View drop-down list arrow again to select the SQL view.

To create action queries, you use the appropriate menu command or toolbar item.

To explore an action query:

1. Use the **View** drop-down list arrow to return to the Design view of the qryAdmittedProspects query.

2. Click **Query** on the menu bar. Note that the Query menu has commands that change the Design view grid so as to support the development of queries that change a table's data.

3. Close the **Query** menu by clicking elsewhere in the window.

4. Click the **Run** button in the toolbar. The Run button executes an action query.

5. Close the **qryAdmittedProspects** query. If Access prompts you to save the changes, click the **No** button.

In your Access application, tables store the data and queries manipulate the data. Forms, on the other hand, display the data on the screen so that the user can interact with the database.

EXPLORING FORMS

Forms are the primary means by which an end user interacts with an Access application. To see a list of the forms in the Database window, you click the Forms object type in the Database window Object Bar. Like the other objects, forms can be displayed in many views in Access. The Design view allows you to make changes to the form. The Datasheet view displays the datasheet of the query or table that supplies data to the form. End users of an application typically interact with a form in its Form view. As with tables and queries, you can take advantage of different views by using the View flyout.

You can create forms in Design view. Forms are divided into three sections. The **Form Header** contains controls that remain on the top of the form (for example, titles and column headings). The **Detail** section contains the data shown on the form. The **Form Footer** displays information that stays at the bottom of a form (for example, totals). Access allows you to draw a form's contents—buttons, list boxes, text boxes, labels—directly on the form. These items are called **controls**. You choose controls from the toolbar to add instances of them to the form. As shown in Figure 1-13, the form frmProspects displays data from the Prospects table.

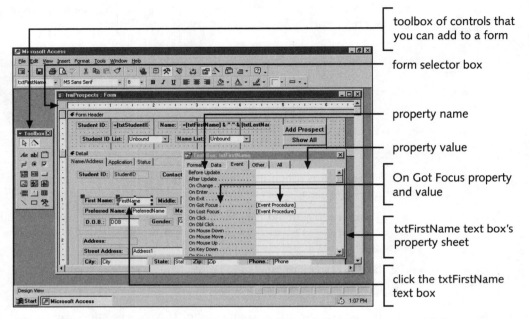

Figure 1-13   Design view of frmProspects and the txtFirstName property sheet

A **text box**, an example of which is in Figure 1-13, displays the current value of some piece of information. You can update text box data by placing the cursor in the text box and typing. Text boxes are named like most objects in Access; the standard prefix for a text box is "txt." The Name property, txtFirstName, identifies the name of the control and is used in queries, macros, and modules to refer to the First Name text box.

Every control on a form has a property sheet. **Property sheets** allow you to modify many of the characteristics of a control, including its colors, border styles, and validation rules. In many cases, Access facilitates the specification of a property through the use of combo boxes or special utilities. You can use the tabs at the top of the property sheet to display properties within a particular category. For example, format properties specify the control's appearance. Data properties control the source of the data. Event properties indicate a macro or procedure that should execute when the event occurs. Other properties contain extra information that affects the control's behavior. When the All tab is selected, every property that the control supports is in alphabetical order.

Forms, as a whole, also have properties. The **form selector** is the box where the rulers meet in the Design view, as shown in Figure 1-13. If you click this box, the entire form becomes the active object and you can then open the form's property sheet, as shown in Figure 1-14.

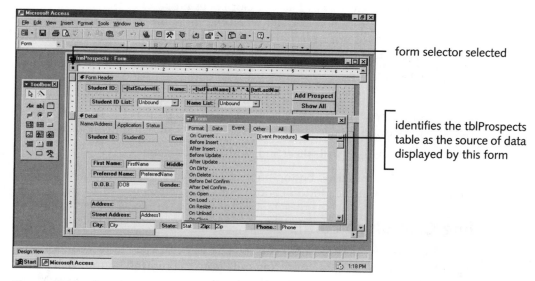

form selector selected

identifies the tblProspects table as the source of data displayed by this form

Figure 1-14   Form property sheet for frmProspects

Like control properties, form properties are also organized by Format, Data, Event, Other, and All tabs. To create a form, you can click the New button in the Database window when forms are listed in the window. Alternatively, you can double-click the "Create form in Design view" list entry or the "Create form by using wizard" list entry. As mentioned earlier, all form names in the MU–DSci application have the prefix "frm."

Exploring frmProspects

You can use the Design view of frmProspects and its associated property sheets to modify the appearance of the form, the data it displays, and the manner in which it displays that information.

To explore the property sheets associated with frmProspects:

1. Display **frmProspects** in Design view.

2. Click the **FirstName** text box.

3. Click the **Properties** button on the toolbar, and then click the **Format** tab. The Text Box: txtFirstName property sheet is displayed.

4. Click the **Back Color** property value field. A Build button appears. Its presence indicates that Access provides a window that helps set this property. In this case, clicking the Build button opens the Color window.

5. Click the **Event** tab. The On Got Focus property of txtFirstName specifies that an event procedure will run when txtFirstName receives the focus—that is, when the cursor is placed in txtFirstName. In this case, the event procedure will cause Access to change the color (Back Color property) of the text box.

6. Click the **All** tab.

7. Click the **form selector** box in the upper-left corner of the form. The form's property sheet displays. The Record Source property of frmProspects identifies the Prospects table as the source of the data shown in frmProspects.

8. Close the property sheet and close frmProspects.

To create a Close command button on frmSwitchboardCopy, you will use the form's Design view and the Command Button control from the toolbox to add a control to the form.

Adding Controls to Forms

Everything you use on a form is a control. The way that you create a control depends on the type of control you want to create. You can create a command button, such as the Close button, to add to the copy of the switchboard on your own, or you can have Microsoft Access create it for you by using a wizard. A **wizard** speeds up the process of creating a command button because it handles all of the basic work automatically.

To create a command button on your own, use the form's Design view and the Command Button control from the toolbox. A command button always has a name; its standard prefix is "cmd." Command buttons generally perform some function when they are clicked, because a macro or program code has been associated with the On Click event property.

So far, object types with which you should already be familiar have been reviewed. The next section describes a new object type in Access. You are not expected to know this object type as well as the table, query, form, and macro object types discussed to this point (or the report object type discussed later in the chapter).

EXPLORING DATA ACCESS PAGES

Data access pages (or just "pages") are new in Access 2000. The **data access page** allows you to manipulate data via the Internet or an intranet. (An **intranet** is a network of networks that can be accessed only by certain people—for example, the employees of a particular organization.) The data involved can be stored in Microsoft Access databases, Microsoft SQL Server databases, or other sources such as Microsoft Excel spreadsheets.

As with forms, you, as the developer, can display pages in Design view while constructing or changing them. Pages are shown in Page view—the view typically seen by end users—when they are being used. To change the views, you use the View drop-down list arrow.

The Design view for pages closely resembles the Design view for forms, except that pages lack the Detail section found on forms. On pages, a **Body object** is divided into two sections: a **Page Header** section and a **Page Navigation** section. The Body object is surrounded by an area that may contain labels and other controls. Above the Body object are two objects: the **HeadingText** object and the **BeforeBodyText** object. The HeadingText object is a static text object where a label can be created for the page. The BeforeBodyText object is a smaller static text object that can hold additional information.

Pages can be designed in much the same manner in which forms are designed. The tools used in the Design View for forms are also available in the Design View for pages. You can choose controls from the toolbar to add them to the Body of the page. Typically, controls will appear in the Header section of the Body object. Access automatically places predefined navigation buttons in the Navigation section when the Header section is bound to data. If the page is not associated with some data source, the Navigation section does not appear. The page pagProspects, shown in Figure 1-15, displays the address data from the tblProspects table in the same manner in which the data are shown in the Name/Address tab section of the form frmProspects.

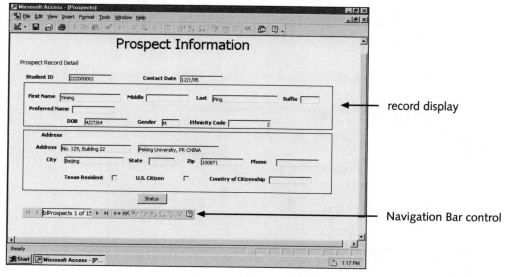

Figure 1-15   pagProspects data access page

Pages, their sections, and their controls are also associated with property sheets, just like forms and their objects. These property sheets function in the same manner as the ones for form objects (and, as you will see later, reports and their objects). A significant difference, however, is that no Event properties exist for pages or their objects. Consequently, pages react to a user in a manner that is different from other Access objects, such as forms and reports. For instance, pages can react through the predefined navigation controls that appear in the Navigation section. They can also react to scripts written by page designers in a language like VBScript or JavaScript when such scripts are connected to the page.

A second difference between pages and other Access objects is the way in which pages are stored. When you create a data access page, the HTML file for the page is stored outside the Access database and a shortcut to the HTML file is embedded in the database window.

The properties for pages are organized by Format, Data, Other, and All tabs. To create a page, you can click the Page shortcut in the toolbar on the left side of the database window and then click the New button. Other options include double-clicking the "Create data access page in Design view" entry in the window or double-clicking the "Create data access page by using wizard" entry. In addition, you can edit an existing Web page. All page names in the MU-DSci application have the prefix "pag." Because pages are still relatively new, a standard prefix has not yet been established.

Exploring pagProspects

To explore the property sheets associated with pagProspects:

1. Display **pagProspects** in Design view.

> **TIP**
> If a window opens, the page has been moved. Use the Locate button to find the new location of the page. If connection problems occur, refresh the table links, save the data access page, and try to open the page again.

2. Click the **txtFirstName** text box, as shown in Figure 1-16.

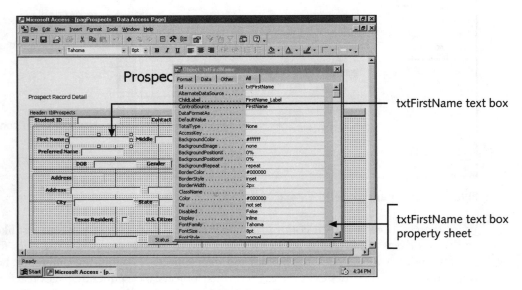

Figure 1-16   pagProspects page in Design view

3. Click the **Properties** button on the toolbar. The Text Box: txtFirstName property sheet is displayed.

4. Click the **FontSize** property value field. A drop-down list button appears. It indicates that Access provides a list of values that help set the property. In this case, the list shows the font sizes available.

5. Click the **All** tab.

6. Click the **Header: tblProspects** header bar. The header's property sheet is displayed, as shown in Figure 1-17.

7. If necessary, scroll to find the **Record Source** property. The Record Source property of pagProspects identifies the Prospects table as the source of the data displayed in pagProspects.

8. Close the property sheet, close **pagProspects**, and then click **No** if asked to save changes.

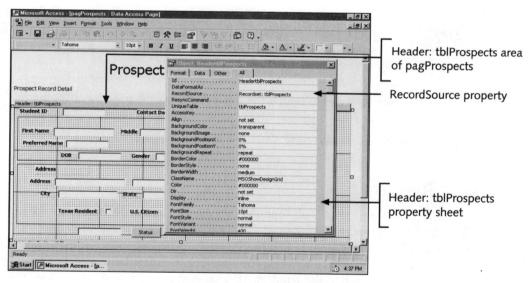

Header: tblProspects area of pagProspects

RecordSource property

Header: tblProspects property sheet

Figure 1-17   pagProspects data access page property sheet

Adding Text Box Controls to Pages

Because page controls do not have events, the text box control will be the most widely used control on most pages. (A limited discussion of scripting comes later in this book in Chapter 13.) Although Access provides a Field list for pages in the same manner that it does for forms, this list looks very different for pages. The Field list for pages has two tabs: a Database tab, which displays a tree structure of the tables in the database, and a Page tab, which displays a tree structure of the pages in the database.

To add a text box control to a page:

1. Open **pagProspects** in Design view.

2. Click the **Field List** button to display the database fields that can be added to the page and, if necessary, click the Database tab.

3. If necessary, expand the tree by clicking on the **plus sign** located to the left of the Tables folder. Locate **tblProspects** in the list, and then expand it by clicking on the plus sign to its left.

4. Select the **MaidenName** field by clicking on the field name. Click the **Add To Page** button to add this field to the page.

5. Close the field list.

6. Click and drag the **MaidenName** field to a position to the right of the PreferredName field.

 If you cannot select the MaidenName field, another field is in front of it. After attempting to select the MaidenName field, go to the Format menu and select Send to Back to move the currently selected object back. You may need to repeat this process more than once before you are able to click the MaidenName field.

7. Format the label to match the other labels on the page by changing its Font weight to **700**.

8. Save and close the page.

EXPLORING REPORTS

Reports format and print data supplied by tables or queries. Property sheets similar to the form and page property sheets control the report, its sections, and its controls. To list reports in the Database window, you click the Reports object type icon in the Object Bar of the Database window. To create a report, you can click the New button of the Database window when reports are listed in the window. Alternatively, you can double-click the "Create report in Design view" list entry or the "Create report by using wizard" list entry.

The Design view of a report includes more sections than the Design view of a form or page. The **Report Header** and **Report Footer** display information at the beginning and end of the report, respectively. The **Page Header** and **Page Footer** appear at the beginning and end of each page, respectively. The **Detail** section contains the data supplied by the report's Record Source. In turn, the **Record Source** indicates the query or table that provides the needed data.

A report can be divided further through the use of Sorting and Grouping. **Sorting and Grouping** allows you to specify groups into which to classify data (for example, Group by the major field). This option enables you to add, delete, and change the fields or expressions on which groups are based, the sort order, and the group properties such as headers and footers. Each group can have its own group header and footer.

Reports are named like most objects in Access; the standard prefix for a report is "rpt". Each report has a **report selector**, just like the form selector on a form. The report selector allows you to select all objects on the report at one time.

A number of ways exist to place a control on a report. For example, you can activate the Report Wizard by clicking the New button in the Database window; this wizard automatically places controls on a report. Likewise, the toolbox, used in the Design view of a report, can be used to create controls.

Besides being shown in the Design view, reports can be displayed as Print Preview or Layout Preview. These two views are similar except that **Print Preview** displays all data in the report's Record Source, whereas **Layout Preview** displays only a sample of the data.

Exploring rptProspectiveStudent

The report rptProspective Student prints a prospect's application. The Design view of a report such as this one is similar to the Design view of a form or page.

To explore the Design view of the rptProspective Student report:

1. Click the **Reports** object type in the Database window Object Bar, click **rptProspectiveStudent** in the Reports list in the Database window, and then click the **Design** button. The rptProspective Student: Report window opens.

2. Click the **First Name** text box, right-click the **text box**, and then click **Properties** on the shortcut menu to display the property sheet for the First Name text box.

3. Click the **report selector** button in the upper-left corner to display the Report property sheet, and then click the **Page Header** bar to display the Section: PageHeader0 property sheet.

4. Close the property sheet.

You can use fields or expressions to organize the rptProspective Student report. These fields and expressions are stored in the Sorting and Grouping window.

To view the Sorting and Grouping information for the rptProspective Student report:

1. Click the **Sorting and Grouping** button in the toolbar. Note that no fields have been set in the Sorting and Grouping window.

2. Close the **Sorting and Grouping** window.

3. Click the **Print Preview** button to display the report as it will be printed.

4. Click the **View** drop-down list arrow. Notice that Layout Preview is dimmed, indicating that it is no longer available.

5. Use the **View** drop-down list arrow to return to Design view.

6. Click the **View** drop-down list arrow. Notice that Layout Preview and Print Preview are both available again.

7. Use the **View** drop-down list arrow to display the Layout Preview. Verify that the Print Preview is now disabled on the View flyout.

8. Close rptProspectiveStudent. Do not save any changes to the report.

Most applications are not complete when the tables, queries, forms, and reports are created. Although they may be ready to accept input, store the data, and display and output the data, something needs to tell each application when to open and close the forms and reports, when to search for specific records, how to update data in tables, and when and what values should automatically be placed in a form or page. Macros and modules perform these types of activities.

EXPLORING MACROS

A **macro** is a named set of actions that manipulates the objects and properties of the Access application. An action performs a single operation on an object or property. For example, the **OpenForm** action displays a form and the **SetValue** action changes the value of some property (for example, the value in a text box). You can have macro objects be listed in the Database window by clicking the Macros object type in the Database window Object Bar. A Macro object may contain more than one macro. Macro object names are preceded by the prefixed "mcr."

The Macro window consists of a series of rows and columns, as shown in Figure 1-18. It always includes the Action and Comment columns. The **Action column** identifies the action to be performed and the **Comment column** is used for documentation. You can display the Conditions and Macro Names columns whenever necessary. The **Conditions column** contains an expression that can be evaluated as True or False. When the expression evaluates to True, the corresponding action is executed. When the expression is False, the action is not executed. The **Macro Names column** is used to write several macros in the same Macro window.

In the Macro window, the actions of a macro start on the first line that contains the macro name and end on the line prior to the line that contains a new macro name. The full name of a macro includes the name of the Macro object followed by a period and the name in the Macro Names column. For example, in Figure 1-18, mcrProspect is the name of the macro object and NewProspect is the name that appears in the Macro Names column. Thus, mcrProspect.NewProspect refers to the macro that moves to a new record in the frmProspects form. When the Macro Names column is not used, the Macro object name is used as the name of the macro.

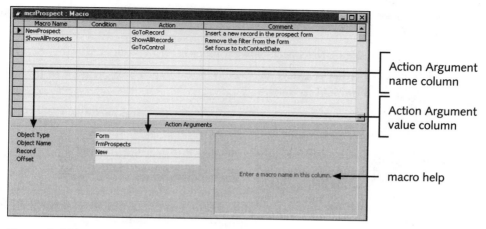

Figure 1-18 mcrProspect Macro window

Most actions require values to be placed in the **Action Arguments** section of the Macro window. For example, the GoToRecord action needs to know to which record it should move. The **Object Type** argument indicates that the move occurs on a form. The **Object Name** argument identifies the specific form involved. The Record argument indicates which record to make the current record. The optional Offset argument provides more precise instructions about the destination record.

A macro named AUTOEXEC automatically executes when an application opens. This macro offers another way to control the startup features of your application.

Macros are executed in a variety of ways, including clicking a menu command or toolbar button. In many cases, they are executed in response to events. To execute an event-related macro, the macro name must appear in an event property of an object.

Exploring mcrProspect

The mcrProspect macro object in MU-DSci contains macros used to move to a new record for entering new data and for resetting the frmProspects form to display all Prospect records.

To view the mcrProspect macro object:

1. Click the **Macros** object type in the Database window Object bar, and then open **mcrProspect** in Design view.

If the Macro Names and Conditions columns are not visible in your Macro window, your Access environment is configured differently. To display the Conditions column, click the View menu and then click Conditions, or click the Conditions button on the toolbar. To display the Macro Names column, click View and then click Macro Names, or click the Macro Names button on the toolbar.

The mcrProspect macros are triggered by the On Click events of the command buttons located on frmProspects.

To explore where the mcrProspect.NewProspect macro is executed:

1. Close the **mcrProspect** Macro window. Do not save changes to the macro if you are prompted to do so.

2. Click the **Forms** object type on the Database window Object Bar, and then display **frmProspects** in Design view.

3. Display the property sheet for the Add Prospect button, and then click the **Event** tab in the property sheet.

4. If necessary, use the scroll bar to locate the **On Click** event property, and then click in the property value column. The On Click property of the Add Prospect command button identifies the mcrProspect.NewProspects macro, as shown in Figure 1-19.

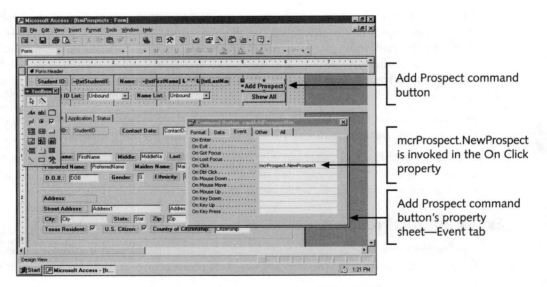

Figure 1-19   Event properties of the Add Prospect command button

 TIP   You can click the Build button to open the Macro window directly from the property sheet.

5. Close the Add Prospect command button's property sheet.

You can test the mcrProspect.NewProspect macro by clicking the Add Prospect button on the Prospects form in Form view.

To test the mcrProspect.NewProspect macro:

1. Display **frmProspects** in Form view.

2. Click the **Add Prospect** button. Notice that the form moves to a new record.

3. Close frmProspects.

In addition to executing macros through events, you can use the Run button in the Database window or the Run button in the Macro Design toolbar. Macros, however, often perform an action that manipulates or requires information from an open form. If the form is not open while the macro is running (for example, if frmProspects is not open while mcrProspects.Add Prospect is running), an error will occur. You can use the Run button to execute the AUTOEXEC macro in the MU-DSci application without generating an error because it does not require that any forms or reports be open already.

Using Macros to Open a Different Form at Startup

The form frmSwitchboard is displayed automatically when MU-DSci opens. You would like frmSwitchboardCopy to open instead. You must therefore modify the AUTOEXEC macro to open frmSwitchboardCopy so that you can use the new Close command button.

To modify the AUTOEXEC macro:

1. Click the **Macros** object type icon in the Database window Object Bar, and then display **AUTOEXEC** in Design view. The Macro window displays the OpenForm action.

2. Click in the value column of the Form Name action argument, and then locate and select **frmSwitchboardCopy**.

3. Click the **Save** button on the toolbar.

4. Close the AUTOEXEC Macro window.

You can test the AUTOEXEC macro by highlighting AUTOEXEC macro and clicking the Run button in the Database window or by closing and reopening the MU-DSci application.

To test the AUTOEXEC macro:

1. Highlight the AUTOEXEC macro, and then click the **Run** button with the macros listed in the Database window. The new switchboard, frmSwitchboardCopy, opens.

2. Click **File** on the menu bar, and then click **Close** to close frmSwitchboardCopy and return to the Database window.

Besides macros, you can use modules to manipulate objects in Access. Modules are different from macros in that they are written in the **Visual Basic for Applications (VBA)** programming language. Using VBA to write modules is more difficult than using macros, but VBA is a more capable language, so modules can accomplish more complex tasks within Access.

EXPLORING MODULES

A **module** is a collection of VBA declarations and procedures stored together as a unit. **Procedures** use and manipulate the objects of an Access application. **Declarations** name a variable, constant, or procedure; they can specify a data type for use in an Access application.

Access supports several types of modules. **Standard modules** contain subroutines and functions and can be run at any time, as long as the application is open. To see a list of standard modules in the Database window, you click the Modules object type in the Database window Object Bar. **Class modules** are associated with the definition of a new object.

Class modules can contain properties as well as procedures. Two types of class modules are possible. **Independent class modules** are listed in the Database window along with standard modules. This type of class module can be invoked at any time while the application is open. **Form** and **report class modules** are connected to a form or report and can be opened or invoked only when the form or report is open. Figure 1-20 shows the Module window.

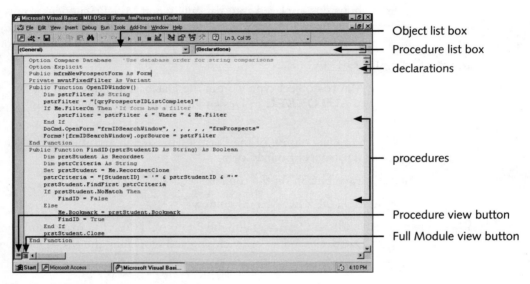

Figure 1-20   Module window

The **Procedure list box** displays all of the procedures within a module that are associated with a certain object. The **Object list box** names the object. In a form and report class module, the object corresponds to controls, the form or report as a whole, or sections in the form or report.

You can use the New button to create a new standard module when the Module appears in the Database window. To modify an existing module, click the Design button. To create a new independent class module, click the Insert menu, and then click Class Module. Module names are prefixed with "bas" (Basic) in Access.

The programming environments for the various types of modules are similar. That is, the menus and toolbar associated with modules always allow you to edit, debug, and compile VBA code.

Objects—whether a form, report, table, query, or module—have many properties (for example, color, contents, and size). These properties can be manipulated through macros and modules, which are themselves triggered by events that occur in the application. For this reason, the Access environment is called **object-based** and **event-driven**. You must understand objects and events to successfully program with modules or macros.

Exploring and Creating Modules in MU-DSci

Like most Access applications, MU-DSci uses a variety of standard modules and class modules.

To view the modules used in MU-DSci:

1. Click the **Modules** object type in the Database window Object Bar. Modules marked with a Code icon are class modules. The other modules are standard modules.

2. Click the **Forms** object type in the Database window Object Bar, and then display the Design view of **frmProspects**.

3. Click the **Code** button on the toolbar. The class module associated with frmProspects displays. The active menus and toolbar buttons support the development of VBA code. You can use the Insert menu to create new procedures.

4. Click the list arrow of the **Procedure** drop-down list box, which is in the upper-right corner of the screen, and then click **OpenIDWindow**. The OpenIDWindow function displays.

5. Close the **VB** window. Do not save any changes to this module.

6. Close **frmProspects**. Do not save any changes to this form.

Wizards, browsers, builders, and Help windows make it easier for you to work in the more complex activities when you develop an Access application. The Expression Builder and Access Help, for example, are available in a variety of development windows.

APPLICATION DEVELOPMENT HELP

The **Expression Builder**, shown in Figure 1-21, supports the development of various types of Access expressions, including references to controls on forms, references to reports, and function calls. These expressions can be placed in the control source on forms, in macros, and in procedures.

The bottom portion of the Expression Builder displays the expression elements in three boxes. The first box refers to the type of object. The second box generally refers to a control or field found inside the object. The third box usually refers to a property of the control or object.

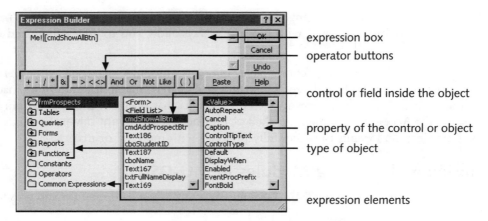

Figure 1-21   Expression Builder

The Access Help menu is similar to the Help menu associated with any other Windows application. Access Help provides steps to accomplish a particular goal, advice, object and property descriptions, legal syntax, and examples. It permits you to search for help on a particular subject using English-like sentences. The What's This command on the Help menu lets you point to an item in the Access environment about which you have questions. In addition, Microsoft provides help at *http://www.microsoft.com/*. A number of other Access Help sites are available on the Internet as well.

Expression Builder

You can invoke the Expression Builder via a number of mechanisms. The Build button in the property sheet and the Build button located on several toolbars open either the Expression Builder or the Choose Builder window, which allows you to select the Expression Builder, the Code Builder, or the Macro Builder. Alternatively, you can select the Expression Builder from the shortcut menu.

Exploring Access Help

Access Help can provide assistance with the objects, events, properties, and methods you have used in the MU-DSci application. It not only provides reminders about the syntax used when performing some operation, but it also serves as an information source that provides clues about how to accomplish a particular task.

To explore Access Help:

1. Click **Help** on the menu bar, and then click **Microsoft Access Help**.

2. In the Microsoft Access Help window, click the **Contents** tab. The Access Help categories are displayed in the Help Topics window.

3. Find and expand the **Visual Basic Language Reference**, and then expand the **Events** topic.

4. Click **Activate Event**. The Help window for the Activate and Deactivate Events opens, as shown in Figure 1-22.

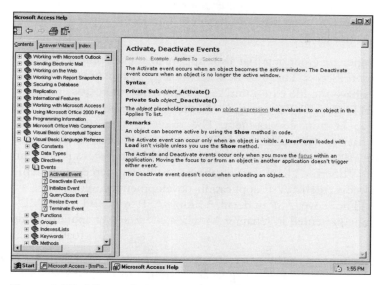

Figure 1-22 Microsoft Access Help window

5. Right-click in the **Help** window to display the shortcut menu. You can take advantage of the shortcut menu to print the Help window for a topic you will be using as you develop an application.

6. Close the Help window.

STARTING A NEW DATABASE

Many issues must be addressed when you are starting a new database. Will the database be used by one person at a time or by several people concurrently? How large is the database likely to grow in terms of number of records? Will new tables be needed to reflect an expanded database scope? Another question concerns the applicability of a client/server implementation as opposed to a single-user workstation implementation. Can the Jet database engine handle the load expected with your application? Will a more powerful database engine like SQL Server be needed later? These issues are just a few of the points to be resolved in choosing the appropriate approach for creating a new database.

There are three ways to create database applications that use Microsoft Access. This book focuses primarily on database applications that utilize the features delivered in Microsoft Access 2000, and specifically on the objects described earlier in this chapter—tables, queries, forms, pages, reports, macros, and modules—and the Jet database engine. As you have already seen, the tables used in an Access application may reside in an Access file that is different from the one containing the forms, pages, and other components. The process of placing the tables in an Access database on a server and installing the forms, reports, and other objects in an Access file that resides on a client computer is one of the simplest ways to implement a client/server-like approach using Microsoft Access. The client application then need only link to the tables on the server.

Two new technologies are emerging that also support the development of database applications using Microsoft Access. The first new technology is the **Active Server Page (ASP)** approach. ASP files have the file extension ".asp." **Active Server Pages** are files that contain a combination of HTML and VBScript code. **VBScript** is a derivative of Visual Basic that supports Web-based application development. The resulting application can connect to a Microsoft Access database through the ASP support embedded in Microsoft's Internet Information Server (IIS). When you use this approach, the interface is programmed entirely in HTML code and VBScript. The Access database must be registered as a system data source on the server. Full coverage of ASP application development would require a book of its own, so this text will not cover ASP in detail. A simple ASP front end to the MU-DSci database will, however, be presented in Chapter 13 when client/server application development is discussed.

The second new technology is the Microsoft Access project. A **Microsoft Access project** is a new Access file type that has been specially designed to facilitate access to Microsoft SQL Server databases. Such a file has the extension "adp". This approach is intended to facilitate the development of client/server applications. When you work with an Access project, you create forms, pages, reports, macros, and modules just as you would when working in Access alone. You create your tables, however, by using SQL Server technology. Once you connect to the SQL Server database, you can view, create, modify, and delete tables using the SQL Server Design Tools. These tools are similar to the tools available in Microsoft's Visual InterDev and Visual Basic environment. Access projects can also offer Form, Page, and Report Wizards that you can use to quickly develop an application.

Access projects take advantage of a new Microsoft database engine called the **Microsoft Database Engine (MSDE)**. MSDE, which provides local data storage that is compatible with SQL Server 7.0, is intended to be a client/server data engine alternative to the Jet database engine used in Access. MSDE is designed and optimized for use on smaller computer systems (single-user systems or small workgroups). For example, it has a 2 GB database size limit. Because it is based on the same data engine as SQL Server, however, applications will typically run in either environment without requiring alterations. (MSDE is available with Access 2000 but is not installed automatically.)

You should consider using Access projects and MSDE if you are developing an application for a small workgroup that has the potential to grow. If you anticipate that the application will ultimately require a full-fledged SQL Server environment, then an Access project using MSDE can provide a path to the SQL Server implementation. Access projects also provide a means to develop and test an SQL Server client/server application on a single computer or workstation. Once the application is ready, you can easily change the Access project connection information to connect to an SQL Server database on a remote server for final tests.

1

CHAPTER SUMMARY

- ❏ DBMS applications represent an important part of an organization's information system. These applications are responsible for storing and retrieving the vital day-to-day transactions that occur in a business. In addition, DBMS applications retrieve and update information that supports critical decisions.

- ❏ Microsoft Access is a software tool that supports the development of DBMS applications. Access applications consist of many different objects. Database objects such as tables and queries are managed by the Jet database engine (a component of Access) or by some other ODBC-compliant DBMS. The application side of Access manages form, page, report, macro, and module objects.

- ❏ Many Access objects support at least two views. The Design view facilitates the development and modification of the object. Other views (for example, Form view, Page view, Layout Preview, Datasheet view) give the end user's view of the object. The graphical nature of the Design view greatly eases system development. Property sheets are integral aspects of this view. Property sheet values specify the data used by the object or change the object's display.

- ❏ A significant portion of Access's success can be attributed to its ease of use. The graphical environment enables relatively inexperienced computer users to quickly build tables, forms, pages, and reports. These same users can then insert, update, and delete data through these new forms and pages. Nevertheless, macros and modules are still needed to create applications that automatically open forms in response to a user action, fill in portions of a form automatically, or change the contents of a form or report in response to the user's current needs.

- ❏ Although the development of macros and modules requires advanced software skills, Access provides many tools that can help you when you are learning to program. These tools include the Expression Builder and Access Help.

- ❏ This book focuses on the development of Access applications. The remaining chapters will cover the knowledge and skills necessary to develop Access applications in detail.

REVIEW QUESTIONS

1. What are the major characteristics of a database application?
2. Name at least three applications that could use a DBMS.
3. What types of objects comprise an Access application?
4. What is the purpose of the Database window?
5. When you are developing an application, hold down the _____ key while the application opens to make normal menu items available.
   a. Ctrl
   b. Alt
   c. Shift
   d. Esc

6. When do you issue the Repair Database command?

7. What is the purpose of the Compact Database command?

8. What is Datasheet view? Which Access objects support this view?

9. The _____ is used to refresh linked tables in an Access application.

   a. overridden normal startup activities

   b. opened the Linked Table Manager

   c. placed the database application in a new directory

   d. executed the links

10. What information displays in a property sheet?

11. What is the difference between a standard module and a class module?

12. What is the difference between a module and a procedure?

13. What columns are available in the Macro window?

14. By default, the _____ window is the first window displayed in an application.

    a. Tools

    b. Database

    c. Current

    d. Table

15. What is the purpose of the Conditions column in the Macro window?

16. What is the purpose of the Action column in the Macro window?

17. What triggers a macro's execution in Access?

18. What is the purpose of the Expression Builder?

19. Using Access Help, describe the purpose of the SetValue action.

20. Using Access Help, describe the purpose of the Beep action.

HANDS-ON PROJECTS

Project 1-1

Natural Parent International. Natural Parent International (NPI) is a support group for parents with infant children. Local chapters of NPI conduct monthly programs that are led by NPI leaders. Monthly program topics include "Preparing for the new baby," "Bringing the new baby home," "A new baby and its siblings," and "Feeding the new baby." Monthly programs are part of a four-program series. Although programs within a series do not repeat, similar or identical programs can appear in different series. Some new parents attend a single series. Other parents are members of NPI for many years. In addition to conducting the monthly programs, NPI maintains a library from which members of NPI can check out books. Books are due in one month, but can be renewed. Members of NPI are encouraged to pay annual dues, but are not required to do so. Dues-paying members receive a monthly NPI magazine.

The leaders of NPI would like a database system that maintains information about members, library holdings, loaned books, programs, and attendance at programs. Besides storing this information, the system should:

- Display a list of programs that were attended by a particular member.
- Indicate when the NPI magazine subscription expires.
- Display a list of members who attended a particular program.
- Print mailing labels for members.
- Print series and program announcements.

The system does not need to record the dues payment details (that is, amount paid and check number).

Complete these steps:

1. List the names of at least four tables that would likely appear in the NPI system.
2. Describe the contents and capabilities of at least four forms that would likely appear in the NPI system.
3. Describe at least one report that would likely appear in the NPI system.

Project 1-2

Metropolitan Performing Arts Company. The Metropolitan Performing Arts Company (MPAC) is a small organization supported through civic and federal grants. It sponsors plays and musical performances during a 40-week season. Plays generally have a 4- to 5-week run. The actors are people with an interest in performing plays. They are not acting professionals; they have other full-time jobs. Similarly, musical performances usually involve a community symphony and local chorus.

Performances take place at the Metropolitan Performing Arts House. This small theater contains four sections: Floor (15 rows), East Wing (5 rows), West Wing (5 rows), and Balcony (8 rows). The number of seats per row varies between 10 and 20. The performance, date, and section selected determine the ticket price. Some complimentary tickets are given away as well.

A small office staff handles the administrative details related to promoting and conducting the performances. MPAC needs a database system to support its operations. Interviews with the Theater Manager and the Symphonic Director have identified the following needs:

- The system should record ticket sales. Recording ticket sales requires maintaining the status of seats and storing sales information. Credit cards, cash, and checks can be used to pay for tickets.
- The system should support ticket returns.

❑ The system should display information about performances, including the date, time, director, and performers. Eventually, this information should be placed on the World Wide Web (WWW).

❑ The system must support multiple ticket agents, but only the manager is allowed to change price and performance information.

❑ The system should print reports that list total sales and returns per performance.

Complete these steps:

1. List the names of at least four tables that would likely appear in the MPAC system.

2. Describe the contents and capabilities of at least three forms that would likely appear in the MPAC system.

3. Describe at least one report that would likely appear in the MPAC system.

Project 1-3

Foreign Language Institute, Inc. Foreign Language Institute, Inc. (FLI) supplies educational materials for learning foreign languages. Long recognized as a leader in the field of training materials by educational institutions, FLI's business has grown exponentially in the last year because of the increasing globalization of world markets. Whereas its customers were once only educational institutions, they now include major corporations, branches of federal and state governments, and individuals. FLI therefore needs a database to support its business needs.

FLI's primary offerings comprise textbooks and software programs used in teaching foreign languages. The company currently offers products at various levels in French, Spanish, Russian, German, and Japanese. Both textbooks and software come with workbooks containing projects and exercises. Products may be classified into three categories: beginner, intermediate, and advanced. (Not all languages have products at all levels.) Software products are available on disk or CD-ROM. All products require at least 4 MB of RAM, 10 MB of free disk space, and a color monitor. Some of its software is written in C, some is written in an object-oriented language named Eiffel, and some is written in HyperCard. The CD-ROM software also requires a CD drive, speakers, and a microphone; it contains recordings of native speakers. For each recording, FLI maintains the name, address, and phone number of the person whose voice was recorded so that the same person might be contacted when updates become necessary.

FLI tracks all of its sales. The company includes a postage-prepaid registration card in every product package that buyers fill out and return to FLI. Customers are then notified when new versions of textbooks or software are created. In addition, FLI tracks all interactions with customers made through the company's toll-free telephone number. It categorizes calls as comments, complaints, technical service requests, and specific product suggestions.

FLI advertises only in magazines. The company wants the database to include information such as the magazine's name and address and who to contact regarding placement of an ad. FLI frequently places several ads in a magazine issue; some are small, whereas others are two pages wide. The company needs to track the issue date on which an ad appears, the page number on which it appears (or the first page of the ad in the case of a multiple-page ad), and the rate paid for the ad.

The management of FLI would like a system that can handle information about products, customers, sales, sales people, calls from customers, and the speakers used in the recordings. Besides storing this information, the system should:

- Display a list of products that were developed with a particular speaker.
- Display a warning if a product has more than two technical complaints associated with it.
- Display information about specific advertisements of products in magazines.
- Display a list of purchases made by a particular customer.
- Display detailed sales information when purchases are made.

The system does not need to calculate the salaries of sales people or their commissions.

Complete these steps:

1. List the names of at least four tables that would likely appear in the FLI system.
2. Describe the contents and capabilities of at least four forms that would likely appear in the FLI system.
3. Describe at least one report that would likely appear in the FLI system.

Project 1-4

King William Hotel. The King William Hotel has five floors, four of which contain ten rooms each. The first floor is dedicated to the lobby and hotel offices. The second floor has a small tearoom in which tea, coffee, breakfast, and light snacks are served each morning and evening. Currently, the tearoom operates on a cash-only (or credit card) basis. The hotel management would like to be able to charge a customer's room account directly. The desired system would allow for direct charges to a hotel patron's bill.

The hotel's location ensures a high occupancy rate throughout the year, but the hotel management describe several problems. For example, the reservation system is manual. Although minimal problems occur in booking a reservation when the reservation data do not change, if a reservation is changed (either the dates of the reservation are altered or the reservation is canceled), then sometimes the record is not modified correctly. These errors lead to overbooking and underbooking of rooms. In the worst case, a customer may cancel a reservation but never receive a refund of his or her deposit, or a potential customer may be denied a room because customers are erroneously expected.

Sometimes rooms aren't ready when customers arrive, even though they arrive after the official check-in time of 1:00 P.M. The hotel staff should be alerted if a room is not ready for check-in. They also need to be able to change the rates for a room category easily. In addition, the same system interface should be utilized throughout the hotel because the front-desk personnel occasionally substitute for the tearoom personnel, and vice versa.

The management of the King William Hotel would like a system that maintains information about reservations and room charges. Besides storing this information, the system should:

- Simplify the process of reserving a specific type of room.

- ☐ Simplify the process of changing the price of a category of rooms.

- ☐ Display summary and detailed information about a customer's bill at check-out time.

- ☐ Print a report of the charges associated with a specific customer (that is, print a bill for the customer's stay in the hotel).

Complete these steps:

1. List the names of at least four tables that would likely appear in the King William Hotel system.

2. Describe the contents and capabilities of at least four forms that would likely appear in the King William Hotel system.

3. Describe at least one report that would likely appear in the King William Hotel system.

Project 1-5

Workers' Compensation Commission System. Hazelwood & Swanzy (H & S) is a large health maintenance organization (HMO) operating in Georgia. H & S owns a large hospital in Atlanta and operates "clinics" in other cities in the state. In addition to providing routine preventive care, the clinics specialize in treating "on-the-job injuries." This department is called the Occupational Medicine Department (OMD). Each patient admitted to the OMD is eligible for supplementary compensation from the state Workers' Compensation Commission (WCC). To receive this compensation, each patient's clinic visit must be documented on one of three forms. The OMD needs a database to help manage the processes related to documenting patient visits and filing the WCC forms.

When a patient is admitted to the OMD, the clinic submits Form A to the WCC. The OMD submits a new Form A each time a patient is admitted to the clinic. In other words, if a worker is injured on Monday and subsequently taken to the clinic, then a Form A is generated documenting that injury. Should the patient return to work on Tuesday but then suffer a new injury requiring another trip to the clinic, then a new Form A will be generated for this patient's new problem.

A Form B is generated upon each visit to the clinic after the first one. If a patient is receiving treatment for injuries that occurred on different dates, the following rule is used: If the visit is clearly related to only one of the injuries, then the date of that injury is specified on Form B. If the visit involves treatment of multiple injuries, it doesn't matter which "date of injury" is specified on Form B.

When a patient is discharged from the OMD after his or her treatment ends, the clinic generates Form C. In some cases, however, a patient may be transferred to another department or clinic for treatment. In this case, the OMD is no longer responsible for filing with the WCC, and the last form generated by the OMD for this patient will be the Form B for the visit that involves the transfer.

The three forms rely on two sets of standard codes for documenting injuries and treatments: the ICD-9 codes and the CPT codes. It is very important that these codes be entered correctly. Erroneous codes result in significant delays in the compensation process.

1

All doctors referenced on the forms are H & S physicians with the following exception: the "new treating doctor" entered on Form B may be a doctor outside the H & S system. The H & S system includes approximately 50 doctors.

The management of the OMD would like a system that maintains information about patients, companies, doctors, and forms filed with the state. Besides storing this information, the system should:

- Simplify the process of data entry for patients and WCC forms.

- Alert the user when a patient has more than two incidents of Form A in the system.

- Automate the creation of the forms submitted to the WCC (that is, print these forms as reports).

Complete these steps:

1. List the names of at least four tables that would likely appear in the WCC system.

2. Describe the contents and capabilities of at least four forms that would likely appear in the WCC system.

3. Describe at least one report that would likely appear in the WCC system.

2

REVIEWING TABLES AND QUERIES

The Foundation of an Access Application

In this chapter you will:

♦ Identify the steps required to develop an Access application

♦ Specify the characteristics of a well-designed table

♦ Create a new Access table with its corresponding fields, keys, indexes, validation rules, input masks, and formats

♦ Create relationships between tables

♦ Create select queries, totals queries, and action queries

♦ Create queries in SQL view

Access stores data in the form of tables. Access queries retrieve and update data. The tables and queries are the foundation for Access applications. Indeed, poorly functioning applications can often be traced back to poor table and query design. As an Access application developer, you must know how to develop tables and queries, understand the development process, and implement the design considerations that lead to well–designed tables and queries.

This chapter first presents an overview of the Access application development processes. It then focuses on two critical objects of an Access application: tables and queries. Properly designed tables protect the integrity of the database by support- ing the entry of valid data and facilitate the development of other Access objects. In addition, the use of well–designed queries simplifies VBA programming.

The Access Application Development Process

Access application development is not governed by one development procedure. Rather, the size and complexity of the application determine the approach taken. For instance, large applications, for which Access might be one of many software tools used to develop the system, may follow a structured systems development approach. The **structured systems development** approach includes a formal requirements specification phase, followed by the creation of an application blueprint (that is, systems design) and then by programming. Smaller applications, on the other hand, are likely to follow a prototyping approach. The **prototyping** approach requires the developer to build an initial system quickly, with a shorter requirements and design phase. The Access visual orientation (for example, forms and reports are designed by pointing and clicking) makes it particularly suitable for a prototyping approach.

Figure 2-1 illustrates a common Access application development procedure. As the developer moves from the interior of the spiral to the outside, the system becomes more complete.

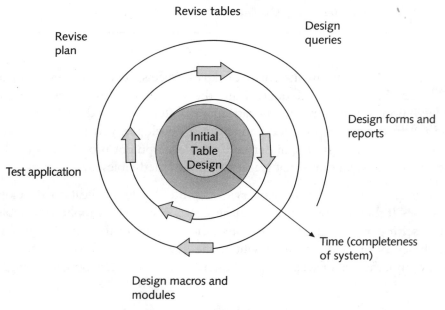

Figure 2-1   Access application development process

Table Development

Table design begins with the specification of the application's objective. This objective determines the application's storage needs, and hence the design of the table. For example, a transcript application must keep track of a student's enrollment history. Thus, tables might store student data (for example, name and student ID), class data (for example, course name and number), and grades. A complete advising system must contain data about majors and course requirements as well.

In addition to determining the data that the tables will store, a system developer needs to know the data constraints. **Data constraints** are the valid values for the data. Examples of data constraints include "all students must have a unique student ID number," "the leveling courses assigned to a student must be contained in the university catalog," and "all phone numbers must be in the form (###) ###-####." Many data constraints can be enforced through the design of the Access tables and relationships.

Terminology and Rules of Table Design

Access stores data in tables. Each table represents a unique subject (students, customers, orders, classes). A well-designed table contains information that *relates* only to that subject.

Each table consists of a set of fields and rows. A row in a table represents a specific and unique instance of the table's subject (for example, a specific student, an enrollment, and sale transaction). A field (that is, a column) represents a particular attribute of the subject (for example, a student's major, the date of a sale). When developing an Access application, you must determine the tables necessary to meet the storage needs of the application, the fields defined in the tables, the data constraints, and the events that will populate the rows. The choice of tables and the assignment of fields to tables significantly influence the ease with which the rest of the application can be developed.

To illustrate good table design, you will now look at three tables from MU-DSci, based on the following syntax:

Syntax

TableName(FieldName1, FieldName2, FieldName3, FieldNameN)

Syntax Dissection

The *TableName* is any valid table in the Tables tab of your Database window.

FieldName1 through *FieldNameN* are the names of the fields in the table; an underline specifies the primary key.

With this syntax in hand, you are ready for a discussion of the Design view of the tblCurrentStudents table:

```
tblCurrentStudents(StudentID, FirstName, LastName,LPhone,
Program,…)
```

In this case, tblCurrentStudents is the table's name. The names inside the parentheses are the table's field names. (Because tblCurrentStudents contains many field names, only the first few fields are presented here; normally, all field names will appear in the parentheses.) Figure 2-2 shows the Design view of tblCurrentStudents.

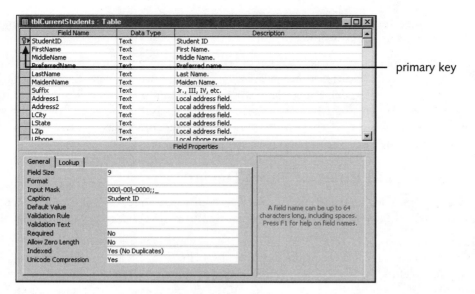

primary key

Figure 2-2   Design view of tblCurrentStudents

The underlined field, StudentID, represents the primary key. A **primary key** is a field or a combination of fields that always contains a value that uniquely identifies a row in a table. That is, a particular value in the primary key field will appear only once in the table. In tblCurrentStudents, each student has a unique StudentID. Because several students may have the same LastName, LastName cannot serve as the primary key.

The next table that you will examine is tblCourses:

      `tblCourses(`<u>`AreaCode`</u>`,` <u>`CourseNo`</u>`, Title, Description,…)`

For this table, two fields are underlined in the table specification because one field alone will not define a unique value. For example, several courses use DSCI as a value for AreaCode. In addition, several subject areas use 641 as a course number. No subject area, however, uses the same course number more than once. When a primary key consists of two or more fields, it is called a **composite key** or a **multiple-field primary key**. To be consistent with Access Help, the latter term will be used in this book.

The third MU–DSci table is tblLevelingNeeded, which contains rows that indicate the leveling courses needed by different students:

      `tblLevelingNeeded(`<u>`LCourseID`</u>`, StudentID, AreaCode, CourseNo,`
      `Needed)`

The StudentID field in tblLevelingNeeded contains values that are also contained by the StudentID field in tblCurrentStudents. The AreaCode and CourseNo fields contain values that are also contained in tblCourses. These fields are called foreign keys. A **foreign key** is a field or a combination of fields that contains values that are also contained by a primary key (usually, *but not always*, located in another table). A foreign key may also be null. The

StudentID field in tblLevelingNeeded is a foreign key because the only values permitted to appear in the StudentID field are values that also appear in tblCurrentStudents. Similarly, the composite key, which comprises AreaCode and CourseNo, is a foreign key that references the corresponding fields in tblCourses.

As noted earlier, the proper design of a table is critical to Access application development. A short-sighted developer may have used separate tables for each major, as follows:

```
tblMISYStudents(StudentID, FirstName, LastName, LPhone, …)
tblPOMAStudents(StudentID, FirstName, LastName, LPhone, …)
tblSTATStudents(StudentID, FirstName, LastName, LPhone, …)
```

This design, however, has several disadvantages. First, if you don't know the major, or Program field, of a student you are trying to find, you must search three tables to find the LPhone, for example, of that particular student. Second, a foreign key relationship cannot be created for StudentID in tblLevelingNeeded, because a foreign key must identify a single primary key that contains all valid values.

Another short-sighted option eliminates the tblLevelingNeeded table, as shown in the code following this paragraph. The first leveling course needed by a student is listed in LevelingAreaCode-1 and LevelingCourseNo-1, the second leveling course needed is listed in LevelingAreaCode-2 and LevelingCourseNo-2, and so on.

```
tblCurrentStudents(StudentID, FirstName, LastName,
LPhone, LevelingAreaCode-1,
LevelingCourseNo-1, LevelingAreaCode-2,
LevelingCourseNo-2, LevelingAreaCode-3, LevelingCourseNo-3,…)
```

This design also has disadvantages. First, tblCurrentStudents requires fields for the maximum number of leveling courses needed. The values of many of these fields will remain blank for most students. All leveling courses needed could not be stored, however, if a student requires more leveling courses than allowed by the number of Leveling fields in tblCurrentStudents. Second, some queries are more complex compared with corresponding queries that are used with the proper table design.

To illustrate the problems created by this design, consider Figure 2-3 and Figure 2-4. Figure 2-3 shows the Design view of a well-designed query that asks for all Student IDs who must take MKTG 641. The query uses a single Criteria row. Figure 2-4 shows the same query for the modified tblCurrentStudents table. The query must test all LevelingAreaCode and LevelingCourseNo fields, because MKTG 641 could appear in any of the fields. As you can see, the more LevelingAreaCode and LevelingCourseNo fields contained in tblCustomers, the more tedious the writing and maintenance of the query.

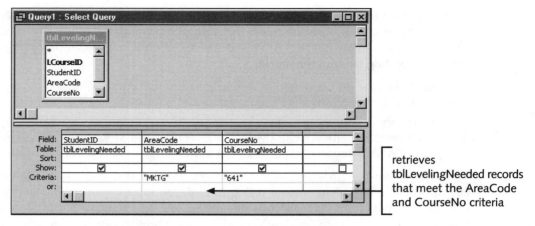

retrieves tblLevelingNeeded records that meet the AreaCode and CourseNo criteria

Figure 2-3   Query that retrieves students who need MKTG 641 (good table design)

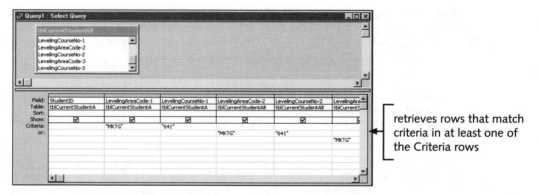

retrieves rows that match criteria in at least one of the Criteria rows

Figure 2-4   Query that retrieves students who need MKTG 641 (poor table design)

When you construct tables, you should keep the following points in mind:

- When two or more tables contain the same fields, consider collapsing the multiple tables into a single table. This table should contain all common fields shared by the original tables plus a new field that represents the attribute identified by the names of the original tables. For example, tblMISYStudents, tblPOMAStudents, and tblSTATStudents existed in a previous version of the current application. They were collapsed into one table, tblCurrentStudents, based on this guideline.

- When a table contains several similar fields, perhaps distinguished by an attached number (for example, LevelingAreaCode-1, LevelingAreaCode-2), consider creating another table that contains the primary key of the original table (for example, StudentID) plus a single field that combines the similar fields of the original table (for example, LevelingAreaCode). The tblCurrentStudents table that includes LevelingAreaCode-# and LevelingCourseNo-# is an example of this problem. The data in this case are better represented in two tables: tblCurrentStudents and tblLevelingNeeded.

2

- If the values of two or more fields always appear together in different rows, whether in the same or different tables, consider creating a new table that contains the related fields. This creation process is called normalization (discussed later in the chapter). For example, the Leveling Needed table in the prototype used the following initial design:

```
tblLevelingNeeded(LCourseID, StudentID, AreaCode, _
        CourseNo, Title)
```

In this version of tblLevelingNeeded, Title is the title of the course. When analyzing the tblLevelingNeeded table, the developers noted that the AreaCode and CourseNo always dictate the Title that appears. For example, no matter what the StudentID is, MKTG 641 is always the area code and course number for Introduction to Marketing. Consequently, the developers constructed a new table, tblCourses, that contains the AreaCode, CourseNo, and Title fields. Now, because of the creation of this new table, tblLevelingNeeded does not need to contain the Title field.

Normalization

Normalization is a process that involves splitting tables into more than one table in an effort to control data redundancy. Such redundancy can cause data validity problems. For example, in the original design, changing the course title required changing each row where the title appeared. In the preferred design, the change is made in only one row.

Database normal forms guide aspects of table design. The normal forms include first, second, and third normal forms. In general, the higher the normal form, the more desirable the table design. The normal forms reflect the concept of dependency. A **dependency** exists between fields when a field or fields determine the value of another field. In these examples, AreaCode and CourseNo determine the value of Title. Table 2-1 summarizes the normal forms.

Table 2-1   Normal form summary

Normal Form	Definition	Original Table	Normalized Tables
First Normal Form (1NF)	A table is in 1NF when repeating groups do not appear in a table (that is, a row column intersection contains only one value).	**tblEmployee** ID Name Children 100 Parker Bob, Sally 101 Smith Martha, Ted	**tblEmployee** ID Name 100 Parker 101 Smith **tblChildren** ID Child Name 100 Bob 100 Sally 101 Martha 101 Ted

Table 2-1   Normal form summary (continued)

Normal Form	Definition	Original Table	Normalized Tables
Second Normal Form (2NF)	A table is in 2NF when it is in 1NF and no attribute is dependent on only part of the primary key.	**tblCourseDetails** Dept. Course Credits College MIS 320 3 Business MIS 428 5 Business Chem 320 5 Science	**tblCourse** Dept. Course Credits MIS 320 3 MIS 428 5 Chem 320 5 **tblDeptCollege** Dept. College MIS Business Chem Science
Third Normal Form (3NF)	A table is in 3NF when it is in 2NF and a non-key attribute is not transitively dependent on the primary key.	**tblCourseSection** Index Instructor Office 123 100-4 M 355 124 101-6 B 424 150 100-4 M 355 160 210-8 B 434 567 101-6 B 424	**tblCourseSection** Index Instructor 123 100-4 124 101-6 150 100-4 160 210-8 567 101-6 **tblInstructor** Instructor Office 100-4 M 355 101-6 B 424 210-8 B 434 100-4 M 355

TIP   Although Access provides the Table Analyzer to help with the analysis of table designs, it is no substitute for the developer's knowledge and experience.

Constraints in the Design View of a Table

When the developer specifies constraints in the Design view of a table, those constraints will be enforced whenever a module, macro, query, or form attempts to update data stored in the table. If the developer does not specify constraints, the data in the table are at the mercy of the many different queries, forms, modules, and macros that interact with that table. If any of these objects fails to validate the data prior to storing that information in the table, then the data will violate the constraints.

Figure 2-2, displayed earlier, shows the Design view of the tblCurrentStudents table. In this view, you can see constraints in action. For instance, after you read the name of the field in the **Field Name** column, note that the **Data Type** column identifies the kind of data that can be stored in the field. That is, the data type enforces a constraint. For example, alphabetic characters cannot be stored in a field declared as an Integer data type. Also, note that the **Field Size** property specifies how many characters (in the case of a Text field) or the type of number (for a Numeric field) that can be contained in the field. This specification provides an additional constraint that validates the entry of data into a field.

Table 2-2 lists additional data types supported by Access. It mentions two data types that are somewhat unusual. The first data type, **AutoNumber**, tells Access to generate a value for the field automatically. Access developers frequently use AutoNumbers as primary keys when a large multiple-field primary key is the only other alternative. Developers use the second data type, **ReplicationID**, when copies of a table are kept on more than one computer (that is, the database is replicated). ReplicationIDs ensure that the value generated for the field is unique across different computers. A unique value may be necessary when merging tables on different computers.

The existence of a primary key also enforces a constraint. Access will automatically verify that primary key fields contain unique values. For example, it displays a warning when a user attempts to add a Current Student with a StudentID equal to a StudentID that already exists for another student. In addition to the uniqueness constraint, Access will not allow any part of a primary key to contain a null value (that is, no value).

Table 2-2   Data types supported by Access

Data Type	Subtype (Field Size)	Bytes	Description
AutoNumber	Long Integer	4	If the NewValues property equals Increment, the new value will follow in order. If NewValues equals Random, a random number is generated.
AutoNumber	ReplicationID	16	Generates a unique number across replicated databases. It is used only when a database is replicated.
Currency	None	8	Fixed decimal point number with 15 digits to the left of the decimal and 4 digits to right. Specializes in storing monetary amounts.
Date/Time	None	8	Used for storing dates and times.
Hyperlink	None		Used for storing World Wide Web page addresses. Maximum of 64,000 characters.
Lookup Wizard			Not a data type, but still accepted in the data type column. It triggers a wizard that establishes a foreign key relationship to another table.
Memo	None	Variable	Maximum of 64,000 characters. Cannot be indexed.
Number	Byte	1	Integer between 0 and 255.
Number	Decimal	12	Maximum of 29 digits, 28 of which can be used to the right of the decimal. The range is -7.9×10^{28} to 7.9×10^{28}.
Number	Double	8	15-decimal-place real number between -1.798×10^{308} and -4.941×10^{-324} for negative values and between 4.941×10^{-324} and 1.798×10^{308} for positive values.

Table 2-2   Data types supported by Access (continued)

Data Type	Subtype (Field Size)	Bytes	Description
Number	Integer	2	Integer between –32,768 and 32,767.
Number	Long Integer	4	Integer between –2,147,483,648 and 2,147,483,647.
Number	ReplicationID	16	Value generated by Windows to ensure uniqueness across computers. It is used when a database is replicated.
Number	Single	4	7-decimal-place real number between -3.4×10^{38} and -1.40×10^{-45} for negative numbers and between 1.40×10^{-45} to 3.4×10^{38} for positive numbers.
OLE Object			Sometimes called a Blob. Used for storing bit maps, formatted text, spreadsheets, sound files and so on. Maximum of 1 GB can be stored.
Text	Integer indicating maximum size of string (maximum is 255)	Same as field size	Any string of alphanumeric characters.
Yes/No	None		Logical (Boolean) field. Values are True (Yes) or False (No). True is represented by –1 or any other non-zero number. False is represented by zero.

TIP   In the case of a multiple-field primary key, hold the control button to highlight all fields in the key. Then click the Primary key.

Specifying the Design of a Single Table in the Swim Lessons Application

Metropolitan University administers swimming lessons at several pools across the city. The Swim Lessons application will track class enrollment, payments, and student progress. It will also display financial reports that show the profitability of offering swimming lessons at particular swimming pools.

Swim Lessons already contains several tables. It still needs a table, however, to record payment information. You will help design this table, which is named tblPayment. The summary syntax for tblPayment is as follows:

```
tblPayment(PaymentNo, PaymentType, PaymentDate, FirstName,
MiddleInitial, LastName, Phone, AmountPaid, CheckNo)
```

Table 2-3 lists the design specifications for tblPayment. Before you create the table, you must load the Swim Lessons application to a hard disk or network drive. Then you will be ready to create your table.

Table 2-3 Design specifications for tblPayment

Field Name	Data Type	Field Size	Description
PaymentNo	AutoNumber	Long Integer, New Values: Increment	A unique number assigned to payment
PaymentType	Number	Byte	1=Cash, 2=Check
PaymentDate	Date/Time		Date of Payment
FirstName	Text	20	First name of payer
MiddleInitial	Text	1	Middle initial of payer
LastName	Text	20	Last name of payer
Phone	Text	10	Telephone number of payer
AmountPaid	Currency		Amount paid
CheckNo	Number	Long Integer	Check Number

To create tblPayment:

1. Open Microsoft Access, if necessary, and then open **SwimData.mdb**.

2. If tables are not displayed in the database window, click the **Tables** object type in the Object Bar (located in the Database Window).

3. Double-click the **Create table in Design view** shortcut (located in the Database window).

4. In the first row of the Table Design window, type **PaymentNo** in the Field Name column, click in the **Data Type** column, select **AutoNumber** from the combo box, click in the **Description** column, and then type **A unique number assigned to payment**.

5. In the second row of the Table Design window, type **PaymentType** in the Field Name column, select **Number** as the Data Type, and type **1=Cash, 2=Check** in the Description column.

6. Click in the **Field Size** text box, and then select **Byte** from the combo box.

7. Create names and data types for the remaining fields listed in Table 2-3.

8. To assign a primary key to PaymentNo, click **PaymentNo** in the Field Name column, and then click **Primary Key** in the toolbar.

9. Click the **Save** button on the toolbar, type **tblPayment** in the Save As dialog box, and then click **OK**. The table design is saved. Figure 2-5 shows the Design view of tblPayment.

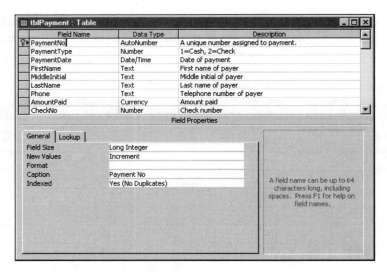

Figure 2-5   Design view of tblPayment

Once you have designed your table, it is useful to add a few rows of test data.

To add test data to tblPayment:

1. Click the **View** button on the toolbar or, if tblPayment is closed, double-click **tblPayment** in the Database window. You are now in Datasheet view.

2. Press the **Tab** key to move to the PaymentType field, and then type **1**. PaymentNo is automatically incremented to 1.

3. Type the following data into the fields: PaymentDate: **6/6/2001**; FirstName: **Sally**; MiddleInitial: **M**; LastName: **Garcia**; Phone: **4182938477**; AmountPaid: **30**; CheckNo: **0**. The reason why Access displays a two-digit year when you type a four-digit year will be explained in a forthcoming series of steps.

4. Move the insertion point to the second row and type the following data into the appropriate fields: PaymentType: **2**; PaymentDate: **6/10/2001**; FirstName: **William**; MiddleInitial: **J**; LastName: **Phillips**; Phone: **4182934199**; AmountPaid: **30**; CheckNo: **412**. The table now contains two records.

5. Close **tblPayment**. The tblPayment table is displayed with the list of tables in the Database window.

Additional Field Properties for Constraint Enforcement and Formatting

Beside keys and data types, other constraints can be specified. For example, you can specify the non-null constraint for non-key fields by choosing Yes in the **Required** field property. A **non-null constraint** requires that all records contain a value for that field. One valid value is a zero-length string. A **zero-length string** is defined as "" (that is, quotes with nothing between them). Choosing No in the **Allow Zero Length** field property prevents the use of zero-length strings.

As another example of a constraint-enforcing mechanism, consider the index. Indexes in a database are similar to indexes in the back of a textbook. An **index** maintains a sorted list of the current values of a field or fields. The items in the list point to the records that have the identified value. Indexes are created automatically for primary keys.

The Indexes window in Figure 2-6 shows the indexes for the tblLevelingNeeded table. Clicking Indexes in the table design toolbar displays the Indexes window. The definition of an index begins with the row containing an index name and ends with the row prior to the next index name. The primary key index is listed automatically in the Indexes window; its default name is PrimaryKey. Although indexes speed data retrieval, they should be defined with care because they increase the database size. In addition, because indexes are updated whenever a table's data are updated, indexes reduce the speed of data insertions, updates, and deletions.

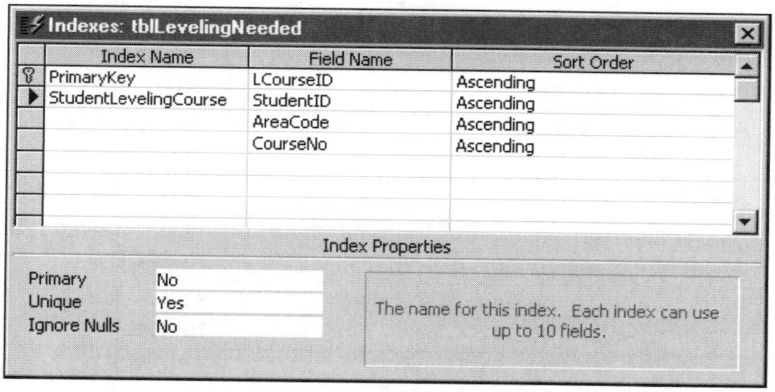

Figure 2-6   Indexes window of tblLevelingNeeded

Validation Rules and Validation Text Field Properties

Developers can also specify a data constraint with the Validation Rules and Validation Text field properties. A **validation rule** is a condition that the corresponding field must satisfy. If this condition is not satisfied, the **validation text** is displayed. The syntax for a validation rule looks like one-half of a conditional expression. As you may recall, a **conditional expression** is any statement that can be evaluated as True or False. Conditional expressions commonly use the operators < (less than), > (greater than), <= (less than or equal to), >= (greater than or equal to), and < > (not equal to).

Table Properties Validation Rule

When a constraint requires a comparison of the contents of two or more fields in the same table, a **Table Properties validation rule** is required. This validation rule is typed in the Table Properties sheet. The conditional expression in a table-level validation rule can contain the names of two or more fields in the table. If a field name contains a blank, you place brackets around the field name. If the table requires more than one constraint, the conditions must be connected with "And."

Access allows the creation of fairly complex validation rules. For instance, it supports several operators that return True or False values: **Between**, **In**, and **Like**. In addition, the **DLookup** function can be used in a table-level validation rule to compare a value to values found in another table. For more information on these items, consult Access Help.

Once created, a validation rule will check whether data obey the constraint prior to writing the data to the table. An **input mask**—another constraint mechanism—guides users as they type input; it prevents users from typing incorrect values. Access supplies an **Input Mask Wizard** that helps set up input masks. Table 2-4 lists some of the special symbols used in input masks.

Table 2-4   Input Mask symbols

Symbol	Function	Example
0	Number or sign required.	00000 allows -9456
#	Number, space, or sign.	##### allows 92 34
9	Number or space (sign not allowed).	9999 allows 156
L	Letter (A–Z) required.	LLLL allows ABcd
A	Any letter or number.	AAA/AA/LLLL allows s12/3G/sjhe
&	Any character or space.	&&&& allows A-Bc
>	All characters to the right of the symbol are converted to uppercase.	>LLLL converts Abcd to ABCD
<	All characters to the right of the symbol are converted to lowercase.	<AAAA converts Abcd to abcd
!	Fills mask from right to left; must be Text data type.	$#,###.##! types $456.00 from right to left

As a final example of a constraint, consider the **Default Value** field property, which specifies the initial value of the corresponding field. For instance, the default value for citizenship in tblCurrentStudents is "USA." This value is displayed in the citizenship field until the user types a new value.

Properties Used for Formatting

Many field properties influence the design of a form or report. For example, the **Caption** property refers to the heading or prompt that will initially appear on a form or report when the corresponding field is included. The default type of control (for example, text box, combo box) that appears on a form or report is specified through the **Display Control** combo box, which is located in the **Lookup** tab in the Field Properties section of the table's Design view. The **Description** column affects a form by placing the value of the Description column as the default status bar text.

Developers use the **Format** field property to indicate how stored data should be displayed. Table 2-5 gives some of the symbols used in the format box and their meaning. If the data type of the field is Number, Currency, Yes/No, or Date/Time, the developer can select from a set of predefined formats. The Format and Input Mask properties are similar. In fact, if an Input Mask is declared, it is usually unnecessary to set the Format field property.

Table 2-5   Symbols used in the Format property

Symbol	Function	Example
0	Displays digit if one exists, or a zero if none exists.	00000 displays 00543
#	Displays digit if one exists, or a space if none exists.	##### displays 543
$	Places a dollar sign at the beginning of the display.	$###,### displays $5,431
m,d,y	Displays month, day, year, respectively.	mmmm/dd/yy displays March/15/96
@	Indicates required string or numeric character.	@@@-@@-@@@@
&	Optional character.	(&&&) @@@-@@@@ displays () 951-2929 if area code does not exist
>	Converts all to right to uppercase.	>@@@@@ displays ABCDE
<	Converts to lowercase.	<@@@@@ displays abcde
; and [color]	Separates positive and negative number formats. [color] indicates color for display.	$###,###.00;$(###,###.00) [red] displays –143 as $(143.00) in red

Adding Field and Table Properties to tblPayment

At this point, you will add several field and table properties to tblPayment. These properties will ensure that the data in tblPayment are valid. The properties will also facilitate data retrieval and formatting when the data are displayed in a datasheet or form. In addition, because payment information must sometimes be accessed by check number or name, you will establish nonprimary key indexes.

To create an index on check number:

1. Click (do not double-click) **tblPayment**.

2. Click the **Design** button in the Database window. The Design view of tblPayment will appear.

3. In the Field Name column, click **CheckNo**. Field properties associated with CheckNo will appear in the Field Properties section.

4. Click the **Indexed** field property.

5. Select **Yes (Duplicates OK)** from the combo box. Because checks will come from different bank accounts, duplicate check numbers may be used. An index is created on CheckNo.

6. Click the **Save** button in the toolbar to save the new design of the table.

The name index requires two fields: LastName and FirstName. Consequently, the Index window must be used.

To create a multiple-field index on LastName and FirstName:

1. Make sure that tblPayment is open in Design view, and then click the **Indexes** button on the toolbar. The Indexes:tblPayment window appears.

2. Move the insertion point to a blank row, and then type **indName** in the Index Name column. It is the name of the index.

3. Click in the **Field Name** column, click **LastName** from the combo box, and then make sure that Sort Order displays **Ascending**.

4. Verify that the Index properties for LastName are as follows: Primary Key: **No**; Unique: **No**; Ignore Nulls: **No**. These properties apply to the entire index, indName.

5. Click in the **Field Name** column in the next row, select **FirstName** in the combo box, and verify that the Sort Order displays **Ascending**. Index properties will not be displayed. FirstName is part of the index.

6. Close the **Indexes** window, and then click the **Save** button in the toolbar to save the table. The indexes are now in effect.

The PaymentType field has only two legal values: 1 or 2. A validation rule should be created to enforce this restriction. In addition, the current default value of 0 is not a legal value; therefore, the default value should be changed to 1 (that is, cash).

To create a validation rule and change the default value for PaymentType:

1. Click somewhere in the **PaymentType** row, and then change the **Default Value** field property to 1.

2. Place the insertion point in the **Validation Rule** text box, and then type **1 Or 2** in the Validation Rule text box.

3. Click in the **Validation Text** text box, and then type **You must enter a 1 for Cash or a 2 for Check**.

4. To save the changes to the table design, click the **Save** button. You will receive a message that says data integrity rules have been changed. Click **Yes** in the dialog box.

The Phone and PaymentDate fields require Input Mask and Format properties to facilitate data entry and display. The input mask for the Phone field can be created through the Input Mask Wizard. Because a four-digit year is required to alleviate year 2000 difficulties, the input mask will be customized for PaymentDate.

2

To create input masks and formats for Phone and PaymentDate:

1. Click in the **Phone** row, and then click the **Input Mask** property.

2. Click the **Build** button that is next to the Input Mask property. If an Input Mask Wizard dialog box opens and asks you to save the table, click **Yes**. The Input Mask window is displayed. (If you receive an error message, the Input Mask Wizard was not installed. In this case, type the value specified in Step 5 into the Input Mask text box.)

3. If the Phone Number row is not highlighted, click on the row, and then click **Next**.

4. Click **Next** on all displays, until the Next button no longer has the focus. The default values will be used for all arguments to the input mask.

5. Click the **Finish** button. Make sure the Input Mask property reads as follows: !(999) 000-0000;;_.

6. Click in the **PaymentDate** row, and then start the **Input Mask Wizard** for PaymentDate, saving the table if prompted to do so.

7. Click **Short Date** in the Input Mask Wizard list box, and then click **Next**.

8. Try typing **05/15/2001** in the Try It text box. The number cannot be entered.

9. Modify the input mask to state **99/99/0099**. Try typing **05/15/2001** again. This date can now be entered. Click **Next**.

10. Click **Finish**. The following value is entered into the input mask: 99/99/0099;;_. This value states that a two- or four-digit year can be entered.

11. Click the **Format** property for PaymentDate, and then type **m/d/yyyy** in the Format property. A four-digit year will be displayed. If this value is not entered, Access displays a two-digit year even when a four-digit year was entered.

12. Click the **Save** button.

Finally, the Caption property should be updated for all fields that have a field name that consists of two concatenated words. For example, the Caption property for PaymentType should be Payment Type.

To create a Caption property that applies to the tblPayment fields:

1. Click in the **Caption** property associated with PaymentType, and then type **Payment Type** in the Caption text box.

2. Using the same caption pattern, repeat Steps 1 and 2 for PaymentDate, FirstName, MiddleInitial, LastName, AmountPaid, and CheckNo.

3. Click the **Save** button.

Before leaving tblPayment, at least one more sample data record should be added. You will use this record to test the input masks, validation rules, and so on.

To test the field properties of tblPayment:

1. Display the Datasheet view of **tblPayment**, if necessary.

2. Place the insertion point in the bottom row and type the following record. As you type, occasionally make a few mistakes to test the properties. The final version of the record should be typed correctly: Payment Type: **2**; PaymentDate: **06/05/2001**; FirstName: **Martha**; MiddleInitial: **B**; LastName: **Smith**; Phone: **4182683948**; AmountPaid: **30**; CheckNo: **101**.

3. Close the table and, if prompted, click **Save**.

The tblPayment table is now complete. The table itself facilitates the entry of legal data values.

Multiple Table Relationships

When more than one table is used, relationships between tables become important. You maintain relationships between tables through the use of **foreign keys**. For example, tblLevelingNeeded contains the StudentID field. StudentID is the primary key of the tblCurrentStudents table, and StudentID in tblLevelingNeeded is the foreign key. The leveling courses associated with a student can be found by matching the common StudentID values. The process of matching common attribute values is called **joining** the tables.

Besides facilitating data retrieval across multiple tables, foreign keys support referential integrity. **Referential integrity** is a constraint on data values that forces the value of a foreign key to either (1) match a primary key value that is contained in a row of the related table or (2) equal null.

In Access, once common attributes exist between two tables, no other step is necessary to retrieve information from more than one table. Retrieval efficiency is enhanced and referential integrity can be enforced, however, if relationships are explicitly identified. Explicit relationships also facilitate the use of **subdatasheets**, which allow you to display related records that are nested within the datasheet of a table. Explicit relationships are created in the Relationships window, as shown in Figure 2-7.

Prior to using the Relationships window to join tables, you should check the Design view of all tables to be used in the Relationships window for compatibility. The data type and field size of foreign key fields must match the data type and field size of the related primary key. For example, the data type and field size of StudentID in tblCurrentStudents are Text 9. Similarly, the data type and field size of StudentID in tblLevelingNeeded are Text 9.

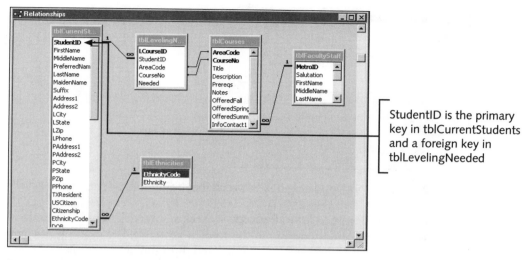

Figure 2-7   Some of the relationships in the Relationships window for MU-DSci

    A slight deviation from this "matching" rule occurs when a primary key field has been defined as an AutoNumber. In this case, the corresponding foreign key field should be defined as a Number data type. If the field size of the AutoNumber is Long Integer, the field size of the foreign key should be Long Integer. If the field size of the AutoNumber is declared as ReplicationID, the field size corresponding to the Number data type should be ReplicationID.

To construct a relationship in the Relationships window, first click and drag the primary key (hold the Control key to select more than one field) from the table in which it is defined to the table that contains the corresponding foreign key. Next, use the Relationships dialog box shown in Figure 2-8 to set or change the type of relationship. In this dialog box, the Table/Query column and the Related Table/Query column should be checked to verify that the correct fields are related. You use the combo boxes in each column to select the related fields. Finally, referential integrity between the primary key and foreign key is enforced by placing a check mark in the **Enforce Referential Integrity** check box.

In the Relationships dialog box, when **Cascade Update Related Fields** is checked, changes in the primary key value are automatically propagated to the corresponding foreign key value. For example, if a current student changes his or her StudentID, Access will automatically update the StudentIDs in the tblLevelingNeeded table. If Cascade Update Related Fields is not checked, no changes can be made to a StudentID in tblCurrentStudents unless a related record does not exist in tblLevelingNeeded.

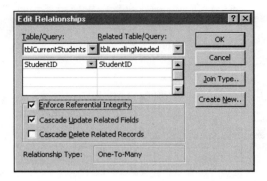

Figure 2-8   Relationships dialog box between the tblCurrentStudents and tblLevelingNeeded

When **Cascade Delete Related Records** is checked, row deletions in the primary key table will cause deletions of related rows in the foreign key table. For example, if Cascade Delete Related Records is checked and a row is deleted from tblCurrentStudents, Access will automatically delete the rows in tblLevelingNeeded that contain that student's Student ID. If Cascade Delete Related Records is not checked, a row in tblCurrentStudents cannot be deleted when rows in the tblLevelingNeeded contain the student's Student ID. If the deletion was allowed, the value in tblLevelingNeeded would no longer refer to a valid value in tblCurrentStudents and referential integrity would no longer exist.

After you define a relationship, a line will connect the tables in the Relationship window. The numeral 1 and an infinity symbol (∞) are used to indicate cardinalities of "one" and "many," respectively. A **one-to-one relationship** (indicated by a 1 on each side of the line) indicates that a value of the primary key can exist in only one row as a foreign key. A **one-to-many relationship** indicates that a value of the primary key can exist in more than one row as a foreign key.

To delete a relationship from the Relationships window, click once on the line connecting the tables, and then press the Delete key. To modify a relationship, double-click the line connecting the tables. This action will open the Relationships dialog box originally used to construct the relationship.

In addition to the Relationships window, Access creates relationships between tables through the Lookup Wizard. For more information on the Lookup Wizard, see Access Help.

Creating Multiple Table Relationships in the Swim Lessons Application

Many of the tables and relationships used by the Swim Lessons application have already been created. Open each of the following tables in turn to explore its contents: tblStudents, tblStaff, tblPool, tblLevel, tblClasses, and tblEnrollment.

You will now relate the tblPayment table to the tblEnrollment table so that the swimming staff can associate a payment with a particular student and class. This relationship is valuable because parents frequently pay for several children and lessons and they occasionally need to know which children and lessons were covered by a particular payment. Creating a relationship between tblPayment and tblEnrollment is a two-step process. First, a compatible field must be created in tblEnrollment.

To create a compatible field in tblEnrollment:

1. Click **tblEnrollment** in the Database window, and then click the **Design** button in the Database window.

2. Click in the **Field Name** column of the first empty row, and then type **PaymentNo**.

3. Select **Number** as the Data Type. Verify that the Field Size is **Long Integer**. PaymentNo is an AutoNumber in tblPayment. Relationships can be established between AutoNumbers and Long Integers.

4. Type **Payment No.** in the Caption text box, delete the 0 from the Default Value text box, click the **Save** button, and then close the **tblEnrollment: Table** window. The table is updated.

Next, the Relationships window will be used to define a relationship between tblPayment and tblEnrollment.

To create a relationship between tblPayment and tblEnrollment:

1. Click the **Relationships** toolbar button. The Relationships window opens.

2. Click the **Show Table** toolbar button. The Show Table window is displayed.

3. Click **tblPayment**, and then click the **Add** button. The tblPayment table will be added to the Relationships window. (You may have to move the Show Table window to see the addition.)

4. Click the **Close** button on the Show Table window.

5. Use the scroll bar in tblEnrollment to make **PaymentNo** visible, click **PaymentNo** in tblPayment, hold down the mouse button, and then drag **PaymentNo** in tblPayment on top of **PaymentNo** in tblEnrollment. Release the mouse button. The Edit Relationships window appears.

6. Verify that **PaymentNo** appears in both list boxes, **tblPayment** appears at the top of the left list box (which is dimmed), and **tblEnrollment** appears at the top of the right list box (which is dimmed). If necessary, use the list boxes to make corrections.

7. Check the **Enforce Referential Integrity** check box. If a PaymentNo is added to tblEnrollment, it should match a stored payment.

8. Check the **Cascade Update Related Fields** check box. If the PaymentNo in tblPayment changes for any reason, the change will be propagated to tblEnrollment. Do not check Cascade Delete Related Records.

9. Click the **Create** button. The relationship is drawn in the Relationships window. Move and resize the boxes until they match Figure 2-9.

10. Close the **Relationships** window, and then answer **Yes** to saving the layout.

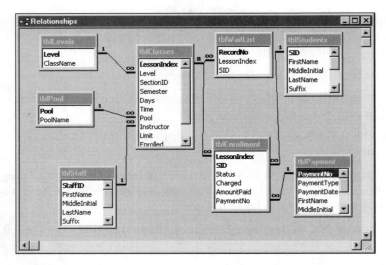

Figure 2-9   Relationships window for the Swim Lessons application

As always, you should test the relationship. In this situation, you will test whether you can add a PaymentNo in tblEnrollment that does not match tblPayment.

To test the relationship:

1. Open **tblPayment** in Datasheet view.

2. For reference, write down the **PaymentNo** for Sally M. Garcia, and then close tblPayment.

3. Open **tblEnrollment** in Datasheet view.

4. Locate the **tblEnrollment** row for LessonIndex 8 and SID 222-11-1116. Click in the corresponding **PaymentNo** field.

5. Type **165** in the PaymentNo field, and then press the **Tab** key. You will receive an Error message stating that a match was not found in tblPayment. Click **OK**. Delete **165** from PaymentNo.

6. Type the number you wrote down in Step 2 into PaymentNo, and then press the **Tab** key. An error does not occur and the value is recorded. Access has enforced referential integrity.

7. Close **tblEnrollment**, and then open the datasheet for tblPayment.

8. Click the **plus sign** that appears next to Sally M. Garcia's payment. The subdatasheet displays the tblEnrollment records that are related to the payment. See Figure 2-10.

9. Close all open datasheets.

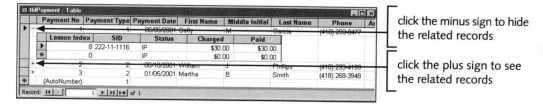

click the minus sign to hide the related records

click the plus sign to see the related records

2

Figure 2-10   Displaying tblEnrollment through the subdatasheet for tblPayment

Linked Tables

If a programmer is to modify a program without interfering with the user's ability to change the data, the data and the program must be separated. You use linked tables to separate the data from the forms, reports, queries, macros, and modules that manipulate the information. To use linked tables, you must develop table definitions and table data in one database (the **source database**) and develop the queries, forms, reports, pages, macros, and modules in a different database (the **container database**).

When using linked tables, note that the container database remembers an absolute path to the source database. That is, if the directory or drive of the source database changes, the container database can no longer find the source database. The Linked Table Manager helps you and your user find and refresh the linked tables. Distributed Access applications that use linked tables should contain program code that searches for source databases and refreshes the link automatically.

Linking Tables and Refreshing Links in the Swim Lessons Application

The Swim Lessons application uses linked tables. For this application, **SwimReg.mdb** is the container database and **SwimData.mdb** is the Source database. The links in **SwimReg.mdb** must be refreshed and the new table, tblPayment, must be linked to **SwimReg.mdb**.

To refresh the links and link new tables in **SwimReg.mdb**:

1. If not closed, close **SwimData.mdb**, and then open **SwimReg.mdb**.
2. On the menu bar, click **Tools**, point to **Database Utilities**, and then click **Linked Table Manager**.
3. Click **Select All**. Check marks are placed in the check boxes next to the tables.
4. Check the **Always prompt for new location** check box. This option forces Access to display the File Browse window after you click OK.
5. Click **OK**, locate and highlight **SwimData.mdb** in the window, and then click **Open**. The data are refreshed.
6. Click **OK** in response to the dialog box, and then close the **Linked Table Manager** window.

7. On the database menu, click **File**, point to **Get External Data**, and then click **Link Tables**. The Link dialog box will appear.

8. Click SwimData.mdb, and then click the **Link** button. A Link Tables dialog box opens.

9. Click **tblPayment**, and then click the **OK** button. The tblPayment table is linked to SwimReg.mdb and the table is displayed in the Database window.

Adding Data to Tables

It is advisable to add some test data after developing the table and relationship specifications. Test data allow the developer to see preliminary results of a query, form, report, page, macro, or procedure. Access's Datasheet view is ideal for adding such test data. The system developer should change the test data systematically to test the system under different situations.

Once the application is complete, it's time to tackle the real data. Loading data into an Access application can be a time-consuming process. The Import features available on the Access file menu can help. For more tips on importing data, see Access Help.

QUERY DEVELOPMENT

Once the tables and relationships have been specified, it is time to begin constructing major sections of the application. When one section of the Access application requires data that differ in some way from the data contained by a single table, a query or several queries should likely be developed. **Queries** provide an efficient and easy method of retrieving, manipulating, and summarizing data. Like many database management systems, Access queries are specified in the Structured Query Language (SQL). Fortunately, Access provides a visual design grid that facilitates the creation of queries without explicitly using SQL. As the query is visually designed, Access automatically creates the corresponding SQL code to execute the query. Nevertheless, SQL code is sometimes created within a VBA procedure; therefore, developers must have at least a basic understanding of SQL to develop complex applications.

The Design view of a query supports many query types, as shown in Figure 2-11. Select and crosstab queries retrieve data. Make-table, update, append, and delete queries are called **action queries** because they change the contents of the database.

Queries retrieve and modify data that are stored in tables. Before you can specify the retrieval or manipulation criteria, however, you must identify the tables that will provide the data. The Show Table dialog box is used to select the tables and queries. If relationships have been declared between tables or if Access can guess relationships between tables, relationships—called **join lines**—are predrawn between the selected tables in the query's Design view, as shown in Figure 2-12. You can also create join lines by dragging a field from one table to a field in another table, similar to the Relationships window.

2

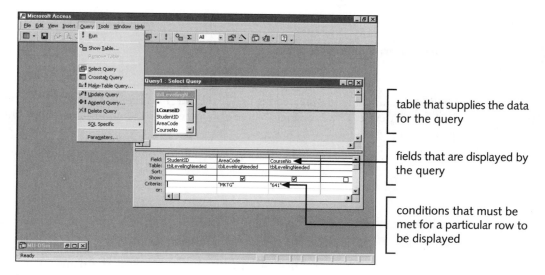

table that supplies the data for the query

fields that are displayed by the query

conditions that must be met for a particular row to be displayed

Figure 2-11   Access Query menu and design grid

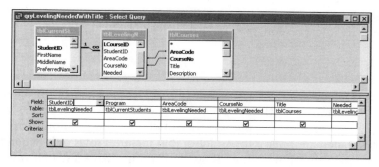

Figure 2-12   Query showing the leveling courses needed by each current student

Select and Crosstab Queries

Most applications use many **select** queries to retrieve data from other tables or queries. Forms and reports frequently display the result of a select query in a user-friendly format.

The design grid of a select query contains several columns and rows. Each column corresponds to a field that will be displayed or tested. The field names appear in the **Field** row of the grid. You can place field names in the Field row by double-clicking the field in the table portion of the Design view, by dragging the field from a table to the design grid, or by using the combo box in the Field row.

The **Criteria** row of the grid limits the displayed rows to those that meet a specified condition. This row contains any statement that evaluates to True or False. These statements can contain a literal (for example, 5 is equivalent to =5, abc is equivalent to = "abc"), field names, and operators. Commonly used operators include < (for example, <5), > (for example, >5), >=, <=, < >, And, Or, Not, Between, In, Like, and Is Null. After you create the query, the Datasheet view displays the query's result. Besides field names, the Field row can contain an expression.

Syntax

NewFieldName: Expression

Definition

- *NewFieldName* is a name created by the developer. This name is used to reference the field in VBA code. The NewFieldName also appears as the column heading when the query is displayed.

- *Expression* can include mathematical operators, string operators, and built-in Access functions.

Code Example

The following expression returns a column that concatenates a first name and a last name:

```
PersonName: [FirstName] & " " & [LastName]
```

FirstName and LastName are fields in a table. PersonName is the name of the new field returned by the expression. The & (ampersand) symbol concatenates the value in FirstName with a space and the value in last name. For a particular row, if Robert is the value of FirstName and Smith is the value of LastName, PersonName is "Robert Smith". When field names are used within an expression, they must be placed inside brackets.

Joins

Join lines between tables are a critical portion of the Design view of the query. Access supports three types of joins, which are specified through the Join Properties dialog box shown in Figure 2-13. On most occasions, you will choose the first join type. This join type (the default) is called an inner join. An **inner join** includes rows only when the fields being compared contain matching values. Rows that do not have a match (for example, a current student without an entry in tblLevelingNeeded) are not included in the result.

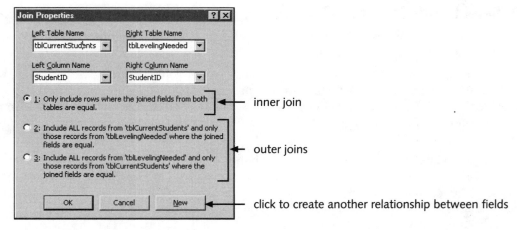

Figure 2-13   Join Properties dialog box

The other join types provide more data in the result. You can choose to include all rows from one table regardless of whether the field being compared contains a matching value. For example, you may choose to have all tblCurrentStudents rows in the result, regardless of whether the student has a tblLevelingNeeded row. This type of join is called an **outer join**. Both of the last two join types in Figure 2-13 produce outer joins. To change the type of join between tables, right-click the join line and then click Join Properties from the shortcut menu.

Total Queries

In addition to retrieving rows of data that meet some criteria, queries can summarize data by aggregating amounts across multiple rows. Select queries that aggregate values are called **totals queries**. Clicking the Totals button in the Query Design toolbar adds a Total row. The list box in the Total row lists the available aggregate functions (for example, Sum, Avg, Min, Max). The **Group By** item in the Total list box tells Access to aggregate the other fields per each unique value within the Group By field (for example, the number of courses per department). A **Where** specification in the Total row states that the field will be tested for a criterion before it is included in the aggregations specified by the other columns.

A **crosstab** query is similar to a totals query, except that the former requires at least two Group By fields. At least one Group By field is identified as a Row Heading and at least one is identified as a Column Heading. In the resulting display, the aggregated field is placed at the intersection of the corresponding row and column in a spreadsheet-like format.

TIP

A frustrating aspect of any database development environment is figuring out certain syntax requirements that are not part of standard SQL. The following list identifies some of the nuances in Access:

- Dates in Access are surrounded by pound signs (for example, #10/14/99#). Usually, the pound signs are placed around a date automatically when you leave a cell in the query's design grid.
- Field names that are used in expressions or in the Criteria row should be placed within brackets. For example, to test whether the quantity-in-stock field is less than the reorder point field in an inventory table, you would type quantity-in-stock in the Field row and < [reorder point] in the Criteria row. Otherwise, Access will treat the criteria as a constant—for example, < "reorder point."
- Query Design view does not easily support SQL subqueries. To simulate a subquery in Design view, create a query that represents the subquery, then create a new query and select the first query (the subquery) from the Show Table dialog box.
- Access supports relational algebra operators such as Union and Intersect. However, these operators are supported only in SQL view.

Creating Select and Crosstab Queries in the Swim Lessons Application

The Swim Lessons application needs to print class lists and other enrollment information for each class. In preparation for the forms and reports that will display the information, you need to create queries. One query will display class lists for summer 2001 classes. It requires the tblClasses, tblStudents, and tblEnrollment tables.

To create a query that lists students in each summer 2001 class:

1. If it is not already open, open **SwimReg.mdb**.

2. If necessary, click the **Queries** object type in the Database window Object Bar.

3. Double-click the **Create query in Design view** shortcut.

4. Hold down the **Ctrl** key, and then click **tblClasses**, **tblEnrollment**, and **tblStudents** in the Show Table dialog box. Click the **Add** button. All three tables are added to the Query Design view. The join lines between the tables should also be displayed.

5. Close the **Show Table** dialog box.

6. Place **Level**, **SectionID**, **Semester**, **Days**, and **Time** from tblClasses into the Field row of the design grid by double-clicking each field name in the table.

7. Click in the **blank column** next to the Time column, and then press **Shift+F2**. The Zoom window opens.

8. Type **Name: [LastName] & ", " & [FirstName] & " " & [MiddleInitial]** in the Zoom window, and then click the **OK** button. Remember that the ampersand is the operator that concatenates text data. The comma and spaces between quotation marks place these characters between the various parts of the person's name.

9. Specify **Ascending** in the Sort row of the Name column (the column in which you are currently working). Also specify **Ascending** in the Level and SectionID columns. These choices will cause Access to sort by Level, then by SectionID, and finally by Name (Access sorts the leftmost sorted field first).

10. Type **01b** in the Criteria row of Semester. This values restricts the query to displaying only rows that have Semester equal to 01b.

11. Save the query as **qryClassRoster**, and then close the query.

12. Display the **Datasheet** view of the query to see the results. Notice that each row contains fields from tblClasses and tblStudents. The Name column concatenates the values from the appropriate fields. If Access prompts you for a value, one of the fields in the Name expression is probably incorrect. If this occurs, enter Design view and place the insertion point in the Field row of the Name expression, and press **Shift+F2**. Double-check that the expression matches Step 8 and repeat Steps 9 through 12.

13. Close and save the query.

As currently designed, the query finds only those majors that have students enrolled. You want to display all of the classes, even if no corresponding records from tblEnrollment exist. You can do so by creating a query in which Join properties display all records from tblClasses.

To display all records from tblClasses in qryClassRosters:

1. Create a new **query** in Design view.

2. Add **tblClasses** from the Show Table dialog box. Do the same for **tblEnrollment**. Note that Access outer joins work best when only two tables are included in the query. Close the Show Table dialog box.

3. Place **Level**, **SectionID**, and **Semester** from tblClasses in the Field row. Place **SID** from tblEnrollment in the Field row.

4. Place **01b** in the Criteria row for Semester.

5. Right-click on the **join line** between tblClasses and tblEnrollment.

6. Click **Join Properties** from the shortcut menu.

7. Click the **Include ALL records from 'tblClasses' and only those records from 'tblEnrollment' where the joined fields are equal** option button.

8. Click **OK** to close the Join Properties dialog box.

9. Display the **Datasheet** view. The rows now include classes that do not have students.

10. Save the query as **qryAllClassEnrollment**.

11. Close the query.

You can use a totals query to retrieve aggregate information about classes. This type of query can be used to quickly indicate the enrollment count.

To count the number of students per level in the summer 2001 classes:

1. Create a new query using the Design view, add **tblClasses**, and then add **tblEnrollment** from the Show Table dialog box. Close the **Show Table** dialog box.

2. Click the **Totals** button in the Query Design toolbar. The Total row appears in the design grid.

3. Place **Level** from tblClasses and **SID** from tblEnrollment in the Field row, and then make sure the Total row for Level states **Group By**.

4. Select **Count** in the Total combo box for SID.

5. Save the query as **qryStudentsPerLevel**, and display it in Datasheet view to see the results of the query. The results should list the levels in one column and the number of levels in another column, as shown in Figure 2-14.

6. Close the datasheet.

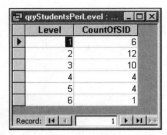

Figure 2-14   Datasheet view of the qryStudentsPerLevel Totals query

Managers of the swimming program may want to see enrollment trends by semester and level. To accomplish this goal, a crosstab query could be used.

To create a crosstab query that counts the number of students per level and semester:

1. Create a new query using the Design view, and then select and add **tblClasses** and **tblEnrollment**. Close the Show Table dialog box.

2. Click **Query** on the menu bar, and then click **Crosstab Query**. The Total and Crosstab rows appear in the design grid.

3. Place **Level** and **Semester** from tblClasses and **SID** from tblEnrollment in the Field row.

4. Set up the Total row so that it contains **Group By** values for Level and Semester and **Count** for SID.

5. Set up the Crosstab row so that Level is a **Column Heading**, Semester is a **Row Heading**, and SID is a **Value**, as shown in Figure 2-15.

6. Save the query as **qryStudentTrends**.

7. Display the Datasheet view to see the results of the crosstab query.

8. Close the datasheet.

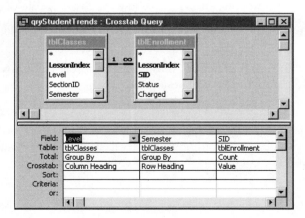

Figure 2-15   Design view of the qryStudentTrends crosstab query

Action Queries

Action queries are a powerful tool for changing the data stored in Access tables. Figure 2-16 displays the action query used to delete denied prospects from the tblProspects table in MU-DSci. This query contains one column. The query is invoked by VBA code that is triggered by the Clear Denials button on frmSwitchboard.

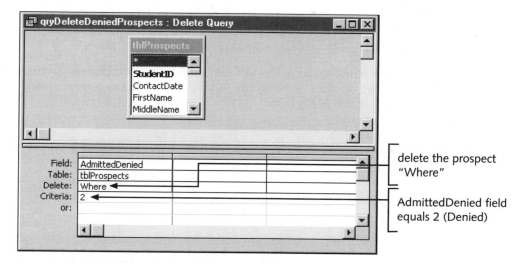

delete the prospect
"Where"

AdmittedDenied field
equals 2 (Denied)

Figure 2-16   Design view of qryDeleteDeniedProspects

You can start action queries by selecting the desired action query from the Query menu in Query Design view. Access supports four types of action queries: delete, make-table, update, and append. **Delete queries** remove rows from a table. In Figure 2-16, Access will delete all Prospects that have an AdmittedDenied field equal to 2 (Denied). **Make-table queries** are similar to select queries, except that the query results are physically stored in a new table. **Append queries** are similar to make-table queries, except that the results of the select query are appended to an existing Access table. **Update queries** change field values in existing rows in a table.

Creating Action Queries for the Swim Lessons Application

Frequently, the swimming classes offered in one semester are similar to those offered in a previous semester. The Append query can be used to quickly create new tblClasses records.

To create a query that appends new class records for 02b based on the values for 01b:

1. Create a new query in Design view that uses tblClasses.

2. Click **Query** on the menu bar, and then click **Append Query** in the menu.

3. Select **tblClasses** from the Table Name list box, and then click **OK**.

4. Place all fields in tblClasses, except LessonIndex, into the Field row of the query design grid. The Append To row is filled in automatically.

5. Delete **Semester** from the Append To row in the Semester column. The Semester column will be used to ensure that only classes that were offered in 01b are added to the table. The new semester, however, will be 02b.

6. Type **"01b"** in the Criteria row for Semester (The quotation marks are necessary, but if you do not add them yourself, Access will add them for you when the focus leaves the text box.), click in a blank column, and then type **"02b"** in the Field row of the new blank column. After you move the insertion point, "Expr1:" will be added to the row.

7. In the same column, select **Semester** in the Append To row.

8. Click the **Run** button in the toolbar. A message will appear indicating the number of rows to add. If the number of new rows added appears reasonable (<30), click **Yes** in the dialog box.

9. Save the query as **qryNewClasses**.

10. Check **tblClasses** to see whether the new rows were added. View the table.

11. Close the window.

To update the price of a new class, you can use an Update query.

To increase the price of classes offered in 02b to $35:

1. Create a new query in Design view that uses **tblClasses**.

2. Click **Query** on the menu bar, and then click **Update Query**. The Update To row is added to the query design grid.

3. Place **Price** in the Field row, and then type **35** in the Update To row of Price.

4. Place **Semester** in the Field Row, and then type **02b** in the Criteria row of Semester. Figure 2-17 illustrates the Design view.

5. Click **Run** in the toolbar. If the dialog box displays a realistic number of row updates (<30), then click **Yes** to run the query.

6. Save the query as **qryUpdatePrice**.

7. Close the dialog box, and then display the Datasheet view for tblClasses to see the results.

8. Close the window.

Parameter Queries

Access applications frequently contain code that references or triggers a query. A particular query can be used more often when certain values in the query can be modified. **Parameter queries** use parameters to substitute for the constant values that are placed in the query grid. VBA code can then substitute new values for the parameter values. If VBA or an Access form does not set the parameter value before running the query, then Access will prompt for the needed value.

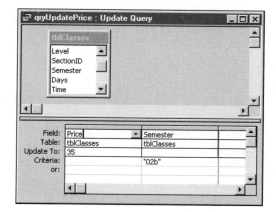

Figure 2-17   Design view of the qryUpdatePrice update query

Using a Parameter Query with qryClassRoster in the Swim Lessons Application

Currently, qryClassRoster displays class rosters for semester 01b. A parameter in the qryClassRoster query can be used to display rosters for any semester.

To update qryClassRoster to contain a parameter:

1. Display **qryClassRoster** in Design view.

2. Click **Query** on the menu bar, and then click **Parameters**. The Parameter window will open.

3. Type **prmSemester** in the Parameter column, and select **Text** from the combo box in the Data Type column. Your Query Parameters window should resemble the one shown in Figure 2-18. Click **OK** to close the window.

4. Delete **01b** from the Criteria row in the Semester column, and type **[prmSemester]** in its place.

5. Click the **View** button on the toolbar. Access will prompt you for prmSemester.

6. Type **01a** at the prompt, and then click **OK**. The datasheet is displayed with 01a as the semester.

7. Save the query and then close the Datasheet view.

8. Close the database window and exit Access.

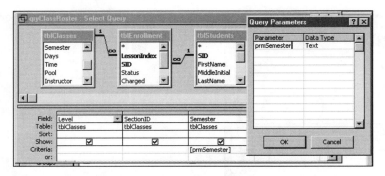

Figure 2-18   Design view and Parameter window of the qryClassRoster parameter query

SQL Syntax

If you do not already know SQL syntax, the Access query design facility can help you understand and learn it. SQL syntax is sometimes used within a VBA module. Clicking SQL view
in the View drop-down list arrow displays the SQL statement that Access generated from the
query design grid. If you need an SQL statement within a VBA module, you can create the
query in Query Design view and then copy and paste the necessary SQL syntax. The basic
syntax for a select statement follows.

Syntax

SELECT *<field list>*
FROM *<table list>*
[WHERE *<criteria>***]**
[GROUP BY *<group by fields>***]**
[ORDER BY *<fields to sort>***]** ;

Dissection

- SELECT *<field list>* is the list of fields, separated by commas, that will be displayed. The
  field list corresponds to the fields found in the Field row that have the Show row
  checked in the query design grid.

- FROM *<table list>* is the list of tables, separated by commas, from which the data are
  retrieved. The table list may also contain the join conditions. The tables in the table list
  correspond to the tables displayed in the Query Design view.

- The optional WHERE *<criteria>* are the conditions that a row in the table(s) must meet
  before data from the row will be displayed. The criteria correspond to the Criteria row
  of the query design grid. If the query contains more than one column with a Criteria
  specification, then the criteria in the SQL statement are connected with the AND
  operator. If the query uses more than one Criteria row, then the criteria are connected
  with the OR operator. Join conditions can also be specified as criteria.

- The optional GROUP BY *<group by fields>* is the list of Group By fields that are speci-
  fied in the Total row of a Totals query.

■ The optional ORDER BY <*fields to sort*> indicates the sort order. The same fields are used in the Sort row in the query design grid.

The SQL view for the query displayed in Figure 2-11 is:

Code Example

```
SELECT tblLevelingNeeded.StudentID, tblLevelingNeeded.AreaCode,
tblLevelingNeeded.CourseNo

FROM tblLevelingNeeded

WHERE (((tblLevelingNeeded.AreaCode)="MKTG") AND
((tblLevelingNeeded.CourseNo)="641"));
```

One possible SQL syntax for the query displayed in Figure 2-12 is the following:

```
SELECT n.StudentID, s.Program, n.AreaCode, n.CourseNo,
c.Courses.Title, n.Needed

FROM tblCurrentStudents s, tblLevelingNeeded n, tblCourses c

WHERE c.CourseNo = n.CourseNo AND c.AreaCode =
n.LevelingNeeded.AreaCode AND s.StudentID = n.StudentID;
```

Although this syntax differs from the syntax that is automatically produced by Access, Access will still understand it. The above SQL statement specifies the join condition in the WHERE clause. The letters that prefix the field names are abbreviations for the tables; they are specified in the FROM statement.

SQL statements for action queries are similar to the SQL syntax for the SELECT statement. For example, the following SQL statement was generated for the delete action query displayed in Figure 2-16.

```
DELETE tblProspects.AdmittedDenied

FROM tblProspects

WHERE (((tblProspects.AdmittedDenied)=2));
```

You should explore the SQL view of several queries to understand the various components of an SQL statement.

CHAPTER SUMMARY

❏ The major focus of most database applications is the retrieval and updating of data; therefore table and relationship specification is commonly the first major step in Access application development. Queries, forms, reports, macros, pages, and modules display or manipulate the data contained in the tables.

❏ Applications should attempt to ensure data integrity (that is, enforce data constraints) through table and relationship design. Primary keys, input masks, validation rules, and referential integrity can all be used to enforce data constraints. In addition, the proper design of the tables is vital to data integrity and can facilitate the creation of other Access objects.

❑ Queries are closely related to tables. Select queries to retrieve data from one more or tables. Totals and crosstab queries aggregate data stored in the tables. Action queries update data in the tables. Like tables, queries are commonly used by forms, reports, pages, macros, and modules. Well-designed tables and queries are a requirement of well-designed applications. In contrast, poorly designed tables and queries can lead to significant problems.

REVIEW QUESTIONS

1. What is prototyping? Which Access features support a prototyping development process?

2. What types of objects are usually developed first in an Access application? Why?

3. A(n) _____ is a field or fields that contain values that uniquely identify a record in a table.

4. A(n) _____ is a field or fields that contain values that are also contained in a field that serves as the primary key for some table.

5. Which of the following field properties does not help prevent invalid data?

    a. Verification Rule

    b. Input Mask

    c. Data Type

    d. Format

6. What is the purpose of the Format field property?

7. What is the purpose of an input mask?

8. A one-to-one relationship between tables A and B is created when the foreign key in table B matches the primary key in table A, and the foreign key in table B is also the primary key in table B. True or False?

9. When Cascade Delete is specified, what happens to a row in a referencing table when you delete the row being referred to (the table containing the primary key)?

    a. The value of the foreign key field is converted to null.

    b. The value of the foreign key field is converted to an empty string.

    c. The row in the referencing table is deleted.

    d. Nothing happens; the deletion is disallowed.

2

10. When Cascade Update is specified, what happens to a row in a referencing table when the row being referred to changes the value of its primary key?

    a. The row in the referencing table is deleted.

    b. Nothing happens; the change to the primary key value is disallowed.

    c. The value in the referencing table is changed to null.

    d. The value of the foreign key in the referencing table changes, too.

11. What is the difference between an inner join and an outer join?

12. Identify four types of action queries.

13. What is the purpose of the Group By value in the Total row of a select query?

    a. It places the Group By fields next to each other.

    b. It causes the totals function to determine a new amount per value of the Group By fields.

    c. It sorts the Group By fields from left to right.

    d. It initiates the use of a subdatasheet.

14. A(n) _____ places a summarized value within grid that contains a row heading and a column heading.

    a. crosstab query

    b. totals query

    c. insert query

    d. select query

15. The following expression will concatenate three fields and two string expressions. How would the expression be used in a query to define a new field named CityState?

    ```
    [City] & ", " & [State] & " " & [Zipcode]
    ```

16. The original design of a nursery inventory system contained the following tables: Flowers(PlantID, PlantDescription, Price, AmountInStock), Tree(PlantID, PlantDescription, Price, AmountInStock). Propose an alternative design.

17. The original table design of a library contained the following tables: Fiction (ISBN, Title, Year, Author-1, Author-2, Author-3, Author-4), NonFiction (ISBN, Title, Year, Author-1, Author-2, Author-3, Author-4). Propose an improved design.

18. Write an input mask that helps the user specify an eight-character equipment ID. The first and last character of the equipment ID must be a letter. The middle six characters are numbers.

19. Write an SQL statement, on paper, that displays the FirstName and LastName for all students who are majors in MISY (that is, for whom the Program field equals MISY). The table tblCurrentStudents in MU-DSci contains the fields that you need.

20. Write an SQL statement, on paper, that displays the Title of all courses offered by the DSCI department in MU-DSci. This information is contained in the tblCourses table.

HANDS-ON PROJECTS

Project 2-1

Natural Parent International

After discussing the information requirements of the Natural Parent International system with several NPI leaders, you determined that the following tables are required:

❏ **tblMembers**(<u>MemberID</u>, FirstName, LastName, SpouseName, Address, City, State, PostalCode, EmailAddress, HomePhone, DateUpdated, MembershipStatus, PaidDate, MembershipDue, MemberType)

- tblMembers contains basic information about people who attend NPI meetings. PaidDate is the date on which a dues payment was made. MembershipDue is the date on which the membership expires. DateUpdated is the date when the record was last updated.

❏ **tblProgram**(<u>SeriesNo, ProgramNo</u>, Description, Date, Time, Address, City, State)

- A tblProgram record exists for each NPI program. Programs occur once per month. SeriesNo is a Long Integer. ProgramNo is an Integer. Together, these fields form the primary key.

❏ **tblProgramsAttended** (<u>MemberID, SeriesNo, ProgramNo</u>, Attended)

- This table stores program attendance information. The key is MemberID, SeriesNo, and ProgramNo.

- The data type of Attended is Yes/No. The value is Yes when the member attended the program.

❏ **tblBooks**(<u>BookID</u>, Title, Publisher, Edition)

- This table records the books in the library.

❏ **tblAuthors**(BookID, LastName, FirstName, MiddleName)

- tblAuthors records the authors of a book.

❏ **tblBookCategory**(<u>Category</u>, Description)

- Books are categorized as B (Breastfeeding), H (Health), M (Miscellaneous), N (Nutrition), or P (Parenting). A book can belong to more than one category.

❏ **tblCategoryOfBook**(<u>BookID, Category</u>)

- This table indicates the category of a book. A book can have more than one category.

❏ **tblCheckOut**(<u>CheckOutID</u>, BookID, MemberID, DateCheckedOut, DateReturned)

- tblCheckOut indicates the member who checked out a book.

- CheckOutID is an AutoNumber/Long Integer.

- BookID is a foreign key with BookID in tblBooks.

- MemberID is a foreign key with MemberID in tblMembers.
- DateCheckedOut and DateReturned are Date/Time fields. A format and input mask should be specified that support four-digit years.
- The DateReturned field must be null, or greater than or equal to DateCheckedOut.

All of the tables except tblCheckout have already been created. You must create this table and add sample data. In addition, several queries will be created in preparation for creating future forms and reports.

Complete these steps:

1. Obtain, install, and open **NPI.mdb**.
2. Create **tblCheckOut** within **NPI.mdb**. Add the input masks and formats that were specified above.
3. Create a table-level validation rule for tblCheckOut to enforce the constraint on DateReturned and DateCheckedOut.
4. Create relationships between tblCheckout and the other tables specified in the tblCheckout description. The relationships with tblCheckout should enforce referential integrity. All the relationships should support Cascade Update. The relationship with tblBooks should also support Cascade Delete.
5. Add sample data to tblCheckout.
6. Create a query that uses tblMembers. The query should display the MemberID and Name for all members. The Name field in the query concatenates [LastName] and [FirstName] (for example, Smith, Anna). Name the query **qrycboNameList**.
7. Create a query that displays checkout information in descending order of CheckOutID. The query requires the use of tblCheckout. This information will be used later to display the most recent checkout information. Name the query **qryCheckOutDescending**.
8. Create a query that displays all fields in tblMembers. The records should be sorted in ascending order on LastName and then FirstName. Name the query **qryMemberLastNameSort**.
9. Create a query that counts the number of times that a particular Title of Book has been checked out. Name the query **qryBookCheckoutCount**.
10. Save your work.

Project 2-2

Metropolitan Performing Arts Company

After discussing the requirements of the Metropolitan Performing Arts Company system, you believe the following tables are required:

❏ **tblPaymentMethods**(PaymentType, Description)

- tblPaymentMethods lists the legal types of payment.

- PaymentType is a four-character text field and the key to tblPaymentMethods. For example, the symbol AE means American Express.

- The Description 20-character text field provides a more detailed description (American Express).

❑ **tblSales**(<u>OrderNo</u>, Date, PaymentType, CheckNo, ApprovalCode, Total)

- tblSales records information about a sale.

- OrderNo is the key. The data type of OrderNo is AutoNumber/Long Integer.

- Date is the date on which the sale was made. The data type for Date fields is Date/Time. A format and input mask should be specified so that the date is displayed with a four-digit year. The default value is today's date.

- PaymentType must match the PaymentType field in tblPaymentMethods.

- CheckNo is a text field that is used to store the check number for those customers paying with checks.

- ApprovalCode is the approval number that is obtained when a credit card is verified with a credit agency. ApprovalCode is a text field because some codes contain dashes and letters.

- Total is a currency field that indicates the total due and paid (payment must be made in full).

❑ **tblPerformance**(<u>PerformanceID</u>, PerformanceName, StartDate, EndDate, Director, Comment)

- tblPerformance records general information about a play or concert.

❑ **tblPerformanceDate**(<u>PerformanceID, DateTime</u>)

- tblPerformanceDate lists the dates and times of the performances.

❑ **tblSections**(<u>Section</u>)

- tblSections lists the sections in the Metropolitan Performing Arts House (for example, Floor, Balcony).

❑ **tblRows**(<u>Section, Row</u>, NumberOfSeats)

- Section and Row form the key. Row is a Long Integer that represents the seat row number.

- NumberOfSeats is a Long Integer that represents the number of seats in the corresponding row.

❑ **tblSectionPrice**(<u>PerformanceID, DateTime, Section</u>, Price)

- tblSectionPrice indicates the price for a seat given a performance, time, and section.

- **tblSeatAvailability**(PerformanceID, DateTime, Section, Row, Seat, Status, OrderNo)

  - PerformanceID, DateTime, and Section match the corresponding rows in tblSectionPrice.

  - Row is a Long Integer that represents the row number.

  - Seat is a Long Integer that represents the seat number.

  - Status is a text field. Legal values for Status are Available, Unavailable, and Complimentary.

  - OrderNo matches the OrderNo in tblSales.

- **tblReturn**(PerformanceID, DateTime, Section, NumTickets, DollarReturn)

  - tblReturn keeps track of the number and dollar value of tickets that were returned.

- **tblPerformer**(PerformerID, FirstName, MiddleName, LastName)

  - tblPerformer contains information about performers.

- **tblPerformanceOfPerformer**(PerformanceID, DateTime, PerformerID)

  - tblPerformanceOfPerformer indicates the performer who is performing at a particular time.

Complete these steps:

1. Obtain, install, and open **MPAData.mdb**. All of the tables except **tblSales** have been created. In addition, the validation rules and relationships for tblSeatAvailability have not been created.

2. Create the **tblSale.mdb** tables described above. Add the input masks, formats, and default values that were described.

3. Create a field-level validation rule for Status (in tblSeatAvailability).

4. Create the relationship between tblSales and tblSeatAvailability. Create a relationship between tblSeatAvailability and the other tables described above. The following relationships should use Cascade Update, but not Cascade Delete: tblSales and tblSeatAvailability, tblPaymentMethods and tblSales. The remaining relationships should use Cascade Update and Cascade Delete.

5. Add sample data to tblSales, and update the OrderNo field for some of the sold seats in tblSeatAvailability.

6. Create another database to hold the forms, queries, reports, macros, and VBA code. Name the new database **MPA.mdb**. Link the tables in **MPAData.mdb** to **MPA.mdb**.

7. Create a query called **qryPerformanceDateDetail**. The query should display the PerformanceID, DateTime, PerformanceName, and Director of all performances. This query will be used in future chapters.

8. Create a query called **qrySeatsForPerformance**. This query should display all fields in tblSeatAvailability plus the Price for the seat. It requires the tblSectionPrice and tblSeatAvailability tables.

9. Create a query called **qryTotalPerPerformance**. This query should display the PerformanceID, PerformanceName, DateTime, and the Total Revenue for the performance. Summing the Price for all seats that are unavailable will determine the total revenue.

10. Save your work.

Project 2-3

Foreign Language Institute

After discussing the information requirements of the Foreign Language Institute system with several FLI leaders, you determined that the following tables are required:

◻ **tblAdvertisements**(<u>AdID</u>, MagazineID, AdDate, Page, AdCost)

- AdID is the key. The data type of AdID and MagazineID is Number/Byte. MagazineID is a foreign key with MagazineID in tblMagazines.

- AdDate is the date on which an advertisement is placed in a magazine. The input mask and format should display a four-digit year.

- Page is a Number/Integer that specifies the page number where the ad appears.

- AdCost is a Currency field.

◻ **tblCalls**(<u>CallID</u>, CustomerID, CallCategory, ProductID, CallDate, CallTime, Detail)

- tblCalls contains product information, the call date and time, and details about each call made by a customer. CustomerID is a Number/Byte that refers to the CustomerID in tblCustomers.

◻ **tblCustomers**(<u>CustomerID</u>, FirstName, LastName, CompanyName, CompanyType, Address, City, State, PostalCode, Country, PrefCustomer, PhoneNumber, FaxNumber, Note)

- This table stores general customer information.

◻ **tblLanguage**(<u>LanguageID</u>, Language)

- tblLanguage records the languages used.

◻ **tblMagazines**(<u>MagazineID</u>, MagazineName, Address, City, State, PostalCode, ContactName, ContactPhone)

- tblMagazines records the magazines in which ads are placed.

◻ **tblProducts**(<u>ProductID</u>, ProdDesc, ProdType, ProdCategory, Language, SpeakerID, QuantityOnHand, Medium, ImpLanguage, Requirements, Price)

- ProductID is the primary key. The data type is Number/Byte.

- ProdDesc is a description of the product. It is a Text field, holding a maximum of 50 characters.

- ProdType (1 = Textbook, 2 = Software), ProdCategory (1 = Beginner, 2 = Intermediate, 3 = Advanced), Medium (1 = Disk, 2 = CDROM, 3 = Book), and SpeakerID are Number/Byte fields.

- Language matches LanguageID in tblLanguage.

- QuantityOnHand is a Number/Integer.

- ImpLanguage describes the implementation language. It is a Text field, holding a maximum of 10 characters.

- Requirements is a Memo field.

- Price is a Currency field.

❑ **tblSales**(<u>SaleID</u>, CustomerID, DateOfSale, SalesPerson, DateFilled, DatePaid)

- tblSales contains general information about the customer and date of sale.

❑ **tblSalesDetail**(<u>SaleID</u>, <u>LineNo</u>, ProductID, QtyPurchased, Disposition)

- This table maintains the detailed sales data for a particular row in tblSales.

- SaleID and LineNo together form the primary key.

- Disposition is a Number/Byte. It has the following values: 1 = Filled, 2 = Backordered.

❑ **tblSalesPeople**(<u>SocialSecurityNumber</u>, FirstName, MiddleName, LastName, Title, EmailName, Extension, Address, City, State, PostalCode, HomePhone, WorkPhone, Birthdate, DateHired, Salary, Deductions, SpouseName)

- tblSalesPeople stores information about sales employees.

❑ **tblSpeakers**(<u>SpeakerID</u>, FirstName, LastName, Address, City, State, PostalCode, PhoneNumber, Note)

- tblSpeakers stores information about the people who provide native voices on the products. The key is SpeakerID.

All of the tables except tblAdvertisments have already been created. In addition, constraint mechanisms have not been developed to enforce the ProdType, ProdCategory, Medium, and Language fields in tblProducts.

Complete these steps:

1. Obtain, install, and open **FLI.mdb**.
2. Create **tblAdvertisements**. Add the input mask and format specified above.
3. Create relationship(s) to tblAdvertisements that were described above. The relationship(s) should support Cascade Update and Cascade Delete.
4. Add sample data to tblAdvertisements.
5. Create mechanisms to enforce the constraints on ProdType, ProdCategory, and Medium in tblProducts.
6. Save your work.

Project 2-4
King William Hotel

After discussing the information requirements of the King William Hotel system with several managers, you determined that the following tables are required:

- **tblCafeBillDetail**(<u>BillNo</u>, LineNo, ItemNo, TransactionDate, Amount, RoomNo)

  - BillNo is the key. The data type is Number/Long Integer.

  - LineNo is a sequential value numbering the line item on the bill. The data type of LineNo is Number/Long Integer. LineNo and BillNo together make up the composite key for tblCafeBillDetail.

  - ItemNo is a Number/Long Integer. It refers to the items on the menu, stored in tblCafeMenu.

  - TransactionDate is the date on which an item was purchased. The input mask and format should display a four-digit year.

  - Amount is a Currency field.

  - RoomNo is a Number/Long Integer. It refers to tblRoom.

- **tblCafeMenu**(<u>ItemNo</u>, ItemName, ItemDesc, Price)

  - tblCafeMenu contains a record for each item on the menu.

- **tblCustomer**(<u>CustomerNo</u>, LastName, FirstName, MI, Address, City, State, Zip, Phone, CreditCardNumber, CardExpDate)

  - tblCustomer stores information about customers.

- **tblHouseKeeping**(<u>TaskNo</u>, RequirementDesc, RoomNumber, Status)

  - This table records tasks that the Housekeeping department needs to perform in rooms.

  - Status is a Yes/No field. Yes implies that the task has been completed.

- **tblReservation**(<u>ReservationNo</u>, RoomNo, StartDate, EndDate, Amount, CustomerNo)

  - This table records the reservations.

  - ReservationNo is the primary key. The data type is AutoNumber.

  - RoomNo is the room reserved. It refers to tblRoom.

  - StartDate and EndDate are the beginning and ending dates of the reservation. They are Date/Time fields. The input mask and format should display a four-digit year.

  - Amount is a Currency field. It will eventually store the total charge associated with the reservation.

  - CustomerNo is a Number/Long Integer. It refers to tblCustomer.

2

❑ **tblRoom**(<u>RoomNo</u>, Category, Unavailable, NeedsCleaning)

- tblRoom describes the room.

- Unavailable is a Yes/No field. Yes implies that the room is unavailable.

- NeedsCleaning is a Yes/No field. Yes implies that the room needs cleaning.

❑ **tblRoomDes**(<u>Category</u>, CategoryDesc, Rate)

- tblRoomDes describes a particular kind of room. Category is the primary key and has the values Economy, Deluxe, or Suite.

All of the tables except tblReservation and tblCafeBillDetail have already been created. You must create these two tables and any corresponding relationships. Sample data should be added. In addition, several queries will be created in preparation for creating future forms and reports.

Complete these steps:

1. Obtain, install, and open **KWH.mdb**.

2. Create the **tblReservation** and **tblCafeBillDetail** tables. Add the input masks, formats, and validation rules as specified.

3. Create relationships between the tables described above. All of the relationships should support Cascade Update and Cascade Delete.

4. Add sample data to tblReservation and tblCafeBillDetail.

5. Create a query based on tblReservation. Place the RoomNo, StartDate, and EndDate in the query. Name the query **qryReservedRooms1**.

6. Create a query based on qryReservedRooms1 and tblRoom. Place the RoomNo from both data sources in the query. Add the Unavailable and Category attributes from tblRoom to the query. Change the join type to an outer join that includes all rows from tblRoom. (*Hint*: Double-click the line connecting the two data sources.) Name the query **qryReservedRooms2**.

7. Create a query based on tblCafeBillDetail. Place all of the attributes in the query. Name the query **qryCafeDetailFilter**.

8. Close all open windows.

9. Save your work.

Project 2-5

Workers' Compensation Commission System

After discussing the information requirements of the Workers' Compensation Commission (WCC) system with several managers, you determined that the following tables are required:

- **tblCompany**(Company Name, <u>Comp Account Number</u>, Address, City, State, Zip Code, Phone Number, Insurance Carrier)

    - tblCompany contains information about the companies that use WCC.

- **tblCPT**(<u>CPT Code</u>, Description)

    - tblCPT provides information that is located in a medical report.

- **tblDoctor**(<u>Physician's License Number</u>, Doctor's Name, Doctor's Title, Doctor's Mailing Address, Doctor's City, Doctor's State, Doctor's Zip, Doctor's Phone Number)

    - This table stores information about doctors.

- **tblICD-9**(<u>ICD-9 Code</u>, Description)

    - ICD-9 Code is a code placed in a medical record.

- **tblPatient**(<u>Medical Record Number</u>, Patient's Name, Date of Birth, Patient's Mailing Address, Patient's City, Patient's State, Patient's Zip Code, Patient's Phone Number, Physician's License Number, Social Security Number, Comp Account Number)

    - This table stores patient information. The key is Medical Record Number.

    - Medical Record Number is a Text field, holding a maximum of 50 characters.

    - Date of Birth is a Date/Time field. The input mask and format should display a four-digit year.

    - The following are Text fields (size is in parentheses): Patient's Name (30), Patient's Mailing Address (40), Patient's City (20), Patient's State (2), Patient's Zip Code (10), Patient's Phone Number (15), Social Security Number (15).

    - Physician's License Number is a Text field, holding a maximum of 10 characters. It refers to tblDoctor.

    - Comp Account Number is a Text field, holding a maximum of 15 characters. It refers to tblCompany.

- **tblWCCA**(<u>Medical Record Number</u>, <u>Date of Visit</u>, TWCC #, Carrier's Claim #, Physician's License Number, Date of Injury, Diagnosis 1, Diagnosis 2, Diagnosis 3, CPT Code 1, Diagnosis Reference 1, CPT Code 2, Diagnosis Reference 2, CPT Code 3, Diagnosis Reference 3, CPT Code 4, Diagnosis Reference 4, Anticipated Date - Limited, Anticipated Date - Max Improv, Anticipated Date - Full Time, History of Occupational Injury or Illness, Significant Past Medical History, Clinical Assessment

Findings, Test Results, Treatment Plan, Referrals/Change of Doctor, Referral/Change Detail, Medications or Durable Medical Equipment, Prognosis, Printed)

- This table records all of the data associated with a Form A for a patient for a specific injury.

❑ **tblWCCB**(<u>Medical Record Number</u>, <u>Date of Visit</u>, TWCC #, Carrier's Claim #, Physician's License Number, Date of Injury, Diagnosis 1, Diagnosis 2, Diagnosis 3, Treatment at This Visit, CPT Code 1, Diagnosis Reference 1, CPT Code 2, Diagnosis Reference 2, CPT Code 3, Diagnosis Reference 3, CPT Code 4, Diagnosis Reference 4, Anticipated Date – Limited, Anticipated Date – Max Improv, Anticipated Date – Full Time, Reason Rep Subsequent, Reason Rep Released, Limited/Normal Activity, Reason Rep Date, Changing Treating Doctors, Name of New Treating Doctor, Address of New Doc, Professional License of New Doc, Date Changing Treating Doctors, Discharge from Name of Hospital, Discharge Date, Changes in Injured Employee's Condition, Treatment Plan, Referrals, Medications or Durable Medical Equipment, Prognosis, Compliance by Injured Employee with Recommended Trmt, Printed)

- This table records all of the data associated with a Form B for a patient for a specific injury.

❑ **tblWCCC**(<u>Medical Record Number</u>, <u>Date of Visit</u>, TWCC #, Carrier's Claim #, Physician's License Number, Date of Injury, Diagnosis 1, Diagnosis 2, Diagnosis 3, Max Med Improv Date, Maximum Medical Improvement, Impairment Rating, Doctor Type, Required Medical Exam Doc, Date of This Report, Treating Doctor's Review, Printed Name of Treating Doctor, Printed)

- This table records all of the data associated with a Form C for a patient for a specific injury.

All of the tables have been created except tblPatient. You must create this table and establish relationships between tblPatient and the other relevant tables. Sample data should be added. In addition, several queries will be created in preparation for creating future forms and reports.

Complete these steps:

1. Obtain, install, and open **WCC.mdb**.

2. Create **tblPatient** as it was described above. Add the input masks and formats specified.

3. Create the relationships between tblPatient and the necessary tables. All of the relationships should enforce referential integrity. The relationships should also support Cascade Update and Cascade Delete.

4. Add sample data to the table.

5. Create a query based on tblCompany. Place the Company Name and the Comp Account Number in the query. Sort the Company Name in ascending order. Name the query **qrySortCompanies**.

6. Create a query based on tblDoctor. Place the Doctor's Name and the Physician's License Number in the query. Sort the Doctor's Name in ascending order. Name the query **qrySortDoctors**.

7. Create a query based on tblPatient. Place the Patient's Name and the Medical Record Number in the query. Sort the Patient's Name in ascending order. Name the query **qrySortPatients**.

8. Create a query that joins tblWCCA, tblPatient, and tblCompany. Place all attributes in the query. Set the criteria for the Printed attribute in tblWCCA equal to No. Name the query **qryWCCA**.

9. Make a copy of qryWCCA and name it **qryWCCASingleRecord**.

10. Create a query that joins tblWCCB, tblPatient, and tblCompany. Place all attributes in the query. Set the criteria for the Printed attribute in tblWCCB equal to No. Name the query **qryWCCB**.

11. Make a copy of qryWCCB and name it **qryWCCBSingleRecord**.

12. Create a query that joins tblWCCC, tblPatient, and tblCompany. Place all attributes in the query. Set the criteria for the Printed attribute in tblWCCC equal to No. Name the query **qryWCCC**.

13. Make a copy of qryWCCC and name it **qryWCCCSingleRecord**.

14. Create an update query that joins tblWCCA, tblPatient, and tblCompany. Place only the Printed attribute from tblWCCA in the query. Set the Update value to Yes. Set the criteria for the Printed attribute in tblWCCA equal to No. Name the query **qryWCCAPrintedUpdate**.

15. Create an update query that joins tblWCCB, tblPatient, and tblCompany. Place only the Printed attribute from tblWCCB in the query. Set the Update value to Yes. Set the criteria for the Printed attribute in tblWCCB equal to No. Name the query **qryWCCBPrintedUpdate**.

16. Create an update query that joins tblWCCC, tblPatient, and tblCompany. Place only the Printed attribute from tblWCCC in the query. Set the Update value to Yes. Set the criteria for the Printed attribute in tblWCCC equal to No. Name the query **qryWCCCPrintedUpdate**.

17. Close all open windows.

18. Save your work.

3

REVIEWING FORMS, REPORTS, AND DATA ACCESS PAGES

The Interfaces to an Access Application

In this chapter you will:

♦ Design easy-to-use forms and data access pages that facilitate the entry of valid data

♦ Bind forms, reports, and data access pages to tables and queries

♦ Create expressions that display the result of calculations

♦ Create groups within the database window that contain related forms, reports, and data access pages

---

Once you are comfortable with storing and retrieving data, it is time to learn how to display it in a user-friendly way. In addition to table and query datasheets, Access offers three ways to display data: forms, reports, and data access pages. Most end users of an Access application will not interact with tables and queries directly. Instead, they will interact with the database through forms, reports, and data access pages. To end users, forms *are* the application when they access an application located on their own PC or local area network. Similarly, pages *are* the application when the user is accessing an application through the World Wide Web (WWW), and reports *are* the application when the data must be printed on paper.

This chapter will teach you how to create and modify well-designed forms, reports, and data access pages that (1) prevent the end user from entering invalid data and (2) display the data that the user may access. As you will discover, each of these objects contains **sections** (for example, header and detail sections in forms, page headers and group headers in reports, and captions and headers in pages) and **controls** (for example, text boxes and check boxes).

In addition, you will see that forms, reports, data access pages and their corresponding sections and controls have properties. A **property sheet** is a window in which you can modify the properties of an object. Programmers use property sheets to specify the format of an object (for example, colors and type of scroll bars) and to specify valid input.

Also in this chapter, you will learn how use, add, and manipulate sections and controls and their properties. Finally, you will create useful and aesthetically pleasing interfaces according to general style conventions.

FORMS, CONTROLS, AND PROPERTIES

Access applications designed by nonprofessionals often require the user to enter and view data through table and query datasheets. This method can prove difficult for the end user to master because datasheets cannot be customized to complement other documents in the user's work environment. For example, entry of a prospect's application (in MU-DSci) is facilitated when the layout of the data entry screen is similar to the application submitted by the student. Professionally styled Access applications have users enter and view data through forms (or pages on the Web). Forms can be customized to mirror other documents in the work environment. In addition, they help enforce data integrity by restricting the data that the user may enter.

To become a competent professional who designs effective forms, you must understand which components make up a form, how bound and unbound forms differ, how to choose the best type of control for a given situation, how to use properties effectively, and how to design an easy-to-use form. Each of these subjects will be discussed in the following subsections. Only then will you begin working with the actual forms.

Components of a Form

Access forms consist of the Form Header, Detail, and Form Footer sections. Each section may contain many controls. A **control**, as it relates to forms, refers to any object that is placed on the form, including text boxes, combo boxes, and command buttons (see Figure 3-1).

Controls in a **Form Header** appear at the top of the screen. The Form Header frequently contains column headings for a form. The contents displayed in the Form Header usually do not change, no matter what record the user is viewing. Controls that appear in the **Form Footer** are shown at the bottom of the screen. This section frequently contains controls that summarize values that appear in the **Detail** section (for example, the total number of students in a class). The values displayed through the controls located in the **Detail** section change depending upon the record that is currently being viewed. Sliding the scroll bar and clicking the navigator buttons at the bottom of the form cause a form to advance to another record.

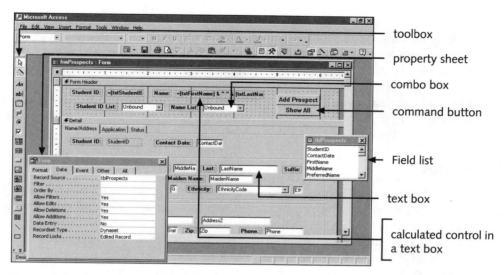

Figure 3-1   Design view of frmProspects

Unbound and Bound Forms

Access forms can be classified into two types: bound and unbound. A **bound form** is a form that is tied to, or associated with, either a table or query. The table or query with which the form is associated—that is, the source of the data—is the record source. The **record source** of a form is identified by the form's RecordSource property. The **RecordSource** property is listed in the Data tab of the form's property sheet. It may contain the name of a table, the name of a query, or an SQL statement. A query is used as a record source when data must be processed before being displayed. For example, some bound forms require data from more than one table. When a bound form is open, the data of the record source is displayed. Most of the forms in MU-DSci, including frmProspects, are bound forms.

An **unbound form** is a form that is not tied to any table or query; that is, it does not have a record source. An example of an unbound form is a **splashscreen,** which displays one or more brief messages to the user that automatically appear and disappear. For example, a splashscreen with a logo often appears when software is loading. Another type of unbound form is the **switchboard.** Switchboards do not display data, but rather contain command buttons that open reports or other forms.

Controls

A control on a bound form is tied to a field in the record source through the control's **ControlSource** property, which is located in the Data tab of the control's property sheet. Normally, the ControlSource property contains the name of a field in the record source. When a user types a new value in the control, the value of the corresponding field in the record source changes. Controls that do not have a value for their control source property are called **unbound controls.** Unbound controls sometimes supply data to a VBA module that the module uses to find a record matching the value of the unbound control.

Regardless of whether the controls are bound or unbound, a major issue faced by a designer is choosing the type of controls that will appear on the form. Access developers have many controls from which to choose. The major consideration when choosing the control type is the number of valid values. Text box controls are used when numerous valid values exist. A check box control is used when a value is either "Yes" or "No." Option buttons are used when the user can select from a few possible values (for example, Gender is either "Male" or "Female"). Finally, combo boxes are used when the legal values can be specified, but many values exist. This issue will be explored further later in this chapter.

Properties

Forms, the sections of a form, and the controls in a form all have property sheets. A property sheet contains five tabs. Properties in the **Data tab** specify the record or control source. In addition, these properties can be used to validate and lock a control—users cannot enter data into a locked control. Properties in the **Format tab** control the aesthetics of the object. Properties in the **Event tab** are used to link an object to a VBA procedure or macro. The **Other tab** contains miscellaneous properties such as the name of the object. The **Name** property is used in VBA procedures and macros to refer to the object. Finally, the **All tab** displays all of the properties specified.

Many properties are common across the various controls, sections, and forms. Some types of controls (for example, the combo box), however, possess properties that many other types do not possess. As you will discover in this chapter and many others, manipulating properties is a key ingredient for successful Access application development.

Form Style

Users of your Access application will likely judge the quality of the application based on their reaction to the design of your forms. When you, as an end user, declare an application to be friendly or unfriendly, you are reacting to the style of the interface. Consequently, the programmer must carefully plan the design. Like the application itself, form design should be thoroughly reviewed with a group of users before the application is released for general use.

The following tips facilitate good form style:

- Use a consistent color and formatting scheme across related forms that distinguishes between locked controls and unlocked controls. Also, use a consistent color and formatting scheme that identifies places on the form that can be clicked.

- Use a consistent button, menu, and toolbar scheme across related forms. Whenever possible, locate menu items, toolbars, and buttons in approximately the same place on each form. Also, keep the icons or text prompts the same when the function of the button, menu, or toolbar button is the same.

- Restrict the amount of text and pictures on a form to a volume that a user can easily comprehend. A rule of thumb is that most people have difficulty comprehending more than nine pieces of information at one time. If the form contains more than nine controls, for example, try to group them into logical units (for example, with boxes).

- Use a soft coloring scheme that is easy to look at for long periods of time. Commonly used schemes are white text on a blue background, blue or black text on a white background, and black text on a tan or gray background. Examine other user interfaces to determine color schemes that worked or did not work.

- Build an application that helps the user remember valid data entries. For example, use combo boxes instead of text boxes when a user can select from a list of valid values. Do not force the user to memorize information located on one form in order to type the information into a different form.

- Test the user interface for understandability of the graphics (for example, icons on toolbars) and for cultural sensitivity. Many professional developers show a graphic to a potential user (without a textual display) and ask the user what he or she thinks the graphic depicts. If users readily understand the meaning of the graphic, the graphic is approved.

- Determine the type of monitors that will be used in conjunction with your application. Different monitors display forms in slightly different ways. A form that fits on the screen of one monitor may not fit on another monitor, for example. Likewise, color schemes and fonts that look good on one monitor may be unusable on another monitor.

- Use shortcut keys or access keys to allow the selection of menus, toolbars, and command buttons through keystrokes. A **shortcut key** is a keystroke that executes a menu item or command immediately. An **access key** moves the focus to an item in the menu. Although most users will use a mouse with the application, some users prefer a keyboard (for example, when using a laptop), and other users, such as visually impaired users, prefer other accomodations. Shortcut keys and access keys can be specified as properties of an object.

WORKING WITH FORMS

Conceptually, creating a form is a five-step process. First, you tell Access that you would like to create a new form (for example, click New in the Forms tab of the Database window). Second, if you are creating a bound form, you place the name of the record source, or an SQL statement, in the form's RecordSource property. Third, you place the controls on a form. If the control is to be bound, the name of the field must be placed in the control's ControlSource property. Fourth, you set various properties of the forms, sections, and controls. For example, you can place a background image on a form by specifying the path to a picture in a form's **Picture** property. Background colors of controls and form sections are set through the **BackColor** property. The text color of a control is set using a control's **ForeColor** property. Finally, you move the form boundaries, section boundaries, and controls to create an aesthetically pleasing and useful form. Table 3-1 summarizes how you can accomplish some common form design tasks.

Table 3-1   Common form design tasks

Task	Steps
Add or change the record source of a form	Select a table or query in the combo box located in the form's RecordSource property. *Or* Click the Build button next to the RecordSource property and create a query in the query design grid.
Change the control source of a control	Select a field from the ControlSource property combo box located on the control's property sheet.
Add a bound control to a form	Drag the desired field from the Field list.
Add an unbound control to a form	Click a control on the toolbox and drag the size of the control in the desired location on the form.
Change a control to a different type	Right-click the control, and then move the cursor to Change To on the pop-up menu and select the desired type of control.
Change the tab order for controls	Click View in the menu and then click Tab Order. Click Auto Order or drag the controls to the desired sequence. Alternatively, change the Tab Index property (located in the Other tab).
Remove a control from the tab order	Change the control's Tab Stop property to No.
Make selected controls have the same height or width	Hold the Shift key while selecting the desired controls. Click Format and then select Size. Click the desired option.
Create equal space between controls	Hold the Shift key while selecting the desired controls. Click Format and then select Horizontal Spacing or Vertical Spacing. Click Make Equal.
Align controls on left, right, top, or bottom boundaries	Hold the Shift key while selecting the desired controls. Click Format and then select Align. Click the desired option.
Move a control and its label	Click the control, place the cursor in the middle of the control, and drag the control to the desired location.
Move a control or label separately	Click the control or its label, place the cursor over the move handle (located in the left corner), and drag the control or label.
Move a label to the Header section of a form	Click the label and then click Cut. Paste the label into the Header section.
Change a form so that it displays one record at a time or multiple records at a time	Change the Default View property of the form to Single Form to display one record at a time. Change the Default View property to Continuous Forms to display more than one record at a time.

The primary difference between the creation of bound forms and the creation of unbound forms is that for an unbound form you will not set the RecordSource and ControlSource properties. In addition, because unbound forms do not display records in a table or query, it is common practice to remove the navigation buttons that appear on the bottom of the form and the record selector that appears on the side of the form. You can remove these items by selecting No in the form's **NavigationButtons** and **RecordSelector** properties, respectively.

Fortunately, Access provides several wizards that facilitate the creation of bound forms. These wizards first ask you to identify a record source and then ask you to select a form style. After you select these items, the RecordSource property is set automatically, the controls are placed on the form with their ControlSource properties set, and the various color properties are defined. Using a wizard to create an initial version of a form can save valuable time. Once the wizard creates the form, you can modify the features of the form in the form's Design view. Table 3-2 summarizes the features of the form wizards.

Table 3-2   Form design wizards

Wizard	Features	Comments
Create form by using wizard shortcut.	Prompts for one or more tables or queries. Based on the tables and fields selected, the wizard determines the possible types of forms and prompts the developer to select a type.	This approach is a good method for creating a first-cut form. If so prompted, select Columnar form to create a form with a Default View of Single Form (one record is displayed at a time) or select Tabular to create a form with a Default View of Continuous Forms (more than one record is displayed at a time). The wizard may create an SQL statement to obtain data for the form. A wizard prompt may ask whether the developer would like to create a main/subform.
Click New, select Form Wizard, but do not select a table or query from the combo box.	Same as the features for creating a form from the shortcut.	
Click New, select Form Wizard, and select a table or query from the combo box.	Same as the features for creating a form from the shortcut, but the table or query selected in the combo box is automatically selected on the wizard's first screen.	This approach is a good technique for creating a form that is based on a single table or query.
Click New, then select AutoForm: Columnar, AutoForm: Tabular, or AutoForm: Datasheet. Select a table or query from the combo box.	Creates a form with a default value of Single Form, Continuous Forms, or Datasheet, respectively. Does not prompt for more information.	

Table 3-2 Form design wizards (continued)

Wizard	Features	Comments
Click New, select Chart Wizard, and select a table or query from the combo box.	Creates a form with a chart object located on the form. Prompts for the type of chart and the various axes.	In Design view, double-click the chart to modify any aspect of the chart. To make the chart bigger, double-click the chart and resize the chart in the Chart Editor.
Click New, and then click Pivot Table Wizard.	Creates a form with an Excel pivot table object placed on the form.	A pivot table is similar to a cross-tab query, except that the user is allowed to select the rows and columns at runtime. The user of the application can also specify how the cells within the pivot table are aggregated. Frequently used for decision support applications.

TIP Form design wizards sometimes place an SQL statement in the form's RecordSource property. This SQL statement may select all fields and rows from a single table or query. When an SQL statement is placed in the RecordSource property, Access runs the SQL statement before the form is opened. Running an SQL statement is unnecessary, however, when you are simply retrieving all rows and columns from a particular table or predefined query. In such a case, you should use the combo box located in the RecordSource property to select the original table or query and remove the SQL statement.

Creating a Form for tblPayment

Now it's time to apply the information you've learned so far to the task at hand. In this book, you are designing the Swim Lessons application, a system to support swimming lessons. The corresponding file name is **SwimReg.mdb**. You need to create a form to facilitate the entry and display of payment information. This form will be named frmPayment and will be bound to the table tblPayment.

To create frmPayment:

1. Open **SwimReg.mdb**, refresh the table links if necessary, and then click the **Forms** object type.

2. Double-click the **Create form by using wizard** button in the Database window, and then select **Table: tblPayment** in the Tables/Query combo box.

3. Move all fields in Available Fields to Selected Fields, and then click **Next**.

4. Ensure that the option button indicating a **Columnar** form is selected, and then click **Next**.

5. Select the **Standard** style, if necessary, and then click **Next**.

6. Change the title of the form to **frmPayment**.

7. Click the **Modify the form's design** option button, and then click **Finish** to open the form in Design view.

8. If necessary, click the **Properties** button on the toolbar to open the property sheet for the form. If the property sheet is not labeled "Form," click the **Form** selector on the form.

9. If the Format tab is not already active, click the **Format** tab, and then change the Caption property to **Payment**.

10. Click and drag the **right boundary** of the form to enlarge the form.

11. Move, align, and resize the controls so that the form looks like that shown in Figure 3-2.

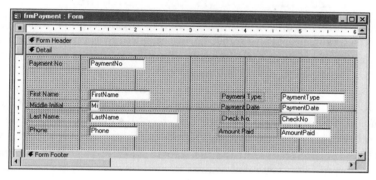

Figure 3-2   Design view of frmPayment

12. Click **View** on the menu bar, and then click **Tab order** to open the Tab Order window. Change the tab order so that the order matches that shown in Figure 3-3, and then click **OK**.

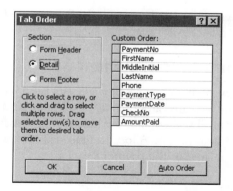

Figure 3-3   Tab order of frmPayment

13. Click the **View** button in the toolbar to switch to Form view. In Form view, use the mouse to drag any **form boundary** to display all data and to eliminate any large blank spaces on the sides or bottom of the form. If necessary, resize the text box controls in Design view.

14. Close and save the form.

WORKING WITH CONTROLS

As you can see, working with forms requires working with controls. Access provides several types of controls. Some controls are used to organize other controls; some are used to display or facilitate the entry of data.

Controls That Organize: Tab Controls and Subforms

The tab control and subform controls are widely used to organize other control instances. When you use a **Tab Control** control instance to organize controls on a form, the user can click a tab to display the controls that are located within the particular tab. A **subform** control instance allows a form (referred to as the **main form**) to display the contents of another record source. The subform control instance contains a form that is displayed within the context of the main form. The form frmStudentQDrops in MU-DSci, for example, is a main form that contains a subform (frmQDrops). The record source of this main form is qryCurrentStudentNameList, and the table tblQDrops is the record source of the subform. The relationship between the records in the main form and the records in the subform is similar to a primary key/foreign key relationship.

As shown in Figure 3-4, the property sheet of the subform identifies the fields that link the main form (**Link Master Fields** property) to the subform (**Link Child Fields** property). The **Source Object** property contains the name of the form that is displayed by the subform. The subform in frmStudentQDrops displays the Q Drops of the student whose record is currently displayed in the main form.

You can create subforms by using a form wizard or by dragging a form from the Database window inside the Design view of another form.

Adding a Tab Control and a Subform to frmPayment

Users of frmPayment would like to see the enrollment records that are associated with a particular payment. To facilitate the display of the allocated amounts to enrollment, frmPayment will use a tab control. One tab within the control will contain the payment information and a second tab will display the allocation information. The Allocation tab will contain a subform listing the enrollment records that are related to the payment.

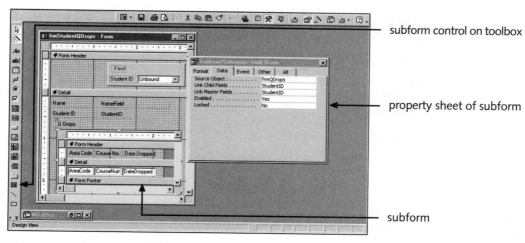

subform control on toolbox

property sheet of subform

subform

Figure 3-4   frmStudentQDrops with subform

To add a tab control to frmPayment:

1. Display **frmPayment** in Design view.

2. Click **Edit** on the menu bar, and then click **Select All** to select all controls.

3. Click **Edit** on the menu bar, and then click **Cut** to cut all of the controls.

4. Click the **Tab Control** control in the toolbox and drag the control so that it covers most of the Detail section. Two tabs should appear within the tab control.

5. If it is not already visible, display the property sheet for the tab on the left, click the **Format** tab, and then type **Payment** in the Caption property. Then, click the **Other** tab and type **tabPayment** in the Name property.

6. Click the **tab** on the right. Type **Allocation** as the Caption property, type **tabAllocation** as the Name property, and then close the property sheet. (If the tab on the right does not appear, right-click the tab control and click Insert Page on the pop-up menu.)

7. Click the **Payment** tab, click **Edit** on the menu bar, and then click **Paste** to paste the controls on the first tab.

8. Close and save frmPayment.

The subform that appears in the Allocation tab will be based on a query that is centered on the tblEnrollment table. In addition to the fields in tblEnrollment, the query should contain the semester of the class (from tblClasses), the student's name (from tblStudents), and a calculated field called AmountDue.

To create the query that will be used as the record source:

1. Create a new query that uses **tblStudents**, **tblClasses**, and **tblEnrollment**. Make sure that join lines exist between the tables.

2. Add all of the fields in tblEnrollment to the Field row of the query design grid.

3. In a blank column in the Field row, type **AmountDue: [Charged]– [AmountPaid]**. This value is a calculated field.

4. Add the **Semester** field from tblClasses to the Field row.

5. In a blank column in the Field row, type **PersonName: [FirstName] & " " & [LastNames]**. This value is a calculated field that concatenates the first and last name.

6. Display the query in Datasheet view to test the query.

7. Save the query as **qryAllocation**. Close qryAllocation.

The next step is to create a form that uses qryAllocation as its record source.

To create a form that displays allocation amounts:

1. Click the **Forms** object type, and then double-click **Create form by using wizard**.

2. Select **Query: qryAllocation** as the query in the Tables/Queries combo box. Move all the fields except PaymentNo to the SelectedFields. PaymentNo will not be displayed on the form, but Access will remember the value for each row.

3. Click **Next**, and then select **Tabular** as the style.

4. Click **Next**, select the **Standard** background style, and then click **Next**.

5. Name the form **frmAllocationSub**, and then click **Finish**.

6. Open the query in Design view, and then adjust the sizes of the text boxes and labels so that the values are visible. To do so, you must also make the form itself wider. Change the caption of PersonalName_Label to **Name**. Change the caption of LessonIndex_Label to **Index**. Reorder the text boxes and labels to match the order shown in Figure 3-5.

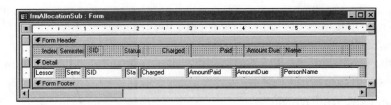

Figure 3-5   frmAllocationSub in Design view

7. Close and save the form.

Next, you need to make frmAllocationSub become a subform in frmPayment.

To create a subform in frmPayment:

1. Display **frmPayment** in Design view.

2. Click the **Allocation** tab.

3. Move **frmPayment** so that the Database window is visible.

4. Drag the **frmAllocationSub** icon from the Database window into the Detail section of frmPayment. A subform box will be displayed.

5. Move and adjust the size of the subform so that all controls are displayed.

6. Delete the label **frmAllocationSub** that is located above the upper-left corner of the subform. This label is not necessary.

7. Display the property sheet for the subform. Notice that the Link Child Fields property and the Link Master Fields property refer to the PaymentNo. PaymentNo links the two forms together. The Source Object property identifies frmAllocationSub as the form to display through the Subform Control.

8. Display **frmPayment** in Form view. The payment of Maria Garcia is shown. The Allocation tab shows the enrollments associated with the payment (see Figure 3-6).

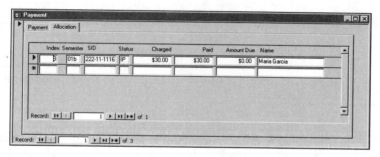

Figure 3-6 Allocation tab view of frmPayment

9. Resize the form in Form view, if necessary, to see all of the data.

10. Close and save the form.

The current version of frmPayment can be used to record payments and view allocations.

Controls That Display and Update Data

Most data in a form are displayed and updated through a text box. Sometimes, however, other controls are a better choice. You can enforce data validity and improve the ease of data entry through the selection of an appropriate type of control. For example, if the data type of a control source is Boolean, you can use a check box that accepts only checks (True) or an empty box (False). If you use a text box instead, you would include a verification rule or VBA code to ensure that the user types a 1 (signifying True) or 0 (signifying False). Clearly, the check box is a better choice in this situation. Table 3-3 summarizes the data entry and display controls that are supplied with Access.

When you modify a form or create an unbound form, you can place controls on a form by clicking a control on the **toolbox** and then dragging the mouse on the form to indicate the location and size of the control. (If the toolbox is not displayed, click the **Toolbox** button in the toolbar.) If the control is supposed to be bound, you must set the ControlSource property. A quicker way to create a bound control is to drag a field from the Field list onto the form. The **Field list** contains a list of the fields in a form's record source. The type of control created depends upon the type specified in the field's display control under the Lookup tab in the table's Design view. Controls created from the Field list automatically have their ControlSource property set. In addition, a label, corresponding to the field's Caption property, is automatically placed on the form.

Table 3-3   Data entry and display controls in Access

Control	Uses
Bound Object Frame	Displays the contents of an OLE field (for example, a picture stored in a table).
Check Box	Indicates a value of True or False. When the item is checked, the value is True; otherwise, the value is False.
Combo Box	Similar to a List Box, but allows the user to type a value or select from the list. A combo box drops down when the user clicks the arrow key; thus the control takes up less room on the form.
List Box	Allows the user to select from a list of possible legal values. The list is usually longer than the possible values of an option group.
Option Button	Typically used in conjunction with an option group. When the button is filled in, the option is True (selected). When the button is not filled in, the option is False.
Option Group	Contains several option buttons, check boxes, or toggle buttons. The option group allows only one of the buttons or boxes to be True. Used when a few valid values exist (for example, Male or Female; Beginner, Intermediate, Advanced). The control source of an option group must be a number.
Text Box	Displays any type of data. Primarily used when a list of valid values cannot be predetermined.
Toggle Button	Button is pressed or not pressed. When the button is pressed, the value of the field is True. When the button is not pressed, the value is False.

Besides a reference to a field in the form's record source, the ControlSource property of a text box can contain an expression. A control with an expression is called a **calculated control**. The expression is similar to an expression that is placed in the query design grid. For example, if a form contains a list of students, a calculated control could count the number of students on the form. The value of the ControlSource in this case is:

```
= Count([StudentID])
```

Note the equals sign, which must appear in front of this type of expression. StudentID is a field in the form's record source.

One disadvantage of a calculated control is that, because the control is not associated with a particular field in the record source, it cannot be used to update data in a field. You can, however, place expressions in a control's DefaultValue property. The value calculated by the expression can then be used to update a value of the control's control source.

After a text box and a label control, the combo box is probably the next most widely used control. To set up a combo box, you must specify several properties. The **RowSource** property contains an SQL statement or the name of a table or query that contains the values to be displayed in the combo box. A row source may return more than one field (for example, the StudentID and the name of the student). The **BoundColumn** property identifies the field that will become the value of the combo box after the user selects an item. It contains an integer that corresponds to the order of the columns (1 is the column farthest to the left). The **ColumnWidths** property indicates the size of the fields to be displayed within the combo box. Occasionally, a width is set equal to zero. This value allows the application to access the value of the column, but hides the column from the user. This technique is frequently used when the database must store information in terms of codes, but the user needs to see the complete description. A combo box wizard, which is activated automatically when you click the Control Wizards button on the Toolbox, facilitates the process of creating the combo box.

ActiveX Controls

In addition to its own controls, Access supports ActiveX controls. **ActiveX controls** are similar to the Access controls discussed previously, except they have been developed for other applications (for example, Excel). Clicking **More Controls** in the toolbox displays a list of ActiveX controls. Most ActiveX controls were created by Microsoft, obey a standard set up by Microsoft, and can be inserted into an Access form just like the controls that come with Access. Organizations can also create their own custom controls.

An example of an ActiveX control is a spin button. A **spin button** allows a user to click on an arrow to increase or decrease the value of a field. This type of control could be used, for example, to increment the quantity sold of an item that is located on a sales form. Spin buttons are often used to specify the number of copies of a document to print. The field increased or decreased is specified in the spin button's ControlSource property. The amount of the increase is set up in the control's **SmallChange** property. In addition, the SpinButton control contains **Maximum** and **Minimum** properties that restrict the valid values that can be entered.

Many ActiveX controls exist. The controls displayed when you click More Controls will depend on the other applications installed on your system.

Modifying frmPayment to Contain an Option Group and a Calculated Control

For the Swim Lessons application, two legal values are allowed for Payment Type: Cash and Check. Because only two values are allowed and the values correspond to integers, an **option group**, which displays a group frame containing toggle buttons, option buttons, or check boxes, should be used to select the payment type. This option group ensures that the user will select a valid value.

To create an option group for Payment Type:

1. Display **frmPayment** in Design view.

2. Click the **PaymentType** text box, and then press the **Delete** key. The text box PaymentType and its corresponding label disappear.

3. Verify that the Control Wizards button is depressed on the toolbox. It must be depressed for the Option Group Wizard to be activated in Step 4.

4. Click the **Option Group** button on the toolbox and drag the mouse on the form to indicate the place and size of the control, as shown in Figure 3-7. The Option Group Wizard appears.

5. Type **Cash** in the first row of Label Names and **Check** in the second row of Label Names, and then click **Next**.

6. Select **Check** as the Default choice, and then click **Next**. A table will appear with the column headings Label Names and Values.

7. When tblPayment was created, it was determined that 1 would represent Cash and 2 would represent Check. Make sure that the correct values are identified in the table, and then click **Next**.

8. Click the **Store the value in this field** check box, select **PaymentType** from the combo box, and then click **Next**.

9. Select **Option buttons** as the type of control and **Sunken** as the style, and then click **Next**.

10. Type **Payment Type** as the caption, and then click **Finish** to create the option group.

11. Move the Payment Type option group and the other controls so that the form, when opened in Form view, looks like Figure 3-7.

12. Return to Design view. Verify that the Payment tab is selected. Click **View** on the menu bar, and then click **Tab Order**. Reorder the tab order so that the option group row appears after the Phone text box.

13. Display the Form view of frmPayment and, working in Design view, fix any problems with control sizes or alignment.

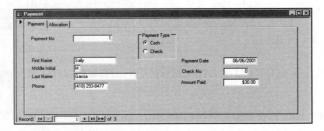

Figure 3-7   frmPayment after moving option group and other controls

14. Close and save frmPayment.

In addition to the option group, you should create a calculated control that sums the amount allocated for a payment. This control will discourage the user from overallocating the payment.

To create a calculated control that sums allocations:

1. Display **frmAllocationSub** in Design view.

2. Place the cursor at the bottom of the Footer section bar. Drag the **Footer** boundary to create room for a text box.

3. Click the **TextBox** control in the toolbox and create a text box in the footer section under AmountPaid. The text box and a label will appear.

4. Using the property sheet, change the Name property of the text box to **txtTotal** and its corresponding label to **Total Allocated**. Resize the label, if necessary.

5. Using the property sheet, type **=Sum([AmountPaid])** in the Control Source property of txtTotal. Then, set the Format property of txtTotal to **Currency**. The form will automatically sum the AmountPaid column when the form is displayed in Form view.

6. Display frmAllocationSub in Form view to see the results.

7. Close and save the form.

WORKING WITH PROPERTY SHEETS TO ENFORCE DATA VALIDITY

Controls and property sheets specify a form's capabilities and appearance. To the maximum extent possible, you should design the form so that it helps protect the validity of the data. Property sheets of forms and controls play a significant role in supporting data validity. Some of the most important properties are located in the Data tab of a form's property sheet. To allow users to change the data on a form, you must set the form's **AllowEdits** property to Yes. Users cannot change the data when AllowEdits is set to No. Similarly, set **AllowDeletions** to Yes to allow users to delete records and **AllowAdditions** to Yes to allow users to add new records.

Controls possess complementary properties. To change the value displayed through a control, set the **Locked** property to No and the **Enabled** property to Yes. The Locked property specifies whether the data can be changed. The Enabled property specifies whether the cursor can be placed in the control. Controls that are locked or disabled should have a different appearance from controls that are not locked and are enabled. The appearance signals to the user, before he or she attempts to type, that a value cannot be changed. One way to distinguish a locked or a disabled control is to change the BackColor property. Another way to distinguish the control is to change the **BackStyle** property to transparent.

 TIP Some queries do not support changes to the data they display. To change data that are included in a query, Access must determine which table and row to update. If the primary key of a table is not included in the query, Access cannot determine the row and therefore does not support updating of the data. If the query is a record source for a form, the form will not allow updating, no matter what values the AllowEdits, Locked, and Enabled properties have. If this effect is not desired, you must modify the query used as the record source for the form.

Input Mask, Validation Rule, Validation Text, and **Default Value** are also important properties in the Data tab of a control. These properties are similar to the field properties with the same names found in a table's Design view. Access automatically uses the input mask, validation rule, validation text, and default value when these values are set as field properties within the control's ControlSource property.

Modifying frmPayment to Enforce Data Validity

The PaymentNo text box on frmPayment is an autonumber that the user cannot modify. Consequently, the user should not be able to update or even place the cursor in this field. The form frmAllocationSub displays allocations of the payment. Because deletions of records in frmAllocationSub would actually delete enrollment records, you will make changes that prevent a user's deletion or insertion of enrollment records and the modification of all but the AmountPaid field.

To lock and disable PaymentNo:

1. Display **frmPayment** in Design view.

2. If the property sheet is not open, right-click the **PaymentNo** text box, and then click **Properties**. The property sheet for PaymentNo will appear. If the property sheet is already open, click the PaymentNo text box.

3. Click the **Data** tab.

4. Change the value of Enabled to **No** and Locked to **Yes**.

5. Click the **Format** tab.

6. Change the Back Style property to **Transparent**. The background color of PaymentNo will appear gray.

7. Click the **Other** tab.

8. Change the value of Tab Stop to **No**.

9. Display frmPayment in Form view. Notice that the cursor skips PaymentNo and moves straight to Payment Type.

10. Close and save frmPayment.

Next, you will modify frmAllocationSub to keep the user from deleting or adding records.

To modify frmAllocationSub so that records cannot be deleted or added:

1. Display **frmAllocationSub** in Design view or, if frmPayment is open, click inside the subform of frmPayment (which allows you to change properties of frmAllocationSub from within frmPayment).

2. Open the property sheet of frmAllocationSub, if necessary, and click the **Data** tab. Change Allow Additions and Allow Deletions to **No**. Close the Property Sheet window.

3. Hold down the Shift key and click **LessonIndex**, **Semester**, **Status**, **AmountDue**, **PersonName**, **SID**, and **txtTotal**. Display the property sheet. "Multiple Selection" will appear in its header.

4. Set the Locked property to **Yes**, Enabled to **No**, Back Style to **Transparent**, and Tab Stop to **No**. These choices will set the properties of the selected controls.

5. Close and save the form.

The possible changes made through frmAllocationSub are now controlled.

CREATING CONDITIONAL FORMATS

In the previous section, you set properties that helped a user enter valid data. Properties can also bring certain characteristics of the data to the user's attention. For example, a class that has achieved its enrollment limit could be displayed in red. The user should not attempt to add more students to the class or increase the enrollment limit. **Conditional formats** change properties of text boxes and combo boxes while the application is being used.

The **Conditional Formatting** dialog box, which is opened from the Format menu, specifies the conditional formats. To specify a conditional format, you highlight one or more text boxes or combo boxes, open the Conditional Formatting dialog box, and then select the type of condition from the Condition combo box. Three types of conditions can be set. The **Field Value Is** condition sets the format when the value of the corresponding control meets certain conditions (for example, set the ForeColor to red when the control's value is greater than the limit). The **Expression Is** condition allows you to change the properties of one control while testing the values of different controls (for example, change the ForeColor of the course title when [enrollment] = [limit], where enrollment and limit are text boxes on the form). The **Field Has Focus** condition allows you to change properties when the user places the cursor in the control. This condition highlights the place where the user can currently type. The **ForeColor, BackColor,** and **Enabled** properties can be changed when the condition is True. The dialog box can also indicate whether the text should be bold, italicized, or underlined. If you create more than one condition for a control and a conflict exists between the conditional formats, the first format is used.

Creating Conditional Formats for frmPayment

Users of frmPayment would like the system to highlight the text box that currently has focus. In addition, they would like the AmountPaid text box to be displayed in a different color when the total allocated equals the amount paid.

To create conditional formats for frmPayment:

1. Open **frmPayment** in Design view.

2. Hold down the **Shift** key and select all text boxes on frmPayment except PaymentNo.

3. Click **Format** on the menu bar, and then click **Conditional Formatting**. The Conditional Formatting dialog box will open.

4. Select **Field Has Focus** in the Condition 1 combo box (on the far left).

5. Click the **Fill/Back Color** drop-down list arrow and select the lightest blue color.

6. Click **OK**.

7. Click on the form to clear the selection of all controls, and then click the **AmountPaid** text box.

8. Click **Format** on the menu bar, and then click **Conditional Formatting**. The conditional format for AmountPaid appears.

9. Click **Add**. The dialog box will display Condition 2.

10. Verify that the combo box displays **Field Value Is**. In the second combo box of the group, select **less than or equal to**, and then type **[frmAllocationSub].[Form]![txtTotal]** in the adjacent text box. This expression is a reference to the txtTotal text box located in the frmAllocationSub form.

11. Click the **Font/Fore Color** drop-down list arrow and select a maroon color. The Conditional Formatting dialog box should appear as shown in Figure 3-8.

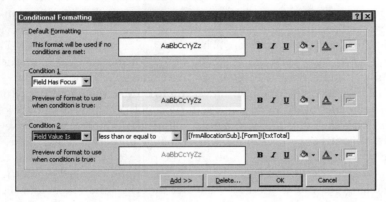

Figure 3-8   Conditional Formatting dialog box for txtTotalPaid

12. Click **OK**, and then display the Form view of frmPayment. The amount paid by Sally Garcia for Maria Garcia should display in a maroon color when the text box does not have the focus. Click in any text box. The back color turns blue in the text box with the focus.

13. Save and close the form.

FORM DESIGN CONSIDERATIONS THAT INFLUENCE MAINTENANCE

As any smart application developer will tell you, organization and standards are half the battle when creating easy-to-maintain systems. One standard that facilitates programming and maintenance is consistent use of object naming conventions. These naming conventions require tags to appear in front of all object names. Form names, for example, are prefixed with the "frm" tag, and text box names are prefixed with the "txt" tag. When these objects are referenced in VBA code, developers immediately recognize the type of object being used. Also, groups in the Database window organize forms, subforms, and their record sources. Groups contain shortcuts to the objects contained in the group.

Using Naming Conventions and Groups to Support frmPayment

To facilitate the maintance of frmPayment, naming conventions and groups should be used.

To rename the controls in frmPayment and frmAllocationSub:

1. Open **frmPayment** in Design view. Click the **Payment** tab, if it is not already selected.

2. Click the **PaymentNo** text box, display the property sheet, if necessary, and then change the Name property to **txtPaymentNo**.

3. Add the **txt** tag to the front of **FirstName** (txtFirstName), **MiddleInitial** (txtMiddleInitial), **LastName** (txtLastName), **Phone** (txtPhone), **PaymentDate** (txtPaymentDate), **CheckNo** (txtCheckNo), and **AmountPaid** (txtAmountPaid).

4. Change the name of the option group for PaymentType to **fraPaymentType**.

5. Click the **Allocation** tab, and then click and change the names of the text boxes in the subform of frmPayment so that each text box name is prefixed with **txt**.

6. Close and save both forms.

The form frmPayment contains a subform and the subform is based on a query. Maintenance becomes easier if the forms and record sources are placed within a group.

To create a group for frmPayment:

1. Click the **Group** bar in the Object window.

2. Right-click under the Group bar, and then click **New Group** in the shortcut menu.

3. Type **frmPayment Objects** in the New Group dialog box, and then click **OK**.

4. Drag **frmPayment**, **frmAllocationSub**, **qryAllocation**, and **tblPayment** to the frmPayment Objects group located under the Groups bar. Shortcuts are created to each of these items, as shown in Figure 3-9.

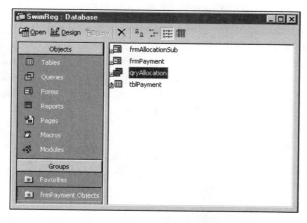

Figure 3-9   Groups on the Database window

CREATING REPORTS

Like forms, reports provide access to data in tables and queries. They differ from forms in that a report provides read-only access to the data. **Read-only** access means that the report cannot modify data in its record source. Normally, reports are printed on paper.

Designing reports is very similar to designing forms. You use property sheets to manipulate the appearance and content of the report. The RecordSource property identifies the table or query that provides data to the report. The ControlSource property identifies the field in the table or query that will be displayed through a particular control. Like controls on a form, controls on a report can contain expressions. In addition, reports can contain subreports, which are similar to subforms.

Fortunately, the toolbox, menus, and toolbars used to design reports are virtually identical to the toolbox, menus, and toolbars used in a form's Design view. The Conditional Formatting dialog box is identical to the dialog box used with a form. The primary difference between the tools and techniques used to design reports is that reports permit more sections.

Report Sections

Reports contain several sections. Controls in the **Report Header** appear once at the beginning of the report. Controls in the **Report Footer** appear at the end of the report. **Page Headers** and **Page Footers** display controls at the beginning and end of the page, respectively.

The sections of a report that differ most dramatically from those on a form are the Group Headers and Footers. A **report group** is a set of records that share a common value for a particular field. Controls in a **Group Header** appear at the beginning of a report group. Controls in the **Group Footer** appear at the end of a report group. Many Group Headers and Footers can appear in a report.

Figure 3-10 shows a report that uses groups. Figure 3-11 shows the Design view of the same report. In this case, the report is grouped on CompanyName. Each time the CompanyName changes, the name of the company and its address are printed. The text box in the CompanyName Footer counts the number of employees at the company.

You add the Report Header/Footer and Page Header/Footer to a report through the View menu. Clicking the Sorting and Grouping option displays the Sorting and Grouping dialog box. This dialog box allows the developer to specify whether Group Headers and Footers are desired. Group On and Group Interval specify how Access should recognize common groups. For example, to group all values that start with the same letter, Group On should equal Prefix characters and Group Interval should equal 1.

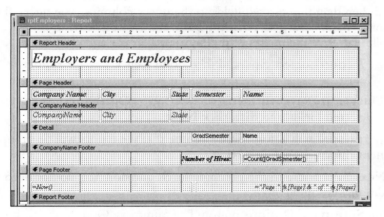

Figure 3-10   rptEmployer

Figure 3-11   rptEmployer in Design view

Report Wizards

The simplest way to create a report is through report wizards. These wizards are very similar to form wizards. The wizard that is available from the shortcut menu prompts for the tables and queries for the record source. Next, a View dialog box may appear. If the screen displayed on the View dialog breaks the fields into groups, the wizard will create a group section. It then asks for any additional grouping levels. Each grouping level that you add will create a group section in the report's Design view. Once the group levels are set, the wizard prompts for sort orders. You can place summaries in the Report Footers by clicking Summary Options in the Sort Order dialog box. The wizard also formats the report. Once it finishes, you can make final touches to the report in Design view.

Other wizards are also available. The Label Wizard produces reports that can be printed on mailing labels. The Chart Wizard produces a report with a graph. The AutoReports Wizard generates reports automatically when the user selects a record source. It does not, however, prompt for additional information.

Creating a Report to Display Payments and Their Allocations

Users of the Swim Lessons application would like to see a printout of payments and their allocations to enrollment.

To create a report that shows payment and allocations:

1. Create a query that uses **tblPayment** and **tblEnrollment**. A join line should appear between the respective PaymentNos.

2. Right-click the join line, and then click **Join Properties** in the pop-up menu.

3. Click option button **2**, and then click **OK**.

4. Double-click the title bar of tblPayment so that all fields are listed in the Field row, and then drag the selected fields to the query columns. The query should also contain **SID**, **Charged**, **AmountPaid**, and **LessonIndex** from tblEnrollment. Save the query as **qryPaymentDetails** and close it.

5. Click the **Reports** object type, and then double-click **Create report by using wizard**.

6. Select **Query: qryPaymentDetails** in the Tables/Queries combo box. Move all fields to Selected Fields, and then click **Next**.

7. The report wizard will automatically assume that the report will be grouped by tblPayment Information. Click **Next**.

8. Click **Next** in response to the grouping levels question. You do not need to add any additional grouping levels.

9. Click the **Summary Options** button. The Summary Options dialog box opens.

10. Click the **Sum** check box in the second row. This choice will generate a sum at the end of the payment group. Click **OK**, and then click **Next**.

11. Select the **Stepped** Layout, if necessary. Click **Next**.

12. Choose the **Corporate** style, if necessary, and then click **Next**.

13. Change the name of the report to **rptPayment** and click the **Modify the report's design** option button. Click **Finish**. The Design view of the report will be displayed.

14. Change the title in the Report Header to **Payment Details**. Change the sum in the text box in the report footer so that it reads **–Sum([tblPayment].[Amount Paid])**.

15. Click the **View** button on the toolbar. The report will be displayed on the screen. In Design view, resize, move, delete, and align the controls, if necessary, to make the report look like the report in Figure 3-12.

3

16. Close and save the report.

Payment Details

No.	Type	Date	First Name	Middle	Last Name	Phone	Check	Amount Paid
1	1	06/06/2001	Sally	M	Garcia	(418) 29	0	$30.00

222-11-1116 $30.00   30.00
Summary for 'PaymentNo' = 1 (1 detail record)
Sum   30.00

| | 2 | 2 | 06/10/2001 | William | J | Phillips | (418) 29 | 412 | $30.00 |

Summary for 'PaymentNo' = 2 (1 detail record)
Sum

Figure 3-12   rptPayment

DATA ACCESS PAGES

The World Wide Web is becoming a popular way to interact with databases. Web-based interfaces are familiar to many users, and the Web supports remote access. A **data access page** is a special Web interface supported by Access. It is stored as an HTML file—that is, the type of file that is commonly displayed through Web browsers. Unlike forms and reports, HTML files do not physically reside inside an Access mdb file. Instead, the icons within the Page tab of the Database window point to the HTML file. The HTML file, in turn, contains a reference back to the database.

You can make a database accessible through the Web by placing the data access page (that is, the HTML file) on a Web server, which is a computer set up to provide information to Web users. The server must also have access to the tables or queries used to support the HTML file. The Access database can reside on the Web server, or it can reside on another computer that is connected to the server through a local area network. Data access pages can also work independently of the Web. For example, a user can display the HTML file as long as his or her PC can find the HTML file, the database, and a Web browser in its own resources or on a LAN that is connected to the PC itself.

Data access pages contain features that are not easily supported in forms and reports. For example, a data access page can incorporate Expand controls, which allow the user to look at data in summarized and aggregated form. For this reason, data access pages can be included in an application as a reporting tool used for decision support purposes. Such pages update data, but have a significant disadvantage: they do not validate data as soon as it is typed.

Creating a Data Access Page

The creation of a data access page is similar to the creation of a report. That is, the developer specifies one or more sections that contain controls; the controls, in turn, are tied to fields in a table or query. All data access pages have a body and at least one Header section. **Header**

sections display records from a table or query. The Header section resides inside a body object. A HeadingText object and a BeforeBodyText object precede the first Header section and primarily contain miscellaneous text or graphics. These objects are not displayed in Page view unless they contain some object text or graphics. Header sections are associated with property sheets. One property of a Header section, the **RecordSource** property, identifies the table or query used to supply data to the section, much like the RecordSource properties for forms and reports. (If the section obtains data from more than one table or query, only one of the tables or queries is identified).

Many of the controls used in a section are similar to form controls; however, several other controls exist. The **bound HTML control**, for example, is similar to a locked text box (that is, you cannot update the data), but is preferred because it displays data more efficiently. Controls that display or update data have a **ControlSource** property.

You can add bound controls to a section by dragging a field from the **Field List** window. The Field List window is different in a data access page than it is in forms and reports, as shown in Figure 3-13. The Database tab of the window shows all of the tables and queries used in the database. The Page tab shows all the fields currently used in the data access page. If you drag a field from a table or query that is not in the record source, Access attempts to determine how the field is related to the record source.

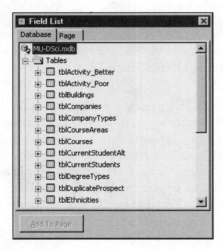

Figure 3-13   Field List window of a data access page

The data access page stores the location of the database. If the database is moved, you can update the location by opening the Field List window, right-clicking the database icon, selecting Connection from the pop-up menu, and then browsing for the database through the Data Link Properties window. This window automatically pops up when Access cannot find the database. If Access cannot find the HTML file when a data access page is opened, it will prompt for the new location.

Like reports, data access pages can use more than one group and therefore can contain multiple Header sections. Groups are defined as records that share the same (or similar) values for a particular field. They can be located within other groups. If a Group Header contains an Expand control, groups that are physically located after the Group Header are displayed only when the Expand control is clicked. Figure 3-14 displays the Page view of pagCitizenships. This page groups students according to their citizenship. Figure 3-15 displays the Design view of pagCitizenship.

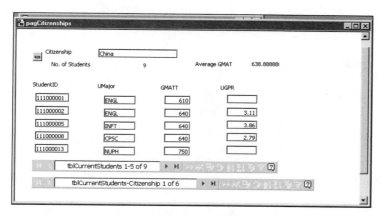

Figure 3-14   Page view of pagCitizenships

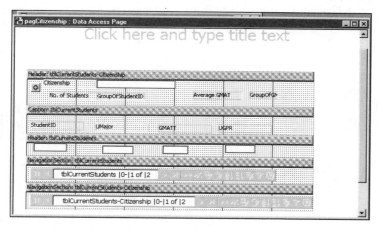

Figure 3-15   Design view of pagCitizenship

In addition to a Header, each group can have a **Footer** that is displayed at the end of a group, a **Caption** that contains labels that appear prior to the data in the Header, and a **Navigation section** that contains controls that allow the user to navigate through the various displayed records. The **Sorting and Grouping** window, which you open by clicking Sorting and Grouping in the toolbar, specifies whether these sections are created (see Figure 3-16). The **Data Page Size** text box located in the Sorting and Grouping window indicates the number of records that should be displayed at one time. Because data access pages display records more slowly than forms do, 1 is the recommended value of Data Page Size. Refer to Access Help to review the other features available in the Sorting and Grouping window.

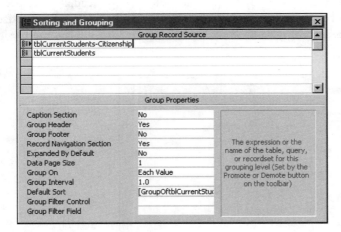

Figure 3-16   Sorting and Grouping window

To create new groups and their corresponding sections, you promote controls or tables that are located in an existing group section. To create a new group, you click the control to promote it and then click **Promote** or **Group by Table** in the toolbar. Group by Table creates a section that will contain all of the fields in the table. Clicking **Demote** removes a section.

The easiest way to create a data access page is to use the Data Access Page Wizard. This wizard is very similar to the report wizards. Access prompts you for the record source, the fields to include in the page, and the groups. Wizards can also convert an existing Web page (not included in Access) into a data access page.

Using the Page Wizard to Create a Data Access Page for Swim Lessons

To facilitate inquiries concerning swimming lessons, you will create a data access page. This data access page will reference the respective mdb file. At a future date, it will be posted on the Web. To facilitate the retrieval of information, the data access page should group classes by semesters and levels.

To create a data access page that displays swimming lessons:

1. Click the **Pages** object type, and then double-click **Create data access page by using wizard**.

2. Select **Table: tblClasses** in the Table/Queries combo box.

3. Move all available fields to the selected fields, and then click **Next**.

4. Adjust the grouping levels to group the classes, first by **Semester**, and then by **Level**. You can use the **<** button and the **>** button to remove and specify grouping levels, respectively. Click **Next**.

5. Sort the fields by **SectionID** in ascending order. Click **Next**.

6. Name the page **pagClasses**. Make sure that the **Modify the page's design** option button is selected, and then click **Finish**. The Design view of pagClasses will appear.

7. Click **View** on the menu bar, and then click **Sorting and Grouping**. The Sorting and Grouping window opens.

8. Click the **tblClasses** row in the Sorting and Grouping window. Next, change Caption Section to **Yes** and Data Page Size to **All**. Close the Sorting and Grouping window. The Caption section will appear.

9. Cut and paste the labels in the Header: tblClasses section to the Caption section. Move the bound HTML controls in Header: tblClasses under the appropriate label. Answer **OK** to any warning or information message boxes. Change the sizes of the controls and the section, if necessary.

10. Click the **Header: tblClasses** section. Use the handles surrounding the section to make the length of the section smaller (that is, reduce the blank space under the controls). Change the labels so that they match Figure 3-17.

11. Save the page as **pagClasses.htm** in the same directory as your Access application. Display the page in Page view.

12. Use the navigation buttons and the Expand control to test the page. You should see results similar to Figure 3-17.

13. Close the page.

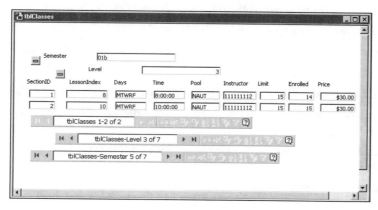

Figure 3-17   tblClasses in Page view

CHAPTER SUMMARY

❑ Forms, reports, and data access pages *are* the system from an end user's point of view. Forms are the principal interface of an application. They display data and allow the user to update data. To the greatest extent allowed, forms should be designed to help the user enter valid data. Reports support printed reports, and data access pages support interaction through the Web.

❑ Most forms, reports, and data access pages are bound to a table or query through the RecordSource property. The ControlSource property identifies the field in the table or query that is displayed and updated through the control.

❑ Wizards are frequently used to create an initial version of a form, report, and data access page. However, an application developer must nevertheless be familiar with property sheets and sections to customize the interface.

❑ In addition to supporting data validity checks, forms, reports, and data access pages should obey proper design characteristics. A well-thought-out design will pay off by streamlining the programming, testing, and maintenance phases of system development.

REVIEW QUESTIONS

1. What is a record source?

   a. A field that is bound to a control

   b. A table that supplies data to a query

   c. A table or query that supplies data to a form, report, or data access page

   d. A section with a report

2. What is a control source?

   a. A field that is bound to a control

   b. A field that supplies data to a query

   c. A table or query that supplies data to a form, report, or data access page

   d. A section within a report

3. Bound forms have a value listed in their RecordSource property. True or False?

4. List three types of controls that can be used to limit the possible values entered by the user.

5. A(n) _____ control can be placed inside a form to display records from a related record source.

6. When should tab controls be used?

7. Control prefixes are used:

   a. to facilitate VBA programming and maintenance.

   b. to create labels for a control on a form.

   c. to supply data to a control.

   d. to disable a control.

8. The Detail section of a form displays different values depending on the record that is currently being viewed. True or False?

9. Describe the relationship between a background color of a control and its Locked and Enabled properties.

10. The _____ can be used to adjust the tab order of the controls on a form.

11. What property (or properties) prevent a user from modifying the value in a control?

    a. Locked

    b. Enabled

    c. Allow Edits

    d. All of the above

12. The _____ for a report allows the user to create new Group Headers and Footers.

13. A Page footer is displayed only at the end of a report. True or False?

14. Write an expression that can be placed in the ControlSource property for a text box. The expression displays the sum of the field Sales.

15. ControlSource properties that contain an expression can be used to update the value in a field. True or False?

16. A(n) _____ changes the background color of a control when the control has focus.

17. A data access page can be used to:

    a. allow access through the Web.

    b. provide decision support through a grouping mechanism.

    c. update data in a database.

    d. All of the above.

18. What is an Expand control?

19. Data access pages are stored in:

    a. the Access mdb file.

    b. an HTML file.

    c. a report

    d. a form.

20. How are new groups created in the Design view of a data access page?

3

HANDS-ON PROJECTS

Project 3-1

Natural Parent International. The first section of the NPI system to be developed will update and display member and book information. Several forms and reports must be created. A form related to members should allow the entry and update of member data. This form should also contain a tab that displays books checked out by the member. The book form will support updating the books found in NPI's library. This form will contain two subforms: one that supports the entry of category information, and one that supports the entry of author information.

Complete these steps:

1. Open **NPI.mbd**. Create a query that uses tblCheckout and tblBooks. This query should display the Title, DateCheckedOut, DateReturned, BookID, and MemberID for books that have not been returned. Books that have not been returned contain a Null value in the DateReturned field. Use the **Is Null** condition in the Criteria row of the DateReturned field to display unreturned books. Sort the query on DateCheckedOut. Name the query **qryMembersCheckOut**.

2. Create a continuous (that is, tabular) form that uses qryMembersCheckOut as the record source. Disallow edits, deletions, and additions in this form. The form should display the Title and DateCheckedOut (the other fields in qryMembersCheckOut need not be displayed). The MemberID and BookID, however, must be included in the Field list. Use color combinations in the form to indicate that the data cannot be updated. Make sure that the text boxes use a txt prefix in the Name property. Name the form **frmMembersCheckOut**.

3. Create a "Single Form" (that is, a Columnar form) that uses qryMemberLastNameSort as its record source. Name the form **frmMembers**. The form should contain a tab control that displays two tabs: Members and Books Out. The Members tab should display all fields in qryMemberLastNameSort, except MemberID and Paid Date. MemberID should appear in the Field list, however. The Books Out tab should contain the subform frmMembersCheckOut. To create this subform, drag **frmMembersCheckOut** into the Books Out tab. Verify that the property sheet for the subform identifies MemberID as the value for the Link Child Field and Link Master Field properties. The name box in the header of the form contains a control source that concatenates the values in the First Name and Last Name text boxes. Use the appropriate prefix for each control. Finally, create a conditional format that highlights a text box when it has the focus.

4. Create a form called **frmLibrary**. The control source is tblBooks. The form should contain two subforms (frmCategory and frmAuthors). You may need to create additional queries to support the subforms. The color pattern and conditional formatting should be the same as that used in the previous forms.

5. Create a report and query (if necessary) that print member names, addresses, and phone numbers. The report should sort members by last name. In addition, the first and last names should be concatenated. The city and state should also be concatenated (for example, Racine, WI). Name the report **rptMembersAddress**.

6. Create a report that lists books by category. Each category should also display the number of books that are classified within that category. Some books may appear in more than one category. Name the report **rptBooksByCategory**. You will need to create a query that will be used as the record source of the report.

7. Save your work.

Project 3-2

Metropolitan Performing Arts Company. The first section of the MPAC system to be developed will display performance-related information. In particular, one form must be designed to facilitate the entry of performance information and a second form should be created that displays seat availability information. Eventually, the second form will be used to facilitate sales. In addition to the forms, a report should be created that displays the amount earned per performance. A data access page should be displayed that shows the various dates of the performances.

Complete these steps:

1. Open **MPA.mdb**. Create a form that uses tblPerformance as the record source. The form will be used to display and update the fields in this table. The caption of the form is Performance. The name of the form is **frmPerformance**.

2. Add a tab control to frmPerformance. The first tab will contain the controls created in Step 1. The second tab should contain a subform that lists the specific dates and times of the performance. The record source of the subform is tblPerformanceDate. The name of the subform is **frmPerformanceDate**.

3. Create a form called **frmPerformanceDateSeats**. This form should contain a subform named **frmSeatsAvailableSubform**. The record source of the main form is qryPerformanceDateDetail. The record source of the subform is qrySeatsForPerformance. The form wizard can be used to create both forms at the same time.

4. Delete the Status textbox from frmSeatsAvailableSubForm and replace the status with a combo box that allows selection of "available", "unavailable", and "complimentary". Name the combo box **cboStatus**.

5. Create a report that uses qryTotalPerPerformance as the record source. The report should group performances by the PerformanceID. A sum in the footer should display the total per Performance. Name the report **rptTotalPerPerformance**.

6. Create a data access page that uses qryPerformanceDateDetail as the record source. Create groups for the PerformanceName. Name the page **pagPerformanceDates**.

7. Adjust your forms and reports to use proper naming conventions and back color displays.

8. Save your work.

Project 3-3

Foreign Language Institute. The first steps in creating this application put the basic forms in place. (Use appropriate naming conventions.) Several forms must be created. A form for customers is needed that will allow entry and modification of customer data. A form is also needed for the maintenance of product data. In addition, you will need forms to support the customer call process.

Complete these steps:

1. Open **FLI.mdb**. The first form to create is a switchboard that will provide access to the rest of the system. Create a blank form and place a label on it that reads "Foreign Language Institute Information System". Change the background color of the form to a color of your choice. Name this form **frmSwitchboard**.

2. Use the wizard to create forms based on tblCustomers (**frmCustomers**), tblCalls (**frmCalls**), tblMagazines (**frmMagazines**), tblProducts (**frmProducts**), tblSales (**frmSales**), tblSalesPeople (**frmSalesPeople**), and tblSpeakers (**frmSpeakers**). Arrange the fields in a format that you find attractive.

3. Create a tabular form based on tblAdvertisements and named **frmAdsSubform**.

4. Create a tabular form based on tblProducts and named **frmProductSubform**. Change the control source for the product type, product category, language, and medium to Unbound. You do not need a SpeakerID control.

5. Create a tabular form based on tblSalesDetail and named **frmSalesDetail**. Change the control source for Disposition to Unbound.

6. Create a Form/Subform relationship with frmSales as the main form and frmSalesDetail as the subform. Create a Form/Subform relationship with frmMagazines as the main form and frmAdsSubform as the subform. Create a Form/Subform relationship with frmSpeakers as the main form and frmProductsSubform as the subform. Name the control on the main form that contains the subform **frmProductsList**.

7. Place command buttons on the forms as specified in Table 3-4. Give the buttons the names specified.

8. Insert the controls specified in Table 3-5. Place the control in the Details section of the form unless otherwise indicated. For combo boxes, use the wizard to create a combo box that retrieves data from the appropriate table.

9. Save your work.

3

Table 3-4   Specifications for command buttons in Hands-on Project 3-3

Form	Button	Action	Object Name
frmSwitchboard	Calls	Open the Calls form	cmdCalls
	Customers	Open the Customers form	cmdCustomers
	Magazines	Open the Magazines form	cmdMagazines
	Products	Open the Products form	cmdProducts
	Sales	Open the Sales form	cmdSales
	Sales People	Open the Sales People form	cmdSalesPeople
	Speakers	Open the Speakers form	cmdSpeakers
	Exit Application	Exit the application	cmdQuit
frmCustomers	Purchases	Open the Sales form	cmdPurchases
	Close	Close the form	cmdClose
frmCalls	Close	Close the form	cmdClose
frmMagazines	Close	Close the form	cmdClose
frmProducts	Close	Close the form	cmdClose
frmSales	Close	Close the form	cmdClose
frmSalesPeople	Close	Close the form	cmdClose
frmSpeakers	Close	Close the form	cmdClose
	Show Detail	Show frmProductList subform	cmdDetail

Table 3-5   Forms and their controls in Hands-on Project 3-3

Form	Control	Action	Object Name
frmAds Subform	Magazine combo box	Sets value of magazine	cboMagazine
frmCustomers	Customer Look Up combo box (in header)	Searches for customer	cboCustomer
	Customer Type option group	Sets value of customer type	fraCustomerType
frmCalls	Product combo box	Sets value of product	cboProduct
	Customer combo box	Sets value of customer	cboCustomer
	Category option group	Sets value of call category	fraCategory
frmProducts	Language combo box	Sets value of language	cboLanguage
	Speaker combo box	Sets value of speaker	cboSpeaker
	Category option group	Sets value of product category	fraProdCategory
	Type option group	Sets value of product type	fraProdType
	Medium option group	Sets value of product medium	fraMedium
frmSales	Sales Person combo box	Sets value of salesperson	cboSalesPerson
	Customer combo box	Sets value of customer	cboCustomer

Project 3-4

King William Hotel System. The first steps in creating this application put the basic forms in place. (Use appropriate naming conventions.) Several forms must be created. A form for customers is needed that will allow entry and modification of customer data. Another form is needed for the maintenance of reservation data. You will also need forms to support the checkout process, which requires summary charges and detailed cafe charges. You also need a form to support posting of the cafe charges to a specific room.

Complete these steps:

1. Open **KWH.mdb**. The first form to create is a switchboard that will provide access to the rest of the system. Create a blank form and place a label on it that reads "King William Hotel Information System". Change the background color of the form to a color of your choice. Name this form **frmSwitchboard**.

2. Use the wizard to create forms based on tblCustomer (**frmCustomer**), tblReservation (two forms: **frmCheckIn** and **frmChargeSummary**), and tblCafeBillDetail (**frmCafeBillPost**). In frmChargeSummary, create three unbound text boxes named txtCafeTotal, txtRoomTotal, and txtAmount. In frmCafeBillPost, create an unbound text box named txtPrice. Arrange the fields in a format that you find attractive.

3. Create a form that is not bound to a record source. Name it **frmMakeReservation**. Specify the control source for txtCustomerNo as follows:

   ```
   = [Forms]![frmCustomer]![txtCustomerNo]
   ```

4. Create a tabular form based on qryCafeDetailFilter named **frmCafeBillDetail**. Hide the ItemNo and RoomNo fields. Add an unbound text box named txtItemDesc. Label it "Item".

5. Create a Form/Subform relationship with frmChargeSummary as the main form and frmCafeBillDetail as the subform. Name the control on the main form that contains the subform **frmCafeBillDetail**.

6. Place command buttons on the forms as specified in Table 3-6. Give the buttons the names specified.

7. Insert the controls on the forms, as specified in Table 3-7. Place the control in the Details section of the form unless otherwise indicated. For combo boxes, use the wizard to create a combo box that retrieves data from the appropriate table.

8. Save your work.

Table 3-6   Forms and their command buttons in Hands-on Project 3-4

Form	Button	Action	Object name
frmSwitchboard	Enter System	Open Customer form	cmdEnter
	Exit System	Exit the application	cmdQuit
frmCustomer	Make Reservation	Open form to add a reservation for this customer	cmdReservations
	Check In	Open reservation for this customer and make any changes necessary	cmdCheckIn
	Check Out	Open form that summarizes room and cafe charges for this customer during this stay	cmdCheckout
frmCharge Summary	Show Detail	Shows/hides details of cafe bills	cmdDetail
frmMake Reservation	Save Reservation	Saves the reservation	cmdSave
frmCafeBillPost	Post Item	Saves current line item on café bill and increments line number	cmdPostItem
	New Bill	Saves current line item, increments bill number, and resets line number	cmdNewBill
	Close	Deletes records with no item number specified and closes the form	cmdClose

Table 3-7   Forms and their controls in Hands-on Project 3-4

Form	Control	Action	Object Name
frmCustomer	Customer Look Up combo box (in header)	Searches for customer	cboCustomerLookUp
frmCafeBillPost	Item Number combo box	Sets value for item	cboItem
frmMake Reservation	Category combo box	Sets value for room category	cboRoomType
	Room Number combo box	Sets value for room number. Only rooms available and in the appropriate category should be displayed in this list.	cboRoom

Project 3-5

Workers' Compensation Commission. The first steps in creating this application put the basic forms in place. (Use appropriate naming conventions.) Several forms must be created. A form for patients is needed that will allow entry and modification of patient data. Another form is needed for the maintenance of Form A, Form B, and Form C data. For completeness, you will create forms to maintain data for companies and doctors, too.

Complete these steps:

1. Open **WCC.mdb**. The first form to create is a switchboard that will provide access to the rest of the system. Create a blank form and place a label on it that reads "State Workers' Compensation Commission Information System". Change the background color of the form to a color of your choice. Name this form **frmSwitchboard**.

2. Use the wizard to create forms based on tblPatient (**frmPatients**), tblDoctor (**frmDoctors**), and tblCompany (**frmCompany**). Arrange the fields in a format that you find attractive.

3. Create a form to support the maintenance of data for Form A. Base the form on tblWCCA and name it **frmWCCA**. Create unbound text boxes to display the three ICD-9 code descriptions and the four CPT code descriptions. Name these text boxes **txtICD91D, txtICD92D, txtICD93D, txtCPT1D, txtCPT2D, txtCPT3D**, and **txtCPT4D**.

4. Create a form to support the maintenance of data for Form B. Base the form on tblWCCB and name it **frmWCCB**. Create unbound text boxes to display the three ICD-9 code descriptions and the four CPT code descriptions. Name these text boxes **txtICD91D, txtICD92D, txtICD93D, txtCPT1D, txtCPT2D, txtCPT3D**, and **txtCPT4D**.

5. Create a form to support the maintenance of data for Form C. Base the form on tblWCCC and name it **frmWCCC**. Create unbound text boxes to display the three ICD-9 code descriptions. Name these text boxes **txtICD91D, txtICD92D**, and **txtICD93D**.

6. On frmWCCA, frmWCCB, and frmWCCC, specify the Default value for txtMedical Record Number as follows:

   `=[Forms]![frmPatients]![txtMedicalRecordNumber]`

   Specify the Default value for txtPhysician's License Number as follows:

   `=[Forms]![frmPatients]![txtPhysician'sLicenseNumber]`

7. Create a tabular form based on tblPatient named **frmPatientListSubform**. Hide the Physician's License Number field.

8. Place command buttons on the forms as specified in Table 3-8. Give the buttons the names specified.

Table 3-8   Forms and their command buttons in Hands-on Project 3-5

Form	Button	Action	Object Name
frmSwitchboard	Enter/Review Patient	Open Patient form	cmdPatient
	Add a New Doctor	Open Doctor form	cmdDoctor
	Add New Company	Open Company form	cmdCompany
	Print WCC Form A	Prints all previously unprinted Form As	cmdPrintA
	Print WCC Form B	Prints all previously unprinted Form Bs	cmdPrintB
	Print WCC Form C	Prints all previously unprinted Form Cs	cmdPrintC
	Quit System	Exit the application	cmdQuit
frmPatients	Form A	Open new Form A for this patient	cmdFormA
	Form B	Open new Form B for this patient	cmdFormB
	Form C	Open new Form C for this patient	cmdFormC
	Add Doctor	Open Doctor form to a new record	cmdDoctor
	Add Company	Open Company form to a new record	cmdCompany
	Add Patient to Database	Save the patient record	cmdAddPatient
	Close	Close the form	cmdClose
frmWCCA	Close	Close the form	cmdClose
	Print	Print the current Form A	cmdPrint
frmWCCB	Close	Close the form	cmdClose
	Print	Print the current Form B	cmdPrint
frmWCCB	Close	Close the form	cmdClose
	Print	Print the current Form C	cmdPrint
frmCompany	Close	Close the form	cmdClose
frmDoctors	Close	Close the form	cmdClose

9. Insert the controls specified in Table 3–9. Place the controls in the Details section of the form unless otherwise indicated. For combo boxes, use the wizard to create a combo box that retrieves data from the appropriate table.

Table 3-9 Forms and their controls in Hands-on Project 3-5

Form	Control	Action	Object Name
frmPatients	Patient Look Up combo box (in header)	Searches for patient	cboPatient
	Doctor combo box	Sets value of Doctor	cboDoctor
	Company combo box	Sets value of Company	cboCompany
frmWCCA	Physician's License Number combo box	Sets value of Physician's License Number	cboDoctor
	CPT Code combo box (four)	Sets value of CPT code	cboCPT1, cboCPT2, ...
	ICD-9 Code combo box (three)	Sets value of ICD-9 code	cboICD91, cboICD92, ...
frmWCCB	Physician's License Number combo box	Sets value of Physician's License Number	cboDoctor
	CPT Code combo box (four)	Sets value of CPT code	cboCPT1, cboCPT2, ...
	ICD-9 Code combo box (three)	Sets value of ICD-9 code	cboICD91, cboICD92, ...
frmWCCC	Physician's License Number combo box	Sets value of Physician's License Number	cboDoctor
	ICD-9 Code combo box (three)	Sets value of ICD-9 code	cboICD91, cboICD92, ...

10. Create a Form/Subform relationship with frmDoctors as the main form and frmPatientListSubform as the subform. Name the control on the main form that contains the subform **frmPatientList**.

11. Save your work.

4

THE FUNDAMENTALS OF VBA, MACROS, AND COMMAND BARS

Commonly Used Tools and Techniques

In this chapter you will:

♦ Specify the fundamental structure of a VBA procedure

♦ Open forms and reports with VBA, macros, and command bars

♦ Create statements that declare variables and constants

♦ String together WHERE conditions used in the process of opening forms and reports

♦ Write code that uses assignment and If...Then...Else statements

♦ Use the VBA debugging facility

♦ Create custom menus and toolbars

Most users of an Access application will have little experience with the Access development environment, which is how it should be. Instead, the application should be specialized to support the tasks of the user's work environment. As an example of this specialization, consider a university. If advisors routinely require reports listing their advisees and those advisees' GPAs, they should not be required to develop their own queries and reports. At the click of a button, the application should prompt for the advisor's identification information and then generate the report.

Developing Access applications that support and resemble the user's work environment almost always requires the use of macros or Visual Basic for Applications (VBA). In addition, menus and toolbars are often customized to identify the particular features of the application. The use of macros, VBA, and custom menus and toolbars is a hallmark of professionally developed Access applications.

In your quest to develop professional applications, you will explore VBA and macros in detail in this chapter. For instance, you will use OpenForm and OpenReport to display data through forms and reports, respectively. To realize the full capabilities of OpenForm and OpenReport, you will write other commonly used statements. These statements include variable declarations, constant declarations, assignment statements, If...Then...Else conditional expressions, and WHERE condition strings. In addition, you will use the VBA debugger as you develop, debug, and test VBA code.

INTRODUCTION TO VBA

Visual Basic for Applications (VBA) is the programming language used in Access to develop complex applications. Programmers use VBA to create procedures that open forms and reports in response to a user's actions. They also use VBA to calculate complex equations (for example, the discounted price of an item) and to validate field values before storing records. Macros—another programming language supported by Access—perform similar tasks. Although macros are easier to develop, they cannot perform as many tasks as VBA.

Most programming languages utilize procedures that are similar to recipes. A recipe typically has a name, ingredients, and steps, as shown in Figure 4-1. When a cook follows a recipe, he or she produces a desired result. Similarly, when a computer follows the VBA procedure, the Access application performs the desired actions. The code in Figure 4-2, for example, opens the frmCompanies form and displays companies of the type selected in the cboCompanyType combo box.

```
Strawberry Banana Cooler                        (Makes: 4 cups)

1 cup strawberries              1 cup milk
1 banana, peeled                ½ cup light corn syrup
1 pint vanilla ice cream

1. Slice banana
2. Make ice cream (see p. 234)
3. In blender, place strawberries, banana, ice cream, milk, and corn syrup
4. Cover blender and blend on high speed for 30 seconds or until well blended

(Blueberry Banana Cooler—same as above, except substitute blueberries for strawberries)
```

Figure 4-1   Recipe for strawberry banana cooler

This VBA "recipe" deserves further investigation. Like a recipe, a procedure has a name. The name of the procedure in Figure 4-2, cmdFilter_Click, identifies the code so that it can be found easily by programmers and referenced by other procedures. The Dim statement at the beginning of the procedure identifies items that will be used in the procedure (like the ingredients in a recipe). **Dim** statements (that is, dimension statements) declare variables. **Variables** are named locations in memory that are used to store data of the type declared in the Dim statement (for example, String, Integer). The type declared determines how much memory will be reserved.

```
Private Sub cmdFilter_Click()
'Filter frmCompanies to show only those companies of the
'selected type.
    Dim pstrCriteria As String
    If IsNull([cboCompanyType]) Then
        MsgBox "Must enter a company type"

    Else
        pstrCriteria = "[CompanyTypeCode] = " & [cboCompanyType]
        DoCmd.OpenForm "frmCompanies", , , pstrCriteria
    End If
End Sub
```

Figure 4-2   cmdFilter_Click() event procedure

The statements following the Dim statements contain the step-by-step instructions that will be followed to produce the desired result. In particular, the steps in cmdFilter_Click verify that the user entered a value for cboCompanyType. If cboCompanyType does not contain a value, the user is shown a message. If cboCompanyType contains a value, frmCompanies opens and the desired companies are displayed. The result of cmdFilter_Click can be seen by opening frmSelectCompanyType in MU-DSci and clicking the Filter command button.

As an Access application developer, you must write the instructions that tell the computer what to do. Your instructions are contained within a named VBA procedure or macro. The instructions will declare variables that are used by the procedure and specify syntactically correct program statements. Keep an eye on the "recipe" in Figure 4-2. This code and basic features of VBA will be explored in more detail in the following sections.

Functions and Sub Procedures

Procedures have a beginning and an end. In Figure 4-2, the procedure begins with Private Sub cmdFilter_Click() and ends with End Sub. It is a special type of procedure called an **event procedure**. The code inside an event procedure executes when the user or the system performs an action (that is, an event). In this case, cmdFilter_Click() executes when the user clicks the command button cmdFilter.

In addition to event procedures, other types of procedures include functions and general sub procedures. **Functions** and **general sub procedures** are not tied to one particular event; rather, the programmer specifies when the procedure executes. For example, a programmer could create a GPA function that supplies the GPA to a student form when it is opened and to a transcript report when it is printed. The primary distinction between a sub procedure and a function is that a function usually returns a value and a sub procedure usually does not return a value.

To illustrate this distinction, consider the IsNull function used in Figure 4-2. Access provides this function (functions provided by Access are called **built-in functions**). After IsNull executes, it returns a value of True when the item inside parentheses does not contain a value (for example, when the combo box is empty). IsNull returns False when the item contains a value. The IsNull function is not directly tied to a user's action. Instead, the programmer invokes IsNull whenever the code needs to know whether a particular item has a value.

All procedures are contained within modules. Modules help organize procedures so that a procedure can be found easily. Several types of modules exist. In a form class module, procedures are stored with a form and can be executed only when the form is opened. In a standard module that is located in the Database window, procedures can be executed at any time.

Functions and sub procedures share a common syntax:

Syntax

[**Private**|**Public**] [**Sub**|**Function**] *ProcedureName* ([*ArgumentList*])

Syntax Dissection

- **Private** indicates that the procedure can be invoked only by other procedures in the same module.

- **Public** indicates that the procedure can be invoked by procedures located in any module.

- **Sub** declares a sub procedure. Sub procedures usually do not return a value.

- **Function** declares a function procedure. Functions usually return a value. Menus, toolbars, and other form and control properties can invoke functions.

- *ProcedureName* is the name of the procedure. Access creates the name automatically when an event procedure is created. Event procedure names should not be changed. The developer specifies the name of functions and general sub procedures.

- *ArgumentList* is a list of variables that are passed to the function or sub procedure.

The method for creating procedures depends on the type of procedure. To create an event procedure, you click the Build button located next to the Event property on a form, control, or report's property sheet. To create a function or general sub procedure, you open the Design view of a module, click Insert, and then click Procedure on the menu. Standard modules are located on the Database window. Form class modules are displayed by clicking Code in the toolbar when the form is in Design view.

OpenForm and OpenReport

OpenForm and **OpenReport** are instructions that are included in a procedure and that cause Access to open forms and open reports, respectively. In VBA, OpenForm, OpenReport, and almost all other instructions are called methods.

Opening forms and reports is a common task in Access applications; consequently, these instructions are one of the first types that you should master. Like VBA procedures, OpenForm and OpenReport are associated with arguments. The arguments specify which form or report to display. They also indicate how to display the form or report. The syntax for OpenForm and OpenReport in VBA is as follows:

Syntax

DoCmd.OpenForm *formname* [*,view*] [*,filtername*] [*,wherecondition*] [*,datamode*] [*,windowmode*] [*,openargs*]

Syntax Dissection

- **DoCmd** is an object capable of manipulating forms, reports, and controls.

- **OpenForm** is a method of DoCmd that opens a form. DoCmd methods cause some action to occur.

- The *formname* argument is a string expression that gives the name of the form to open. It is the only required argument of OpenForm.

- The *view* argument is the view of the form to display. The following are legal values of *view*: acDesign (display the form in Design view), acFormDS (display the form in Datasheet view), acNormal (display the form in Form view), and acPreview (display the form in Print Preview mode). If you omit this argument, the form displays in acNormal.

- The *filtername* argument is a string expression that is the name of a query to apply to the form before it opens. A filter limits the records displayed to those that meet the criteria specified in the query. The query must have the same columns as the form's record source.

- The *wherecondition* argument is a string expression that is an SQL WHERE clause (without the word WHERE); it limits the records displayed. Like the Criteria row in a query, wherecondition limits the data displayed to those records that meet a specified condition. It allows a form to display different data depending on the situation.

- The *datamode* argument specifies whether and how the data can be changed. The following are its legal values: acFormAdd (a blank screen is displayed for the entry of new data), acFormEdit (data in the record can be changed), acFormReadOnly (data in the form cannot be changed), and acFormPropertySettings (the *datamode* is determined by the property settings specified in the form's property sheet). For this argument, acFormPropertySettings is the default value. The value of the *datamode* argument overrides the form's AllowEdits, AllowDeletions, and AllowAdditions properties, which were set in the form's property sheet; consequently, VBA allows the same form to be used for a variety of purposes.

- *windowmode* indicates how the form opens. Its possible values are acDialog (the form displays on top of all other forms and the user must close the form before using any other form), acHidden (the form is opened, but not visible), acIcon (the form is minimized), and acWindowNormal (the form displays according to the properties specified in the form's property sheet).

- *openargs* is a string expression that is passed to the form that is opened.

Syntax

DoCmd.OpenReport *reportname*[, *view*][, *filtername*][, *wherecondition*]

Syntax Dissection

- The *reportname* argument is a string expression that is the name of the report to open.

- The *view* argument indicates how to display the report. Its legal values are acViewNormal (prints the report immediately), acViewPreview (displays the report in Print Preview mode), and acViewDesign (displays the form in Design view).

- The *filtername* argument is the same as *filtername* in OpenForm.

- The *wherecondition* argument is the same as *wherecondition* in OpenForm.

You should notice that the OpenForm and OpenReport methods are attached to a DoCmd object. In VBA, almost all instructions belong to some object. The object is the thing that knows how to perform the instruction indicated by the method. The DoCmd object possesses many methods that perform actions on other objects (for example, on forms and reports).

Now that you know the syntax of the two methods, you will look at some examples. Start with OpenForm:

```
DoCmd.OpenForm "frmCurrentStudents"
```

This code causes Access to display frmCurrentStudents in Form view.

Next, you look at an example of OpenReport. In this example, the code prints the rptEmployers report:

```
DoCmd.OpenReport "rptEmployers"
```

 TIP   In VBA, the name of the form or report must be placed in quotation marks.

The previous code causes Access to send rptEmployers to the printer. If the report should be displayed in Print Preview mode, however, the *view* argument is used:

```
DoCmd.OpenReport "rptEmployers", acViewPreview
```

To create a "read-only" form so that users cannot change the data, use the *datamode* argument.

```
DoCmd.OpenForm "frmCurrentStudents",,,,acDataReadOnly
```

Access expects the arguments to appear in order; consequently, several commas are used to place acDataReadOnly in the correct spot. Alternatively, you can use the following notation:

```
DoCmd.OpenForm formname:="frmCurrentStudents", _
datamode:=acDataReadOnly
```

The previous code uses **named arguments**. The advantage of this approach is that the string of commas is not necessary and a specific order is not required. The names of the arguments are specified in the OpenReport and OpenForm syntax. If a VBA instruction will not fit on one line, the **continuation character**, which is a space followed by an underscore (_), is used to indicate that the instruction continues on the next line. The continuation character is commonly used when an entire line cannot be seen in the VBA window.

Two additional items are worth pointing out in the previous line of code. The first item is acDataReadOnly, which is an intrinsic constant. An **intrinsic constant** is a keyword that represents some particular value (usually an integer). For example, acNormal represents the integer 0 and acPreview represents the integer 2. These integers are the values actually passed to OpenForm. The application becomes easier to maintain, however, when the OpenForm instruction uses more descriptive intrinsic constants. The second item is the *wherecondition* argument. In using this argument, you will learn about variable declarations and control referencing.

Procedure Ingredients: Objects and Variables

Like a recipe, a procedure uses and manipulates "ingredients." Ingredients that are manipulated by a procedure include the control, form, report, query, table, and page objects that make up an Access application. For example, a procedure may obtain the current value of a text box to calculate a value to be placed in another text box. In addition to objects, procedures use variables and constants. You next examine controls and variables in detail.

Controls

Many procedures use or update the current value of a control on a form. A **value** is usually a number (for example, 152 and 7.5) or a string ("100 Elm Street"). The current value of a text box is displayed on a form, report, or data access page. The current value of a combo box refers to the value of the bound column. Consider the sub procedure in Figure 4–2 once again. It refers to the value of the cboCompanyType combo box. This value changes whenever the user selects a different item in the combo box. The cboCompanyType combo box contains two columns: the CompanyType and the CompanyTypeCode. The bound column, identified by the BoundColumn property in the cboCompanyType property sheet, is CompanyTypeCode. If a form displays more than one record, the value of control is determined by the record containing the insertion point (that is, the current record).

VBA procedures require a special syntax to refer to the value of a control. Although Access supports a variety of notations, a commonly used notation is the **bang notation**. Its syntax is as follows (note that Forms! indicates that the entity following the ! is a form):

Syntax

Forms![*formname*]![*controlname*]

Syntax Dissection

■ The *formname* argument refers to the name of an open form that contains the control.

■ The *controlname* argument refers to the name of the control as specified in the control's property sheet.

A standard procedure that refers to the value of cboCompanyType could use the following notation (the form must be opened before the code can execute):

```
Forms![frmSelectCompanyType]![cboCompanyType]
```

A procedure that is located in a form's class module can use an abbreviated syntax to refer to controls on its form. In such a case, only the name of the control is required. If the control name contains a space, square brackets must be placed around the name (for example, [txtFirst Name]). By convention, most programmers place square brackets around control names even when they do not contain any spaces. In Figure 4-2, the current value of cboCompanyType was obtained through the following syntax:

```
[cboCompanyType]
```

Variables

As noted earlier, **variables** are named locations in the computer's memory. They are key ingredients in a VBA procedure because they store values that are needed to complete the steps in the procedure.

Although it is not absolutely necessary, variables are usually declared before they are used. Declaring a variable tells Access that you intend to use a variable and that it should reserve a spot for the variable in memory. You declare a variable to hold a particular type of data (that is, the data type). When Access knows the data type of a variable, processing can take place more efficiently. For example, if an equation uses an undeclared variable, Access must verify that the value in the variable is numeric before the result of the equation can be determined. Because programmers do not like to search for variable declarations when they are trying to modify procedures, most variables are declared within the first few lines of a procedure. Variable declarations can become complex. Most, however, use the following syntax:

Syntax

Dim *varname* [**As** *datatype*]

Syntax Dissection

- **Dim** is used to start a variable declaration inside the scope of a procedure (for example, a sub procedure or function).

- The *varname* argument is any valid name given to the variable. Variable names must start with a letter. They cannot use a space, period, exclamation mark, or the characters @, &, $, and #. Also, they cannot use the same name as any built-in function, constant, or other reserved word. A reserved word is a word that Access already uses to signal some operation (for example, DoCmd).

- The optional *datatype* identifies the type of data stored in the variable. If you omit the *datatype* argument, by default its type is Variant. Variant data types can store almost all types of values. They do not store or retrieve data as efficiently as other data types, however.

To facilitate the maintenance of a system, prefixes and tags should be placed on variable names, although this naming convention is not required for the procedure to work. The prefix indicates the scope of the variable, and the tag indicates the type of data that the variable can store. Variables declared inside the scope of a procedure should begin with the letter "p". The "p" states that the variable is private; that is, other procedures cannot use the variable. The "p" should be followed by the data type tag.

Let's look at an example of a variable declaration. The following statement declares one variable that will store only integer values:

```
Dim pintSeatsAvailable As Integer
```

As another example, note that the procedure in Figure 4-2 used the following declaration to declare a string variable:

```
Dim pstrCriteria As String
```

More than one variable can be declared with the same Dim statement. The following statement declares two variables of different data types:

```
Dim psngGradePoint As Single, pdblAverageGPR As Double
```

A variable that is defined without a data type declaration, such as

```
Dim pvntTestValue
```

has the Variant data type by default.

Variables do not need to be declared before they are used. When Access encounters a name that it does not recognize, it automatically creates a Variant variable. The danger, of course, is that a misspelling can result in the creation of a new variable. For example, if you declare the variable pintQuantity and then later accidentally type pintQuantiy, a new variable will be created. This variable will be assigned a value, and the code will likely produce incorrect results. To fix this problem, you can force Access to check for undeclared variables by placing an Option Explicit statement in the Declarations section of a module.

The Declarations section appears at the top of a module, outside the scope of any procedure. It specifies how the code should be compiled and processed. If the Declarations section contains the statement Option Explicit, Access will display an error message when it finds undeclared variables. Option Explicit is the default when the Options dialog box has a check next to Require Variable Declarations. Because of the numerous problems that are encountered when variables are not declared, good programming practice requires the use of Option Explicit.

Assignment Statements

Variables are useful only when they contain values. They obtain their values through assignment statements that are located within a procedure. **Assignment statements** are instructions that tell Access to place a value in a particular location. Once a variable has a value, it can be used in any expression or placed in any argument that requires a value that is consistent with the variable's data type. The syntax for assigning values to variables is as follows:

Syntax

[**Let**] *variable* = [*value* | *expression*]

Syntax Dissection

- **Let** is an optional word that indicates the start of the assignment statement. The word **Let** is almost always omitted.

- The *variable* argument is the name of the variable that will receive the value. When the Declarations section of the module contains the phrase Option Explicit, the variable must be declared before it can be used in an assignment statement.

- The *value* argument represents the value to be assigned; it can consist of a number, text, or date. Text values must be enclosed in quotation marks. Date values must be enclosed in pound (#) signs.

- The *expression* argument refers to any combination of constants, variables, operators, references to controls, and functions that result in a value that is consistent with the data type of the variable designated to receive the value. Legal operators include + (addition), - (subtraction), * (multiplication), / (division), ^ (exponent), \ (integer division), and & (string concatenation).

The following code illustrates several different types of assignment statements:

```
Public Sub CalculateDue()
'Illustrates assignment statements and calculates total due
    Dim pcurTotal As Currency, pcurSub As Currency
    Dim psngTaxRate As Single
    Dim pstrMessage As String
    psngTaxRate = .05 'place .05 in psngTaxRate
    'Place the value that is currently in the control,
    'txtSubTotal
    'located on the form frmSales, in the pcurSub variable.
    pcurSub = Forms![frmSales]![txtSubTotal]
    'Calculate the total due and place in the variable
    'pcurTotal
    pcurTotal = pcurSub + (psngTaxRate * pcurSub)
    'Construct a message and place the message in
    'pstrMessage
    pstrMessage = "Amount Due: $" & pcurTotal
    MsgBox pstrMessage
End Sub
```

The MsgBox built-in function at the end of the program code causes Access to display the value of the variable pstrMessage on the screen. If the initial value of txtSubTotal was $100, the message box would display "Amount Due: $105."

Basic wherecondition Arguments

Assignment statements that use the concatenation operator (&) are frequently used to form **wherecondition arguments,** which programmers use to add additional criteria to a record source before the data are displayed or retrieved. The wherecondition argument must be a string (that is, text). Referring back to Figure 4-2, the following assignment statement formed the string that will be used in the wherecondition argument of the OpenForm method:

```
pstrCriteria = "[CompanyTypeCode] = " & [cboCompanyType]
```

The location of the quotation marks in the assignment statement is critical. The code concatenates the string "[CompanyTypeCode] = " with the value in the combo box. If the user selects "Chemical Processing" from the combo box in frmSelectCompanyType (see Figure 4-3), pstrCriteria will store the following value:

```
[CompanyTypeCode] = 20
```

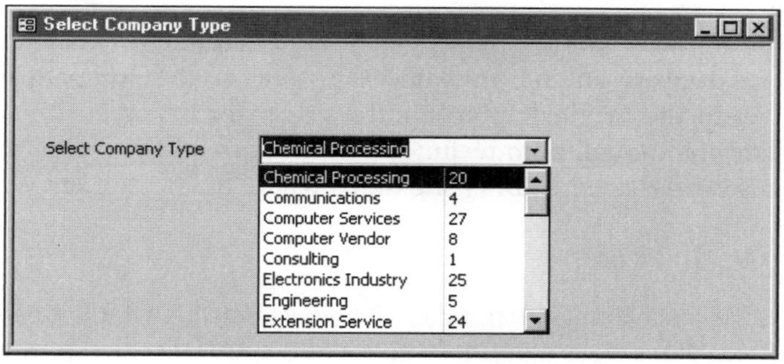

Figure 4-3 Selecting Chemical Processing from the combo box

Moving to the next line of code in Figure 4-2, you can see that frmCompanies is opened through the OpenForm method. The record source for frmCompanies is the table tblCompanies. Normally, frmCompanies will display all the records in tblCompanies. Here, however, the wherecondition argument that was created in the previous line has added another criterion.

Conceptually, adding the wherecondition criterion to the tblCompanies table has the same effect as the query illustrated in Figure 4-4.

As usual, a developer has more than one way to write code to accomplish a particular goal. Rather than the previous assignment statement, for example, the following assignment statement could also be used to restrict the data displayed in frmCompanies:

```
pstrCriteria = _
"[CompanyTypeCode] = " & _
"Forms![frmSelectCompanyType]![cboCompanyType]"
```

The value of pstrCriteria is then

```
[CompanyTypeCode] =
Forms![frmSelectCompanyType]![cboCompanyType]
```

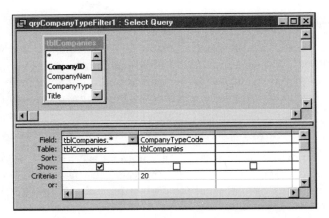

Figure 4-4 Query equivalent to adding a wherecondition to the record source of frmCompanies

The difference between the values of the two wherecondition arguments is subtle. With the second approach, the Jet database engine must find the value of cboCompanyType when frmCompanies opens. With the original approach, the value (for example, 20) was sent as part of the wherecondition. Although both techniques work correctly, you need to be aware of the differences because you may encounter situations where one technique works better than another.

> **TIP** A common mistake made by many beginning VBA programmers is to include bang notation on the left side of the equal sign. The left side of the equals sign must refer to a field in the record source; the right side can use bang notation, if desired.

whereconditions That Do More

You can make powerful whereconditions. For instance, if the data in a form must obey more than one new criterion, the **AND** operator is strung into the wherecondition. If the data must obey at least one criterion, the **OR** operator is used. Parentheses can also be used to specify how the wherecondition should be evaluated (for example, Code =1 AND (Dept = 1 OR Dept= 2)). In addition, operators such as <, >, <=, and >= can be used instead of the equals sign. The wherecondition argument can contain any string that could appear after the word WHERE in an SQL statement.

More power is nice, but you must take care when the value for a field is text or a date. Text fields must be compared to text (that is, strings). Microsoft Access expects strings to be enclosed in quotation marks. In Query Design view, Access automatically places quotation marks around textual criteria. These quotation marks must also be strung into the wherecondition string. Textual data can be surrounded by single quotes rather than double quotes.

As an example of a complex wherecondition, assume that our client would like to generate a report that prints all prospects that were admitted or denied in a certain semester. The user will enter the semester desired in a text box called txtSemester; the semester is a string value. The user will also indicate whether the report should print admitted or denied prospects. This is a numeric value selected from an option group called fraAdmission. The form is named frmAdmitSpecs. The following code segment could be used:

```
Dim pstrCriteria As String
pstrCriteria = "[AdmittedDenied] = " & _
Forms![frmAdmitSpecs]![fraAdmission] _
& " AND [EntryDate] = '" _
& Forms![frmAdmitSpecs]![txtSemester] & "'"
DoCmd.OpenReport "rptAdmissions",,,pstrCriteria
```

If fraAdmission is equal to 1 and txtSemester is equal to 01A, then pstrCriteria is equal to the following:

```
[AdmittedDenied] = 1 AND [EntryDate] = '01A'
```

TIP You can place the Msgbox function in your code temporarily to help you determine whether the wherecondition has been created correctly. For example, MsgBox pstrCriteria will display the value stored in pstrCriteria.

As a final example of a more complex wherecondition, assume that you want to find all students who were born after a certain date entered in a text box called txtDOB. The text box is located on the form frmAge. Access expects dates to be surrounded by pound signs. The following statements could be used:

```
pstrCriteria = "[DOB] >= #" & Forms![frmAge]![txtDOB] & "#"
DoCmd.OpenForm "frmCurrentStudents",,,pstrCriteria
```

If the user enters 1/1/1980 into the text box, pstrCriteria contains the value

```
[DOB] >= #1/1/1980#
```

and frmCurrentStudents will display only students born after 1/1/1980.

In addition to OpenForm and OpenReport, whereconditions are used with many other built-in functions and methods. For instance, **domain aggregate functions** return values or statistical information from the records in a table or query. Consider the following statement, which will return the number of companies of the type selected in the cboCompanyType combo box:

```
=DCount("[CompanyTypeCode]","tblCompanies", _
"[CompanyTypeCode] = " & [cboCompanyType])
```

The wherecondition string is the third argument in the function. Rather than using a variable, the string is formed within the parentheses. The preceding statement can be placed in the ControlSource properly of a text box, forming a calculated control. The text box will display the value that is returned by DCount. Alternatively, the statement could be placed in a function or sub procedure. In that case, a variable will appear on the left side of the equals sign. Like an OpenForm and OpenReport method, the wherecondition could be placed in a string variable and then the string variable could be used in the third argument as well.

Conditional Execution

Often blocks of code need to be executed under some conditions but not executed under others. The **If...Then...Else statement** in VBA supports conditional execution. It has the following syntax:

Syntax

If *Condition* **Then**
     Instructions-1
[**ElseIf** *Condition-n*
     ElseIfInstructions]
[**Else**
     ElseInstructions]
End If

Syntax Dissection

- *Condition* is an expression that evaluates to True or False. The expression may contain =, >, <, >=, <=, <>(not equal), And, Or, Not, and many other types of operators. The Not operator reverses the remaining expression's truth value. The expression may also contain built-in functions like IsNull.

- *Instructions* are VBA statements that are executed when the condition is True.

- *Condition-n* is similar to *Condition*, but is tested only when the previous conditions are not true.

- *ElseIfInstructions* are VBA statements that are executed when the corresponding ElseIf condition is true.

- *ElseInstructions* are VBA statements that are executed when none of the conditions is true.

The sub procedure in Figure 4-2 uses a conditional expression. You now have enough information to understand a detailed discussion of this code. The first line of the code specifies the name of the sub procedure. The next two lines are comments. Programmers use **comments** to document the code; these lines are not executed as a part of the steps necessary to produce the procedure's goals. Placing a single quote in front of a statement creates a comment. The line following the comments declares a string variable. Next, a conditional expression is encountered. The IsNull function evaluates the contents of cboCompanyType. If IsNull returns True, a message box is displayed. If IsNull returns False, pstrCriteria is loaded with a string that concatenates a constant with the value in cboCompanyType. Next, frmCompanies is displayed and pstrCriteria is sent as the wherecondition argument.

Printing Payment Reports in the Swim Lessons Application

The rptPayment report in the Swim Lessons application prints all payment records in the database. Receipts should be generated to print the payment information for each single payment. You are to create a command button on frmPayment that prints, in Print Preview mode, the payment information for the payment that is currently displayed on the screen.

To create code in VBA that prints payment information for a single payment:

1. Open **SwimReg**, refresh the links, if necessary, and then open **frmPayment** in Design view.

2. If the Payment tab is not selected, click the **Payment** tab.

3. Create a command button in the upper-right corner of the detail section (within the Payment tab). Cancel the Command Button Wizard, if it appears.

4. Display the property sheet for the command button, and, if necessary, click the **All** tab. Type **cmdReceipt** in the Name property and **Receipt** in the Caption property.

5. Click the **Event** tab in the property sheet, and then click the **On Click** event property. A build button should appear next to the text box.

6. Click the **build** button, click **Code Builder**, and then click **OK**. The Sub procedure cmdReceipt_Click() displays.

7. Verify that **Option Explicit** is located under the phrase Option Compare Database, but prior to the beginning of the Sub procedure. If it does not appear there, type **Option Explicit** under Option Compare Database.

8. Place the insertion point in the first blank row within the Private Sub cmdReceipt_Click() procedure, and then type the boldface code so the procedure looks like the following:

```
Private Sub cmdReceipt_Click()
'Print a receipt for this payment
    Dim pstrCriteria As String
    pstrCriteria = "[PaymentNo] = " & [PaymentNo]
    DoCmd.OpenReport "rptPayment", acViewPreview, , _
    pstrCriteria
End Sub
```

9. Close the VBA window, display the Form view of frmPayment, and then click the **Receipt** command button. The report rptPayment should preview payment information for the payment displayed on the screen.

10. Close and save frmPayment.

Users of the Swim Lessons applications would also like to print payments that occur between two dates. This printout will accompany deposits to the bank. You will need to create a new form to specify the dates, and a VBA procedure to display the correct records in the report.

To create a report that prints payments between two dates:

1. Create a new unbound form that contains two text boxes. One text box is for the beginning date and the other is for the ending date. Name the textboxes **txtBegin** and **txtEnd**, respectively, and make the captions of the accompanying labels **Beginning Date:** and **Ending Date:**, respectively.

2. Save, but do not close, the form, name the form **frmPrintDeposits**, and then type **m/d/yyyy** in the Format properties for both text boxes.

3. Create an input mask for each text box with the specification **99/99/0099;1;_** .

4. Place a command button on frmPrintDeposits. Cancel the wizard if it appears. Name the command button **cmdDeposits**. Make the caption **Print Deposits**. In Form view, your form should resemble Figure 4-5. You may have to resize some of the control instances to achieve an exact match.

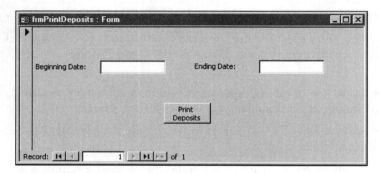

Figure 4-5   frmPrintDeposits form

5. Create an event procedure for the On Click event of cmdDeposits.

6. Write code so that the VBA module appears as follows:

```
Option Compare Database
Option Explicit

Private Sub cmdDeposits_Click()
'Print all payments between the two dates.
    Dim pstrCriteria As String

    'If legal dates are entered, form criteria, and print
    If IsDate([txtBegin]) And IsDate([txtEnd]) Then
        pstrCriteria = "[PaymentDate] >= #" & _
            [txtBegin] & "# AND [PaymentDate] <= #" _
            & [txtEnd] & "#"
        DoCmd.OpenReport "rptPayment", acViewPreview, , _
            pstrCriteria
    'If legal dates are not entered, send message
    Else
        MsgBox "You must enter two dates"
    End If
End Sub
```

7. The IsDate function returns True when the values entered are dates. Display frmPrintDeposits in Form view, enter two dates (for example, **1/1/2001** and **6/6/2001**), and click the **Print Deposits** button. Verify that the report is correct.

8. If an error occurred, type **MsgBox pstrCriteria** after the assignment statement in the event procedure created in Step 6. Test the form again and verify that the string displayed in the message box is correct. Correct any errors.

9. Close and save the form.

Now that you understand some of the basic components of a VBA procedure and their importance for application development, you can appreciate the nuances of the Visual Basic Editor, which is discussed next.

THE VISUAL BASIC EDITOR

Efficient programming in VBA requires familiarity with the **Visual Basic Editor (VBE)**. The VBE allows you to quickly access modules, procedures, possible intrinsic constants, and other objects that could be used in a VBA procedure. In addition, it has many tools that help the programmer create syntactically correct statements. The VBE also contains debugging tools that help a programmer find and fix the errors that will inevitably occur in the process of developing the application.

As illustrated in Figure 4-6, the VBE consists of several windows and list boxes. The Project Explorer window contains references to all modules in the application. To open a module with the VBE, click on the module in the Project Explorer and then click the View Code button located in the Project Explorer window.

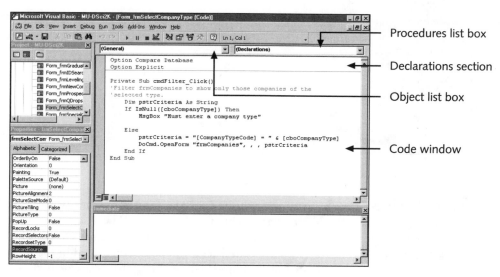

Figure 4-6   Visual Basic Editor

The Properties window displays properties of the form, report, or module that is highlighted in the Project Explorer. To display the current property values for a particular control on the form or report, you click the control in the Properties window list box. In order for the properties to be displayed, however, the object (for example, form or report) must be open. If the object is open, you can use the VBE Properties window to edit the properties' values.

You use the Code window to create, display, and edit VBA code. Although you can use the scroll bar to find various procedures within a module, it is sometimes quicker to use the Object and Procedures list boxes located at the top of the Code window. In the case of a form or report class module, the Object list box lists all controls on the form or report. The Procedures list box lists all event procedures that are activated by the control currently highlighted in the Object list box. When (General) is selected in the Object list box, the Procedures list box shows general procedures that are not associated with a control.

As you type in the Code window, you will notice that Access attempts to help you build syntactically correct code. For example, it prompts for arguments and often presents a list box of possible values.

The **Object Browser** is an additional source of help. Clicking Object Browser in the toolbar displays the Object Browser window. All of the objects recognized by VBA, Access, the database engine, and any other application with which you are working will then appear in the Object Browser, as shown in Figure 4-7.

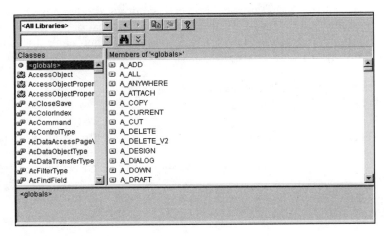

Figure 4-7   Object Browser

Within the Object Browser, you can use the Libraries list box to narrow your search for an object by identifying the library responsible for that object. The Classes window, which is located within the Object Browser, lists objects that contain other objects. The Members window lists objects or properties associated with the object identified in the Class window. Most of the intrinsic constants can be found within the globals class or within classes that begin with Ac or Vb.

Debugging Tools

Programming is an activity in which mistakes will inevitably occur. Even experienced programmers make mistakes and must debug their code. If you do not find any errors during your application development, you probably have not performed adequate tests.

Errors can be classified into three categories: compilation errors, runtime errors, and logic errors. **Compilation errors** occur before the code is run. Prior to running code, Access must translate the code into a language that the computer will understand. If a syntax error has been made, Access will not be able to translate the code. Access will normally catch syntax (compilation) errors while you are typing or during the compilation process. **Runtime errors** cause a running procedure to abort. Invalid or unexpected data can cause this type of error. For example, in Figure 4-2, if pstrCriteria was declared as an Integer, the program would abort when the assignment statement was executed. **Logic errors** do not abort execution, but rather produce incorrect results. For example, the application might calculate the incorrect amount due or display the incorrect customer record. Debugging tools are especially useful for helping you diagnose runtime and logic errors.

Immediate Window

The **Immediate window** holds commands that will be executed as soon as the programmer presses the Enter key. For instance, entering a question mark, followed by the name of a variable or control, will display the value of the variable or control:

```
?pstrName
```

The Immediate window can also display values that are in a form, but that are not referenced in the aborted procedure.

Besides displaying variables, programmers can use the Immediate window to test new or revised expressions. For example, the following code, when typed into the Immediate window, displays the result of a discount equation:

```
?psngPrice — (psngPrice-[txtCouponTotal])*[txtDiscount])
```

Locals Window

Once a procedure aborts, you can use the **Locals window** to display information about all variables, forms, reports, or controls used in the aborted procedure. If an item in the Locals window has a plus sign (+) next to it, clicking + will display more information about the item. The Locals window can also be displayed through the Debug toolbar. If this toolbar does not appear on the screen, click the View menu, point to Toolbars, and then click Debug to make it visible.

Breakpoint

Unfortunately, the line of code that Access believes to have caused the error is not always the line of code that actually caused the error. Frequently, it is useful to step through code, line-by-line, until the error occurs. This approach is particularly beneficial when certain lines of code are executing (or not executing) unexpectedly.

Setting a breakpoint suspends the execution of a program. To set a breakpoint, you place the insertion point on the line where execution should stop and then click Breakpoint in the Debug toolbar. A quicker way to set or remove a breakpoint is to click the Margin Indicator Bar at the line of code where you wish to add or remove the breakpoint.

Debug Toolbar

Once program execution is suspended, you can click the following buttons on the Debug toolbar:

- Step Into causes the highlighted line to execute and moves the insertion point to the next line that should execute, even if it is in another procedure.

- Step Over causes the highlighted line to execute. If this line invokes another procedure, that procedure executes in its entirety, and then processing is suspended at the next executable line.

- Step Out causes the entire procedure to finish executing. Control is suspended again in the procedure that invoked the currently highlighted procedure.

- Continue causes the procedure to run until it is finished, aborts, or encounters another breakpoint.

- Break causes a running procedure to stop.

- Reset causes the program, even in its suspended state, to stop running.

Several other debugging tools exist, including Watch Expressions and Call Stacks. See Access Help for more information about these tools.

Testing and Debugging the Receipt Procedure

The Swim Lessons procedure that printed a receipt for an individual payment has not been adequately tested. What happens when the user clicks the Receipt command button before entering a payment? Work through the following steps to find out.

To test and debug the receipt procedure:

1. Open **frmPayment** in Form view.

2. Use the record navigator to move to a new record.

3. Click the **Receipt** command button. An error dialog box will appear.

4. Click **Debug**. The cmdReceipt_Click() procedure is displayed and the DoCmd line is highlighted, as shown in Figure 4-8.

```
Private Sub cmdReceipt_Click()
'Print a receipt for this payment
    Dim pstrCriteria As String
    pstrCriteria = "[PaymentNo] = " & [PaymentNo]
    DoCmd.OpenReport "rptPayment", acViewPreview, , pstrCriteria
End Sub
```

Figure 4-8   Highlighted line in cmdReceipt_Click()

5. Move the insertion point over pstrCriteria. The value of pstrCriteria is displayed.

6. Move the insertion point to the Immediate window. If the Immediate window is not visible, click the **View** menu and then click **Immediate Window**.

7. Type **?pstrCriteria** in the Immediate window, and then press **Enter**. [PaymentNo]= is displayed.

8. Click the **Reset** button on the toolbar. The highlighted lines are removed.

9. The cause of the problem may be the fact that PaymentNo is Null in a new record. You must therefore correct the code so that it recognizes Null values. Add the boldface lines of code and adjust the indenting so that cmdReceipt_Click() looks as follows:

```
Private Sub cmdReceipt_Click()
'Print a receipt for this payment
    Dim pstrCriteria As String
    If Not IsNull([PaymentNo]) Then
        pstrCriteria = "[PaymentNo] = " & [PaymentNo]
        DoCmd.OpenReport "rptPayment", acViewPreview, , _
            pstrCriteria
    End If
End Sub
```

To ensure that the code works correctly, you will next place a breakpoint on the If line. Then, you will step through the code to monitor its effect.

To set a breakpoint and watch the code run:

1. Click the line that begins with "If."

2. Click **View** on the menu bar, point to **Toolbars**, and then click **Debug**. The Debug toolbar is displayed.

3. Click the **Toggle Breakpoint** button on the toolbar. The "If" line is highlighted.

4. Click **File** on the menu bar, and then click **Close and Return to Microsoft Access**.

5. Display **frmPayment** in Form view, and then move to a new record.

6. Click the **Receipt** button. The cmdReceipt_Click() procedure will be displayed and suspended at the "If" line.

7. Click the **Step Into** button on the Debug toolbar. Control will pass to the "End If" line.

8. Click the **Continue** button. The procedure will stay on the screen but the code will finish executing.

9. Close the VBE window and repeat steps 1–8 for a record that does have a PaymentNo. Use the Step Into button to move through the procedure until the report is displayed. (You will need to click the Microsoft Access button at the bottom of the screen to see the report.)

10. Return to VBE, and then click the **Continue** button on the Debug toolbar to finish the procedure.

11. On the menu bar, click **Debug**, and then click **Clear All Breakpoints** to remove the breakpoint.

12. Close the VBE, click **OK** in the resulting dialog box and then close frmPayment. If prompted to do so, save frmPayment, and then close the Payment Details window.

You have now written, tested, and debugged a VBA procedure. Next, you will use your knowledge of VBA programming to understand macro programming.

MACROS

A **macro** is a sequence of actions that automates a task. Like code in a procedure, actions perform many tasks, including opening forms, previewing reports, and setting values. Although most advanced Access applications use VBA rather than macros, professional developers know how to create macros and may employ them to perform simple tasks. From a beginning programmer's standpoint, macros offer an advantage because legal actions are selected from a combo box and Access then prompts for the value of any necessary arguments (for example, the arguments for the OpenForm macro action). Figure 4-9 shows a macro that performs the same task as the VBA code in Figure 4-2. This macro will be discussed in more detail in the following sections.

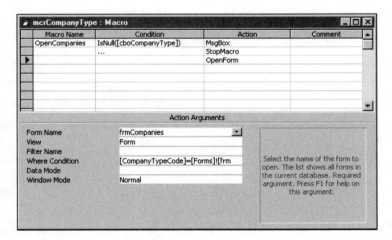

Figure 4-9   Macro equivalent to cmdFilter_Click()

Macro Groups

The first column that you should notice in Figure 4-9 is the Macro Name column. When you use the Macro Name column, Access creates a macro group. A **macro group** refers to a macro that contains other macros. The mcrCompanyType macro shown in the Database window is actually a macro group that contains the OpenCompanies macro.

Figure 4-10 shows another example of a macro group. In this case, the mcrExit macro group contains two macros: To Access and To Windows. Macro groups are similar to modules that contain procedures. Programmers use macro groups to organize their macros into categories that facilitate finding the macro when it needs to be updated.

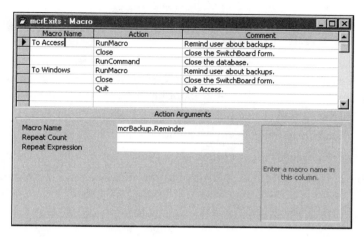

4

Figure 4-10   mcrExits

Condition Column

The Condition column is similar to a VBA If…Then…Else statement. When the expression in the Condition column evaluates to True, the action in the Action column executes. The expression placed in the Condition column is identical to the If…Then…Else condition used in VBA.

In Figure 4-9, the IsNull function determines whether cboCompanyType has a value. Although the bang notation introduced previously could have been used to refer to cboCompanyType, this longer notation was not necessary. When bang notation is not used, Access searches the form that has the focus in an effort to find a field that has the specified name (for example, cboCompanyType).

The ellipsis in the second row of Figure 4-9 tells Access to execute the corresponding action when the condition contained in the previous row is True. Consequently, when IsNull returns a value of True, Figure 4-9 displays a message box and stops the query. If cboCompanyType contains a value, the actions in the first two rows are not executed, but the third row does execute.

Action Column

The action selected from the combo box located in the Action column tells Access to perform some task. As with VBA methods, most actions require the use of an action argument. The arguments for the OpenForm action are almost identical to the arguments used by the VBA OpenForm method. The Where Condition argument contains the same type of string that was discussed earlier. That is, the left side of a comparison expression refers to a field in the form's record source and the right side of the expression is frequently bang notation that refers to a control on a form. The Where Condition in Figure 4–9 contains the following expression:

```
[CompanyTypeCode] = _
Forms![frmSelectCompanyType]![cboCompanyType]
```

Creating a Macro for Swim Lessons

Occasionally, parents will ask for a list of all payments that they made to Metropolitan University for swim lessons. To meet this request, you will place another command button on frmPayment that prints payments based on the phone number that is currently displayed in frmPayment. This time you will create a macro.

To create a macro that prints payments based on a phone number:

1. Click the **Macros** object type, and then click **New**.

2. On the toolbar, click the **Macro Names** button, and then click the **Conditions** button. The Macro Name and Condition columns will appear.

3. In the first row, type **PhonePrint** in the Macro Name column, and then type **IsNull([txtPhone])** in the Condition column.

4. In the first row, select **MsgBox** in the Action column, type **A phone number must be entered** for the Message action argument, and then, in the first row, type **Print based on phone number** in the Comment column.

5. In the second row, enter **Not IsNull([txtPhone])** in the Condition column, and then select **OpenReport** in the Action column.

6. Enter **rptPayment** as the Report Name action argument, and then enter **Print Preview** as the View action argument.

7. Enter **[Phone] = Forms![frmPayment]![txtPhone]** in the Where Condition text box, and then save the macro as **mcrPayment**. Close the Macro.

8. Open **frmPayment** in Design view, if necessary, and place a command button on frmPayment. Cancel the wizard, if necessary.

9. Name the command button **cmdPhone**, and type **Customer Payments** as the caption.

10. Use the combo box to assign **mcrPayment** to the **On Click** property of cmdPhone.

11. Display **frmPayment** so that a record with a phone number is shown on the screen, and then click the **Customer Payments** command button.

12. Close the report, and then move frmPayment to a new record.

13. Click the **Customer Payments** command button. If an error message appears, you may have entered the IsNull or Where Condition statements incorrectly. Correct any errors.

14. Close and save the form.

COMMAND BARS

So far, you have used command buttons to trigger VBA procedures and macros. Command bars are a very popular supplement and possible alternative to command buttons. **Command bars** is the collective name given to menu bars, toolbars, and shortcut menus.

Command bars are common in many Windows-based applications. Command bar controls (that is, items in a menu, toolbar, or shortcut menu) can open forms, print reports, move the cursor to a new record, delete records, and perform many other operations. Menus and toolbars offer an advantage over command buttons in that they do not take up space on a form. In fact, some system designers believe that command bars should be used instead of command buttons, because forms should be used almost exclusively to display data. Regardless of whether you agree with this philosophy, it is important to know how to build custom command bars that supplement your application.

Strategies and Tools for Developing Menu Bars and Toolbars

The first rule of good menu bar and toolbar design is to adhere to industry norms. For example, users expect to see the File menu on the far left, followed by Edit. The far right of the menu bar should contain the Window menu and a Help menu.

The second rule in developing command bars is to be consistent. For example, the Add New Record menu item should not be located under the Insert menu in one menu bar and under the File menu in another menu bar.

When you are ready to create menu bars, it is a good idea to determine the features common to all menu bars. Next, you should create a menu bar that contains these common features. You can then copy and modify this menu bar to fit the unique needs of the various forms and reports. Finally, you should use the standard Access menu controls whenever possible. Even in a custom menu bar, Access automatically disables the menu controls it recognizes when the control is not applicable. Custom controls must be disabled and enabled in VBA procedures.

As with the development of a form or report, Access provides point-and-click techniques that you can use to create menu bars, menus, and controls. The Customize dialog box is used to create toolbars, menu bars, and shortcut menus. When this dialog box is open, you can drag new menus and commands (that is, controls) into any portion of the menu or toolbar. Likewise, you can remove controls or menus by dragging the control or menu off the menu bar or toolbar.

Like other objects used in an Access application, menu bars and toolbars and their controls have names and properties. To facilitate program maintenance, menu names are prefixed with the tag "mnu" and toolbars are prefixed with the tag "tbr." Table 4-1 summarizes the properties of menu bar and toolbar controls.

Table 4-1   Properties of menu bar and toolbar controls

Property	Description
Caption	The text that will appear on the toolbar. A letter preceded by & will be underlined and will serve as an access key.
HelpFile	The name of the file that contains Help information related to this command.
HelpContextID	The location of Help within the Help file.
OnAction	An alternative way to associate a macro or function with the command or button. If OnAction contains a value, it overrides the value in the Parameter property. Use the list box to select a macro or type =*FunctionName()* to trigger a function.
Parameter	Usually indicates the macro to perform when the button is clicked. If the OnAction property is used, Parameter can contain miscellaneous information that can be used by a VBA procedure.
ShortcutText	Contains shortcut text that can be used to activate the macro associated with the button. When the Ctrl key is typed in conjunction with the shortcut text, the menu command is activated.
Style	Indicates whether the command should display only text, an image, or text and an image.
Tag	Contains any miscellaneous information.

After a menu and toolbar are created, they should be assigned to one or more forms. The MenuBar property of a form, located in the Other tab of a form's property sheet, contains the name of the menu that should be used when the form is open. Similarly, the Toolbar property contains the name of the toolbar that should be displayed.

 It is easy to make a mistake when designing menu bars and toolbars. These mistakes may affect your default menus. You can always recover from such a mistake by first right-clicking on any command bar and then clicking Customize on the shortcut menu that appears. Next, in the Customize dialog box, highlight the command bar to be fixed and then click Reset.

Creating a Menu Bar and a Toolbar for frmPayment

You need to create a menu bar and toolbar that supports frmPayment. In addition to supporting the default form commands, the menu bar should contain a Report menu that lists the types of reports that can be produced from frmPayment. The toolbar should contain a button that prints the receipt. Normally, a toolbar button and a command button (already located on frmPayment) do not perform the same operation. It is common practice, however, to experiment with the "look and feel" of the application during the development process.

Unfortunately, the receipt is created through a private sub procedure. Command bar controls cannot trigger these types of procedures. Thus you must create a public function prior to creating the command bars.

To create a public function in the frmPayment class module:

1. Display **frmPayment** in Design view, and then click the **Code** toolbar button. The VBE displays.

2. Click **Insert**, and then click **Procedure** in the VBE menu bar. The Add Procedure dialog box opens.

3. Type **PrintReceipt** in the Name text box, click the **Function** option button, make sure that the Scope is **Public**, and do not check All Local variables as Statics. Finally, click **OK**. A public function is created.

4. Copy and paste the contents of **cmdReceipt_Click()** into the **PrintReceipt** function. Copying and pasting procedures is not normally good design practice, but the goal in this case is to create a public function quickly so that you can learn how to use it in a command bar.

5. Close the VBE.

6. Close and save frmPayment.

Next, the menu bar can be created.

To create a menu bar for frmPayment:

1. On the menu bar, click **View**, point to **Toolbars**, click **Customize**, and then click the **Toolbars** tab, as shown in Figure 4-11.

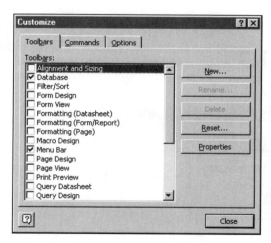

Figure 4-11   Customize dialog box

2. Click the **New** button, and then type **mnuPayment** as the name for the menu. Click **OK**. A small toolbar will appear.

3. Click the **Properties** button. In the Toolbar Properties dialog box, change the Type to **Menu Bar**, as shown in Figure 4-12, and then click **Close**.

Figure 4-12   Toolbar Properties dialog box

4. Move the Customize dialog box and mnuPayment so that you can see both at the same time. On the Commands tab, click **Built-in menus** from the Categories list box. Drag **File**, **Edit**, **View**, **Insert**, **Records**, **Window**, and **Help** to mnuPayment. The menu now contains the default menus for File, Edit, View, Insert, Records, Window, and Help. Move the dialog box and mnuPayment so that they match the placements shown in Figure 4-13. A Window menu should always be included in menu bars. Access automatically displays the name of open windows within this menu.

 The items inside default menus should not be deleted or modified. Modifications to these items change the default built-in menus for all applications!

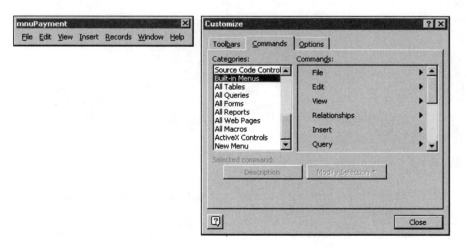

Figure 4-13   mnuPayment and the Customize dialog box

5. Click **New Menu** in the Categories list box, and then drag New Menu to mnuPayment, as shown in Figure 4-14. Right-click **New Menu** in mnuStudent and change the name to **Reports**.

Figure 4-14   New Menu in mnuPayment

6. Right-click **Reports**, and then click **Properties**. Change the Caption property to **Re&ports** (this also changes the Name property). The "p" is now underlined in Reports. The keystroke Alt+P becomes an access key that will cause the focus to shift to the Reports menu.

7. Close the Properties dialog box, and then click **All Forms** in the Categories list box. Drag **frmPrintDeposits** to and then under the Reports menu. An icon for frmPrintDeposits will appear under Reports. When the menu bar is used, this item will automatically open frmPrintDeposits.

8. Right-click the **frmPrintDeposits** control, and then change the name to **Deposits**.

9. Right-click **Deposits**, and then click **Properties**. Change the name of the Caption to **&Deposits**. Change the ScreenTip to **Print payments between two dates**, as shown in Figure 4-15. The ScreenTip appears when the insertion point is placed over the Deposit control. Close the Properties box.

Figure 4-15   Deposits menu bar control properties

10. Click **All Macros** in the Categories list box. Drag **mcrPayment.PhonePrint** to the Reports menu. When the menu is used, clicking this command bar control will execute mcrPayment.PhonePrint.

11. Change the Caption of mcrPayment.PhonePrint to **&Customer Payments** and the ScreenTip to **Print payments coming from this phone number**.

12. Click **All Reports** in the Categories list box, and drag **rptPayment** to Reports. Right-click **rptPayment**, and click **Copy Button Image**. Right-click **Customer Payments** under Reports. To paste the image, click **Paste Button Image**. The Customer Payments image changes from the macro icon to the report icon. The change in the image does not affect the macro, but the report image is a better representation of what the customer will view on the screen.

13. Click **rptPayment** within the Reports menu, and then drag **rptPayment** off the menu into a blank spot on the screen. This removes rptPayment from the menu. This control was used only temporarily in order to copy its button image in Step 12.

14. Click **File** in the Categories list box, and then drag **Custom** to the bottom of the Reports menu.

15. Right-click **Custom**, click **Properties**, and change the Caption to **&Receipt** and the ScreenTip to **Print Receipt**. Change the Style to **Image and Text**. Leave the Control Properties window open.

16. Type **=PrintReceipt()** in the On Action property, as shown in Figure 4-16. This function will be invoked when the user clicks the menu item and frmPayment is open. Close the property window.

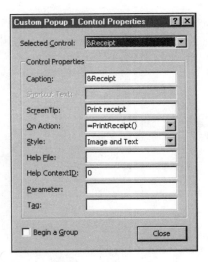

Figure 4-16   Control properties for the Receipt control

17. Copy the button image from Customer Payments and paste it into Receipts by right-clicking each control. The mnuPayment menu bar should look like Figure 4-17.

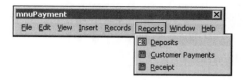

Figure 4-17   mnuPayment

18. Close the Customize dialog box. The menu bar is now ready for use.

You should also create a toolbar to support frmPayment. This toolbar should look like the default form toolbar, but also contain a control to print the receipt.

To create a toolbar for frmPayment:

1. Open **frmPayment** in Form view. The default toolbar for forms appears at the top of your screen. The same toolbar would appear regardless of which form you opened.

2. Click **View** on the menu bar, point to **Toolbars**, and then click **Customize**. The Customize dialog box opens.

3. Click the **Toolbars** tab, click the **New** button, and then type **tbrPayment** as the name for the toolbar. Click **OK**. A small toolbar appears.

4. Move the **tbrPayment toolbar** so that it is close to the default form toolbar.

5. Hold down the Ctrl key and drag the **drop-down list arrow** to tbrPayment. This will copy the drop-down list arrow to the new toolbar. Repeat this process for all toolbar controls on the Form view toolbar up to the Properties control (do not include the Properties control).

6. As many times as necessary, right-click the controls and click **Begin a Group** to place group lines at the appropriate spots.

7. If mnuPayment is not displayed, check **mnuPayment** under the Toolbars tab of the Customize dialog box.

8. Holding the **Ctrl** key, drag **Receipt** from the Reports button from mnuPayment to tbrPayment, placing it between Print Preview and Spell Check.

9. Right-click **Receipt** in tbrPayment, and then click **Default Style** in the pop-up menu. To be consistent with the other toolbar controls, the report icon will be displayed without the text, as shown in Figure 4-18.

button to print the receipt

Figure 4-18   tbrPayment

10. Remove the check marks next to tbrPayment and mnuPayment from the Toolbars tab of the Customize dialog box. Close the Customize dialog box. The new command bars will disappear from the screen.

Finally, you must assign the new menu bar and toolbar to frmPayment.

To assign mnuPayment and tbrPayment to frmPayment:

1. Display the Design view of **frmPayment**.

2. Display the property sheet for the form, if necessary.

3. Under the Other tab, assign **mnuPayment** to the Menu Bar property.

4. Assign **tbrPayment** to the Toolbar property.

5. Open **frmPayment** in Form view, and then drag **mnuPayment** to the top of the screen until it takes the form of a menu bar.

6. Drag **tbrPayment** to a position under mnuPayment, and then click the **Print Receipt** button in tbrPayment. The receipt should print in Preview mode.

7. Close and save frmPayment.

You have successfully developed a custom menu and toolbar.

WIZARDS AND THE SWITCHBOARD MANAGER

You can build—or at least partially build—many simple Access applications with the techniques described so far. In addition to employing the coding techniques that you have learned, you should be aware that Access wizards can help you develop very simple procedures automatically. The Command Button Wizard, for instance, can generate code that uses a wherecondition in the process of opening a form. The Combo Box Wizard can generate similar code.

The Switchboard Manager Wizard found under the Tools, Database Utilities menu creates a form with buttons that open forms, reports, tables, queries, and macros. The code generated by the Switchboard Manager Wizard also allows the end user to add new buttons to the form. The code generated by the wizard is located in the newly created Switchboard form.

For more information on wizards and the Switchboard Manager, see Access Help.

CHAPTER SUMMARY

◻ Macros and VBA are the hallmarks of professionally developed applications. Access supports both macros and VBA. Although macros are easier to use, experienced Access developers prefer to work with VBA because it is a more capable language.

◻ Like other programming languages, VBA procedures and macros require a name, objects to work with, and a set of instructions that cause actions to occur. The name of a Macro consists of the name specified in the Save As dialog box, followed by the name listed in the Name column of the Macro window. The name of a VBA procedure is specified in a sub or function statement. Both macros and procedures can refer to values of controls on a form or report. VBA procedures can also declare variables that can be used within the context of the procedure. Each variable has a name and can store data of a certain data type.

❑ Many macros and VBA procedures use the OpenForm and OpenReport actions or methods. These two instructions use a number of arguments. The wherecondition argument restricts the data that are displayed in the form or report to those records that meet the specified criteria.

❑ The Visual Basic Editor (VBE) facilitates the development of VBA procedures. The debugger allows the developer to create breakpoints. In addition, the developer can watch the execution of VBA code on line-by-line basis.

❑ An Access developer must know how to create custom command bars (that is, menu bars, toolbars, and shortcut menu bars). Like command buttons, the controls on command bars can invoke a number of operations. The advantage of command bars is that they do not take up space on the form.

REVIEW QUESTIONS

1. What is a difference between a function and a sub procedure?

   a. Functions are located in form class modules and sub procedures are contained in standard modules.

   b. Functions usually return a value and sub procedures usually do not.

   c. Functions are a type of event procedure.

   d. Sub procedures have a name and functions do not.

2. The Macro Name column is used to create a macro group. True or False?

3. What is the purpose of Option Explicit?

4. What is a variable?

5. Write bang notation to refer to the value of the txtPosition text box located on the form frmEmployee.

6. Write a statement that declares an integer variable with the name pintCounter.

7. Write a statement that declares a string variable that will hold a person's last name.

8. Write a statement that declares a variable that will hold the result of a calculation that determines a person's gross pay. The variable should hold monetary amounts.

9. What is an intrinsic constant?

   a. A named location in memory that can contain a variety of values during the execution of a VBA procedure

   b. An instruction that is associated with the DoCmd object

   c. A name that is supplied by Access (or a library referenced by Access) that can be used to refer to some constant value

   d. A property of a form

10. What is an assignment statement?

11. The _____ column in a macro is similar to the If...Then...Else VBA statement.

12. What is the purpose of the wherecondition argument in an OpenForm or OpenReport method?

13. A form named frmW4 must be opened to display tax information related to an employee whose record is displayed in frmEmployee. The form frmW4 contains a text box called txtSocSecNumber; the control source for txtSocSecNumber is SSN. The form frmEmployee contains a text box named txtSSN; the control source of txtSSN is SSN. What OpenForm wherecondition argument can be used to open frmW4 to the correct employee record?

14. What is a breakpoint?

    a. A line of executable program code that has been flagged by the programmer and that tells Access to suspend processing when it reaches the flagged line of code

    b. A line of code that causes a runtime error

    c. A type of compiler error

    d. An error message that is sent to the user

15. Which toolbar buttons are useful for stepping through code line by line?

16. What is the purpose of the Immediate window?

17. Which window contains a list of all the intrinsic constants?

    a. Project Explorer window

    b. Code window

    c. Properties window

    d. Object Browser

18. List three types of command bars.

19. The _____ window must be open before you can modify a command bar.

20. In relation to a command bar control, what is the purpose of the On Action property?

HANDS-ON PROJECTS

Project 4-1

Natural Parent International. The NPI system must use menus, toolbars, command buttons, and other techniques for opening forms and reports. Users should be able to open one form from another form. For example, double-clicking a record in a form that lists all members should display more detailed information about that member in frmMembers. Similarly, frmLibrary should display the relevant information about a book when a book name is double-clicked in frmMembers.

Besides specifying that these capabilities be added, leaders of NPI have requested a form that displays the lent books. Lent books are books that are currently checked out. The desired form will list the member, title, day checked out, and number of days since the book was checked out. The days out text box should be highlighted in red when the book has been out for more than 35 days.

Complete these steps:

1. Open **NPI4.mdb**. Develop a query that will be used as the record source for the Lent Books form. The query should contain the name of the member, MemberID, Title, BookID, DateCheckedOut, DateReturned, and Days field. The query should use the IsNull condition to list books that have not been returned. The Name field should concatenate the first and last names of the member. The Days field should use the DateDiff function to determine the number of days between the DateCheckedOut and today's date. The format for DateDiff is DateDiff("d",*EarlierDate*,*LaterDate*). The Date() function can be used to determine today's date. The letter "d" represents "days between the dates" (versus years or months). Name the query **qryLentBooks**.

2. Develop a continuous form called **frmLentBooks** that uses qryLentBooks as its record source. Use the Conditional Format feature to specify the color of the Days field.

3. Create a macro that opens frmMembers and displays the member whose record is double-clicked in frmLentBooks. The macro should be placed inside a macro group called OpenForms. Name the macro **GetMember**. The Where Condition in the macro should reference MemberID. Assign OpenForms.GetMember to the double-click event of the Name text box in frmLentBooks.

4. Create a macro that opens frmLibrary when a title in frmLentBooks is double-clicked. Name the macro **OpenForms.GetBook**.

5. Write a VBA procedure for the double-click event of the txtTitle text box in frmMembersCheckOut. The procedure should open frmLibrary to the book that is double-clicked in frmMembersCheckOut. Note that frmMembersCheckOut is a sub-form of frmMembers.

6. Create a new continuous form called **frmMemberSummary**. The record source of frmMemberSummary is qryMemberLastNameSort. The form should display the member's FirstName, LastName, SpouseName, EmailAddress, and HomePhone.

7. Create a public function inside the form frmMemberSummary. Name the function **GetMemberDetail**. This function should open frmMembers so that frmMembers displays the record of the person double-clicked in frmMemberSummary. Type **=GetMemberDetail()** in the double-click events for all of the text boxes in frmMemberSummary. You can accomplish this task by selecting all the text boxes (holding down the Shift key) and then displaying the property sheet.

8. Create command bars called **mnuNPI**, **mnuMembers**, **mnuMemberSummary**, and **mnuLoanedBooks**, all of which are menu-type command bars. Create mnuNPI first. It should contain the following menus: File, Edit, View, Insert, Records, Tools, Forms, Reports, Window, Help. Construct the File, Edit, View, Insert, Records, and Help menus by creating new menus and then copying the items from the standard form menu. These menus will be modified later, so do not drag the entire File menu, for example, to mnuNPI. Instead, the items in the File menu must be dragged individually. You can drag the entire Tools and Window menus to mnuNPI. The Forms menu should contain items that open frmMembers, frmLentBooks, frmLibrary, and

frmMembersSummary. The Reports menu should open the reports that have been created so far. The mnuMembers menu is similar to mnuNPI except the Forms menu does not reference frmMembers. The menu mnuMemberSummary should contain an item that triggers GetMemberDetail. To accomplish this task, place **=GetMemberDetail()** in the On Action property of the menu item. The menu mnuLoanedBooks should contain menu items in Forms to trigger the macros created earlier.

9. Create a **Switchboard** form with buttons that open frmMembers, frmLentBooks, frmLibrary, and frmMembersSummary. The Switchboard form should also display the reports in Print Preview mode. You can use the Switchboard Manager to create the switchboard. Use Access Help, if necessary, to help you design the switchboard.

10. Save your work.

Project 4-2

Metropolitan Performing Arts Company.   The MPAC system must contain menus, toolbars, and command buttons that allow the user to display data in one form that is based upon the data in another form. For example, a command button in frmPerformance should open frmPerformanceDateSeats so that it displays only the shows for the performance displayed in frmPerformance. In addition, frmPerformanceDateSeats should use a menu and toolbar that contain controls that open frmPerformance and a form that displays performers who are scheduled to appear on a particular date.

Complete these steps:

1. Open **MPA4.mdb**. Create a query named **qryPerformerJobs** that displays the PerformerID, name of the performer (concatenate the first and last name), the PerformanceID, and the DateTime of the performance. The query uses fields from tblPerformer and tblPerformanceOfPerformer.

2. Create a continuous form named **frmPerformerJobs** that uses qryPerformerJobs as its record source.

3. Create a macro group named **mcrPerformance**. It should contain a macro named DisplaySeats that opens frmPerformanceDateSeats. This macro should use a Where Condition so that only the performances that have the same PerformanceID as the current record in frmPerformance are displayed. Assign the macro to the On Click event of a command button located in the Header section of frmPerformance.

4. Create a menu bar (**mnuPerformanceSeats**) that will be assigned to frmPerformanceDateSeats. The menu should contain all of the menus typically used by a form (for example, File, Edit, Records). In addition, the menu bar should contain a menu for Forms. One of the commands in the Forms menu should open frmPerformance.

5. Create a public function in the form class module of frmPerformanceDateSeats. The function should be named **OpenfrmPerformerJobs**. It should open frmPerformerJobs so that the performers for the PerformanceID and DateTime that are currently displayed in frmPerformanceDateSeats are shown.

6. Create a control located in the Forms menu of mnuPerformanceSeats that triggers OpenfrmPerformerJobs.

7. Create a toolbar named **tbrPerformanceSeats** that contains the items typically found in a form's toolbar as well as controls for the commands in the Forms menu of mnuPerformanceSeats.

8. Save your work.

Project 4-3

Foreign Language Institute System. Now that the tables and forms are in place for this project, you can begin to refine the system by adding more functionality.

Complete these steps:

1. Open **FLI4.mdb**. You are now ready to write VBA code for all of the Close buttons in the system. Open the Properties window for each button. Set the On Click property to [Event Procedure], and click the build button. Enter the following line of code:

```
Docmd.Close
```

2. Compile and save each procedure.

3. Write VBA code for the button on the opening screen that exits the system. Open the Properties window for the button. Set the On Click property to [Event Procedure], and click the build button. Enter the following line of code:

```
Application.Quit
```

4. Write VBA code to open each form indicated on the opening screen. Open the Properties window for each button. Set the On Click property to [Event Procedure], and click the build button. Use the OpenForm method of the DoCmd object. Be careful to enclose the names of forms in quotation marks so that Access will recognize them as strings.

5. Save your work.

Project 4-4

King William Hotel System. Now that the tables and forms are in place for this project, you can begin to refine the system by adding more functionality. This system should constrain much of its processing to specific dates. For example, when calculating cafe charges for a room, the charges processed should be only the charges for the current reservation.

Complete these steps:

1. Open **KWH4.mdb**. To filter the cafe charges correctly, modify the qryCafeDetailFilter query by placing the following constraint criteria on the TransactionDate:

```
Between [Forms]![frmChargeSummary]![txtStartDate] And
[Forms]![frmChargeSummary]![txtEndDate]
```

2. When a user is making a reservation, the system must display only rooms in the proper category and only rooms that are not already reserved on the relevant dates. Two queries are needed to get the correct list of rooms for cboRoom on frmMakeReservation. First,

modify qryReservedRooms1 to add the following criteria in the first criteria row for the StartDate attribute:

```
<=[Forms]![frmMakeReservation]![txtStartDate]
```

3. Add the following criteria in the first criteria row for the EndDate attribute:

```
>=[Forms]![frmMakeReservation]![txtEndDate]
```

4. Add the following criteria in the second criteria row for the StartDate attribute:

```
>=[Forms]![frmMakeReservation]![txtStartDate] And
<=[Forms]![frmMakeReservation]![txtEndDate]
```

5. Add the following criteria in the second criteria row for the EndDate attribute:

```
>=[Forms]![frmMakeReservation]![txtEndDate]
```

6. Add the following criteria in the third criteria row for the StartDate attribute:

```
<=[Forms]![frmMakeReservation]![txtStartDate]
```

7. Add the following criteria in the third criteria row for the EndDate attribute:

```
>=[Forms]![frmMakeReservation]![txtStartDate] And
<=[Forms]![frmMakeReservation]![txtEndDate]
```

8. The previous criteria combine to select all rooms that are reserved during a requested reservation time. You still need to limit the rooms to the proper category, however. To do so, add the following criteria to the qryReservedRooms2 query for the Category attribute:

```
[Forms]![frmMakeReservation]![cboRoomType]
```

9. Add IsNull to the criteria for the Room No attribute coming from the qryReservedRooms1 query (not the one coming from the tblRoom table).

10. Connect qryReservedRooms2 to the Row Source property of cboRoom on frmMakeReservation.

11. Write VBA code for all of the Close buttons in the system. To do so, open the Properties window for each button. Set the On Click property to [Event Procedure], and click the build button. Enter the following line of code:

```
Docmd.Close
```

12. Compile and save each procedure.

13. Write VBA code for the button on the opening screen that exits the system. Open the Properties window for the button. Set the On Click property to [Event Procedure], and click the build button. Enter the following line of code:

```
Application.Quit
```

14. Write VBA code to enter the system using the button indicated on the opening screen. Open the Properties window for the button. Set the On Click property to [Event Procedure], and click the build button. Use the OpenForm method of the DoCmd object to open frmCustomer. Be careful to enclose the name of the form in quotation marks so that Access will recognize it as a string.

15. Save your work.

Project 4-5

Workers' Compensation Commission System. Now that the tables and forms are in place for the WCC project, you can begin to refine the system by adding more functionality. The next step is to create macros to handle some of the printing requirements. One part of the printing requirements involves setting a flag in the tables that provide data for Forms A, B, and C to indicate when a particular record has been printed. As the user should not be bothered with superfluous warning messages, you should hide the messages that Access generates when the flag is updated.

Complete these steps:

1. Open **WCC4.mdb**. Create reports for Forms A, B, and C. Name the report for Form A **rptFormA** and base it on qryWCCA. Base **rptFormB** on qryWCCB, and base **rptFormC** on qryWCCC. On rptFormA and rptFormB, create unbound text boxes to display the three ICD-9 code descriptions and the four CPT code descriptions. Name these text boxes **txtICD91D**, **txtICD92D**, **txtICD93D**, **txtCPT1D**, **txtCPT2D**, **txtCPT3D**, and **txtCPT4D**. On rptFormC, create unbound text boxes to display the three ICD-9 code descriptions. Name these text boxes **txtICD91D**, **txtICD92D**, and **txtICD93D**.

2. Create a macro named **mcrFormAReports**. This macro must perform several actions. The first step is to open the report for Form A, but only for those records that have not yet been printed; use the Where Condition argument to specify this constraint. The second step is to close the report. Next, the macro should update the database to reflect the fact that each Form A has now been printed. The third step in the macro is therefore to turn off the warnings that Access generates when updates occur in the database. The fourth step is to execute the qryWCCAPrintedUpdate query from the macro. The fifth step is to turn the warning messages back on.

3. Create macros named **mcrFormBReports** and **mcrFormCReports** that function similarly to mcrFormAReports.

4. Attach these macros to the proper command buttons on the opening screen. Use the On Click event property.

5. To print a specific Form A report, the qryWCCASingleRecord query must be modified to specify which record to print. Modify this query by placing the following criteria in the Medical Record Number field:

   `[Forms]![frmWCCA]![Medical Record Number]`

6. Create a macro named **mcrPrintSelectedFormA** that will print a Form A report for a specific patient. The first step is to open the report for the appropriate record. Use the Filter Name argument of the Open Report action to specify that the qryWCCASingleRecord query will be the filter. Finally, close the report in the macro. Make sure your code turns system messages on and off.

7. Make similar modifications to the qryWCCBSingleRecord and qryWCCCSingleRecord queries. Create two more macros named **mcrPrintSelectedFormB** and **mcrPrintSelectedFormC** as described in Step 6.

8. Attach the mcrPrintSelectedFormA macro to the Print button on Form A. Make similar connections between the other two macros and Form B and Form C, respectively.

9. Connect the qrySortPatients query as the data source to the cboPatient combo box on frmPatients. Use the Row Source property to do so. Make a similar connection between qrySortDoctors and cboDoctor and between qrySortCompanies and cboCompany.

10. You should now write VBA code for all of the Close buttons in the system. To do so, open the Properties window for each button. Set the On Click property to [Event Procedure], and click the build button. Enter the following line of code:

```
Docmd.Close
```

11. Compile and save each procedure.

12. Write VBA code for the button on the opening screen that exits the system. Open the Properties window for the button. Set the On Click property to [Event Procedure], and click the build button. Enter the following line of code:

```
Application.Quit
```

13. Write VBA code to open the Patient, Doctor, and Company forms as indicated on the opening screen. Open the Properties window for each button. Set the On Click property to [Event Procedure], and click the build button. Use the OpenForm method of the DoCmd object. Be careful to enclose the names of forms in quotation marks so that Access will recognize them as strings.

14. Save your work.

5

USING OBJECTS AND PROPERTIES

Manipulating Objects in VBA

In this chapter you will:

♦ Define and explain the roles of objects and properties in an Access database

♦ Describe the differences between Microsoft Access objects, Data Access Objects (DAO), and ActiveX Data Objects (ADO)

♦ Write dot and bang notation that retrieves and updates object properties in a macro and module

♦ Create a query with a criterion that references a control on a form

♦ Modify the properties of a form through a macro or VBA statement

♦ Modify the properties of a linked table

♦ Create recordsets in a VBA procedure

♦ Find and describe properties related to many objects, including forms, reports, tables, commands, controls, fields, databases, and recordsets

---

Access is a relational database environment that is built around objects and collections of objects. It maintains descriptions of the objects in an Access application in data items called **properties**. Many properties can be set through the property sheet that is associated with an object. Property sheets not only specify the appearance of an object (for example, the color of a label on a form or report), but also establish rules that validate data.

As you work through this chapter, you'll find that property sheets have a significant limitation: Although Access application developers may use property sheets to set the initial values of a property (for example, Default Value, Back Color), the values of some properties change after the application is delivered to the user or as the application is running. To retrieve and change properties automatically, you will learn how to use macros, modules, and queries to identify the correct object and property to use in a given situation.

THE WORLD ACCORDING TO OBJECTS

The Access objects with which you are most familiar are probably tables, forms, and reports. There are many other objects in the Access environment, however. For instance, the fields in a table are objects, as are the definitions of queries, the controls that appear on forms, and the databases you create.

Each object has **properties**, which are data items that describe the objects. In addition to properties, objects have other characteristics. One characteristic is that objects can contain other objects. For example, in Access, Form objects contain Control objects, and Table objects contain Field objects.

A second characteristic is that objects have methods. **Methods** are the capabilities or procedures that the objects can perform. In Access, a Form object has the ability to go to a certain page (in a multipage form) with a GoToPage method. Another object may ask a particular form to go to a certain page by sending it a message that contains the method to invoke.

A third characteristic is that related objects can be grouped. Many development environments call a group of related objects a class. Access calls a group of related objects a collection. In Access, a particular form (for example, frmProspects in MU-DSci) has the same type of properties and methods as other forms. All open forms are part of the Forms collection.

Sometimes a group of objects, called a **subclass**, is a subset of another group of objects, called a **superclass**. For example, all automobiles belong to the superclass vehicles. The vehicles superclass also includes subclasses of motorcycles and trucks. Objects in vehicles have certain properties in common (for example, wheels). When a new subclass, such as trains, is placed inside a superclass, objects within that subclass inherit the properties of the superclass (for example, all trains have wheels). This process is called **class inheritance**.

When an application development environment uses objects that have the features just described, the development environment is called **object-oriented**. Most experts agree that Access is not object-oriented because it does not support class inheritance, which is fundamental to an object-oriented development environment. Nevertheless, Access does support object properties, object methods, collections, and objects that contain other objects. For this reason, it is frequently referred to as an **object-based** development environment.

OBJECTS AND COLLECTIONS IN ACCESS

What types of objects does Access allow? Generally speaking, three major categories of objects exist: Microsoft Access objects, Data Access Object (DAO) objects, and ActiveX Data Objects (ADO). **Microsoft Access objects** are created and maintained by the Access programming environment and primarily relate to the user interface and modules. Forms and reports are examples of Microsoft Access objects. **DAO objects** are created and managed by the Jet database engine and primarily involve objects related to data storage and retrieval. Tables and queries, referred to as **TableDef** and **QueryDef** objects, are examples of DAO objects. **ADO objects** are similar to DAO objects. In the ADO model, the **Table** object replaces the TableDef object used in DAO and the **Command** object replaces the QueryDef DAO object. The ADO model, however, can do more with the Table and Command objects than the DAO model can do with the TableDef and QueryDef objects.

As data access methods matured, Microsoft began moving toward a concept it called Universal Data Access, in which one data model will be used for all Microsoft products. The ADO model will be the basis of Universal Data Access. That's why the overlap exists between DAO and ADO. This book will focus on the Microsoft Access objects and the ADO objects, because ADO is being phased in to eventually replace DAO.

Most Microsoft Access, DAO, and ADO objects are grouped into predefined collections. A **collection** is an object that contains related objects. For example, the **Tables** collection (or TableDefs in DAO) contains definitions of all Table objects. The **Forms** collection contains all open forms (that is, all forms that are loaded). Objects may own (that is, incorporate) collections. For example, each TableDef object owns a **Fields** collection that in turn contains the Field objects in the table. Each Form object owns a **Controls** collection that contains all of the controls in the form. Collections, like other objects, have properties and methods. For instance, the **Count** property of a collection indicates the number of objects in the collection.

VBA, macros, and queries identify an object by specifying the collection in which it belongs. Many tables, for instance, contain a StudentID field. To specify the StudentID in tblProspects, VBA tells Access to search in the Columns collection of the tblProspects object. It also tells Access that the tblProspects object is located in the Tables collection.

Figures 5-1, 5-2, and 5-3 summarize the relationships among some of the collections and objects in Access. In Figure 5-2, each box with a shaded box behind it is a collection; each shaded box is an object.

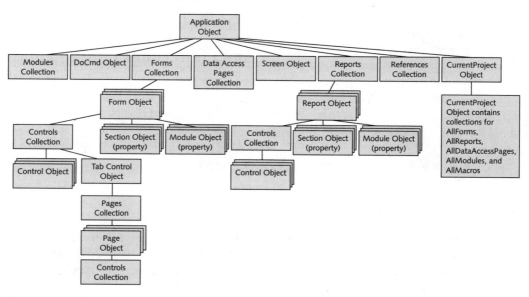

Figure 5-1   Some of the relationships among Microsoft Access objects

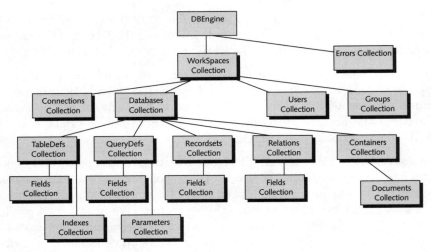

Figure 5-2   Relationships among DAO objects

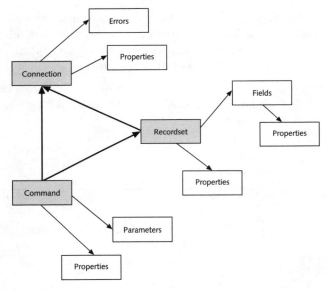

Figure 5-3   Relationships among ADO objects

OBJECTS AND PROPERTIES IN ACCESS

The easiest way to change properties is through the property sheets associated with forms, pages, reports, tables, and queries. Property sheets are available only during the design of an application; VBA, macros, and queries must use a notation that identifies the objects and properties to manipulate while the application is open.

The syntax used by VBA, macros, and queries is called dot notation. **Dot notation** uses the dot (.) operator to indicate that what follows is an item defined by Microsoft Access. For example, you would use the dot operator to refer to a property of a form, page, report, or control. Some form of dot notation is used in many object-based languages. In this notation, a dot is used to construct identifiers that reference specific objects or properties.

As an example of dot notation, consider the sequence of steps you undertake to change a property of a control. First, you open the Design view of the form that contains the property. Second, you click the desired control. Third, you open the property sheet for that control. Finally, you locate the property in the property sheet and change the value of the property. Dot notation provides a path to the desired property by identifying an initial object, identifying the desired object that may be contained in the initial object, and then identifying the property using the following notation. The names of the path parts (the initial object, the desired object contained in the initial object, and so forth) are separated by a dot, as shown in the following syntax:

Syntax

ObjectIdentification*.PropertyCollection(Index)*

Syntax Dissection

- ***ObjectIdentification*** is a path that identifies the desired object. Components of the path are separated by a dot. In its most complete form, *ObjectIdentification* requires that the collection containing the object and the object ID within the collection be specified.

- *PropertyCollection* identifies the particular property collection to be accessed.

- *Index* can be the ordinal location of the specific property in the collection to access (for example, 0, 1, 2, 3, . . .) or the name (for example, "Default" or "AutoIncrement").

Access uses the same dot notation to refer to both objects and properties. In addition, all objects have two unique identifications: the name specified with the Save command when the object is saved and an index (that is, an integer). Indexes in Access are zero-based; that is, they begin counting with the number zero.

As an example of dot notation, consider the following syntax, which references the BackColor property of the form frmProspects:

```
Forms("frmProspects").BackColor
```

If you know that the frmProspects form is the third form in the collection, you could write

```
Forms(2).BackColor
```

Remember that with zero-based indexes, the first three forms in the collection have indexes 0, 1, and 2, respectively. The third form will therefore be referenced by index number 2. To reference the background color property of the txtFirstName text box, you would write

```
Forms("frmProspects").Controls("txtFirstName").BackColor
```

As you can see, dot notation can result in long paths. Fortunately, default collections and properties can reduce the length of the identifiers. For example, Controls is the default collection of a form; therefore the word "Controls" does not need to appear in the notation. To determine the default collections for other objects, check Access Help.

The following two statements are equivalent to the preceding statement. Note the exclamation point in the second statement.

```
Forms("frmProspects")("txtFirstName").BackColor
```

or

```
Forms![frmProspects]![txtFirstName].BackColor
```

The notation using the exclamation point (!) is called bang notation. **Bang notation** can be used in place of dot notation when the collection referenced by an object is the default collection. The brackets are required only when the object name contains a space. By convention, however, brackets are almost always placed in syntax. Any form of dot and bang notation can be used in the same application. Access encourages developers to use bang notation because it is a little shorter.

The disadvantage of bang notation is that it is not as flexible as dot notation. For example, in VBA a variable can be substituted for the constant name enclosed in quotes when dot notation is used. In other words, if a variable named strFormName contains the value "frmProspects", then the code above could be written as follows:

```
Forms(strFormName).BackColor
```

Keywords can be used to shorten object property paths. For instance, VBA can use the word **Me** inside a form or report class module to refer to the form or report that contains the module (for example, Me![txtFirstName].BackColor). A form or report class module can use the word **Parent** to refer to a form or report that contains another form or report. In a form that contains a subform, Parent refers to the main form (not the subform). For example, frmQDrops in MU-DSci is used as a subform in frmStudentQDrops. VBA in the class module associated with frmQDrops can refer to the value in txtNameField (located in the main form) as Parent![txtNameField].Value.

Creating the Record Source for frmStudentsAndClasses

The frmStudentsAndClasses object is a main/subform in the Metropolitan University's Swim Lessons application that displays data from the tblStudent table in the main form and displays class schedule information in the subform. The Source object of the subform is frmStudentEnrollment. Currently, frmStudentsAndClasses displays schedule information for all students. You need to adjust the record source of frmStudentsAndClasses so that the form will display only the student currently shown in frmStudent.

To create a new record source for frmStudentsAndClasses:

1. Open **SwimReg.mdb** while overriding its startup procedures by pressing the **Shift** key as you open the database, refresh the links, if necessary, and create a new query that is based on the tblStudents. Restore the visible menus to the default settings.

2. Place **SID**, **FirstName**, **MiddleInitial**, and **LastName** in the Field row of the query, and then click the **Criteria** row under the **SID** column.

3. Click the **Build** button ... in the toolbar. The Expression Builder opens.

4. In the first column of the Expression Builder, double-click **Forms**, double-click **All Forms**, and then click **frmStudent** (use the scroll bars to find the correct form).

5. In the second column of the Expression Builder, click **txtSID** and then click the **Paste** button. The bang notation referring to the txtSID text box in frmStudent is displayed, as shown in Figure 5-4.

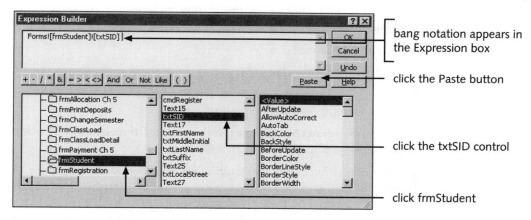

Figure 5-4   Expression Builder referring to txtSID in frmStudent

6. Click **OK**, save the query as **qryMainStudentsAndClasses**, and then close it.

Next, the result of the query should be tested.

To display the query results:

1. Display the Form view of **frmStudent**, and then use the navigation buttons to find **Jenny G. First**.

2. Click **Window** on the menu bar, and then click **SwimReg: Database** to return to the Database window.

3. Click the **Queries** object type, and then double-click **qryMainStudentsAndClasses**. The datasheet for qryMainStudentsAndClasses displays the record of Jenny G. First.

4. Close both the qryMainStudentsAndClasses query and frmStudent.

The criteria in qryMainStudentsAndClasses tell Access to find the student that has an SID that matches the SID displayed in txtSID in frmStudent. Next, qryMainStudentsAndClasses should be defined as the record source for frmStudentsAndClasses.

To change the record source for frmStudentsAndClasses:

1. Display the Design view of **frmStudentsAndClasses**.

2. Display the **Form** property sheet, if it is not already visible, and then click the **Data** tab if it is not already on top.

3. Click in the **Record Source** property, use the combo box to select **qryMainStudentsAndClasses**, and then save and close the form. The form frmStudentsAndClasses should display the data retrieved by qryMainStudentsAndClasses.

To test frmStudentsAndClasses:

1. Open **frmStudent** in Form view and move the focus to **Jenny G. First**.

2. Use the Database window to open **frmStudentsAndClasses** in Form view. Jenny G. First's record should be displayed.

3. Close **frmStudentsAndClasses**, and then click **frmStudent** to make it the active window, if it is not already active.

4. Use the navigation buttons in frmStudent to move to the record for **Craig T. Jones**, and then use the Database window to open **frmStudentsAndClasses** in Form view again. The record corresponding to this student should be displayed.

5. Close both forms.

CHANGING PROPERTY VALUES

VBA can change the value of a property by using the **assignment statement** in a VBA procedure. An assignment statement that changes the value of a property has the following syntax:

Syntax

PropertyPath = NewValue

Syntax Dissection

- *PropertyPath* is the dot or bang notation that identifies the property.

- *NewValue* is the desired value of the property.

As an example of this syntax, consider a line of code in a procedure within the frmProspects class module that makes cmdShowAllBtn invisible:

```
Me![cmdShowAllBtn].Visible = False
```

When the Visible property equals True, the control is displayed.

When VBA is used to reference object properties, it is important to select variables and new values that are consistent with the data type of the property. VBA supports several data types, including Integer (a relatively small integer), Long (a larger integer), Single (a real number), Double (a real number that offers twice as much storage space, and hence precision, as a Single), String (a series of characters or numbers), Boolean (True or False), and Variant (can contain anything). The data types of the properties are mentioned here for easy reference. Table 5-1 lists the various Microsoft Access objects.

Table 5-1   Microsoft Access objects

Object	Description	Typical Use	Example Notation
Form	An open form	To change properties of the user interface	Forms![frmProspects]
Report	An open report	To change properties of a printed report	Reports![rptStudent Data]
Control	A control in an open form or report	To change properties of the control	Forms![frmProspects]![txtQDrop].ForeColor
Page	A member of the Pages collection that is owned by a Tab control	To contain controls under different tabs of a form	Forms![frmCustomer]![tbcCustInfo].Pages(1)
ItemsSelected	A collection object that lists items (not objects) selected in a list or combo box	To identify the items selected by the user	Forms![frmOrder]![lstItems].ItemsSelected
Application	The running application	To set the default menu	Application.MenuBar
Screen	The active form or report	To identify the active form	Screen.ActiveForm
Property	A user-defined or datasheet property of a form, report, or control	To store user-defined properties	Forms![frmProspects].Properties!DataSheet FontWeight
Module	An open module	To determine the type of module (for example, Class module or standard module) that is running	Modules(0).Type
Reference	Identifies a library that contains other objects that are referenced by this application (for example, Excel objects)	To support the development of VBA code that interacts with other applications	References(1).Kind
DoCmd	An object that executes actions that change the user interface; no properties are associated with DoCmd	To open and close windows	

5

Macros change property values through the SetValue action. The SetValue action requires two action arguments: the **Item** argument, which contains the dot or bang notation that identifies the property, and the **Expression** argument, which contains the new value. Figure 5-5 shows a macro in MU-DSci that uses the SetValue action to make a Form Header invisible.

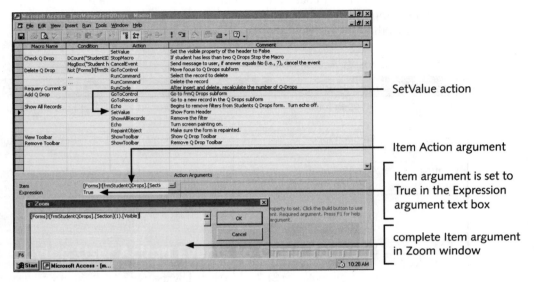

Figure 5-5   Macro action that shows a form's Form Header

You must set the values of properties carefully. Some properties can be set only under certain conditions. Many properties can only be assigned a value that comes from a valid set of values. For example, the possible values of Visible are True and False. You should consult Access Help to determine legal values for a property and the conditions under which a property can be set. The values listed in a property sheet are not always the legal values that are used in a VBA statement or macro.

A good way to preview the properties of an object is to examine the property sheet associated with the object, if one is available. Property names used in VBA and macros are frequently the same as those shown in the property sheet, except the spaces are eliminated. For example, "Control Source" in the form's property sheet is referred to as "ControlSource" in VBA and macros.

MICROSOFT ACCESS OBJECTS AND PROPERTIES

Many macro actions and VBA statements manipulate the properties of Microsoft Access objects. Much of the code you write will manipulate the properties of objects that are directly associated with the user interface and reports. Commonly used Microsoft Access objects and properties are examined in the following sections. As the properties are described, the data types of the properties are mentioned.

TIP For detailed information on labeling conventions, see Appendix A of this book.

The Application Object and Properties

The **Application** object represents the Access application that is currently running. It is used primarily to set up default values for certain items in the application. For example, **MenuBar** identifies the default menu that will be displayed when the application opens. The following code changes the default menu bar to mnuStandardMenuBar:

```
Application.MenuBar = "mnuStandardMenuBar"
```

Table 5-2 lists some of the properties associated with the Application object. The legal values for a few of these properties are specified by intrinsic constants. An **intrinsic constant** is a name used by Access to represent a particular integer.

Table 5-2   Some Application object properties

Property	Data Type	Legal Values	Description
CurrentObjectName	String		The name of the active form, report, macro, module, query, or table
CurrentObjectType	Long	An intrinsic constant (for example, acTable, acForm)	The type of object that is currently active
MenuBar	String		The name of the default menu bar
ShortcutMenuBar	String		The name of the ShortcutMenuBar that is displayed when the right mouse button is clicked

Properties associated with the Application object are not used often. Instead, properties associated with other objects frequently provide the same information. In addition, the Startup window can be used to set the MenuBar and ShortcutMenuBar properties.

The Screen Object and Properties

The **Screen object** refers to the form, report, or control that is currently active on the screen. Several Screen object properties are widely used, including the ActiveForm and ActiveControl properties that identify the form or control that has the focus, respectively. Often a macro or VBA statement will manipulate the properties of the object that currently has the focus. For example, the following code changes the background color of the control with the focus:

```
Screen.ActiveControl.BackColor = RGB(0, 255, 255)
```

This code is triggered each time the insertion point is placed in a new control. The advantage of this approach is that a separate line of code does not need to be written for each control on the form. Legal values for the BackColor property are long integers, with different integers representing different colors. The RGB function calculates the long integer based on the amounts of red, green, and blue that are specified, respectively, in the RGB arguments.

Table 5-3 lists additional screen properties. Some screen properties are **read-only**—that is, macros and VBA statements can read the current value but cannot change it.

Table 5-3   Important Screen properties

Property	Data Type	Legal Values	Description
ActiveForm	Form object		A read-only property that identifies the form with the focus
ActiveControl	Control object		A read-only property that identifies the control with the focus
MousePointer	Integer	0, 1, 3, 7, 9, 11	Determines the type of mouse pointer displayed on the screen; each integer corresponds to a different pointer (for example, 11 specifies the hourglass)
PreviousControl	Control object		A read-only property that identifies the control that last had the focus

Although Screen properties are useful, they can also be a source of errors. For example, if the code listed earlier was accidentally triggered when a command button had the focus, Access would display an error message because the command button control does not support the BackColor property.

Opening frmStudentsAndClasses from Other Forms

For the convenience of the Swim Lessons users, clicking a button on frmStudent should open frmStudentsAndClasses. When the system is complete, several forms in the Swim Lessons application will contain a txtSID control. You will develop a macro that opens frmStudentsAndClasses from any form that has a txtSID control. These copies are used to test several variations of the Student Data Form. Here you will develop a macro that opens frmStudentsAndClasses from any copy of frmStudent.

To create a macro that opens frmStudentsAndClasses:

1. Open the **mcrOpens** macro object in Design view, click in the **Macro Name** column below the ShowAllStudents entry, and then type **OpenStudentClass**.

2. Use the combo box in the Action column to select **OpenForm**.

3. In the Action arguments section, use the Form Name combo box to click **frmStudentsAndClasses**.

4. Save the macro and close it.

Next, you will place a button on frmStudent. When the user clicks the button, the mcrOpens.OpenStudentClass macro will run.

To create a button that opens frmStudentsAndClasses:

1. Display the Design view of **frmStudent**.

2. Add a command button control instance under the Reset button. Cancel the wizard if it is activated.

3. Use the **Size** and **Align** commands in the Format menu to give the button a size and alignment consistent with the other buttons.

4. If it is not already displayed, display the property sheet of the command button control instance, and then type **cmdStudentClasses** as the Name property and **Student's Classes** as the caption. Resize the button, if necessary, so that all of the caption is visible.

5. Click the **Event** tab, click the **On Click** property's value column, and then select **mcrOpens.OpenStudentClass** in the combo box. This choice tells Access to run mcrOpens.OpenStudentClass when the button is clicked.

6. Save and close frmStudent.

7. Open **frmStudent** in Form view. Use the navigation buttons to move to the record of **Jenny G. First**. Click the **Student's Classes** button. The frmStudentsAndClasses form should open to the correct student.

8. Close both forms.

Next, you will modify qryMainStudentsAndClasses to operate with any form containing a control named txtSID.

To adjust qryMainStudentsAndClasses to apply to any form with a txtSID control:

1. Display the Design view of the query **qryMainStudentsAndClasses**.

2. Modify the Criteria in the SID column to become **[Screen].[ActiveForm]![txtSID]**. If you desire, you can press **Shift+F2** when your insertion point is in the Criteria row to use the Zoom window and thereby see the whole statement you type. If you do so, click the **OK** button when you have finished modifying the criteria.

3. Save and close the query.

4. Open **frmStudent** in Form view. Use the navigation buttons to move to the record of **Jenny G. First**. Click the **Student's Classes** button. The frmStudentsAndClasses form should open to the correct student.

5. Close both forms.

Objects and Properties Related to Forms, Reports, and Controls

Properties associated with forms, pages, reports, and controls can be used to change the user interface in response to data values and a user's actions. Form, Page, and Report objects exist for each open form, page, and report, respectively. Each of these objects owns a controls collection. Forms, pages, reports, and controls are associated with many properties. Tables 5–4 and 5–5 list some of the properties that are commonly used in conjunction with VBA statements and macros.

Table 5-4   Commonly used properties associated with format or appearance

Property	Objects	Values	Description
BackColor	Form sections, report sections, controls	A long integer typically calculated through the RGB function	Changes the background color of some object. The background color of a control is commonly used to indicate the status of a control (for example, locked, enabled).
Caption	Forms and reports	String	The title displayed in the title bar.
ForeColor	Controls	A long integer typically calculated through the RGB function	Changes the text color. The text color commonly indicates the status of a particular value (for example, illegal values are indicated in red).
SpecialEffect	Controls, form sections, report sections	The integers 0–5	Changes the "look" of a control or section (for example, sunken or raised). Special effects are often used to indicate the status of a control (for example, a sunken control tells a user that the value can be updated).
Visible	Forms, form sections, reports, report sections, controls	True, False	Hides or displays an object on the screen.

Table 5-5   Commonly used properties associated with updating data

Property	Objects	Values	Description
AllowAdditions	Forms	Boolean	Specifies whether a user can add a new record to the table. Access 2.0 does not support the Boolean data type, but uses the Variant data type to recognize True and False values.
AllowDeletion	Forms	Boolean	Specifies whether a user can delete a record. Access 2.0 does not support the Boolean data type, but uses the Variant data type to recognize True and False values.
AllowEdits	Forms	Boolean	True indicates that saved records can be updated. False indicates that the user cannot change the data through the form. Access 2.0 does not support the Boolean data type, but uses the Variant data type to recognize True and False values.
CurrentRecord	Forms	Long Integer	The record number of the current record being viewed in the form. If the record number equals zero, the form may not contain any records.
DataEntry	Forms	Boolean	A value of True indicates that the form is for the entry of new records only; it cannot be used to display previously entered records. Access 2.0 does not support the Boolean data type, but uses the Variant data type to recognize True and False values.
Dirty	Forms	Boolean	True indicates that the current record has been modified since it was last saved. Access 2.0 does not support the Boolean data type, but uses the Variant data type to recognize True and False values.
Enabled	Controls	Boolean	Specifies whether the insertion point can be placed in a control. Access 2.0 does not support the Boolean data type, but uses the Variant data type to recognize True and False values.
Filter	Forms and reports	A string that specifies a criterion	Limits the data displayed to those records in the record source that meet the criterion. Not supported in Access 2.0.
FilterOn	Forms and reports	Boolean	Indicates whether the filter specified in the Filter property is in effect.

Table 5-5 Commonly used properties associated with updating data (continued)

Property	Objects	Values	Description
LimitToList	Combo boxes	Boolean	True indicates that a value typed in the combo box must match a value in the list. Access 2.0 does not support the Boolean data type, but uses the Variant data type to recognize True and False values.
Locked	Controls	Boolean	True indicates that the value of a control cannot be changed. Access 2.0 does not support the Boolean data type, but uses the Variant data type to recognize True and False values.
NewRecord	Forms	Boolean	True indicates that the current record is a new record. Not supported in Access 2.0.
OldValue	Controls	Depends on the type of control	The value displayed in a control before the user changed the value.
RecordSource	Forms and reports	A string that specifies a table name, query name, or SQL statement	The source of the data that will be displayed by a form or report.
RowSource	Combo boxes and list boxes	The value depends on the setting of the RowSourceType property; if RowSourceType equals Table/Query, RowSource is a string that identifies the table, query or SQL statement	The source of the data that will be displayed by the combo box or list box.
Text	Text box and combo box	String	The value that currently is displayed in the text box or combo box. The value may or may not have been saved.
Value	Controls	Depends on the type of control	The last saved value of the control. A value is saved after it is entered and the user moves to a new control.

As an example of these properties' uses, consider a segment of code contained in frmProspects. Primarily, frmProspects is used to display and enter Prospect records. Secondarily, a second copy of frmProspects is used as part of an error message that is displayed when a user types the StudentID of a prospect that already exists in the Prospects table. In this case, the copy of frmProspects displays the record of the existing prospect with the identical StudentID. Unlike the original frmProspects, the copy should not be used to enter data or search for other prospects.

The following code segment, contained in frmProspects and executed when a copy of frmProspects is displayed, changes the properties of controls and forms to accommodate these requirements.

```
Public Property Let oprFixedFilter _
    (ByVal pstrNewValue As String)
    Dim pobjProspectsMenu As New cmoProspectsMenuBar
    'Set the filter
    mvntFixedFilter = pstrNewValue
    Me.Filter = pstrNewValue
    Me.FilterOn = True
    'Hide the command buttons and combo boxes
    Me![cmdShowAllBtn].Visible = False
    Me![cmdAddProspectBtn].Visible = False
    Me![cboStudentID].Visible = False
    Me![cboName].Visible = False
    'Set the caption
    Me.Caption = "Prospects Duplicate Student"
    Me.AllowAdditions = False
    pobjProspectsMenu.CreateSingleRecordVersion
End Property
```

5

The four VBA statements that change the **Visible** property to False hide the Show All command button, the Add New Prospects command button, the Student ID combo box, and the Name combo box. The value of the **Caption** property is changed to distinguish the previously opened frmProspects form from the newly opened copy. A form's Caption property displays text in the title bar of the form. Setting **AllowAdditions** to False prohibits the entry of new records.

In the code, the **Filter** property is slightly more complex. When the **FilterOn** property equals True, the Filter property restricts the rows that the form displays to those rows that meet the criteria. The term on the left side of the equals sign (for example, [StudentID]) identifies a Field in the record source of the form. On the right side of the equals sign is a value with which to compare the Field. In the preceding code, StudentID is compared with the current value of txtStudentID in the original (that is, not the copy) frmProspects form.

 TIP Although both code segments are written in class modules here, they could also be written with a series of SetValue actions in a macro.

Manipulating Record Sources and Row Sources

The RecordSource property of forms and reports and the **RowSource** property of combo and list boxes play important roles in user interface design. A row source specifies a table or query that contains the values listed in the combo or list box. A record source identifies the table or query that supplies data to the entire form, page, or report. Changing the value of a record source or row source in a module or macro changes the data that are displayed by the form, page, report, combo box, or list box.

The frmIDSearchWindow form in MU-DSci is an example of a form that is used to display different data depending on the situation. This form contains a combo box, named cboStudentID, which is used to locate student IDs. When an ID is selected from the combo box, the application finds and displays the corresponding student in frmProspects, frmCurrent Students, or frmGraduates, depending on which form invoked frmIDSearchWindow. The row source of cboStudentID changes depending on whether it is used to find a prospect, a current student, or a graduate. The following statement is similar to one found in MU-DSci:

```
Forms![frmGraduates]![cboStudentID].RowSource _
    = "qryGraduatesIDList"
```

The qryGraduatesIDList query retrieves IDs and names from the tblGraduates table. The line is executed when frmIDSearchWindow is invoked from frmGraduates. The RowSource property is set to a different query when frmIDSearchWindow is invoked from frmCurrentStudents.

The query associated with a row source can also be created in a way that adjusts the data displayed in a combo or list box automatically, depending on the values of other controls in the form. For example, consider the form frmClassLoad in SwimReg. It contains two combo boxes: one combo box that lists semesters (cboSemester), and another combo box that lists instructors (cboInstructor). The list of items in the cboInstructor combo box depends on the value selected in the cboSemester combo box. This form shows the classes taught by a particular instructor in a particular semester.

Figure 5-6 shows the Design view of the query that is the row source of the cboInstructor combo box. This query states that the class name must equal the value of the cboSwimClass combo box in the schedule form. Using row sources that reference the value of other controls helps the user enter valid data combinations.

Nuances of Forms, Reports, and Controls Notation

In most cases, dot or bang notation that refers to properties of forms, reports, and controls is relatively straightforward. Nevertheless, two problems are frequently encountered. First, it is important to remember that the Forms and Reports collections contain only *open* forms and reports, respectively. Dot and bang notation cannot be used to refer to a form or report that is not open. (Typically, an open form is one that is displayed on the screen, but a form could also be open and not visible.) Fortunately, Access recognizes a time period between opening a form and displaying a form (for example, between the Open and Load events). Properties that must be changed prior to displaying the form can be updated during this time period.

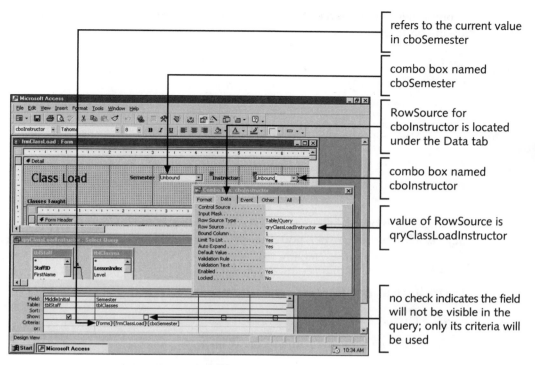

refs to the current value
in cboSemester

combo box named
cboSemester

RowSource for
cboInstructor is located
under the Data tab

combo box named
cboInstructor

value of RowSource is
qryClassLoadInstructor

no check indicates the field
will not be visible in the
query; only its criteria will
be used

Figure 5-6   Creating a hierarchical sequence of combo boxes

Sometimes a user closes a form or report earlier than the programmer expected. For example, an error is generated when frmCurrentStudents in MU-DSci is closed before a student ID is selected from the cboStudentID combo box in frmIDSearchWindow. The frmIDSearchWindow contains code that causes frmCurrentStudents to locate a particular record. To prevent a user from closing frmCurrentStudents prematurely, the property sheet of frmIDSearchWindow can be used to declare frmIDSearchWindow a modal and pop-up form. When the **Modal** property of a form is True, a user cannot perform an operation on any other form until the current, or **modal**, form is closed. When the **PopUp** property of a form property is True, Access places the current form in front of all other open forms. Thus, the combination of PopUp and Modal causes a form to open and be placed in front of all other forms and prevents the user from interacting with any other part of the system until the modal, pop-up form is closed.

A second problem with dot and bang notation concerns referencing the properties of a subform. A subform is a control on a main form. Like all controls, the subform has properties associated with the control (for example, Visible) that can be referenced through a property sheet, VBA statements, and macros. A subform, through the SourceObject property, references another form, however. (Similarly, a subreport references another report.) The Source object of a subform (and subreport) contains its own controls and has its own form properties. Because VBA and macros must be able to refer to properties of the subform control as well as properties of the Source object, dot and bang notation must be used as shown in the following syntax:

Syntax

Forms![*FormName*]**!**[*SubformName*].*Property*

Syntax Dissection

- *FormName* refers to the name of the main form.
- *SubformName* refers to the name of the subform control.
- *Property* refers to the name of property of the subform control.

When a macro or module must refer to the property of the form or report that is the Source object of a subform or subreport, the **Form** and **Report properties** are used, respectively.

Syntax

Forms![*FormName*]**!**[*SubformName*].[*Form* | *Report*].*Property*

Syntax Dissection

- *FormName* refers to the name of the main form.
- *SubformName* refers to the name of the subform control.
- *Form* or *Report* is the property that points to the form or report that serves as the source object.
- *Property* is a form property of the source object form.

For example, to find the RecordSource of the frmQDrop subform that is located inside frmStudentQDrops, you use the following statement:

```
Forms![frmStudentQDrops]![frmQDrops].Form.RecordSource
```

To find the value of the txtCourseNumber text box inside frmQDrops, you use the following statement:

```
Forms![frmStudentQDrops]![frmQDrops].Form![txtCourseNumber]
```

Remember, Value is the default property and does not have to be referenced explicitly.

An important corollary to the subform notation is that macros and modules that work when a form is opened as a main form may not work when the form or report is embedded as a subform. For example, when frmStudentQDrops is opened on its own, Forms![frmQDrops]![txtCourseNumber] refers to the value of txtCourseNumber. When frmQDrops is opened as a subform, the identifier Forms![frmStudentQDrops]![frmQDrops].Form![txtCourseNumber] must be used to refer to the value of txtCourseNumber in frmQDrops. Class modules for frmQDrops can use Me (for example, Me![txtCourseNumber]) to create a robust VBA statement that will work when frmQDrops is opened by itself or within frmStudentQDrops.

Modifying frmStudentsAndClasses with Property Sheets and VBA

The frmStudentsAndClasses and frmStudentEnrollment forms need some changes to refine the way in which they operate. For example:

- The subform should list only courses that correspond to a semester entered in the main form. This change should not be permanent, but rather should take place only when the forms are running together.

- The main form and subform should not allow additions, deletions, or updates. The background color of all controls except the Semester text box should be changed to gray, and the controls should be disabled so that the user cannot place the insertion point in the control.

- The total number of courses that the student takes should appear above the subform.

- The total number of courses should not appear inside the subform. This change should not be permanent, but rather should take place only when the forms are running together.

The changes that will be permanent can be accommodated by changing properties on the property sheet. To change properties temporarily, you will use VBA statements.

To modify the property sheets of the forms to meet these objectives:

1. Display the Design view of **frmStudentEnrollment**, open the **Properties** window for the form, if necessary, click the **Data** tab, if necessary, and then change the Form properties as follows: Allow Edits = **No**, Allow Deletions = **No**, and Allow Additions = **No**.

2. Select all text boxes on frmStudentEnrollment. Click the **Format** tab in the Properties window and change the property as follows: Back Style = **Transparent**. Click the **Data** tab and change the properties as follows: Enabled = **No** and Locked = **Yes**.

3. Save and close frmStudentEnrollment.

4. Open **frmStudentsAndClasses** in Design view.

5. Change the form's properties so that additions and deletions are not allowed.

6. Add a text box named **txtCourses** to the main form of frmStudentsAndClasses to the right of the student's last name and above the subform.

7. The label corresponding to txtCourses should be **Number of Courses**.

8. Select all text boxes on frmStudentsAndClasses and change the disabled, locked, and background color properties to be the same as the form. Make any necessary changes.

You have now added a text box that will hold the course total in frmStudentsAndClasses. Next, you need to bind the text box to the text box in frmStudentEnrollment that has this information.

To add the code to place the total number of courses from frmStudentEnrollment into frmStudentsAndClasses:

1. Select **txtCourses**, click the **Data** tab, click the **Control Source** property field, and then open the **Expression Builder**.

2. Double-click **frmStudentsAndClasses** at the top of the first column. The form frmStudentEnrollment will appear under this heading.

3. Click **frmStudentEnrollment**. The controls of frmStudentEnrollment are visible in the second column.

4. Click **txtCourseCount** in the second column, and then click **Paste**.

5. Click **OK** to close the Expression Builder. The expression =[frmStudentEnrollment].Form![txtCourseCount] is entered in the Control Source property. The value of this control is obtained from the subform. Notice that Forms![frmStudentsAndClasses] is not prefixed to this expression. The Forms prefix is assumed when the control references another control in the form.

6. Save and close frmStudentsAndClasses.

7. Test frmStudentsAndClasses by opening **frmStudent**, navigating to the record for **Samone R. Lia**, and then clicking the **Student's Classes** button. You should see an #Error message in txtCourses because Samone R. Lia is not enrolled in any courses. This message is normal and will disappear for students that have courses.

8. Close frmStudentsAndClasses.

9. Test frmStudentsAndClasses again by navigating to the record for **Jerremy Williams** in frmStudent, and then clicking the **Student's Classes** button. Jerremy Williams's schedule appears in frmStudentsAndClasses and the proper value appears in txtCourses.

10. Close both forms.

Next, you will prepare a new record source for frmStudentEnrollment. This record source will contain criteria stating that the Semester must match the txtSemester text box in frmStudentsAndClasses. The query qryRosters_Part1 is the record source of frmStudentEnrollment. You will modify the record source by changing a copy of this query.

To create a new record source that lists courses according to the semester in another form:

1. Open **frmStudentsAndClasses** in Design view.

2. Add a text box named **txtSemester** to frmStudentsAndClasses. The text box should have a white background and be enabled and unlocked. The label should be **Semester**. Place txtSemester to the right of txtSID.

3. Save and close the form.

4. Display the queries in the Database window. Click **qryRosters_Part1**.

5. Click **Edit** on the menu bar, and then click **Copy** to copy the query.

6. Click **Edit** on the menu bar, and then click **Paste**. Type **qryClassesBySemester** in the Query Name text box in the Paste As dialog box, and then click **OK**.

7. In Design view, modify **qryClassesBySemester** so that the Criteria row of the Semester column references **txtSemester** in **frmStudentsAndClasses**. (Use the Expression Builder to help you with the correct notation, if necessary.)

8. Save and close the query.

Finally, you will develop VBA code that hides the Number of Courses text box in frmStudentEnrollment and changes the record source to the semester found in the qryClassesBySemester query. VBA code will change these properties temporarily while the forms are open at the same time. Only the properties you've changed in the property sheets will be in effect when frmStudentEnrollment is used independently from frmStudentsAndClasses.

To create VBA code that changes the properties of frmStudentEnrollment:

1. Display the Design view of **frmStudentsAndClasses**.

2. In the property sheet's Event tab, click the **On Load** property field, and then open the **Code Builder**.

3. Type the following statements:

```
'Change the RecordSource property and
'hide the form footer of the subform

Me![frmStudentEnrollment].Form.RecordSource _
    = "qryClassesBySemester"
Me![frmStudentEnrollment].Form.Section(2).Visible _
    = False
```

4. Click **Compile SwimReg** from the Debug menu.

5. Save the procedure and close the Visual Basic window, and then save and close frmStudentAndClasses.

6. Test the code by opening **frmStudent** in Form view, navigating to the record for **Jenny G. First**, and then clicking the **Student's Classes** button.

7. Type **00a** in the Semester text box. In the Records menu, click **Refresh** to update the display. You should see the classes for this student in semester 00a.

8. Close both forms.

5

DATA ACCESS OBJECTS AND THEIR PROPERTIES

The object properties described to this point characterize the objects managed by the Microsoft Access application environment. Many of these properties are used to manipulate the user interface. As mentioned earlier, two other object models are currently supported in Microsoft Access: the Data Access Objects (DAO) model and the ActiveX Data Objects (ADO) model.

Although DAO is supported in Access 2000, there are currently no plans to update this model. The DAO model contains more than 50 objects, but for our purposes many of them are subsumed in the newer ADO model.

This section will discuss only the commonly used DAO objects that do not have corresponding ADO objects: the DBEngine object and the Workspace object. The DAO Database object will also be discussed because it works closely with the DBEngine and Workspace objects. Table 5-6 lists commonly used DAO objects. In the table, "db" refers to a Database object variable.

Table 5-6   Commonly used DAO objects

Object	Description	Typical Use	Example Notation
Connection	A connection to an ODBC database	To retrieve the path to the database	DBEngine(0). Connections(0).Name
Container	An object that groups documents of the same type	To establish default permissions for a type of object	db.Containers!Forms. Permissions
Database	A representation of one open database (that is, a file)	To provide access to tables, queries, and recordsets that are defined within the database	DBEngine(0)(0) CurrentDb()
DBEngine	The object representing the Jet database engine that stores and retrieves data	To provide access to other DAO objects	DBEngine
Document	Information about one instance of an object (for example, Form)	To access ownership of an object	db.Containers.Forms! [frmProspects].Owner
Error	An error discovered by the Jet database engine	To identify the type of error that occurred	DBEngine.Errors(0). Description
Field	A representation of a field in a table, query, recordset, or index	To change or access the value of a field	db.TableDefs! [Prospects]! [GMATT].Default
Group	Identification of a group of users that has the same permissions	To establish permissions for a group	DBEngine(0).Groups ("Admin").PID

Table 5-6   Commonly used DAO objects (continued)

Object	Description	Typical Use	Example Notation
Index	A representation of an index on a table	To create a new index	db.TableDefs![Prospects]. Indexes![PrimaryKey]. Foreign
Parameter	An argument supplied to a query	To define arguments that are supplied to frequently run queries	db.QueryDefs.Parameters! [PDate]
QueryDef	A representation of a query	To execute an action query	db.QueryDefs! [QDropList].SQL
Recordset	A copy of the data retrieved from a table or query	To retrieve a value from a field in a table	rstStudents![StudentID] rstStudents is an object variable declared through a Set statement.
Relation	A representation of a relationship between tables	To create a new referential integrity relationship between tables	db.Relations(1).Table
TableDef	A representation of a table	To change the properties of the table's design	db.TableDefs![Prospects] .ValidationRule
User	A user account	To establish permissions of a user	DBEngine(0).Users(0). Name
Workspace	A session managed by the DBEngine	To provide a space used to record operations on one or more databases; these operations can be rolled back (that is, undone) if desired	DBEngine(0)

DBEngine, Workspace, and the Database Objects

Databases are the reason why Access exists. The DAO Database object includes several collections. A **Database** object represents an open database and is managed within the context of a Workspace. A **Workspace** object defines how an application interacts with data. It contains information about the connection to the database, the database, and users of the application. A default Workspace object is automatically created when an application is opened.

The database engine, or **DBEngine** object, manages workspaces. The DBEngine comprises the built-in procedures that retrieve and update data in response to a user's request and is automatically started when an Access application is opened. A DBEngine requires space to record some of its operations.

Unlike Microsoft Access objects, which are identified without reference to the highest object in the hierarchy (that is, the Application object), the notation that references DAO objects must start from the DBEngine. The notation for the DBEngine is simply DBEngine. The default Workspace object is referred to in the following manner:

```
DBEngine.Workspaces (0)
```

That is, the default Workspace is the first object in the Workspaces collection. Most Microsoft Access and DAO collections (and ADO collections) are zero-based, so the first object in the collection is referenced by 0. The notation for the default Workspace can therefore be abbreviated as DBEngine(0).

The notation for the default database can be abbreviated as DBEngine(0)(0). A special function, CurrentDb(), references the database that is automatically opened when an Access application is opened. Use of CurrentDb() is now preferred over DBEngine(0)(0).

The DBEngine, Workspace, and Database objects have several properties. Many of these properties relate to the security and current user of the application (for example, DBEngine.DefaultUser, DBEngine.DefaultPassword, and DBEngine.Workspaces(0) .UserName) and are used in environments where more than one user is working with the application. Other properties are related to overhead information. For example, DBEngine.Workspaces(0).LoginTimeout specifies the length of time to wait before abandoning an attempt to open another database.

ActiveX Data Objects and Properties

The ActiveX Data Objects model (ADO) is not hierarchical like the DAO model. In fact, the ADO model has several parts. Data manipulation is provided by a part known as the ActiveX Data Objects Database model (ADODB). Data definition and security is provided by a part named ADO Extensions for DDL and Security (ADOX). Replication issues are handled in a third part named the Jet Replication Objects model (JRO). This book refers to the three parts collectively as the ADO model. These models are illustrated in Figures 5-7, 5-8, and 5-9 respectively. Note that in Figure 5-8, each of the Table, Index, and Column objects also has a standard ADO Properties collection.

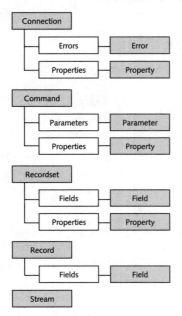

Figure 5-7   ActiveX Data Objects Database Data Model (ADODB)

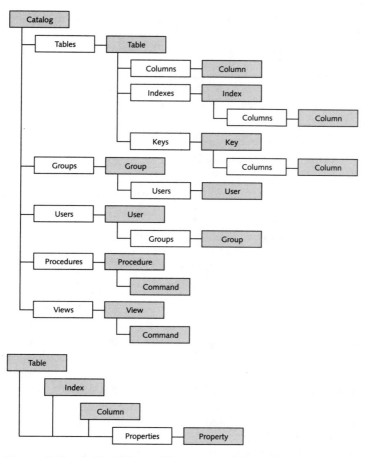

Figure 5-8   ActiveX Data Objects Extensions for DDL and Security Data Model (ADOX)

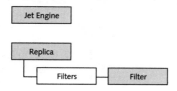

Figure 5-9   ActiveX Data Objects Jet Replication Objects Data Model (JRO)

Libraries

The libraries needed to support ADOX and JRO are not automatically loaded by Access for the programmer. To use these objects, a programmer must go to the Tools menu in the Visual Basic window and add the following references: "Microsoft ADO Ext. 2.1 for DDL and Security" and "Microsoft Jet and Replication Objects 2.1 Library."

The ADODB library is automatically referenced when a new database is created. It is not referenced when an earlier version of an Access application is upgraded to Access 2000, however. In this case, you must add a reference to "Microsoft ActiveX Data Objects 2.1 Library" as well.

If a programmer uses both DAO and ADO objects in an Access project, then he or she should explicitly specify which library to use when declaring objects because DAO and ADO include several objects with the same names (for example, Recordsets). The following lines of code illustrate the difference:

```
Dim rstADO as ADODB.Recordset
Dim rstDAO as DAO.Recordset
```

If the qualifier is omitted, then VBA will use the object from the first model it encounters in the references list.

The fundamental component of the ADO model used in connecting to the database is the Connection object. Programmers use the Catalog, Table, and Index objects to create tables. Queries are created and executed using the Command object. Data manipulation occurs in recordsets, which are created and manipulated using the Recordset object.

Connection Object

The Connection object establishes a connection to the database (or more generally, a data source) and defines a session in which a user interacts with the data. Although the ADO model is not hierarchical in structure, in a sense the Connection object appears at the top of the list of ADO objects because you must establish a connection to the database before you can do anything else. After you have established a connection to a database, it can be used with multiple recordsets. Table 5-7 lists commonly used ADODB Connection object properties.

Table 5-7   Commonly used ADODB Connection object properties

Property	Type	Default	Attributes	Description
ConnectionString	adBStr	" "		Contains all information needed to connect to the database. If specified, it can include the values for the Provider, DataSource, UserID, and Password properties, among others.
DataSource	adBStr	" "	adPropRead, adPropWrite, adPropRequired	The path and name of the database to which to connect.
ExtendedProperties	adBStr	" "	adPropRead, adPropWrite, adPropRequired	A string containing connection information for opening external databases.

Table 5-7   Commonly used ADODB Connection object properties (continued)

Property	Type	Default	Attributes	Description
Mode	adInteger	adSharedMode DenyNone	adPropRead, adPropWrite, adPropRequired	A bitmask specifying access permissions.
Password	adBStr	" "	adPropRead, adPropWrite, adPropRequired	The password to be used when connecting to the data source.
Provider	adBStr	" "		The database engine, typically Microsoft.Jet.OLE DB.4.0.
UserID	adBStr	"Admin"	adPropRead, adPropWrite, adPropRequired	The user ID to be used when connecting to the data source.

Opening a Connection object requires declaring a variable as an ADODB.Connection, setting it to a value, and then opening the connection. The Connection object is declared using a Dim statement:

```
Dim Conn as ADODB.Connection
```

The Connection object is instantiated using a Set statement:

```
Set Conn = New ADODB.Connection
```

Next, you must open the Connection object. The Open method of the Connection object requires a connection string. Other optional parameters that can be specified include a user ID and a password. The simplest way to supply the optional parameters is to use the Connection property of the CurrentProject object. This object and property supply information in the same manner as the CurrentDb function in the DAO model (illustrated earlier). The following line of code illustrates the required statement:

```
Conn.Open CurrentProject.Connection
```

When connecting to another database, however, you will need to specify the Provider and the DataSource properties with the following code. Note that this code uses the With statement, in which all properties or collections preceded by a dot or bang symbol apply to the object identified in the With statement. It allows you to use a shorter notation and highlights the fact that subsequent properties or collections apply to the object, which in turn facilitates maintenance.

```
Dim Conn as ADODB.Connection
With Conn
    .Provider="Microsoft.Jet.OLEDB.4.0;"
    .DataSource="pathname\filename"
    .Open
End With
```

Catalog and Table Objects

A **Catalog** object represents a database. In most cases, you will simply open a catalog and reference objects in it. Occasionally, you may append new objects (such as a table) to the catalog. A **Table** object contains the definitions that define the table structures in the database. Table objects are used to access properties of the table's design. Although tables can be created and modified through VBA, they are developed more frequently through Table Design view.

Table 5-8 summarizes some of the properties associated with tables. The values for many of these properties can be set through the Table property sheets that can be displayed when the table is highlighted in the Database window or displayed in Design view.

Table 5-8   Commonly used Table object properties

Property	Type	Default	Attributes	Description
Temporary Table	adBoolean	False	adPropRead, adPropRequired	Indicates whether the table is destroyed when the connection is released
Jet OLEDB: Create Link	adBoolean	False	adPropRead, adPropWrite, adPropRequired	Indicates whether the table is a linked table
Jet OLEDB: Link Datasource	adBStr	" "	adPropRead, adPropWrite, adPropRequired	A string containing the name of the external database to which to link
Jet OLEDB: Table Validation Rule	adBStr	" "	adPropRead, adPropWrite, adPropRequired	Sets or returns an expression that is used to validate data when a record is changed or added to the table
Jet OLEDB: Table Validation Text	adBStr	" "	adPropRead, adPropWrite, adPropRequired	Sets or returns a String that specifies the text of the message to be displayed to the user when the validation rule is violated

You can update Table object properties through VBA code. Just as the Design view cannot update some properties of a linked table, however, VBA cannot update some linked table properties. The following code will update the Validation Text property of the Prospects table in MU-DSci, assuming the current connection opens Data.mdb.

```
Dim catMyDatabase as ADOX.Catalog
Set catMyDatabase = New Catalog
catMyDatabase.ActiveConnection = CurrentProject.Connection
catMyDatabase.Tables("Prospects").Properties_
    ("Jet OLEDB Table Validation Text") _
    = "Need First or Last Name"
```

Some properties are optional. That is, the database engine manages these properties only when they are created in VBA code or set by the system developer through the Design or

Datasheet view of an object. An example of this type of property is the **Description** property. The Description property is created by Microsoft Access (not the database engine) through the Table property sheet. Optional properties are referenced through the Properties collection.

Syntax

CatalogReference.Tables.(*TableIndex*).Properties.(*PropertyIndex*)

Syntax Dissection

- *CatalogReference* is a valid reference to a catalog.

- *CatalogReference*.Tables. references the Tables collection of the database referenced.

- *TableIndex* refers to the table contained in the Tables collection.

- *TableIndex* may be the ordinal index (0, 1, 2, . . .) of the table in the collection or the name of the table enclosed in quotes. It must be enclosed in quotes.

- *Properties* references the Properties collection of the table.

- *PropertyIndex* refers to the property contained in the Properties collection.

- *PropertyIndex* may be the ordinal index (0, 1, 2, . . .) of the property in the collection or the name of the property enclosed in quotes. It must be enclosed in quotes. Datasheet properties must be referenced through the Properties collection.

Field Objects and Properties

Every Table object owns a Columns collection. The properties of a Column object correspond with the names of Field Properties identified in the Design view of a table. As you append columns to the Columns collection, you specify the information needed for the **Data Type**. In the case of character data, you also specify the length of the attribute. For example,

```
Columns.Append "FirstName", adWChar, 20
```

is equivalent to Data Type equal to Text and Size equal to 20. The statement

```
Columns.Append "CustomerNo", adInteger
```

sets the Data Type to Integer.

Microsoft Access creates the Format, InputMask, and CaptionField properties. Therefore these properties must be referenced through the Properties collection. An example that specifies a Caption property follows:

```
Dim catMyDatabase As ADOX.Catalog
Dim tbl As ADOX.Table
Set catMyDatabase = New ADOX.Catalog
catMyDatabase.ActiveConnection = CurrentProject.Connection
Set tbl = dbMyDatabase.Tables("tblProspects")
tbl!StudentID.Properties("Description") = "Student ID"
```

In contrast, the AutoIncrement property for a field is defined by the database engine. It is specified as follows:

```
Dim catMyDatabase As ADOX.Catalog
Dim tbl As ADOX.Table
Set catMyDatabase = New ADOX.Catalog
catMyDatabase.ActiveConnection = CurrentProject.Connection
Set tbl = dbMyDatabase.Tables("tblProspects")
tbl.StudentID.Properties.AutoIncrement = True
```

Properties that require use of the Properties collection can be set on a linked table. Properties created by the database engine cannot be updated on a linked table.

Index Objects and Properties

Besides a Columns collection, most tables own an Indexes collection and a Keys collection. **Indexes** are fields that are used to find and sort records in a table. Other fields can be made indexes as needed through VBA or through the Indexes window. Each index created through a table's Design view is an Index object. **Keys** are either primary keys or foreign keys. An index whose PrimaryKey property is True, for example, is a primary key.

Many of the properties associated with an Index object are displayed in the Indexes window (for example, Primary and Unique). Other properties can be accessed only through VBA. Table 5-9 describes some of the commonly used Index properties.

Table 5-9 Commonly used ADOX Index properties

Property	Type	Default	Attributes	Description
AutoUpdate	adBoolean	True	adPropRead, adPropRequired	Indicates whether the index is maintained automatically when changes are made to the corresponding base table
IndexNulls	adInteger	adIndex NullsDisallow	adIndexNulls Disallow, adIndexNullsIgnore, adIndexNullsAllow	Indicates whether the index may accept null values
Name	adBStr	" "		Indicates the name of the index
PrimaryKey	adBoolean	False		Indicates whether the index serves as the primary key of the table

If you need to create tables from within a VBA procedure, the process is simple in ADO. The first step is to establish a connection with an Access catalog object. You follow the fundamental process illustrated several times earlier. That is, you declare a Catalog object using a Dim statement and then set the value of its ActiveConnection property, as follows:

```
Dim cat as ADOX.Catalog
Set cat = New ADOX.Catalog
cat.ActiveConnection = CurrentProject.Connection
```

Once the Catalog object is established, you declare a Table object, specify its structure, and append it to the catalog. The table's ParentCatalog property should be set to the current catalog. Its Columns property can then be used to define the attributes of the table.

Let's walk through an example. First, assume that you want to create a table named tblMenu that has three attributes. The first attribute, the primary key, is named ItemNo and is an Autonumber. The second and third attributes are named ItemName and ItemDescription, respectively, and are both character strings. The following statements declare the needed object variables, create the table, create the attributes, and append the table to the catalog (these statements assume the prior statements have been used to establish the catalog connection):

```
Dim tbl As ADOX.Table
Dim idx As ADOX.Index
'create the table
Set tbl = New ADOX.Table
With tbl
     .Name = "tblMenu"      'name the table
     Set .ParentCatalog = cat    'add to the catalog
'add the attributes to the table
     .Columns.Append "ItemNo", adInteger
     .Columns("ItemNo").Properties("AutoIncrement") = True
     .Columns.Append "ItemName", adWChar
     .Columns.Append "Calories", adWChar
End With
cat.Tables.Append tbl      'append the table to the catalog
```

The next step is to create the primary key. It is done in the following code:

```
Set idx = New ADOX.Index
With idx
     .Name = "PrimaryKey"
     .Columns.Append "ItemNo"
     .PrimaryKey = True
     .Unique = True
End With
tbl.Indexes.Append idx     'append to the indexes collection
```

ADO also provides a Key object that can be used to establish a primary key (or a foreign key). The preceding statements could be reduced to one statement, by utilizing the Key collection as follows:

```
tbl.Keys.Append "PrimaryKey", adKeyPrimary, "ItemNo"
```

You will now practice these concepts.

Changing the Semester Default Value in the Enrollment Table

Several forms in the Metropolitan University's Swim Lessons application will display data related to the current or upcoming semester. The value for the current semester is stored in the Semester table. This value must be updated once per semester. In addition to updating the value in the Semester table, the default value of the Semester field in the Enrollment table should be updated. This default value is used when students register for new courses. The Enrollment table is a linked table. Because VBA cannot update the Default property of a linked table, the procedure must open the SwimData.mdb database.

To update the semester in the Semester table:

1. Create a new form called **frmChangeSemester**, and make **tblSemester** the record source of the form.

2. Add a text box control instance to the form called **txtSemesterID**. Make **SemesterID** the control source of txtSemesterID.

3. Make the label corresponding to txtSemesterID read **Semester ID**, and then change the form properties of **frmChangeSemester** so that additions and deletions are not allowed.

Because txtSemesterID is bound to SemesterID, changes to the text box are written to the SemesterID field in the Semester table. You will write VBA code to update the default value of the Semester field in the Enrollment table. This code will be triggered when txtSemesterID is updated in the new frmChangeSemester.

To create a procedure that updates the Default property of the SemesterID field in the Enrollment table:

1. Open the properties window for txtSemesterID, and then click the **Events** tab, if necessary.

2. Select **[Event Procedure]** for the After Update property of txtSemsterID, and then click the **Build** button.

3. Click **Tools** on the Visual Basic menu bar, click **References**, select **Microsoft ADO Ext. 2.1 for DDL and Security**, and then click **OK**. Display the property sheet for txtSemesterID, click the **Event** tab, click the **AfterUpdate** property field, and open the **Code Builder**. The insertion point appears in the Private Sub txtSemesterID_AfterUpdate() procedure.

4. Type the statements shown below into the procedure. If SwimData.mdb is stored in a different drive and/or folder on your computer or network, substitute the correct drive and directory in the cnnSwimData.Open statement in the code.

```
'Update the default value of the Semester field
'in tblEnrollment
Dim cnnSwimData As ADODB.Connection
Dim tbl As ADOX.Table
Dim cat As New ADOX.Catalog
```

```
Set cnnSwimData = New ADODB.Connection
cnnSwimData.Open "Provider=Microsoft.Jet.OLEDB.4.0;" & _
"Data Source=C:\My Documents\AccessApps\Swim\SwimData.mdb;"

Set cat.ActiveConnection = cnnSwimData
Set tbl = cat.Tables("tblClasses")
tbl.Columns("Semester").Properties("Default") = _
    Chr(34) & Me![txtSemesterID] & Chr(34)
cnnSwimData.Close
End Sub
```

5

The object variable cnnSwimData contains a connection pointer to an object. The Open statement is a built-in method of the Connection object that opens a connection to another database. SwimData.mdb can be opened even though you are in SwimReg.mdb (it is not displayed on the screen, however). After a database connection and catalog are opened, the tables can be referenced. From the perspective of the database, Semester is not linked, so the table's properties can be modified.

The Default property is made equal to the value typed in txtSemesterID. Because SemesterID is a Text data type, the value stored in the Default property must include quotation marks. Chr(34) is a built-in function that returns quotation marks. The & operator is used to create a string that has quotation marks surrounding the value placed in txtSemesterID (for example, "99a" with the quotation marks is stored in the DefaultValue property). The statement cnnSwimData.Close causes SwimData.mdb to close.

5. Click **Compile SwimReg** in the Debug menu, save the procedure, save the open forms, and then close the Visual Basic window.

6. Save and close frmChangeSemester, open **frmChangeSemester** in Form view, type **99a** into the text box, and then close frmChangeSemester.

7. Open the Design view of the **tblClasses** table. Click the **Yes** button in response to the message box indicating that you cannot modify some of the properties in the table. The DefaultValueField argument for Semester should state "99a". Unlike Microsoft Access object properties, which revert back to the value typed into the property sheet after the object is closed, VBA permanently changes the value of a Table property.

8. Close the tblClasses table.

In the next section, you'll see that a very similar process is used to create a new query.

Command Object

A Command object can contain information needed to define a query. You can manipulate the queries listed under the Queries tab of the Database window with Command objects. A Command object can be used to create new queries, execute action queries, and create views.

Command objects are associated with several descriptive properties, as shown in Table 5-10.

Table 5-10 Commonly used ADODB Command properties

Property	Type	Default	Description
ActiveConnection	adBStr	" "	A string specifying the currently active database connection
Jet OLEDB: Link Datasource	adBStr	" "	A string containing the name of the external database to which to link
CommandText	adBStr	" "	A string containing the command to be executed (often an SQL query)
CommandType	adInteger		Indicates whether the command is a stored procedure (adCmdStoredProc, for Jet 4.0) or is treated as a table (adCmdTable, for earlier versions of Access)

Command objects own a Parameters collection. Parameter objects in this collection represent the data needed by the command to execute an action.

In the same manner in which you add a table definition by creating the table, creating the attributes, and appending the table to the catalog, you can create a new query by creating the query, creating the SQL command that implements the query, and appending the query to the catalog. This process uses the Command object. As in creating the table definition, the first step establishes the Catalog object:

```
Dim cat as ADOX.Catalog
Set cat = New ADOX.Catalog
cat.ActiveConnection = CurrentProject.Connection
```

TIP

Queries created through the ADO model will not appear in the Database window in Access 2000 because Access 2000 mixes the DAO and ADO models. Queries created through the wizards and Design view of a query are saved in an older format (a DAO format). In addition, the record sources of forms and reports are DAO objects. Microsoft will not display queries that are created in ADO in the Database window because you cannot use these queries as record sources for forms and reports. If you place the query in the Views collection, however, the VBA code can refer to the queries again.

After establishing the Catalog connection, the next step is to declare a Command object, specify the SQL command structure it will use, and append it to the catalog. The query's CommandText property is used to define the SQL command. Assume that you want to create a query named qryAllMenuData that will access all rows in the tblMenu table. The following statements declare the needed object variables, create the query, create the SQL command, and append the query to the catalog (these statements assume the prior statements have been used to establish the catalog connection):

```
Dim cmd As ADODB.Command

Set cmd = New ADODB.Command
cmd.CommandText = "SELECT * FROM tblMenu;"
cat.Views.Append "qryAllMenuData", cmd
cat.Views.Refresh
```

Recordset Objects and Properties

Connection, Table, Command, Column, and Index objects represent the *definitions* of database connections, tables, commands, columns, and indexes, respectively. **Recordset** objects, on the other hand, provide access to the actual data stored in and retrieved from the database. Stated more precisely, a Recordset object represents a copy of the data stored in a table or retrieved from a query.

ADO recognizes four general types of recordsets, which are determined by the CursorType property setting. The allowed values—adOpenDynamic (Dynamic), adOpenKeySet (KeySet), adOpenForwardOnly (Forward Only), and adOpenStatic (Static)—are described below.

- **Dynamic** cursors are fully scrollable. You can use methods such as MoveFirst (finds the first record in a recordset) and MoveLast (finds the last record in a recordset) to access records in a Dynamic recordset. All changes to the recordset by other users are visible. Dynamic cursors consume the most system resources, as they provide a "live" view of the data.

- **KeySet** cursors are also fully scrollable, but do not offer the capability of seeing changes made by other users.

- **Forward Only** cursors are not scrollable. A programmer can use only methods like MoveNext—not methods like MovePrevious. No changes by other users are visible, and updates to the data are allowed only one record at a time. Forward Only cursors, the default type used, consume the fewest system resources.

- **Static** cursors are fully scrollable. They do not offer the option of seeing changes made by anyone in a Static cursor.

All of these cursors allow the data to be updated. The specific update capability, however, depends on the setting of the LockType property. A programmer can specify one of the following values for the LockType property: adLockReadOnly (the default), adLockPessimistic, or adLockOptimistic. Table 5-11 lists the supported CursorType and LockType property value combinations.

Table 5-11   Allowed CursorType/LockType combinations in ADO

CursorType	LockType/Options	DAO Equivalent
adOpenFOrwardOnly	adLockReadOnly	dbOpenSnapShot, dbForwardOnly
adOpenKeySet	adLockReadOnly	N/A
adOpenKeySet	adLockPessimistic	dbOpenDynaset
adOpenKeySet	adLockOptimistic	dbOpenDynaset
adOpenKeySet	adLockBatchOptimistic	dbOpenDynaset
adOpenStatic	adLockReadOnly	dbOpenDynaset
adOpenDynamic	adLockOptimistic, adCmdTableDirect	dbOpenTable

A recordset is automatically created when a bound form is opened. This recordset contains all of the records that are displayed through the bound form. Recordsets of bound forms are DAO recordsets. You can also define a recordset independently of a form. For example, in MU-DSci the procedure that moves records from the tblProspects table to the tblCurrentStudents table declares and initializes a recordset. Figure 5-10 shows a section of the procedure containing the relevant code.

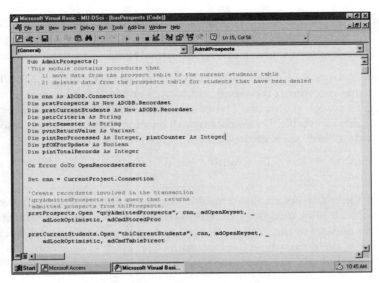

Figure 5-10   Prospect processing module section

In this code, prstProspects and prstCurrentStudents are declared as Recordset object variables. The prefix "p" indicates that the variable will be used only in the current procedure; that is, it is a **procedure-level** or **local variable**. The prefix "rst" indicates that the object variable is a Recordset object. The Open method is used to define a recordset. The default type of recordset in ADO has the characteristics of CursorType set to adOpenForwardOnly and the characteristics of LockType set to adLockReadOnly. In this code, the object variable prstProspects refers to a dynaset-type recordset that contains data from the qryAdmittedProspects query; prstCurrentStudents is a dynaset-type recordset that contains data from the tblCurrentStudents table.

Many properties are available that can facilitate recordset processing as illustrated in Table 5-12. In addition to the properties listed in Table 5-12, recordsets use many of the same properties associated with the recordset's table or query. For example, the ValidationRule property of a recordset contains the same value as the ValidationRule of the table used to create the recordset.

Table 5-12 Commonly used Recordset properties

Property	Type	Default	Attributes	Description
BOF	adBoolean			Equals True when the Bookmark property points to a position prior to the first record
Bookmark	adBStr	" "		A pointer to the current record in the recordset
EOF	adBoolean			Equals True when the Bookmark property points to a position after the last record
LockType	adInteger	adLockRead Only	adLockBatchOptimistic, adLockOptimistic, adLockPessimistic, adLockReadOnly	Specifies the type of record locking to use when a value is to be updated
RecordCount	adInteger			The number of records accessed in a recordset

Recordset objects own a Fields collection. Fields are used to retrieve or update a particular value. The value of a field in a recordset is obtained through the following syntax:

Syntax

RecordsetObject![*FieldName*]

Syntax Dissection

RecordsetObject refers to an object variable that has been defined through a Set statement.

FieldName refers to the name of the field in the table or query used to generate the recordset.

An example of a reference to a field's value follows:

```
prstProspects![FirstName]
```

This notation returns the FirstName of the current record of the recordset. Like a table or query, a recordset contains multiple rows. At any point in time, however, only one of the rows is identified as the current record. The **Bookmark** property of a recordset points to the current record (for example, prstProspects.Bookmark). Recordsets have methods that are capable of moving the bookmark (for example, MoveNext and Find). The values of some recordset properties are determined after one of these methods executes. For example, the **EOF** property equals True when a previously executed Find method does not find a record that matches a specified criterion. Likewise, the **EOF** property equals True when the bookmark advances past the last record in the recordset, such as when a MoveNext method executes after the bookmark points to the last record in the recordset.

When an empty recordset is returned, both the BOF and EOF properties are True. Testing both properties is used to determine whether the recordset is indeed empty. In addition, when using VBA code, if the bookmark is located prior to the beginning of a recordset or after the end of a recordset, any action other than moving back to a record will cause a runtime error.

As in the earlier ADO examples, the basic process involves establishing a connection to the recordset and then opening it with parameters that correspond to the actions you intend to execute. To illustrate, suppose you want to open tblMenu in order to process the records in it. The following code is needed:

```
Dim Conn As ADODB.Connection
Dim rst As ADODB.Recordset
'establish the objects
Set Conn = New ADODB.Connection
Set rst = New ADODB.Recordset
'establish the connection
Conn.Open CurrentProject.Connection
rst.Open "tblMenu", Conn, adOpenKeyset
```

The four types of recordsets (Dynamic, KeySet, Forward Only, and Static) are specified by the third parameter on the Open method in the code above. The constant used with KeySet cursors is adOpenKeySet. With Static cursors, the constant is adOpenStatic; with Read Only, it is adOpenReadOnly.

OBJECTS DEFINED BY OTHER APPLICATIONS

Although most of the objects used by an Access application are classified as DAO or ADO objects or Microsoft Access objects, objects managed by other applications can be used as well. For example, Access frequently uses the Err object. This object is managed by VBA and is available to any application that uses VBA as its programming language.

Many Access applications also use the CommandBar object and CommandBars collection. Microsoft Office manages the CommandBar object. Menu bars and toolbars are CommandBar objects, for example. CommandBar objects own a Controls collection. This Controls collection contains an object for any item on the menu bar or toolbar. Properties associated with CommandBar objects and controls allow the programmer to change the display of a menu bar or toolbar. For example, to disable the Format &Report control on the &File menu of the mnuStudents, you would use the following code:

```
CommandBars("mnuStudents").Controls("&File"). _
Controls("Format &Report").Enabled = False
```

If you want to write code that uses objects from another application, the Microsoft Access References collection must contain an object that identifies the other application.

CHAPTER SUMMARY

❏ Access is an object-based database environment—that is, it uses objects as fundamental building blocks. Tables, queries, forms, reports, and even databases are objects. Other objects that support data access activities are recordsets and workspaces.

❏ Access maintains hundreds of data items, called properties, that describe the objects in an Access database. The objects themselves are grouped into collections, and collections are in turn associated with the user interface (Microsoft Access objects) or with the database engine (Data Access Objects and ActiveX Data Objects). Programmers can modify many aspects of an Access application and database by manipulating object properties.

❏ Some properties simply provide information to the programmer. Most of the properties for applications and indexes fall into this category. The properties for the other objects—controls, forms, pages, queries, reports, tables, fields, and so on—define a wide range of characteristics. These characteristics include font descriptions, colors and styles, record sources, formats and masks, validation characteristics, window characteristics, default values, and much more.

❏ Generally speaking, properties can be examined and changed by opening the property sheets associated with the object. Not all objects use property sheets, however. In addition, not all properties are listed on property sheets.

❏ Most properties can be manipulated through VBA. Macros and VBA allow the programmer to change object properties while the program is running. Effective Access applications can be developed by creating objects and changing their properties either in Design view or in runtime mode with a VBA procedure or macro.

REVIEW QUESTIONS

1. Why is Access described as object-based rather than object-oriented?

2. What is a collection?

3. What are Microsoft Access objects? What are ADO objects? Identify at least three objects in each category.

4. How can an object own a collection?

5. The word _____ is used by a form class module to refer to a form that contains another form.

6. What property indicates whether a control can be seen?

7. What properties can be used to prevent a user from entering a value in a text box?

8. What property indicates the source of a bound form?

9. A(n) _____ represents a particular integer in Access.

   a. intrinsic constant

   b. application object

   c. screen constant

   d. read-only variable

10. What does it mean when a form's Modal property is set to Yes?

11. When the Modal property of an object is set to False, a user cannot perform an action on any other object until the current object is closed. True or False?

12. What object and property can be used to refer to the form that is currently active?

13. What object and property can be used to refer to an open connection in the current project?

14. _____ cursors are not scrollable.

   a. Dynamic

   b. Static

   c. KeySet

   d. Forward Only

15. What is the difference between Dynamic, Static, Forward Only, and KeySet curors?

16. What is the purpose of the Properties collection? What objects own a Properties collection?

17. Workspaces manage DBEngine objects. True or False?

18. How are catalog objects used?

19. What is the purpose of a bookmark?

20. In a project using both the DAO and ADO object models, if a variable is declared as follows:

    ```
    Dim precStudent as Recordset
    ```

    what object model will be used to define precStudent?

Hands-on Projects

Project 5-1

Natural Parent International. Two additional features must be added to the library portion of the NPI system. First, a form must be created that records the dates on which books were checked out and returned. The caption of this form should display the title of the book being processed. The second feature is an enhancement to a capability that was developed in Chapter 4. As a result of work performed in Chapter 4, frmLibrary displays details of the book that was double-clicked in the subform of frmMembers. An equivalent menu item was not developed for this capability because menu items cannot find a public function that is contained in a subform. Consequently, a public function must be developed in frmMembers that opens frmLibrary to the book that is currently selected in the subform of frmMembers. This function must refer to the BookID that is located in the subform of frmMembers. In addition, because an error will occur when a member does not have any checked-out book, the function must verify that a book is currently selected in the subform before executing the code that opens frmLibrary.

Complete these steps:

1. Open **NPI.mdb**. Develop a form named **frmCheckOut**. The record source for the form is qryCheckoutDescending. frmCheckOut is a continuous form that displays the Member, Date Out, and Date Returned. The Member should be selected with a combo box, called cboMember, that displays the name of the member. The row source for the combo box is qrycboNameList. The combo box should update the MemberID field.

2. Place a command button called **cmdCheckout** on frmLibrary. Develop VBA code that opens frmCheckOut so that checkout/checkin records related to the book selected in frmLibrary are displayed. The VBA code should change the caption of frmCheckOut so that the title of the selected book is displayed. The DoCmd.Open form statement should pass the BookID of the book to be checked out to frmCheckout through the use of an OpenArgs argument.

3. Write the following code in the After_Update event of cboMemberID:

```
Private Sub cboMember_AfterUpdate()
'The OpenArgs property contains the BookID that was used
'to filter the form. Place this value in BookID for the form
'after the MemberID is updated.
    If IsNull(Me.OpenArgs) Then
        MsgBox "Unknown book. Please open the form from " & _
            "the library form or the book list.", _
            vbInformation, "Unknown Book"
    Else
        Me!BookID = Me.OpenArgs
    End If
End Sub
```

The BookID is not displayed in frmCheckout; therefore VBA code must update the BookID based on the value of the OpenArgs property.

4. Create code that places the current date—(Date())—in the Date Out and Date Returned text box when each text box is double-clicked.

5. Create a function named **GetBookFromSub** in frmMembers. The function should open frmLibrary so that the record in frmLibrary corresponds to the currently selected book in the subform of frmMembers. If a member does not have any books, the CurrentRecord property equals zero. Test the value of the CurrentRecord property prior to executing the statement that opens frmLibary. Create a menu item inside the Forms menu of mnuMembers that triggers GetBookFromSub().

6. If you have not already done so, associate mnuMembers with frmMembers, mnuMemberSummary with frmMemberSummary, mnuLoanedBooks with frmLentBooks, and mnuNPI with frmLibrary.

7. Save your work.

Project 5-2

Metropolitan Performing Arts Company. To enhance the usability of the MPAC system, two enhancements should be made. First, the caption of frmPerformerJobs should depend on the performance that is being displayed. For example, the caption should state "Performers for Gone With the Wind at 8/10/01 9:00:00 PM" when that performance is displayed in frmPerformanceDateSeats. Second, clicking a toolbar button should filter frmPerformance DateSeats so that only available seats are displayed. Clicking the toolbar button again should reset frmPerformanceDateSeats to display all seats. A label frmPerformanceDateSeats, the ToolTip of the toolbar, and the image on the toolbar should reflect the current status of the filter.

Complete these steps:

1. Open **MPA.mdb**. Add code to the function OpenfrmPerformerJobs so that the caption of frmPerformerJobs displays the performance name, date, and time of the performance.

2. Create a label on frmPerformanceDateSeats that says **Showing available seats**. Name the label **lblAvailableSeats**. Set the visible property to **No**.

3. Create a function named **FilterAvailable** in the class module of frmPerformanceDateSeats. If the visible property of lblAvailableSeats is False, the function should filter the subform of frmPerformanceDateSeats so that only available seats are displayed. In addition, lblAvailableSeats should be made visible. If the lblAvailableSeats is already visible, the filter should be turned off and lblAvailableSeats should become invisible. You will need to use the Filter and FilterOn properties to filter the form.

4. Add a toolbar button to tbrPerformanceSeats to run FilterAvailable( ). Name the button **Available Seats**. Type **Show available seats only** in the ScreenTip property. Copy the button image for "Apply Filter" and paste the button image to "Available Seats." Use the Button Editor to change the colors on the button (so that it is distinguished from Apply Filter).

5. Modify **FilterAvailable** so that the ScreenTip states **Show all seats** when the subform is filtered. The tip should display **Show available seats** only when the subform is not filtered. In addition, the image of the toolbar button should appear to be pressed down when the subform is filtered and should appear not to be recessed when the subform is not filtered. Before constructing this procedure, you should select Microsoft Office Object Library in the Reference window. You will need to use the TooltipText and State properties of a command bar control. The state property can be set to the intrinsic constants **msoButtonDown** and **msoButtonUp**.

6. Save your work.

Project 5-3

Foreign Language Institute System. When viewing the product purchases made by a customer, the button on the frmCustomers form that opens the frmPurchases form should ensure that only the purchases for the appropriate customer are displayed. You will now write VBA code to open frmSales when the Purchases button on frmCustomers is clicked.

Complete these steps:

1. Open **FLI.mdb**. Open the **Properties** window for the cmdPurchases button, set the OnClick property to **[Event Procedure]**, click the **Build** button, and then enter the following line of code:

```
DoCmd.OpenForm "frmSales", acNormal,, "[CustomerID]=" & _
Me![txtCustomerID]
```

The criterion in the WhereCondition argument of the OpenForm method ("[CustomerID]=" & Me![txtCustomerID]) ensures that the form opens to the proper customer record.

2. Save your work.

Project 5-4

King William Hotel. When a customer contacts the hotel to make a reservation, the customer's data are first entered into the system. Next, the frmMakeReservation form is accessed to set up a reservation. You will now write VBA code to open frmMakeReservations when the Make Reservations button on frmCustomer is clicked.

Complete these steps:

1. Open **KWH.mdb**. Open the **Properties** window for the cmdReservations button, set the OnClick property to **[Event Procedure]**, click the **Build** button, and then enter the following line of code:

```
DoCmd.OpenForm "frmMakeReservation", acNormal
```

2. In a similar manner, the Check In button should open the frmCheckIn form and the Check Out button should open the frmChargeSummary form. In both of these cases, however, the form being opened should display records for the appropriate customer. Open the **Properties** window for the cmdCheckIn button, set the OnClick property to **[Event Procedure]**, click the **Build** button, and then enter the following line of code:

```
DoCmd.OpenForm "frmCheckIn", acNormal,, "[CustomerNo]=" & _
Me![txtCustomerNo]
```

The criterion in the WhereCondition argument of the OpenForm method ("[CustomerNo]=" & Me![txtCustomerNo]) ensures that the form opens to the proper customer record.

3. Repeat the process for the cmdCheckOut button. Open the **Properties** window for the cmdCheckOut button, set the OnClick property to **[Event Procedure]**, click the **Build** button, and then enter the following line of code:

```
DoCmd.OpenForm "frmChargeSummary", acNormal,,
        "[CustomerNo]=" & Me![txtCustomerNo]
```

4. Save your work.

Project 5-5

Workers' Compensation Commission System. The patients form is the center of much of the processing in this system. From this form, users need to get to Form A, Form B, and Form C. You should now add VBA code to the command buttons on frmPatients that open the forms.

Complete these steps:

1. Open **WCC.mdb**. Open the **Properties** window for the cmdFormA button. Set the OnClick property to **[Event Procedure]**, click the **Build** button, and then enter the following line of code:

```
DoCmd.OpenForm "frmWCCA"
```

2. Repeat the process in Step 1 for the cmdFormB and cmdFormC buttons, changing the form name as needed. Be careful to enclose the form names in quotation marks so that Access will recognize them as strings.

3. Save your work.

6

EVENT-DRIVEN PROGRAMMING AND ACCESS EVENTS

Using Events to Display and Update Payment and Registration Data

---

In this chapter you will:

♦ Learn the advantages and disadvantages of event-driven programming

♦ Trigger macros, functions, and event procedures through an Access event

♦ Develop a macro that highlights the control that has focus

♦ Distinguish between the various user actions, data retrieval, and data update events

♦ Determine the most appropriate event to use in a particular situation

---

In this chapter, you will consider events. **Events** are actions recognized by an object. In event-driven programming environments, you can define a response to events as they occur. Events include button clicks, keystrokes in text boxes, the opening of forms, and record deletions. When an event occurs, a macro or VBA procedure defines the response to that event. This response might be the program opening or closing a form, manipulating properties of objects, or performing complex calculations. For example, a macro that opens a form may execute in response to a button click. In another example, a VBA procedure that changes the background property of a control may execute in response to a change in cursor position.

As you go through the chapter and place the role of events in perspective, consider the ingredients of an Access application. The most basic ingredients are the tables, forms, pages, reports, and queries that are defined in their respective Design views. The next ingredients are the macros and procedures that use dot or bang notation to manipulate the properties of the tables, forms, pages, reports, and queries. You will eventually see that a vital ingredient is still missing: the ingredient that controls when the macros and procedures execute. Obviously, they cannot be randomly executed. Random execution may result in a very interesting effect, but would lead to a very confusing (and worthless) application.

To resolve this problem, programming languages provide a number of ways to control or time the execution of program code. Historically, many languages have used a management/subordinate approach to executing code. That is, a particular piece of program code (the subordinate) executes when another piece of program code (the management) tells it to execute. The management/subordinate approach is commonly used in "older" languages such as COBOL, FORTRAN, C, and traditional Basic. VBA—and, to a limited extent, Access macros—support this type of execution.

Another, more modern approach uses the concept of events. That is, code is associated with some action or change in the system's environment. The code executes when the event occurs. Access uses this type of programming, called **event-driven programming**, and this is the main focus of this chapter.

EVENT-DRIVEN PROGRAMMING

Event-driven programming is a powerful Access feature. This type of programming supports the creation of systems that can react to a wide range of user actions. Unlike the management/subordinate approach to controlling execution, event-driven programming does not require the development of management components that anticipate the variety of user actions that can occur. In a Windows environment, the sequence of actions (for example, opening multiple windows, using menus, using toolbars, resizing a form, moving to a new record in a form) is almost impossible to anticipate. With event-driven programming, the system developer identifies important events and associates macros and procedures with them. The macros and procedures may execute in a variety of sequences, depending on the actions of the user.

Unfortunately, event-driven programming can also be a source of frustration for the beginning programmer and for those who must maintain the code. Sources of frustration include the following:

- Events occurring outside an anticipated sequence
- Anticipated events that do not occur
- Events occurring at an inappropriate time
- Events occurring more than once
- Timing problems between events
- Difficulty in locating relevant code
- Difficulty in understanding how the system executes

When performing program maintenance, a programmer may find it difficult to determine the event and associated code that is causing a result. Experience plays a large role in overcoming programming and maintenance difficulties.

THE WORLD ACCORDING TO EVENTS

From a human perspective, events change us or the environment that surrounds us. Frequently, this change causes an action to take place. For example, while you are driving a car, a stoplight changes from green to yellow. The stoplight change is an event that triggers a procedure. The procedure instructs you to remove your foot from the accelerator and press the brake.

If someone wanted to automate the car-stopping procedure in response to a stoplight's green-to-yellow event, the car object could be given an event property that identifies the procedure to execute. An **event property** is an object property that associates a procedure or macro with an event that is recognized by the object. If the event occurs, the macro or procedure identified by the event property executes. In terms of the car-stopping example, the property and procedure assignment might look like the following:

```
Cars("Bob's Car").OnGreenToYellow = "StopProcedure"
```

Cars is a collection that contains car objects. "Bob's Car" is a particular car in the Cars collection. OnGreenToYellow is an event property that identifies a procedure or macro to be executed when the Green To Yellow event occurs. "StopProcedure" is the name of the procedure or macro to execute.

Sometimes you need to account for sequences of events that may be related in complex ways. For example, consider the car event properties OnTurnGreen, OnBrakeRelease, and OnSiren. A car's OnTurnGreen event property identifies code that causes the car to release the brake and accelerate when the light turns green. Releasing the brake causes code associated with OnBrakeRelease to execute. This code may turn off the brake lights. The OnSiren event property identifies code that causes the car to stop and pull over. The Siren event should cancel the execution of code associated with the OnTurnGreen event property if it occurs prior to the light turning green.

OVERVIEW OF EVENTS IN ACCESS

In a manner similar to the approach depicted in the previous car scenarios, Access recognizes a set of events. An event is associated with a form, report, or control object through an event property. Usually, the name of the event property begins with On and is followed by the event name.

Syntax

OnEventName

Syntax Dissection

EventName is the name of a built-in Access event. The value of an object's event property is the name of a macro or a VBA procedure to run when the event occurs.

For example, consider the **OnClick** property associated with the button cmdProspectBtn on frmSwitchboard that identifies the macro mcrOpens.Prospects shown in Figure 6-1. This macro executes when the user clicks the Prospects button. mcrOpens.Prospects opens frmProspects in Form view.

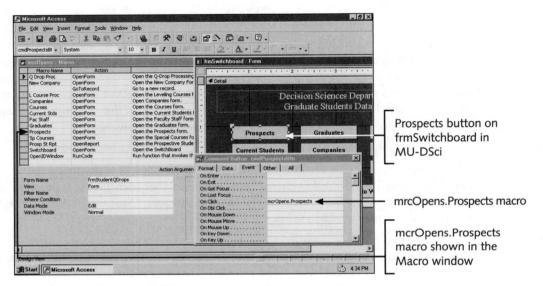

Figure 6-1   Using an event property to trigger a macro that runs frmProspects

VBA procedures are identified by the key phrase **[Event Procedure]** or by an equals sign followed by a function name. An **event procedure** is a subroutine contained within a form or report class module that is closely associated with an event. The name of the subroutine uses the following syntax:

Syntax

Form_*EventName*

or

Report_*EventName*

or

ControlName_EventName

Syntax Dissection

Access uses **Form_***EventName* when the procedure is associated with one of the form's event properties. It uses **Report_***EventName* when the procedure is associated with a report's event property. In addition, it uses *ControlName_EventName* when the procedure is associated with a control's event property. *EventName* is the name of an Access event. It matches the event name in the object's associated event property. *ControlName* is the name of the control as identified by the control's Name property.

MU-DSci uses several event procedures. You can see sample event procedures by displaying the form property sheet of frmProspects, clicking the Event tab, clicking OnCurrent, and then clicking the Build button located next to the OnCurrent property. When you execute these actions, Access displays the subroutine Form_Current, as shown in Figure 6-2. This procedure executes each time a form's record selector moves to a new record.

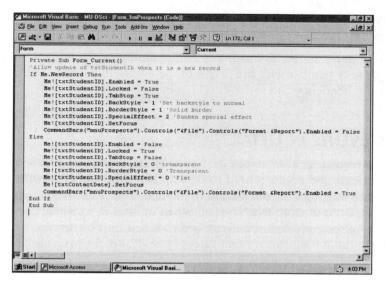

Figure 6-2   Form_Current event procedure for frmProspects

As an alternative to using an event procedure, you can use the following syntax:

Syntax

= *FunctionName()*

Syntax Dissection

The equals sign allows the property text box to accept the function as its value. FunctionName is the name of the function that is contained in a standard or form class module.

Programmers frequently use this syntax when more than one event triggers the same VBA code. For example, if the function OpenGrades displays the frmGrade form for a particular class, the statement =OpenGrades() can be placed in the OnClick event property of a button named cmdGrade and in the OnDblClick event property of a text box named txtCourseID. In this case, either clicking the cmdGrade button or double-clicking in the txtCourseID text box will open frmGrade.

In another similarity to the car scenario, one event in Access can trigger many related events, and these events can influence one another. For example, if the user clicks cmdProspectsBtn, the Click event of cmdProspectsBtn occurs. In addition, when frmProspects opens, the following sequence of events occurs: Open event for the form, Load event for the form, Activate event for the form, Current event for the first record in the form, Enter event for txtFirstName (the first control on the form), and GotFocus event for txtFirstName. Although the technique was not used in frmProspects, code associated with an Open event can cancel the opening of a form, which will also prevent subsequent events from occurring.

Successful programming in an event-driven programming environment requires the programmer to be very familiar with the details of the events. In particular, close attention must be paid to the frequency and order in which events occur.

EXPLORING ACCESS EVENTS IN DETAIL

In general, Access recognizes three types of events: events related to user actions, events related to data retrieval, and events related to data updates. **User action events** occur primarily in the application's user interface. **Data retrieval events** occur when data are placed in a form or report. **Data update events** occur when updates in a form are propagated to the form's record source. Although the events are classified into categories, events in one category frequently cause events in another category. Several more commonly used events are discussed in the following sections.

Events Related to User Actions

Events that primarily recognize user actions and manipulate the user interface are one category of events. These events encompass mouse actions, window manipulation, and keystrokes. When a user presses the Tab key to move the cursor from the last control in a record to the first control in the next record in a form, for example, several events occur:

- An Exit event occurs for the control that the cursor is leaving.
- A **LostFocus** event occurs for the control in the old record that no longer has the cursor.
- If changes were made in the previous record, the cursor movement to a new record causes the changes to be saved. In this case, **BeforeUpdate** and **AfterUpdate** events for the record being saved occur.
- A **Current** event for the form occurs when the new record becomes the one (currently) being manipulated.
- An **Enter** event occurs for the control to which the cursor is moving.
- A **GotFocus** event occurs for the control that contains the cursor in the new record.

Although multiple events occur as a result of a user action, only those events that are associated with a macro or procedure (through an event property) are of any consequence. Without a macro or procedure, Access does not respond to an event.

Table 6-1 summarizes many of the user action events. In most cases, these events are straight-forward. You must, however, pay special attention to slight differences between the events, actions that cause multiple events, and the interaction between an event and the active form and control. For example, the Change event of a control occurs whenever data in the control are changed—that is, with every keystroke. The Change event is often confused with the BeforeUpdate and AfterUpdate events for a control, which occur only once. When the Tab key moves the cursor from one control to another, the Enter, Exit, LoseFocus, and GetFocus events occur. Finally, some controls are unknown to Access during the Load event for a form, but they become known after the Activate event. For example, the ActiveControl property of the Screen object, which in this case is the form, is not known during the initial loading of the form.

Table 6-1   User action events

Event	Description	Related Events	Notes
Activate	Occurs when a form or report receives focus.	Usually followed by the GotFocus and Enter events for the first control on the form.	Commonly used to display toolbars or forms that must be displayed with the form that is active.
Click	Occurs when a user presses and releases the left mouse button while the cursor is over a control or form.	The MouseDown, MouseUp, and Click events occur in sequence.	Frequently used with command buttons to open forms or reports. The Click event procedure cannot determine whether the Shift, Alt, or Ctrl key is being held down.
DblClick	Occurs when a user presses and releases the left mouse button twice while the cursor is over a control or form.	The sequence of events depends on the control; normally, causes the MouseDown, MouseUp, Click, and DblClick events, in that order.	Not normally used with a command button. Frequently used with a text box as an alternative to a menu, toolbar, or command button click to open another related form.
Deactivate	Occurs when a form or report loses focus.	Normally causes a LostFocus event.	Does not occur when focus switches to a PopUp form. Commonly used to close toolbars or other forms that are displayed only when the deactivated form is displayed.

Table 6-1   User action events (continued)

Event	Description	Related Events	Notes
Enter	Occurs just before a control on the form receives focus.	Always followed by a GotFocus event.	Activated when a control is the first control to receive focus on a newly opened form.
Exit	Occurs just before a control loses focus.	Always followed by a LostFocus event.	Activated when a form is closed. Program code can cancel the Exit event, leaving the cursor in the control. Code associated with an Exit event may check the validity of data. Also used to set the cursor in a portion of a form that depends on the user's entry. For example, if the user enters Married in a marital status control, code in the Exit event can place the cursor in a control that inquires about the spouse's name.
GotFocus	Occurs when a control or form receives focus.	Frequently preceded by an Enter event.	Applies to a form on when all controls on the form are disabled or invisible.
KeyDown	Occurs when a user presses a key while a form or control has focus.		Typically used to recognize pressing of special keys, such as function keys and the Ctrl key. Once a function key is recognized in a VBA procedure, code can be executed that corresponds to the function key.
KeyPress	Occurs when a user presses and releases a key while a form or control has focus.	The KeyDown, KeyPress, and KeyUp events occur in sequence.	Typically used to recognize pressing character or numeric keys, not function keys.

Table 6-1   User action events (continued)

Event	Description	Related Events	Notes
KeyUp	Occurs when a user releases a key while a form or control has focus.		Typically used to recognize special keys, such as function keys and the Ctrl key. Once a function key is recognized in a VBA procedure, code can be executed that corresponds to the function key.
LostFocus	Occurs whenever a control or a form loses focus.	Frequently preceded by an Exit event.	Applies to a form only when all controls are disabled or invisible.
MouseDown	Occurs when the user presses a mouse button.		The MouseDown event procedure can identify which mouse button is pressed and whether the Shift, Alt, or Ctrl key is being held down. Can be used with MouseUp and MouseMove events, with some fancy coding, to build a drag-and-drop interface that supports the movement of data.
MouseMove	Occurs when the user moves the mouse.		Applies only to forms, form sections, and controls on a form, not controls on a report. Moving a form can trigger a MouseMove event even if the mouse is stationary.

6

Table 6-1 User action events (continued)

Event	Description	Related Events	Notes
MouseUp	Occurs when the user releases a mouse button.		The MouseUp event procedure can identify which mouse button is pressed and whether the Shift, Alt, or Ctrl key is being held down in conjunction with the mouse event. Can be used with MouseDown and MouseMove events, with some fancy coding, to build a drag-and-drop interface that supports the movement of data.

Focus

The concept of **focus** is fundamental to many of the user action events. Generally speaking, when an Access object becomes the object of attention, it has "received focus." For example, when a user activates a form (by opening or clicking), the form "receives focus." When a user places the cursor in a control to modify the contents of the value displayed, the control also "receives focus." In an analogous fashion, as the attention moves from one object to another, the object that had focus "loses focus" to the next object that is receiving the focus. The **Activate, Deactivate**, Enter, Exit, GotFocus, and LostFocus events, accordingly, are related to the processes associated with moving from one object to another. These processes, including pressing the Enter key, pressing the Tab key, clicking the mouse, executing macros, and executing procedures, can change focus, thereby triggering focus events.

The frmCurrentStudents and frmProspects forms in MU-DSci illustrate several focus events. For example, code associated with the OnGotFocus and OnLostFocus event properties changes a control's background color. This code executes when the GotFocus event occurs:

```
Screen.ActiveControl.BackColor = RGB(0, 255, 255)
```

This code changes the color to cyan. The following code executes when the LostFocus event occurs:

```
Screen.ActiveControl.BackColor = RGB(255, 255, 255)
```

This code changes the background color to white.

Besides GotFocus and LostFocus, frmCurrentStudents and frmProspects use the Activate and Deactivate events. A form's Activate event occurs whenever the form receives focus. A form's Deactivate event occurs whenever the form loses focus to a non-PopUp form. The frmCurrentStudents form, for example, uses these events to add and remove a toolbar. In particular, an event procedure associated with the OnActivate event property displays the toolbar, and an event procedure corresponding to the form's OnDeactivate event property removes the toolbar from the screen.

The process of reacting to events can be demonstrated by opening frmCurrentStudents and frmProspects. When frmCurrentStudents has focus, the toolbar displays. When frmProspects has focus, the toolbar is not displayed. Similarly, frmProspects uses an Activate event. An event procedure associated with this event enables and disables items on the menu bar so that the menu bar is consistent with the needs of frmProspects.

Event Timing

Events related to focus demonstrate the importance of understanding event timing. A LostFocus event occurs for txtFirstName when the cursor leaves the text box and enters txtMiddleInitial, and txtMiddleInitial receives the focus. Recall that Screen.ActiveControl refers to the control that currently has focus. Why doesn't Screen.ActiveControl.BackColor = RGB(255,255,255), triggered by the LostFocus event of txtFirstName, work on the background color of txtMiddleInitial and leave txtFirstName alone? It doesn't happen because, when the cursor moves from txtFirstName to txtMiddleInitial, the following activities occur in the order specified:

1. The LostFocus event occurs for txtFirstName.

2. The ActiveControl is set to txtMiddleInitial (that is, txtMiddleInitial receives focus).

3. The GotFocus event occurs for txtMiddleInitial.

This sequence of events makes toggling background colors easy. If the LostFocus event for txtFirstName needs to know which new control will receive the focus, however, Screen.ActiveControl will not provide the correct answer. Figure 6–3 illustrates the typical order of control focus events.

When the cursor is in Control X and the user clicks Control Y or tabs to Control Y, the following sequence of events occurs: Exit of previous control, LostFocus of previous control, Enter of new control, GotFocus of new control.

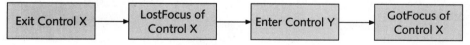

Figure 6-3   Order of control focus events

When the cursor is in Control X in Figure 6–3 and the user clicks Control Y or tabs to Control Y, the following events occur:

1. The Exit event for Control X

2. The LostFocus event for Control X

3. The Enter event for Control Y

4. The GotFocus event for Control Y

Other user action events are mouse clicks and keypresses. For instance, programmers commonly use the Click event in conjunction with a command button. Access activates a **DblClick** event when the user clicks the mouse twice. By convention, DblClick is rarely used with a command button; rather, users expect to double-click over a text box, list box, or combo box. Many Click and DblClick events trigger procedures or macros that open forms. Click and DblClick events are related events. In fact, a DblClick event activates both a Click event and a DblClick event. Only rarely would you add code to both the Click event and the DblClick event for the same object.

> You can use keypresses to simulate command button clicks. In particular, laptop computer users frequently appreciate the ability to use keypresses instead of mouse clicks to trigger a command button. By default, the Enter key causes a mouse click whenever a command button has focus. In addition, an access key can be established by placing & (ampersand) in front of a letter in the Caption property. The & causes the letter to be underlined. Pressing the Alt key in conjunction with the underlined letter causes a Click event. Do not use the same letter more than once per form (for example, do not use Alt+F for Faculty and Alt+F for File); Access will perform only one operation—the first one it recognizes.

Employing User Action Events to Open Forms

Throughout this chapter, you will modify several forms to implement the registration and payment process for the Swim Lessons application. The processes for registration and payment are described in the following paragraphs.

All activity in the database begins with a user adding the student to the database. Once the student is in the database, a user may register the student for classes. Payment for registrations may be made at the time of registration or later. Because a parent may be making a payment that will cover lessons for several children, the system must be able to allocate a single payment to multiple registrations. In this application, partial payments for a registration are not allowed and you don't have to worry about overpayment situations.

To begin creating the proper interface, you must add buttons to several forms that will open other forms.

To add command buttons to frmStudent that will be used to process payments and registrations:

1. Open **SwimReg.mdb**, refresh the links, if necessary, and then open **frmStudent** in Design view.

2. Place a **command button** under the one labeled Student's Classes. If the wizard launches, click the **Cancel** button to stop it.

3. Open the **Properties** window for the command button, if necessary, click the **Other** tab, if necessary, and then name the command button **cmdPayment**.

4. Click the **Format** tab, and then change the caption to **Payment**.

5. Click the **Event** tab, select **[Event Procedure]** from the drop-down list for the On Click property, and then click the **Build** button on the Form Design toolbar.

6. Enter the following code in the event procedure:

```
'If the record has changed, save it before opening the
'Payment form
If Me.Dirty Then DoCmd.RunCommand acCmdSaveRecord
DoCmd.OpenForm "frmPayment", , , _
    "[SID]=[Forms]![frmStudent]![txtSID]"
```

7. Save the procedure and close the Visual Basic window.

8. Place another **command button** below cmdPayment on frmStudent. If the wizard launches, click the **Cancel** button to stop it.

9. Open the **Properties** window for the command button if it isn't already open, click the **Other** tab, and then name the command button **cmdRegister**.

10. Click the **Format** tab, and then change the caption to **Register**.

11. Click the **Event** tab, select **[Event Procedure]** from the drop-down list for the On Click property, and then click the **Build** button.

12. Enter the following code in the event procedure:

```
'If the record has changed, save it before opening the
'Registration 'form
If Me.Dirty Then DoCmd.RunCommand acCmdSaveRecord
DoCmd.OpenForm "frmRegistration", , , _
    "[SID]=[Forms]![frmStudent]![txtSID]"
```

13. From the Debug menu, select **Compile SwimReg**.

14. Resize the buttons to a common size and align them in a straight line.

15. Save the procedure and close the Visual Basic window.

16. Save and close frmStudent.

The frmRegistration form also needs a button to open frmPayment as well as a button to close frmRegistration.

To add a button to open frmPayment:

1. Open **frmRegistration** in Design view.

2. Place a **command button** on frmRegistration. If the wizard launches, click the **Cancel** button to stop it.

3. Open the **Properties** window for the command button, if it is not already open, click the **Other** tab, and then name the command button **cmdPayment**.

4. Click the **Format** tab, and make the caption **Payment**.

5. Click the **Event** tab, select **[Event Procedure]** from the drop-down list for the On Click property, and then click the **Build** button.

6. Enter the following code:

```
'Open the Payment form
DoCmd.OpenForm "frmPayment", , , _
    "[SID]=[Forms]![frmStudent]![txtSID]"
```

7. From the Debug menu, select **Compile SwimReg**.

8. Save the procedure and close the Visual Basic window.

Next, you will add a close button to frmRegistration.

To add a button to close frmRegistration:

1. Place a **command button** on frmRegistration. If the wizard launches, click the **Cancel** button to stop it.

2. If necessary, open the **Properties** window for the command button. Click the **Other** tab, and then name the command button **cmdClose**.

3. Click the **Format** tab, and make the caption **Close**.

4. Click the **Event** tab, select **[Event Procedure]** from the drop-down list for the On Click property, and then click the **Build** button.

5. Enter the following code:

```
'Close the Registration form
DoCmd.Close acForm, "frmRegistration"
```

6. From the Debug menu, select **Compile SwimReg**.

7. Save the procedure and close the Visual Basic window.

8. Save and close frmRegistration.

Finally, you will add buttons on frmPayment to open both frmRegistration and a new form named frmProcessPayment. You will also modify the database to include the student ID field in the payment table so that a payment can be allocated to a student's charges.

To add buttons to frmPayment to open frmRegistration and frmProcessPayment:

1. Open **frmPayment** in Design view.

2. Place a **command button** on the form. If the wizard launches, click the **Cancel** button to stop it.

3. Open the **Properties** window for the command button, if necessary, click the **Other** tab, and then name the command button **cmdRegister**.

4. Click the **Format** tab. Make the caption **Register**.

5. Click the **Event** tab, select **[Event Procedure]** from the drop-down list for the On Click property, and then click the **Build** button.

6. Enter the following code:

```
'If the record has changed, save it before opening the
'Registration 'form
If Me.Dirty Then DoCmd.RunCommand acCmdSaveRecord
DoCmd.OpenForm "frmRegistration", , , _
     "[SID]=[Forms]![frmStudent]![txtSID]"
```

7. From the Debug menu, select **Compile SwimReg**.

8. Save the procedure and close the Visual Basic window.

9. Place another **command button** on the form. If the wizard launches, click the **Cancel** button to stop it.

10. Open the **Properties** window for the command button, if necessary, click the **Other** tab, and then name the command button **cmdProcessPay**.

11. Click the **Format** tab. Make the caption **Process Payment**.

12. Click the **Event** tab, select **[Event Procedure]** from the drop-down list for the On Click property, and then click the **Build** button.

13. Enter the following code:

```
'If the record has changed, save it before opening the
'Process Payment form
If Me.Dirty Then DoCmd.RunCommand acCmdSaveRecord
DoCmd.OpenForm "frmProcessPayment", , , _
     "[SID]=[Forms]![frmStudent]![txtSID]"
```

14. From the Debug menu, select **Compile SwimReg**.

15. Save the procedure and close the Visual Basic window.

16. Save and close frmPayment.

17. Close the **SwimReg.mdb** database and open the **SwimData.mdb** database.

18. Open **tblPayment** in Design view, add **SID** as a field name, and then make the Data Type Text with a Field Size of **9**.

19. Use the **Build** button to create an input mask appropriate for a Social Security number, and then change the caption to **Student ID**.

20. Save the changes and close the Design view window.

21. Close the **SwimData.mdb** database and open the **SwimReg.mdb** database.

User action events allow programmers to respond to actions executed by a user. In the next section, you turn your attention to events that occur when Access retrieves data.

Events Related to Data Retrieval

Unlike the user action events, most data retrieval events are not defined by the different ways in which a user interacts with the system. Rather, data retrieval events are defined by their role in placing data on and removing data from forms and reports. In fact, two actions instigate most of the data retrieval events: the opening and closing forms and reports. Table 6-2 summarizes many of the data retrieval events.

Table 6-2 Data retrieval events

Event	Description	Sequence	Notes
ApplyFilter	Occurs when the user tells Access to enforce the filter created when the Filter event occurred.	Result of a user action, once a filter has been prepared.	Used to manipulate the properties of a form. For example, menu items or command buttons that help find a record may be made invisible when one record is the outcome of the filter. Not supported in Access 2000.
Close	Occurs when a form is closed and removed from the screen.	Normally preceded by Unload and Deactivate events.	Frequently used to remove other related forms from the screen.
Current	Occurs when focus moves to a new record.		Can be caused by opening a form, a user action, a macro, or a procedure. Used to adjust form properties based on the active record.
Filter	Occurs when the user creates a new filter for a form. A filter limits the records displayed through a form to those that meet some criteria.	Normally, but not necessarily, followed by an ApplyFilter event.	Sometimes used to set a default filter for the user. Used to disable or enable controls that could facilitate the filter. Not supported in Access 2000.
Format	Occurs for each report section, just prior to formatting and displaying the section's data.	Occurs after a report's Open event.	Used to change properties of controls in a section based on the data in the section.
Load	Occurs when a form is opened and its data are displayed.	Occurs after a form's Open event.	Used to adjust properties of a form based on the data displayed. For example, the form caption could be adjusted based on field values in the first record. Cannot be canceled.

Table 6-2   Data retrieval events (continued)

Event	Description	Sequence	Notes
NoData	Occurs in a report when the underlying recordset does not contain any data.	Occurs after a Format event, but before a Print event.	Used to cancel printing a report when the report contains no records. In Access 2000, the DCount function can be used in the Format event to determine whether data exist in a report.
Open	Occurs when a form or report is opened but before data are displayed on the screen.	Normally followed by a Load event.	Used to change the properties of a newly displayed form or report. These properties can include Record Source, Control Source, and Row Source. Canceling prevents the form from being displayed.
Print	Occurs for each section of a report, after it is formatted but before it is displayed.	Preceded by a Format event.	Used to perform complex calculations based on the data in a form section.
Unload	Occurs after a form is closed but before it is removed from the screen.	Followed by Deactivate and Close events.	Canceling prevents the form from being removed from the screen.

6

Figure 6-4 displays the sequence of events that occur when a form is opened and closed.

This sequence includes both data retrieval and user action events. Data retrieval events are vital because they are often the first events that provide an opportunity for the programmer to make adjustments to the properties of newly opened forms or reports. Because the Forms and Reports collections contain only open forms and reports, respectively, dot notation cannot be used to change a property until the form or report is opened. The events corresponding to the opening of a form and a report can trigger event procedures to change these properties.

Programmers commonly use three data retrieval events. **Open** occurs when a form is opened but before the first record displays. Similarly, Open occurs when a report is opened but before the first record is previewed or printed. **Load** occurs after a form is opened, after the first record is read from the database but just prior to the first record being displayed. The **Current** event occurs when focus moves to a new record (making it the **current record**) and when the form opens.

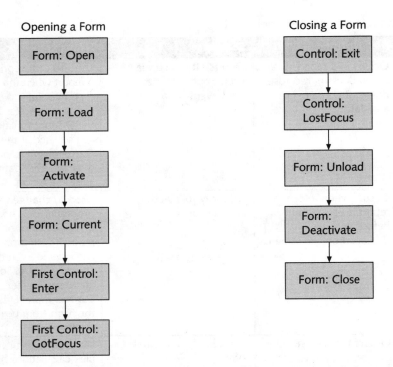

Figure 6-4 Sequence of events caused by opening and closing a form

You can find an example of the Current event in frmCurrentStudents in MU–DSci. When a new record displays in the form (that is, when a new record becomes the current record), a VBA procedure executes and checks the value of txtQDrops. If this value is 2 or greater, which it is in one of the records toward the end of the form, the procedure highlights txtQDrops by adjusting its ForeColor, FontWeight, and FontUnderline properties. The value property of a control (for example, Me![txtQDrops]) always refers to the value in the current record.

The frmCurrentStudents and frmProspects forms also use the Current event to adjust the properties of txtStudentID. The Form_Current event procedure checks the NewRecord property of the form (that is, Me.NewRecord). When NewRecord is true, the application can adjust the properties of txtStudentID to support data entry (for example, enable it). You can verify the triggering of these events by opening frmCurrentStudents and using the navigation buttons to move from one student to the next.

Although the forms in MU–DSci do not use Open and Load events, programmers frequently use these events. One use of an Open event is to trigger a VBA procedure or macro that changes the properties of the form prior to its being displayed. For example, one form might be used to display the results of several different queries. A programmer could change the record source of the form in the Open event so as to identify the query to display. Alternatively, the form might hide certain fields or buttons based on which user is logged into the application. A programmer can also change the row source of combo boxes and the control source of controls during this event.

Technically, the Open event occurs before the Load event. In many cases, however, code that could be placed in the Load event could be placed in the Open event, and vice versa. Even though the Open event occurs before data are loaded, it can still access the values of data in the first record. Similarly, even though the Load event occurs after the data have been read from the database, the record source can still be changed in this event. It is probably more efficient to change record sources in the Open event, however. The knowledge that code can be placed in either the Open or Load event is useful. If two separate actions need to occur when the form is opened, you can place one procedure in the Open event and the other in the Load event. Although having a choice of events is sometimes advantageous, some of the most important decisions you will make involve choosing the best event to trigger a VBA procedure or macro. Your choice will influence the number of actions supported by your user interface and the maintainability of your application.

The frmProspects form illustrates an important design choice. The Add Prospects command button (that is, cmdAddProspectBtn) triggers an event procedure that displays a blank Prospects record. A user can use this record for data entry. The form uses the NewRecord property in the Form_Current event procedure to determine whether txtStudentID should be made available for data entry. An alternative to using the Current event is to change the properties of txtStudentID in the event procedure associated with the Click event of cmdAddProspectBtn. Because cmdAddProspectBtn causes the form to advance to a new record, the NewRecord property does not need to be checked.

The biggest problem with this alternative is that other user actions display a new record as well. The user can move to a new record through menu commands, toolbar buttons, and the navigation buttons at the bottom of the form. None of these actions triggers the Click event for cmdAddProspectBtn. In general, whenever more than one event could be used to trigger the same code, try to associate the code with the event that is triggered by most of the user actions. From this perspective, it is usually a better choice to associate the code with a data retrieval event than with a user action event.

The frmCurrentStudents form provides another example involving a choice of where to place code. As discussed earlier, the Current event of this form updates the ForeColor property of txtQDrops based on the number of dropped courses. You could have also placed this code in the OnEnter event property of the first control (that is, txtFirstName). Each time a new record displays on the screen, focus is automatically set to the first control. This alternative has several problems, however. First, the Enter event is also triggered when a user changes focus based on mouse clicks. Because there is no reason to execute this code more than once per record, a data retrieval event is preferred over a user action event. Second, and more importantly, other programmers would not expect the code to be located in the Enter event.

Sometimes object considerations help in determining where the code should be located. In the case of manipulating the properties of txtQDrops, it makes more sense to associate the code with the entire record (which includes txtQDrops) than to associate it with txtFirstName, which has nothing to do with the number of Q Drops. Ideally, the color control code could be placed with txtQDrops itself. There is no event associated with a control that would accomplish this goal. Executing code from the object most associated with the code facilitates the process of finding code when it needs to be updated.

Data Update Events

Once the application retrieves data from the database and places it on a form, the user may change the data through any of the available user actions (for example, typing and clicking). Data update events occur when the user enters new data or changes data in a record. A sequence of data update events is triggered as the data are sent from the form and placed permanently in the form's underlying table(s). Table 6-3 summarizes the data update events.

Table 6-3   Data update events

Event	Object	Description	Notes
AfterDelConfirm	Form	Occurs after the delete confirmation message and after the record is deleted.	Commonly used to update another table that may be affected by the deletion.
AfterInsert	Form	Occurs after a new record is written to a database.	A new record is written when the user saves the record or moves focus to a different record. Cannot be canceled. Commonly used to update other affected tables.
AfterUpdate	Control, form	Occurs after a user changes the value in any control on a record and the change has been written to the current record buffer (for a control) or the record has been written to the database (for a form).	Cannot be canceled. Commonly used to determine default values for other controls on the same record and to update values in other tables that may be affected by the change.
BeforeDeleteConfirm	Form	Occurs after a record is deleted but before the delete confirm message is displayed.	Commonly used to display a custom delete-confirm message box.
BeforeInsert	Form	Occurs as soon as the first character is typed on a form.	Can be canceled. Commonly used to place default values in a new record.
BeforeUpdate	Control, form	Occurs after a user changes a value but before the value is written to the current record buffer (for a control) or before the record is moved to the database (for a form).	Canceling writes the original value back to the control or record. Commonly used to determine the validity of a value or a combination of values in a record. A Save command, closing the form, or shifting focus to another record initiates a form's BeforeUpdate event.

Table 6-3   Data update events (continued)

Event	Object	Description	Notes
Change	Control	Occurs for each keystroke in a text box or combo box.	Rarely used.
Delete	Form	Occurs after a user attempts to delete a record but before the deletion occurs.	Canceling will cancel the deletion of the record. Commonly used to verify that a deletion should occur.
NotInList	Combo box	Occurs when a user types a value that is not currently in the combo box.	LimitToList property must be set to Yes for this event to occur. Commonly used to update values in a list box.

6

Figure 6–5 illustrates the general sequence of data update events. One difference between data update events and other events is that the former are triggered by user-entered changes to data.

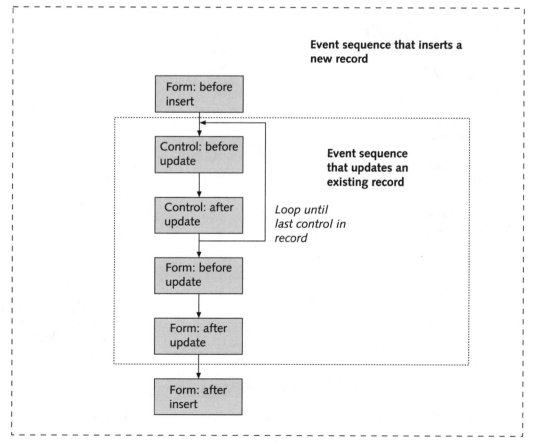

Figure 6-5   Sequence of events for inserting and updating records through a bound form

Many data update events use the concepts of before and after (for example, BeforeUpdate and AfterUpdate). At least two before events and two after events are triggered before changes made to a bound form are propagated to the database, as shown in Figure 6-6.

Access writes user-entered changes to a control (for example, the value of a text box) into a **current control buffer.** The current control buffer is a storage area that contains the displayed value of the control with focus. Access considers the change complete when focus moves to another control. When focus moves in this way, a BeforeUpdate event executes that allows a procedure to analyze the data. If code in the BeforeUpdate event procedure does not cancel the event, Access writes the data to the **current record buffer** and Access triggers an AfterUpdate event.

The current record buffer stores values for all bound controls in a form. Values in the current record buffer are not written to the database until the user clicks Save in the File menu, changes focus to a new record, or closes the form. If one of these actions occurs, it triggers the form BeforeUpdate event. This event allows a procedure to analyze the data for the entire record. If the BeforeUpdate event is not canceled by an event procedure, the data are written to the form's recordset and the relevant form after the events (that is, AfterInsert and AfterUpdate) are triggered.

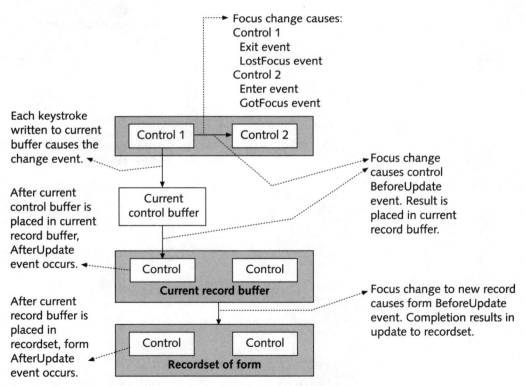

Figure 6-6   Focus changes before and after update events and buffers

BeforeUpdate occurs for a control when the user finishes adding or changing data in the control. This event takes place prior to the data being written to the current record buffer. One of its uses is to analyze the changed data prior to actually updating the database. For example, if a user attempts to add a course to a student's schedule, the course prerequisites could be checked before allowing the course to be updated.

A common property used with BeforeUpdate is **OldValue**. The OldValue property of a control allows the system to compare the user-typed value with the previous value of the control. This verification might be useful in a payroll form that checks to ensure that a new salary is not more than 15% higher than the old salary. Part of the code to check this salary follows:

```
If Me![Salary] > 1.15 * Me![Salary].OldValue Then ...
```

In this code example, Me![Salary] refers to the recently typed salary (in the current control buffer) and Me![Salary].OldValue is the previous value (in the current record buffer).

AfterUpdate occurs after Access writes changed data in a control to the record buffer. txtStudentID in frmProspects uses the AfterUpdate event to determine whether the student already has an entry in the database. If a match is found, a copy of frmProspects is displayed containing the data of the matched record. Access uses the AfterUpdate event property of txtStudentID instead of the AfterUpdate event property of the form so that the duplicate is found just after the user enters the value for txtStudentID. Using the AfterUpdate event for the control is a better choice than using the AfterUpdate event for the form, because other controls on the form could receive data before something occurred to trigger the form's AfterUpdate event. In that case, a user might be required to reenter data or change data already entered. This choice prevents data from being entered into the other controls unnecessarily.

The **NotInList** event occurs when a user enters a value in the text box portion of a combo box, but that value is not in the combo box list. For example, the NotInList event occurs in frmCurrentStudents. When a user enters a university name that does not already appear in the list, the NotInList event occurs and a VBA procedure executes to capture the new university and add it to the list.

Like controls, forms use a series of events that have either a before or an after characteristic. **BeforeInsert** occurs when the user types the first character in a new record, but before the record is actually created. **AfterInsert** occurs after changes to the record are completed (that is, focus changes to a different record) and written to the database. **BeforeUpdate** occurs before changed data, either edited or new, are written from the current record buffer to the database.

Like the control's before and after updates, a programmer can use these form events to validate data before the information is sent to the database and to update other tables when the data are actually changed in the database. For example, if the system keeps track of enrollment in a course, VBA code or a macro connected to the AfterUpdate event could recalculate the enrollment after a new student has registered. A programmer can also use the events to generate necessary data for a table that are not entered by the user. For example, the BeforeUpdate property of frmGraduates uses an event procedure that sets the Date Updated field to the system's current date.

TIP

> The BeforeUpdate and AfterUpdate events for controls and records occur only when data have been changed in a control and record, respectively. On some occasions, a procedure other than those associated with BeforeUpdate and AfterUpdate needs to know whether the data in a record have changed. The Dirty property exists for this purpose. The Dirty property of a form is set to True when the record has been changed but not saved. It is set to False if the record has not changed since the last save. A Dirty event can be used to trigger an event procedure to respond to record changes.

Besides adding or changing records, a user may delete a record. The **Delete** event occurs when a user performs any action that causes a record to be deleted (for example, clicks a menu item, the Delete button, or a Delete toolbar button). It occurs prior to actually deleting the record. Closely related to the Delete event are the BeforeDelConfirm and AfterDelConfirm events. **BeforeDelConfirm** occurs after the user deletes records but before Access displays a dialog box requesting delete confirmation. **AfterDelConfirm** occurs after a user confirms a deletion and the records are actually deleted or the deletions are canceled. As you can see, Access has several events that programmers can use to help users avoid deleting records by accident.

If the Delete event is not canceled by a VBA procedure, the record is deleted but also written to a buffer so that it can be restored. The BeforeDelConfirm event provides the opportunity to restore the record. If this event is not canceled, the record is deleted. The AfterDelConfirm event can check whether the record was actually deleted.

Like the other after events, the AfterDelConfirm event allows the system to update tables or forms that might be affected by the deletion. For example, if a student drops a course through the frmCourseEnrollment form, the class total enrollment should decrease. If the class total enrollment is stored in a table (the Class table) that is not part of the record source for frmCourseEnrollment, a programmer can use the AfterDelConfirm event to write the new enrollment amount to the class table. It does not make sense to use the Delete or BeforeDelConfirm event to update the table, because the user could cancel the deletion in either of these events.

As with data retrieval events, a programmer can sometimes use more than one data update event to trigger a VBA procedure or macro. For example, if a programmer places a Drop command button on frmCourseEnrollment, a Click event could execute a procedure that both deletes the current record and reduces the total enrollment in the class table. The problem with this approach is that the user has many ways to delete a record, including pressing the Delete key and using a menu item. If the code has been associated with the Drop command button, the enrollment will not be updated as a result of using the Delete key. To counteract this problem, you should use the event most closely associated with the conditions for dropping a class: AfterDelConfirm. This event is triggered no matter how the record is deleted; thus you can always test it to verify that the user did not cancel the deletion.

Programmers often use message boxes to confirm that a user wants to change or delete a record. A **message box** is a window that displays a brief message and then waits for the user to click a button. The **MsgBox** action displays a message box. The MsgBox function can also be used in VBA code.

In general, if code can be associated with either a data update event or a user action event, the data update event is usually the better choice. This guideline is not a universal rule, however. As you add code to your program, you should think carefully about which event most closely matches the conditions under which the VBA procedure or macro should execute.

Using Events to Process Payments

Earlier in this chapter, you made it easier to navigate the Swim Lessons application by adding buttons that allow the user to open forms from several places. The user can open either frmPayment or frmRegistration from frmStudent. The user can also open frmPayment from frmRegistration, and vice versa. Now, you will add code to process payments that will execute when certain events occur. First, you need to add a feature to frmPayment that will allow a payment to be applied to any student. The approach will use a combo box to select the student. The combo box will display the student's identification number. An additional text box will be added to display the student's entire name.

To add a combo box and a text box to frmPayment to display the student associated with the payment:

1. Open **frmPayment** in Design view.

2. From the toolbox, add a **combo box** to frmPayment. Put it to the right of the Payment Type option group. Execute the following options in the wizard:

   - Select **I want the combo box to look up the values in a table or query**.

   - Select **tblStudents** as the table providing values to the combo box.

   - Select **SID**, **LastName**, **FirstName**, and **MiddleInitial** from the Available Fields list.

   - Deselect the **Hide key column (recommended)** check box.

   - Accept **SID** as the value to store in the database.

   - Store the **value** in the field named SID.

   - Make the label **Payment for Student:**.

3. After the wizard finishes, open the **Properties** window for the combo box, if necessary, name it **cboSID**, set the Default Value property to **[Forms]![frmStudent]![txtSID]**, and then adjust the label to fit the form.

4. Use the toolbox to add a **text box** to the form. Place the text box under the combo box. Make it long enough to display a student's entire name.

5. Delete the **label** by clicking on the label and pressing the **Delete** key, and then use the Properties window for the text box to name it **txtPersonName**.

6. Display the **Properties** window for the cboSID, click the **Event** tab, select **[Event Procedure]** from the drop-down list for the After Update property, and then click the **Build** button.

7. Enter the following code:

```
Me![txtPersonName]=DlookUp("[Lastname]", "tblStudents", _
    "[SID]='" & Me![cboSID] & "'")
```

8. From the Debug menu, select **Compile SwimReg**.

9. Save the procedure and close the Visual Basic window.

10. Save and close frmPayment.

The preceding actions created a combo box that displays a list of students currently in the database. By setting the default property to reference the student ID displayed in frmStudent, you force the combo box to display (initially) the name of the student being processed in frmStudent. If the name in the combo box is changed, however, the AfterUpdate event will occur and the code associated with that event's event procedure will execute, constructing a new name to display in txtPersonName. Because the CheckNo field on the form applies only when payments are made by check, you will modify the form to display that field only when the Check payment option is selected.

To modify the Option Group to hide the CheckNo field if cash is paid:

1. Open **frmPayment** in Design view.

2. Open the **Properties** window for the option group named fraPaymentType.

3. Click the **Event** tab, select **[Event Procedure]** from the drop-down list for the After Update property, and then click the **Build** button.

4. Enter the following code:

```
'Show or hide the CheckNo field based on the Payment Type
Me![txtCheckNo].Visible = (fraPaymentType = conCheck)
```

5. Use the left drop-down menu at the top of the window to select **(General)** to move to the Declarations section of the module.

6. Add the following three lines of code after the Option Compare Database statement (you may skip the Option Explicit statement if it is already there):

```
Option Explicit
Const conCash=1  'Symbolic constant for the cash payment
'option
Const conCheck=2 'Symbolic constant for the check
'payment option
```

7. From the Debug menu, select **Compile SwimReg**.

8. Save the procedure and close the Visual Basic window.

9. Save and close frmPayment.

The code in the AfterUpdate event procedure for fraPaymentType takes advantage of the fact that the Visible property can have only two values: True and False. That is, the expression in parentheses will evaluate to either True or False. If the value of fraPaymentType is equal to the value of conCheck, the expression is equal to True. Otherwise, the expression is equal to False. Because multiple payments may be applied to a particular student (for example, when a student has taken multiple lessons) and because the payments may be any combination of cash or check, you need to modify the form so that the CheckNo field displays at the appropriate time.

To modify frmPayment to display the check number field:

1. Open **frmPayment** in Design view.

2. Open the **Properties** window for the form if it is not already open.

3. Click the **Event** tab, if necessary, select **[Event Procedure]** from the drop-down list for the OnCurrent event property, and then click the **Build** button.

4. Enter the following code:

```
'Show or hide the CheckNo field based on the Payment Type
 Me![txtCheckNo].Visible = (fraPaymentType = conCheck)
```

5. From the Debug menu, select **Compile SwimReg**.

6. Save the procedure and close Visual Basic window.

7. Close and save frmPayment.

The program code in the Open event procedure determines whether a student ID was passed to the form via the OpenArgs parameter. If so (that is, if the OpenArgs parameter is not null), the ID is used to display the student's name in txtPersonName. The code in the Current event displays or hides the CheckNo field using the same expression seen earlier in the AfterUpdate event procedure for fraPaymentType.

Next, you will build a new form named frmProcessPayment. This form is needed to support the flexibility you want to have in allocating payments. The new form should be capable of partitioning a payment over multiple lessons and multiple students.

To create frmProcessPayment:

1. Open a new form in Design view based on tblEnrollment.

2. Add **LessonIndex**, **SID**, **Status**, **Charged**, **AmountPaid**, and **PaymentNo** to the Details section. Move all of the labels for these controls to the Header section. If you do not see the Header section on your screen, click **View** on the menu bar, and then click **Form Header/Footer**. Arrange the controls across the Details section in a single horizontal row. You must use Cut and Paste to move labels from the Details section to the Header section.

3. Add the prefix **txt** to each control name.

4. Make all the controls (except txtPaymentNo) locked and disabled. Make the Background Style of these controls transparent.

5. Add an **unbound text box** to the Header section, and then name it **txtPersonName**. Change its Enabled property to **No** and its Locked property to **Yes**. Change its label to **Student Name** and make the Background style transparent.

6. Add a second **unbound text box** to the Header section, and then name it **txtPaymentToProcess**. Change its Enabled property to **No** and its Locked property to **Yes**. Change the label to **Payment No. Being Processed** and make the Background style transparent.

7. Add a **combo box** to the Header section and execute the following in the wizard:

   - Select **I want the combo box to look up the values in a table or query**.
   - Select **tblStudents** as the table providing values to the combo box.
   - Select **SID** from the Available Fields list.
   - Adjust the column width to display the entire SID, and then select remember the value for later use when prompted.
   - Make the label **Student:**.

8. After the wizard finishes, open the **Properties** window for the combo box, if necessary, name the combo box **cboSID**, and then set the Default Value property to **[Forms]![frmStudent]![txtSID]**. Adjust the label to fit the form.

9. Open the **Properties** window for the form, click the **Event** tab, select **[Event Procedure]** from the drop-down list for the OnOpen property, and then click the **Build** button.

10. Enter the following code:

```
'Declare local variables for constructing name.
'Variants must be used because DLookup can return a null
'value
Dim varFirstName As Variant
Dim varLastName As Variant
Dim varMI As Variant
'Set the value of the Payment number to display
Me.txtPaymentToProcess = _
[Forms]![frmPayment]![txtPaymentNo]

'Look up and construct the name
varFirstName = DLookup("[FirstName]", "tblStudents", _
    "[SID]='" & [Forms]![frmStudent]![txtSID] & "'")
varLastName = DLookup("[LastName]", "tblStudents", _
    "[SID]='" & [Forms]![frmStudent]![txtSID] & "'")
varMI = DLookup("[MiddleInitial]", "tblStudents", _
    "[SID]='" & [Forms]![frmStudent]![txtSID] & "'")

Me.txtPersonName = varLastName & ", " & varFirstName & _
        " " & varMI
```

11. When cboSID is used to select a new student for the payment allocation, the form needs to update the name displayed. Select **cboSID** from the Object combo box at the upper-left of the Visual Basic window. Select **AfterUpdate** from the event combo box at the upper-right of the Visual Basic window.

12. Enter the following code:

```
'Declare local variables for constructing name.
'Variants must be used because DLookup can return a null
'value
Dim varFirstName As Variant
Dim varLastName As Variant
Dim varMI As Variant

'Filter the form according to the value of cboSID
If IsNull(Me![cboSID]) Then
    Me.Filter = "[PaymentNo is Null]"
    Me.FilterOn = True
    Me.txtPersonName = ""
Else
    Me.Filter = "[SID] = '" & Me![cboSID] & "'" & _
        " And [PaymentNo] Is Null"
    Me.FilterOn = True
    'Look up and construct the name
    varFirstName = DLookup("[FirstName]", "tblStudents", _
        "[SID]='" & Me![cboSID] & "'")
    varLastName = DLookup("[LastName]", "tblStudents", _
        "[SID]='" & Me![cboSID] & "'")
    varMI = DLookup("[MiddleInitial]", "tblStudents", _
        "[SID]='" & Me![cboSID] & "'")
    Me.[txtPersonName] = varLastName & ", " & _
            varFirstName & _ " " & varMI
End If
```

13. From the Debug menu, select **Compile SwimReg**.

14. Save the procedures, name the form **frmProcessPayment**, and close the Visual Basic window.

Finally, you need to add code to check whether the payment is enough to cover the amount charged. You must also verify that the payment has not been applied to more charges than it can cover. You will use the BeforeUpdate and AfterUpdate events of txtPaymentNo to check these conditions.

To add code to the txtPaymentNo text box to process the application of the payment:

1. Open the **Properties** window for txtPaymentNo, click the **Event** tab, select **[Event Procedure]** from the drop-down list for the Before Update property, and then click the **Build** button.

2. Enter the following code:

```
Dim curTotalAllocation As Currency
Dim varTotalAllocation As Variant
Dim curPaymentAmount As Currency
```

```
'Look up the Payment Amount in the payment table
curPaymentAmount = _
    DLookup("[AmountPaid]", "tblPayment", "[PaymentNo]=" _
        & Me![txtPaymentToProcess])
'Sum the lesson payments (if any) to which this payment
'has already been allocated
varTotalAllocation = _
    DSum("[AmountPaid]", "tblEnrollment", "[PaymentNo]=" _
        & Me![txtPaymentToProcess])
If IsNull(varTotalAllocation) Then
    curTotalAllocation = 0
Else
    curTotalAllocation = varTotalAllocation
End If


'Check for overapplication of payment
If curTotalAllocation > curPaymentAmount Then
    MsgBox "Allocation exceeds payment amount.", _
        vbOKOnly + vbCritical + vbDefaultButton1, _
        "Payment Allocation"
    SendKeys "{ESC}"   'Erase entry in txtPaymentNo
    Cancel = True
    Exit Sub
End If


'Check for underpayment - partial payments are not allowed
'in this system
If Me![txtCharged] > _
        curPaymentAmount - curTotalAllocation Then
        MsgBox "Not enough remaining in payment " & _
          "to cover entire amount.", _
          vbOKOnly + vbCriticial + vbDefaultButton1, _
          "Payment Allocation"
        SendKeys "{ESC}"   'Erase entry in txtPaymentNo
        Cancel = True
        Exit Sub
End If
```

3. Use the right drop-down menu at the top of the window to select **AfterUpdate** to move to the AfterUpdate event procedure for this control in the module.

4. Enter the following code:

```
'BeforeUpdate checks must have been OK,
'so update the displayed value of Amount Paid
Me![txtAmountPaid] = Me![txtCharged]
```

5. From the Debug menu, select **Compile SwimReg**.

6. Click the **Save** button.

7. Close the Visual Basic window.

8. Save and close frmProcessPayment.

9. Test the application by entering various combinations of students, payments, and registrations.

The code in the BeforeUpdate event procedure uses the DLookup domain function to find the amount of the payment associated with the payment number being processed. Next, all enrollments that have been paid for using this payment are summed to find the total amount that has been allocated out of the payment. If the sum of the allocations exceeds the amount to be allocated, then the application sends the value of Escape key to the application to cancel the attempted allocation entry.

Finally, the frmPayment form must be requeried, if it is open, so that it reflects the payment processing.

1. Open the **Properties** window for the Form. Click the **Event** tab, select **[Event Procedure]** from the drop down list for the **AfterUpdate** property, click the **Build** button, and then enter the following code:

```
'If frmPayment is open, requery the allocation subform
    Dim pobjProject As CurrentProject
    Set pobjProject = Application.CurrentProject
    If pobjProject.AllForms("frmPayment").IsLoaded Then
        Forms![frmPayment].UpdateAllocations
    End If
```

2. From the Debug menu, select **Compile SwimReg**.

3. Save the procedures and close the Visual Basic window.

Finally, the code in the procedure checks whether an allocation of a payment fully covers the charge for the lesson. Partial payments are not allowed in this application. As with the overallocation situation, underpayment causes the procedure to send the value of the Escape key to the application, thus canceling the attempted allocation entry.

Time and Error Events

Access recognizes several other events besides those classified as user actions, data retrievals, and data updates. The **Timer** event, for example, occurs in forms at regular intervals when a specified amount of time has passed. The amount of time is specified in the form's **TimerInterval** property. You can use the Timer event to create a splashscreen that appears when you open a database. This screen is simply a form that has its Timer property set to 4000 (the time is specified in milliseconds; 4000 milliseconds = 4 seconds). The first time that the Timer Event occurs, a macro attached to the On Timer event property closes the form, as shown in Figure 6-7.

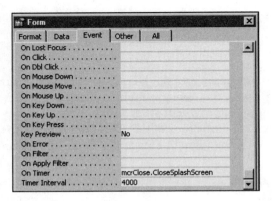

Figure 6-7   Event properties of frmSplashScreen

The **Error** event is another useful event. An event procedure attached to the **OnError** event property of a form specifies VBA code to execute when an error is detected on a form. Access produces its own error message for the user, but the VBA code can be used to display a more "user-friendly" message and guide the user through the problem. Examples of problems caught by the OnError event property include duplicate primary keys, violations of validation constraints, and violations of foreign key constraints.

CHAPTER SUMMARY

◻ Event-driven programming is a powerful Access feature. An event is triggered by a change in an Access object, a change in the environment surrounding an object, or a user action. Common events include mouse clicks, form activation, control focus changes, and text box updates. Each event recognized by Access is associated with an event property of an object. The value of an event property identifies the macro, function, or event procedure that should execute when the event occurs. For example, the value of the OnClick event property of a cmdClose button indicates the code that should execute when the user clicks cmdClose.

◻ Access events can be classified into several categories. Events related to user actions center on interactions with the user interface. Focus events are an important type of user action event that occurs when the cursor moves from one control to another. Data retrieval events are associated with the display of data in a form or report. They include Open, Close, Load, Unload, and Current. Data update events respond to user-caused changes to the values of some control. They include BeforeUpdate, BeforeInsert, AfterUpdate, AfterInsert, and Delete. Many user actions generate several other events.

◻ Although event-driven programming allows the development of code that can respond to a wide variety of events, event timing and event interaction sometimes make program debugging and maintenance difficult. To facilitate program debugging and maintenance, macros and VBA procedures should be associated with the objects and events that are most closely aligned with the code's results and conditions for execution. Because many different user action events can cause the same data retrieval and update events, it is advantageous to associate macro and VBA procedures with data retrieval or update events if possible.

REVIEW QUESTIONS

1. Events are actions recognized by a(n) ——————————.

2. Event-driven programming requires the development of management components. True or False?

3. Describe the relationship between an event, an event property, and a macro.

4. Describe the relationship between an event, an event property, and a function.

5. Describe the relationship between an event, an event property, and an event procedure.

6. A(n) —————————— event occurs for a control that a cursor is leaving.

   a. Exit

   b. LostFocus

   c. Leave

   d. Encompass

7. Identify at least one use for a Click event.

8. How do a control's Change, BeforeUpdate, and AfterUpdate events differ?

9. A(n) —————————— event occurs for the control to which the cursor is moving.

10. Which events occur when the cursor on a form is moved to another record?

11. Does the Delete event occur before or after a record is actually deleted? Explain your answer.

12. The Deactivate event is related to the processes associated with moving focus from one object to another. True or False?

13. What does it mean to "get focus"? Describe some ways that a control or form can get focus.

14. How do the GotFocus and Enter events differ?

15. How do the Load event and the Activate event for a form differ?

16. The —————————— event occurs for a control when the user finishes adding or changing data in the control.

   a. CurrentControl

   b. BeforeUpdate

   c. AfterInsert

   d. OldValue

17. What sequence of events occurs when a form opens?

18. What sequence of events occurs when a form closes?

19. The AfterUpdate event occurs when a user enters a value in the text box portion of a combo box, but that value is not in the combo box list. True or False?

20. The New property of a form is set to True when the record has been changed, but not saved. True or False?

HANDS-ON PROJECTS

Project 6-1

Natural Parent International. Three features should be added to the NPI system. First, an "On Loan" label on frmLibrary should be displayed when the book is currently checked out. Second, the frmMember form should display a combo box that lists the names of members. When a name is selected, the code should find the corresponding record in frmMember. Third, the Book Details command in the Form menu of mnuMembers should be disabled when a member does not have any books.

Complete these steps:

1. Open **NPI.mdb**. Place an "**On Loan**" label on frmLibrary. Name the label **lblLoanFlag**.

2. Create an event procedure that displays the "On Loan" flag only when a book is on loan. A book is on loan when a tblCheckOut record exists for the book and the DateReturned field equals Null. You will need to use the DCount or DLookup function to determine whether the appropriate record exists. The criteria in the DCount or DLookup function will need to include the statement **[DateReturned] Is Null**. In addition, you should verify that the current record is not a new record (Me.NewRecord). If the current record is a new record, do not display the "On Loan" flag and execute the Exit Sub statement prior to executing the DCount or DLookup statement. Depending on how you design the procedure, you may need to use the **IsNull** function.

3. Place a combo box on frmMembers that uses qrycboNameList as its RowSource. After a name is selected, the form should find and display the corresponding member. One way to implement this procedure is to use the ListIndex property of a combo box to find the number of the item selected in the combo box (the first item starts with 0). Next, use **DoCmd.GoToRecord, , acGoTo,** *recordnumber* to move to the record. Prior to executing these statements, you will need to make sure that the FilterOn and OrderByOn properties of the form are set to False.

4. Create an event procedure that enables and disables the Book Details command in mnuMembers depending on whether a member has a book. You will need to check the Microsoft Office 9.0 Object Library in the References window prior to writing VBA code that manipulates command bars. Similar to the VBA code written in the GetBookFrom Sub procedure written earlier, the CurrentRecord property can be used to determine whether the member has checked out a book.

5. Save your work.

Project 6-2

Metropolitan Performing Arts Company. You are ready to start the sales section of the MPAC system. The sales section requires a sales form, toolbar, and menu. The sales form will contain the amount due and payment information. Customers can pay with cash, a check, or a credit card. A check number text box in the sales form is enabled only when check (the payment ID for a check is chck) is selected as the payment type. The authorization text box is enabled only when a credit card is selected. Prior to constructing the sales form, however, you must finish one more feature of frmPerfomerJobs. This form should display the message, "Sorry, the performers have not been scheduled at this time" whenever the form does not display a single performer.

Complete these steps:

1. Open **MPA.mdb** and refresh the links. Change frmPerformerJobs so it does not allow edits, deletions, or additions.

2. Add a label named **lblNoPerformers** to the Header section of frmPerformerJobs. The caption should contain the message described above.

3. Create code in the Open or Load event of frmPerformerJobs that determines whether the form displays any records. (*Hint*: Consider using the CurrentRecord property of the form.) If the form does not display records, lblNoPerformers should be visible and other controls on the form should not be visible.

4. Create a form named **frmSales**. This form should contain all of the fields contained in tblSales. A combo box (named **cboPaymentType**) should be used to select the payment type. The row source of cboPaymentType is tblPaymentMethods. The CheckNo text box should be named **txtCheckNo** and the Approval Code text box should be named **txtApprovalCode**.

5. Create a menu and toolbar (named **mnuSales** and **tbrSales**, respectively) for frmSales. The menu should contain all menus and commands in mnuPerformanceSeats, except that the Forms menu should not contain a command that opens frmPerformerJobs. The mnuSales menu should contain a command that opens frmPerformanceDateSeats, however. The toolbar is the same as tbrPerformanceSeats, except that it does not contain a command to open frmPerformerJobs or a command to open frmPerformance. A command on tbrSales should open frmPerformanceDateSeats, however.

6. Create VBA code that manipulates the Enabled property of txtCheckNo and txtAuthorization. When cboPaymentType is cash, both should be disabled. When cboPaymentType equals check, txtCheckNo should be enabled. When cboPaymentType is a credit card, txtAuthorization should be enabled. If a value has not been placed in cboPaymentType, txtCheckNo and txtAuthorization should not be enabled.

7. Save your work.

Project 6-3

Foreign Language Institute System. A common feature of database applications is an ability to easily locate and display a record. The users of the FLI system need the ability to easily locate and display a customer's data. You can provide this capability through the customer lookup combo box on the customer form.

Complete these steps:

1. Open **FLI.mdb**. Open the **Properties** window for the cboCustomer combo box on frmCustomers. Set the AfterUpdate property to **[Event Procedure]**, and click the **Build** button. Use the OpenForm method of the DoCmd object to reopen the frmCustomer form in this event. The form will reposition to the correct record if you place the following criteria in the WhereCondition argument of the OpenForm method:

   ```
   "[CustomerID]=" & Me![cboCustomer]
   ```

Be careful to enclose the name of the form in quotation marks so that Access will recognize it as a string.

2. As an additional touch, clear out the value in the combo box after the form has been reopened. The following line of VBA code after the statement to open the form will perform this task:

   ```
   Me![cboCustomer] = Null
   ```

3. Save your work.

Project 6-4

King William Hotel System. A common feature of database applications is an ability to easily locate and display a record. The users of the King William Hotel system need the ability to locate and display a customer's data easily. You can provide this capability through the customer lookup combo box on the customer form.

Complete these steps:

1. Open **KWH.mdb**. Open the **Properties** window for the cboCustomerLookUp combo box on frmCustomer. Set the AfterUpdate property to **[Event Procedure]**, and click the **Build** button. Use the OpenForm method of the DoCmd object to reopen the frmCustomer form in this event. The form will reposition to the correct record if you place the following criteria in the WhereCondition argument of the OpenForm method:

   ```
   "[CustomerNo]=" & Me![cboCustomerLookUp]
   ```

Be careful to enclose the name of the form in quotation marks so that Access will recognize it as a string.

2. As an additional touch, clear out the value in the combo box after the form has been reopened. The following line of VBA code after the statement to open the form will perform this task:

   ```
   Me![cboCustomerLookUp] = Null
   ```

3. Save your work.

Project 6-5

Workers' Compensation Commission System. A common feature of database applications is an ability to easily locate and display a record. The users of the WCC system need the ability to locate and display a patient's data. You can provide this capability through the patient lookup combo box on the patient form.

Complete these steps:

1. Open **WCC.mdb**. Open the **Properties** window for the cboPatient combo box on frmPatient. Set the AfterUpdate property to **[Event Procedure]**, and click the **Build** button. Use the OpenForm method of the DoCmd object to reopen the frmPatients form in this event. The form will reposition to the correct record if you place the following criteria in the WhereCondition argument of the OpenForm method:

```
"[Medical Record Number]=[Forms]![frmPatients]![cboPatient]"
```

Be careful to enclose the name of the form in quotation marks so that Access will recognize it as a string.

2. As an additional touch, clear out the value in the combo box after the form has been reopened. The following line of VBA code after the statement to open the form will perform this task:

```
Me![cboPatient] = Null
```

3. Save your work.

6

7

VBA MODULES, FUNCTIONS, VARIABLES, AND CONSTANTS

The Power of VBA

In this chapter you will:

♦ Design VBA code that is organized into standard modules, independent class modules, and form and report class modules

♦ Determine when each type of module is appropriate

♦ Develop simple sub procedures, functions, and property procedures

♦ Determine when a sub procedure or a function is most appropriate

♦ Declare arguments, variables, and constants

♦ Invoke procedures and pass arguments between procedures

♦ Cancel and manage events through VBA

Microsoft Access supports two approaches for developing program instructions: macros and Visual Basic for Applications (VBA). We reviewed macros earlier in this book. Like macros, VBA can be used to modify an object's properties and perform actions such as opening forms, finding data, and moving the cursor.

Compared with macros, however, VBA provides many more capabilities. For example, it can update rows in tables that are not currently displayed in a form. In addition, VBA supports a wider variety of conditions than the Condition column of a macro, performs repeated execution of code within a procedure, and supports extensive error handling. Because VBA is a more capable language than macros are, most advanced Access applications use VBA.

This chapter will focus on VBA and how to write procedures that can be used with multiple inputs and that can be used throughout an Access application. We begin our discussion with a high-level view of modules and procedures.

MODULES

A **procedure** is a collection of VBA statements combined in a manner to accomplish a processing task. You can group procedures related to a specific process into a **module** to make maintaining the application easier in the long run. Modules can contain one or more procedures. They can also contain definitions needed throughout the application.

VBA recognizes three types of modules: form and report class modules, standard modules, and independent class modules. Figure 7-1 shows the placement of procedures within these modules. **Form** and **report class modules** include code for all event procedures triggered by events occurring on a specific form or report, or the controls on that form or report. Additionally, a form or report module can contain other sub or function procedures that relate to it.

Form and report class modules are associated with forms and reports, respectively. If a form or report is copied and pasted, its associated class module is copied and pasted as well. If a form or report is deleted, the class module associated with it is deleted too. A form or report must be opened before the procedures inside its associated class module can be executed or modified. Form and report modules exist only when VBA code has been written to provide some processing capability to the form or report. That capability may be a response to an event, a calculation to provide a value to a control, or any other processing needed in the form or report. Consequently, some forms and reports will not have a corresponding module because no code has been written specifically for the form or report.

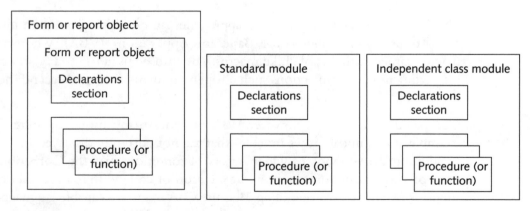

Figure 7-1   Procedures within modules

Standard modules are similar to form or report class modules except that they are not associated with a form or report. A **standard module** is a module in which you can place sub and function procedures and declarations that you want to make available to other procedures throughout your application. Access can execute the procedures in a standard module whenever the application is running. A standard module typically contains procedures that are used by more than one form, report, or procedure. Procedures that manipulate properties as well as procedures that validate public variables can be placed in standard modules.

Like standard modules, **independent class modules** are not connected to a form or report. Procedures inside an independent class module can be executed as long as the application is open. All class modules can define properties. In a sense, an independent class module is a custom-made object whose properties can be referenced and manipulated.

Selecting Module Types

The selection of the best module type for a procedure depends on the runtime efficiency of the application and the amount of primary memory expected on the computer executing the application. Standard modules and independent class modules are loaded into primary memory when the application is initially opened. Standard and independent class modules use primary memory even when they are not needed, but the time needed to load the module into primary memory occurs only once. Form and report class modules are loaded into primary memory when the form or report opens. Although they do not use primary memory until the form or report is opened, the form or report takes longer to open because the module must be loaded into primary memory.

The number of forms and reports that use a procedure also influences the selection of the module type. If more than one form or report uses the same procedure, the code could be located in a standard or independent class module, where all forms and reports can access it. If only one form or report needs the code, the procedure probably belongs in the form's or report's class module.

The most important factor to consider when selecting a module type is the object that the procedure manipulates. Object-based systems are easier to maintain when the program code used by an object is associated with that object. If the procedure tends to manipulate properties of a single form or report, then it belongs with that form or report. If the procedure manipulates properties of an object that are not part of a form or report (for example, a toolbar or recordset) and other procedures are also related to this same object, then you should consider grouping all of these procedures in an independent class module.

MU-DSci reflects design decisions made by the authors of this book. For instance, this application uses an independent class module called cmoProspectsMenuBar to manipulate the properties of the menu bar associated with frmProspects. It also contains a standard module named basUtilities, which contains procedures that provide a number of general, miscellaneous processing capabilities.

PROCEDURES

Three types of procedures exist in Access: sub procedures, functions, and property procedures. They are distinguished by how programmers invoke and use them.

Sub Procedures

Sub procedures are containers for programming code. All of the programming code in a procedure should be aimed at accomplishing a specific processing task, such as responding to an event or calculating a specific value.

A programmer can invoke a sub procedure at any time by writing a statement within a different procedure to invoke the necessary sub procedure. A sub procedure is invoked simply by placing its name and, if needed, the values for its arguments on a line within the invoking procedure. For example, the following line of code invokes the AdmitProspects procedure:

```
AdmitProspects
```

This procedure, which is located in the basProspects module of MU-DSci, does not use arguments. This sub procedure moves the admitted prospects from the tblProspects table to the tblCurrentStudents table.

Functions

Unlike sub procedures, **functions** return a value. You can invoke a function by simply placing it in an expression or using it as a value to display in a control. Your application can then use the value returned by a function in the expression. For example, the following line is contained in the LevelingStatus function located within the basLevelingRoutines module:

```
pstrCriteria = LevelingCriteria(pvntStudentID, pvntAreaCode, _
    pvntCourseNo)
```

LevelingCriteria is a function that produces a Where Condition string that is assigned to the variable pstrCriteria.

 TIP You can also invoke a function by placing the function name and any arguments on a single line, although the return value is discarded in this case.

Property Procedures

A **property procedure** defines a property that is attached to an object through dot notation. Assigning or using the value of a property activates the procedure. For example, the OpenIDWindow function in the class module associated with frmCurrentStudents uses the following line of code:

```
Forms![frmIDSearchWindow].oprSource = pstrFilter
```

The oprSource portion of the statement is a property procedure of frmIDSearchWindow. The preceding statement sends the value placed in the variable pstrFilter to oprSource. The VBA code of oprSource will use pstrFilter to assign a value to the row source of a combo box.

Determining which type of procedure to use depends on your intent. If the procedure will correspond to something that could be a property, you should use a property procedure. Otherwise, you should use a function when a value needs to be returned, and a sub procedure when a returned value is not required.

CREATING AND USING SUB PROCEDURES

ErrorTrap is an example of a sub procedure that is invoked by several procedures. ErrorTrap is located in the basUtilities standard module in MU-DSci, and it processes error messages. When a procedure encounters an error, the error-handling capability of Access executes a statement that invokes ErrorTrap.

The alternative to using ErrorTrap is to let each procedure record and display its own errors. The advantage of the sub procedure is that error messages become standardized. That is, the user of the system will not see different window formats for errors. In addition, if the error-handling process must be modified, you can make changes in only one procedure.

The syntax for the first statement in a sub procedure is as follows:

Syntax

[Private | Public] [Static] Sub *ProcedureName* **[(***ArgumentList***)]**

Syntax Dissection

- **Private** indicates that the sub procedure can be invoked only by other procedures in the same module.

- **Public** indicates that the sub procedure can be invoked by procedures located in any module. Public is the default declaration.

- **Static** indicates that variables declared within a procedure maintain their values after the procedure finishes executing. Otherwise, variables are reset to empty or zero each time the procedure is invoked.

- *ProcedureName* is the name given to the sub procedure.

- *ArgumentList* is a list of variables called **formal arguments** that are used to provide information to the sub procedure. Variables in *ArgumentList* are separated by commas. The argument list may also contain additional information about an argument.

Possible variations of the *ArgumentList* can be complex. The complete syntax for *ArgumentList* follows.

Syntax

[Optional][ByVal | ByRef][ParamArray]*ArgumentName***[( )][As** *DataType*]

[= *DefaultValue*]

Syntax Dissection

- The **Optional** keyword indicates that a value for the argument does not need to be supplied by the invoking procedure.

- The **ByVal** keyword specifies that the sub procedure will be sent a copy of the argument's value rather than the address of the value. The **ByRef** keyword specifies that the sub procedure will be sent the address of the argument's value rather than a copy of the value.

- The **ParamArray** keyword indicates that the argument will consist of an unspecified number of indexed variables.

- *ArgumentName* refers to the name of the argument as it will be used in the sub procedure. The argument is a variable that contains values used in the procedure.

- *DataType* identifies the type of data that will be passed to the argument. It is similar to a field's data type. Access can perform operations with an argument (for example, add, compare to other arguments) more easily when it knows something about the type of data stored by the argument. Table 7-1 describes the available VBA data types and their corresponding data types in Access table fields.

- *DefaultValue* specifies the value that the argument will assume if it is not specified by the programmer.

Table 7-1 Data types in VBA and their corresponding types in Access tables

VBA	Description	Data Type Used in Access Table	Notes
Boolean	True or False. Internally True is represented as –1 and False is represented by 0.	Yes/No	Not supported in Access 2.0; use Integer for Boolean data
Byte	Integers. Range: 0 to 255.	Number (Byte)	Not supported in Access 2.0; use Integer for Byte data
Currency	Numbers that represent monetary amounts. Contains a fixed decimal point. Range: –922,337,203,685,477.5808 to 922,337,203,685,477.5807	Currency	
Date	Dates and times	Date/Time	Not supported in Access 2.0; use Variant for a Date/Time data
Double	Double-precision floating-point numbers (that is, the decimal point can move). Range: 1.79769313486232E308 to –4.94065645841247E-324 for negative values; 4.94065645841247E-324 to 1.79769313486232E308 for positive values	Number (Double)	

Table 7-1   Data types in VBA and their corresponding types in Access tables (continued)

VBA	Description	Data Type Used in Access Table	Notes
Integer	Integers. Range: −32,768 to 32,767	Number (Integer)	
Long	Integers. Range: −2,147,483,648 to 2,147,483,647	Number (Long Integer) AutoNumber (Long Integer)	In Access 2.0, the Long data type should be used to represent Counter data in VBA.
Object	A reference to an Access application or DAO object		Any type of more specific object can also be used as a data type, including Form and Textbox. In addition, the name of a form can be used as the data type of a variable (for example, [frmCurrent Students]).
Single	Single-precision floating-point numbers. Range: −3.402823E38 to −1.401298E-45 for negative values; 1.401298E-45 to 3.402823E38 for positive values	Number (Single)	
String	A set of alphabetic, numeric, and special characters. Maximum string length for variable-length string (that is, length not pre-specified) is 65,400 characters. Fixed-length strings can be 2 billion characters.	Text Memo Number (Replication ID) AutoNumber (ReplicationID)	OLE objects are represented by String data in Access 2.0, and Replication IDs are not supported.
Variant	Data of an unspecified type. Variant data types can be used to store numeric, date, string, and null values.		
Array of Byte	Not actually an array of byte data, but the best way to represent an OLE object	OLE object	

An argument list normally consists of a set of variable names and their corresponding data types. For example, the code in ErrorTrap is defined as follows:

```
Public Sub ErrorTrap(pstrMessage As String)
MsgBox pstrMessage, vbOKOnly + vbExclamation + _
    vbDefaultButton1, "Error Detected."
End Sub
```

The pstrMessage argument of ErrorTrap expects the invoking statement to provide a String value whenever ErrorTrap is invoked. The MsgBox function displays the value in pstrMessage on the screen. The other arguments of the MsgBox function place buttons and icons in the message box, specify the default button, and give a title to the message box, respectively. (These arguments are intrinsic constants, which were introduced earlier in this book.) All sub procedures end with the End Sub statement.

Passing Arguments by Reference and by Value

By default, Access passes arguments by reference. Likewise, arguments are passed by reference when the ByRef keyword is used. When arguments are processed **by reference**, the memory address containing the value to be used is "referenced" by the argument. Therefore, arguments processed by reference will reflect any changes made to their value in that procedure in the actual arguments as well. The danger of this technique is that values in the invoking procedure could be changed accidentally. For example, if you use

```
Surcharge_Calculation Me.txtTuition, _
Me.txtStateSurchargeRate, _
Me.txtSurchargeTotal, Me.txtDiscountAmount
```

to invoke Surcharge_Calculation and the following alternate form of Surcharge_Calculation is used, then the value of Me![txtTuition] will change, as will the value of Me![txtSurchargeTotal]:

```
Sub Surcharge_Calculation (pcurFee As Currency, _
psngSurchargeRate As Single, pcurTotal As Currency, _
pcurDiscount As Currency)
pcurFee = pcurFee - pcurDiscount
'Reduce Fee by Discount amount
pcurTotal = pcurFee * psngSurchargeRate
End Sub
```

You can also pass arguments **by value**. When a programmer wants the values in the arguments to be processed by value, he or she uses the ByVal keyword. When Access processes arguments by value, a copy of the value, instead of a reference to the memory location containing the value, is supplied to the procedure. Consequently, if the procedure alters formal arguments processed by value, those changes are not reflected in the original arguments because the changes were made to the copy of the value, rather than to the original value stored in the memory location.

To specify that the arguments will be processed by value, change the sub statement as follows:

```
Sub Surcharge_Calculation (ByVal pcurFee As Currency, _
ByVal psngSurchargeRate As Single, pcurTotal as Currency, _
ByVal pcurDiscount As Currency)
```

Some programmers believe that sub procedures should not modify values in arguments passed by reference. Such modifications are called "side effects" because the change occurs outside the procedure. To prevent side effects, you should pass all arguments by value. Side effects are difficult to find when debugging an application and difficult to detect later when maintaining the application. An advantage to using passing by reference, however, is that it is more efficient in terms of storage space and processing time than is the practice of passing arguments by value, which requires copying the value in the arguments.

The Optional Keyword

The **Optional** keyword can be used with arguments and offers some conveniences to the programmer. It specifies that the invoking procedure does not need to provide a value for the argument. Usually, when Optional is used, a programmer provides a default value. For example, the sub statement for Surcharge_Calculation can be declared as follows:

```
Sub Surcharge_Calculation (pcurFee As Currency, _
psngSurchargeRate As Single, pcurTotal As Currency, _
Optional pcurDiscount As Currency = 0)
```

If a student does not have a discount, the following notations can be used to invoke the procedure:

```
Surcharge_Calculation Me.txtTuition, _
    Me.txtStateSurchargeRate, _
    Me.txtSurchargeTotal

Surcharge_Calculation pcurFee:=Me.txtTuition, _
    psngSurchargeRate:=Me.txtStateSurchargeRate, _
    pcurTotal:=Me.txtSurchargeTotal
```

In both cases, zero will be used as the Discount. The second technique, however, makes an explicit connection between the control containing the value to be used in the Surcharge_Calculation procedure and the variable using that value. This approach is called the **named arguments** approach. The advantage of this technique is that the arguments can be placed in any order and commas do not have to be used to represent blank arguments. A problem with named arguments is that the invoked procedures cannot change the names of their formal arguments without influencing the Call statements that are used in various locations throughout the application.

Nuances of Argument Use

A sub procedure can produce different results depending on the values supplied by the invoking procedure. As an example of the many variations of argument use, consider the following sub procedure:

```
Private Sub Surcharge_Calculation (pcurFee As Currency, _
    psngSurchargeRate As Single, pcurTotal As Currency,_
    pcurDiscount As Currency)
    pcurTotal = (pcurFee - pcurDiscount) * psngSurchargeRate
End Sub
```

7

This procedure needs three pieces of information: the fee of the student registering for classes, the discount (if any) given to the student, and the surcharge rate that should be applied. The result is placed in the pcurTotal variable. The value placed in the pcurTotal variable will be available to the procedure that invoked Surcharge_Calculation.

The following statement invokes Surcharge_Calculation:

```
Surcharge_Calculation Me.txtTuition, _
Me.txtStateSurchargeRate, _
Me.txtSurchargeTotal, Me.txtDiscountAmount
```

The arguments pcurFee, pcurDiscount, psngSurchargeRate, and pcurTotal are **formal arguments**. Statements inside Surcharge_Calculation can use or update pcurFee, pcurDiscount, psngSurchargeRate, and pcurTotal.

The Value properties of Me.txtTuition, Me.txtDiscountAmount, Me.txtStateSurchargeRate, and Me.txtSurchargeTotal are **actual arguments**. The first three arguments provide the values that will be used for pcurFee, pcurDiscount, and psngSurchargeRate. Whatever the value of Me.txtTuition, that value will be used for pcurFee in Surcharge_Calculation. Whatever the value of Me.txtDiscountAmount, that value will be used for pcurDiscount in Surcharge_Calculation. Whatever the value of Me.txtStateSurchargeRate, that value will be used for psngSurchargeRate in Surcharge_Calculation.

In this code, the pcurTotal argument and Me.txtSurchargeTotal work in reverse directions. When Surcharge_Calculation reaches its End Sub statement, the value of Me.txtSurchargeTotal will equal the value placed in pcurTotal. In this case, the actual arguments consist of controls on a form. The programmer also could have declared variables through Dim statements. When variables are used, the value of the variable corresponding to the pcurTotal argument would change when pcurTotal is updated.

Whenever a programmer invokes a procedure, it must be invoked using the same number of actual arguments as there are formal arguments in the sub statement, unless optional arguments (described later in this chapter) are used. Also, the actual arguments will supply values for the formal arguments in the order in which they are listed (unless named arguments are used), so the data types must be compatible. For example, given the sub statement shown earlier, if you use the statement

```
Surcharge_Calculation Me.txtDiscountAmount, Me.txtTuition, _
Me.txtStateSurchargeRate, Me.txtSurchargeTotal
```

in a procedure, the invoked procedure would use the value of Me.txtDiscountAmount for pcurFee and the value of Me.txtTuition for pcurDiscount. The procedure would perform the calculation, but the result would be incorrect.

Using the Call Statement to Invoke Sub Procedures

Programmers execute, or invoke, sub procedures by using a Call statement. The syntax for the Call statement is as follows:

Syntax

[**Call**] **Sub** *ProcedureName* [(*ArgumentList*)]

Syntax Dissection

- **Call** is an optional word that can be placed in front of **Sub** *ProcedureName*. If **Call** is used, *ArgumentList* is surrounded by parentheses. If **Call** is not used, *ArgumentList* is not surrounded by parentheses. Placing **Call** in front of **Sub** *ProcedureName* has no effect on the performance of the application. The advantage of using this optional word is that, to someone who needs to update the program, the statement is immediately recognizable as invoking a sub procedure.

- **Sub** *ProcedureName* is the name of the sub procedure to be invoked.

- *ArgumentList* is the list of actual arguments to be passed to the sub procedure. Actual arguments must match the order and data type of the formal arguments in the sub procedure invoked unless named arguments are used. Almost any item that evaluates to a value can be passed to a sub procedure, including constants (for example, numbers, strings between quotes), variables, expressions, and properties of objects.

The following statements invoke the ErrorTrap procedure (statements similar to these are located in the basProspects module of MU-DSci):

```
Call ErrorTrap("Error in clearing denied prospects.")
ErrorTrap "Error in clearing denied prospects."
ErrorTrap "Error moving " & precProspects.StudentID & _
    " to Current Students."
```

Access uses pstrMessage to refer to the string following ErrorTrap. The first two statements accomplish the same thing. The third statement creates a string by concatenating three strings. The precProspects![StudentID] argument is the Student ID of the student in a Recordset object.

Event Procedure Arguments

Event procedures are special types of sub procedures located in form and report class modules. They execute whenever a particular event occurs, provided that the event property for the event has been set to the value [Event Procedure].

Although most event procedures do not take arguments, some have one or more predefined arguments. Access uses these arguments to provide information to the programmer that is relevant to the event that has occurred. The arguments also contain values that Access evaluates during and after the procedure executes to determine how to continue the application's processing. Arguments used in this manner are called **flags**. As an Access application programmer, you write the code for event procedures in the same manner that you write other sub procedures.

Table 7-2 identifies many of the event procedures that use a single argument to cancel the event that invoked the procedure. Setting the Cancel argument to True cancels the event. In other words, a programmer can write VBA code to detect a situation that calls for the event to be stopped and force Access to stop the event by setting the Cancel argument to the value of True and exiting the event procedure. For example, if an invalid (that is, illogical) combination of values occurs in a record, code in a form's BeforeUpdate event procedure could stop the update from occurring by assigning True to the Cancel argument and exiting the event procedure.

Table 7-2   Event procedures with single arguments

Event Procedure Name	Result of True
BeforeInsert (Cancel As Integer)	Record is not saved and cursor remains in the saved record
BeforeUpdate (Cancel As Integer)	Prevents update and keeps cursor in the control
DblClick (Cancel As Integer)	Cancels the event
Delete (Cancel As Integer)	Restores the original value
Exit (Cancel As Integer)	Sets focus back to the object
NoData (Cancel As Integer)	Prevents report from printing
Open (Cancel As Integer)	Stops form or report from opening
Unload (Cancel As Integer)	Prevents closing a form

 TIP   Use care in setting Cancel to any nonzero value in the Unload event for a modal form. This action prevents the form from being unloaded and closed. Depending on the circumstances, you may not be able to return control to the rest of the application.

Table 7-3 lists many of the event procedures that take multiple arguments or arguments that specify actions other than canceling events. Many of the arguments use an Integer data type. Access uses **intrinsic constants** to represent the legal values for these arguments. You've learned that an intrinsic constant is a keyword that represents some particular value (usually an integer). For example, the word **True** is an intrinsic constant that represents value −1, which is the internal representation for True.

Table 7-3   Event procedures with multiple or special arguments

Event Procedure Name	Arguments	Notes
AfterDelConfirm (Status As Integer)	Status indicates whether the deletion was performed.	When Status equals acDeleteOK, the record was deleted. When Status equals acDeleteCancel or acDeleteUserCancel, the record was not deleted.
ApplyFilter (Cancel As Integer, ApplyType as Integer)	Cancel set to True prevents filter from occurring. ApplyType indicates the action taken to cause the filter.	
BeforeDelConfirm (Cancel As Integer, Response As Integer)	Cancel equal to True cancels the deletion, restores the record, and prevents the deletion confirmation dialog box from being displayed. Response tells Access whether to display the deletion confirmation dialog box.	When Response is set to acDataErrContinue, the dialog box is not displayed. When Response equals acDataErrDisplay, the default dialog box is displayed.
Error (DataErr As Integer, Response As Integer)	DataErr identifies the error code for the error that triggered the event. Response is set by the programmer to indicate whether Access should display the default error message.	
Filter (Cancel As Integer, FilterType As Integer)	Cancel indicates whether the filter window should be opened. FilterType specifies the filter window the user was trying to open.	
KeyDown (KeyCode As Integer, Shift As Integer)	KeyCode identifies the key pressed. Shift indicates whether the Shift, Alt, or Ctrl key was pressed.	
KeyPress (KeyAscii As Integer)	KeyAscii identifies the key pressed. It can also be set to change the key sent to the object.	
KeyUp (KeyCode As Integer, Shift As Integer)	See the description for KeyDown.	
MouseDown (Button As Integer, Shift As Integer, X As Single, Y As Single)	Button identifies the mouse button pressed. Shift indicates whether Shift, Alt, or Ctrl was also pressed. X is the horizontal coordinate of the current mouse location. Y is the vertical coordinate of the current mouse location.	

Table 7-3 Event procedures with multiple or special arguments (continued)

Event Procedure Name	Arguments	Notes
MouseMove (Button As Integer, Shift As Integer, X As Single, Y As Single)	Button identifies the mouse button pressed. Shift indicates whether Shift, Alt, or Ctrl was also pressed. X is the horizontal coordinate of the current mouse location. Y is the vertical coordinate of the current mouse location.	
MouseUp (Button As Integer, Shift As Integer, X As Single, Y As Single)	Button identifies the mouse button pressed. Shift indicates whether Shift, Alt, or Ctrl was also pressed. X is the horizontal coordinate of the current mouse location. Y is the vertical coordinate of the current mouse location.	
NotInList (NewData As String, Response As Integer)	NewData is the String entered into the text box portion of the combo box. Response is provided by the programmer to tell Access how the event was handled.	The LimitToList property must be set to Yes for the NotInList event to occur. Use NewData to update the list in the combo box or to produce a custom error message. When Response is set to acDataErrDisplay, Access displays the default "not in list" message to the user. When Response is set to acDataErrContinue, the default message is suppressed. Response is set to acDataErrAdded, which tells Access that the combo box has been updated and the default "not in list" message should not be displayed, and Access automatically requeries the combo box so that the new data value is displayed.
Updated (Code As Integer)	Code indicates how an OLE object was updated.	

Many of the combo boxes in MU–DSci have code written in their NotInList event procedures. For instance, the NotInList event procedure for cboGDegreeType and cboUDegreeType located on frmProspects and frmCurrentStudents contains a single line of code. The example from cboGDegreeType is as follows:

```
Private Sub cboGDegreeType_NotInList(NewData As String, _
    Response As Integer)
    Call NewDegreeType(NewData, Response)
End Sub
```

Because the NotInList event procedure processing is identical for each of the combo box objects, we created a sub procedure in the basUtilities standard module. This sub procedure asks users whether they want to add the contents of NewData to the table that serves as the row source of the combo box. If a user answers "yes," the event procedure uses several VBA statements to insert the value into the table. Then, NewDegreeType sets the Response variable to the value represented by acDataErrAdded, an intrinsic constant. When Access detects that the Response variable is equal to the value of acDataErrAdded, the default error message is surpressed. If the user does not want to add the data, the Response variable is set to the value of the intrinsic constant acDataErrContinue. Because Response is the argument name in the sub statement and in the NewDegreeType Call statement, Access communicates the value of Response returned by NewDegreeType to Access.

Using Event Procedures to View and Hide the frmClassLoad Detail

The frmClassLoad form in the Swim Lessons application displays the classes taught by an instructor in a particular semester. In its current implementation, the form has a few problems. First, no detail data display when the form opens, because a semester and instructor haven't been selected yet. Second, the detail information remains on the screen when a new semester is selected until the time that the user selects an instructor. Because an instructor might also teach in the second semester selected, this implementation could inadvertently lead to an erroneous interpretation of the data displayed on the screen.

As an example of the second problem, suppose the user selects both a semester and an instructor and then views the (correct) data. Next, suppose the user changes the semester value, but is distracted from her work before she changes the instructor value. When her attention returns to the screen, she may not remember that she did not reselect the instructor to update the detailed information shown. A better design—one that automatically resets the instructor combo box when changes occur in the semester combo box—would avoid this problem.

To hide and view the frmClassLoadDetail information:

1. Open **SwimReg**, refresh the links, and then open **frmClassLoad** in Design view.

2. Open the **Properties** window for the cboSemester combo box, if it is not already open. Click the **Event** tab, if necessary, click in the **AfterUpdate** event property field; Select **[Event Procedure]** from the property combo box, click the **Build** button, if necessary, and then enter the following lines of code:

```
Me.frmClassLoadDetail.Visible = False
Me.cboInstructor.Requery
```

3. Close the Visual Basic window, and display the **Properties** window for the cboInstructor combo box. Click the **Event** tab, if necessary. Click in the **AfterUpdate** event property field. Select **[Event Procedure]** from the property combo box, click the **Build** button, and then enter the following lines of code:

```
Me.frmClassLoadDetail.Visible = True
Me.frmClassLoadDetail.Requery
```

4. From the **Debug** menu, select **Compile SwimReg**, save your code, and then close the Visual Basic window.

As the form should open with the details hidden, you will next add a line of code to hide the detail information when the form opens.

5. Display the **Properties** window for the form. Click the **Event** tab, if necessary. Click in the **OnOpen** event property field. Select **[Event Procedure]** from the drop-down menu list. Click the **Build** button, and then enter the following line of code:

```
Me.frmClassLoadDetail.Visible = False
```

6. From the **Debug** menu, select **Compile SwimReg**.

7. Save and close the Visual Basic window.

8. Save and close frmClassLoad.

9. Test the form by opening it in Form view, typing **98a** for the semester value, and then selecting **Voss** as the instructor. Next, use **01b** as the semester value and select **Crist** as the instructor. The form should work as expected. Close the form.

Writing a NotInList Event Procedure for frmClassesBrief

We created the cboLimitSemester combo box in frmClassesBrief to allow a user to easily filter frmClassesBrief to show only those courses offered in the semester indicated. The row source of cboLimitSemester is a query that returns all semesters stored in the tblClasses table. We created a NotInList event procedure that displays a message box whenever someone types in a value that is not displayed in cboLimitSemester. When this error occurs, Access displays its own message as well. You will now modify the message with more information. Also, you'll add code to reset the combo box to a null value and then suppress the message displayed by Access.

To modify the NotInList event procedure for cboLimitSemester:

1. Open **frmClassesBrief** in Form view, type **99G** into the **Limit Semester** combo box, and then press the **Enter** key.

Two error messages, one following the other after you click Enter, will be displayed to indicate that the input is not valid.

2. Delete **99G**, and then close the form. Respond to any messages by indicating that you want to continue closing the form, and then open **frmClassesBrief** in

Design view. Modify the **NotInList** event procedure of cboLimitSemester so that it looks like the following:

```
Private Sub cboLimitSemester_NotInList(NewData As String,_
    Response As Integer)
MsgBox "We do not maintain records for ", & NewData, _
    vbOKOnly + vbCritical + vbDefaultButton1,
    "Limit Semester"
Me.cboLimitSemester = Null     'Reset the combo box
Response = acDataErrContinue
End Sub
```

MsgBox uses a string that is concatenated with the data entered by the user; the user's input is stored in the NewData argument. The Response argument is set equal to the value of acDataErrContinue, which turns off other Access messages.

3. From the Debug menu, select **Compile SwimReg**.

4. Save the code and close the Visual Basic window.

5. Open **frmClassesBrief** in Form view. Type **99G** in the combo box, and then press the **Enter** key.

   The error message you created should be displayed. Click **OK** to close the message box.

6. Save and close frmClassesBrief.

Almost all of the concepts that apply to sub procedures also apply to function procedures. In the next section, we'll discuss the features that differ or are unique to function procedures.

CREATING AND USING FUNCTIONS

Function procedures, usually referred to as just functions, are very similar to sub procedures. They use formal arguments, can be declared as Public or Private, and can contain variable and constant declaration statements. The syntax for the Function statement is as follows:

Syntax

[**Public** | **Private**] [**Static**] **Function** *FunctionName* [*(ArgumentList)*] [**As** *DataType*]

Syntax Dissection

- **Public**, **Private**, **Static**, and *ArgumentList* are the same as defined for a sub procedure.

- *DataType* refers to the data type of the value that will be returned by the function. Legal values of *DataType* are the same as those identified for arguments. By default, the data type of a function is Variant when the data type is omitted from the function statement. The *DataType* argument distinguishes a function from a sub procedure.

- *FunctionName* is the name that will be used to invoke the function.

The Surcharge_Calculation sub procedure, described earlier in this chapter, is a function. The function specification for this procedure is as follows:

```
Function Surcharge_Calculation (pcurFee As Currency, _
    psngSurchargeRate As Single, _
    pcurDiscount As Currency) As Currency
Surcharge_Calculation = (pcurFee - pcurDiscount) * _
    psngSurchargeRate
End Function
```

In a function procedure, the function name is assigned a value. This assignment of a value is the fundamental difference between sub procedures and functions. You would use a statement such as the following to invoke the function:

```
pcurTotalCharge =Surcharge_Calculation (Me.Tuition, _
    Me.psngStateSurchargeRate, Me.DiscountAmount)
```

The result of the function is placed in pcurTotalCharge. Normally, functions are used only when a value is to be returned to the invoking procedure or object. However, the RunCode macro action and the OnAction property of a command bar control cannot invoke sub procedures. To accommodate macros and command bars, functions may be written without explicitly setting a return value.

Programmers can invoke functions in response to an event (for example, the GotFocus event) by placing the proper statement in the property. Normally, event procedures should be used rather than functions. Functions are useful, however, when several different events must invoke the same code.

Using a Function to Create a Name String

You've already worked with several forms to implement the payment and registration process. A few of these forms—frmPayment, frmRegistration, frmProcessPayment, and frmAllocationSub—contain code to build a person's name for display purposes. Suppose you wanted to change the way the name is displayed—for example, by including the [Suffix] information in tblStudent. You would need to find every place that the name is constructed and modify the code that builds the name. A better approach is to write a function that will build the name and then use this function wherever you need to build a name.

To create a function that constructs a person's name:

1. Create a new module, and then enter the following line of code if it was not created for you automatically:

```
Option Explicit
```

2. Select **Procedure...** from the Insert Module list, name the function **PersonName**, set the Type to **Function**, and, if necessary, set the Scope to **Public**. Make sure there is no check in the check box that sets all local variables to Statics. Click **OK**.

3. The cursor will be placed between the Function statement and the End Function statement. Enter the following code. Be careful to modify the Function statement as shown.

```
Public Function PersonName(varID As Variant) As String
'Declare local variables for constructing name.
'Variants must be used because DLookup can return a null
'value
Dim varFirstName As Variant
Dim varLastName As Variant
Dim varMI As Variant

On Error GoTo PersonNameError

'Check for null ID
If IsNull(varID) Then
    PersonName = ""
Else
    'Look up and construct the name
    varFirstName = DLookup("[FirstName]", "tblStudents", _
            "[SID]='" & varID & "'")
    varLastName = DLookup("[LastName]", "tblStudents", _
            "[SID]='" & varID & "'")
    varMI = DLookup("[MiddleInitial]", "tblStudents", _
            "[SID]='" & varID & "'")
    PersonName = varFirstName & " " & (varMI + ". ") & _
            varLastName
End If
Exit Function

PersonNameError:
PersonName = ""
End Function
```

4. Select **Compile SwimReg** from the **Debug** menu, save the module, name it **basUtilities**, and close the Visual Basic window.

You may have noticed that the name is constructed using both concatenation operators: & and +. Although & is generally used for concatenation, + is needed in this case to properly evaluate a potentially null middle initial. Using & instead of + would result in a period occurring in the middle of a name when no middle initial exists. The + operator eliminates the period when the middle initial is null.

Next, you will modify frmPayment to use the name-building function.

To modify frmPayment to use the PersonName function:

1. Open **frmPayment** in Design view, open the **Properties** window for the form, if it is not already open, click in the **OnOpen** event property field, click the **Build** button, select **Code Builder**, and then click **OK**.

2. Enter the following code in the **Form_Open** procedure:

```
Me.txtPersonName = PersonName (Me.cboSID)
```

3. Close the Visual Basic window, and display the **Properties** window for cboSID. Click in the **AfterUpdate** event property field, and then click the **Build** button.

4. Replace all code in the **cboSID_AfterUpdate** event procedure with the following code:

```
Me.txtPersonName = PersonName (Me.cboSID)
```

5. Select **Compile SwimReg** from the **Debug** menu, save your code, close the Visual Basic window, and then close the form.

To ensure that the name is displayed the same way throughout the application, other places that build a person's name should use the PersonName function as well.

To change frmProcessPayment to also use the PersonName function:

1. Open **frmProcessPayment** in Design view, open the **Properties** window for the form, if it is not already open, click in the **OnOpen** event property field, and then click the **Build** button.

2. Replace the code in the **Form_Open** procedure that constructs the name with the following code:

```
'Look up and construct the name
Me.txtPersonName = PersonName (Forms.frmStudent.txtSID)
```

3. Select **Compile SwimReg** from the **Debug** menu, save the procedure, and close the Visual Basic window.

4. Close the form.

The Registration form uses a different approach to build the person's name. In this form, the control source of txtPersonName contains a formula to build the name. The formula can also be replaced by the function.

To use the PersonName function in the control source of txtPersonName on frmRegistration:

1. Open **frmRegistration** in Design view, open the **Properties** window for txtPersonName, and then click the **Data** tab.

2. Delete everything in the ControlSource property, and then enter the following code into the ControlSource property:

```
=PersonName([txtSID])
```

3. Save and close frmRegistration.

You can now test the forms by entering a new person into the system and registering that person for classes. If you wanted to modify the way in which a person's name is displayed, you could now make the change once, and all of the places where the person's name is displayed would automatically reflect the change.

Another benefit of writing this general function is that more than one form can use it. In this case, frmPayment, frmRegistration, and frmAllocationSub all use the name-building function. Also, any argument that references a student identification number can be passed to the function. In this example, the txtSID field on frmStudent and the cboSID field on frmPayment both served as input values to the function and produced the proper result.

PROPERTY PROCEDURES—LET, SET, AND GET

Like a sub procedure, Property Let and Set procedures accept information from an invoking procedure, but do not return a value. Like a function, a Property Get procedure returns a value to the calling procedure.

Property Let and Get (and also Set and Get) usually appear in pairs. Property Let is used to specify a new value for a property, and Property Get supplies the property's value on request. The frmIDSearchWindow form uses Property Let and Get. To the procedures outside frmIDSearchWindow, the oprSource property identifies the filter that is in effect for the Window at the current moment. When oprSource is assigned a value, the Property Let procedure is used to construct a new filter for the combo box. Figure 7-2 displays the property procedures for frmIDSearchWindow.

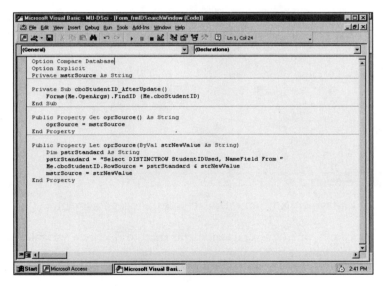

Figure 7-2   Property procedures for frmIDSearchWindow

The following statement triggers the Property Let procedure:

```
Forms.frmIDSearchWindow.oprSource = pstrFilter
```

Access places the value of pstrFilter into strNewValue in the Property Let statement. This value is concatenated to another longer string that is, in turn, placed in the row source of the combo box. The value is also stored in mstrSource. When a procedure asks for the current value of oprSource, the Get statement retrieves the value from mstrSource. The advantage of the Property Let statement is that an outside procedure does not need to know the details of how the row source is created. It simply needs to know something about the value that the Property procedure requires. Program maintenance is enhanced when the majority of the code needed to perform an operation on an object is associated with the modified object.

DECLARING VARIABLES

Variables define memory locations that store values used in an application's processing. **Dim statements** define variables that will be used within procedures. For example, the txtPaymentNo_BeforeUpdate event procedure from frmProcessPayment, illustrated in Figure 7-3, begins with two Dim statements. Variables are frequently used to store intermediate results as execution of the procedure moves from one line to another.

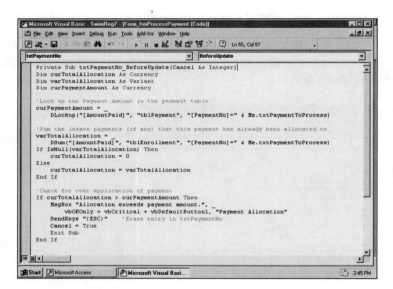

Figure 7-3 Part of txtPaymentNo_BeforeUpdate in frmProcessPayment

The Dim statement is only one of several statements used to declare a variable. The general syntax for declaration statements is as follows:

Syntax

DeclarationType [**WithEvents**] *varname*[([*subscripts*])] [**As** [**New**] *datatype*]

Syntax Dissection

- *DeclarationType* indicates the scope and life of the variable. **Dim** is used in a procedure or in the Declarations section of a module to declare variables that are used only within the module or procedure. **Private** is used in the Declarations section of a module to declare variables that are used only within the procedures contained by the module. **Public** is used in the Declarations section to declare variables that can be used by any procedure in any module. **Static** is used in a procedure to declare variables that retain their values even after the procedure finishes executing. Static variables may be declared only within procedures.

- **WithEvents** is an optional keyword used to specify that a variable should respond to events triggered by an ActiveX object. **WithEvents** is beyond the scope of this book.

- A *varname* is any valid name given to the defined variable. Variable names must start with a letter. They cannot use a space, period (.), exclamation mark (!), or the characters @, &, $, and #; they also cannot use the same name as any VBA built-in function, constant, or other reserved word.

- Optional *subscripts* are used to define an array. An array is an indexed set of variables of a similar data type.

- The **New** keyword indicates that the variable represents a new instance of an object. It can be used with many objects, including catalogs, tables, commands, and user-defined objects. It is frequently used to create a second copy of a form or report.

- The optional *datatype* identifies the type of data stored in the variable. Legal values for *datatype* are the same as the data types used by arguments.

As mentioned earlier in this book, programmers typically declare variables within the first few lines of the procedure in which they are used. This practice allows for easy program maintenance because variable declarations can be found quickly (that is, they are not buried in the lines of code). Table 7–1 lists the data types used in VBA. One of those data types, the Variant, deserves additional attention.

The Variant Data Type

The Variant data type is very flexible. It can contain almost any type of data, including numbers, strings, and dates. Variant is the only data type in VBA that can store null and empty values.

Sometimes a Variant variable is required rather than optional. For example, suppose a control on a form labeled "Extra Fees" can contain the phrase "To Be Determined" when the fee is unknown and a currency value when the extra fee is known. A procedure that references the control must use a Variant variable to refer to both possible values.

A programmer can determine the type of data stored in a Variant by using the **VarType** built-in function with the following syntax:

Syntax

VarType (*Variable*)

Syntax Dissection

- *Variable* is a Variant variable.

Other functions also check the data type of a Variant variable. Table 7-4 indicates the values returned by the VarType function and the functions that check for the specified type. These functions return the value True when the Variant is of the corresponding type.

Table 7-4   Values returned by VarType and variable testing functions

Data Stored in Variant Variable	Value Returned by VarType	Intrinsic Constant	Function That Tests for Type
Empty (no value stored)	0	vbEmpty	IsEmpty
Null	1	vbNull	IsNull
Integer	2	vbInteger	IsNumeric
Long	3	vbLong	IsNumeric
Single	4	vbSingle	IsNumeric
Double	5	vbDouble	IsNumeric
Currency	6	vbCurrency	IsNumeric
Date	7	vbDate	IsDate
String	8	vbString	—
Object	9	vbObject	IsObject
Error	10	vbError	IsError
Boolean	11	vbBoolean	—
Byte	17	vbByte	IsNumeric

The flexibility of the Variant data type requires additional care on the part of the programmer. The program should confirm that the content of the variable is, in fact, numeric before performing arithmetic operations on a Variant variable. Otherwise, an error will occur and the procedure may abort.

Processing is always more efficient when the program uses a specific data type (non-Variant) in declaring a variable because Access is not required to handle all possible values in the variable. For this reason, Variant variables should be used with care. Access also allows programmers to define their own data types.

The User-Defined Type

Besides using predefined data types, VBA provides a way to create a **user-defined type** with a **Type** statement. This statement allows you to define a complex data structure. The Type statement is placed in the Declarations section of a module using the following syntax:

Syntax

[Public | Private] Type *UserType*

    ElementName **As** *TypeName*

    [ElementName **As** *TypeName]*

End Type

Syntax Dissection

- **Public** indicates that the user-defined type is available to procedures in all modules. It is the default in standard modules.

- **Private** indicates that the user-defined type is available only to procedures within the module where the declaration was made. Private is the only option available in class modules and must precede the Type statement.

- *UserType* is the name for the data type you wish to define.

- *ElementName* is an element or component of the structure you are defining.

- *TypeName* is the data type of the element. *UserType* and *ElementName* must follow all of the rules for valid variable names. *TypeName* must be a valid VBA data type.

7

The following is an example of a user-defined type:

```
Type StudentRecord
    Name As String
    Address As String
    Major As String
    GPR As Single
End Type
```

This declaration defines a type named StudentRecord. Subsequently, a variable in a procedure could be declared as follows:

```
Dim pudtStudent As StudentRecord
```

Programmers can reference elements in the pudtStudent variable using dot notation, as follows:

```
pudtStudent.Name = "Suzanne Voss"
```

User-defined types are useful when the values of many similar variables need to be copied to other variables. For example, if pudtStudent contains values for each of its elements, all the values could be copied to another set of variables as follows:

```
Dim pudtPreviousStudent as StudentRecord
pudtPreviousStudent = pudtStudent
```

Although the need for an array in a relational database environment can often be satisfied with a table structure, Access nevertheless provides an array data structure that programmers can use. An array requires just a small amount of additional attention—that is, specifying the size of the array and the particular location in the array that you want to access. In the next section, we discuss those details.

Single- and Multiple-Dimension Arrays

When programmers require a large or uncertain number of variables, arrays may be useful. **Arrays** are collections of variables given a single name but indexed by one or more values. For example, you might store the names of the 50 states in an array called States that has 50 locations. To use an array, the size, name, and data type must be declared with the following syntax:

Syntax

Dim *ArrayName*([*lowerbound* **To**]*upperbound*) **As** *DataType*

Syntax Dissection

- The **Dim** statement uses the same form as a variable declaration.
- *ArrayName* is the name of the array. It takes one argument, the bounds of the array. If you do not specify the optional *lowerbound*, *lowerbound* is automatically set to 0.

Array indexes, like object and property indexes, begin at zero. For example, if you are storing the names of the states, you would have the first state name in State(0), the second state name in State(1), and so forth up to the last state name, which would be in State(49). The declaration in this case is:

```
Dim State(49) As String
```

Here, 49 defines the largest index used in the array, or the upper bound.

Suppose, however, that you really want the first state name to be stored in State(1), the second in State(2), and so forth up to the last state name, which would be in State(50). In this case, you can use the following declaration:

```
Dim State(1 To 50) As String
```

In fact, you can specify any lower and upper bound. If you want to force all of your arrays to begin with location 1, you can place the **Option Base 1** statement in the Declarations section of the module.

Multiple-dimension arrays follow the same rules as single-dimension arrays do, with the additional dimensions specified separated by commas. (You can have a maximum of 60 dimensions.) For example, if you had test data for students such that you had two tests for each of 50 students, you might declare the following:

```
Dim TestData (1 to 50, 1 to 2) As Single
```

This declaration provides for 50 rows and 2 columns of test data. To refer to the first test of student 25, the following statement is used:

```
TestData(25, 1)
```

Sometimes, it is desirable to leave the size of the array unspecified until runtime. The **ReDim** statement can change the size of the array. For example, the following statements change the size of the array depending on the number of dependents:

```
Dim Dependents() As String
Private Sub ListDependents(NumDependents As Integer)
    ReDim Dependents(NumDependents)
End Sub
```

Practically speaking, the ability to work directly with records in tables removes much of the need to work with arrays. If you do use an array, you should declare only as much array space as you need. Access allocates the space for an array based on the values of the indexes, so unnecessarily large arrays result in wasted memory.

Declaring Variables to Support the Update of frmClassDetails

The frmClassDetails 2 form in the Swimming Lesson database contains a text box that allows the enrollment limit for a course to be modified. Occasionally, users make mistakes. A mistake may occur, for instance, when a user enters a limit that is less than the current enrollment. To guard against the possibility of a mistake, you will create a BeforeUpdate procedure that displays a message box when a user enters a too-low value. The event procedure requires variables that determine the difference between the current enrollment and the limit. The MsgBox function is used to assign a value to a variable indicating the user's choice.

To create a BeforeUpdate event procedure that verifies the course limit:

1. Display **frmClassDetails 2** in Design view, open the **Properties** dialog box, if necessary, click **txtLimit**, click the **Event** tab in the Properties window, click the **BeforeUpdate** field, click the **Build** button, select **Code Builder**, and then click **OK**.

2. Type the statements shown in bold in the event procedure.

```
Private Sub txtLimit_BeforeUpdate(Cancel As Integer)
'Verifies the new value of Limit
Dim pintNewLimit As Integer
Dim pintEnroll As Integer
Dim pintDifference As Integer
Dim pstrMessage As String
Dim pintReturned As Integer

'Get new Limit and current Enrollment values
pintNewLimit = Me.txtLimit
pintEnroll = Me.txtEnrolled

If pintNewLimit < pintEnroll Then
    'Determine difference between enrollment and limit
    pintDifference = pintEnroll - pintNewLimit
    'Create an appropriate message
    pstrMessage = "The new limit is less than the " & _
        "enrollment by "
    pstrMessage = pstrMessage & pintDifference
    'add carriage return
    pstrMessage = pstrMessage & "." & Chr(13)
    pstrMessage = pstrMessage & "Do you want the " & _
        "limit set to "
    pstrMessage = pstrMessage & pintNewLimit & "?"

    'Display message and get user choice
    pintReturned = MsgBox(pstrMessage, vbQuestion + _
        vbYesNo + vbDefaultButton2, "Limit Confirmation")

    'If user answers no, restore the old value and cancel
    'the event
```

```
        If pintReturned = vbNo Then
                SendKeys "{ESC}"
                'OldValue property not applicable here
                Cancel = True
        End If
End If
End Sub
```

This sub procedure uses several variables. pstrMessage contains the message displayed in the message box. The message is constructed by concatenating messages to the previous value of pstrMessage. MsgBox is a function that returns the value 7 when the user clicks No. The returned value is placed in an integer variable called pintReturned. vbNo is an intrinsic constant, supplied by Access, that represents the value 7. Finally, the program uses pintLimit, pintEnroll, and pintDifference to hold the limit, enrollment, and difference, respectively.

pintLimit and pintEnroll are not absolutely necessary. Me![txtLimit] and Me![txtEnrolled] could be used anywhere pintLimit and pintEnroll are used, respectively. When a value is used more than once in a procedure, however, it is slightly more efficient to place the value in a variable. Otherwise, Access must retrieve the value from the form each time it is needed.

3. Click **Compile SwimReg** on the Debug menu to check for syntax errors, save your code, close Visual Basic, and then close the form.

4. Display **frmClassDetails 2** in Form view and modify the Enrollment Limit of one of the classes to a number less than the Number Currently Enrolled. Use the **Tab** key to move to another control. The message box is displayed.

5. Click **No** in response to the message box. The old value is restored and the cursor remains in txtEnrolled.

6. Save and close the form.

Scope, Life, and the Dim Statement

Although programmers declare most variables by using the Dim statement, variables can also be declared using the Public, Private, and Static statements. Variables may be declared at either the module level in the Declarations section or at the procedure level. Where and how they are declared determine which other procedures can use the variable (the **scope** of the variable) and how long the variable actually exists (the **life** of the variable). Table 7-5 shows the prefixes used to convey scope information in variable names.

Variables declared with the Dim or Private statement in the Declarations section are available only to procedures in that module. Within the Declarations section, the Dim and Private statements are equivalent. The Private statement is favored over the Dim statement because it highlights the fact that the declared variable is not available to procedures outside the module.

Table 7-5   Variable and constant scope prefixes

Scope	Prefix	Example
Public or Global	g	gintAmount
Module	m	mintAmount
Local or Private	p	pintAmount
Constants	c	cdblPI

The frmCourses form in MU-DSci uses a variable declared in the Declarations section to set the txtAreaCode value to the value entered in a previous record. Data entry clerks often enter several records consecutively. The entered records frequently have some values in common. In MU-DSci, new course records are often entered for the same department; consequently, txtAreaCode is the same from record to record. To accommodate this situation, the code shown in Figure 7-4 is used.

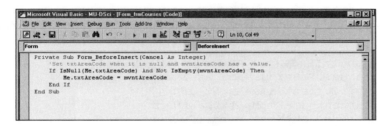

Figure 7-4   Procedure that facilitates the reuse of values

When a new record is inserted, Form_AfterInsert() sets mvntAreaCode to Me.txtAreaCode (a field entered by the user). Upon inserting the next record, a different procedure, Form_BeforeInsert(), uses the value of mvntAreaCode to automatically set the value of Me.txtAreaCode.

The application fills Me.txtAreaCode automatically when two conditions are met. First, mvntAreaCode must have a value. The mvntAreaCode variable will not have a value if this record is the first one inserted after the form is opened. Second, the user must not have already typed something into Me.txtAreaCode.

With modules external to a particular class module (for example, a form or report), the class module's public variables are treated as properties of the class (for example, a property of a form). For example, if the Declarations section of frmCustomer declares a public variable named gdtmOpenTime, a programmer can reference the value for the variable through the statement Forms![frmCustomer].gdtmOpenTime. Dot or bang notation is not needed to reference public variables declared in standard modules; the name of the variable is all that is required.

Any variable declared in the Declarations section of a module maintains its stored value as long as the application continues to run (in the case of standard and independent class modules) or as long as the form or report remains open (in the case of form and report class modules). Variables declared with the Dim statement in a procedure are available to that procedure only as long as the procedure is running. When the procedure finishes, the memory used by the variable is reclaimed and reused, thus destroying the value that was stored there.

Scope, Life, and the Static Statement

Unlike variables declared with the Dim statement, variables declared with the Static statement in a procedure continue to exist after the procedure finishes. If the procedure is used again (without the application being halted between procedure executions), Access will use the value from the prior execution as the current value of the variable.

Programmers frequently use static variables to determine whether a newly entered value is the same as a previous value. For example, assume that a sub procedure needs to know whether the last name of a newly entered person is the same as the one entered previously. If it is the same, another sub procedure is invoked. The following sub procedure (not found in MU-DSci) uses a static variable to hold the value of the previously entered last name. When a new last name does not match sstrPreviousName, the program updates sstrPreviousName so that it is used the next time the sub procedure is invoked. If sstrPreviousName was declared with a Dim statement, the value stored in sstrPreviousName disappears when the sub procedure finishes.

```
Private Sub txtLastName_AfterUpdate ()
    Static sstrPreviousName As String
    Dim pstrCurrentName As String
    pstrCurrentName = Me.txtLastName
    If sstrPreviousName = pstrCurrentName Then
      'Set address field to same address as prior person
        Call SameAddress
    Else     'Set sstrPreviousName to the new last name
        sstrPreviousName = pstrCurrentName
    End If
End Sub
```

Filtering frmClassesBrief

The frmClassesBrief form in the Swim Lessons application needs a filter to be applied after a user clicks a semester in cboLimitSemester. If a semester was set prior to closing the form, the filter should be reapplied when the form is opened again. However, it should be removed when the user exits the application.

To create the VBA code that causes frmClassesBrief to be filtered by semester:

1. Display **frmClassesBrief** in Design view, open the **Code Builder** for the **AfterUpdate** event property of **cboLimitSemester**, and then type the following code (shown in bold) into the event procedure:

```
Private Sub cboLimitSemester_AfterUpdate()
Dim pstrFilterSemester As String
pstrFilterSemester = "[Semester] = " & Chr(34) & _
    Me.cboLimitSemester & Chr(34)
DoCmd.ApplyFilter, pstrFilterSemester
End Sub
```

When assigning a value to a variable, Access expects to see the name of a field in the form's record source on the left side of the equals sign. The right side of the equals sign contains the value in cboLimitSemester. Because the Semester field is text, quotation marks must surround the cboLimitSemester value. Chr is a built-in function that returns characters based on an ASCII code value; 34 is the ASCII code for double quotes. The Chr function is necessary because double quotes signify constants in VBA. Double quotes are included because FilterSemester expects quotation marks around all string constants. DoCmd.ApplyFilter is similar to the ApplyFilter action.

2. Click **Compile SwimReg** in the **Debug** menu and correct any errors. Save your code and exit the Visual Basic window.

3. Display **frmClassesBrief** in Form view. Type **00c** into the Limit Semester combo box, and press the **Enter** key. The frmClassesBrief form should display only courses for the semester 00c.

4. Save and close frmClassesBrief.

Next, you need to develop a Form_Open event procedure that applies the filter, if any, when the form is opened.

To develop a Form_Open procedure that applies a semester filter:

1. Display **frmClassesBrief** in Design view and open the **Code Builder** for the OnOpen event property of the form.

2. Type the following boldface code into the Form_Open event procedure:

```
Private Sub Form_Open(Cancel As Integer)
If pstrFilterSemester <> "" Then
    DoCmd.ApplyFilter , pstrFilterSemester
End If
End Sub
```

3. Click **Compile SwimReg** in the **Debug** menu. A compile error occurs because pstrFilterSemester does not exist. The scope of pstrFilterSemester does not include the Form_Open procedure. The scope and location of the FilterSemester variable must be defined properly, at the module level, for this event procedure to work.

4. Go to the Declarations section of the **frmClassesBrief** class module by selecting **General** from the object combo box in the upper-left portion of the window and **Declarations** (if necessary) from the procedure combo box in the upper-right portion.

5. Type the following code in the Declarations section:

```
Dim mstrFilterSemester As String
```

6. Change the Form_Open procedure to use **mstrFilterSemester** instead of pstrFilterSemester. Do the same for the cboLimitSemester_AfterUpdate procedure. Delete the **Dim** statement in cboLimitSemester_AfterUpdate.

7

7. From the **Debug** menu, select **Compile SwimReg**.

   No error should occur; mstrFilterSemester is available to all procedures in the class module.

8. Save the procedures, close the Visual Basic window, and open **frmClassesBrief** in Form view. Select a semester using **cboLimitSemester** to filter the form.

9. Close frmClassesBrief then reopen **frmClassesBrief** to see whether the filter is still applied.

   It is not. Although mstrFilterSemester is available to the procedures, it loses its value as soon as the form is closed.

10. Save and close frmClassesBrief. Open the **basUtilities** standard module, located in the Modules listing of the Database window, in Design view and type the following statements below the Option Explicit statement in the Declarations section:

```
'Filter for frmClassesBrief
Public gstrFilterSemester As String
```

11. Save the code and close the Visual Basic window, and then open **frmClassesBrief** in Design view.

12. For the form, change **mstrFilterSemester** to **gstrFilterSemester** in the Form_Open and cboLimitSemester_AfterUpdate event procedures. Delete the **Dim** statement in the form's Declarations section.

13. Save the code, close the Visual Basic window, and then open **frmClassesBrief** in Form view. Test frmClassesBrief by clicking a semester and then closing and reopening the form. The same classes displayed when you close the form should be displayed when the form opens the second time. Close the form.

Now the procedure needs a few finishing touches. The filter should be removed when cmdAllBtn is clicked and when Remove Filter is clicked in a menu or toolbar.

To remove the semester filter in frmClassesBrief:

1. Display **frmClassesBrief** in Design view and type the following boldface code into the Visual Basic window for the Click event procedure for cmdAllBtn:

```
Private Sub cmdAllBtn_Click()
DoCmd.ShowAllRecords
Me.cboLimitSemester = Null
End Sub
```

2. Type the following boldface code into the Visual Basic window for frmClassesBrief's ApplyFilter event procedure:

```
Private Sub Form_ApplyFilter(Cancel As Integer, _
    ApplyType As Integer)
If ApplyType = acShowAllRecords Then _
    gstrFilterSemester = ""
End Sub
```

The ApplyFilter event occurs whenever the user clicks in the menu or when the DoCmd.ShowAllRecords statement executes. Access passes the value of ApplyType automatically; acShowAllRecords is an intrinsic constant that indicates that a Remove Filter or DoCmd.ShowAllRecords statement triggered the event.

3. From the **Debug** menu, select **Compile SwimReg**, save your code, and then close the Visual Basic window.

4. Test the procedures by opening **frmClassesBrief** in Form view, filtering the form through **cboLimitSemester**, and clicking the **All semesters** button. You should verify that frmClassesBrief maintains its filter until you click the All Semesters button on the form or the Remove Filter button on the toolbar.

5. Save and close frmClassesBrief.

7

INTRINSIC AND SYMBOLIC CONSTANTS

A **constant** is a named item that retains the same value throughout the execution of a program. VBA frequently requires the use of integer values that have some particular meaning. These values are **intrinsic constants**; they make programming easier for the developer and facilitate program maintenance. For example, the MsgBox function returns the value seven when a user clicks a No button displayed in a MsgBox. A programmer is not required to remember this value, however, because Access supplies an intrinsic constant named vbNo that has the value of seven. So, instead of comparing the value returned by the MsgBox function with the value seven to determine whether a user clicked a No button, a programmer can simply compare the value returned by the MsgBox function to the intrinsic constant named vbNo. The programmer does not need to memorize this value (or hundreds of others), and the code is easier to understand, too.

In contrast to an intrinsic constant, a **symbolic constant** is a constant that is defined by the programmer (as opposed to the intrinsic ones predefined by Access). A symbolic constant retains a constant value throughout the execution of a procedure. It is similar to a variable except that its value is specified as soon as the constant is declared. Symbolic constants assign a meaningful name to some value that is used throughout a procedure. Meaningful names facilitate long-term maintenance of the procedure. The syntax for declaring a symbolic constant is as follows:

Syntax

[**Public**|**Private**] **Const** *ConstantName* As *DataType* = *value*

Syntax Dissection

- [**Public**|**Private**] indicates the scope of the constant. Public constants can be used by procedures located in other modules. Private constants can be used only in the procedure or module where they are declared.

- **Const** indicates that a constant is being declared.

- *ConstantName* is the name of the constant. The name must obey the variable naming rules. The tag "con" should be used as a prefix to the constant name to facilitate maintenance of the application.

- *DataType* specifies how the data will be stored. Its values are the same as those for a variable declaration.

- The *value* argument indicates the permanent value of the constant.

Examples of symbolic constant declarations can be found in the Declarations section of the basUtilities module in the MU-DSci application, as shown in Figure 7-5. The Public keyword makes them available to all procedures throughout the application.

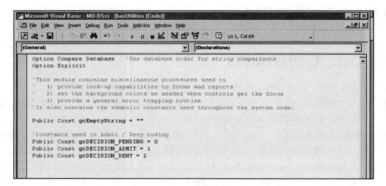

Figure 7-5   Public constants in the Declarations section of the basUtilities module

Declaring a Constant for Double Quotes

Earlier in this chapter, you used the Chr(34) function in cboLimitSemester_AfterUpdate. Unless someone knows that Chr(34) is a double quote (that is, the character formed from two consecutive apostrophes), the string expressions using this function are confusing. This problem may make future maintenance of the code difficult. To alleviate this problem, a symbolic constant can be declared and used instead.

To create and use a symbolic constant for double quotes:

1. Display the **Declarations** section of the basUtilities module.

2. Type the following code in the Declarations section:

```
'Declare DblQuote to equal a double quote
Public Const gcDblQuote = """"
```

   VBA recognizes four quotes in a row to be equal to one double quote.

3. From the **Debug** menu, select **Compile SwimReg**, save the code and close Visual Basic, and then display the code for **frmClassesBrief**.

4. Replace **Chr(34)** in cboLimitSemester_AfterUpdate with the constant **gcDblQuote** in both places, save the procedures, and then close the Visual Basic window.

5. Open **frmClassesBrief** in Form view to verify that the semester filter works correctly, and then save and close frmClassesBrief.

The Declarations section can be used for more than declaring variables. It is also a good place to document the purpose of the procedures within a module. Documentation is a vital component of any well-developed application. In the next section, we'll discuss how a programmer can influence how Access processes certain situations.

CONTROLLING PROCESSING IN THE DECLARATIONS SECTION

The Declarations section may declare certain rules that govern how Access analyzes and executes your code. It is usually the first section to appear when you enter the Design view of a module.

One statement for controlling processing is the **Option Compare** statement, which is automatically included in the Declarations section. This statement defines the default method to use when comparing text data. The general form is as follows:

Syntax

Option Compare *Method*

Syntax Dissection

- *Method* is Binary, Text, or Database.

- If a programmer specifies the **Binary** method, comparisons will be case-sensitive. When comparisons are case-sensitive, a "K" is not considered equivalent to a "k". The relative order of characters under this setting is determined by the character's relative order of appearance in the ANSI character set.

- When a programmer specifies **Text**, comparisons will not be case-sensitive. In this case, "K" will be considered equivalent to "k". The relative order of characters is based on the Country setting in the International section of the Microsoft Windows Control Panel.

- The **Database** option is the comparison method included automatically by Access. This approach compares text based on the characters' relative positions according to the sort order specified when the database was created or compacted. The Options window displayed from the Tools menu of the Database window illustrates the possible sort orders (look under the General tab).

If the Declarations section of the module containing the procedure contains an **Option Explicit** statement, variables must be explicitly defined prior to their use. If the Declarations section does not contain an Option Explicit statement, variables do not need to be declared before they are used. That is, any legal and unrecognized word used in an expression is assumed to be a variable. This approach is a dangerous practice, however. Misspelled variables and constants can produce unexpected results.

Option Explicit is automatically placed in the Declarations section of new modules. When it is used, the compiler activated when the programmer clicks Compile Loaded Modules finds undeclared variable names.

Chapter Summary

❏ VBA statements are written inside function procedures, sub procedures, and property procedures. All three types of procedures are stored in modules.

❏ Standard modules can contain functions and sub procedures and are loaded into memory as soon as the application opens. Form and report class modules can contain all three types of procedures, as can independent class modules.

❏ Functions differ from sub procedures in two ways. First, a function returns a value. Second, a function has an associated data type. Although a sub procedure can usually be written to perform any action that a function performs, a function should be written in cases where a value is being returned.

❏ All procedures may have arguments. Argument values can be passed by reference or by value. When arguments are passed by reference, changes made to the value passed into the procedure are reflected in the environment where the procedure was originally invoked. Arguments that are passed by value make a copy of the actual argument value available to the procedure. Although changes may be made to the copy passed into the procedure, these changes are not carried back into the environment that invoked the procedure.

❏ Variables can be local, meaning they are available only to the procedure in which they are declared, or they can be public, available everywhere. Variables are usually available only while the code in which they have been declared is executing. Afterward, they are deleted from memory unless they have been declared as static. Variables may be declared as one of a number of different data types.

❏ Access also provides for arrays, which are collections of indexed variables with a common name, and user-defined types, which allow programmers to create their own data structures. In addition, Access allows users to define constants. Constants help make the program code more understandable. Finally, Access allows the programmer to control processing in the Declarations section.

Review Questions

1. What is the difference between an independent class module and a form or report class module?

2. A standard module cannot contain declarations. True or False?

3. What are the roles of the Declarations section?

4. How is DoCmd related to a macro action?

5. What VBA statement is equivalent to the Condition column in a macro?

6. What is the difference between a function and a sub procedure?

7. Independent class modules must be connected to a form or a report. True or False?

8. What is the difference between passing arguments by reference and passing them by value?

9. A(n) _____ procedure defines a property that is attached to an object through dot notation.

10. When should a Variant data type be used?

11. Write the statements that make the following declarations:

    a. A function named Taxes takes one argument, Value. Taxes returns a Currency value. Value is Currency that is passed by value.

    b. A variable named FullName is a string variable.

    c. A variable named ZipCode can be used by any module in an application. ZipCode is a string variable.

    d. A variable named CurrentBalance is a Currency value. It should maintain an accurate current value even when the procedure in which it is declared is not being executed.

12. What is an array?

13. Write a statement that defines a private array that holds a maximum of 10 integers. The values correspond to the project IDs of projects under construction during the current month.

14. The _____ keyword specifies that a sub procedure will be sent the address of an argument's value.

    a. ByParam

    b. ByRef

    c. ByData

    d. ByValue

15. What is an intrinsic constant?

16. Use Access Help find the intrinsic constant used to specify that a form should be open in read-only mode.

17. How is a Property Let procedure invoked?

18. What is the difference between a built-in function and an API procedure?

19. True or False? Property Let supplies a property's value on request.

20. What is the purpose of Option Explicit?

HANDS-ON PROJECTS

Project 7-1

Natural Parent International.   One more library procedure must be created for NPI's application. This procedure verifies that a book is not being checked out prior to the book's return to the library. That is, two members cannot check out the same book at the same time. This situation may occur when a leader or librarian (designated by the leader) forgets to update the system for a book return.

After this procedure is developed, a new section of the program will be created. A form will be developed that facilitates entry of program information. Program information includes the title of the program and the program's location. Location information should be entered automatically based on the previous entry. For example, if the previous entry was in the city of Racine, the default city for the next entry is Racine. The defaults for the series and program numbers should be developed as well. If the program number is less than 4, the default series is the same as the last record entered. If the program number is equal to 4, the default series is 1 plus the previous series number. The program numbers are incremented by 1 until 4 is reached. After 4, by default the next program is 1.

Complete these steps:

1. Open **NPI.mdb**. Create an event procedure in frmCheckOut that verifies that a book to be loaned is not currently recorded as being checked out. You will need to use DCount or DLookup to determine whether the book has not been returned. If the book is supposedly checked out, a message box should ask the user whether the book should be checked out anyway. If the user answers "No," the Update event should be canceled.

2. Create a "tabular" (Single Form) form named **frmProgram** that uses tblProgram as its record source. Typically, all programs in a series are entered in one sitting. These programs are often located at the same address. Write procedures that set the default values of the address, city, and state. These default values should equal the values that were entered in the previous record. Default values will not exist when frmProgram first opens. Consider using module-level variables and an AfterUpdate procedure to create this feature. The default value can be set in a number of ways. For example, the default value property can be set equal to a function (=DefaultCity()) that returns the correct value. The default value property could also be set in the OnCurrent event procedure.

3. Place the following function in the class module of frmProgram:

```
Private Function DefaultSeries() As Long
'Determine the Default Series
Dim plngLastSeries As Long
Dim pintLastProgram As Integer
Dim pstrCriteria As String
'Nz returns a one when DMax returns a Null
plngLastSeries = Nz(DMax("SeriesNo", "tblProgram"), 1)
pstrCriteria = "[SeriesNo] = " & plngLastSeries
```

```
'Nz returns a zero when DMax returns a Null
pintLastProgram = Nz(DMax("ProgramNo", "tblProgram"), 0)
If pintLastProgram = 4 Then
    DefaultSeries = plngLastSeries + 1
Else
    DefaultSeries = plngLastSeries
End If
End Function
```

4. Type **=DefaultSeries()** in the Default Value property of the Series Number text box.

5. Create a function that calculates the default program number. This function is similar to, but has fewer lines of code than, the DefaultProgram function. The DMax criteria should reference the Series Number text box. The DMax function should be placed inside the Nz function. DMax will return a Null value when the series number text box refers to a series value that does not yet have a program saved in tblProgram.

6. Save your work.

Project 7-2

Metropolitan Performing Arts Company. The sales portion of the MPAC system will determine the total due and record the method of payment. The frmPerformanceDateSeats form and the frmSales form must be opened to record a sale. Specific requirements of the system include the following:

❏ frmPerformanceDateSeats should not allow edits of the seat status unless frmSales is open and displays a record that has the ApprovalCode equal to Pending. The appropriate back styles should be used to signal the enabled and locked status of the cboStatus control.

❏ When the status of a seat is changed to unavailable, the price of the seat should be added to the total in frmSales. In addition, the order number from frmSales should be placed in the subform of frmPerformanceDateSeasts.

❏ When the status of a seat is changed from unavailable to available or complimentary, the price of the seat should be subtracted from the total in frmSales (this change indicates that a customer has changed his or her mind). This operation is allowed only when OrderID in the subform is equal to OrderID in frmSales.

Complete these steps:

1. Open **MPA.mdb**. Change the properties of frmPerformanceDateSeats and frmSeatsAvailableSubform so that edits, deletions, and additions are not allowed. Also, change the BackStyle properties of the controls to provide a visual indication to the user that a change cannot be made.

2. Create a private subprocedure called **SupportEdits** that modifies the properties of the subform and any relevant controls to allow changes to be made. Create another subprocedure called **StopEdits** that modifies these properties so that edits are not allowed.

3. Create a property procedure called **AllowStatusEdit**. When the value received by the property is equal to True, SupportEdits should be invoked. When AllowStatusEdit is equal to False, StopEdits should be invoked.

4. Place the following code in the Open event procedure of frmPerformanceDateSeats:

```
Private Sub Form_Open(Cancel As Integer)
'If frmSales is open and ApprovalCode is Pending, edits are
'supported
    If CurrentProject.AllForms("frmSales").IsLoaded Then
        If Forms![frmSales]![txtApprovalCode] = _
        "Pending" Then
            SupportEdits 'Call the procedure
        End If
    End If
End Sub
```

5. Create a sub procedure in frmSales called **UpdateSeatEditStatus**. The code should set the value of the frmPerformanceDateSeats property, AllowStatusEdit. The value set by the code should depend on the current value of txtApprovalCode.

6. Create a button on frmSales and name it **cmdStart**. Place the following code in the OnClick event procedure, which causes Access to save the record. The record must be saved so that edited records in frmSeatsAvailableSubform do not experience a foreign key violation.

```
Private Sub cmdStart_Click()
    If Not Me.NewRecord Then
        DoCmd.GoToRecord acDataForm, "frmSales", acNewRec
    End if
    Me.txtApprovalCode = "Pending"
    DoCmd.RunCommand acCmdSaveRecord
    IfCurrentProject.AllForms_
            ("frmPerformanceDateSeats").IsLoaded Then
        UpdateSeatEditStatus
    End If
End Sub
```

7. Modify the current event procedure of frmSales so that UpdateSeatEditStatus is called. You will need to test whether frmPerformanceDateSeats is open.

8. Write code for the BeforeUpdate event procedure for cboStatus in frmSeatsAvailableSubform. The update from unavailable to available (or complimentary) should not be allowed unless the order IDs in frmSales and frmSeatsAvailableSubform match. You may need to use the OldValue property of a combo box.

9. Write code that adds the price of a seat to the total field in frmSales. This code will be triggered by an AfterUpdate event for cboStatus. To facilitate data entry, cboStatus should be set to unavailable whenever the user double-clicks the combo box. The total should be decreased when the status changes from unavailable to available or complimentary. You will need to use the OldValue property of a combo box. In addition, your code may need to use the DoCmd.RunCommand acCmdSaveRecord statement within this procedure. Be sure to test your procedure under a variety of circumstances. Verify that the total is being calculated correctly.

10. Save your work.

Project 7-3

Foreign Language Institute System. A database application should respond to conditions reflected in the data stored in the database. The users of the FLI system need to know when customers have called in more than two technical complaints about a product. This product may need to be reviewed and modified before further sales occur.

You can enhance the FLI system to alert users when a product has three or more technical complaints. This condition can be detected by counting the number of calls in the database for the product that are in the technical complaint category and displaying an appropriate label on the frmProducts form if necessary.

Complete these steps:

1. Open **FLI.mdb**. Create a label on the form that reads: **X technical complaints exist concerning this product**. Name the label **lblWarning**. Make the text red or some other attention-grabbing color.

2. Set OnCurrent to **[Event Procedure]**, and then add the following code to the OnCurrent event for the form:

```
Dim intTechCalls As Integer
intTechCalls = DCount("[CallID]", "tblCalls", _
 "[ProductID]=" & Me![txtProductID] & " AND [CallCategory]=3")
If intTechCalls > 2 Then
      'display warning if >2 technical calls
    Me![lblWarning].Caption = intTechCalls & _
     " technical complaints exist concerning this product."
    Me![lblWarning].Visible = True
Else
    Me![lblWarning].Visible = False
    End If
```

3. The next enhancement will standardize the error messages that appear to the user. A general error-processing routine is needed. Write the following code in a general module and save the module as **basUtilities**:

```
Sub ErrorTrap(ErrorLoc As String)
    Dim strRLF As String, strMsg As String
    Const L1 = "An error occurred in "
    Const L2 = "This is a program error."
    Const L3 = "A change is needed in the program code."
    Const L4 = "Contact your system administrator."
    strRLF = Chr(13) & Chr(10)     'Return and line feed
    strMsg = L1 & ErrorLoc & "." & strRLF & L2 & strRLF & _
     L3 & strRLF & L4
    MsgBox strMsg, vbOKOnly + vbCritical + vbDefaultButton1, _
     "Error trapped in code."
End Sub
```

4. Save your work.

Project 7-4

King William Hotel System. A database application should respond to conditions reflected in the data stored in the database. The users of the King William Hotel system need to know when a customer is about to check into a room that needs cleaning or is otherwise unavailable. The King William clerk can then change the assigned room or otherwise accommodate the customer by offering a free snack in the cafe while the room is prepared for occupancy.

You can enhance the King William Hotel system to alert users when a room needs cleaning or is unavailable. This condition can be detected by looking at the room's attributes in the database and displaying an appropriate label on the frmCheckIn form if necessary.

Complete these steps:

1. Open **KWH.mdb**. Create a label on frmCheckIn that reads: **Room needs cleaning or is unavailable**. Name the label **lblWarning**. Make the text red.

2. Set OnCurrent to **[Event Procedure]**, and then add the following code to the OnCurrent event for the form:

```
Dim blnWarning As Boolean
'Display warning if room needs cleaning or is unavailable
blnWarning = DLookup("[NeedsCleaning]", "tblRoom", _
     "[RoomNo]=" & Me![RoomNo]) Or _
     DLookup("[Unavailable]", "tblRoom", "[RoomNo]=" & _
     Me![RoomNo])
lblWarning.Visible = blnWarning
```

3. Write the following code in a general module and name the module **basUtilities**:

```
Sub ErrorTrap(ErrorLoc As String)
    Dim strRLF As String, strMsg As String
    Const L1 = "An error occurred in "
    Const L2 = "This is a program error."
    Const L3 = "A change is needed in the program code."
    Const L4 = "Contact your system administrator."
     strRLF = Chr(13) & Chr(10)      'Return and line feed
     strMsg = L1 & ErrorLoc & "." & strRLF & L2 & strRLF & _
          L3 & strRLF & L4
     MsgBox strMsg, vbOKOnly + vbCritical + vbDefaultButton1, _
          "Error trapped in code."
    End Sub
```

4. Save your work.

Project 7-5

Workers' Compensation Commission System. A database application should respond to conditions reflected in the data stored in the database. The users of the WCC system need to know when a patient has been admitted more than two times. This patient may be trying to take advantage of the workers' compensation laws.

You can enhance the WCC system to alert users when a patient has more than two admissions. This condition can be detected by counting the number of Form As in the database for the patient and displaying an appropriate label on the frmPatients form if necessary.

Complete these steps:

1. Open **WCC.mdb**. Create a label on the form that reads: **Patient has X admissions in the system**. Name the label **lblWarning**. Make the text red or some other attention-grabbing color.

2. Set OnCurrent to **[Event Procedure]**, and then add the following code to the OnCurrent event for the form:

```
Dim intA As Integer
intA = DCount ("[Medical Record Number]", "tblWCCA", _
    "[Medical Record Number]='" & _
    Me![txtMedicalRecordNumber] & "'")
'Notify user if patient has > 2 prior admissions
If intA > 2 Then
admissions
    Me![lblWarning].Visible = True
    Me![lblWarning].Caption = "Patient has " & intA & _
    " admissions in the system."
Else
    Me![lblWarning].Visible = False
End If
```

3. Write the following code in a general module and save the module as **basUtilities**:

```
Sub ErrorTrap(ErrorLoc As String)
    Dim strRLF As String, strMsg As String
    Const L1 = "An error occurred in "
    Const L2 = "This is a program error."
    Const L3 = "A change is needed in the program code."
    Const L4 = "Contact your system administrator."
    strRLF = Chr(13) & Chr(10)     'Return and line feed
    strMsg = L1 & ErrorLoc & "." & _
      strRLF & L2 & strRLF & L3 & _
      strRLF & L4
    MsgBox strMsg, vbOKOnly + vbCritical + vbDefaultButton1,_
      "Error trapped in code."
End Sub
```

4. Save your work.

8

OBJECT-BASED PROGRAMMING
IN VBA

Effective Use of Object Variables and Methods

In this chapter you will:

- ♦ Declare and use object variables
- ♦ Create procedures that use built-in form methods
- ♦ Find and manipulate data with recordset objects
- ♦ Execute parameter queries in VBA
- ♦ Communicate with other applications with Automation objects
- ♦ Find methods through the Object Browser
- ♦ Create class modules
- ♦ Open multiple form instances with user-defined objects
- ♦ Describe the features of a well-designed, object-based application

---

Creating and using objects are fundamental operations in Visual Basic for Applications (VBA). Programmers use properties of objects to change the user interface. In addition to properties, objects possess methods. Methods perform actions, such as opening forms, changing the cursor location, and deleting records. Access provides more than 100 built-in methods.

To develop applications that perform actions for an end user, Access application developers must understand the most widely used built-in methods. They must also take advantage of Access Help and the Object Browser to find other methods that may be necessary to meet the special needs of a particular application. In addition, to build easy-to-maintain systems, Access developers must understand the philosophy of object-based programming and recognize how to create their own user-defined objects and methods.

This chapter explores object-based programming in VBA. The concept of a method is introduced, objects are identified with object variables, and commonly used built-in methods are explored in detail. The chapter also explores the Object Browser, which allows less commonly used methods—including methods from other Windows applications (that is, Automation objects)—to be identified. Finally, the chapter describes user-defined objects and methods and explains how these concepts can be used in a "well-designed" Access application.

THE WORLD ACCORDING TO METHODS

Access uses objects and properties because people understand and use objects and properties in their daily lives and thus can easily apply the concepts to programming. For example, people recognize that a car is an object. They also recognize that a car object has color, seating capacity, and a current speed—all of which are properties.

Access uses methods to take this analogy one step further. A **method** is a procedure or action that belongs to an object. For example, a particular car not only has a current speed property, but can also stop and accelerate. Stopping and accelerating are methods that are associated with the car object.

You can use the following notation to refer to the Year property of a car: Cars("Bob's Car").Year. In this notation, "Cars" is the collection, "Bob's Car" is the object, and "Year" is the property. As with properties, programmers use dot notation to invoke a method. The following are examples in our hypothetical, non-Access, "car" world:

```
Cars("Bob's Car").Stop
Cars("Bob's Car").AccelerateToSpeed:=65, Rate:=5
pintHowOld = Cars("Bob's Car").Age
Cars("Bob's Car").ReleaseAirBag
```

The first example causes "Bob's Car" to stop. The second example invokes a method that uses arguments—"Bob's Car" is to accelerate to 65 mph at a rate of 5 mph/second. The third example invokes a method that calculates the age of the car. The final example demonstrates a method that influences objects other than "Bob's Car"; ReleaseAirBag not only changes properties of "Bob's Car," but also influences the body position property of a driver object.

Once you understand the "Bob's Car" example, you can extend the analogy into the Access world. In that world, the objects used in VBA correspond to Microsoft Access, ADO, and DAO objects, and methods correspond to actions of these objects.

Overview of Access Methods

Like the methods just illustrated, Access methods perform actions. The syntax for invoking a method is similar to the dot notation syntax for a property:

Syntax

Object.Method [[*ArgumentName1* :=]*argument1*] [,[*ArgumentName2* :=] *argument2*] [,[*ArgumentName* :=] *argument*] [,...]]

Syntax Dissection

- *Object* is any valid object.

- *Method* is any valid method for that object.

- The *argument* is a value that programmers pass to the method for processing. When the method returns a value, parentheses must be placed around the list of arguments. Similar to the syntax of a function or procedure call, arguments must be placed in order, separated by commas.

- Alternatively, *ArgumentName* followed by := can precede an argument. In that case, the arguments can be provided in any order.

MU-DSci uses methods in many procedures. For instance, the NewDegreeType procedure in the basUtilities module in Figure 8-1 has five methods. A user invokes this procedure whenever he or she types a degree type into a combo box that is not currently stored in the tblDegreeTypes table (that is, the NotInList event is activated). The procedure then asks the user whether the newly entered degree type should be placed in tblDegreeTypes. If the user answers Yes, the degree type is added. If the user answers No, the degree type is not added. Degree type combo boxes are displayed in frmProspects and frmCurrentStudents.

```
Sub NewDegreeType(NewData As String, Response As Integer)
'This routine enables entry of a new degree type in the
'Degree Types table.


    Dim pstrTitle As String

    Dim pstrMessage As String

    Dim pctrCurrentField As Control

    Dim cnn As ADODB.Connection

    Dim  prstDegreeTypes As ADODB.Recordset


'Remember which combo box has the control. This allows the
'routine to be used for any combo box on the form that references
'Degree Types.
    Set pctrCurrentField = Screen.ActiveControl


'If user has deleted an old entry, just clear field and return
    If NewData = "" Then

        pctrCurrentField.Value = Null

        Response = acDataErrContinue

        Exit Sub

    End If
```

Figure 8-1 NewDegreeType procedure

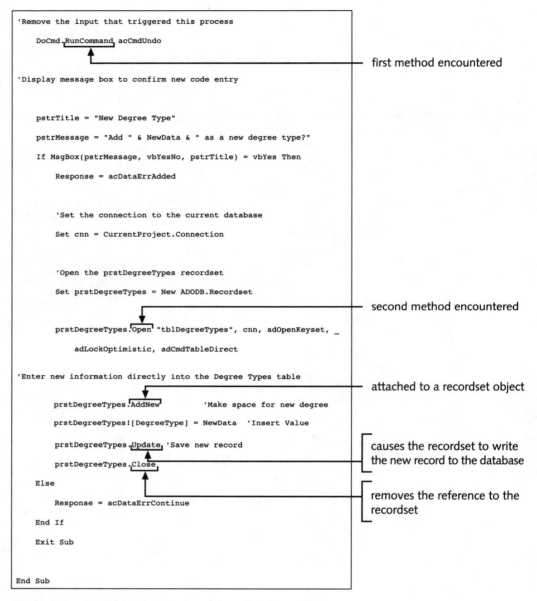

```
'Remove the input that triggered this process
    DoCmd.RunCommand acCmdUndo                                    ─── first method encountered

'Display message box to confirm new code entry

    pstrTitle = "New Degree Type"
    pstrMessage = "Add " & NewData & " as a new degree type?"
    If MsgBox(pstrMessage, vbYesNo, pstrTitle) = vbYes Then
        Response = acDataErrAdded


        'Set the connection to the current database
        Set cnn = CurrentProject.Connection


        'Open the prstDegreeTypes recordset
        Set prstDegreeTypes = New ADODB.Recordset
                                                                  ─── second method encountered

        prstDegreeTypes.Open "tblDegreeTypes", cnn, adOpenKeyset, _
            adLockOptimistic, adCmdTableDirect

'Enter new information directly into the Degree Types table
                                                                  ─── attached to a recordset object
        prstDegreeTypes.AddNew           'Make space for new degree
        prstDegreeTypes![DegreeType] = NewData   'Insert Value
        prstDegreeTypes.Update  'Save new record                  ─── causes the recordset to write
        prstDegreeTypes.Close                                         the new record to the database
    Else
        Response = acDataErrContinue                              ─── removes the reference to the
                                                                      recordset
    End If
    Exit Sub


End Sub
```

Figure 8-1 NewDegreeType procedure (continued)

Note the following facts about the methods:

- The first method encountered in the procedure is RunCommand. Like most DoCmd methods, RunCommand is similar to the RunCommand macro action. **DoCmd.RunCommand acCmdUndo** erases the user's most recent entry from the form.

- The second method is Open. When Open is applied to a recordset object, the recordset can access data in the table or query that is specified in the Source argument.

- The AddNew method (that is, prstDegreeTypes.AddNew) is attached to a record-set object. AddNew is an example of a method that performs an action on the object; it causes a recordset to create space for a new record.

- Related to the AddNew method, the Update method causes the recordset to write the new record to the database.

- The Close method (that is, prstDegreeTypes.Close) removes the reference to the recordset. The NewDegreeType sub procedure will be explained in more detail throughout the chapter.

OBJECT VARIABLES

You have seen that objects have methods. To invoke a method, the associated object must be referenced. The dot and bang notations allow the identification of specific forms, reports, controls, tables, or fields. These same notations can also be used when invoking a method. For example, to set the focus to the txtAreaCode control located in the frmQDrops sub-form of frmStudentQDrops, you can use the following notation:

```
Forms![frmStudentQDrops]![frmQDrops].Form![txtAreaCode] _
.SetFocus
```

Consider the following syntax:

Syntax

*Object.***SetFocus**

Syntax Dissection

- The **SetFocus** method places the cursor in a form or control.

- *Object* is a reference to any form or control that can receive the focus; that is, the object's Enabled property must equal True.

Dot and bang notations have two disadvantages:

- First, as evident in the preceding code, dot and bang notations can be long. From the typing and ease-of-reading standpoints, it would be nice to abbreviate the syntax.

■ Second, when used repeatedly, dot and bang notations are not very efficient. Each time VBA encounters the notation, it locates the object or property by following the path of the notation from left to right. In the code shown earlier, VBA first finds the Forms collection, and then finds the frmStudentQDrops form. Next, it locates the subform control frmQDrops, and then finds txtAreaCode in the Controls collection of frmQDrops. This process is repeated each time this syntax is encountered.

In contrast to dot and bang notations, VBA can use object variables. **Object variables** are variables used in VBA procedures that contain a pointer (that is, reference) to the item of interest. Once the object variable is set, the path to the object need not be retraced. In addition to providing an efficient reference to Access application objects, object variables must be used to reference DAO and ADO objects.

Declaring and Setting Object Variables

Declaration statements declare variables as String, Long, Integer, and so on. The VBA statements are similar to those found in many other procedural languages. In VBA, however, the data types used in declaration statements can also include objects. Programmers can declare variables that will point to objects, as shown in the following syntax:

Syntax

DeclarationType VariableName[([*subscripts*])] [**As** [**New**] *ObjectType*]

Syntax Dissection

■ *DeclarationType* refers to Dim, Public, Private, or Static statements.

■ *VariableName* is any valid variable name. As with variables in other languages, VBA programmers commonly use name prefixes to facilitate the identification of the variable's object type.

■ The *subscripts* argument declares an array.

■ *ObjectType* is any valid object, including an ADO object, DAO object, or Microsoft Access object. If DAO and ADO objects are used in the same application, the object type must be prefixed with ADODB to refer to objects in the standard ADO library, with ADOX to refer to the extended ADO library (for creating new tables, for example), with JRO to refer to replication objects, and with DAO to refer to DAO objects. *ObjectType* can refer to specific types of controls, such as TextBox, ComboBox, and Label.

■ An object variable can also be declared generically as an **Object** (for example, Dim pobjX As Object); it can then contain any type of object. Just as Variant type variables are less efficient than a more specific data type, Object type variables are not as efficient as more specific object types.

■ **New** causes Access to create a new object of the type declared in *ObjectType* the first time the variable is used. When the object is created, a value is placed in the *VariableName* that points to the object type. New can also be used in the Set statement (discussed next). Access runs more efficiently when New is used in the Set statement.

In most cases, once you declare an object variable, you will want to assign a value to the variable. Programmers use the Set statement to assign a value.

Syntax

Set *VariableName* = [[**New**] *ObjectExpression* | **Nothing**]

Syntax Dissection

- The **Set** statement assigns a value to the *VariableName*. The value is a pointer to the same object identified by the *ObjectExpression*.

- *VariableName* identifies an object variable or property. Like other variables, object variables should be defined in a declaration statement (for example, Dim, Public) prior to their use.

- *ObjectExpression* refers to dot or bang notation, an object variable, a function, or a method that returns an object. The object returned by *ObjectExpression* must have an object type that is consistent with the object type of *VariableName*.

- **New** creates a new instance of an object. The pointer assigned to *VariableName* identifies the new instance. If a variable is defined with the New keyword in a declaration statement, the Set statement should not be used.

- **Nothing** discontinues the association between *VariableName* and any previously assigned object. Its use releases the memory used to store the reference to the object.

In the following example of object declaration and Set statements, the object variable pctrArea points to txtAreaCode.

```
Dim pctrArea As Control
Set pctrArea = _
Forms![frmStudentQDrops]![frmQDrops].Form![txtAreaCode]
```

As a result of these statements, pctrArea could be used anywhere that Forms![frmStudentQDrops]![frmQDrops].Form![txtAreaCode] is used. For example, the statement

```
pctrArea.SetFocus
```

sets the focus to Forms![frmStudentQDrops]![frmQDrops].Form![txtAreaCode]. In addition, a new value can be displayed in txtAreaCode with

```
pctrArea = "ACCT"
```

Another Technique for Setting Object Variables

Figure 8-1 demonstrates a slightly different technique for setting object variables. The following nonadjacent lines from Figure 8-1 declare a control object variable and then set

the object variable to the control that currently has the focus. This control is identified by
the ActiveControl property of the Screen object.

```
Dim pctrCurrentField As Control
Set pctrCurrentField = Screen.ActiveControl
```

Programmers use this technique when a procedure can work with whatever control
has the focus. In the code in Figure 8-1, several forms use a cboDegreeType combo box.
Consequently, this code will work with a combo box regardless of the form.

Besides using Dim and Set statements to define and set the values of object variables, programmers can define object variables as formal arguments in the sub and function statements. They pass references to objects when a procedure invokes the subroutine or function.
For example, the following statements could be used to create a cyan-colored background
in a control:

```
Sub Cyan_Background(pctrCurrent as Control)
    pctrCurrent.BackColor = RGB(0, 255, 255)
End Sub

Private Sub txtFirstName_GotFocus()
    Cyan_Background Me!txtFirstName
End Sub
```

BUILT-IN METHODS RELATED TO MICROSOFT ACCESS OBJECTS

Now that you know the basics of methods and variables, it is time to turn your attention to
Microsoft Access objects. These objects—which include forms, reports, and applications—
support many built-in methods. Some objects—such as forms, reports, and independent class
modules—also support the creation of custom methods.

Any public subroutine or function that belongs to a form, report, or independent class module is considered a method of its associated object (that is, a method of the form, report, or
independent class module). The syntax for invoking custom methods is exactly the same as
the syntax for invoking built-in methods.

As you investigate the built-in methods used by Microsoft Access objects, it is important to
remember that Access, like any development environment, continues to evolve with each
new version. Access still possesses remnants of its non-object-based past. If you cannot find
a built-in method to perform a certain task, a built-in function may handle it. In addition,
check the methods of the DoCmd object, which contains many methods that manipulate
other objects. We'll look at these methods next.

DoCmd Methods

The DoCmd object is an unusual object: It is never manipulated by its methods, but those
methods frequently manipulate another object. For example, the OpenForm and OpenReport
methods with which you are already familiar open forms and reports, respectively.

A DoCmd method exists for almost every action that can be selected from a macro's action column. The method's name matches a macro action, and the method's arguments usually correspond to the macro's action arguments. A method associated with another object sometimes performs the same operations as a DoCmd method. For example, DoCmd.GoToControl and a control's SetFocus method both move the cursor to a specified control.

You should avoid using DoCmd methods whenever another similar method can serve the same purpose because form, report, and control methods are more efficient. Table 8-1 lists several DoCmd methods that do not have an equivalent form, control, or report method.

Table 8-1   Commonly used DoCmd methods

DoCmd Method	Operation	Example	Notes
ApplyFilter [*FilterName*] [,*WhereCondition*]	Sets a filter on a form	DoCmd.ApplyFilter, "[SID] = [Forms]! [CurrentStudent]! [SIDEntry]"	*FilterName* is the name of the query, and *WhereCondition* is a string that specifies an SQL WHERE condition. Triggers the ApplyFilter event. The Filter and FilterOn properties of a form can be used instead of this method.
Close [*ObjectType*, *ObjectName*], [*Save*]	Closes an open form, report, table, or query	DoCmd.Close acForm, "frmProspects"	*ObjectType* is an intrinsic constant that specifies the type of object, *ObjectName* is a string that indicates the name of the object, and *Save* is an intrinsic constant that indicates whether the object should be saved. Closes the active form when arguments are not provided. Will trigger Close, Unload, LostFocus, and Deactivate events.

8

Table 8-1   Commonly used DoCmd methods (continued)

DoCmd Method	Operation	Example	Notes
FindRecord *FindWhat* [, *Match*][, *MatchCase*][, *Search*][, *SearchAsFormatted*][, *OnlyCurrentField*][, *FindFirst*]	Finds a record in a form	DoCmd.FindRecord [Forms]! [CurrentStudent]! [SIDEntry]	*FindWhat* is an expression that indicates the value to find, *Match* indicates the part of the field to search, *MatchCase* specifies whether the search is case-sensitive, *Search* specifies the direction of the search, *SearchAsFormatted* specifies whether to search the field as it is formatted on the screen or as it is stored in the database, *OnlyCurrentField* indicates the fields to search, and *FindFirst* specifies where to start the search.
GoToRecord [*ObjectType*, *ObjectName*][, *Record*][, *Offset*]	Moves to another record	DoCmd.GoToRecord acNewRec	*ObjectType* and *ObjectName* indicate the type and name of object that contains the record, respectively, *Record* is an intrinsic constant that indicates where the cursor should be placed, and *Offset* is an integer that indicates the absolute or relative record number. Triggers a Current event.
Maximize	Maximizes a form	DoCmd.Maximize	
OpenForm *FormName*[, *View*][, *FilterName*][, *WhereCondition*][, *DataMode*][, *WindowMode*][, *OpenArgs*]	Opens a form	DoCmd.OpenForm "frmProspects", , , "[StudentID] = '111-22-3333'", , "IDWindow"	The first six arguments are the same as the macro's arguments. *OpenArgs* is used to pass data to the opened form. The value of *OpenArgs* is placed in the object's OpenArgs property. OpenForm triggers Open and Load events.
OpenReport *ReportName* [, *View*] [, *FilterName*] [, *WhereCondition*]	Opens a report	DoCmd. OpenReport "rptStudent Data"	

Table 8-1   Commonly used DoCmd methods (continued)

DoCmd Method	Operation	Example	Notes
Printout [*PrintRange*][, *PageFrom, PageTo*][, *PrintQuality*][, *Copies*][, *CollateCopies*]	Prints the active object	DoCmd.Printout	
Restore	Restores a form to previous size	DoCmd.Restore	
RunCommand acCmdSelectRecord	Selects an entire record in a tabular form	DoCmd. RunCommand acCmdSelectRecord	Also a method of the Application object.
RunCommand acCmdDeleteRecord	Deletes a record in a form	DoCmd. RunCommand acCmdDeleteRecord	Also a method of the Application object.
RunCommand acCmdSaveRecord	Saves the current record in a form	DoCmd. RunCommand acCmdSaveRecord	Also a method of the Application object.
RunCommand acCmdSizeToFitForm	Resizes a form so that all controls are shown (resizes to fit form in Window menu)		Also a method of the Application object.
RunCommand acCmdUndo	Rolls back the changes in a control	DoCmd. RunCommand acCmdUndo	Also a method of the Application object.
ShowAllRecords	Removes a filter from a form	DoCmd. ShowAllRecords	

The RunCommand Method and Its Intrinsic Constants

As shown in Table 8-1, the action performed by the RunCommand method depends on the value of its command argument. Programmers use intrinsic constants to specify that value. An intrinsic constant exists for almost all of the controls listed in the Access built-in menu bars.

To prevent errors or to reduce the number of mouse clicks required to perform an operation, programmers sometimes create procedures that automatically perform several menu operations. As an example, consider the form frmStudentQDrops (see Figure 8-2). This form contains a subform that lists the dropped courses for a particular student. If special VBA code had not been written, the user would have been forced to click the record in the subform and then click the Delete Record command in the Edit menu. A user might forget to click the subform when he or she selects a student from the combo box and then notice that the record selector in the subform already points to the course he or she wishes to delete. If the user does not click the subform first, Access will attempt to delete the student rather than the course.

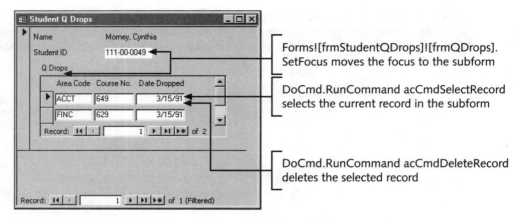

Figure 8-2   Deleting a record from frmStudentQDrops

The following sample VBA code sets the focus to the subform, selects the current record in the subform (if a record was not selected), and then deletes the record. A toolbar button that triggers the following code will cause Access to delete the class record identified by the record selector.

```
Public Function DeleteQDrop()
'Delete the current class in frmStudentQDrops
     Forms![frmStudentQDrops]![frmQDrops].SetFocus
     DoCmd.RunCommand acCmdSelectRecord
     DoCmd.RunCommand acCmdDeleteRecord
End Function
```

Other intrinsic constants can be found in the Object Browser and in Help. In Help, you should search for the RunCommand method and then click RunCommand Method Constants.

Form and Control Methods

Form and control objects support several methods related to the content and appearance of a form. Some of these methods keep displayed data up-to-date. The data shown on a form might not be current for at least three reasons:

- The recordset generated for the form may not reflect recent changes to the database. In Access terms, the recordset behind the form must be refreshed or requeried to reflect the recent changes. **Refreshing** a recordset refers to the process of updating the fields of all records currently in the recordset. Refreshing does not add records that are new to the database or delete records that should no longer be part of the recordset (that is, caused by Add and Delete operations carried out by another user or form). **Requerying** a form completely regenerates the recordset; that is, fields are updated and records are added and deleted.

- A calculated control (that is, a control that has an expression as its control source) may not recalculate its expression after the value of a control used in the expression changes. In Access terminology, the calculated control should be **recalculated**.

- The form may know the correct values that should be displayed, but because Access is executing other procedures, it does not have time to display the correct values on the screen. In Access terminology, the form needs **repainting**.

Figures 8-2 through 8-4, which are taken from MU-DSci application, graphically illustrate these concepts. In MU-DSci, the user opens frmStudentQDrops through frmCurrentStudents. The text box txtQDrop, located on frmCurrentsStudents, reflects the number of Q-dropped courses. After a course is added or deleted in frmStudentQDrops, txtQDrop will not reflect the correct number of Q Drops. That is, the recordset for frmCurrentStudents will no longer be current. This recordset must be requeried, the value in txtQDrop must be recalculated, and the new value must be repainted on the screen.

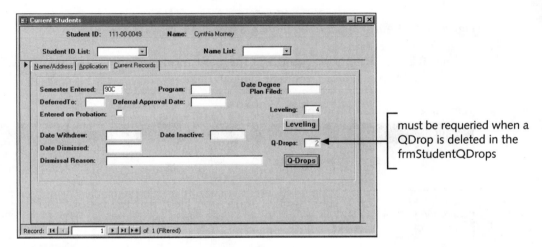

Figure 8-3 frmCurrentStudents and txtQDrops

Methods that Update Displayed Data

Access automatically refreshes, recalculates, and repaints forms at Access-defined intervals. The **refresh interval** is specified in the database's Options window. On occasion, however, the screen is not updated when the programmer or user desires. In such a case, the programmer can use a form's **Refresh** method to refresh the recordset, its **Recalc** method to cause a recalculation of the form's calculated controls, or its **Repaint** method to force the system to repaint the screen.

Unlike with the refreshing process, Access does not automatically requery the database after a specified interval. Instead, you must use the **Requery** method to force Access to regenerate a recordset. Consequently, a Requery method is used in MU-DSci to force frmCurrentStudents to display the correct number of Q Drops. Combo boxes, list boxes, and text boxes that use domain aggregate functions can be requeried as well. Requerying causes the form to be refreshed, recalculated, and repainted. Similarly, refreshing causes recalculation and repainting.

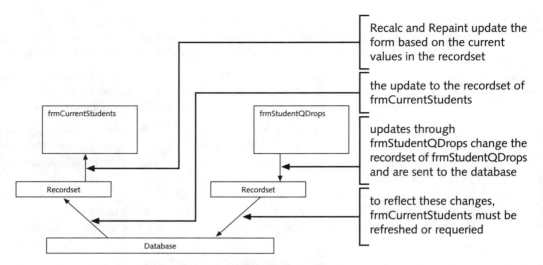

Figure 8-4   Refreshing and requerying a form

Besides Refresh, Recalc, Repaint, and Requery, forms and controls support several other methods. Table 8-2 summarizes these built-in methods.

Table 8-2   Form and control methods

Method	Operation	Applies to	Example	Notes
DropDown	Forces a combo box to drop down	Combo box control	Me![cboStudentID]. DropDown	Possibly used when combo box receives the focus
GoToPage *pagenumber*[, *right*][,*down*]	Moves the cursor to a specified page	Form	frmProspects.GoTo Page 2	Arguments are the same as the similar macro action
Recalc	Forces all controls to rerun the calculations listed in their control sources	Form	Forms! [frmProspects]. Recalc	The entire form must be recalculated
Refresh	Forces the form to update field values for all records in its recordset	Form	Me.Refresh	
Repaint	Causes the system to perform any pending screen updates	Form	Forms! [frmProspects]. Repaint	

Table 8-2   Form and control methods (continued)

Method	Operation	Applies to	Example	Notes
Requery	Causes the form to rerun the query that generates the recordset	Form, list box, combo box, subform controls	Me.Requery	If Requery is issued on a control other than the combo boxes, list boxes, or subforms, the entire form is requeried
SetFocus	Moves the cursor to a specified form or control	Form control	Me.txtSteet.SetFocus	Causes GotFocus and Enter events
SizetoFit	Resizes a control so that all of the text is displayed	Control	Me![txtStreet].SizeToFit	
Undo	Changes the value of the object back to a previous value	Form control	Forms![frmProspects].Undo	

Using the Requery Method to Update cboLessonIndex and frmRegistration

The Swim Lessons application requires at least two new procedures. First, VBA code should be written to update cboLessonIndex in the subform of frmRegistration. The frmRegistration form is used to register students for classes, and cboLessonIndex specifies the particular class. The row source of cboLessonIndex refers to the value in cboSemester and cboLevel, so that only classes that match the level indicated in cboLevel and the semester indicated in cboSemester are displayed. Currently, cboLessonIndex does not display the correct data when the Semester and Level combo boxes are updated (see Figure 8-5).

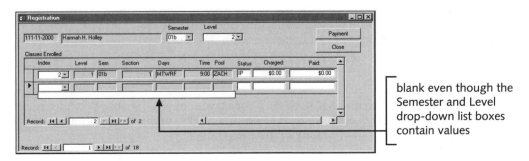

Figure 8-5   Need to requery cboLessonIndex in frmRegistration

To create code that requeries cboLessonIndex:

1. Start **Access**, open **SwimReg.mdb**, refresh the links, if necessary, and display **frmRegistration** in Form view.

2. Without selecting a semester or level, click the **Index drop-down list arrow** in the second row. A blank row should be displayed in the combo box.

3. Select a **semester** and a **level**. Click the **Index drop-down list arrow** again. A blank row is still displayed.

4. To remedy this problem, add the following line of code to the AfterUpdate event procedures for the form's cboSemester and cboLevel combo boxes:

```
Me!frmClassesEnrolled_subform.Form.cboLessonIndex.Requery
```

5. Save your work, and then close the Visual Basic window.

6. Open **frmRegistration** in Form view and test the code. The Index drop-down list box will contain different rows depending on the selected semester and level.

7. Close the form.

A similar problem occurs with the Allocations tab of frmPayment. After an allocation is made through frmProcessPayment, it is not immediately listed in frmPayment.

To create code that requeries the subform in frmPayment:

1. Open **frmStudent** in Form view, and then find **Jenny First**. Click the **Payment** button. Advance to a new payment record, and then type **$30** as the amount paid. Note the payment number for reference.

2. Click the **Process Payment** button, and then allocate the payment to Lesson Index 12 by typing in the current payment number.

3. Close the form, and then click the **Allocation** tab. The tab does not reflect the payment. Close all open forms.

4. Display **frmPayment** in Design view.

5. Add the following code to the frmPayment's class module:

```
Public Sub UpdateAllocations()
'This procedure updates the subform when a change is made
'in the allocations on another form
    Dim pctrAllocationSub As Control
    Set pctrAllocationSub = Me!frmAllocationSub
    pctrAllocationSub.Requery
End Sub
```

The Dim and Set statements identify an object variable, pctrAllocationSub, that points to a subform. A single line of code—Me!frmAllocationSub.Requery—could be used instead of the three lines.

6. Save your work, close the Visual Basic window, and then display **frmProcessPayment** in Design view.

7. Write the following code in the **AfterUpdate** event procedure of frmProcessPayment:

```
'If frmPayment is open, requery the allocation subform
    Dim pobjProject As CurrentProject
    Set pobjProject = Application.CurrentProject
    If pobjProject.AllForms("frmPayment").IsLoaded Then
        Forms![frmPayment].UpdateAllocations
    End If
```

The IsLoaded property of an object in the AllForms collection is used to determine whether frmPayment is open. The line following the If statement invokes the UpdateAllocation procedure written earlier. Because UpdateAllocations is a public sub procedure, it is a method of frmPayment.

8. Save your work, close the Visual Basic window, and open **frmStudent** in Form view.

9. Add a **$30** payment and allocation for **David B. Smith** to test the sub procedure. The Allocations tab of frmPayment should be updated after a record is updated in frmAllocation (remember updates are triggered when the cursor moves to a different record).

10. Close all open forms.

Report, Module, and Application Methods

Methods associated with the Form, Control, and DoCmd objects are used in almost all Access applications. Once you become familiar with these methods, it is fairly easy to find and use the methods of many other Access application objects. An easy way to discover other methods is to identify the object that needs to be manipulated, find the object in Access Help, and then click the Methods hyperlink. For example, if you look up the methods associated with a Report object, you will find many methods that are capable of adding objects to a report in VBA code. If you look up methods associated with the Module object, you will find methods that are capable of modifying or inserting lines of code in a VBA procedure.

Another object that is frequently used in Access applications is the Application object. As shown in Table 8-3, methods of the Application object perform a variety of tasks. As an example, consider the Echo method, which is frequently used in conjunction with DoCmd's **HourGlass** method. The **Echo** method turns screen updating off while several changes occur to the form. Rather than watch the changes flicker on the screen, updating stops until all of the changes are made. If the user must wait for some period of time, the cursor should change to an hourglass so that the user is aware of the time-consuming process. The following code segment switches the cursor into an hourglass, halts screen updating, makes several changes to the screen (the ellipsis signifies many lines of code), turns on screen updating, and sets the cursor back to a pointer:

Table 8-3 Commonly used Application object methods

Method	Operation	Example	Notes
AccessError(*ErrorNum*) • *ErrorNum* is the number of the error for which a description is desired.	Returns a string that describes the error represented by the error number	AccessError(18) or Application. AccessError(18)	Err.Description returns the description of the current error. AccessError is used when you want to look up a particular error that occurred at another time. The word "Application" is optional.
BuildCriteria(*Field, Fieldtype, Expression*) • *Field* is the name of the field to be tested. • *Fieldtype* is the data type of the field. • *Expression* is the statement to be tested.	Returns a string that is in the correct format for a Where Condition	Application. BuildCriteria ("AppDate, dbDate, "> 1.1.97")	
CloseCurrentDatabase	Closes the database shown in the database window	Application.Close CurrentDatabase	
Echo *EchoOn[, StatusbarText]*	Turns screen updating on or off	Application.Echo False	Frequently used when a number of changes happen to a form at one time.
Quit [*option*]	Exits Microsoft Access	Application. Quit acSaveYes	
Run *Procedure* [*arg*] [*,arg*] [*,arg*]…	Runs a function or subroutine	Application.Run FindID	Normally used when you are running Access from another application.
RunCommand *Command*	Runs a command based from the menu	Application. RunCommand acDeleteRecord	Same as the RunCommand method of the DoCmd object.
SetOption *OptionName, Setting*	Changes a global option that affects how Access processes other objects	Application. SetOption "Default Field Type", 5	Can be specified in the Options window.
SysCmd(*action[, text][, value]*) • *action* is the action to perform on the status bar. • *text* is the string to display in the status bar. • *value* is a numeric value that controls the progress meter.	Performs a variety of tasks, including updating the progress meter on the status bar; also can be used to test whether a form is open	`varReturn = SysCmd(acSysCmd InitMeter, "Running", 100)`	

```
DoCmd.HourGlass True
Application.Echo False
. . .
Application.Echo True
DoCmd.HourGlass False
```

Another type of commonly used Access Application object is a user-defined class module (for example, a class module that is created within the Modules tab). Methods of a user-defined class module are invoked like any other methods. First, the module is identified through an object variable. Next, the method is invoked through dot notation. Many of the ADO and DAO examples in the following section will be contained within user-defined class modules.

ADO AND DAO METHODS

Methods related to ActiveX Data Objects (ADO) and Data Access Objects (DAO) perform many important operations, including connecting to databases, executing queries, and updating data that are not currently displayed in a form. For example, an ADO recordset object and its methods were used to add new degrees to the tblDegreeTypes table, as shown in Figure 8-1. As another example, the MU-DSci application uses ADO methods to generate a list of possible leveling courses for a student just before frmLeveling opens.

ADO is replacing DAO as the standard method for manipulating data in Microsoft products. Consequently, as a programmer you need to understand ADO objects and their methods. Unfortunately, the recordsets that are created for bound forms and reports are still DAO objects. To manipulate these recordsets, you must also understand DAO. This discussion will therefore focus on manipulating data through ADO objects and methods; DAO objects and methods will be introduced when ADO will not perform the necessary task.

Methods of the Connection Object

Almost all procedures that use ADO objects require a Connection object (one of the ADO objects). The Connection object identifies and opens the database that contains the tables and queries that are used within the procedure. The user of the application does not see a new database on the screen. Rather, the Connection object establishes a connection to a database that will be manipulated in VBA code.

In most cases, the database that contains the tables and queries is the same database that the user has already opened. A Connection object variable can point to this connection through the following code:

```
Dim cnn As ADODB.Connection
Set cnn = CurrentProject.Connection
```

Sometimes VBA needs to use tables or queries that are not contained in the current database. In addition, some properties of linked tables cannot be manipulated in the database that contains the links. In these situations, the Connection object must use the Open method to connect to the desired database directly. The syntax for the Open method follows:

Syntax

*Connection.***Open** *ConnectionString, UserID, Password, Options*

Syntax Dissection

- *Connection* is an expression or object variable that refers to a Connection object.

- **Open** is a method of a Connection object that opens the database so that it can be used.

- *ConnectionString* is an optional argument that contains a string that will be passed to the source database. Many parameters can be passed in this string, including the path to the desired database, a name for an ODBC data source, user IDs, and passwords. The exact connection string depends on the type of data source (for example, SQL Server, Jet, Oracle). You must look in the manual for the data source to determine the required parameters.

- *UserID* is an optional argument that refers to the user ID that will open the database. Alternatively, the ID can be placed in the connection string.

- *Password* is an optional argument that contains a password that will open the database. Alternatively, the password can be placed in the connection string.

- *Options* contains an intrinsic constant that tells Access to wait for the desired database to open or to continue processing even when the database has not finished opening.

Most of the arguments used in the Open method are also properties of the connection object. If the properties are set before the Open method executes, the arguments do not need to be passed. The following lines of code can connect to **Data.mdb** from **MU-DSci.mdb**:

```
Dim cnn As New ADODB.Connection
cnn.Open "Provider=Microsoft.Jet.OLEDB.4.0;" & _
"Data Source=C:\My Documents\AccessApps\MU-DSci\Data.mdb;"
```

To understand the effects of this code, you must understand the Connection object in detail. It is actually a pathway between a procedure and a data source. A Connection object variable points to the path. Every database has a pathway (that is, a connection) to itself. The CurrentProject.Connection object and property point to that path.

When CurrentProject.Connection is used, the Dim or Set statement for the Connection object variable does not need the New argument because the path already exists. The New argument is used when a new pathway must be created. This new pathway does not identify a source database, however, until the ConnectionString property is set (until the ConnectionString property is set, the path leads nowhere). The Open method may set the ConnectionString property and clear the path of obstacles (for example, user IDs and passwords), thereby allowing data and commands to flow through the connection.

You can display the connection string for the current database by typing ?CurrentProject.Connection.ConnectionString in the Immediate window of the VBE Editor. You can then cut and paste this connection string into your VBA code. Another way to facilitate the writing of a connection string is to create a Data Source file. To create this file, you click File, point to Get External Data, click Link Tables, and then select ODBC databases in the File Type combo box. When the Select Data Source window pops up, click New. This action will start a wizard that asks a series of questions about the data source. When you are finished, the wizard asks for a filename. The appropriate parameters are stored in this file. To incorporate these parameters into the ConnectionString property, include the phrase DSN=*filepath* inside the string.

A Connection object possesses many other methods. For example, the **Close** method shuts down the pathway to the database. The **Execute** method can be used to execute queries, although the combination of the Execute method with Command objects offers more options.

8

Executing Queries in VBA Through the Command Object

The **Execute** method associated with the Command object in VBA causes a query to run. A Command object is analogous to a car that carries commands through the pathway. Programmers of the MU-DSci application used the Execute method in the ClearDeniedProspects subroutine (located in the basProspects module) to delete all the denied prospects. The query qryDeleteDeniedProspects, shown in Figure 8-6, is a query located under the Queries tab.

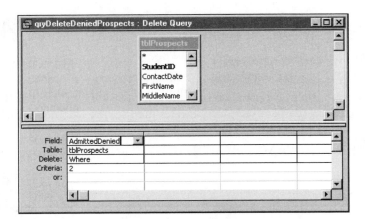

Figure 8-6   qryDeleteDeniedProspects

The ClearDeniedProspects subroutine is triggered from a command button located on frmSwitchboard. Consider the following lines of code, which were extracted from ClearDeniedProspects:

```
Dim cnn As ADODB.Connection
Dim cmd As New ADODB.Command
Dim plngRecordsAffected As Long
Set cnn = CurrentProject.Connection
cmd.ActiveConnection = cnn
cmd.CommandText = "qryDeleteDeniedProspects"
cmd.Execute plngRecordsAffected
```

The first two lines declare the object variables. The New argument is used because the Command object does not already exist. The fourth line sets cnn to the current connection. The next line tells the Command object which connection points to the database that holds the data and the query. The sixth line sets the CommandText property of the Command object; this property contains either an SQL statement or the name of a query (qryDeleteDeniedProspects) to execute. The last line causes the query to run. After the query is run, the database will place the number of records that were deleted in the plngRecordsAffected argument.

Query Parameters

Frequently, action queries triggered in VBA code use parameters. The advantage of parameters is that the query will retrieve or update different data depending on the parameters' values. To execute a parameter query in VBA, the values of the parameters must be supplied.

The second argument of the Execute method can be used to pass parameter values. This method expects the parameters to be passed in the form of an array. Consequently, the Array function can be used to create this argument. An example of the Array function follows:

```
cmd.Execute plngNum, Array(1, 5, "ACCT" )
```

This Array function returns an array containing the values 1, 5, and ACCT. These values correspond to the first, second, and third parameters, respectively, that are specified in the query Design view. The example in the next section illustrates the use of a parameter query.

Executing an Update Query to Reduce Enrollment

The table tblClasses contains a field that stores the number of students currently enrolled in a class. If a student drops a class, the value in the enrolled field must be reduced by 1. You can use an update query to reduce the enrollment amount. Here, you will execute the query in VBA code. The procedure to execute the query will be placed in a class module called cmoEnrollment.

To create and execute an action query that reduces enrollment:

1. Create a new query that uses **tblClasses**.

2. Click **Query** on the menu bar, and then click **Update Query**. The Update To row is added to the query Design view.

3. Right-click in a blank area in the query Design view, and then click **Parameters** in the pop-up menu. The Query Parameters dialog box will appear.

4. Type **parLesson** in the Parameter column, and select **Long Integer** in the Data Type column. Click **OK**.

5. Design the query so that it has the information shown in Figure 8-7. Save the query as **qryReduceEnrollment**, and then close it.

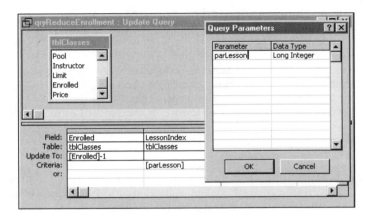

Figure 8-7   qryReduceEnrollment

6. Click **Insert** on the toolbar, click **Class Module**, and then enter the following code:

```
Public Sub ReduceEnrollment(plngLesson As Long)
'Reduce Enrollment field in Classes by one
    Dim cnn As ADODB.Connection
    Dim cmd As ADODB.Command
    Set cnn = CurrentProject.Connection
    Set cmd = New ADODB.Command
    'Identify the location of the query
    cmd.ActiveConnection = cnn
    'Identify the query
    cmd.CommandText = "qryReduceEnrollment"
    'Execute the query, sending the parameter through
    'the parameter argument.
    cmd.Execute , Array(plngLesson)
End Sub
```

7. Save the class module as **cmoEnrollment**, close the Visual Basic window, and then close any open forms.

8. Display **frmClassesEnrolled_subform** in Code view. This form, a subform of frmRegistration, is used to register a student for a class or drop a student from a class. Place the following code in the Declarations section:

```
Private mlngSavedLessonIndex As Long
```

9. Make the **Delete** and **AfterDelConfirm** event procedures match the following code:

```
Private Sub Form_Delete(Cancel As Integer)
    'Do not delete if Status is not equal to IP
    If [txtStatus] <> "IP" And Not IsNull(txtStatus) Then
        MsgBox "The course is complete, you cannot delete"
        Cancel = True
    Else
        'Save the lesson index for deletion
        mlngSavedLessonIndex = [cboLessonIndex]
    End If
End Sub
Private Sub Form_AfterDelConfirm(Status As Integer)
    Dim pcmoEnrolled As New cmoEnrollment
    'Call the method that reduces enrollment
    pcmoEnrolled.ReduceEnrollment mlngSavedLessonIndex
    'Clear the saved index
    mlngSavedLessonIndex = 0
End Sub
```

To invoke the ReduceEnrollment method of cmoEnrollment, an instance of cmoEnrollment is created (pcmoEnrolled). The Dim and New keywords create this instance. The ReduceEnrollment method is similar to a public sub procedure.

10. Save the code, close the Visual Basic window, and then close the form.

11. Open **tblClasses** in Datasheet view and note the value in the Enrolled column for Lesson Index 10. Close tblClasses.

12. Open **frmStudent** in Form view, find the record for **Craig T. Jones**, and then click the **Register** button. The Registration form will appear.

13. Delete the record with Index **10** for Craig T. Jones.

14. Open **tblClasses** to verify that the number currently enrolled was reduced by 1. Close any open forms. Close tblClasses.

Consider the results of the code that you just typed. The Delete event procedure disallows a deletion when the student has already completed the course. If the course can be dropped (that is, deleted), the Delete event procedure saves the LessonIndex in a module-level variable. Access automatically places a Null value in cboLessonIndex after the Delete event procedure executes. The AfterDelConfirm event procedure needs the LessonIndex to invoke the ReduceEnrollment method. The line pcmoEnrolled.ReduceEnrollment mlngSavedLessonIndex invokes the procedure that reduces enrollment by 1.

Opening Recordsets

In addition to queries, programmers can use recordsets to locate and update data. Although action queries are usually superior when it comes to updating multiple records in a database, recordsets can be used to perform more complex tasks.

Before using recordsets, you must declare and set a recordset object variable. Normally, you must also open a pathway to the table or query that contains the data through the Open method. The syntax for the Open method follows:

Syntax

recordset.**Open** *Source, ActiveConnection, CursorType, LockType, Options*

Syntax Dissection

- The *recordset* object refers to a recordset object variable.

- The **Open** method makes the data in the query or table available.

- *Source* is a string that specifies a table name, query name, or SQL statement that is the data source for the recordset. *Source* can also refer to a Command object.

- *ActiveConnection* contains the name of a Connection object that points to the database containing the desired data.

- *CursorType* and *LockType* indicate how the recordset will be used.

- *Options* contains an intrinsic constant that indicates how the provider should evaluate the *Source* argument. The value **adCmdTableDirect** indicates that the source is a table, **adCmdText** indicates that the source is an SQL statement that is to be evaluated, and **adCmdStoredProc** indicates that the source is a stored procedure or query. Other intrinsic constants exist as well.

You already saw an example of an Open method—in NewDegreeType in Figure 8-1. The Open method in that procedure provides access to the data in the tblDegreeTypes table. Before the Open method was used, a recordset variable was declared and a new instance of the recordset was created through the Set statement. The instance of a recordset can be envisioned as a container that will keep track of properties and hold the data of the recordset. The data are placed in the container through the Open method.

In addition to using data that come directly from tables (as in Figure 8-1), several other methods are available for creating recordsets. For instance, the following code uses an SQL statement in the Open method:

```
Dim rst As Recordset
Dim pstrQuery As String
pstrQuery = _
"Select * FROM tblCurrentStudents WHERE [Program] = '" _
    & [cboProgram] & "'"
Set rst = New Recordset
rst.Open pstrQuery, CurrentProject.Connection, adOpenKeyset, _
    adLockOptimistic, adCmdText
```

The advantage of using an SQL statement rather than using the name of table, as in Figure 8-1, is that the procedure retrieves only the needed records.

Recordset objects can be created from other recordset objects through the Clone method as well the Open method. The Clone method creates a new recordset object that points to the same data as the recordset object that is being cloned. It automatically creates the recordset object and associates data with the recordset; as a result, this method does not require the New keyword. Copies of recordsets are useful whenever you need to keep track of more than one record at a time. The following code demonstrates the syntax of a statement that uses the Clone method:

```
Set prstEmployee2 = prstEmployee.Clone
```

The Execute method can also be used to create a recordset. You should check Access Help to obtain additional information about this technique.

Finding Records in a Recordset

Once a recordset is open, several methods can be used to move from record to record. In general, only one record in a recordset can be manipulated at any given time. The Bookmark property of a recordset is a string expression that uniquely identifies the current record. The **AbsolutePosition** property is a long integer that contains the ordinal position of the current record. Methods that modify the current record also change the values of the Bookmark and AbsolutePosition properties.

Simple movement to new records can be accomplished with the **MoveFirst**, **MoveLast**, **MovePrevious**, and **MoveNext** methods. A similar method, named **Move**, is used in conjunction with a long integer to move the specified number of records forward (positive number) or backward (negative number). Examples of the syntax follow:

```
prstStudent.MoveFirst
prstStudent.MoveLast
prstStudent.MovePrevious
prstStudent.MoveNext
prstStudent.Move 3
```

Besides moving sequentially through the rows, recordsets support several methods for locating rows based on some criteria. As an example, the Find method is frequently used to find a row based on a single criterion. The syntax for the Find method follows:

Syntax

*recordset.***Find** *Criteria, SkipRows, SearchDirection, Start*

Syntax Dissection

- The *recordset* object is a recordset object variable.

- **Find** locates a record that is consistent with the *Criteria*.

- *Criteria* is a where condition (without the word WHERE) that does not contain AND or OR as part of the condition.

- *SkipRows* is an optional argument that specifies an offset from the current row to start the search (the default is zero). If the current record already meets the criteria, SkipRows should equal 1.

- *SearchDirection* indicates whether the search should go forward (adSearchForward) or backward (adSearchBackward).

- *Start* is an optional bookmark value that indicates where to begin the search.

Recordsets also support the **Seek** method and the **Filter property** to find records that match a specified criterion. The Seek method is an efficient way to search a recordset through the primary key or indexes. The Filter property is similar to a form's filter property.

BOF and EOF

The BOF (Beginning of File) and EOF (End of File) properties are frequently used in conjunction with the movement methods. BOF (for example, prstStudent.BOF) is True when the bookmark points to a position located prior to the first record in the recordset. EOF (for example, prstStudent.EOF) is True when the bookmark points to a position located after the last record in the recordset. If a Find method does not find a record that meets the criteria, BOF and EOF equal True.

8

Using a Find Method to Locate Default Data for a Particular Class

Users of the Swim Lessons application register for a course by selecting a lesson index in the subform of frmRegistration. After a lesson index is selected, the application should find the default price and place this amount in the Charged column.

To place a price in the Charged column:

1. Open **cmoEnrollment** in Design view.

2. Create the following function inside cmoEnrollment:

```
Public Function DefaultPrice(plngLesson As Long) As Currency
'Retrieve the default price
    Dim prstClass As ADODB.Recordset
    Dim cnn As ADODB.Connection
    Dim pstrCriteria As String
    Set cnn = CurrentProject.Connection
    'Open the recordset
    Set prstClass = New ADODB.Recordset
    prstClass.Open "tblClasses", cnn, adOpenKeyset, _
     adLockReadOnly, adCmdTableDirect
    'Form the criteria
    pstrCriteria = "[LessonIndex] = " & plngLesson
    'Find record that matches criteria
    prstClass.Find pstrCriteria
    'If found set the price
```

```
            If prstClass.EOF Then
                DefaultPrice = 0
            Else
                DefaultPrice = prstClass!Price
            End If
            prstClass.Close
        End Function
```

3. Save cmoEnrollment, close the Visual Basic window, and then display **frmClassesEnrolled_subform** in Design view.

4. Write the following code in the **AfterUpdate** event procedure of **cboLessonIndex**:

```
'Get the default price from cmoEnrollment
Dim pcmoEnrollment As New cmoEnrollment
If Not IsNull([cboLessonIndex]) Then
    Me!txtCharged = _
pcmoEnrollment.DefaultPrice([cboLessonIndex])
End If
```

The cboLessonIndex is sent to the DefaultPrice method. This method returns a value that is placed in txtCharged.

5. Save the code, close the Visual Basic window, and then close any open forms.

6. Open **frmStudent** in Form view, locate **Hannah Holly**, and then click the **Register** button.

7. Select **02b** as the semester and **2** as the level. Next, select Index **37** as the new record of the subform. The price will appear automatically.

8. Close any open forms.

Editing, Deleting, and Updating Data in a Recordset

Programmers frequently use recordsets to edit, delete, and update records. Recordset methods specify how the data are to be updated. The recordset must be opened with a LockType that permit updating of the database (for example, adLockOptimistic, adLockPessimistic). The following syntax specifies the methods used to update data:

Syntax

recordset.[**AddNew** | **Delete** | **Update** | **UpdateBatch** | **CancelUpdate** | **CancelBatch**]

Syntax Dissection

- The *recordset* is a recordset object variable.

- The **AddNew** method tells Access to move the bookmark to a new record. Assignment statements following AddNew place values in the record's fields.

- The **Delete** method deletes the current record in the recordset. An optional *AffectedRecords* argument tells Access to delete all or part of the records in the recordset. Before execution of the Delete method, the EOF and BOF properties should be checked to verify that the record targeted for deletion exists.

- The **Update** method tells Access to write the new record or changed record to the database.

- The **UpdateBatch** method writes all pending recordset updates to the database. It is used when the recordset lock type is adLockBatchOptimistic. It ensures that several records will be updated, with the updated records being put into a buffer that will be written to the database when the UpdateBatch method is encountered.

- The **CancelUpdate** method is used when an error occurs. It aborts an update operation.

- The **CancelBatch** method is executed instead of UpdateBatch when the program recognizes an error.

  Field values are changed in a recordset by using an assignment statement that places new values in one or more fields. The updates are written to the database when the VBA code moves the current record to a different record or when an Update method executes.

8

The assignment statements have the following syntax:

Syntax

Recordset!FieldName = Expression

Syntax Dissection

- *Recordset* is a recordset object variable.

- *FieldName* is a field in the table that is referenced by the recordset.

- *Expression* is any VBA expression that returns a result that is consistent with the data type of *FieldName*.

Figure 8-1 illustrated the operation of the AddNew and Update methods by using them to insert a new record into the tblDegreeTypes table. In this case, only the DegreeType field needs to be updated. Normally, an assignment statement is used for each field in the recordset. However, AutoNumber fields are set automatically by Access and should not be updated in VBA.

You now possess the knowledge necessary to understand the nuances of NewDegreeType, which appeared in Figure 8-1. Let's review what you know:

- The first several lines declare the string, integer, and object variables.

- The Set pctrCurrentField = Screen.ActiveControl statement sets a pointer to the combo box that triggered this sub procedure. If the sub procedure was triggered because a user deleted the old value in the combo box, the first If statement will detect this condition, send a message to Access through the Response argument, and exit the sub procedure. If an entry was made, the DoCmd.RunCommand acCmdUndo method will remove the input from the combo box.

- Next, a message is displayed asking whether the new data should be added to the table. If the user answers "yes," the application sets the Connection object and opens the recordset.

- The AddNew method is then used to indicate that a new record will be added, the new value is inserted into the DegreeType field, and the Update method causes the new record to be written to the database. In addition, the Response argument is set to acDataErrAdded. This intrinsic constant tells Access to requery the combo box so that the combo box will display the new degree type.

You will now see how to edit a record in the Swim Lessons application.

Adding One to the Enrolled Field Through a Recordset

Before a student can enroll in a course, the enrolled value must be compared with the limit. If the number of students enrolled is less than the limit, the student can be enrolled in the class and the enrollment should increase by 1.

This process should be relatively simple, but building procedures that facilitate additions and deletions reveals another decision that must be made: Should students be allowed to change the value of the LessonIndex once they are enrolled? If so, the enrollment should decrease by 1 for the old LessonIndex and increase by 1 for the new LessonIndex. If not, you must disallow changes to the LessonIndex value; to change classes, a student must therefore drop a class and add another class.

You will write code that verifies the enrollment, increases the enrollment count by 1, and disallows changes to the LessonIndex when the LessonIndex contains a value.

To verify enrollment and increase the Enrolled field value by 1:

1. Type the following code into the cmoEnrollment class module:

```
Public Function AddToEnrollment(plngLesson As Long) As Bool
ean
'Add 1 to enrollment if room is available
    Dim prstClass As ADODB.Recordset
    Dim cnn As ADODB.Connection
    Dim pstrSelect As String
    Set cnn = CurrentProject.Connection
    'Form the criteria
    pstrSelect = _
      "Select * FROM tblClasses WHERE [LessonIndex] = " _
      & plngLesson
    Set prstClass = New ADODB.Recordset
    'Open the recordset
    prstClass.Open pstrSelect, cnn, adOpenKeyset, _
      adLockOptimistic, adCmdText
    'If found and enrolled < limit, increase enrolled;
```

```
            'otherwise, set value to False to inform user
            'that capacity has been reached or the class
            'does not exist.
            If prstClass.RecordCount = 0 Then
                AddToEnrollment = False
            ElseIf prstClass!Enrolled >= prstClass!Limit Then
                'No more room
                AddToEnrollment = False
            Else
                'Add 1 to total enrolled
                prstClass!Enrolled = prstClass!Enrolled + 1
                prstClass.Update
                AddToEnrollment = True
            End If
            prstClass.Close
        End Function
```

2. Save the code, close the Visual Basic window, and then add the following code to the **BeforeUpdate** event procedure of **frmClassesEnrolled_subform**:

```
'If this is a new record, verify that enrolled < limit
'and add 1 to the enrollment.
    Dim pcmoEnrolled As New cmoEnrollment
    If Not Me.NewRecord Then
        Exit Sub
    End If
    If pcmoEnrolled.AddToEnrollment([cboLessonIndex]) = _
False Then
        'There is no room in the class
        MsgBox "Sorry this class is full"
        Me.Undo 'Undo the record
        Cancel = True 'Cancel the update
    End If
```

The If statement invokes AddToEnrollment and then checks the value returned.

3. To disallow updates to the value of cboLessonIndex after the record is inserted, add the following code to the module of frmClassEnrolled_subform:

```
Private Sub Form_Current()
        'Lock cboLessonIndex when this is not a new record.
        'Locking will prevent users from changing classes.
        'Users must delete and then add a new class to make a
        'change.
        If Me.NewRecord Then
            Me![cboLessonIndex].Locked = False
        Else
            Me![cboLessonIndex].Locked = True
        End If
End Sub
```

4. Save the code, close the Visual Basic window, and then close any open forms.

5. Open **tblClasses**, and note the Limit and Enrolled in rows 37 and 38. Close tblClasses.

6. Open **frmStudent** in Form view, and find **Sarah J. Thomas**. Click the **Register** button. The Registration form will appear. Select **02b** as the semester and **2** as the level.

7. Select **37** in the Index drop-down list box. The price should appear. Advance to a new record. A message box will appear stating that the class is full.

8. Select **38** in the Index drop-down list box, and then advance to a new record. The new record is allowed. Close the forms.

9. Open **tblClasses** to verify that the enrollment for row 38 has been increased by 1. Close tblClasses.

Using DAO Recordsets

Access automatically creates a DAO recordset whenever a bound form or report is opened. This recordset contains the data that are displayed through the form or report. Because the recordset is a DAO recordset, you must use DAO methods when manipulating it through VBA code. In the MU-DSci application, a DAO recordset is used when the user clicks All Courses in frmLeveling. This action executes code that moves through the form's recordset and checks all of the chkNeeded boxes.

The methods of a DAO recordset are similar to the methods of an ADO recordset. For example, a DAO recordset supports **FindFirst, FindNext, FindPrevious,** and **FindLast** methods, which are similar to ADO's Find method. In the case of ADO, the programmer sets the search direction through the SearchDirection and SkipRows arguments. With DAO, the choice of method determines the search direction. The FindFirst, FindNext, FindPrevious, and FindLast methods take a Criteria argument. The value of this Criteria argument is the typical SQL WHERE condition, which has been illustrated many times previously in this book. Unlike the ADO's Find method, the Criteria argument can incorporate AND and OR.

The methods that update data in a DAO recordset are also similar to the corresponding ADO methods. The **AddNew, Update,** and **Delete** methods are almost identical to their ADO counterparts. One difference is that, unlike with ADO, a record is not written to the database in DAO when a Move or Find method changes the current record. In fact, the insertion will be lost if an Update method does not execute before the current record moves. A second difference is that a DAO **Edit** method must be executed before values in an existing record are changed. After the Edit method executes, assignment statements are used to alter the values. Like the AddNew method, the Edit method requires a partner Update method to write changes to the database.

The following code illustrates the creation and use of a DAO recordset object. This procedure finds a record that has a StudentID equal to the value that is passed to the function. It is used in frmCurrentStudents, frmGraduates, and frmProspects in MU-DSci.

```
Public Function FindID(pstrStudentID As String) As Boolean
    Dim prstStudent As Recordset
    Dim pstrCriteria As String
    Set prstStudent = Me.RecordsetClone
    pstrCriteria = "[StudentID] = '" & pstrStudentID & "'"
    prstStudent.FindFirst pstrCriteria
    If prstStudent.NoMatch Then
        FindID = False
    Else
        Me.Bookmark = prstStudent.Bookmark
        FindID = True
    End If
    prstStudent.Close
End Function
```

8

In the preceding code, prstStudent is set to equal the recordset that underlies the form. The **RecordsetClone** property of a form returns a pointer to this recordset. The FindFirst method is used to find the desired record. A DAO recordset utilizes a **NoMatch** property to indicate whether the previous Find method failed to find a match. If the FindFirst method is successful, the Bookmark property of the recordset will point to the desired record. A form also has a Bookmark property. Setting the form's Bookmark property equal to the recordset's Bookmark property causes Access to display the found record in the form.

ADO and DAO Methods—Some Final Thoughts

Many additional ADO and DAO methods exist. Over time, you will become comfortable with the process of searching for the methods you need through Access Help and the Object Browser. One such method is the **CompactDatabase** method, which is associated with the JetEngine object. It performs the "compact database" operation that appears in the Access menu. Compacting a database makes the database smaller. Because many users forget to compact the database manually, the CompactDatabase method can be executed periodically through VBA code.

Another method, **Append**, places newly created objects in a collection. For example, you can add a new field to a table by appending the field to the table's Fields collections. Once the field appears in the Fields collection, the new object is saved and is available whenever the application is open. Conversely, the **Delete** method of a collection object removes an object from the collection. As you explore Access and other applications, you will find that many objects utilize the Append (or similar method) and Delete methods.

USING OBJECTS AND METHODS FROM A VARIETY OF OBJECT LIBRARIES

Besides the methods that are supplied with or custom-built inside Access, VBA can take advantage of methods that are supplied by other object libraries. For example, Access can use Excel methods to manipulate Excel worksheets. The major requirement for using objects within these libraries is that the library must be checked in the References window and therefore listed in the Object Browser.

Like Access methods, methods supplied through other object libraries provide information about an object or perform actions that create or manipulate objects. Programmers can search through manuals, Help, and the Object Browser to find the methods that best meet their needs.

The Object Browser

The Object Browser is available in the Visual Basic Editor (VBE)—see Figure 8-8. To find and paste a method from the Object Browser into the program window, you must perform a series of steps. For detailed information on these steps, see the respective topic in Access Help.

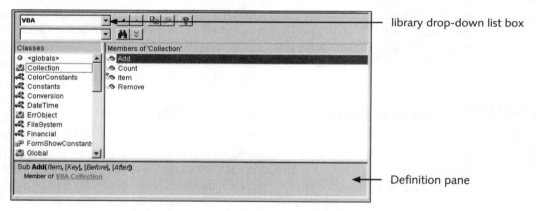

Figure 8-8   Object Browser for VBA Collection Add method

Automation Object Variables and Methods

A major advance in application development over the last few years is the greater ease with which one development environment can reference objects and methods used by another environment. For example, VBA in Access can reference an Excel spreadsheet object (assuming that Excel is installed). The properties and methods normally used in Excel can also be used within Access. To illustrate this idea, the following code sets xbook to an Excel workbook (that is, a spreadsheet file) and xsheet to an Excel worksheet. The code then displays the contents of cell A1 in a message box by using a worksheet's Range method.

```
Dim xbook As Excel.Workbook
Dim xsheet As Excel.Worksheet
Set xbook = GetObject("c:\MIS3201.xls")
```

```
Set xsheet = xbook.Worksheets(1)
MsgBox xsheet.Range("A1")
```

To reference another application, object variables must be defined and set. In addition, the References window should contain a check that identifies the application (for example, Microsoft Excel 9.0 Object Library) to be referenced.

The Dim statements in the earlier code use dot notation to identify the application (Excel) and the type of object in the application (a workbook or a worksheet). The first Set statement identifies the file that contains the objects of interest. The **GetObject** function returns a pointer to objects in another Windows application (called the **source application**). Once a file has been identified, the Set statements follow the object hierarchy found in Excel. Any variable that references an object contained in another application is called an **Automation object variable**.

A programmer can create new applications in Access by using the **CreateObject** function (some applications also support the New keyword). The following code creates a new Excel application, creates a workbook, places a number in a cell, and then saves the workbook:

```
Dim X As Excel.Application
Dim ExcelWB As Excel.Workbook
Set X = CreateObject ("Excel.Application")
Set ExcelWB = X.Workbooks.Add
ExcelWB.Worksheets(1).Range("A1") = 5
ExcelWB.SaveAs "c:\temp\demo.xls"
X.Quit
Set X = Nothing
Set ExcelWB = Nothing
```

Excel.Application refers to the highest object in the Excel hierarchy. To close the Application object, the code uses Excel Quit method (for example, X.Quit). If the Quit method does not execute, other users cannot use the spreadsheet. You can view the spreadsheet in Excel. After Access saves a spreadsheet, however, the spreadsheet typically remains hidden. To view the spreadsheet, click Windows and then Unhide after opening the spreadsheet.

Executing a Word Merge Document to Create a Confirmation Letter

In our application, a confirmation letter should be generated for a new registration. The Microsoft Word document, **confirm.doc**, is a merge document that uses the query qrySingleForWord as its data source (see Figures 8-9 and 8-10).

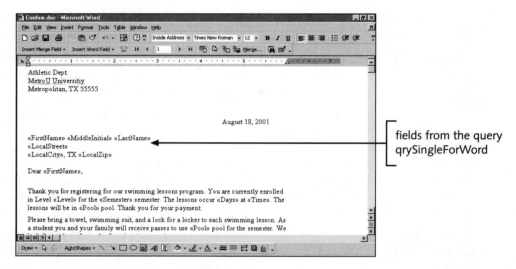

Figure 8-9   Merge document Confirm.doc

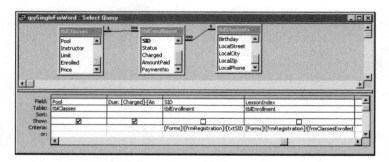

Figure 8-10   Data source for Confirm.doc

As shown in Figure 8-10, the criteria row for qrySingleForWord references frmRegistration. The query lists the registration detail for the current student and class displayed in frmRegistration. The MS Word document was created by opening qrySingleForWord, clicking Tools, Office Links, and then clicking Merge It with Microsoft Word in the menu. As a programmer, you must create VBA code to execute the merge operation and display the resulting document. Before you do so, however, you must go through a few steps to ensure that **Confirm.doc** can find the database.

To confirm that **Confirm.doc** can find the database:

1. Close Access and save any changes. Close all open programs.

2. Open **Confirm.doc** in Word, click the **Find Data Source** button, and then browse to find and select **SwimReg.mdb** (you'll need to switch file types).

3. Click the **Queries** tab, click **qrySingleForWord**, and then click **OK**.

4. Enter the value **111112000** at the first dialog box prompt, press **Enter**, enter **2** at the next dialog box prompt, and then press **Enter**. (Opening Confirm.doc opened Access; you may have to toggle between Word and Access to find the dialog box prompts.)

5. Click the **View Merged Data** button on the Mail Merge toolbar in Word.

6. Exit Word, saving your work if prompted to do so.

Now, let's write that code.

To write VBA code that executes a Microsoft Word document and displays the resulting form:

1. Open SwimReg.mdb in Access. Create a new module, click **Tools** on the menu bar, and then click **References**. The References window will open.

2. Check the **Microsoft Word 9.0 Object Library** check box in the References window. (If this library is not available, check the latest Microsoft Word object library). Click **OK**.

3. Insert the following public function procedure into the module:

```
Public Function WriteToWord()
'Execute a mailmerge so that a confirmation letter is
'generated
    Dim pobjWord As Word.Document
    Dim pobjMerge As Object
    Dim pstrPath As String
    pstrPath = CurrentProject.Path & "\confirm.doc"
    'Open the Word document. Word is open but not visible.
    Set pobjWord = GetObject(pstrPath)
    'Set a pointer to mailmerge object that controls merges
    Set pobjMerge = pobjWord.MailMerge
    'The destination for the merge is a new document
    pobjMerge.destination = wdSendToNewDocument
    'Execute the merge and create a new document
    pobjMerge.Execute
    'Make MS Word appear in Windows
    pobjWord.Application.Visible = True
    'Close the confirm.doc so the user does not see the
    'merge fields. The new document remains open.
    pobjWord.Close
    'Remove the pointers to the MS Word objects.
    Set pobjMerge = Nothing
    Set pobjWord = Nothing
End Function
```

4. Click **Debug** on the menu bar, and then click **Compile SwimReg**. Save the module as **basMailMerge**.

5. Display **frmRegistration** in Design view. Display the property sheet and toolbox, if they are not already open. Place a new command button on the form. Close the wizard if it opens. Name the button **cmdLetter**. Type **Letter** in the Caption property of cmdLetter.

8

6. Type **=WriteToWord()** in the OnClick event property of cmdLetter. It will trigger the above function when the user clicks the cmdLetter.

7. Display **frmRegistration** in Form view, find **Hannah Holley**, and then click the **Letter** button. The confirmation letter for Hannah H. Holley appears (see Figure 8-11).

8. Close Word. Close VBE.

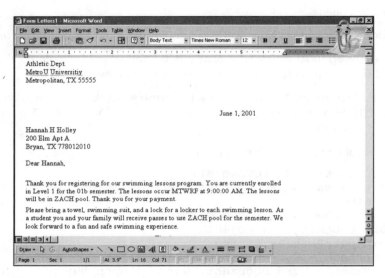

Figure 8-11   Result of executing the merge document

THE OBJECT-BASED APPROACH TO APPLICATION DEVELOPMENT

Successful Access application developers will not only understand the syntax of the VBA language, but also be able to use VBA to construct procedures that are easy to maintain and reuse. The object-based philosophy of Access provides some guidance as to how an application should be organized. Consider these facts:

- Many objects make up an Access application. Most of these objects possess the ability to test or manipulate their own features. For example, a field in a table uses an index, default values, and validation rules to control the data that can be stored within it. With this approach, other objects do not need to perform these operations for the field.

- Other objects such as collections and forms possess abilities (that is, methods) that perform certain operations on themselves. Procedures outside the object need to know only which methods are available and what the methods do. The procedures do not need to understand exactly how the Append method works, for example. In fact, the code used internally to implement an Append operation could change, but the modification would not affect a procedure unless the purpose of the Append method changes as well.

- Another benefit of locating methods with the objects that they manipulate is that many objects can use the same method. If the code used to implement an Append method was not centralized, for example, each procedure that interacts with a Collection object would need to implement its own Append code.

The object-based philosophy used by the built-in Access objects and methods should extend to your own custom objects and procedures. It suggests the following "rules of thumb" for designing Access applications:

1. Organize procedures based on the object being manipulated. For example, in the Swim Lessons application, an Enrollment object contains all procedures related to enrollment. Likewise, procedures that manipulate a form should be located in the form's class module. Organizing procedures in this fashion aids in maintenance because the procedures that influence an object are easy to find.

2. Try to build objects that can be reused. In the case of a form, small differences between forms that depend on the user or the use of the information in the form should not necessarily prompt the creation of two or more nearly identical forms. Instead, use VBA code to update the form according to its current purpose. The disadvantage of creating duplicate forms is that changes made to one form may need to be made to all duplicate forms so that they will continue to have the same appearance.

3. Build objects that are not highly coupled with other objects. That is, one object should not depend significantly on the internal components of another object. In the case of a form, procedures in the form's class module should avoid referencing controls or properties on another form. The problem with a high degree of coupling is that one object cannot be changed without affecting other objects.

These rules of thumb are not meant to govern all situations. Other factors may influence the design. For example, highly coupled forms are appropriate when one form will always be opened in conjunction with another form. Nevertheless, you should consider these rules when developing the architecture of your applications.

Opening Multiple Instances of a Form

Occasionally, two or more copies of a form must be opened at the same time. For instance, the MU-DSci application opens a second copy of frmProspects when a user enters a Student ID that matches a Student ID in the database. The second copy of frmProspects displays information about the matched student. The user can then confirm whether a duplicate entry was about to be made.

One way to create multiple copies of a form is to copy and paste a form into the Database window. This technique violates one of the "rules of thumb" mentioned earlier, however. An alternative to the copy-and-paste approach is to open multiple instances of the same form; thereby eliminating the maintenance problem.

To open multiple instances of a form, you must use a different notation for forms (and reports). Previously, we referenced forms by referring to the form collection (for example,

Forms![frmProspects]). The alternative notation is based on the concept of a user-defined object. A **user-defined object** is a class object that can be used to create other objects. A **class object** is a model of an object. For example, Table is a class object because it specifies the basic properties and collections that all tables instantiate. Objects that are based on a class are called **instances** of the class object. In an earlier chapter, a new instance of a table was created with the following code:

```
Dim tbl As ADOX.Table
Set tbl = New ADOX.Table
```

Every form that you create in Access is a class object. The class object name for a form is specified with the following syntax:

Syntax

Form_*formname*

Syntax Dissection

- **Form** indicates the object type being referenced.

- The *formname* is the name of the form.

- If the *formname* contains spaces, place brackets around the above syntax.

- To use this syntax, the form must have a class module. That is, the HasModule property of the form must equal True.

The class object name for a form is the name displayed in the Object Browser. Properties of a form can be updated and retrieved using this alternative syntax. For example, the RecordSource property of frmProspects is referenced as follows:

```
Form_frmProspects.RecordSource
```

This type of notation can be used even when frmProspects is not open. The reference to Form_frmProspects.RecordSource temporarily opens the form with the Visible property set to False.

A similar notation is used for reports. To refer to the RecordSource of rptStudentData, use the following notation:

```
Report_rptStudentData.RecordSource
```

Similarly to the technique employed in the table example, a new instance of a form can be created by using the New keyword. The following code opens a new instance of frmProspects. Each time the code runs, a new instance of frmProspects will be displayed.

```
Public mfrmNewProspectForm As Form_frmProspects
Set mfrmNewProspectForm = New Form_frmProspects
mfrmNewProspectForm.Visible = True
```

Two idiosyncrasies exist in the preceding code. First, an object that is created with the New keyword ceases to exist when the life of the object variable ends. That is, mfrmNewProspectForm must be declared in the Declarations section of a module. Second, when the New keyword is used to open a form or report, the object cannot be identified by name in the Forms and Reports collections. That is, the objects belong to the collections, but notations that refer to the name inside the Forms or Reports collection will not work. Procedures inside the form should use the Me notation to refer to the form.

Opening Multiple Instances of frmClassDetails

The form frmClassesBrief lists summary information about each class. The form frmClassDetails contains more detailed information. Users of frmClassesBrief should be able to double-click the lesson index to display frmClassDetails for that lesson. If the user double-clicks more than one lesson index, multiple frmClassDetails should appear. When the user closes frmClassesBrief, all open frmClassDetails should be closed as well.

To create code that opens multiple instances of frmClassDetails:

1. Display **frmClassesBrief** in Code view, and then add the following code in the Declarations section of the module:

```
'Store forms that are opened by frmClassesBrief
Private mcolOpenedForms As New Collection
```

A Collection object is an object supported by VBA. It is similar to other collections (for example, a Tables collection), except for two points: it can store any type of object, and the Add method is used to place an object in the collection instead of using the Append method.

2. Close the Visual Basic window.

3. Display the property sheet of txtLessonIndex, click in the field of the **On Dbl Click** event property, open the Code Builder, and then enter the following code (new code is shown in bold):

```
Private Sub txtLessonIndex_DblClick(Cancel As Integer)
    'Open a copy of frmClassDetails
    Dim pfrmClass As Form_frmClassDetails
    Set pfrmClass = New Form_frmClassDetails
    'Display the correct data in the form
    pfrmClass.Filter = "[LessonIndex] = " & [txtLessonIndex]
    pfrmClass.FilterOn = True
    pfrmClass.Caption = pfrmClass.Caption & " for " & _
        [txtLessonIndex]
    'Add the form to the collection so that the form remains
    'on the screen after the sub procedure ends.
    mcolOpenedForms.Add pfrmClass
    'Display the form on the screen
    pfrmClass.Visible = True
End Sub
```

4. Close the Visual Basic Editor.

8

5. Type **Double-click to see more details** in the ControlTip Text property of txtLessonIndex.

6. Save frmClassesBrief.

7. To test the procedures, open **frmClassesBrief** in Form view. Double-click any index. The form frmClassDetails should appear in Form view. Double-click another index. Move the forms and use the Windows menu to verify that multiple instances of frmClassDetail are displayed.

8. Close frmClassesBrief. All instances of frmClassDetails will close, because the mcolOpenedForms collection object ends its life.

Now that you have experience with form user-defined objects, let's look at independent class modules, a type of user-defined object that was employed throughout this chapter.

Creating and Using Independent Class Modules

Like other modules, independent class modules contain sub procedures and functions. They can also contain Let and Get property procedures. The difference between a class module and a standard module is that the former type of module is treated as an object. For example, public variables of a class module are properties of the user-defined object and public sub and function procedures are methods.

As you learn more about object-based programming in Access, you will discover that class modules can also invoke events. Because a class module is an object, instances of the object can be created (through the New keyword). In the Swim Lessons application, you invoked the necessary procedures by creating an instance of the cmoEnrollment object and then called the necessary methods. Using objects to manage one aspect of a database (for example, enrollment) facilitates maintenance. That is, other programmers will understand that cmoEnrollment is the object with expertise related to enrollment data.

CHAPTER SUMMARY

◻ In VBA, objects and properties are manipulated and created by methods. Access supplies numerous built-in methods for manipulating objects. In addition, you can create your own methods by developing public procedures for forms, reports, and independent class modules. Organizing your application according to the object-based style can significantly improve the maintenance and reusability of your code.

◻ The syntax for invoking a method is Object.Method. In VBA, objects can be identified through the dot and bang notations. The use of object variables, however, shortens this notation. Such variables contain a value that points to a particular object. Object variables can be declared as any recognized ADO, DAO, or Microsoft Access object type. Objects that are outside Access but included in the Object Browser can also be used in the declaration statement. The Set statement assigns a value to the object variable.

❏ Form objects are associated with several built-in methods. The Requery method tells the form to regenerate its recordset. Recalc, Refresh, and Repaint ensure that Access is displaying the correct data on a form. The SetFocus method moves the screen's cursor. In addition to form methods, the DoCmd object offers many methods for manipulating data on a form.

❏ Recordsets can be created with several methods and properties. Recordsets methods, such as Find, locate data in a table or query. Methods such as AddNew, Delete, and Update change data located in a table. Filling parameters and executing an action query in VBA code constitute another powerful technique for updating data.

❏ Automation object variables allow VBA in Access to use and manipulate objects in other languages such as Word and Excel. The syntax for using Automation objects is the same as the syntax for using Access objects.

❏ Access generates user-defined objects whenever forms and reports are created. The combination of the New keyword with a user-defined object can be used to open multiple form instances. The lives of these objects last only as long as the lives of the variables that reference them. Assigning an object to a persistent collection prolongs the object's life. The VBA Collection object is frequently used to manage multiple instances of a form.

8

REVIEW QUESTIONS

1. What is the purpose of an object variable?

2. Which of the following Dim statements will create the most efficient object variable?

   a. `Dim X As Object`

   b. `Dim X As Control`

   c. `Dim X As Listbox`

   d. `Dim X As Variant`

3. Write the Dim statement and the Set statement to create an object variable that refers to the txtTuition text box on the frmTotalFees form.

4. What is the purpose of the Reference window opened from the VBE Tools menu?

   a. The window identifies properties that can be used in a procedure.

   b. The window is used to create relationships between tables.

   c. The window identifies libraries containing objects that can be used in the procedure.

   d. The window allows you to copy and paste methods into a procedure.

5. Write the code that sets the cursor to the txtTuition text box in the frmRegister form.

6. What is the difference between the Refresh and Requery form methods?

   a. Refresh updates a form display by checking the field values in the form's current recordset; Requery updates the field values and regenerates the recordset so that deleted records are removed and new records are added.

   b. Requery causes the form to recalculate calculated controls; Refresh writes pending screen updates to the screen.

   c. Requery is periodically performed by Access automatically; Refresh is not automatically performed.

   d. Refresh can be applied to a text box; Requery cannot.

7. Which statements (and methods) would open a recordset variable named rstNewMoney (as a keyset) that contains records stored in a table named tblDeposits that is located in the current project?

8. Which statement would create a recordset that refers to the underlying recordset of the frmTotalFees form?

9. Which statement would position a recordset named prstStudentTable to the first record in the set?

10. Which statement would position a recordset named prstStudentTable to the first record in the set that has the value 4.00 in a field named GPR?

11. ADO recordsets use Edit and Update methods to alter a value in a recordset. True or False?

12. SQL statements can be created and used in VBA to retrieve records that satisfy a certain condition. True or False?

13. Other than a recordset object and method, what object and method can be used to alter data in a database?

14. Programmers of an Access application do not need to know about DAO objects. True or False?

15. Write two alternative statements that will open the form called frmStudentFees.

16. Users of the frmCustomer form can change the color of the form to fit their desires. Supported color combinations include the following: (1) Standard: gray form background, white control background, black control foreground; (2) Patriotic: blue form background, white control background, red control foreground; and (3) Ocean: blue form background, light green control background, aqua control foreground. Which type of procedure would you use to create this feature?

   a. Property Let procedure

   b. Property Get procedure

   c. A function in a standard module

   d. A sub procedure in a standard module

17. Write the statements to set an object to the first sheet of an Excel spreadsheet located at c:\statistics\sales\regionA.xls.

18. What is the purpose of the Object Browser? How is it related to the References window?

19. Forms that do not have a procedure are examples of user-defined objects. True or False?

20. You can set an object variable to an instance of an independent class module. True or False?

Hands-on Projects

Project 8-1

Natural Parent International. So far, frmProgram does not set default values when the form opens initially. You need to write an Open event procedure that sets the default time, address, city, and state to the values of the last entry in tblProgram. If records do not exist in tblProgram, the procedure should obtain default time, city, and state values from a default table.

In addition to default information, frmProgram should be associated with a menu or command button that, when clicked, generates a Word document that advertises the currently displayed program.

Complete these steps:

1. Open **NPI.mdb**. Create a new table called **tblDefault**. This table should contain text fields for City and State. It should also contain a Date/Time field to hold the default time.

2. Create a tabular (that is, Single Form) form, called **frmDefault**, that supports the entry of tblDefault data.

3. Write an Open event procedure for frmProgram that uses a recordset to look up the values of the last record in tblProgram. These values will be used to set the module-level variables created in Chapter 7. If tblProgram does not contain any records, another recordset should be used to find the first record in tblDefault. The values in tblDefault are used to set the module-level variables.

4. Create a query, called **qryFlyer**, that contains parameters that refer to the current Series and Program Numbers in frmProgram. The qryFlyer query should display all fields in frmProgram.

5. Create a merge document in Word that references qryFlyer.

6. Create a procedure that opens the Word document and initiates the merging process.

7. Trigger the procedure created in Step 6 with a command button or menu item.

8. Save your work.

8

Project 8-2

Metropolitan Performing Arts Company. The manager of MPAC would like a simple mechanism for recording returns. You will place a toolbar button for returns on tbrPerformanceSeats. The button will be enabled when the current record in the subform of frmPerformanceDateSeats has a status of Unavailable or Complimentary. If the user clicks the Return toolbar button, the tblReturn table should be updated. This table contains a row for each performance (identified by PerformanceID and DateTime) and seat section. Each row contains the number of returns and total dollar amount of the returns for that performance and section. The dollar amount returned when a complimentary ticket is returned is zero; otherwise, the dollar amount matches the price of the ticket. Because tickets are rarely returned, refunds are paid in cash. A form should be created to total the amount to give to the customer.

Complete these steps:

1. Open **MPA.mdb** and refresh the links.

2. Create an unbound form called **frmReturns**. This form will contain a text box called txtReturnAmount. Format the text box to hold currency, and give it a default value of 0.

3. Place a command button, called **cmdClear**, on frmReturns. Clicking the command button should place a zero in txtReturnAmount.

4. Create a private function named **ReturnPrice** in the form class module of frmPerformanceDateSeats. If the current record in the subform has a status of Complimentary, ReturnPrice is zero. Otherwise, ReturnPrice is the price listed in the subform.

5. Create a public function called **ReturnTicket** in the form class module of frmPerformanceDateSeats. This procedure should verify that the user wants to return a ticket (use a message box). The procedure should also open frmReturns (if it is not already opened) and add the correct price to txtReturnAmount. In addition, it should update or insert a record in tblReturn. If a record for a PerformanceID, DateTime, and Section already exists, the return price should be added to DollarReturn and NumTickets should be increased by 1. If a record does not exist, the application should insert a new record. You will probably need to use a recordset object for this procedure. You may want to use an SQL statement as the source of the recordset object. The SQL string for the source is as follows (you may need to adjust the field names to correspond to the names you chose as you developed the application):

```
pstrSelect = "Select * From tblReturn WHERE " & _
        "[PerformanceID] = '" & Me.PerformanceID & "'" _
        & " AND " & _
        "[DateTime] = # " & Me.DateTime & "#" & _
        " AND " & _
        "[Section] = '" & pctrSubForm.Form!Section & "'"
```

The pctrSubForm object variable refers to the subform of frmPerformanceDateSeats.

6. Create a new toolbar button, called **Return**, on tbrPerformanceSeats. This toolbar button should invoke the function ReturnTicket.

7. Create VBA code that enables and disables the Return toolbar button at the appropriate times.

8. Save your work.

Project 8-3

Foreign Language Institute System. All applications should be designed in a manner that facilitates the work of any user. Although graphical user interfaces make data entry easier than is possible in non–graphical interfaces, the interface may still need enhancements. For example, users with less-than-perfect eyesight might have a difficult time seeing the cursor when they are entering data. Some users might need additional assistance to see which control contains the cursor at any point during the data input process.

You can enhance FLI's system to make data entry easier by adding VBA code that changes the background color of a control when the user is ready to enter data in it. You can use the GetFocus and LoseFocus events to execute VBA code that changes the BackColor property of the control. Due to the manner in which events occur, however, the first control to receive the focus must be handled as a special case.

Complete these steps:

1. Open **FLI.mdb**. Write two subroutines in the frmCustomers form. Name the first subroutine **Highlight_On**. It will change the background color of the currently active control to cyan. An error occurs when Access tries to execute this subroutine for the first control in the tab stop order, due to the timing of the GetFocus event and the setting of the value for the ActiveControl property of the Screen object. The error is handled by referring explicitly to the first control in the tab stop order with the following code:

```
Private Sub Highlight_On()
'Turns background of control to cyan
On Error GoTo Errhandler
Screen.ActiveControl.BackColor = RGB(0, 255, 255)
Exit Sub
Errhandler:
    [Forms]![frmCustomers]![txtCustomerNo].BackColor = _
    RGB(0, 255, 255)
    Resume Next
End Sub
```

2. Name the second subroutine **Highlight_Off**. It changes the background color for the currently active control to white. There is no unusual error situation to handle. The code for this subroutine follows:

```
Private Sub Highlight_Off()
Screen.ActiveControl.BackColor = RGB(255, 255, 255)
End Sub
```

3. To change every control, place a call to **Highlight_On** in the GetFocus event of every control and a call to **Highlight_Off** in the LoseFocus event of every control.

4. Another enhancement for the FLI system is the ability to show or hide detailed data as desired. The frmSpeakers form contains detailed data in a subform and a command button for showing or hiding those data. Modify this form so that the products mentioned by a speaker are displayed when the user clicks a button labeled "Show Detail." When the products are visible, change the label on the button to "Hide Detail." When the button displays the label "Hide Detail," clicking it should hide the detailed data and change the label back to "Show Detail." The form should open with the detail data hidden.

Place the code needed for this enhancement in two places. First, in the Click event for the command button, add the following code:

```
Me![frmProductsList].Visible = Not Me![frmProductsList].Visible
If Me![frmProductsList].Visible Then
    Me![cmdDetail].Caption = "Hide Detail"
Else
    Me![cmdDetail].Caption = "Show Detail"
    End If
```

5. Then, in the Open event for the form, add the following code:

```
Me![frmProductsList].Visible = False
Me![cmdDetail].Caption = "Show Detail"
```

6. Save your work.

Project 8-4

King William Hotel System. All applications should be designed in a manner that facilitates the work of any user. Although graphical user interfaces make data entry easier than is possible in non–graphical interfaces, the interface may still need enhancements. For example, users with less-than-perfect eyesight might have a difficult time seeing the cursor when they are entering data. Some users of the King William Hotel system might need additional assistance to see which control contains the cursor at any point during the data input process.

You can enhance the King William Hotel system to make data entry easier by adding VBA code that changes the background color of a control when the user is ready to enter data in it. You can use the GetFocus and LoseFocus events to execute VBA code that changes the BackColor property of the control. Due to the manner in which events occur, however, the first control to receive the focus must be handled as a special case.

Complete these steps:

1. Open **KWH.mdb**. Write two subroutines in the frmCustomer form. Name the first subroutine **Highlight_On**. It will change the background color of the currently active control to cyan. An error occurs when Access tries to execute this subroutine for the first control in the tab stop order, due to the timing of the GetFocus event and the setting of the value for the ActiveControl property of the Screen object. The error

is handled by referring explicitly to the first control in the tab stop order. The code for Highlight_On follows:

```
Private Sub Highlight_On()
'Turns background of control to cyan
On Error GoTo Errhandler
    Screen.ActiveControl.BackColor = RGB(0, 255, 255)
    Exit Sub
Errhandler:
    [Forms]![frmCustomer]![txtCustomerNo].BackColor = _
RGB(0, 255, 255)
    Resume Next
End Sub
```

2. Name the second subroutine **Highlight_Off**. It changes the background color for the currently active control to white. There is no unusual error situation to handle. The code for this subroutine follows:

```
Private Sub Highlight_Off()
Screen.ActiveControl.BackColor = RGB(255, 255, 255)
End Sub
```

3. To change every control, place a call to **Highlight_On** in the GetFocus event of every control and a call to **Highlight_Off** in the LoseFocus event of every control.

4. It is now time to enhance the form that supports the checkout process. For a given reservation, frmChargeSummary should display the total cafe charges and the total room charge (number of nights in the reservation multiplied by the room rate). Place the code for this process in the OnCurrent event for the form:

```
Dim intDays As Integer,
Dim strCategory As String
Dim curRate As Currency
Dim dbKW As ADODB.Connection
Dim rstReservation As New ADODB.Recordset
On Error Resume Next
Me![frmCafeBillDetail].Visible = False
Me![cmdDetail].Caption = "Show Detail"
'Sum the cafe charges for this reservation
Me![txtCafeTotal] = DSum("[Amount]", _
"tblCafeBillDetail", "[RoomNo]=" & Me![txtRoomNo] & _
" AND ([TransactionDate] Between #" & Me![txtStartDate] & _
"# And #" & Me![txtEndDate] & "#)")
If IsNull(Me![txtCafeTotal]) Then Me![txtCafeTotal] = 0
'Calculate the room charge
intDays = DateDiff("d", Me![txtStartDate], Me![txtEndDate])
strCategory = DLookup("[Category]", "tblRoom", "[RoomNo]=" & _
Me![txtRoomNo])
curRate = DLookup("[Rate]", "tblRoomDes", "[Category]='" & _
strCategory & "'")
Me![txtRoomTotal] = intDays * curRate
'Update the reservation to ensure current data
```

8

```
Set dbKW = CurrentProject.Connection
With rstReservation
    .CursorType = adOpenKeyset
    .LockType = adLockOptimistic
    .Open "tblReservation"
    .Find "[ReservationNo]=" & Me![txtReservationNo]
    ![Amount] = Me![txtRoomTotal] + Me![txtCafeTotal]
    .Update
End With
Me![txtAmount] = rstReservation![Amount]
```

5. Another enhancement for this system is the ability to show or hide detailed data as desired. The frmChargeSummary form contains detailed data in a subform and a command button for showing or hiding those data. Modify this form so that the detailed charges are displayed when the user clicks a button labeled "Show Detail." When the detailed charges are visible, change the label on the button to "Hide Detail." When the button displays the label "Hide Detail," clicking it should hide the detailed data and change the label back to "Show Detail." The code needed to add this enhancement appears in two places. First, in the Click event for the command button, add the following code:

```
Me![frmCafeBillDetail].Visible = _
Not Me![frmCafeBillDetail].Visible
If Me![frmCafeBillDetail].Visible Then
    Me![cmdDetail].Caption = "Hide Detail"
Else
    Me![cmdDetail].Caption = "Show Detail"
    End If
```

6. Then, in the OnCurrent event for the form, add the following lines of code:

```
Me![frmCafeBillDetail].Visible = False
Me![cmdDetail].Caption = "Show Detail"
```

7. The Current event needs to execute when the form opens so as to force an update of the first record. Therefore, add the following line to the Open event of the form:

```
Call Form_Current
```

8. Another bit of functionality is needed for the hotel's system. When posting cafe charges to a room, several scenarios are possible. The frmCafeBillPost contains three buttons to handle these scenarios. The button labeled "Post Item" adds an item to the current bill number and increments the line number in anticipation of adding another item to the same bill number. The button labeled "New Bill" increments the bill number and resets the line number so that the first item on the bill appears on line number 1. The processing behind these buttons creates a situation where a line (the last one created) has no item associated with it. Therefore, the Close button cleans up this small anomaly. To program this process, you need to declare global variables in the Declarations section of the form as follows:

```
Dim intBillNo As Integer
Dim intRoomNo As Integer
Dim intLineNo As Integer
Dim datTransDate As Date
```

9. When the form opens, the following code in the form's Open event sets the stage for the processing:

```
'Set up variables to control date, line number, and bill
'number
DoCmd.GoToRecord acDataForm, "frmCafeBillPost", acLast
intLineNo = 0
datTransDate = Date
intBillNo = DMax("[BillNo]", "tblCafeBillDetail") + 1
Call Form_Current
```

10. You can see that the Current event is called. Enter the following code:

```
If Me.NewRecord Then
'Use same room number, bill number, and transaction date
'Increment line number
Me![txtRoomNo] = intRoomNo
Me![txtTransactionDate] = datTransDate
Me![txtBillNo] = intBillNo
Me![txtLineNo] = intLineNo + 1
intLineNo = intLineNo + 1
End If
```

11. Enter the code for the "Post Item" command button:

```
If Me.txtRoomNo <> 0 Then
'Save room number and transaction date
intRoomNo = Me![txtRoomNo]
datTransDate = Me![txtTransactionDate]
DoCmd.GoToRecord acDataForm, "frmCafeBillPost", acNewRec
Me![txtPrice] = Null 'reset price displayed
End If
```

12. Enter the code for the "New Bill" command button:

```
Dim intCancel As Integer
DoCmd.GoToRecord acDataForm, "frmCafeBillPost", acNewRec
'Reset room number and price
intRoomNo = 0
Me![txtPrice] = Null
Call Form_Open(intCancel)
'Set focus to proper control
Me![txtRoomNo].SetFocus
```

13. Enter the cleanup code in the Close button:

```
On Error Resume Next
'This design causes the last records stored in the table to
have a 'zero item number.
'This bit of code cleans out those records.
Dim qdfDelete As New ADODB.Command
qdfDelete.ActiveConnection = CurrentProject.Connection
qdfDelete.CommandText = _
"DELETE * FROM [tblCafeBillDetail] WHERE [ItemNo]=0;"
```

```
DoCmd.RunCommand acCmdSaveRecord
qdfDelete.Execute
DoCmd.Close
```

14. To begin to populate the control on frmCafeBillPost, open the Properties window for cboItem.

15. If necessary, click the **Events** tab to display the Event Properties.

16. In the AfterUpdate event property, select **[Event Procedure]**, and then click the **Build** button.

17. Enter the following code:

```
'display  price and update table
Me![txtPrice] = _
Dlookup("[Price]", "tblCafeMenu", _
     "[ItemNo]=" & Me![cboItem]) _
Me![txtAmount] = Me![txtPrice]
```

18. Save the procedure, and then close the Visual Basic window.

Project 8-5

Workers' Compensation Commission System. All applications should be designed in a manner that facilitates the work of any user. Although graphical user interfaces make data entry easier than is possible in non-graphical interfaces, the interface may still need enhancements. For example, users with less-than-perfect eyesight might have a difficult time seeing the cursor when they are entering data. Some users might need additional assistance to see which control contains the cursor at any point during the data input process.

You can enhance the WCC application to make data entry easier by adding VBA code that changes the background color of a control when the user is ready to enter data in it. You can use the GetFocus and LoseFocus events to execute VBA code that changes the BackColor property of the control. Due to the manner in which events occur, however, the first control to receive the focus must be handled as a special case.

Complete these steps:

1. Open **WCC.mdb**. Write two subroutines in the frmPatients form. Name the first subroutine **Highlight_On**. It will change the background color of the currently active control to cyan. An error occurs when Access tries to execute this subroutine for the first control in the tab stop order, due to the timing of the GetFocus event and the setting of the value for the ActiveControl property of the Screen object. The error is handled by referring explicitly to the first control in the tab stop order. The code for Highlight_On follows:

```
Private Sub Highlight_On()
'Turns background of control to cyan
On Error GoTo Errhandler
    Screen.ActiveControl.BackColor = RGB(0, 255, 255)
    Exit Sub
```

```
Errhandler:
   [Forms]![frmPatients]![txtMedicalRecordNumber].BackColor = _
   RGB(0, 255, 255)
   Resume Next
End Sub
```

2. Name the second subroutine **Highlight_Off**. It changes the background color of the currently active control to white. There is no unusual error situation to handle. The code for this subroutine follows:

```
Private Sub Highlight_Off()
Screen.ActiveControl.BackColor = RGB(255, 255, 255)
End Sub
```

3. To change every control, place a call to **Highlight_On** in the GetFocus event of every control and a call to **Highlight_Off** in the LoseFocus event of every control.

4. Another enhancement for this system is the ability to show or hide detailed data as desired. The frmDoctors form contains detailed data in a subform and a command button for showing or hiding those data. Modify this form so that the doctor's patients are displayed when the user clicks the button labeled "Show Patients." When the patient data are visible, change the label on the button to "Hide Patients". When the button displays the label "Hide Patients," clicking it should hide the detailed data and change the label back to "Show Patients." The form should open with the detailed data hidden. The code needed to add this enhancement appears in two places. In the Click event for the command button, add the following code:

```
Me![frmPatientList].Visible = Not Me![frmPatientList].Visible
If Me![frmPatientList].Visible Then
    Me![cmdDetail].Caption = "Hide Patients"
Else
    Me![cmdDetail].Caption = "Show Patients"
End If
```

5. In the Open event for the form, add the following code:

```
Me![frmPatientList].Visible = False
Me![cmdDetail].Caption = "Show Patients"
```

6. Save your work.

WRITING, TESTING, AND DEBUGGING ACCESS APPLICATIONS

Enhancing the Swim Lessons Application

In this chapter you will:

- ◆ Write VBA procedures that use a variety of assignment statements
- ◆ Choose and write appropriate conditional execution statements
- ◆ Create program loops
- ◆ Write disk- and file-related statements
- ◆ Invoke error handlers and write error-handling routines
- ◆ Test Access applications
- ◆ Debug Access applications using message boxes and the debugging facilities

---

In this chapter, you will learn about writing VBA statements so that you can develop Access applications that manipulate data in Access databases. You will also learn how to test, debug, and maintain Access applications so that end users receive and continue to use a quality system. When you have completed this chapter, you'll understand why the best programmers consider thorough testing to be an essential part of application development.

We begin our discussion with the details surrounding programming constructs.

FUNDAMENTAL PROGRAMMING CONSTRUCTS

The key to writing, debugging, testing, and maintaining Access applications is the development of well-constructed and well-documented procedures. Before getting into the details of the statements that make up the procedures, let's review the conventions relevant to many VBA statements and procedures.

Operators

Many VBA statements support mathematical, string, and comparison operations. Addition, subtraction, multiplication, and division are indicated by the +, -, *, and / operators, respectively. **Integer division** is indicated by \ (for example, 14 \ 3 evaluates to 4). **Exponentiation** is indicated by the ^ operator (for example, 2 ^ 3 evaluates to 8).

VBA also recognizes a full complement of **comparison operators**: <, <=, >, >=, =, and <>. These operators signify less than, less than or equal to, greater than, greater than or equal to, equal to, and not equal to, respectively. **And** and **Or** are available as logical operators. **Not** is used as a negation operator. And, Or, and Not have the traditional precedence relationships (that is, Not has the highest precedence, followed by And and then Or). Parentheses can be used to control the precedence. For example, Not 2 < 3 And 3 > 4 evaluates to False, whereas Not (2 < 3 And 3 > 4) evaluates to True.

String concatenation, which is the uniting of two or more string values, can be performed using either the + or & operator. The + operator produces a null result when either operand is null; the & operator treats a null operand as a zero-length string. In most cases, & is the desired operator because when it is used, a null operand will not produce a null result, which is typically the preferred outcome.

Figure 9-1 illustrates the use of string concatenation to build an SQL statement that will be executed within VBA. This statement appears in the Form_Open event procedure in frmLeveling. The If statement checks whether the student is enrolled in a program. If the student is not enrolled, the code produces the following SQL statement:

```
Select * FROM tblTracks WHERE
Category='Program Prerequisite' AND (Program = 'ALL')
```

If the student is enrolled in a program—for instance, the DSCI program—then the code constructs the following statement:

```
Select * FROM tblTracks WHERE
Category='Program Prerequisite'
AND (Program = 'ALL' OR Program = 'DSCI')
```

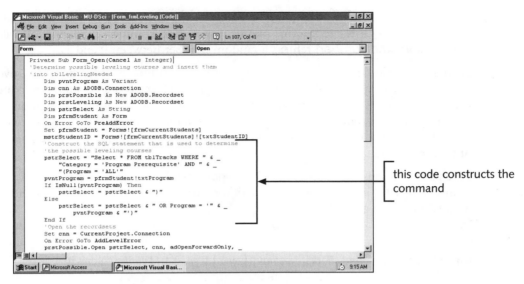

Figure 9-1 Constructing an SQL command by using strings in VBA

9

> In almost all calculations that involve a null value, the result will be null. The only exception to this rule occurs when concatenating string expressions using the & operator.

> Comparing null values results in a null comparison. That is, if you compare two variables (as in X > Y) and either (or both) contains a null value, the comparison evaluates to null. It may seem odd, but if X contains a null value and Y contains a null value, then X is not considered equal to Y (nor is X considered not equal to Y!). The result of the comparison is null. Working with null values is a special feature of working in a database environment.

Comments

Comments are vital to system maintenance because they indicate the purpose of each section of code. The **Rem** statement is used to include explanatory comments in a program. Rem can be—and generally is—represented in code with a single quote (').You can place comments on lines by themselves or append them to lines of code. Comments should increase the understanding of the reader. Try to avoid comments such as

```
Exit Sub     'Exit the Subroutine
```

which provides no additional information.

Built-in Functions

Built-in functions provide built-in functionality to the developer. For example, IsNull and IsEmpty allow If...Then...Else statements to test whether a user has entered a value into a text box. In addition, a programmer can use built-in functions to perform trigonometric calculations (for example, **Cos (***number***)** returns a cosine), financial calculations (for example, **IRR(***array***)** returns the internal rate of return), and common mathematical calculations (for example, **Rnd(***number***)** returns a random number between 0 and 1).

Further examples abound. For instance, many built-in functions handle the conversion of data from one data type to another (for example, **CInt(***expression***)** rounds an expression to the nearest integer and **Str(***number***)** returns the string representation of a number). In addition, programmers commonly use the MsgBox built-in function in VBA statements, and they often use the resulting message boxes as a programming tool to monitor the behavior of their programs.

One particularly useful built-in function is **InputBox**. A programmer can use this function to prompt a user for information. The function returns the user's input. The InputBox function has the following general form:

Syntax

InputBox[$] (*Prompt* [, *Title*][, *Default*] [,*xpos*] [,*ypos*] [,*Helpfile, Context*])

Syntax Dissection

- If the **$** is used, the value returned by the function must be a string.
- *Prompt* is the message displayed in the input box.
- *Title* is the text displayed in the title bar.
- *Default* indicates the value returned by the function when the user does not type anything into the input box.
- *xpos* and *ypos* establish the position of the input box on the screen.
- *Helpfile* and *Context* indicate the location of custom help, designed by the programmer, that is relevant for the input box.

As an example of a built-in function, consider the NewInstitute subroutine (located in the basUtilities module of the MU-DSci database). It uses the InputBox function as part of an assignment statement. The input box asks for the country where the institute is located. In addition, NotInList event procedures associated with combo boxes located in frmProspects invoke NewInstitute.

Adding a Module to Identify Frequent Registrants

Now that you have reviewed statements versus lines, operators, comments, and built-in functions, it is time to pull all of this knowledge together in the exercise of adding a module to identify frequent registrants. The Swim Lessons application will use the procedures in the module to designate certain students for discounted registration fees. The module will organize all the procedures related to this processing in a single place.

We will use a structured approach to construct the procedures. At first, the major purpose of the procedures will be coded and tested. Later, additional statements will be added. Such an approach helps you coherently plan the structure of the program, test individual procedures, and test the interaction between the procedures. The standard basDiscounts module will contain all of the procedures.

To create the basDiscounts module:

1. Open Access, open **SwimReg.mdb**, and then refresh the links, if necessary. Click the **Modules** object type in the Object Bar, and then click the **New** button. Make sure that the Option Explicit statement is included in the Declarations section of the module. Type it there if you do not see it. If it is not included, undeclared variables will not be considered errors.

2. Create a public procedure called **UpdateDiscounts** that contains the following code:

```
Public Sub UpdateDiscounts()
'Determine students with multiple registrations.
'Award discounts at levels specified in the database.

Dim prstDiscount As New ADODB.Recordset
Dim prstStudent As New ADODB.Recordset
Dim psngDiscount As Single
Dim pintDiscountPoint As Integer
Dim psngDiscountAmount As Single
Dim varReturn As Variant
Dim pintProcessCount As Integer
Dim pintStudentCount As Integer

With prstDiscount
    .ActiveConnection = CurrentProject.Connection
    .CursorType = adOpenKeyset
    .LockType = adLockOptimistic
    .Open "SELECT * FROM tblDiscount"
End With

With prstStudent
    .ActiveConnection = CurrentProject.Connection
    .CursorType = adOpenKeyset
    .LockType = adLockOptimistic
    .Open "SELECT * FROM tblStudents"
End With

'Get discount parameters from the database
If prstDiscount.EOF Then
    Exit Sub     'no discounts being offered
Else
    prstDiscount.MoveFirst
    pintDiscountPoint = prstDiscount![DiscountPoint]
    psngDiscountAmount = prstDiscount![Amount]
    prstDiscount.Close
    End If
End Sub
```

9

3. Compile **SwimReg**.

4. Click the **Save** button on the Standard toolbar, save your code as **basDiscounts**, and then close the Visual Basic window. Close frmClassesEnrolled_Subform.

Later in this chapter, you will have an opportunity to add VBA statements to this procedure to complete the programming task.

VBA STATEMENTS

Now that the preliminaries are out of the way, we can examine the formats of individual statements in some detail. The statements supported by VBA are similar to those of many programming languages, and, like most languages, VBA has the ability to assign values to variables, test conditions, and create loops. Each programming language, however, has its own nuances concerning the statement syntax. To build Access applications, you must learn the particulars of VBA.

Assignment and With Statements

Assignment statements are fundamental to most Access applications. These statements change the values of an object's properties. Programmers also use them to update fields in recordsets and to place values in VBA variables. Although you encountered assignment statements earlier in this book, we will now go into more depth so that you can create procedures to handle complex processing tasks.

The **With** statement allows you to abbreviate assignment statements that reference object properties, because the object does not need to be specified. You will find the With statement useful when, for instance, a series of properties is updated for a particular object; the With statement allows a programmer to drop the object portion of the dot or bang notation. Examine its syntax:

Syntax

With *object*
[*statements*]
End With

Syntax Dissection

- The **With** keyword tells Access to concatenate *object* to any notation that begins with a dot. A **With** statement block must end with **End With**.

- The *object* is a valid reference to an object. It includes dot notation, bang notation, and an object variable. The object can also be a user-defined type.

- The *statements* are frequently assignment statements, but they can consist of any valid series of VBA statements, including If…Then…Else statements.

One advantage of the With statement is that it identifies a block of statements that operates on the same object. Blocking statements (that is, grouping related statements) can make statements easier to read and understand; therefore, program maintenance becomes easier. The following sets of statements illustrate this concept:

```
Me![txtQDrop].ForeColor = RGB(255, 0, 0)   'Red
Me![txtQDrop].FontWeight = cBOLD_FONT
Me![txtQDrop].FontUnderline = True
```

is the same as

```
With Me![txtQDrop]
    .ForeColor = RGB(255, 0, 0)   'Red
    .FontWeight = cBOLD_FONT
    .FontUnderline = True
End With
```

Access supports assignment statement formats that are specific to strings. For instance, you can use **Mid** (or Mid$) to replace part of a string with another string. Examine its syntax:

Syntax

Mid [$](*StringVariable, Start* [*,Length*]) = *StringExpression*

Syntax Dissection

- *StringVariable* is the variable receiving the string.

- *Start* indicates where in *StringVariable* to begin the assignment.

- *Length* indicates how many characters should be assigned.

- *StringExpression* represents the string that will be placed inside *StringVariable*.

An example of this assignment statement follows:

```
pstrWholeName = "John K. Smith"
Mid$ (WholeName, 6, 1) = "L"
```

The new value of pstrWholeName is "John L. Smith".

Table 9-1 provides a list of assignment statements.

Table 9-1   Summary of assignment statements

Statement	Definition	Syntax
Let	Assigns a value to a variable or property	[Let] Varname = Expression ■ Varname is any valid variable name or property ■ Expression is any legal expression that returns a value

9

Table 9-1   Summary of assignment statements (continued)

Statement	Definition	Syntax
LSet	Left-aligns a string within a string variable	LSet strVariable = string ■ strVariable is any variable defined as a string ■ string is any expression that returns a string
Mid	Replaces part of a string with another string	Mid[$] (StringVariable, Start [,Length]) = StringExpression ■ StringVariable, Start, Length, and StringExpression are defined in the text
Rset	Right-aligns a string within a string variable	RSet strVariable = string ■ strVariable is any variable defined as a string ■ string is any expression that returns a string
Set	Causes an object variable to point to the same storage location as the object in which it is assigned	Set Objectvar = [[New] ObjectExpression | Nothing] ■ Objectvar refers to a variable declared as some type of object (for example, Control, Form, TextBox) ■ ObjectExpression identifies the object to which Objectvar is assigned (for example, dot or bang notation, a function that returns an object) ■ The New keyword indicates that Objectvar is to point to a copy of ObjectExpression ■ Nothing removes the pointer from Objectvar

Sometimes you'll want different program statements to execute depending on the outcome of one or more conditions. Conditional execution statements allow the specification of these conditions.

Conditional Execution Statements (If Statement)

Often, blocks of code need to be executed under some conditions but not under others. VBA provides several statements for these situations. For instance, the If statement can evaluate multiple conditions and thus selectively execute multiple sections of code. It has the following format:

Syntax

If *Condition1* **Then**
   StatementBlock1
[**ElseIf** *Condition2* **Then**
   StatementBlock2]
[**Else**
   StatementBlockN]
End If

Syntax Dissection

- *Condition#* is any expression that evaluates to True or False. It can contain the comparison and logical operators discussed earlier. It can also use functions and properties that evaluate to True or False, such as IsNull, IsEmpty, and NoMatch.

- *StatementBlock#* contains any valid set of VBA statements, including If statements.

The If statement can also contain multiple ElseIf parts. When it does include such parts, conditions occur for the initial If part and for each ElseIf part. In this form of the If statement, StatementBlock1 is a block of VBA statements that executes if Condition1 is True, StatementBlock2 is a block of VBA statements that executes if Condition2 is True, and so forth. If no condition evaluates to True, the statement block included in the optional Else block executes.

Only one Else block may be included in this type of statement. The statement blocks are usually indented to show that they "belong" to the condition that precedes them. The statement ends with an End If statement, which can be placed anywhere on the line. Some programmers prefer the End If statement to appear in the same column as the If to which it belongs. Another widely used style indents this statement to the same level as the statement blocks to show that the End If is subordinate to the If to which it belongs. Whichever style you adopt, you should be consistent in its use. An example of this statement type follows:

```
If pstrClassType = "Chemistry Lab" Then
    pcurLabFee = 20
    pstrMessage = "Safety Glasses and Lab Coat Required"
ElseIf pstrClassType = "Physics Lab" Then
    pcurLabFee = 15
    pstrMessage = "Safety Glasses Required"
ElseIf pstrClassType = "Lab" Then
    pcurLabFee = 10
    pstrMessage = ""
Else
    pcurLabFee = 0
    pstrMessage = ""
End If
```

The Swim Lessons application has some flaws that you are now ready to address with your greater knowledge of VBA. In the next section, you will apply new techniques to enhance that application.

Using Conditional Branching to Implement a Wait List

Currently, the Swim Lessons application does not allow you to maintain information about students who want to enroll in classes that are already full. The application would be improved if a user could place students on a wait list for classes that are full. You can easily modify the application to accomplish this objective.

To add a student to the wait list table:

1. Open **frmClassesEnrolled_subform** in Design view and then use the Properties window for the form to locate the code for the **Form_BeforeUpdate** event procedure.

2. Modify the code in the procedure to it so that it appears as follows (new code is shown in bold):

```
'If this is a new record, verify that enrolled < limit
'and add one to the enrollment
Dim pcmoEnrolled As New cmoEnrollment
Dim pstrMsg As String
If Not Me.NewRecord Then
    Exit Sub
End If
If pcmoEnrolled.AddToEnrollment([cboLessonIndex]) = _
     False Then
    'There is no room in the class
    pstrMsg = "Sorry this class is full. " &_
         "Add student to wait list?"
    If MsgBox (pstrMsg, vbYesNo + vbInformation + _
         vbDefaultButton1, "Class Limit") = vbYes Then
        'Add the student to the wait list
        pcmoEnrolled.AddToWaitList Parent![txtSID], _
             Me![cboLessonIndex]
    End If  'Yes to add to list
    Me.Undo 'Undo the record
    Cancel = True 'Cancel the update
End If
```

3. Save your work, and close the Visual Basic window.

The code that you added to frmClassesEnrolled_subform contains a reference to a procedure that adds a student to the wait list for this class. You need to add that function to the cmoEnrollment object in the Modules list.

To add the AddToWaitList function to cmoEnrollment:

1. Open **cmoEnrollment** in Design view.

2. Add a new procedure named **AddToWaitList**. Select **Sub** for the procedure type and **Public** for the scope.

3. Add the following code (new code is shown in bold):

```
Public Sub AddToWaitList (strSID As String, _
     lngLessonIdx As Long)
'If student not on the wait list, add student to wait list
    Dim cnn As ADODB.Connection
    Dim prstWaitList As New ADODB.Recordset
    If Not OnWaitList(strSID, lngLessonIdx) Then
        'Add record to wait list table
        Set cnn = CurrentProject.Connection
```

```
        prstWaitList.Open "tblWaitList", cnn, _
            adOpenKeyset, adLockOptimistic, _
            adCmdTableDirect
        With prstWaitList
            .AddNew
            ![LessonIndex] = lngLessonIdx
            ![SID] = strSID
            .Update
        End With
        prstWaitList.Close
    End If  'not already on wait list
End Sub
```

The code that you just wrote contains a reference to a function that determines whether a student is already on the wait list for this class. Now you need to add that function.

To add the OnWaitList function to cmoEnrollment:

1. Insert a new procedure named **OnWaitList**. Select **Function** for the procedure type and **Public** for the scope.

2. Add the following code (new code is shown in bold):

```
Private Function OnWaitList(strSID As String, _
lngLessonIdx As Long) As Boolean
'Returns True if student is already on the Wait List for
'this class
Dim pstrCriteria As String
pstrCriteria = "[LessonIndex]=" & lngLessonIdx _
    & " And [SID]='" & strSID & "'"
OnWaitList = (DCount("[RecordNo]", "tblWaitList", _
        pstrCriteria) > 0)
End Function
```

3. Click **Compile SwimReg** in the Debug menu. Fix any compilation errors, and then close the Visual Basic window.

Conditional Execution Statements (Select Case Statements)

When the same variable is tested for multiple values, the Select Case statement can be used. The syntax for the Select Case statement is as follows:

Syntax

Select Case *TestExpression*
  [**Case** *ExpressionList1*
    StatementBlock1]
  [**Case** *ExpressionList2*
    StatementBlock2]
  [**Case Else**
    StatementBlockN]
End Select

Syntax Dissection

- *TestExpression* is a string or numeric expression to be evaluated.

- *ExpressionList1* and *ExpressionList2* compare the test expression with some other expression.

- *StatementBlocks* are valid VBA statements that execute when the associated *ExpressionList* is True.

The If…Then…Else statement illustrated earlier can be changed to a Select Case statement as follows:

```
Select Case pstrClassType
    Case "Chemistry Lab"
        pcurLabFee = 20
        pstr Message = "Safety Glasses and Lab Coat Required"
    Case "Physics Lab"
        pcurLabFee = 15
        pstr Message = "Safety Glasses Required"
    Case "Lab"
        pcurLabFee = 10
        pstr Message = ""
    Case Else
        pcurLabFee = 0
        pstr Message = ""
End Select
```

In the preceding code, "Lab" is an ExpressionList containing one value: a constant. ExpressionLists need not be constants, and, when you evaluate them, you are not restricted to evaluating for equality. For example, the following statement is valid:

```
Select Case pintTotalHours
    Case Is < 3
        pcurGeneralUseFee = 0
        pstrStatus = "Minimal enrollment"
    Case 4 to 12
        pcurGeneralUseFee = 5 * pintTotalHours
        pstrStatus = "Part-time"
    Case Else
        pcurGeneralUseFee = 60
        pstrMessage = "Full-time"
End Select
```

Like the Else keyword in an If statement, the statements following Else execute when none of the previous conditions is True.

Iterative (Looping) Statements

Statements that cause blocks of statements to repeat are called **iterative** or **looping** statements. MU-DSci uses looping statements in several locations. For example, clicking cmdAllCourses on frmLeveling causes the application to place a check in all possible leveling courses. The VBA code that supports this action iterates the same statement block for each record in frmLeveling.

VBA supports multiple looping statement forms. The Do statement is a commonly used "looping" statement. It has several forms:

Syntax

Do [[**While** | **Until**] *Condition*]
   StatementBlock
   [**Exit Do**]
   StatementBlock
Loop

Syntax Dissection

- *Condition* is an expression that evaluates to True or False. It is tested at the beginning of the **Do** loop.

- **While** causes a block to repeat while a condition is True. If the condition immediately evaluates to False under the While condition, VBA does not execute the statements in the loop.

- **Until** causes a block to repeat until the condition is True. If the condition immediately evaluates to True under the Until condition, VBA does not execute the statements in the loop.

- **Exit Do** causes Access to exit the loop; the code continues executing at the first statement after the Loop statement.

The code at the end of the next paragraph illustrates the Do/Until statement used in the procedure that is activated when the user clicks cmdAllCourses. The cmdAllCourses_Click subroutine cycles through the recordset behind frmLeveling. The RecordsetClone property of the form creates the recordset used by the procedure. The MoveFirst method sets the recordset pointer (that is, the bookmark) to the first record in the recordset. Do Until prstPossible.EOF tells Access to repeat the code between the Do statement and the Loop statement until the bookmark of prstPossible reaches the end of the data. (EOF is a common acronym for *end-of-file*; in this case, however, the data are located in a table.)

Within the looping block, the bookmark of the form is set equal to the bookmark of the recordset. Next, an If statement tests the value of chkNeeded on the form, checking the box if it is not already checked. The next statement calls a procedure to create an array that will allow the user to undo these changes. The last statement in the looping block, prstPossible.MoveNext, moves the bookmark to the next record in prstPossible. If the bookmark moves to a position after the last record in the recordset, Access assigns a True value to the EOF property of the recordset.

```
Private Sub cmdAllCourses_Click()
  'Causes all possible courses to be added to leveling

  Dim prstPossible As Recordset

  'Error code is executed when the Recordset cannot be opened

  On Error GoTo LevelingCourseCloneProblem

  'Turn off screen updating to prevent a fluttering screen.

  Application.Echo False

  'Set precPossible to the Recordset behind the
  'PossibleLevelingForStudent form

  Set prstPossible = Me.RecordsetClone

  'Move the bookmark to the first record

  prstPossible.MoveFirst

  'If an error occurs while processing an individual record
  'nothing special is performed, but the system moves to the
  'next record.

  On Error Resume Next

  'Loop through each record in the recordset
  'Set the Bookmark of the form to the Bookmark of the Recordset.
  'If an x is not in the NeededCheck box, call a subroutine
  'that adds the course to the tblLevelingNeeded table.

  Do Until prstPossible.EOF
    Me.Bookmark = prstPossible.Bookmark
    If Not Me![chkNeeded] Then   'Don't add if already added
      Me![chkNeeded] = True
      CreateUndoArray
    End If
    prstPossible.MoveNext          'Move to the next record
  Loop

  'Turn screen updating on.

  Application.Echo True
  prstPossible.Close
  Exit Sub
```

```
LevelingCourseCloneProblem:
  'Error processing routine when Recordset cannot be created.
  Dim pstrErrMessage As String
  pstrErrMessage = "Cannot add Leveling. " & Err.Description
  Call ErrorTrap(pstrErrMessage)
  Exit Sub

End Sub
```

The following Do While statement could be substituted for the Do Until statement in the previous code:

```
Do While Not prstPossible.EOF
```

This statement tells Access to repeat the code as long as the record pointer is not at the end of the file. If you use this statement, you do not need to change any other lines shown in the previous full code listing.

Table 9-2 lists other forms of the Do statement, as well as other looping statements. No particular looping statement is preferred in all situations. The statement chosen should be the one that best meets the needs of the programmer and that is the easiest to understand.

9

Table 9-2   Looping statements

Statement		Example		Notes
Do [[While|Until]] Condition ... [Exit Do] Loop		Do Until recStudent.EOF ... Loop		*Condition* is tested before the first iteration of the loop
Do ... [Exit Do] Loop [[While|Until]] Condition		Do ... Loop While prec.GPR > 3.0		*Condition* is tested at the end of the loop; at least one iteration of the loop is performed
For Counter = Start to End [Step Increment] ... [Exit For] Next		For i = 0 to precStudent.Count ... Next		Used when the number of iterations is known; frequently used to cycle through all objects in a collection
While Condition ... [Exit Do] Wend		While Not recStudent.EOF ... Wend		The same as a Do While loop; *Condition* is tested at the beginning of the loop

> **TIP** A loop becomes an infinite loop when it never stops executing once it starts. As an example, consider the previous full code listing. If you omit the prstPossible.MoveNext statement inside the loop, an infinite loop occurs. Executing the MoveNext method ensures that each record is processed, ultimately causing the EOF property to be set to True. If you inadvertently create an infinite loop, you can press the Ctrl + Break keys simultaneously to interrupt the loop's execution.

A slightly different type of loop can be set up with a For Next statement. This statement is used whenever the number of loop iterations can be determined prior to the start of the loop. It is commonly used on arrays and collections, where an index can be used to retrieve the items in the collection or array.

Syntax

For *Counter* = *Start* **To** *End* [**Step** *Increment*]
  StatementBlock
  [**Exit For**]
  StatementBlock
Next [*Counter*]

Syntax Dissection

- *Counter* is a variable that indicates which iteration of the For Next loop is being executed.

- *Start* is the first value of *Counter*.

- *End* is the last value of *Counter*.

- *Increment* is the amount to add to *Counter* after iteration through the loop. If the *Step* part of the statement is omitted, *Increment* is assumed to be 1.

The following procedure (which is not actually implemented in the MU-DSci application) uses the ForNext statement to close all forms except the Switchboard form:

```
Sub CloseAllForms ()
    'Close all forms except the Switchboard
    Dim pintFormIndex As Integer
    Dim pfrmTheForm As Form
    For pintFormIndex = (Forms.Count - 1) To 0 Step -1
        Set pfrmTheForm = Forms(pintFormIndex)
        If pfrmTheForm.Name <> "Switchboard" Then
            pfrmTheForm.SetFocus
            DoCmd.Close
        End If
    Next pintFormIndex
End Sub
```

To understand this procedure, recall that a form can be referenced through the use of an index on the Forms collection. Access numbers the open forms in the Forms collection starting with the number 0. The Count property on the Forms collection is equal to the number of open forms in the application. In the loop just shown, the variable pintFormIndex starts with the highest Form index (which is 1 less than the value of Count) and is decreased by 1 each time the Next statement is encountered. The loop quits after pintFormIndex is less than zero.

Creating a Loop to Determine Discounts

Now that you know how loops work, it's time to put the concept to work. In the following steps, you will create a loop to process all of the student records so as to determine which students are eligible for a discount in the future.

To determine which students should be given future discounts:

1. Open **basDiscounts** in Design view, and locate the UpdateDiscounts procedure.

2. Enter the program code shown below just prior to the End Sub statement:

```
'Loop through the student records
prstStudent.MoveFirst

Do Until prstStudent.EOF
    'Calculate number of prior registrations
    If DCount("[SID]", "tblEnrollment", _
    "[SID]='" & prstStudent![SID] & "'") > _
            pintDiscountPoint Then
        psngDiscount = psngDiscountAmount
    Else
        psngDiscount = 0
        End If
    'Update the student record
    If psngDiscount > 0 Then
            With prstStudent
            '.Edit  Edit not needed in ADO
            ![DiscountPct] = psngDiscount
            .Update
        End With
    End If

    prstStudent.MoveNext
Loop
```

3. Compile the code and fix any compilation errors.

4. Save the code, and then close the Visual Basic window.

Assuming that errors do not occur in the database, the system is now capable of counting the courses for which a student has registered and updating the Discount field in tblStudents. In the process of registering a student and evaluating for discounts, however, errors can occur. For example, a table name could be changed or a null value could occur unexpectedly. These potential errors in the database require the use of special Error statements. Error statements and their routines frequently rely on unconditional branching statements.

Unconditional Branching Statements

In VBA, **unconditional branching statements** cause the program to skip execution of code that would have otherwise been executed. You use these types of statements in situations where you always want to skip some section of VBA code.

Programmers commonly use line labels and numbers in the creation of unconditional branching. A line label and number identify a single line of code within a procedure and follow a specific syntax:

- A line label must begin with a letter, end with a colon (:), and follow the same naming conventions as variables. It must begin in the first column of a procedure and must be unique within the module.

- A line number is any combination of the digits 0 through 9 and ends with a colon (:). The maximum line number is 21478483647. It must begin in the first column of a procedure and must be unique within the module.

Labels and numbers accomplish the same purpose, but programmers tend to prefer line labels because they provide a better description of the line of code being marked.

The simplest statement for unconditional branching is the GoTo statement. Its syntax is as follows:

Syntax

GoTo [*LineLabel* | *LineNumber*]

Syntax Dissection

- *LineLabel* is a valid line label in the procedure.
- *LineNumber* is a valid line number.

The following is an example of the use of GoTo:

```
        If plngEntered > 500 Then GoTo InvalidEntry
        MsgBox "Thank you. I will continue processing"
        . . .
        Exit Sub

InvalidEntry:
        Msgbox "The number is not valid"
    End Sub
```

In this example, if plngEntered is greater than 500, the program skips to the Invalid Entry line label. If plngEntered is less than or equal to 500, the message box appears. The Exit Sub statement causes the program to exit a subroutine. **Exit Function** works in the same way as Exit Sub except that it exits a function rather than a subroutine.

Although other unconditional branching statements exist, they can often be replaced with other statements such as Select Case statements, If...Then...Else statements, subroutines, and functions. Programmers generally prefer these statements over unconditional branching statements because the latter statements can make it difficult for maintenance programmers reading the code to follow the sequence of statement execution. Unconditional branching statements should therefore be used only when an alternative does not exist or when the block of code created by an unconditional branch is the best way to facilitate understanding of the code. (An exception to this heuristic is the On Error statement, which is discussed later in this chapter.)

VBA STATEMENTS AND RELATED FUNCTIONS THAT PERFORM ACCESS ACTIONS

9

While VBA supports many of the same statements found in other programming languages, it also provides many statements that may not appear elsewhere. These statements typically perform actions that can be classified as follows:

- Statements that manipulate the Access environment
- Statements that manipulate files
- Statements that reference the Windows environment
- Statements that manipulate other Windows applications

Many of the action-oriented statements are related to one or more functions that return information about the item manipulated by the action. In addition, a programmer can replace some of these statements or functions with other easier-to-use built-in functions.

Statements Related to the Access Environment

Table 9-3 describes several VBA statements that perform actions in the Access environment. The **SendKeys** statement is particularly useful when you want to trigger a series of events. For example, when VBA code updates a text box, Access does not execute the BeforeUpdate and AfterUpdate events. To replace this nonexecution with execution, you can use the SendKeys statement to change the value in the control, thereby simulating a user's typing action. For example,

```
Me![txtPhone].SetFocus
SendKeys "(414) 771-6543"
```

places the phone number in txtPhone and triggers the Change, BeforeUpdate, and AfterUpdate events.

Table 9-3 Statements that perform actions within the Access environment

Statement	Example	Description	Notes
Beep	Beep	Plays a tone on the computer's speaker	The Beep statement is commonly used to notify a user of an error or an unusual screen display. Many typists keep their eyes on a source document. An auditory cue is necessary to alert the typist to an unusual event.
DeleteControl FormName, ControlName	DeleteControl "frmStudents" "cmdClosebtn"	Removes a control from a form	The companion to the CreateControl function.
DeleteReportControl ReportName, ControlName	DeleteReportControl "rptTranscript", "txtSSN"	Removes a control from a report	The companion to the CreateReportControl.
SendKeys key	SendKeys {F2}	Simulates a user's keystroke	The SendKeys statement is similar to the SendKeys action used in a macro. Just as a user's keystrokes can trigger an event, so the SendKeys keystroke can trigger events (for example, OnChange). Alphabetic and numeric keystrokes must be specified as a string (for example, "A", "1"). Special keys must be placed within curly brackets (for example, {+}, {F2}). Commonly used SendKeys statements include • SendKeys {F1} Triggers context-sensitive help • SendKeys {F2} Causes the entire text in a text box to be highlighted • SendKeys {Down} Down arrow; can be used to select the next item in a combo box • SendKeys {Delete} Deletes the highlighted text in a text box • SendKeys {Esc} Undoes the update in the current field

Table 9-3   Statements that perform actions within the Access environment (continued)

Statement	Example	Description	Notes
Erase ArrayName	Erase mstr CourseArray	Sets numeric values to zero and string values to "" in a fixed array; reclaims storage space in dynamic arrays	
Randomize [number]	Randomize	Initializes the random number generator prior to using the Rnd function	Randomize should be used prior to the first use of the Rnd function so that Rnd does not repeat the same list of numbers each time the application is opened.

Windows Disk- and File-Related Statements

Occasionally, an application needs to obtain information about the environment in which it is running. The application may even need to change properties of the environment that influence its execution. VBA provides statements with which the application can accomplish these tasks, listed in Table 9-4. The disk and file statements are similar to the old DOS commands. If a programmer does not specify the full path to a file or directory, the current drive or directory is used. The current drive is changed with **ChDrive**, and the directory is changed with **ChDir**. The **CurDir()** function returns the current directory.

Table 9-4   Disk- and file-related statements

Statement	Description	Example
ChDrive *Drive*	Changes the current disk drive	ChDrive "A"
ChDir *Path*	Changes the current directory	ChDir "c:\mydoc"
MkDir *Path*	Creates a new directory	MkDir "c:\mydoc\reminder"
RmDir *Path*	Removes a directory	RmDir "c:\access\mytmp"
Name *OldFile* As *NewFile*	Changes the name of a file	Name "reminder" as "myrem"
Kill *FileSpec*	Deletes a file	Kill "c:\access\mytmp"

File input/output (I/O) statements, which write or read data that are contained in generic files rather than in Access tables, are useful as well. Generic files might store data concerning error logs, application start and end times, and database change documentation (that is, who updated what, and when). An advantage of generic files is that they can be used by a number of applications. Table 9-5 lists file I/O statements.

Table 9-5   File I/O statements

Statement	Description	Example
Close [*FileNumber*]	Closes the specified file	Close #1
Get [#] *FileNumber*, [*Position*], *Variable*	Reads a record from a random access file; the record is identified with the Position argument or the current record as positioned by the Seek statement	Get #4, 10, TheRecord
Input # *FileNumber*, *VariableList*	Reads values from a file into variables	Input #2 Desc, Num
Line Input # *FileNumber*, *Variable*	Reads an entire line from a sequential file into a variable	Line Input #3 TextLine
Lock [#] *FileNumber* [,*Range*]	Locks a file so others can't use it	Lock #1
Open *File* [**For** Mode] [*Access AccessMode*][**Lock**]**As** [#] *FileNumber* [**Len**=RecLength]	Opens a file; if file does not exist, the file is created Prerequisite to any other file I/O statement	Open "ErrFile" For Output As #1
Print # *FileNumber*, *Expressionlist*	Prints formatted files (for example, columns)	Print #8 Zone1; Tab; Zone2
Put [#] *FileNumber*, [*Position*] *VariableName*	Places a new record in the specified position	Put #4, 12, NewRecord
Reset	Closes all files	Reset
Seek [#] *FileNumber*, *Position*	Moves record pointer for beginning of read operations	Seek #1, 5
Unlock [#] *FileNumber* [,*Range*]	Unlocks a file so others can use it	Unlock #1
Width #*FileNumber*, *Width*	Sets output line width in an already open file	Width #1, 10
Write # *FileNumber* [,*VariableList*]	Writes a line to a sequential file; items in the file are separated by commas	Write #1 Err.Desc, Err.Number

Using Print Statements in an Error Routine

Any program that processes an entire table is likely to encounter an error at some point in its processing. The UpdateDiscounts procedure of the Swim Lessons application must proceed without failure when an error occurs. Notification through message boxes on a user's terminal is not practical, however. Instead, you will design a subroutine that prints errors to a file. Later, this subroutine can be invoked by other procedures.

To create a subroutine that prints errors to a file:

1. Display the **basDiscounts** module in Design view.

2. Add a new procedure by typing in the following code (in the third line, use the path name appropriate for your computing environment; if an errlog file does not already exist, Access will create one):

```
Public Sub PrintError(pstrError As String)
    'Open the Error Report so that data are appended to end.
    Open "c:\path\errlog" _
        For Append As #1

    'Print today's date and time with the error message.
    'Format is a built-in function that formats
    'the date. Tab specifies the print column
    Print #1, Tab(1); Format$(Now(), "General Date"); _
        Tab(20); pstrError

    'Write a blank line to the file
    Print #1,
    Close #1
End Sub
```

3. Click **Compile SwimReg** in the Debug menu, and fix any errors.

4. Type the following code into the Immediate window of the Debug facility:

```
PrintError "This is the first test"
PrintError "This is the second test"
```

When you press the Enter key after typing each line, Access writes to the errlog file.

5. Open the **errlog** file in any word processor (for example, Wordpad, Notepad, or Word). Errlog contains the date, time, and a message.

6. Close the word processor and return to Access. Close the Visual Basic window.

One potential problem with this code is that the path to the errlog file is coded into a VBA statement and therefore cannot be changed by the end user. In some applications, the path to a file depends on the folder in which the application is installed. In these cases, the Access application must determine the path.

Determining and Setting the Applications Operating Environment

Unfortunately, the CurDir() function, reviewed earlier, does not necessarily return the directory path that indicates the location of the application. Typically, CurDir() returns the default path for Access (usually My Documents). Sometimes, an application needs the path to an application's directory so as to create generic files that are stored in a convenient location. The application may also need the path when VBA code refreshes table links.

The application can determine the path to an application by reading the Windows Registry, which contains a variety of settings that support the management of many Windows applications. These settings include associations between file extensions and applications, the locations of windows on the screen, and Help file information. The application can access information about the Registry through the **GetSetting** and **GetAllSettings** functions. Access also provides statements that update the Windows Registry.

Although you do not need to undertake a full-blown study of the Registry, you should know that programmers frequently use the SysCmd function to obtain information that is similar to that found in the Registry. SysCmd also performs a number of other general operations, such as displaying a progress meter, retrieving the directory of the work group controlling Access security, and determining whether a form is open.

Syntax

SysCmd(*action*[, *text*][, *value*])
SysCmd(*action*[, *objecttype*][, *objectname*])

Syntax Dissection

- *action* is an intrinsic constant indicating the action performed by the SysCmd function.

- *text* is a string to display in a status bar.

- *value* is an amount to display in a progress meter.

- *objecttype* is an intrinsic constant that indicates the type of object under scrutiny (for example, acTable, acForm).

- *objectname* is the name of an object (for example, frmCurrent Students).

Table 9-6 describes some commonly used SysCmd specifications.

Table 9-6   Commonly used SysCmd specifications

SysCmd Specification	Description
SysCmd(acSys CmdAccessDir)	Returns the path where Msaccess.exe is located
SysCmd(acSysCmdGetObjectState, acForm, *FormName*)	Returns a nonzero value when the form is opened
SysCmd(acSysCmdGetWorkgroupFile)	Returns the path to the Workgroup file that is associated with Access
SysCmd(acSysCmdIniFile)	Returns the ini file that Access is using
SysCmd(acSysCmdRuntime)	Returns True if a runtime version of Access is running
SysCmd(acSysCmdInitMeter, *Status Bar Title, length*)	Initializes a progress meter
SysCmd(acSysCmdRemoveMeter)	Removes the progress meter
SysCmd(acSyscmdUpdateMeter, *progress value*)	Updates a progress meter

Finding the path to the Workgroup file with SysCmd(acSysCmdGetWorkgroupFile) is useful because this path is frequently (but not necessarily) the same as the path that contains the Access application and any attached database. Consequently, an application can use the path in an attempt to automatically reattach tables in program code. The path, after undergoing some string manipulation to remove the name of the Workgroup file, could also be used in an Open statement.

Using SysCmd to Implement a Progress Meter

A progress meter should be used whenever an operation is expected to take a long time. The last three rows in Table 9-6 provide SysCmd specifications for using a progress meter. Note these facts:

- The acSyCmdInitMeter constant is used to start the progress meter. The length argument is a number that indicates to the user the total time of the planned operation (for example, the total number of records to process, the number of fields to update, and the number of calculations).

- The acSysCmdRemoveMeter constant is used when the operation is complete.

- The acSysCmdUpdateMeter constant is used to show the progress at a given point in time.

As the number of students in the Swim Lessons database grows, the amount of time needed to update the Discount values in the database will increase accordingly. As currently implemented, the application provides no feedback to the user to indicate that anything is happening when the discount values are being updated. A progress meter is an effective way to reassure the user that the system is functioning properly. You will therefore implement one in the next set of steps.

As you go through the steps, remember that the progress meter must know the total number of records that will be processed and that this number can be found by moving to the last record in the table and then checking the RecordCount property. Your code will also effect another outcome: While the procedure is processing, the cursor will change to an hourglass icon as an additional visual cue indicating that the system is busy.

To implement a progress meter:

1. Open **basDiscounts** in Design view.

2. Add the following lines of code to the UpdateDiscounts procedure, just prior to the prstStudent.MoveFirst statement:

```
'Find the number of records to process
prstStudent.MoveLast
pintStudentCount = prstStudent.RecordCount
pintProcessCount = 0

'Set up the progress meter
varReturn = SysCmd(acSysCmdInitMeter, "Processing...", _
        pintStudentCount)
DoCmd.Hourglass True
```

A count of the number of students processed so far must be maintained to determine the progress that has been made.

3. Add the following lines of code just after the prstStudent.MoveNext statement:

```
'Update progress meter
pintProcessCount = pintProcessCount + 1
varReturn = SysCmd(acSysCmdUpdateMeter, pintProcessCount)
```

4. Once all of the records have been processed, the progress meter must be removed from the status bar and the mouse pointer must be changed from the hourglass icon back to the normal pointer. To accomplish this task, add the following lines of code just after the Loop statement:

```
'Remove the progress meter
varReturn = SysCmd(acSysCmdClearStatus)
DoCmd.Hourglass False
Exit Sub
```

5. Compile the procedure and correct any compilation errors.

6. Save your work, and then close the Visual Basic window.

Thus far, you have studied programming techniques that allow a programmer to interact with the operating environment. In the next section, you'll begin to study techniques for addressing problems that arise when you encounter programming errors.

CATEGORIES OF ERRORS

Programming is an activity in which mistakes will inevitably occur. Even experienced programmers make mistakes and must debug their code. The programming task is not complete when the program produces the desired results under typical operating conditions. Errors can still occur during the use of the program, especially under nontypical operating conditions. It is the programmer's duty to create an application that can handle unanticipated errors gracefully.

This section explores three categories of errors: compilation errors due to syntax mistakes, runtime errors due to improper statement use, and logic errors. In the process of the discussion, you will see how to use message boxes and the Debug window to find and fix runtime and logic errors. In addition, you will learn how to use error-handling statements to compensate for unavoidable or unanticipated errors.

Compilation Errors

Before Access can execute any procedure, all procedures that have not been previously compiled must be compiled. Compiling a procedure tells Access to translate VBA code into a format that is efficiently executed by the computer. As has been seen in many previous examples, the developer can force Access to compile all of the procedures within a module by clicking the Compile Loaded Modules button located on the toolbar. This option, as well as the Compile All Modules option, is also available from the Debug menu.

No matter how many compilation options you have (or that you try to use), a procedure will not compile when one or more lines of code violate the syntax rules of VBA. A variety of syntax mistakes can produce a compilation error. For example, if the module includes the Option Explicit statement, then a misspelled variable will cause an "undeclared variable" error upon compilation. Access will display an error message and highlight the offending variable. You can then correct the spelling and restart the compilation process.

Other syntax errors are easily corrected as you construct the procedure because VBA scans each line as you enter the code. When VBA detects an error, Access displays a pop-up window to notify you of the mistake. You can obtain additional information about the error by selecting the Help button in the pop-up window. These error messages are somewhat general in nature, so sometimes they will not be particularly useful. If you find the Help less than helpful, select the OK buttons in the dialog boxes until you get back to the code-writing environment. Then, use Access Help to obtain help for the statement you are trying to write.

Runtime Errors

Even when code compiles cleanly, problems still can occur. The VBA compiler is not capable of checking whether all statement combinations used within a procedure are valid. A statement combination is valid when it implements an executable sequence of processes. When a statement combination is invalid, errors may occur when the procedure executes. These errors are called runtime errors, because they occur when the procedure "runs."

As an example of a runtime error, consider what happens when the Seek method is used on a recordset that has not been opened as a table, as shown in Figure 9-2. This code is in the basRunTimeErrorExample module in the Swim Lessons application.

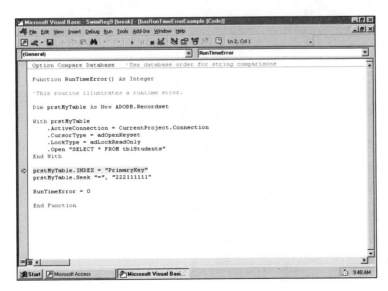

Figure 9-2   Runtime error example

Although a student record exists that has a student identification number (SID) with the value "222111111", this code will produce a runtime error because the Seek method cannot be used with a recordset that has been opened as a dynaset. Seek can be used only with recordsets that have been opened as a keyset with the adCmdTableDirect option.

When such an error occurs, a window pops up to ask whether you want to end or debug the module. (Clicking the Debug button produced the module window shown in Figure 9-2.) If the error requires the adjustment of only the highlighted line of code, you can correct the error, save the code, and continue executing the procedure (click Continue in the Run menu or in the shortcut menu obtained by right-clicking). If the error requires the adjustment of several lines of code, you can reset (or cancel) the procedure by closing the module window and answering "yes" in response to the prompt. You can also reset it by clicking Reset or End in the Run menu.

Other runtime error types exist. For instance, runtime errors can occur when the environment that is expected by a procedure does not exist. For example, a SetFocus method applied to a form that is no longer open will generate a runtime error. In addition, a runtime error can occur when a procedure expects numeric data (for example, 0 in a variable), but the variable contains a null value. When this type of error occurs, Access will detect it and open an error window, as discussed previously.

When runtime errors occur and no error handlers have been written, Access will highlight the line that caused the error. *This line may or may not be the one that needs to be changed.* In some cases, the program logic needs to be analyzed to determine the needed changes.

 TIP   If a message box appears repeatedly on your screen, you may be in an infinite loop. Press Ctrl+Break to quit the routine and then reset your procedure.

Logic Errors

Code that compiles cleanly and does not produce runtime errors may still operate incorrectly due to a logic error. A logic error occurs when a procedure executes successfully but produces an incorrect result. When your program has a logic error, you must analyze it in detail to discover the source of the problem. Common logic errors include the following:

- Procedures are associated with events that do not execute.

- Procedures are associated with events that execute at an unplanned time.

- Events execute in an unplanned sequence.

- The focus of a control, form, or report changes earlier or later than a procedure expects. (This type of error is commonly observed when a programmer misuses the Screen.ActiveForm or Screen.ActiveControl object properties.)

- The value of a control changes earlier or later than an executed procedure expects.

- The criteria string used by a method such as Find, OpenForm, or OpenReport is incorrect.

- An expression that does not accommodate null values or empty strings receives a null value or an empty string.

For example, when procedures are associated with events that do not execute, you will often find that tables in the database are not modified as expected. If tables are not modified correctly, you can go to the code that you expect to modify them and place a MsgBox statement there to print out a message when the procedure executes. If the message never appears, then you can be sure that the event is not executing.

In a similar manner, you can use MsgBox statements to output the value of a control when a procedure executes. If the value is not what you expected, then perhaps it is changing earlier or later than you planned.

When an application is deployed to users, it must be able to handle unexpected runtime errors without stopping execution. The next section discusses how to accomplish that goal.

HANDLING ERRORS

In Access, you can handle runtime and logic errors by placing error-handling statements into the VBA code itself to accommodate errors that cannot be anticipated or avoided. You can also use specific VBA tools to discover and correct the sources of errors. This section discusses the nuances of both approaches.

Error-handling statements are vital to robust programming. Indeed, one of the most challenging and critical tasks that you will face in any programming environment is writing code that handles error conditions gracefully. All programs can fail; procedures that appear to work in every possible test may nevertheless fail when the program is put into daily use. The failure may occur because a user executes an unanticipated series of keystrokes, the underlying network infrastructure changes, shared libraries are deleted or moved, or any number of other events that are outside of the developer's control occur.

Your error-handling statements should account for a variety of situations, such as network failure and unanticipated keystrokes by the user. If your statements do not perform this function, you will find that the Access application you have deployed (that is, the one created when you make an MDE file) can abort and send the user to the Windows interface. Users have little patience with applications that "bomb" and cause a loss of work. Fortunately, VBA provides several statements that facilitate error processing. At least one of these statements should be placed in every procedure.

The On Error Statement

The **On Error** statement is the principal means for controlling error processing in VBA. When VBA encounters an On Error statement, it enables an error handler. An error handler is a mechanism for transferring process control to specific VBA statements when an error occurs.

In a sense, the error handler acts like a supervisor who watches the code as it executes. It remains enabled as the program executes each line of code in the procedure. When VBA encounters an error, the error handler causes Access to perform the action specified by the On Error arguments, the syntax of which follows:

Syntax

On Error [**GoTo** [*LineNumber* | *LineLabel*] | **Resume Next** | **GoTo 0**]

Syntax Dissection

- If the argument contains the **GoTo** statement, the error handler transfers control to the corresponding *LineLabel* or *LineNumber*. Programmers frequently call the lines of code that are executed as the result of an On Error GoTo statement an error-handling routine (which is not the same as the error handler).

- If the argument is **Resume Next**, VBA ignores errors, and control flows to the statement following the one that caused the error.

- The **GoTo 0** argument disables any error handler that has been enabled to that point.

The Resume, Exit, and End Statements

An error-handling routine runs until it encounters a **Resume**, **Exit**, or **End** statement. The Resume statement causes the system to continue processing. The Exit statement (for example, Exit Sub) causes the system to end the error-handling routine. The End statement is the last statement in a procedure (for example: End Sub, End Function).

Syntax

Resume [[**0**] | **Next** | *LineLabel* | *LineNumber*]

Syntax Dissection

- The **Resume** statement must contain at least one of the arguments that follows it in the syntax line above.

- If the statement uses the **0**, control flows to the statement that caused the error, if that statement appears in the same procedure as the error handler.

- **Next** indicates that execution resumes with the statement following the one that caused the error.

- When the statement uses a *LineLabel* or *LineNumber*, program control goes to that line, which must appear in the same procedure as the error handler.

The following code illustrates the use of the On Error Resume Next statement:

```
' This code is in Form_frmCurrentStudents Module
Public Sub RecalcLevelNumber()
    On Error Resume Next
    Me![txtLeveling].Requery
End Sub
```

Let's look at specific lines of this code more closely. An error could occur in the Form_Close procedure if frmCurrentStudents is closed by another process. Although the line of code in Form_Close would generate an error, VBA would ignore the error because the On Error Resume Next statement has been detected. The end user need not worry about this process because your code handled the situation. That is, because the form is not open, the number of leveling courses does not need to be requeried.

 TIP On Error Resume Next should be used sparingly and only in simple processing situations. This approach to error handling can hide problem situations during development that really need to be programmed before the application is delivered to the user.

Advanced Error Handling

Now that you are familiar with the Resume, Exit, and End statements, let's examine more complex error-handling situations, as shown in the combined images in the following code:

```
'This module contains procedures that
' 1) move data from the prospect table to the current
'students table
' 2) deletes data from the prospects table for students that
'have been denied

Sub AdmitProspects()

Dim cnn As ADODB.Connection
Dim prstProspects As New ADODB.Recordset
Dim prstCurrentStudents As New ADODB.Recordset
Dim pstrCriteria As String
Dim pstrSemester As String
Dim pvntReturnValue As Variant
Dim pintRecProcessed As Integer, pintCounter As Integer
Dim pfOKForUpdate As Boolean
Dim pintTotalRecords As Integer

On Error GoTo OpenRecordsetsError

Set cnn = CurrentProject.Connection

'Create recordsets involved in the transaction
'qryAdmittedProspects is a query that returns
'admitted prospects from tblProspects.
prstProspects.Open "qryAdmittedProspects", cnn, adOpenKeyset, _
    adLockOptimistic, adCmdStoredProc
```

```
prstCurrentStudents.Open "tblCurrentStudents", cnn, adOpenKeyset, _
  adLockOptimistic, adCmdTableDirect

pstrSemester = InputBox$ _
("Enter the entering semester code (e.g., 01A):", "Semester Code")

On Error GoTo GetRecordError

pintRecProcessed = 0 'Intialize records processed counter to 0
pintTotalRecords = prstProspects.RecordCount
'Display message in status bar.
pvntReturnValue = SysCmd(acSysCmdInitMeter, "Moving Data...", _
  pintTotalRecords)
prstProspects.MoveFirst 'Get first record

cnn.BeginTrans

'Loop through all admitted prospects
For pintCounter = 1 To pintTotalRecords
  cnn.BeginTrans
  On Error GoTo AdmitTransactionProblem
  pintRecProcessed = pintRecProcessed + 1
  pvntReturnValue = SysCmd(acSysCmdUpdateMeter, pintRecProcessed)
'Update meter.

  'Check to see whether record already exists in CS
  prstCurrentStudents.MoveFirst 'Initialize at beginning
  pstrCriteria = "[StudentID] = '" & prstProspects!StudentID & "'"
  prstCurrentStudents.Find pstrCriteria, , adSearchForward, _
    adSeekFirstEQ

  If prstCurrentStudents.EOF Then
  'No existing record so add a new one
    pfOKForUpdate = True
    prstCurrentStudents.AddNew
    'Move the key
    prstCurrentStudents!StudentID = prstProspects!StudentID

  Else  'Existing record, update it?
    If StudentExistsResponse(prstProspects!StudentID) = vbYes _
    Then
      'User wants to change record even though it is in
      'tblCurrentStudents already
      pfOKForUpdate = True
    Else
      'User does not want to update the record
      pfOKForUpdate = False
    End If
  End If

  If pfOKForUpdate Then 'Record is to be moved
```

```
With prstProspects
   prstCurrentStudents!FirstName = !FirstName
   prstCurrentStudents!MiddleName = !MiddleName
   prstCurrentStudents!LastName = !LastName
   prstCurrentStudents!PreferredName = !PreferredName
   prstCurrentStudents!MaidenName = !MaidenName
   prstCurrentStudents!Suffix = !Suffix
   prstCurrentStudents!USCitizen = !USCitizen
   prstCurrentStudents!Citizenship = !Citizenship
   prstCurrentStudents!EthnicityCode = !EthnicityCode

   prstCurrentStudents!PAddress1 = !Address1
   prstCurrentStudents!PAddress2 = !Address2
   prstCurrentStudents!PCity = !City
   prstCurrentStudents!PState = !State
   prstCurrentStudents!PZip = !Zip

   prstCurrentStudents!PPhone = !Phone
   prstCurrentStudents!TXResident = !TXResident
   prstCurrentStudents!DOB = !DOB
   prstCurrentStudents!Gender = !Gender
   prstCurrentStudents!YrsWorkExp = !YrsWorkExp
   prstCurrentStudents!TypeWorkExp = !TypeWorkExp

   prstCurrentStudents!GMATV = !GMATV
   prstCurrentStudents!GMATQ = !GMATQ
   prstCurrentStudents!GMATT = !GMATT
   prstCurrentStudents!TOEFL = !TOEFL

   prstCurrentStudents!UDegree = !UDegree
   prstCurrentStudents!UMajor = !UMajor
   prstCurrentStudents!UDegreeType = !UDegreeType
   prstCurrentStudents!UDegreeInst = !UDegreeInst
   prstCurrentStudents!UDegreeDate = !UDegreeDate
   prstCurrentStudents!UGPR = !UGPR

   prstCurrentStudents!GDegree = !GDegree
   prstCurrentStudents!GMajor = !GMajor
   prstCurrentStudents!GDegreeType = !GDegreeType
   prstCurrentStudents!GDegreeInst = !GDegreeInst
   prstCurrentStudents!GDegreeDate = !GDegreeDate
   prstCurrentStudents!GGPR = !GGPR

   prstCurrentStudents!Program = !Program
   prstCurrentStudents!EntrySemester = pstrSemester

End With
prstCurrentStudents.Update
prstProspects.Delete 'Remove record from prospects table

'Write transaction results to database
cnn.CommitTrans
```

9

```
      Else 'Do not move record
        cnn.RollbackTrans
      End If

  GetNextRecord:
    On Error GoTo GetRecordError
    prstProspects.MoveNext
  Next
  cnn.RollbackTrans
  'Data moved. Remove progress meter.
  pvntReturnValue = SysCmd(acSysCmdRemoveMeter)

  prstCurrentStudents.Close
  prstProspects.Close
  Exit Sub

  OpenRecordsetsError:
    Call ErrorTrap _
    ("Error prior to move from Prospects to Current Students.")
    Exit Sub

  AdmitTransactionProblem:
    'Error occurred in the transaction, so
    'rollback transaction and get next record
    MsgBox Err.Number & " " & Err.Description
    cnn.RollbackTrans
    Call ErrorTrap _
      ("Error moving " & prstProspects!StudentID & _
      " to Current Students.")
    Resume GetNextRecord

  GetRecordError:
    MsgBox Err.Number & " " & Err.Description
    Call ErrorTrap _
    ("Error reading next Prospect for move to Current Students.")
    prstCurrentStudents.Close
    prstProspects.Close
    pvntReturnValue = SysCmd(acSysCmdRemoveMeter) 'Remove meter
  End Sub
```

The AdmitProspects error handling in the AdmitProspects procedure subroutine moves student data from the tblProspects table to the tblCurrentStudents table. The subroutine uses three error handlers and three error-handling routines. Only one error handler is active at a given time. Each error handler corresponds to a different type of error. The first error handler is enabled prior to opening the recordset. A recordset error can occur if the query that identifies admitted prospects fails or if the tblCurrentStudents table is not found. Such errors could be caused by moving the attached database to some other location. If this type of error occurs, the error handler will jump to the OpenRecordsetsError label. If the query and table open successfully, Access encounters the On Error GoTo GetRecordError statement. From this point, any error that occurs will cause the program to jump to the GetRecordError label; the previous error-handling instructions are no longer enabled. The system will continue to jump to the GetRecordError label on encountering an error until the system reaches On Error GoTo AdmitTransactionProblem.

The AdmitTransactionProblem error handler remains in effect while the data are being transferred from the tblProspects table to the tblCurrentStudents table. Just prior to moving to the next record for processing, however, the procedure invokes the GetRecordError handler. This error handler remains active until the loop continues and reinvokes the AdmitTransactionProcessing error handler at the top of the loop.

Note that if the error-processing routine executes the code at GetRecordError, the recordsets are open. The recordsets should be closed prior to the end of the procedure; therefore, the error handler closes them.

Err is a commonly used error-handling object. The Err object belongs to the Visual Basic for Applications object library, specializes in handling VBA runtime errors (for example, forms that are not open), and is associated with several useful properties and methods:

- The **Description** property of the Err object, which was used in the previous code listing, contains the Access default description of the error that just occurred.

- The **Number** property of the Err object contains the Access internal error number for the most recent error. When the Number property equals zero, an error has not occurred.

- The **Clear** method of the Err object automatically sets the Number property to zero. Resume, On Error, and Exit statements also reset the Number property to zero.

In addition to these methods and properties, the Err object is associated with the **Raise** method, which allows the programmer to invoke an error:

Syntax

Err.Raise *Number* [,[*Source*][, [*Description*][, [*HelpFile*][, [*HelpID*]]]]]

Syntax Dissection

- *Number* is a long integer that determines the error raised. Setting *Number* equal to some number plus the intrinsic constant vbObjectError raises a unique error—one that is unrecognized by VBA.

- *Source* names the object or application that generates the error.

- *Description* allows the programmer to set a unique description that can be referenced by Err.description.

- *HelpFile* is the path to the Help file that contains information about the error.

- *HelpID* is the location within *HelpFile* where the error information can be found.

The following example raises a unique error with a description:

```
Err.Raise 10 + vbObjectError, , _
      "A unique account name must be entered"
```

An error can be deliberately invoked for several reasons:

- Sometimes VBA code contains logic that detects an error that is not recognized by Access. In this case, the program code raises an error to prompt the error-handling routine to run.

- A programmer can use Err.Raise to test error routines that are not normally activated.

- Occasionally, an error is not an anomaly, but something that is anticipated to happen frequently. For example, if the location of an attached database changes, an error will occur when an application attempts to use one of the attached tables. To alleviate this problem, a procedure can be invoked as soon as the application starts. This procedure tries to open the recordset of an attached table. If an error routine is invoked, the programmer knows that the attached database has been moved. The error routine can then attempt to locate the attached database (for example, ask the user) and refresh the links (that is, use the RefreshLink method).

The DAO object library includes an object that is similar to the Err object: Error. Like Err, Error has Number and Description properties. An Error object is created only when a DAO error occurs. DAO errors include any error caused by reading or updating the database. The Error object belongs to an Errors collection. Sometimes a single error spawns multiple errors. In that case, each error is represented by an error object and then placed in the Errors collection.

Handling Runtime Errors in the UpdateDiscounts Procedure

Now that you have studied the tools that you can use for error-handling purposes in your VBA code, it is time to apply your newfound knowledge to the database in this book. To its credit, this database attempts to protect against invalid grades through validation rules and formats. It doesn't protect against everything, however. For example, there may be a time when no discounts are allowed. As currently written, the UpdateDiscounts routine will fail if the tblDiscounts table does not contain any data. You need to fix that specific situation. You also need to protect against other potential general errors, such as the failure of tblStudents. You will now modify the UpdateDiscounts procedure to ensure that it reacts gracefully to unanticipated errors.

To include error-handling capabilities that guard against unanticipated errors:

1. Display **basDiscounts** in Design view. Then, locate the UpdateDiscount() subprocedure.

2. Place the following line of code after the Dim statements and before the assignment statements:

```
On Error GoTo UpdateDiscountsError
```

3. Add the following code after the Exit Sub statement and before the End Sub statement:

```
UpdateDiscountsError:
DoCmd.Hourglass False
Call ErrorTrap (Err.Description, "UpdateDiscounts")
Exit Sub
```

 Make sure that an Exit Sub statement precedes an error-handling routine. The Exit Sub statement prevents Access from executing statements in the error-handling routine after the rest of the procedure code has executed.

4. Compile and save the basDiscounts module, correcting any compilation errors. Close the Visual Basic window.

5. Open the **basErrorTrapping** module in Design view.

6. Locate the **ErrorTrap** procedure and add the following code:

```
'A simple, general Error Reporting routine

Dim pstrRLF As String, pstrMessage As String

Const pcLine1 = "The following error occurred in "
Const pcLine2 = "This is a program error."
Const pcLine3 = "A change is needed in the program code."
Const pcLine4 = "Contact your system administrator."

'Character codes for Return and Line Feed
pstrRLF = Chr(13) & Chr(10)

pstrMessage = pcLine1 & ErrorLocation & ": " & _
        ErrorDescription & pstrRLF & pcLine2 & _
        pstrRLF 7 pcLine3 & pstrRLF & pcLine4

MsgBox pstrMessage, vbOKOnly + vbCritical + _
        vbDefaultButton1, "Error trapped in code."
```

7. Compile and save the basErrorTrapping module, correcting any compilation errors. Exit the Visual Basic window.

This approach will protect users from many problems that cause an application to stop executing. Of course, not all runtime errors occur in this manner. You could have a program logic flaw; in such a case, errors must be actively investigated and solved. Sometimes, this debugging process is quick, easy, and obvious. At other times, the logic and timing of several processes must be analyzed step-by-step to determine the problem.

Handling Logic Errors by Using MsgBox

One of the simplest techniques for understanding the underlying logic of your code is to include MsgBox statements in the code. These MsgBox statements can display the value of variables as the code executes. When the values are displayed, you can see what is actually happening in a procedure and compare that to what you think should be happening. For example, assume that the program is not finding a particular record that it should be able to locate in the recordset. A MsgBox that displays the Criteria string used in the FindFirst method will show the criteria being used. The MsgBox statement could be something like the following:

```
MsgBox "Criteria in Find Module is: " & pstrCriteria
```

When the MsgBox is displayed, the programmer can verify that the criteria contain the correct values and are in the correct format (for example, quotation marks in the correct place). This type of confirmation allows the programmer to rule out a possible problem.

Sometimes events are not activated, even when you believe that you have written code to activate them. Such a problem might happen when you misunderstand the timing of events. In this case, you can also use a MsgBox to ensure that a procedure is actually activated. If the MsgBox never appears, Access has not recognized the event.

Using VBA's Debug Facility to Find and Solve Complex Logic Errors

The Debug facility can interact with VBA procedures. This interaction provides a nice tool for program logic debugging because you can use it to automate some aspects of the debugging process.

The simplest way to interact with the Debug facility is to use the **Print** method in conjunction with the **Debug** object. The Debug object is a special object that allows a program to communicate with the Debug facility. It supports Assert and Print methods. The Assert method is used for debugging, but is not discussed in this book. Arguments sent to the Print method are printed in the Immediate window. For example, the following code, when included inside a subroutine or function, will print the number 5 in the Immediate window:

```
X = 5
Debug.Print X
```

Any expression can be used as an argument. Multiple arguments can be sent to the Print method by placing a comma, space, or semicolon between them.

The Print method has the same purpose as the message boxes described in the previous section. Once a procedure stops running, the Immediate window in the Debug facility can be opened. This window displays the results of the Print method. The advantage of this technique over the MsgBox is that the procedure does not wait until the user clicks OK in the MsgBox window before continuing. In addition, the results of multiple executions of a Print method are displayed one line after another in the Immediate window. Subsequent results do not destroy previous results. In contrast, results displayed in a message box disappear when you click OK.

Besides placing Print methods inside a procedure, you can type them directly in the Immediate window. This option is beneficial because it allows you to check the values of variables and properties in an ad hoc fashion. When a procedure stops because of a runtime error, the procedure causing the error is shown in the Module window. For example, if a stopped procedure contains the object variable precLeveling, the name of the recordset at the point when the runtime error occurred can be displayed by typing the following into the Immediate window:

```
Debug.Print precLeveling.Name
```

In the Immediate window, values of local variables, static variables, and properties can be probed by typing Debug.Print argument in the Immediate window of the Debug facility (see Figure 9-3). Alternatively, Debug.Print can be shortened to simply Print, or abbreviated with a question mark when used in the Immediate window, as follows:

```
? precLeveling.Name
```

The advantage of this approach is that it allows you to analyze the values of variables and properties in detail when a procedure stops. You do not have to prespecify which variables or properties to display.

9

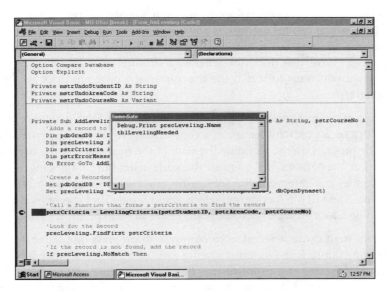

Figure 9-3   The Immediate window of the Debug facility

Printing in the Debug Window to Test the UpdateDiscounts Procedure

The UpdateDiscounts procedure must cycle through each record in the tblStudents table. Before you allow this procedure to actually update tblStudents, you should test the UpdateDiscounts procedure by monitoring it through the Immediate window.

Perform the following steps to create and monitor UpdateDiscounts:

1. Open **basDiscounts** in Design view. Add a Debug.Print statement to UpdateDiscounts that displays the SID and discount amount for each student. The statement should be placed just before the prstStudent.MoveNext statement.

   ```
   Debug.Print prstStudent![SID] & " " & psngDiscount
   ```

2. Call **UpdateDiscounts** from the Immediate window of the Debug facility.

   You should see a line in the Immediate window for each student.

3. Close the Immediate window, and then close the Visual Basic window.

Analyzing output using the Debug facility may be all that is required. Sometimes, however, forced suspension of procedures that can cause logic problems will provide important feedback to the programmer.

Breakpoints, Step Into, and Step Over

Access provides the ability to suspend the execution of a procedure using a **breakpoint**. Once the procedure is suspended, the Print method can be used in the Immediate window to display the values of a procedure's variables. In addition, the **Step Into** and **Step Over** menu items (in the Debug menu) can be used to execute one statement in a procedure at a time. The ability to suspend the execution of a program is particularly important when you are trying to debug a logic error that does not generate a runtime error. Suspending execution is also necessary when you want to watch the execution of a program prior to the generation of any runtime error.

Although you can stop the execution of a procedure by placing a **Stop** statement in the procedure, the VBA **Toggle Breakpoint** feature is a more attractive way to interrupt a program because it allows the programmer to examine the state of the processing at the time when the statement executed. A **breakpoint** is a point in the code where the processing is suspended so that the programmer can intervene for debugging purposes. You can set a breakpoint by placing the cursor on a line of VBA code and selecting the Toggle Breakpoint menu item from the Debug menu. The **Clear All Breakpoints** option clears all breakpoints set previously.

The **Step Into** menu item causes execution to continue to progress one statement at a time inside the invoked procedure. If the statement being executed invokes a procedure or a function, then Step Into will enter that procedure or function, allowing you to debug it as well. The **Step Over** menu item functions much like Step Into, but if the statement being executed invokes a procedure or a function, Step Over does not go into the procedure or function. Instead, control returns to the procedure (the invoked procedure executes without any breaks). At each step of the procedure, you can use the Debug facility to examine the values of variables and see whether the procedure actually performs in the expected way.

To cause Access to run several lines of code before stopping, you can select the **Run to Cursor** menu item in the Debug menu. This entry causes Access to continue processing until it reaches the point where you have placed your cursor. The procedure will then suspend processing. When you select the **Continue** item in the Run menu, Access will continue processing the procedure until it reaches another breakpoint. If additional break-points have not been set, Access will finish executing the code.

Several other options are available from the Run and Debug menus. The **Reset** menu item resets the internal representation of the code so that the execution environment returns to what it would be before the procedure is executed. Using this option terminates the execution of procedures and reinitializes all variables. You should use the Reset menu item when you have altered the code and wish to examine how the revised code will execute.

The **Set Next** Statement option causes the system to move to the statement that currently contains the cursor and makes it the next executable statement. The **Show Next** Statement option displays the next executable statement in the procedure.

Many of these menu options appear as buttons in the Debug toolbar. To access it, select Toolbars from the View menu and then select Debug from the submenu that appears.

Setting Breakpoints in UpdateDiscounts

Setting breakpoints will allow you to analyze the performance of the UpdateDiscounts procedure in detail.

To analyze the procedure using breakpoints:

1. Open **basDiscounts** in the Swim Lessons application in Design view. Locate the procedure named **UpdateDiscounts**.

2. Add a breakpoint to the `precStudent.MoveFirst` statement in the **UpdateDiscounts** procedure in basDiscounts by moving the cursor to that statement and clicking in the gray area to the left of the statement. A red dot will appear, and the statement background will be red.

3. Open the **Immediate** window, and then, if the Debug toolbar is not visible, make it visible on your screen. Call **UpdateDiscounts** from the Immediate window.

4. When the program stops, use the **Step Into** button to move step-by-step through the code. Display the values of **pintProcessCount** and **precStudent![SID]** by placing your cursor over these variables.

5. Experiment with the other Debug commands (for example, Step Over). Then, click **Debug** on the menu bar, click **Clear All Breakpoints**, and click the **Continue** button to continue processing the procedure. At this point you should become satisfied that the procedures are working correctly.

6. Close the Immediate window and close the Visual Basic window.

Using Watch Expressions to Find Logic Errors

The previous illustrations of the Debug facility took place within the Immediate window. Because different logic problems sometimes require different approaches to identify them, the Debug facility has several windows with which you can work: the Immediate window, the Locals window, and the Watch window. The Immediate window was covered in previous sections. It is useful because it provides you with the ability to examine the values of variables and properties during the suspension of an executing procedure. This section will concentrate on the Watch window and the Locals window.

The Watch window allows your code to break on changes in the variable that you want to analyze. This capability is useful when a line of code causes an error that cannot be identified, but the variable that is incorrect can be identified. The Watch window displays the value of watch expressions that are not necessarily being processed in the suspended procedure. Watch expressions are expressions that the programmer has specified be monitored for changes. An easy way to set watch expressions is to highlight the expression you want to watch and then click Quick Watch in the Debug menu. A window will open that displays the watch expression and its value (if any). Click Add to declare the variable as a watch expression. When the procedure is suspended, the Watch window will show the value for this variable even when you are not looking in the procedure that contains the watch expression.

To display more watch expression options, select Add Watch from the Debug menu to open the Add Watch window (see Figure 9-4). An object's properties, a procedure's variables, and any legal expression (for example, X + Y) can be typed into the Expression text box of the Add Watch window. The expression does not have to be part of any procedure. Access fills in the Expression text box automatically when a variable has been highlighted in the procedure prior to clicking Add Watch.

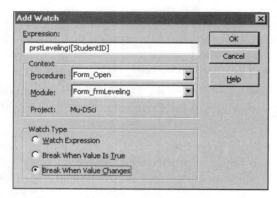

Figure 9-4   The Add Watch window

In addition to the watch expression, the Add Watch window contains Context and Watch Type sections. The Context section indicates the modules and procedures in which Access should "watch" the value of the expression. As a result, expressions can be watched across more than one procedure. If the Procedure box identifies a particular procedure, the expression is watched only when that procedure executes. If the Procedure box states All procedures, the expression is watched and a value displayed (if one exists) for all procedures in the module.

The Watch Type section allows the programmer to select from three alternatives. The first alternative, Watch Expression, tells Access to display the value of the watch expression. The second alternative, Break When Value Is True, tells Access to suspend the execution of the program code whenever the expression evaluates to True. The last alternative, Break When Value Changes, causes Access to suspend execution as soon as the value of the watch expression is updated.

The second and third alternatives provide yet another way to suspend execution of the program code. Note, however, that watch expressions provide useful information only when the code is suspended in some way (for example, by runtime error, by breakpoint, or by Break When Value Changes). The Watch window displays "out-of-context" values for all watch expressions when a procedure finishes executing.

You can change or delete watch expressions by using the Edit Watch menu item. If more than one watch expression is declared, the Edit Watch menu item will open a window to the watch expression that is currently highlighted in the Watch window of the Debug facility. To delete a watch expression, press the Delete button in the Edit Watch window (see Figure 9-5).

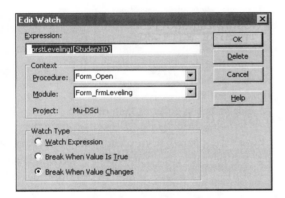

Figure 9-5   The Edit Watch window

The simplest way to view variables is by opening the Locals window (see Figure 9-6). This window displays the current values of all expressions encountered in the procedure that is currently being executed. Placing the cursor over an expression in the suspended code will also display the value.

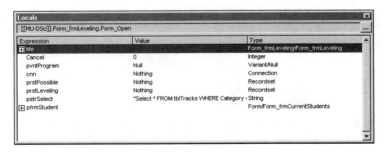

Figure 9-6   The Locals window

Call Stack Window

When you are debugging a procedure, it may not always be clear why or when a suspended procedure was activated. This situation is especially likely in an event-driven environment in which a procedure that executes at an inappropriate time is a frequent error source. Fortunately, the Call Stack window shows the sequence of procedures that were invoked, leading to the suspended procedure (see Figure 9-7).

You can open the Call Stack window from a suspended procedure by clicking the Call Stack button on the Debug toolbar, by selecting Call Stack from the View menu, or by clicking the Build button located on the Debug window. Clicking the Show button in the Call Stack window displays the highlighted procedure.

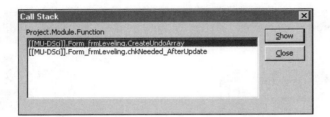

Figure 9-7   The Call Stack window

Setting Watch Expressions in UpdateDiscounts

You've studied the theory. Now it's time to apply what you know. In this section, you will set a watch expression to monitor the number of classes for which a student has been registered. This monitoring will provide some confidence that the discount figures will be updated correctly.

To use a watch expression in UpdateDiscounts:

1. Open **basDiscounts** in Design view, click **Debug** on the menu bar, and then click **Add Watch**. Add a watch expression for **psngDiscount**. Set Watch Type to **Break When Value Changes** in the UpdateDiscounts procedure.

   A window may display an <out of context> message. If the window opens, close it.

2. Click **View** on the menu bar and then click **Immediate Window**. Call **UpdateDiscounts** from the Immediate window.

3. Analyze the value of the watch expression when the procedure stops.

   The Watch expression should display a value for psngDiscount. This value corresponds to the new value that will be written to the Discount field.

4. Use **Step Over** and **Step Into** until you have a feel for what the system is doing.

5. Display the **Locals** window. Select **Continue** from the Debug menu, and then use the Locals window to analyze the values of variables after the procedure stops again.

6. Select **Continue** from the Debug menu a few times. Note the changes in variable values.

7. Delete the watch expression using the **Edit Watch** command in the Debug menu.

8. Click **Run** on the menu bar, and then click **Continue** to finish the procedure.

The procedure should process the student records correctly.

9. Save your work, and then close the Visual Basic window.

Occasionally, an open Debug facility window will cause an error that does not occur when the window is closed. One such error arises when a procedure uses Screen.ActiveForm to identify the form to be read or updated. The Immediate window is itself a form. If the Immediate window is open, it is probably the active form. Therefore, code that attempts to update or read the active form is trying to update or read the Immediate window. When the Immediate window is closed, the code should run normally.

The Debug facilities work properly only when Access is allowed to update the screen. For example, if a procedure executes an Application.Echo False method prior to being suspended, the suspended procedure cannot be displayed. Because screen updating has been turned off, Access does not even update the screen for debugging purposes. Comment out (that is, place a single quote before the statement) Application.Echo False statements when screen updating interferes with debugging.

9

REPAIRING AND COMPACTING A DATABASE

In almost all cases, errors in Access applications are caused by the programmer. In a few cases, Access itself contains the error. Because Access is software, its underlying code contains some bugs. These problems are becoming much rarer as the Access product matures. When Access seems to be the source of the bug, not much can be done except to note the problem and try something else.

Another type of problem occurs when an Access application becomes corrupted. A corrupt application occurs when an error affects the Access internal representation of an application's tables, forms, pages, reports, procedures, and macros. This error can be caused when the system crashes and needs to be rebooted in the middle of an application. It can also be caused by write errors on disk (a common problem when an Access application is stored on a floppy disk). Finally, simply updating code, forms, and procedures can cause a corruption problem. Corruption problems are more common when a number of updates have been made to the code in a short period of time. Although it does not happen often, the underlying representation of an application may differ from the representation displayed to the programmer.

There are two symptoms of a corrupt application. First, Access may recognize when the application is corrupt and notify the user when the application is opened. Second, the application may run in a strange and unpredictable fashion. For example, Access might prompt the user for old fields or variables that no longer exist in the application. As another example, a procedure might be executed as a result of an event, even though the procedure is no longer associated with the event.

The Repair Database command repairs the database. If errors in an application were caused by a corrupt database, this command should fix them. If they are not fixed, continue searching for logic errors using the techniques described earlier in the chapter.

Once a database is repaired, you should consider compacting it. Compacting the database will reduce the disk space required by it. You should always repair a database prior to compacting it; a compact corrupt database may not be repairable. Additionally, the Compact on Close option of Access 2000 provides a way to ensure that a database is compacted routinely.

Chapter Summary

❑ Statements accomplish an objective by organizing the objects, variables, and expressions used in a procedure. They can assign values to properties, influence the execution of a procedure, and change aspects of the Access environment. To build an Access application, a developer must construct statements, order those statements inside a procedure, and determine when the procedure should execute. An Access developer must continuously and effectively test the application to ensure that a quality system is delivered to the user. In addition, he or she must construct statements and the application in general in such a way that they can be maintained over their lifetime.

❑ VBA supports several types of statements. Assignment statements take several forms, depending on the type of variable being manipulated. They use an equals sign to store a value in a variable. Object variables require the Set statement, which assigns a pointer to the variable that identifies the variable's associated object. The With statement is frequently used with assignment statements. It allows the object portion of dot notation to be dropped when a series of statements refers to the same object.

❑ Conditional execution statements are provided in the form of If...Then...Else and If...Else statements. These statements tell VBA to execute a statement block only under certain conditions. The Select Case statement also provides a useful mechanism for choosing between several conditions.

❑ VBA supports several types of looping statements. The For Next loop, the Do While loop, and the Do Until loop provide different ways to control the number of loop executions. Do statements allow the condition controlling the execution of a loop to be placed at either the beginning or the end of the loop.

❑ Because all applications will experience errors, error handling is a vital ingredient of a successful application. The use of the On Error statement establishes error-handling capabilities within a procedure. When an error occurs, program control transfers to the location specified in this statement.

❏ Not all errors can be handled with the On Error statement—some errors must be debugged. VBA provides an excellent debugging environment. Compilation errors are often identified as soon as statements are entered. Runtime errors that have not been caught by an error handler cause Access to display an error message and highlight the line where processing stopped. Logic errors can be debugged as an application is executing by setting breakpoints or watch expressions. Breakpoints suspend execution of an application so that the programmer can step through the statements one at a time, using the Immediate window or Watch window to display the values of the variables. This type of online debugging provides a very efficient means of identifying and correcting errors.

❏ When an Access application operates in a strange way, it is possible that the application has become corrupted. To repair a corrupt database, use the Repair Database menu item. After a database application is repaired, the developer should consider compacting it. Compacting a database can significantly reduce the amount of storage space required by an Access application.

9

REVIEW QUESTIONS

1. Which operators are used for addition, subtraction, multiplication, division, and integer division?

2. What is the difference between using & and + for concatenation?

3. One advantage of the With statement is that it identifies a block of statements that operate on the same object. True or False?

4. Which built-in functions are available for obtaining input from a user and for displaying messages to a user?

5. How are comments inserted into VBA code?

6. What is the purpose of the With statement?

7. What is the role of the GoTo statement?

8. Identify two statements used for conditional branching.

9. When should a Select Case statement be used?

10. When should a For Next statement be used?

11. When should a Do While statement be used?

12. What is the difference between the Do While loop statement and the Do Loop While statement?

13. The If statement cannot evaluate multiple conditions. True or False?

14. _____ statements cause a program to skip execution of code that otherwise would have been executed.

   a. Label execution

   b. Branched execution

   c. Error branching

   d. Unconditional branching

15. Which statement is used to establish an error handler within a procedure?

16. Which objects and properties can be used to display the type of error that has occurred in a procedure?

17. What is the difference between the Err object and the Error object?

18. _____ or looping statements cause blocks of statements to repeat.

19. Which statements are used to create and remove directories on a disk?

20. What is the difference between the Input statement and the Get statement?

HANDS-ON PROJECTS

Project 9-1

Natural Parent International. NPI needs to keep track of attendance at its programs. A new tab should be placed on frmProgram. This tab will contain a subform that lists the names of all members. A check box next to the name will be checked when the member attends the program. A button placed on the subform should generate the list of current members that could attend the program. A second button should filter the subform so that only the members who did attend are displayed. A third button should delete the records in tblProgramsAttended that contain a false value in the Attended check box. In the long run, this procedure will reduce the amount of storage required for the NPI application.

Complete these steps:

1. Open **NPI.mdb**. Create a query called **qryAttendedProgram**. The query should contain all of the fields in tblProgramsAttended and the name of the member that corresponds to the MemberID in tblProgramsAttended. Sort the query on the last and first names of the member.

2. Create a continuous form (that is, a columnar form) that uses qryAttendedProgram as the record source. Name the form **frmAttendedProgram**.

3. Modify frmProgram to include a tab and frmAttendedProgram as a subform.

4. Develop an independent class module called **cmoAttendance**. Create a global sub procedure, called **GenerateAttendanceList**, that requires a series number and program number argument. The procedure should create a record in tblProgramsAttended for each record in tblMembers. It should use an error routine

that is activated when a duplicate record is entered into tblProgramsAttended (the user activates the procedure more than once). The Error Number for a duplicate record is −2147217887. The error procedure should use the CancelUpdate method to cancel the update and then resume processing the next member.

5. Create a query called **qryDeleteNotAttended**. This query deletes all records in tblProgramsAttended, with a specified series and program number, which have the Attended field equal to False. The query requires two parameters: SeriesNo and ProgramNo.

6. Create a global sub procedure in cmoAttendance, called **Compress**, that triggers qryDeleteNotAttended. The procedure requires series number and program number arguments.

7. Place three command buttons on frmAttendedProgram and develop their corresponding On Click event procedures. One command button should save the record in frmProgram and then invoke GenerateAttendanceList. A second command button should invoke the Compress procedure. The final command button should invoke code that filters frmAttendedProgram so that only attendees are displayed (but nonattendees are not deleted from tblProgramsAttended). If the command button is clicked again, the filter should be removed.

8. Save your work.

Project 9-2

Metropolitan Performing Arts Company. Several utilities must be created to support the MPAC system. The first utility should automatically insert records into the tblSeatAvailability table. This table contains a record for every seat at every performance. The status field indicates whether the seat is available, unavailable, or given away as complimentary. In this project, you will create a utility that automatically inserts seats for a particular performance.

Complete these steps:

1. Open **MPA.mdb**. Create a public sub procedure named **GenerateSeatControl**. The procedure should be placed in a standard module named PerformanceManagement. The procedure should accept the PerformanceID and DateTime of the performance as arguments. First, the procedure should verify that the user would like to generate seat records for the performance (use a message box). Second, it should count the number of seats that are already in tblSeatAvailablity for that PerformanceID and DateTime. If this number is equal to the total number of seats at the theater (sum the NumOfSeats field in tblRows), a message box should be displayed that indicates to the user that the seats have already been generated. You can use the DCount and DSum functions to obtain the needed figures. If the count is less than the total number of seats, a sub procedure called InsertSeats should be called.

2. Create a sub procedure called **InsertSeats**. This procedure should also be contained in the PerformanceManagement module. It requires PerformanceID, DateTime, and a total number of seats argument. The procedure should insert seats into tblSeatAvailability for the performance identified by the PerformanceID and

DateTime arguments. One record should be inserted for each seat in the theater. Your code will need to read each record in tblRows. Each of these records identifies the section, row, and number of records in the row. One way to create the procedure is to write a ForNext loop that is contained within a Do loop.

3. Incorporate an hourglass and progress meter into InsertSeats. The progress meter should use the total number of seats argument (the sum of NumOfSeats in tblRows).

4. Write an error-handling routine for each procedure. Occasionally, a particular performance may have some seats in tblSeatAvailability, but not all seats. The error handler should catch the error that occurs when a new record is created for an existing record. The Err.Number property is equal to −2147217887 when a duplicate record (a record with the same primary key) is created. You will need to use the CancelUpdate method when this error occurs.

5. Create a command button, called **cmdGenerate**, on frmPerformance. This command button should trigger the GenerateSeatControl procedure.

6. Save your work.

Project 9-3

Foreign Language Institute System. Your next enhancement to the FLI system will create functions to be used on the Products form to display the product type, product category, product medium, and product language (given the corresponding code stored in the product data).

Complete these steps:

1. Open **FLI.mdb**. Place the following functions in a general module named basProducts:

```
Public Function ProductMedium(MediumCode As Variant) As Variant

If IsNull(MediumCode) Then
    ProductMedium = Null
    Exit Function
End If

Select Case MediumCode
    Case 1
        ProductMedium = "Disk"
    Case 2
        ProductMedium = "CD ROM"
    Case 3
        ProductMedium = "Book"
    Case Else
        ProductMedium = "Unknown"
End Select
End Function

Public Function ProductCategory(CategoryCode As Variant) _
    As Variant
```

```
If IsNull(CategoryCode) Then
    ProductCategory = Null
    Exit Function
End If

Select Case CategoryCode
    Case 1
        ProductCategory = "Beginner"
    Case 2
        ProductCategory = "Intermediate"
    Case 3
        ProductCategory = "Advanced"
    Case Else
        ProductCategory = "Unknown"
End Select
End Function

Public Function ProductLanguage (LanguageCode As Variant) _
    As Variant

If IsNull(LanguageCode) Then
    ProductLanguage = Null
    Exit Function
    End If

ProductLanguage = DLookup("[Language]", "tblLanguage", _
"[LanguageID]=" & LanguageCode)

End Function

Public Function ProductType(TypeCode As Variant) As Variant

If IsNull(TypeCode) Then
    ProductType = Null
    Exit Function
    End If

Select Case TypeCode
    Case 1
        ProductType = "Textbook"
    Case 2
        ProductType = "Software"
    Case Else
        ProductType = "Unknown"
    End Select

End Function
```

9

2. You can invoke the function to determine the product type frmProductSubform by specifying the Control Source of txtProdType as follows:

```
=ProductType([ProdType])
```

The other functions are invoked in a similar manner.

3. The next enhancement to the FLI system will automate the process of adding new languages. Whenever a new language is needed that is not already in the database, the user should be able to add it directly through the combo box used to select the language. This ability utilizes the NotInList event for the combo box. The following code should be placed in a general module named basUtilities to implement this enhancement:

```
Public Sub NewLanguage (NewData As String, _
        Response As Integer, CurrentField As Control)
'This routine enables entry of a new language in the database

    Dim intWantToAdd As Integer
    Dim strNewDesc As String
    Dim dbWCC As ADODB.Connection
    Dim rstLanguage As New ADODB.Recordset

    Const EMPTYSTRING = ""

    On Error GoTo LangNILError

'If user has deleted an old entry, just clear field and return
    If NewData = EMPTYSTRING Then
        CurrentField.Value = Null
        Response = acDataErrContinue
        Exit Sub
    End If

'Remove the input that triggered this process
    DoCmd.RunCommand acCmdUndo

'Display message box to confirm new code entry

    intWantToAdd = MsgBox("Add new language?", _
        vbYesNo + vbQuestion + vbDefaultButton1, _
        "Language not in list.")
    If intWantToAdd = vbYes Then

'Set Response variable to control MS Access error messages
        Response = acDataErrAdded

'Enter new code and description directly into the CPT Codes
table
        Set dbWCC = CurrentProject.Connection
```

```
        With rstLanguage
            .ActiveConnection = dbWCC
            .CursorType = adOpenKeyset
            .LockType = adLockOptimistic
            .Open "tblLanguage"
            .AddNew
            ![Language] = NewData     'Primary Key is Autonumber
            .Update
            .Close
        End With

'Set focus to combo box
        CurrentField.SetFocus

'No need for much ELSE code...when field was cleared above the
 focus
'was set to the combo box field and MS Access will open the
combo box
'automatically

    Else
        Response = acDataErrContinue
    End If
Exit Sub

LangNILError:
    Response = acDataErrContinue
    Call ErrorTrap("Language Not In List in Form")
End Sub
```

4. Place the following lines of code in the NotInList event procedure for the cboLanguage combo box on frmProducts:

```
Dim CurrentControl As Control
Set CurrentControl = Screen.ActiveControl
Call NewLanguage(NewData, Response, CurrentControl)
```

5. Save your work.

Project 9-4

King William Hotel System. Your next enhancement to this project will create a function to be used on the frmCafeBillDetail form to display the item description for an item purchased in the cafe (given the corresponding code stored in the detailed cafe charges data).

Complete these steps:

1. Open **KWH.mdb,** and then make sure the following references are added to your system: Microsoft ActiveX Data Objects 2.1 Library, Microsoft ADO Ext. 2.1 for DDL and Security, and Microsoft Word 9.0 Object Library.

2. Enter the following code in a function in the basMenu module:

```
Public Function GetItemDescription(PrimaryKeyField As _
Control) _
    As String

'Enables display of menu item description on form

    Dim dbKW As ADODB.Connection
    Dim rstMenuItem As New ADODB.Recordset
    Const EMPTYSTRING = ""

    On Error GoTo ItemDescError

    GetItemDescription = EMPTYSTRING
    If IsNull(PrimaryKeyField) Then
        Exit Function
    Else
        Set dbKW = CurrentProject.Connection
        With rstMenuItem
            .ActiveConnection = dbKW
            .CursorType = adOpenKeyset
            .LockType = adLockOptimistic
            .Open "tblCafeMenu"
            .Find "[ItemNo]=" & PrimaryKeyField
        End With
        If Not rstMenuItem.EOF Then
            GetItemDescription = _
                rstMenuItem.Fields("ItemDesc").Value
        End If
        rstMenuItem.Close
    End If
    Exit Function

ItemDescError:
    Call ErrorTrap("Get Item Description in Form")
End Function
```

3. You can invoke the function on one of the forms by specifying the control source of the txtItemDesc text box as follows:

```
=GetItemDescription([txtItemNo])
```

4. The next enhancement to this system will automate the process of adding new menu items. Whenever a new menu item is needed that is not already in the database, the user should be able to add it directly through the combo box used to select the item. This ability utilizes the NotInList event for the combo box. The following code should be placed in a general module to implement this enhancement:

```
Public Sub NewCafeItem(NewData As String, Response As Integer, _
    CurrentField As Control)
'This routine enables entry of a new menu item in the database
```

```
        Dim intWantToAdd As Integer
        Dim curPrice As Currency
        Dim strNewDesc As String
        Dim dbKW As ADODB.Connection
        Dim rstMenuItem As ADODB.Recordset

        Const EMPTYSTRING = ""

        On Error GoTo MenuItemError

'If user has deleted an old entry, just clear field and return
        If NewData = EMPTYSTRING Then
            CurrentField.Value = Null
            Response = acDataErrContinue
            Exit Sub
        End If

'Remove the input that triggered this process
        DoCmd.RunCommand acCmdUndo

'Display message box to confirm new code entry

        intWantToAdd = MsgBox("Add new menu item?", _
            vbYesNo + vbQuestion + vbDefaultButton1, _
            "Menu item not in list.")
        If intWantToAdd = vbYes Then

'Set Response variable to control MS Access error messages
            Response = acDataErrAdded

'Get description for new code. Must use input box to update
'field in form on the fly. Opening a form will not do it.
            strNewDesc = InputBox$("Enter item description (" & _
                NewData & ") . ", "New item description.")
            curPrice = InputBox$("Enter item price (" & _
                NewData & ") ., "New item price.")

'Enter new code and description directly into the Cafe Menu
  table
            Set dbKW = CurrentProject.Connection
            With rstMenuItem
                .ActiveConnection = dbKW
                .CursorType = adOpenKeyset
                .LockType = adLockOptimistic
                .Open "tblCafeMenu"
                .AddNew
                ![ItemName] = NewData 'PK is autonumber
                ![ItemDesc] = strNewDesc
```

```
        ![Price] = curPrice
        .Update
        .Close
    End With

'Set focus to combo box
    CurrentField.SetFocus

'No need for much ELSE code. When field was cleared above
'the focus was set to the combo box and MS Access will open
'the combo box automatically

    Else
        Response = acDataErrContinue
    End If
Exit Sub

MenuItemError:
    Response = acDataErrContinue
    Call ErrorTrap("Menu item Not In List in Form")
End Sub
```

5. Place the following lines of code in the NotInList event procedure for the cboItem combo box on frmCafeBillPost:

```
Dim CurrentControl As Control
Set CurrentControl = Screen.ActiveControl
Call NewCafeItem(NewData, Response, CurrentControl)
```

6. A final enhancement is needed to finish the frmMakeReservation form. This form contains unbound controls because a user will likely make many changes (room type, room number, and so forth) before finalizing the reservation. It also contains a combo box (cboRoom) that has values conditional on the current value of another combo box (cboRoomType). First, place a label on the form that will warn users if a room needs cleaning. Name the label **lblWarning** and choose a color for the text that will get the user's attention. When the form opens, the customer's name should be displayed and the lblWarning warning label on the form should not be visible. The following code in the form's Load event will set up this condition:

```
Me![lblWarning].Visible = False
Me![txtName] = DLookup("[LastName]", "tblCustomer", _
    "[CustomerNo]=" & Me![txtCustomerNo]) & _
    ", " & DLookup("[FirstName]", "tblCustomer", _
    "[CustomerNo]=" & Me![txtCustomerNo])
```

7. Whenever a room category is chosen using cboRoomType, the room rate should be displayed in the txtAmount text box. Any value displayed in cboRoom should be erased because it could be incorrect. The focus should move to the next logical

field—in this case, the txtStartDate text box. The following code in the AfterUpdate event for cboRoomType accomplishes these actions:

```
'If category changes, remove room number
Me![cboRoom] = Null
Me![txtAmount] = DLookup("[Rate]", "tblRoomDes", _
"[Category]='" & Me![cboRoomType] & "'")
Me![txtStartDate].SetFocus
```

8. The cboRoom combo box values depend on the value currently displayed in cboRoomType. Therefore, when cboRoom receives the focus, it should always be requeried to ensure that the proper values will appear in the combo box list. The following code in the GotFocus event of cboRoom will accomplish this task:

```
'Always requery in case dates or room type changed
Me![cboRoom].Requery
```

9. After a room is selected in cboRoom, the system must indicate whether the room needs cleaning. This line of code in the AfterUpdate event of cboRoom takes care of that detail:

```
Me![lblWarning].Visible = DLookup("[NeedsCleaning]", _
"tblRoom", "[RoomNo]=" & Me![cboRoom])
```

10. When the reservation is finally set, the user will click the Save button to save the reservation. Here is the code needed for the Click event of cmdSave:

```
Dim rstReservation As New ADODB.Recordset
With rstReservation
    .ActiveConnection = CurrentProject.Connection
    .CursorType = adOpenKeyset
    .LockType = adLockOptimistic
    .Open "tblReservation"
    .AddNew
    ![CustomerNo] = Me![txtCustomerNo]
    ![StartDate] = Me![txtStartDate]
    ![EndDate] = Me![txtEndDate]
    ![RoomNo] = Me![cboRoom]
    ![Amount] = 0
    .Update
End With
DoCmd.Close
```

11. Save your work.

Project 9-5

Workers' Compensation Commission System. In a database application environment, you often have two ways of obtaining information. First, you can join tables of data on primary and foreign values to create a result that contains all of the data you need in one recordset. Second, you can write a function that will retrieve the desired information.

Your next enhancement to the WCC system will create a function to be used on Form A, Form B, and Form C to display the description for a diagnosis code displayed on the form.

Complete these steps:

1. Open **WCC.mdb**. Place the following function in a general module named basICD9:

```
Public Function Get_ICD9_Description(PrimaryKeyField As _
    Control) As String

'Enables display of ICD-9 code description on form

    Dim rstICDTable As New ADODB.Recordset
    Const EMPTYSTRING = ""

    On Error GoTo WCCICD9DescError

    Get_ICD9_Description = EMPTYSTRING
    If IsNull(PrimaryKeyField) Then
        Exit Function
    Else
        Get_ICD9_Description = DLookup("[Description]", _
"tblICD-9", "[ICD-9 Code]='" & PrimaryKeyField & "'")
    End If

    Exit Function

WCCICD9DescError:
    Call ErrorTrap("Get ICD9 Description in Form")
End Function
```

2. Invoke the function by entering the following code, as indicated:

in frmWCCA, in txtICD91D, in the Control source property, enter:
=Get_ICD9_Description([cboICD91])

in frmWCCA, in txtICD92D, in the Control source property, enter:
=Get_ICD9_Description([cboICD92])

in frmWCCA, in txtICD93D, in the Control source property, enter:
=Get_ICD9_Description([cboICD93])

in frmWCCB, in txtICD91D, in the Control source property, enter:
=Get_ICD9_Description([cboICD91])

in frmWCCB, in txtICD92D, in the Control source property, enter:
=Get_ICD9_Description([cboICD92])

in frmWCCB, in txtICD93D, in the Control source property, enter:
=Get_ICD9_Description([cboICD93])

in frmWCCC, in txtICD91D, in the Control source property, enter:
=Get_ICD9_Description([cboICD91])

in frmWCCC, in txtICD92D, in the Control source property, enter:
=Get_ICD9_Description([cboICD92])

in frmWCCC, in txtICD93D, in the Control source property, enter:
=Get_ICD9_Description([cboICD93])

3. The next enhancement to this system automates the process of adding new ICD-9 codes. Whenever an ICD-9 code is needed that is not already in the database, the user should be able to add it directly through one of the combo boxes used to select the code. This ability utilizes the NotInList event for the combo box. The following code should be placed in a general module to implement this enhancement:

```
Public Sub NewICD9Code(NewData As String, _
      Response As Integer, CurrentField As Control)

'This routine enables entry of a new ICD code in the ICD table
'from any combo box that uses the ICD code table for lookup

    Dim intWantToAdd As Integer
    Dim strNewDesc As String
    Dim rstICDTable As New ADODB.Recordset

    Const EMPTYSTRING = ""

    On Error GoTo ICD9NIL1Error

'If user has deleted an old entry, just clear field and return
    If NewData = EMPTYSTRING Then
        CurrentField.Value = Null
        Response = acDataErrContinue
        Exit Sub
    End If

'Remove the input that triggered this process
    DoCmd.RunCommand acCmdUndo

'Display message box to confirm new code entry

    intWantToAdd = MsgBox("Add new ICD code?", _
        vbYesNo + vbQuestion + vbDefaultButton1, _
        "ICD Code not in list.")
    If intWantToAdd = vbYes Then

'Set Response variable to control MS Access error messages
        Response = acDataErrAdded

'Get description for new code. Must use input box to update
'field in form on the fly. Opening a form will not do it.
    strNewDesc = InputBox$("Enter new code description (" & _
        NewData & "). ", "New code description.")
```

9

```
        'Enter new code and description directly into the ICD Codes
        table
            With rstICDTable
                .ActiveConnection = CurrentProject.Connection
                .CursorType = adOpenKeyset
                .LockType = adLockOptimistic
                .Open "tblICD-9"
                .AddNew
                ![ICD-9 Code] = NewData      'ICD Code (Primary Key)
                ![Description] = strNewDesc
                .Update
                .Close
            End With

        'Set focus to combo box
            CurrentField.SetFocus

        'No need for much ELSE code...when field was cleared,
        'the focus is set to the combo box field and
        'MS ACCESS will open the combo box automatically

            Else
                Response = acDataErrContinue

            End If
            Exit Sub

    ICD9NIL1Error:
        Response = acDataErrContinue
        Call ErrorTrap("ICD9 Code Not In List in Form")
    End Sub
```

4. Place the following lines of code in the NotInList event procedure for the ICD combo boxes:

```
Dim CurrentControl As Control
Set CurrentControl = Screen.ActiveControl
Call NewICD9Code(NewData, Response, CurrentControl)
```

5. Save your work.

10

PROTECTING DATA INTEGRITY IN A MULTIUSER ENVIRONMENT

Transactions, Record Locking, and Replication

In this chapter you will:

♦ Develop code that implements database transactions

♦ Develop code that commits and rolls back transactions

♦ Identify the types of problems that occur when multiple users access a database concurrently

♦ Implement database, recordset, page-level, and record-level locking strategies

♦ Develop error-handling procedures that support concurrent use of a database

♦ Replicate and synchronize replicas and partial replicas of a database

---

You should design your Access applications so as to protect data integrity (that is, the validity of the data stored in tables). Programmers use table verification rules, the specification of referential integrity in the Relationship window, and combo boxes in forms to prevent users from inputting invalid data.

Unfortunately, merely preventing individual users from entering invalid data does not prevent the corruption of data due to a system failure. It also does not account for all errors that can occur in a multiuser environment. In such an environment, two users could each enter valid data, but collectively create an incorrect final result.

In this chapter, you will learn about transactions that protect against system failure. In addition, you will use transactions and locking so as to avoid data integrity problems that might result from multiple concurrent use of the database application. Finally, you will explore database replication.

USING TRANSACTIONS TO PROTECT AGAINST SYSTEM FAILURE

A **transaction** is a logical unit of work. Each of these units of work comprises one or more physical database operations (such as read, insert, and update). The transaction is the key to understanding the recovery from system failure.

As an example of a transaction, consider a banking system that transfers money from one bank account to another. Encompassed in one transaction would likely be the following operations:

- Begin transaction
- Read the first account record
- Deduct the amount to be transferred from the account balance field
- Write the updated record to the database
- Read the second account record
- Add the amount to be transferred to the account balance field
- Write the updated record to the database
- End transaction

If a system failure occurs after the first record has been updated, but before the second one has been updated, the customer loses money. If the transaction is reexecuted, the first account will have the amount deducted twice!

To avoid data integrity problems resulting from system failure that occurs in the middle of a transaction, database applications take an "all or nothing" approach. Either a transaction is completely successful or it completely fails. In the banking example, the amount is deducted from the first account only when the amount is also added to the second account.

When a transaction (which, in this example, includes multiple operations) completes successfully, changes that the transaction made to the database are **committed** to the database. A transaction that does not reach completion aborts. Whenever a transaction aborts, changes that it made to the database before aborting are not committed to the database. In such a case, the changes are **rolled back**; that is, the database fields that contain changes return to their original state.

The key to successful transaction processing is identifying when the transaction begins and when it ends. The methods that programmers use to specify the attributes of a transaction are discussed next.

Transaction Processing in VBA

Programmers use three methods of the Connection object to define the beginning or end of a transaction in VBA. The **BeginTrans** method denotes the beginning of a transaction. The **CommitTrans** method denotes the end of a successful transaction. The **RollbackTrans** method denotes the end of an unsuccessful transaction. These methods have the following syntax:

Syntax

*ConnectionObject.***BeginTrans**
*ConnectionObject.***CommitTrans**
*ConnectionObject.***RollbackTrans**

Syntax Dissection

- *ConnectionObject* is a Connection object variable. For Microsoft Jet databases, the connection object is frequently defined as Set cnn = CurrentProject.Connection.

- The **BeginTrans** method denotes the beginning of a transaction.

- The **CommitTrans** method denotes the end of a successful transaction. When the application executes CommitTrans, all record updates that took place within the confines of *ConnectionObject* will be written to the database.

- The **RollbackTrans** method denotes the end of an unsuccessful transaction. This method is frequently contained in an error-handling routine. That is, when the application detects an error in the middle of a transaction, an error-handling routine is invoked and all updates made since the execution of the BeginTrans method are rolled back.

10

The AddNew, Update, and Delete methods of recordset objects or the Execute method of Connection and command objects is placed after the BeginTrans method. Updates to the database, caused by these methods, remain temporary until the application encounters a CommitTrans method. Only then are the updates permanently written (committed) to the database. If a RollbackTrans method executes before a CommitTrans method executes, the updates are aborted. If the system crashes or the Connection object is closed before a CommitTrans or RollbackTrans method executes, the updates are not made to the database.

Now that we have discussed the concept of committing and aborting in theory, let's apply it to our Swim Lessons application.

Using Transactions in a Wait List Procedure

So far in your project, you have developed procedures that added a student to a wait list when a desired class reached its enrollment limit. Now you will develop and modify procedures that will find the first person on the wait list and then add that person to a class when an enrolled student drops out of the class.

Adding a student from the wait list requires two database updates: The student record must be deleted from tblWaitList and then added to tblEnrollment. A transaction will be defined that includes these two updates so that a system failure does not cause a student to be added to tblEnrollment but not deleted from tblWaitList.

To create a procedure that automatically adds a student to a class from tblWaitList:

1. Open the **SwimReg.mdb** database, and then refresh the links if necessary.

2. Open the **cmoEnrollment** module.

3. Insert the following AddFromWaitList procedure into the module. This procedure adds a student to tblEnrollment and removes the same student from
tblWaitList. A transaction is defined around the AddNew and Delete methods.

```
Public Sub AddFromWaitList(lngLessonIdx As Long)
'Move person from wait list to the course
    Dim pstrSelect As String
    Dim cnn As ADODB.Connection
    Dim prstWaitList As ADODB.Recordset
    Dim prstEnrollment As ADODB.Recordset
    pstrSelect = _
      "Select * From tblWaitList" & _
      "WHERE [LessonIndex] = " & lngLessonIdx
    Set cnn = CurrentProject.Connection
    Set prstWaitList = New ADODB.Recordset
    prstWaitList.Open pstrSelect, cnn, adOpenKeyset, _
        adLockOptimistic, adCmdText
    Set prstEnrollment = New ADODB.Recordset
    prstEnrollment.Open "tblEnrollment", cnn, _
        adOpenKeyset, adLockOptimistic, adCmdTableDirect
    If prstWaitList.RecordCount > 0 Then
        prstWaitList.MoveFirst 'Find first on wait list
        On Error GoTo RollbackWaitListTrans
        cnn.BeginTrans
            prstEnrollment.AddNew
                prstEnrollment![SID] = prstWaitList![SID]
                prstEnrollment![LessonIndex] = _
                   prstWaitList![LessonIndex]
            prstEnrollment.Update
            'Delete record from the Wait List
            prstWaitList.Delete
        cnn.CommitTrans
    End If
    prstWaitList.Close
    prstEnrollment.Close
    Exit Sub

RollbackWaitListTrans:
'Roll back the transaction when an error occurs
    cnn.RollbackTrans
    prstWaitList.Close
    prstEnrollment.Close
End Sub
```

4. Save your code, exit the Visual Basic window, and then open
frmClassesEnrolled_subform in Code view. Modify the **AfterDelConfirm**

event procedure as follows so that it calls AddFromWaitList, and then save your changes (new code is shown in bold):

```
Private Sub Form_AfterDelConfirm(Status As Integer)
    Dim pcmoEnrolled As New cmoEnrollment
    Dim pstrCriteria As String
    Dim pstrMsg As String

    'Check for wait list students
    pstrCriteria = "[LessonIndex]=" & mlngSavedLessonIndex
    If DCount("[RecordNo]", "tblWaitList", pstrCriteria) _
        > 0 Then
        pstrMsg = "Students are on wait list. " & _
            "Move next one to class?"
        If MsgBox(pstrMsg, vbYesNo + vbQuestion + _
            vbDefaultButton1, "Wait List") = vbYes Then
            'Add student from the wait list
            pcmoEnrolled.AddFromWaitList _
                mlngSavedLessonIndex
        Else 'Do not move student
        'Call the method that reduces enrollment
            pcmoEnrolled.ReduceEnrollment _
                mlngSavedLessonIndex
        End If  'Answer to message to add student
    Else 'Nobody on wait list
        'Call the method that reduces enrollment
        pcmoEnrolled.ReduceEnrollment mlngSavedLessonIndex
    End If  'Students on wait list

    'Clear the saved index
    mlngSavedLessonIndex = 0
End Sub
```

5. Save your code, exit the Visual Basic window, close frmClassesEnrolled_subform and then test the procedures by finding **Maria L. Cedeno** in frmStudent in Form view.

6. Click the **Register** button and attempt to add Maria to a class by using **01b** as the semester, **5** as the level, and **35** as the index. After you move the cursor to a new record, the system will prompt you to add Maria to the wait list. Do so, and then close the form.

7. Find **Moses K. Shavers** in frmStudent, click the **Register** button, and then delete his **Semester 01b, Index 35, Level 5** class. The system will ask to move students from the wait list. Click **Yes**. Maria L. Cedeno will now be enrolled in the course.

8. Close all open forms.

9. To test the transaction methods, place the statement **Err.Raise 50** between the prstEnrollment.Update and prstWaitList.Delete statements in the AddFromWaitList procedure in cmoEnrollment. The Raise method forces Access to generate an error.

10

10. Save your code, and then close the Visual Basic window. Open **frmStudent** in Form view.

11. Add **Richard L. Smith** to the wait list of **Semester 01b, Level 5, Index 35**. Then, delete **Semester 01b, Level 5, Index 35** for **Maria L. Cedeno**. An error will be encountered, and Richard L. Smith will not be added to the course or deleted from the waiting list.

12. Remove the **Err.Raise 50** statement from AddFromWaitList.

The transaction defined in the AddFromWaitList procedure successfully prevented a student from being added to tblEnrollment without being deleted from tblWaitList as well. The only problem with the procedure is that when a transaction is rolled back, the ReduceEnrollment method is not invoked in the Form_AfterDelConfirm procedure. This procedure should be invoked, because a new student was not added to the class. Additional error processing must be built into the procedures to handle this situation. This code will be developed in later sections.

Additional Transaction Features and Caveats

Before looking at how transactions are used in a multiuser environment, you should be aware of some additional features and caveats:

- Transactions can surround query executions as well as recordset operations. Rolling back a transaction causes insertions, updates, or deletions caused by the query to be rolled back as well. In addition to using Connection object methods to define and control a transaction, two query properties influence how a query is executed. When the **UseTransaction** property is set to Yes (or True in VBA), a transaction is automatically defined for the query; therefore the BeginTrans and CommitTrans methods are unnecessary. When the **FailOnError** property is set to Yes (or True in VBA), the query results are automatically rolled back when the first error occurs. If FailOnError is No and an error occurs, the query executes in its entirety, and the application or user can decide whether to save the query results. These properties can be set in the query property sheet in query Design view (see Figure 10-1). Note that the Connection methods are more efficient than the UseTransaction and FailOnError property.

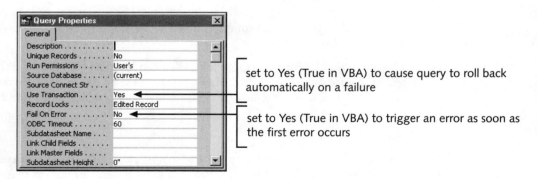

Figure 10-1   Setting the Use Transaction and Fail On Error properties in query Design view

- Access supports a maximum of five levels of nested transactions. The following lines of code nest one transaction within another:

```
cnn.BeginTrans
    . . .
For X = 1 to n . . .
    cnn.BeginTrans
    . . .
    cnn.CommitTrans
Next
If . . . Then
    cnn.CommitTrans
Else
    cnn.RollbackTrans
End If
```

When one transaction is nested inside another, commitments of transactions are temporary until the final CommitTrans method executes. If that method does not execute or the corresponding RollbackTrans method executes, all nested transactions are rolled back.

- The Connection object controls a transaction. Recordsets that use a particular connection (as specified in their Open method or ActiveConnection property) are rolled back when the RollbackTrans method is applied to the Connection object; they are committed when the CommitTrans method is applied. Occasionally, you may want to update some data even when a RollbackTrans method executes. In this case, the record that should not be rolled back must use a different Connection object. This situation occurred in the AdmitProspects and StudentExistsResponse procedure in MU-DSci (located in basProspects).

- When data are updated through bound forms, Access developers have little control over the definition of a transaction. Instead, Access controls these updates. Usually, this situation does not pose a problem. In most cases, a bound form updates a single record, so transactions are not necessary. If an end user notices a mistake, changes can be rolled back through the Undo Current Field/Record or Undo Saved Record commands located on the Edit menu. Programmers can roll back records by canceling, through an event procedure or macro, the Before Update, Before Insert, Delete, and Before Delete Confirm events. Because they do not have as much control over transactions when updates occur through a bound form, some programmers use unbound forms to display and update data. In that case, program code must be written to mimic the behavior of bound forms. That is, you must write code to display data from and write data to an underlying table or query. The advantage is that the programmer exercises complete control over the transaction definitions.

10

Now that you understand the basics of transactions, you can use them in a multiuser environment.

SOLVING CONCURRENT PROCESSING PROBLEMS

Transactions are critical in a multiuser environment because serious problems can arise when two or more **concurrent transactions**—that is, transactions that overlap in time—access the same data. Consider the denial and admittance process in the MU-DSci application. Assume that User A updates the GMAT score from 400 to 600 for a particular prospect, but has not completed all of the operations for that particular transaction. In the meantime, User B pulls up the same prospect's record, sees a Denied status, and sends a rejection letter. In this case, User B has pulled up the old GMAT score and based the rejection decision on inaccurate information. This type of concurrency issue is called the **inconsistent analysis** problem. If User B pulls up the old record, makes a change to a field, and then writes the old record back to the database, the new GMAT score will be lost. This is an example of the lost update problem.

Locking mechanisms prevent more than one transaction at a time from modifying a data object. In Access, you can lock an entire database, a recordset, a page (a page is usually one or more records), or, in some cases, an individual record. The level of locking is referred to as **granularity**. When a transaction is unable to access a record because it is locked, it must wait and attempt to access the record later. Locking at the database level (coarse granularity) generates more waiting situations than locking at the record level (fine granularity), because locking a record still allows other records in the database to be processed.

In addition to setting the level of locking granularity, Access developers can specify several other locking characteristics. For instance, at some granularity levels, you can specify a write lock or a read lock. A **write lock** allows other users to read the locked records, but does not allow the users to update the locked records. This type of locking prevents the lost update problem, but does not prevent the inconsistent analysis problem. A **read lock** prevents other users from reading or writing locked records. It prevents both the inconsistent analysis problem and the lost update problem.

At the page and record levels, the developer can also specify when a lock starts. **Pessimistic locking** locks a page or record as soon as the first field in the record is changed and releases a lock after the record is written (for example, when the transaction is complete). **Optimistic locking** locks a page or record when the Update method is encountered in VBA and releases the lock after the record is written. In the case of a bound form, optimistic locking locks a record just before it is saved. Pessimistic locking locks the record for a longer period of time; once the lock is obtained, however, it guarantees that other users will not interfere with the transaction. If two users will likely access the same record concurrently, pessimistic locking should be used; otherwise, optimistic locking should be used.

As the last option, you can specify an **isolation level**. The isolation level indicates the degree to which the transaction should be independent of other transactions. For example, in some cases, you may want to be able to read the results of uncommitted updates made in another transaction. This capability would result in less waiting. If the other transaction is subsequently rolled back, however, the record read will contain invalid data—a situation called a **dirty read**. To prevent a dirty read, you can specify that your transaction should not read changes made by another transaction until the other transaction is complete.

The granularity, locking type (write or read), locking timing, and isolation level that you specify will depend on the purpose of the procedure and the risk of concurrent use of the same record.

Locking Records at the Database Level

Database-level locking is beneficial when a procedure uses most of the records in the database. For example, procedures that archive old records or back up the database should use a database-level lock.

Several techniques can be used to lock the entire database. One technique locks the database through the Open window, as shown in Figure 10-2.

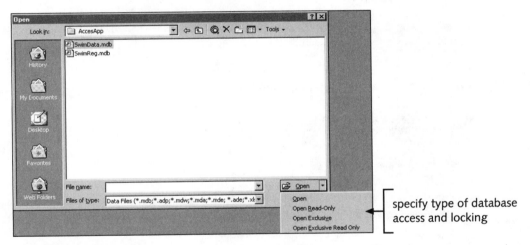

specify type of database access and locking

Figure 10-2   Opening a database in Exclusive mode

If a database is always opened in Exclusive mode, the default open mode for the database should be changed. To change the default open mode, use the Options dialog box, as shown in Figure 10-3.

In addition to using the Open and Options dialog boxes to lock a database, you can lock databases through startup command lines and VBA code. To do so, you place a startup command line in the Target box of the property window that is associated with a Shortcut icon. This icon appears on either the Windows desktop or the Start button taskbar. When the **Excl** option is placed on the command line, the database opens in Exclusive mode. For example, placing "C:\Program Files\Microsoft Office\Office\MSAccess.exe" "C:\AccesApp\MU-DSci\MU-DSci.mdb"/Excl in the Target box of a Shortcut icon, as shown in Figure 10-4, will open **MU-DSci.mdb** in Exclusive mode when the user clicks the shortcut. The advantage of this technique is that end users do not need to open Access prior to opening the database.

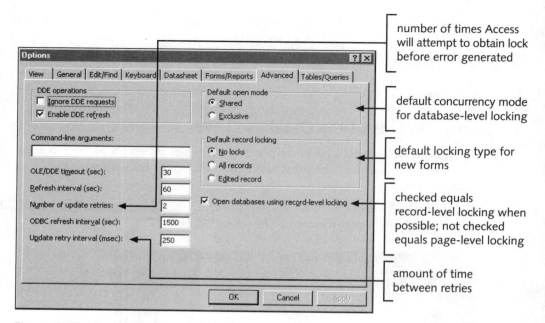

Figure 10-3 Record locking defaults within the Advanced tab of the Options dialog box

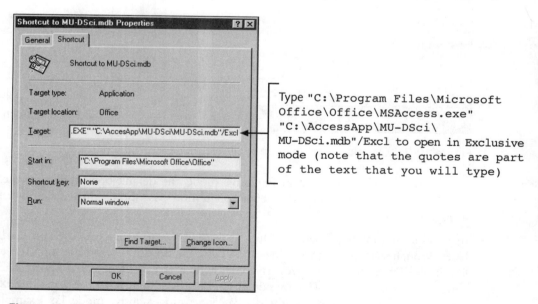

Figure 10-4 Opening a database in Exclusive mode through a shortcut

The last technique involves using the **Mode** property of the Connection object. You use this property to specify whether other users can access the database. When Mode is set to the intrinsic constant **adModeShareExclusive**, other users cannot open a connection to the database. As an example of this technique, the following code segment will prevent other users from opening **Data.mdb**:

```
Dim cnn As Connection
Set cnn = New Connection
cnn.Mode = adModeShareExclusive
cnn.Open "Provider=Microsoft.Jet.OLEDB.4.0; " & _
Data Source=C:\AccesApp\MU-DSci\Data.mdb"
```

Table 10-1 lists other legal values for the Mode property. Note that if the default mode will not be used, the Mode property must be set before the connection is opened.

Table 10-1 Legal values for the Mode property

Intrinsic Constant	Meaning
adModeUnknown	Permissions have not been specified (default)
adModeRead	Procedure will only read data
adModeWrite	Procedure will write data but not read data
adModeReadWrite	Procedure will read and write data
adModeShareDenyRead	Prevents others from opening a connection to the database with read permissions
adModeShareDenyWrite	Prevents others from opening a connection to the database with write permissions
adModeShareExclusive	Prevents others from opening a connection to the database
adModeShareDenyNone	Prevents others from opening a connection to the database with any permissions

10

Setting the Locking Characteristics of Bound Forms

Programmers use the RecordLocks property of a form and the Advanced tab of the Options dialog box to set the locking characteristics of bound forms. Table 10-2 summarizes the various types of locks that are associated with bound forms and the settings required to specify each type of lock.

Table 10-2 Setting the locking characteristics of bound forms

RecordLock Value Property Sheet	VBA Value	Options Dialog Box Setting for "Open database using record-level locking"	Type of Record Lock
All Records	1	Checked or not checked	Recordset-level locking
Edited Record	2	Checked	Record level: pessimistic locking
Edited Record	2	Not checked	Page level: pessimistic locking
No Locks	0	Checked	Record level: optimistic locking
No Locks	0	Not checked	Page level: optimistic locking

Recordset-level locks are specified by setting the RecordLocks property to **All Records** in the form property sheet or to 1 in VBA. When the form is opened with the property set to this value, other users cannot edit, insert, or delete records into the tables that make up the record source of the bound form. Recordset-level locking is very restrictive. This level of locking is typically used when the record source consists of very few records and the user expects to update most of them. The following VBA code sets the RecordLocks property of frmCurrentStudents to All Records:

```
Forms![frmCurrent Students].RecordLocks = 1
```

Edited Record and No Locks provide a less restrictive form of locking. The **Edited Record** option locks a record (or page) as soon as a user begins to change the value of a field (that is, pessimistic locking). The **No Locks** option does not lock the record until all of the changes have been made (that is, optimistic locking). The disadvantage of the No Locks option is that a user may make many changes to a record, only to find that another user has concurrently changed the record. In this case, the changes may need to be rolled back.

 You can change the default record locks value for new forms in the Options dialog box.

When the Options dialog box contains a check next to "Open database using record-level locking," only one record at a time is locked. If this item is not checked, Access locks all records that reside on the same physical page as the current record. Note that while an Access page contains 2 KB (that is, 2048 bytes) of space, because of the overhead associated with a record, only about nine 200-byte records can fit on a page. Also note that although record-level locking is less restrictive than page-level locking, Access requires more overhead space to lock individual records.

 Prior versions of Access did not support record-level locking.

Observing Various Types of Record Locking in the Swim Lessons Application

Prior to implementing your Swim Lessons application in a multiuser environment, you must investigate the various types of locking strategies and decide their levels of appropriateness for the application. To start the process, you will simulate a multiuser environment on your single computer by using copies of the same form.

To observe a pessimistic locking environment:

1. Display the Design view for both **frmClassDetails** and **frmClassDetails 2**. Verify that the RecordLocks property of both forms is set to Edited Record.

2. Open **frmClassDetails** and **frmClassDetails 2** in Form view and display the class **Index 1** (**Semester 00c**) in both forms.

3. On frmClassDetails 2, change the Time to **10:00**, but do not advance to a new record.

4. On frmClassDetails, change the Pool to **CITY**. Notice that Access beeps and the update is disallowed.

5. Close both forms.

When pessimistic locking is used, any change made in one form causes the record to be locked immediately.

To observe an optimistic locking environment:

1. Display **frmClassDetails** and **frmClassDetails 2** in Design view. Set the RecordLocks property of both forms to No Locks.

2. Save both forms.

3. Open **frmClassDetails** in Form view, and then open **frmClassDetails 2** in Form view.

4. Use the navigation buttons on both forms to locate the class identified by **Index 2**.

5. On frmClassDetails 2, change the Time to **10:00**, but do not advance to a new record.

6. On frmClassDetails, change the Pool to **CITY** and advance to a new record.

7. Return to **frmClassDetails 2** and advance to a new record.

8. The warning window shown in Figure 10-5 appears. Click the **Drop Changes** button. If you do not drop the changes, the pool in frmClassDetails is set back to ZACH and the new value for the pool will be lost. Close all open forms.

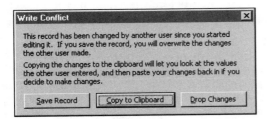

Figure 10-5 Dialog box that appears when two users update the same record under optimistic record locking

Optimistic record locking allows the user to make the changes and then warns him or her when a possible lost update problem occurs.

Finally, you will review recordset-level locking.

To view recordset level locking:

1. Open **frmClassDetails** and **frmClassDetails 2** in Design view. Change the Record Locks property of only frmClassDetails to **All Records**. Save the change.

2. Open **frmClassDetails** in Form view.

3. Open **frmClassDetails 2** in Form view, and try to change the value in any field of any record. Notice that Access beeps and the change is disallowed.

4. Move to a new record in frmClassDetails 2 and try to change a record. Once again, the change is disallowed. Changes in frmClassDetails are allowed, however.

When recordset-level locking is used in a form, other users cannot change any of the tables used by the form. This type of locking is too restrictive for the Swim Lessons application.

To return the environment to pessimistic locking:

1. Set the RecordLocks properties for frmClassDetails and frmClassDetails 2 back to **Edited record**.

2. Save and close both forms.

Although each type of locking has its advantages, pessimistic locking appears to be the most appropriate for frmClassDetails. You do not want another user to update fields such as the Enrolled field when a manager is updating the class details.

Record-Level Locking Techniques in VBA

The locking strategy of recordsets other than those associated with bound forms can be adjusted through the **LockType** property. When the LockType property is set to **adLockPessimistic**, pessimistic locking is employed. When the LockType property is set to **adLockOptimistic**, optimistic locking is employed.

The LockType property is an argument of a recordset's Open method. It can also be set though an assignment statement that is executed before the Open method executes. As an example of its use, the following line of code specifies pessimistic locking for prstCurrentStudents:

```
prstCurrentStudents.Open "tblCurrentStudents", cnn, _
    adOpenKeyset, adLockPessimistic, adCmdTableDirect
```

 The ADO language (used within the context of VBA) does not support recordset-level locks or read locks. The DAO—the primary language for accessing data objects in previous versions of Access—does support these types of locks. To use the DAO language in Access 2000, set a reference to DAO 3.5.

In addition to the LockType property, you may need to consider two other properties that influence how a VBA procedure behaves in a multiple-user environment. We'll discuss them next.

The CursorType Property

Unlike the LockType property, which indicates how others can respond when you make changes, the **CursorType** property indicates how you should respond when others make changes. It is a property of a recordset object.

The two values of CursorType that are relevant for the Jet engine are adOpenStatic and adOpenKeyset. The constant **adOpenStatic** indicates that, once the recordset is created, the recordset should not reflect changes, new records, or deletions made by other users (unless the recordset is requeried or refreshed). The constant **adOpenKeyset** indicates that the recordset will be updated automatically when another user changes or deletes a record.

The IsolationLevel Property

The **IsolationLevel** property can also be used to control how Access behaves in a multiple-user environment. Like the CursorType property, the IsolationLevel property indicates how you should respond when others make changes. It is a property of a Connection object.

The IsolationLevel property specifies when recordsets can view changes by other users. If it is set to **adXactReadUncommitted**, the recordset can view changes by others before they are committed in a transaction; therefore, a dirty read is possible. The constant **adXactReadCommitted** indicates that the transaction cannot view the results of another transaction until the other transaction is committed.

When the Connection object is set to CurrentProject.Connection and Jet is the database engine, IsolationLevel is automatically set to adXactReadCommitted; this value cannot be changed. Table 10-3 specifies the legal values for IsolationLevel.

10

Table 10-3   IsolationLevel values and descriptions

Constant	Value	Description
adXactUnspecified	-1	Provider is using a different IsolationLevel than specified and the level cannot be determined
adXactChaos	16	Cannot overwrite pending changes from more highly isolated transactions
adXactBrowse	256	From one transaction, you can view uncommitted changes in other transactions
adXactReadUncommitted	256	Same as **adXactBrowse**
adXactCursorStability	4096	From one transaction, you can view changes in other transactions only after they've been committed (default)
adXactReadCommitted	4096	Same as **adXactCursorStability**
adXactRepeatableRead	65,536	From one transaction, you cannot see changes made in other transactions, but requerying can bring new recordsets
adXactIsolated	1,048,576	Transactions conducted in isolation of other transactions
adXactSerializable	1,048,576	Same as **adXactIsolated**

Code for IsolationLevel and CursorType

The following code segments set the IsolationLevel and the CursorType properties:

```
Dim cnn As Connection
Dim rstStudent As Recordset
Set cnn = New Connection
cnn.IsolationLevel = adXactReadUncommitted
Set rstStudent = New Recordset
cnn.Open "Provider=Microsoft.Jet.OLEDB.4.0; " & _
       "Data Source=C:\AccesApps\MU-DSci\Data.mdb"
rstStudent.Open "tblCurrentStudents", cnn, adOpenKeyset, _
       adLockOptimistic, adCmdTableDirect
```

Problems with Locking

Although record locking is an important technique in preventing data integrity problems, locking can cause problems of its own. Let's reconsider the banking scenario, except now assuming that two transactions are trying to update Accounts 112 and 114. For convenience, we will label the transactions as A and B. Transaction A locks the record associated with Account 112 and deducts the appropriate amount. Transaction B locks the record associated with Account 114 and changes the amount. It then attempts to lock Account 112, but the account is already locked. This situation puts Transaction B into a "wait" condition. Meanwhile, Transaction A is attempting to access Account 114, but the account is locked. This situation puts Transaction A into a "wait" condition. In this situation, because each transaction is waiting for the other to release a locked resource, neither transaction can finish. This situation is called a **deadlock**. If you do not limit the amount of time that the transactions will wait, the transactions will wait indefinitely.

To prevent deadlock, Access allows you to adjust the Update Retry Interval and the Number of Update Retries. The **Update Retry Interval** is the time, in milliseconds, that Access waits before trying to obtain the record again. The **Number of Update Retries** is the number of times that Access will attempt to obtain the record. These values are set in the Advanced tab of the Options dialog box (see Figure 10-3).

When the number of retries attempted reaches the Number of Update Retries limit, an error condition will occur that should trigger an error procedure. The details of error handling in a multiuser environment are discussed next.

HANDLING CONCURRENCY ERRORS

In a multiuser environment, it is inevitable that some users will be unsuccessful in their attempts to lock and update records. Unsuccessful locks and updates are error conditions. In multiuser environments, error handlers must be created that handle these errors gracefully.

Error-handling routines tend to wait some amount of time and then reexecute the statements that generated the error. The exact statements to reexecute depend on the error detected. For example, if an error handler detects a locked database, recordset, or record, the error-handling routine typically waits and then repeats the statement through the use of the

Resume statement. When the routine repeats the statement and finds that the record has changed since it was originally found, the routine may need to requery the recordset to reflect any changes and then reexecute the code that follows the method that found the record. If the error handler is triggered while executing an Update method, another transaction may have changed or inserted the record first. In such a case, the transaction should abort.

The key to handling errors gracefully is correctly detecting the error in the first place. Several properties in Access indicate the type of error that occurred. The **SQLState** property of an Error object, for instance, returns a value that identifies the error according to the ANSI SQL standard (used by most database engines). Access Help documents these error codes. Table 10-4 lists commonly used values for the SQLState property and their corresponding descriptions.

Table 10-4   Commonly used values of SQLState

SQLState	Error Message
3006	Database *name* is exclusively locked.
3008	Table *name* is exclusively locked.
3009	Couldn't lock table *name*; currently in use.
3046	Couldn't save; currently locked by another user.
3050	Couldn't lock file.
3052	MS-DOS file sharing lock count exceeded. You need to increase the number of locks installed with Share.exe.
3158	Couldn't save record; currently locked by another user.
3167	Record is deleted.
3186	Couldn't save; currently locked by user *name* on machine *name*.
3187	Couldn't read; currently locked by user *name* on machine *name*.
3188	Couldn't update; currently locked by another session on this machine.
3189	Table *name* is exclusively locked by user *name* on machine *name*.
3197	Data has changed; operation stopped.
3202	Couldn't save; currently locked by another user.
3211	Couldn't lock table *name*; currently in use.
3212	Can't lock table *name*; currently in use by user *name* on machine *name*.
3218	Couldn't update; currently locked.
3225	Encountered record locking deadlock while performing Btrieve operation.
3230	Out-of-date Paradox lock file.
3254	ODBC—Can't lock all records.
3260	Couldn't update; currently locked by user *name* on machine *name*.
3330	Record in table *name* is locked by another user.
3418	Can't open *name*. Another user has the table open using a different network control file or locking style.
7752	Can't apply filter if all records are locked.
7787	Write Conflict: The record has been changed by another user since you started editing. (Note: This error occurs only within the On Error Procedure of a bound form.)

10

Consider the following syntax, in which the statement uses the SQLState property to refer to an error:

Syntax

ConnectionObject.**Errors(0).SQLState**

Syntax Dissection

- *ConnectionObject* refers to any Connection object.

- **Errors(0)** refers to the first error listed in the Errors collection. A particular situation may generate more than one error. If so, the Errors collection will contain more than one Error object. However, you can find your error by checking only Errors(0).

- **SQLState** returns a five-character string that identifies the SQL standard error (when comparing the string to a value, the value is not put in quotes).

Unfortunately, SQLState does not always return an informative error. In cases where it does not, you may find that the **Number** property of an Error object provides better information. The Number property returns a long integer that is determined by the database provider and the connection. Access Help does not document these numbers, but you can learn the values of the Number property by testing the code in a multiuser environment. The following code segment illustrates a reference to the Number property:

```
cnn.Errors(0).Number
```

The Number property returned by Errors(0) is temporarily placed in Err.Number. Err.Number is the statement that refers to the most recent Visual Basic error.

The third property, the **Status** property of a recordset object, may also be consulted to gather information about the success or failure of an operation. Table 10-5 lists possible values of the Status property.

Table 10-5   Values of the recordset Status property

Constant	Description
adRecOK	Record was successfully updated
adRecNew	Record is new
adRecModified	Record was modified
adRecDeleted	Record was deleted
adRecUnmodified	Record was not modified
adRecInvalid	Record was not saved because its bookmark is invalid
adRecMultipleChanges	Record was not saved because it would have affected multiple records
adRecPendingChanges	Record was not saved because it refers to a pending insert
adRecCanceled	Record was not saved because the operation was canceled
adRecCantRelease	Record was not saved because of existing record locks

Table 10-5   Values of the recordset Status property (continued)

Constant	Description
adRecConcurrencyViolation	Record was not saved because optimistic concurrency was in use
adRecInvalid	Record was not saved because its bookmark is invalid
adRecMultipleChanges	Record was not saved because it would have affected multiple records
adRecPendingChanges	Record was not saved because it refers to a pending insert
adRecCanceled	Record was not saved because the operation was canceled
adRecCantRelease	New record was not saved because of existing record locks
adRecConcurrencyViolation	Record was not saved because optimistic concurrency was in use
adRecIntegrityViolation	Record was not saved because the user violated integrity constraints
adRecMaxChangesExceeded	Record was not saved because there were too many pending changes
adRecObjectOpen	Record was not saved because of a conflict with an open storage object
adRecOutOfMemory	Record was not saved because the computer ran out of memory
adRecPermissionDenied	Record was not saved because the user has insufficient permissions
adRecSchemaViolation	Record was not saved because it violates the structure of the underlying database
adRecDBDeleted	Record has already been deleted from the data source

You could use the following code in an error routine:

```
ProcessErrors:
Select Case rstCurrentStudents.Status
   Case adRecConcurrencyViolation
       'Code to repeat processing of record
   Case adRecDBDeleted
       'Code to end procedure
End Select
```

Unfortunately, the Status property is sometimes uninformative. Because it is difficult to predict whether the SQLState, Number, or Status property will provide the best information, you must modify and test your code in a multiuser environment.

Adding Multiuser Error-Handling Procedures to the Swim Lessons Application

Several procedures in the Swim Lessons application require error procedures to handle concurrency errors that could arise when two users simultaneously attempt to access the same records:

- The AddToEnrollment procedure may encounter locked or changed records.

- The ReduceEnrollment procedure that is triggered when a student drops a class may encounter locked records when other students are adding or dropping the class.

- The AddFromWaitList procedure will encounter problems when a wait list exists and two students drop a class at the same time. Concurrent use of the AddFromWaitList procedure may add the same student twice.

You will create several procedures to fix these concurrent access problems. Your first creations will be a pause procedure and a message procedure. Both will be used by other procedures.

To add the pause procedure and the message procedure:

1. Open the Design view of the module **basUtilities**.

2. Create the Sub procedure Pause in basUtilities:

```
Public Sub Pause(psngPauseTime As Single)
'Causes program to stop processing for the given
'number of seconds.
    Dim pdtmStart As Date
    On Error GoTo ExitPause
    pdtmStart = Now ' Set start time.
    Do While psngPauseTime > DateDiff("s", pdtmStart, Now)
        DoEvents    ' Yield to other processes.
    Loop
ExitPause:
    Exit Sub
End Sub
```

The Pause sub procedure determines the time between the current time (that is, Now) and the time that the procedure started. If the difference is greater than a specified value, the procedure quits. This procedure causes the system to wait for some amount of time before trying to obtain a lock.

3. Create the following function, which asks whether the user wants to continue waiting for a locked record, in basUtilities:

```
Public Function WantToRetry(pvntErrorNum As Variant, _
    pstrDesc As String) As Integer
'Ask about retry of locked record
    Dim pstrMsg As String
    pstrMsg = "Error: " & pvntErrorNum & " " & pstrDesc & _
        vbCrLf & "The record you are attempting to " & _
        "update appears to be locked." & vbCrLf & _
        "Do you want to retry?"
    WantToRetry = MsgBox(pstrMsg, vbYesNo + vbQuestion, "Lo
cked")
End Function
```

4. Save your work, and then exit the Visual Basic window.

The AddToEnrollment function determines whether a class has achieved the maximum enrollment. If it has not, 1 is added to the enrolled field and the student is allowed to register for the class. If the procedure encounters a locked record that has not been changed, the Update method should be reexecuted until the system successfully updates the record. If the procedure determines that the record has been changed since it compared the number enrolled to the limit, the procedure should get the new value and check whether the class is available.

To add concurrency features to AddToEnrollment:

1. Find **AddToEnrollment** in the cmoEnrollment class module.

2. Modify AddToEnrollment so that the procedure is consistent with the following code (new code is shown in bold):

```
Public Function AddToEnrollment(plngLesson As Long) _
As Boolean
'Add 1 to enrollment if room is available
    Dim prstClass As ADODB.Recordset
    Dim cnn As ADODB.Connection
    Dim pstrSelect As String
    Dim pobjError As ADODB.Error
    Dim pintNumRetries As Integer
    Set cnn = CurrentProject.Connection
    'Form the criteria
    On Error GoTo AddEnrollError
    pstrSelect = "Select * FROM tblClasses " & _
        "WHERE [LessonIndex] = " & plngLesson
    'Open the recordset
    Set prstClass = New ADODB.Recordset
    prstClass.Open pstrSelect, cnn, adOpenKeyset, _
        adLockOptimistic, adCmdText
    'If found and enrolled < limit, increase Enrolled;
    'otherwise, set value to False to inform user
    'that capacity has been reached or the class
    'does not exist.
CheckEnrollment:
    If prstClass.RecordCount = 0 Then
        AddToEnrollment = False
    ElseIf prstClass!Enrolled >= prstClass!Limit Then
        'No more room
        AddToEnrollment = False
    Else
        'Add 1 to total enrolled
        prstClass!Enrolled = prstClass!Enrolled + 1
        prstClass.Update
        AddToEnrollment = True
    End If
    prstClass.Close
    Exit Function
AddEnrollError:
    Set pobjError = cnn.Errors(0)
    Select Case pobjError.SQLState
        Case 3158, 3186, 3188, 3189, 3202, 3218, 3260, 3330
```

```
                         'Record is locked. If the number of retries is less
                         'than 2 attempt to reexecute the Update method.
                         If pintNumRetries < 2 Then
                             Pause Rnd * 3
                             pintNumRetries = 1 + pintNumRetries
                             Resume
                         Else
                         'User has waited for a while. Ask for retry.
                             pintNumRetries = 0
                             If WantToRetry(pobjError.SQLState, _
                                 pobjError.Description) = vbYes Then
                                 Resume
                             Else
                                 MsgBox _
                                 "Enrollment for class was not increased"
                                 prstClass.CancelUpdate
                                 AddToEnrollment = False
                             End If
                         End If
                     Case 3197 'The data changed since last read
                         prstClass.CancelUpdate
                         prstClass.Requery 'Get new data
                         Resume CheckEnrollment 'start over
                     Case Else
                     'Don't understand error. Ask user what to do.
                         If WantToRetry(pobjError.SQLState, _
                             pobjError.Description) = vbYes Then
                             Resume
                         Else
                             MsgBox _
                             "Enrollment for class was not increased"
                             prstClass.CancelUpdate
                             AddToEnrollment = False
                         End If
                 End Select
             End Function
```

3. To watch the concurrency handling of AddToEnrollment, click the **side bar** next to the statement following the CheckEnrollment line. This action will create a breakpoint.

4. Save your work. Next, open **frmClassDetails** in Form view and change the enrollment limit for a class that has not reached its limit, but do not advance to a new record. Note the level, index, and semester information for this class. You'll need it for the next step.

5. Register **Melissa K. Sawyer** for the class that is displayed in frmClassDetails. Move to a new record. The AddToEnrollment procedure will run.

6. Display the Debug toolbar if it is not already displayed. Use the **Step Into** toolbar button to advance line by line through the code. After the procedure pauses once because of a locked record, advance frmClassDetails to a new record.

7. Continue clicking the **Step Into** toolbar button. The procedure will recognize a changed record, restart at CheckEnrollment, and continue processing.

8. Click the **side bar** next to the breakpoint line in AddToEnrollment. This action will remove the breakpoint.

9. Close all open forms and the Visual Basic window.

Let's examine what has happened as a result of your executing the previous steps. First, because the procedure used optimistic record locking, the AddToEnrollment procedure discovered concurrency problems at the Update method. Then, the Resume statement in the error-handling procedure caused Access to retry the Update method, and the Resume CheckEnrollment statement forced Access to restart code execution earlier in the procedure. Notice that a Requery method was used in the code following Case 3197. Thus, although the keyset cursor was used (that is, adOpenKeyset was used in the Open method), the recordset did not reflect changes made by other users unless the recordset was requeried.

A similar error-handling procedure can be created for the reduce enrollment procedure. Recall that this procedure uses an action query to reduce the enrollment field. Thus, encountering locked records is the only major concern.

To add concurrency handling to the ReduceEnrollment procedure:

1. Open **cmoEnrollment** in Design view, and then modify the **ReduceEnrollment** procedure as follows (new code is shown in bold):

```
Public Sub ReduceEnrollment(plngLesson As Long)
'Reduce Enrollment field in Classes by 1
    Dim cnn As ADODB.Connection
    Dim cmd As ADODB.Command
    Dim pobjError As ADODB.Error
    Set cnn = CurrentProject.Connection
    Set cmd = New ADODB.Command
    'Identify the location of the query
    cmd.ActiveConnection = cnn
    'Identify the query
    cmd.CommandText = "qryReduceEnrollment"
    'Execute the query, sending the parameter through
    'the parameter argument.
On Error GoTo ReduceError
    cmd.Execute , Array(plngLesson)
    Exit Sub
ReduceError:
    Set pobjError = cnn.Errors(0)
    If WantToRetry(pobjError.SQLState, _
        pobjError.Description) = vbYes Then
            Resume
```

10

```
      Else
         MsgBox "Enrollment for class was not reduced"
      End If
   End Sub
```

2. Place a breakpoint on the cmd.CommandText line. Test this code by deleting a record for **Melissa K. Sawyer**, making sure that you change frmClassDetails as you have in the previous testing scenarios. Remove the breakpoint when you are finished.

3. Close all open forms and the Visual Basic window.

The previous code used a simpler error handler. This error handler notified the user of the error and gave him or her the option of continuing. As you test this code, you will notice that Access detects concurrency problems in ReduceEnrollment while in the cmd.Execute statement. The Resume statement in the error-handling procedure tells Access to reexecute this statement.

The AddFromWaitList procedure will encounter different types of concurrency problems. Although the procedure may encounter locked records, the greatest concern is that another user may have already added a student to a class from the wait list. In this case, the procedure will encounter a duplicate primary key error. If such an error occurs, the procedure should determine whether the student is still on the wait list. If the student remains on the wait list, he or she should be deleted from it. Next, the procedure should inform the AfterDelConfirm procedure (the procedure that invoked AddFromWaitList) that the student was not added to the class.

To modify AddFromWaitList to handle concurrency errors:

1. Modify **AddFromWaitList** in the cmoEnrollment class module as follows (new code is shown in bold):

```
Public Sub AddFromWaitList(lngLessonIdx As Long)
'Move person from wait list to the course
   Dim pstrSelect As String
   Dim cnn As ADODB.Connection
   Dim prstWaitList As ADODB.Recordset
   Dim prstEnrollment As ADODB.Recordset
   Dim pobjError As ADODB.Error
   Dim pstrSIDToProcess As String
   Dim pstrErrorDescription As String
   pstrSelect = "Select * From tblWaitList WHERE & _
      [LessonIndex] = " & lngLessonIdx
   Set cnn = CurrentProject.Connection
   Set prstWaitList = New ADODB.Recordset
   prstWaitList.Open pstrSelect, cnn, adOpenKeyset, _
      adLockOptimistic, adCmdText
   Set prstEnrollment = New ADODB.Recordset
   prstEnrollment.Open "tblEnrollment", cnn, _
      adOpenKeyset, adLockOptimistic, adCmdTableDirect
   If prstWaitList.RecordCount > 0 Then
      prstWaitList.MoveFirst 'Find first on wait list
```

```
        pstrSIDToProcess = prstWaitList![SID]
        On Error GoTo RollbackWaitListTrans
        cnn.BeginTrans
            prstEnrollment.AddNew
                prstEnrollment![SID] = pstrSIDToProcess
                prstEnrollment![LessonIndex] = _
                    prstWaitList![LessonIndex]
            prstEnrollment.Update
            prstWaitList.Delete
            'Delete record from the wait list
        cnn.CommitTrans
End If
prstWaitList.Close
prstEnrollment.Close
Exit Sub

RollbackWaitListTrans:
'Roll back the transaction when an error occurs
cnn.Roll backTrans
Set pobjError = cnn.Errors(0)
If pobjError.Number = -2147217887 Then 'Already in class
    prstEnrollment.CancelUpdate
    If OnWaitList(pstrSIDToProcess, lngLessonIdx) Then
    'If student is still on the wait list,
    'remove him or her
    'from the wait list.
        prstWaitList.Delete
    End If
    pstrErrorDescription = "Attempted to add person on " _
        & "wait list, but person was already in the class."
Else
    pstrErrorDescription = pobjError.Description
End If
prstWaitList.Close
prstEnrollment.Close
'Trigger another error so that the error procedure in
'AfterDelConfirm will be triggered.
Err.Raise 520 + vbObjectError, , pstrErrorDescription
End Sub
```

2. Save your code, close the Visual Basic window, and then modify **AfterDelConfirm** in frmClassesEnrolled_subform as follows (new code is shown in bold):

```
Private Sub Form_AfterDelConfirm(Status As Integer)
    Dim pcmoEnrolled As New cmoEnrollment
    Dim pstrCriteria As String
    Dim pstrMsg As String

    'Check for wait list students
    pstrCriteria = "[LessonIndex]=" & mlngSavedLessonIndex
```

10

```
            StartEnrollmentProcessing:
            On Error GoTo DeleteConfirmError
            If DCount("[RecordNo]", "tblWaitList", pstrCriteria) _
            > 0 Then
              pstrMsg = _
              "Students are on wait list. Move next one to class?"
              If MsgBox(pstrMsg, _
              vbYesNo + vbQuestion + vbDefaultButton1, _
                "Wait List") = vbYes Then
                pcmoEnrolled.AddFromWaitList mlngSavedLessonIndex
              Else 'Do not move student
                'Call the method that reduces enrollment
                 pcmoEnrolled.ReduceEnrollment _
                    mlngSavedLessonIndex
            End If   'Answer to message to add student
          Else 'Nobody on wait list
               'Call the method that reduces enrollment
               pcmoEnrolled.ReduceEnrollment mlngSavedLessonIndex
          End If   'Students on wait list
          'Clear the saved index
    mlngSavedLessonIndex = 0
    Exit Sub
    DeleteConfirmError:
        MsgBox Err.Description
        If Err.Number = 520 + vbObjectError Then
        'Check wait list again
            Resume StartEnrollmentProcessing
        End If
    End Sub
```

3. Save your work, and then close all open forms and windows.

4. Display the datasheet of tblEnrollment, and find a lesson index for a course that has a status of IP and at least two students enrolled. Write down the Social Security numbers of these students. Close the table.

5. Open the datasheet of tblWaitList, and add one of these students to tblWaitList. You are adding a student to a class for which he or she is already enrolled. Close the table.

6. Open **frmClassesEnrolled_subform** in Code view, and bring **AfterDelConfirm** up on the screen. Place a breakpoint on the assignment statement line for pstrCriteria and close frmClassesEnrolled_subform.

7. Open **frmStudent** in Form view. Find the second student who is registered in the class that you identified and delete the registration for that student.

8. Use the **Step Into** button to follow the logic of the code. You will notice that the error-handling routine in AddFromWaitList is invoked, which causes the error-handling routine in Form_AfterDelConfirm to be invoked. This routine causes Access to check the wait list for another student.

9. Close all open forms and the Visual Basic window.

The code in the previous series of steps used the error number −2147217887, which indicates a primary key violation. If this error occurs, the student may still need to be deleted from tblWaitList. If any error occurs, the procedure warns the invoking procedure (that is, AfterDelConfirm for frmClassesEnrolled_subform) by raising another error. The statement "Err.Raise 520 + vbObjectError" purposely invokes another error with the error number 520 + vbObjectError. (Programmers use the vbObjectError constant so that a programmer-defined error number is not equal to an error number already reserved by Access.)

DATABASE REPLICATION

Concurrent access to a common database is one way for multiple users to update and share data. It requires a reliable, relatively fast connection to the database (for example, a local area network). When this connection is not available, another data-sharing method must be used. One common method is the creation of database files for each user. These users will read, update, and periodically send their copies to a central location, where their updates can be merged with the updates of others.

Although this method sounds simple, care must be taken when merging the results of the data entry efforts. The database files cannot simply be copied from one computer to another, because the copied file will overwrite changes in the file it replaces. To successfully implement this technique, users need a more sophisticated approach to reconciling the contents of individually updated databases. Access supports this goal through database replication and synchronization.

Database replication creates copies of all or part of a database. Each copy can reside on a different computer. Through a process called **synchronization**, you can periodically distribute updates from one copy to other copies of the database.

An Overview of Replication and Synchronization Steps

The first step in the replication process is to prepare the original database for replication. The original database takes on the special status of Design Master. The **Design Master** is the copy of the database that can propagate structural changes (for example, table designs, forms, and reports) to the replica databases (that is, database copies). Once a database is declared as replicable, it cannot be switched back to a nonreplicable database, so creation of a backup copy of the database is advised. In this chapter, you will make a copy of your database. You will then use this copy to perform replication. This strategy will leave your original database intact for use in subsequent chapters.

At least two issues must be resolved during the process of creating the Design Master:

- The design of the database should be analyzed to determine whether it adequately supports replication. For example, tables that use Incremented AutoNumbers as keys will not work in a replication environment, because two copies of the database may derive the same AutoNumber. Access automatically converts Incremented AutoNumbers to random AutoNumbers. Depending on the particular situation, this approach may or may not yield an adequate solution.

10

- You must determine which objects will be replicated. Normally, the programmer is interested in replicating and synchronizing the tables. End users rarely modify forms and reports; consequently, replication and synchronization of forms and reports are unnecessary. In addition, it may be unnecessary to replicate all of the tables. Before creating the first replica, you can identify which tables to replicate.

Once you solve your preliminary issues, you must create the replica sets. The **Design Master replica set** consists of databases that share the same Design Master database. You can create a replica from the Design Master or from another replica. Several types of replicas can be created:

- A **complete replica** contains all of the data from replicable tables.

- A **partial replica** contains only the rows that meet a particular criterion. For example, in MU–DSci, one partial replica may contain only information about students declared as majors in a certain area of study, whereas another partial replica may contain all other students.

You can declare complete and partial replicas to have one of three types of views. **Global replicas** can be used to create other replicas and can be synchronized with any replica (the Design Master is a global replica). Global replicas can also create and then serve as a synchronization **hub** for local replicas. A **local replica** can create only other local replicas and must be synchronized with the global replica that was used to create it. The replicas created from a particular global replica, directly or transitively through a local replica, define a **replica set** (as shown in Figure 10-6).

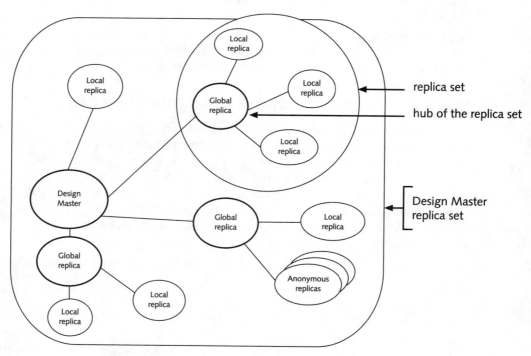

Figure 10-6   Replica sets

TIP Anonymous replicas are similar to local replicas, but the global replica does not keep track of their existence. Programmers use this type of replica when the global replica is publicly available for copying and synchronization.

After you solve your preliminary issues and create your replica sets, the third major step is synchronization. Synchronization of the database is necessary periodically after the replicas are updated individually. Access synchronizes a pair of databases by writing record updates from one database into another (in one or both directions). By default, synchronization is performed at the column (that is, field) level. Records may be inserted, updated, or deleted during the synchronization process.

During synchronization, a **conflict** occurs when the same record and column in two different replicas have been updated. Conflicts also occur when two new records share the same primary key and when one replica deletes a record that has a referential integrity relationship with a record in another replica. When conflicts arise, the update from the replica with the highest priority wins and is written to both replicas. These priorities are set when replicas are created. The "losing" value or action (for example, a deletion) is documented in a conflict table, which is then placed in both replicas.

 TIP In addition to exchanging data, the Design Master, through synchronization, can propagate database design changes.

10

After synchronization ends, conflicts that occurred during the synchronization process must be analyzed and possibly corrected. For example, the user must compare the "losing" data values that were stored in the conflict table with the "winning values" to determine whether the "winning" value chosen by Access is the desired value. After analysis of the conflict table is complete, the conflict table is deleted.

Replicating the Class and Related Tables in the Swim Lessons Database

One of the simplest ways to create and manage replicas is by working through the Access menu. The Replication submenu on the Tools menu, as shown in Figure 10-7, contains the necessary commands. You will use these menu items to create replicas that support the Swim Lessons application.

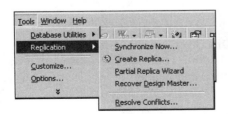

Figure 10-7   Replication menu

Periodically, the tblClasses table in the Swim Lessons application must be updated to include classes for the upcoming year. To facilitate this process, the tblClasses table should be replicated and placed on a laptop computer so that the manager can update the classes. Because tblClasses is related to tblPool, tblLevels, and tblStaff through referential integrity, those tables must be replicated as well. Tables such as tblEnrollment must also be replicated because Access tries to cascade changes in tblClasses to these tables. Because only the data will be replicated, you will work with the SwimData.mdb file.

To make **SwimData.mdb** become a Design Master for use in replication:

1. Close all databases, if any are open. Make a copy of **SwimData.mdb** and place it in another directory. You will work with the *copy* rather than the original database. Once a database is replicable, it cannot be converted to a nonreplicable database.

2. Open the copy of **SwimData.mdb**.

3. Click **Tools** on the menu bar, point to **Replication**, and then click **Create Replica**.

4. Answer **Yes** to the "Close Database" question.

5. If you have room on your disk, answer **Yes** to the "Backup" question. Access will run procedures to make **SwimData.mdb** become a Design Master. **SwimData.mdb** is now replicable.

6. Click the **Cancel** button when the system prompts you for a location for the replica database. Canceling prevents Access from creating the first replica. By default, Access will replicate all tables (and other objects) in the database unless you tell it otherwise. You will indicate the tables to replicate in later steps.

7. Click the **OK** button when the Design Master message box appears. Access displays the Database window. Tables in this window are marked with the Replication icon.

Before creating a replica from SwimData.mdb, you must switch off the Replicable property for those tables that should not be replicated.

To create a replica that contains tblClasses and its related tables:

1. Click **tblClasses** in the Database window, but do not open the table.

2. Click **View** on the menu bar, and then click **Properties** in the Database menu. The property sheet associated with tblClasses appears. (see Figure 10-8).

3. Make sure that the **Replicable** check box is checked. Click **OK**.

4. Open the property sheets for **tblDiscount** and **tblSemester** and make sure that the **Replicable** check box is *not* checked. The rest of the tables are related to tblClasses, so you cannot change the Replicable property. Click **OK** to close any message boxes.

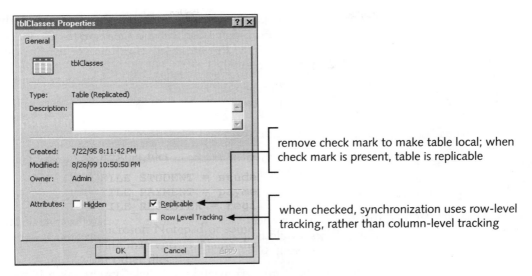

remove check mark to make table local; when check mark is present, table is replicable

when checked, synchronization uses row-level tracking, rather than column-level tracking

Figure 10-8   tblClasses Properties window

TIP If the database contains objects other than tables (for example, forms) and you do not want to replicate these objects, click Database Properties on the File menu. Next, click the Custom tab and select the ReplicateProject property in the Properties box. Finally, click No next to Value and then click Modify.

5. Click **Tools**, point to **Replication**, and then click **Create Replica**. The Location of New Replica dialog box opens, as shown in Figure 10-9.

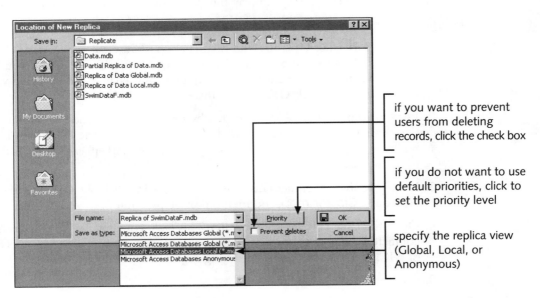

if you want to prevent users from deleting records, click the check box

if you do not want to use default priorities, click to set the priority level

specify the replica view (Global, Local, or Anonymous)

Figure 10-9   Location of New Replica dialog box

6. Name the replica database **Classes.mdb**, select **Microsoft Access Databases Local** in the Save as type drop-down list box, and then save the file in a convenient location. Do not check the Prevent delete check box or the Priority button. Click **OK**. **Classes.mdb** is created.

7. Answer **Yes** to close and reopen the database.

Next, you will perform the synchronization process.

To update and synchronize **SwimData.mdb** and **Classes.mdb**:

1. In **SwimData.mdb**, open the **tblClasses** in Datasheet view. Next, change the price of several classes scheduled for the semester 02b.

2. Close **SwimData.mdb**, and then open **Classes.mdb**.

3. Open **tblClasses** in Datasheet view and change the price for several classes. Some of the classes should be the same as the ones used in Step 1, but the price values should be different. Close the table.

4. Click **Tools**, point to **Replication**, and then click **Synchronize Now**. Click **Yes** in response to any prompt that asks you to close open database objects. The Synchronize Database dialog box opens.

5. Select **SwimData.mdb** from the Directly with Replica drop-down list box, and then click **OK**. Click **Yes** in response to the close database prompt. Access synchronizes the database. Click **OK** in response to the "Synchronization was completed successfully" prompt.

6. Click **No** in response to the "Conflict resolution" question, if one appears. You will not resolve conflicts at this time. Access displays the Database window.

Before resolving conflicts, you will display the tables used to support the replication.

To display system tables that support replication:

1. Click **Tools**, click **Options**, and then click the **View** tab, if necessary. Check the **Hidden Objects** and **System Objects** check boxes, if necessary. If you had to check the check boxes, click the **Apply** button to change the Database window display, and then click **OK** to close the Options window.

2. Look at some of the tables generated by replication and synchronization. Notice that several new tables are displayed. Tables marked with the Replication icon are replicated whenever the database is replicated. MySysReplicas identifies databases in the replica set.

3. If the tblClasses_Conflict table does not appear in the Tables tab, close the database, open **Classes.mdb**, and then repeat Steps 1 and 2.

4. Open the table **tblClasses_Conflict**. This table contains the "losing" records that conflicted with another record during the synchronization process. The contents of tblClasses_Conflict are used during the conflict resolution process.

5. Close tblClasses_Conflict.

After synchronization occurs, conflicts must be resolved.

To resolve conflicts between SwimData.mdb and Classes.mdb:

1. Click the **Tools** menu, point to **Replication**, and then click **Resolve Conflicts**. If the utility is not available or does not appear, close and then reopen Access, and then try again.

2. Make sure that **tblClasses** is highlighted, and then click the **View** button. A window similar to Figure 10-10 will be displayed.

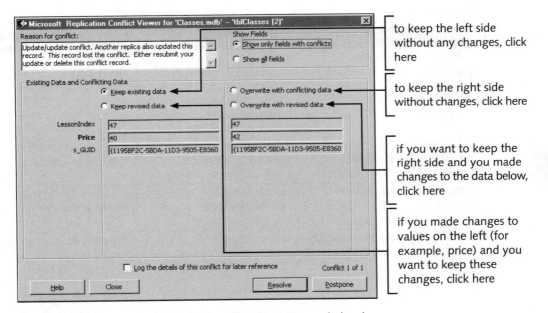

to keep the left side without any changes, click here

to keep the right side without changes, click here

if you want to keep the right side and you made changes to the data below, click here

if you made changes to values on the left (for example, price) and you want to keep these changes, click here

Figure 10-10   Microsoft Replication Conflict Viewer dialog box

3. For each conflict, select an action, and then click **Resolve**.

4. Close the window when you are finished.

5. Open the other database, and repeat Steps 1 through 4 to resolve any conflicts.

6. Synchronize the databases again. The databases are synchronized and the conflicts are resolved.

7. Close all open databases.

Of course, a professionally developed application would not force the user to add data through a datasheet. Instead, the user would likely link Classes.mdb to a front-end application that contained forms, reports, and modules.

Replication Within VBA

As usual, VBA offers the most flexible way to manage database replication. To support replication, it uses objects contained in the **Microsoft Jet and Replication Object Library** (JRO). This library must be checked in the References window before you can use the replication objects.

The objects in the JRO support methods that perform activities similar to the activities carried out when you replicate and synchronize through the menus. Table 10-6 summarizes the methods that support replication. Check Access Help to obtain more details about these methods.

Table 10-6   Replication objects and methods

Method	Example	Description
Replica.**CreateReplica** *ReplicaName, Description* [, *ReplicaType*] [, *Visibility*] [, *Priority*] [, *Updatability*]	rep.CreateReplica "c:\My Documents\Replica \DataRep.mdb", "Read Only Replica", ,jrRepVisibilityLocal, -1, jrRepUpdReadOnly	Creates a replica of the database
Set *ReturnValue = Replica*. **GetObjectReplicability** (*ObjectName, ObjectType*)	Set pblnValue = rep.GetObjectValue ("tblCustomers", "Tables")	Indicates whether an object is set to be replicated
Replica.**MakeReplicable** [*ConnectString*] [, *ColumnTracking*]	rep.MakeReplicable "c:\AccesApps\Data.mdb"	Creates a Design Master database that can be replicated
Replica.**SetObjectReplicability** *ObjectName, ObjectType, Replicability*	rep.SetObjectReplicability "tblQDrops", "Tables", False	Specifies whether an object should be local or replicable; by default, all objects are replicable before the database is made replicable; new objects in a replicable database are local by default
Replica.**Synchronize** *Target* [, *SyncType*] [, *SyncMode*]	rep.Synchronize "c:\My Documents\Replica\ DataRep.mdb", , jrSyncModeDirect	Synchronizes two databases
Filters.**Append** *TableName* [, *FilterType*], *FilterCriteria*	rep.Filters.Append "tblCurrentStudents", JrFltrTypeTable, "[program] = 'MISY'" rep.Filters "tblQDrops", JrFltrTypeRelation, "tlb CurrentStudentstlbQDrops"	Specifies a filter for a table; when the filter is a relation, rows are included only when a foreign key match to the other table in the relationship exists
Filters.**Delete**(*Index*)	Rep.Filters(1).Delete	Removes a filter
Replica.**PopulatePartial** *FullReplica*	rep.PopulatePartial "Provider=Microsoft.Jet. OLEDB.4.0; c:\My Documents\AcessApp\Data. mdb; Mode=Share Exclusive"	Populates the partial replica; also used to synchronize a full and partial replica; code cannot run in the partial replica

As a demonstration of the power and convenience of one of these methods, consider the Synchronize method (the fifth method in Table 10-6). Unlike when synchronizing through the menu, the Synchronize method allows two-way and one-way synchronization. Two-way synchronization copies changes from both directions. One-way synchronization copies changes from Database A to Database B, but not vice versa. One-way synchronization is useful whenever a local replica contains confidential information that cannot be shared with other replicas, yet needs the changes contained in those other replicas.

The following code performs a one-way synchronization with the **Classes.mdb** replica that appears in the Replicate folder. The **jrSyncTypeImport** intrinsic constant placed in the SyncType argument initiates the one-way synchronization. The jrSyncModeDirect intrinsic constant tells Access to use the built-in synchronization procedure as opposed to some other procedure that could be purchased from a third-party.

```
Dim rep As JRO.Replica
Set rep = New JRO.Replica
rep.ActiveConnection = "C:\AccesApps\Data.mdb"
rep.Synchronize "C:\My Documents\Replicate\Classes.mdb", _
jrSyncTypeImport, jrSyncModeDirect
Set rep = Nothing
```

You can create partial replicas by using the **CreateReplica, Append,** and **PopulatePartial** methods. Unlike full replicas, partial replicas are not populated through the CreateReplica method. The PopulatePartial method adds data to the replica. The creation of partial replicas is demonstrated in the following section.

Creating a Partial Replica That Lists Classes and Students for a Particular Instructor

The swimming instructors desire a copy of the database that lists their personal classes and students. To provide these copies, you will create individualized copies of the database as partial replicas. To create the replicas, you will develop a new database that is linked to the copy of **SwimData.mdb** that you created earlier in the chapter. Next, you will develop a form that contains a combo box that lists StaffIDs. After a StaffID is selected, a partial replica is created. This replica will contain the replicable tables of SwimData.mdb. Note that tblStaff will contain only the record for the selected staff member, tblClasses will contain only classes taught by the selected instructor, and the other tables will contain only records that are related to a record in tblClasses.

To develop and test the partial replicas in VBA:

1. Create a new database and name it **RepControl.mdb**. Link this database to the tables that are contained in the copy of the **SwimData.mdb** database that you made earlier.

2. Create an unbound form (that is, don't use a wizard) and name it **frmRepControl**.

3. Place a combo box on frmRepControl using the combo box wizard. The data should be obtained from **tblStaff**. The selected fields should be **StaffID** and **LastName**. When prompted by the wizard, do not hide the StaffID column. The StaffID is the Bound Column of the combo box. Make the label match Figure 10-11. Name the combo box **cboStaffID**. Figure 10-11 shows the final version of frmRepControl after two command buttons (created next) are placed on the form.

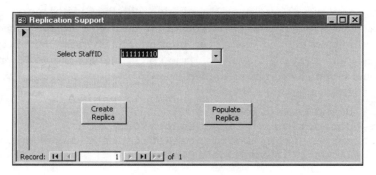

Figure 10-11 frmRepControl

4. Place a command button on frmRepControl (cancel the command button wizard if it appears). Name the command button **cmdCreate**, and make its caption **Create Replica**.

5. Place the following code in the OnClick event procedure for cmdCreate (new code is shown in bold; note that the lines that contain a path name and filename must match the information on your system):

```
Private Sub cmdCreate_Click()
    Dim repMaster As JRO.Replica
    Dim repPartial As JRO.Replica
    Dim pstrFile As String
    Dim pstrFilter As String
    'Specify a path and name for the file
    pstrFile = "C:\AccesApp\Replicate\Staff" & _
        Me.cboStaffID & ".mdb"
    Set repMaster = New JRO.Replica
    Set repPartial = New JRO.Replica
    repMaster.ActiveConnection = _
  "C:\AccesApp\Replicate\SwimData.mdb"
    repMaster.CreateReplica pstrFile, _
        Me.cboStaffID.Column(1), jrRepTypePartial
    Set repMaster = Nothing
    'Set the ActiveConnection of repPartial to the file
    'that was just created.
    repPartial.ActiveConnection = pstrFile
    'Create the WHERE condition filter
    pstrFilter = "[StaffID] = '" & Me.cboStaffID & "'"
```

```
'Add the WHERE condition filter to the Filters collec
'tion
repPartial.Filters.Append "tblStaff", _
    jrFilterTypeTable, pstrFilter

'Use the relationship between classes and tblStaff to
'filter
'classes so that only classes taught by staff in the
'partial replicas tblStaff table are included.
repPartial.Filters.Append "tblClasses", _
jrFilterTypeRelationship, "tblStafftblClasses"

'Include only Pools and Levels that are necessary to
'be consistent with the referential integrity rules
'between tblPool and tblClasses, and between tblLevels
'and tblClasses.
repPartial.Filters.Append "tblPool", _
    jrFilterTypeTable, "False"
repPartial.Filters.Append "tblLevels", _
    jrFilterTypeTable, _
    "False"

'Filter tblEnrollment, tblStudents, and tblPayments so
'that only records related to tblClasses are included.
repPartial.Filters.Append "tblEnrollment", _
    jrFilterTypeRelationship, "tblClassestblEnrollment"
repPartial.Filters.Append "tblStudents", _
    jrFilterTypeTable, "False"
repPartial.Filters.Append "tblPayment", _
    jrFilterTypeTable, "False"
Set repPartial = Nothing
End Sub
```

The filters in the preceding code can be pictured as a series of branches that start with one point, as shown in Figure 10-12. The WHERE condition type filter for tblStaff is the beginning node. The tblStaff table is related to tblClasses through a one-to-many relationship. Consequently, the filter for tblClasses is jrFilterTypeRelationship. This type of filter states that records should be included only when they match a record in the parent node (that is, tblStaff). Because tblClasses is related to tblEnrollment through a one-to-many relationship, a similar type of filter is used for tblEnrollment. The "False" string is reserved for tables that have a different type of relationship with a filtered table. For example, tblPool is the parent of a one-to-many relationship with tblClasses. The "False" filter tells Access to include Pool records only when they are related to a record in tblClasses.

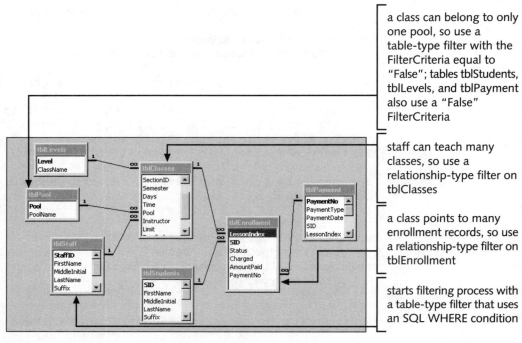

a class can belong to only one pool, so use a table-type filter with the FilterCriteria equal to "False"; tables tblStudents, tblLevels, and tblPayment also use a "False" FilterCriteria

staff can teach many classes, so use a relationship-type filter on tblClasses

a class points to many enrollment records, so use a relationship-type filter on tblEnrollment

starts filtering process with a table-type filter that uses an SQL WHERE condition

Figure 10-12   Relationships and the type of filter

6. Save your work, and then click **Tools** on the menu bar, click **References**, and then select **Microsoft Jet and Replication Objects 2.1 Library**. Click **OK**.

7. Place a second command button on frmRepControl. Name the command button **cmdPopulate** and make its caption **Populate Replica**.

8. Type the following code in the OnClick event procedure for cmdPopulate (new code is shown in bold; note that the lines that contain a pathname and filename must match the information on your system):

```
Private Sub cmdPopulate_Click()
'Put data in the replica. Can also be used to synchronize
'the replica.
    Dim repPartial As New JRO.Replica
    Dim pstrConnect As String
    Dim pstrFilter As String
    On Error GoTo PopulateError:
    'Establish the connection string.
    'The partial rep must be opened in Exclusive mode.
    'If necessary, change the path for your computer.
pstrConnect = "Provider=Microsoft.Jet.OLEDB.4.0;" & _
        "Data Source=C:\AccesApp\Replicate\Staff" & _
        Me!cboStaffID & ".mdb; " & _
        "Mode=Share Exclusive"
DoCmd.Hourglass True
```

```
        repPartial.ActiveConnection = pstrConnect
        repPartial.PopulatePartial _
        "C:\AccesApps\Replicate\SwimData.mdb"
        DoCmd.Hourglass False
        Set repPartial = Nothing
        Exit Sub
PopulateError:
        DoCmd.Hourglass False
        MsgBox "Error: " & Err.Number & " " & Err.Description
    End Sub
```

9. Save your code, close the Visual Basic window, and then open **frmRepControl** in Form view.

10. Select **111111114** in the combo box, and click the **Create Replica** button. The partial replica is created.

 TIP If an error occurs on a relationship filter, open the Relationship window, delete the relationship, and then create the relationship again. Access 2000 names relationships based on the table names. Earlier versions named relationships as Reference#. Deleting and recreating the relationship will cause Access to create the correct name for the relationship. Delete Staff1111111114.mdb and perform Step 9 again.

11. Select **111111114** in the combo box, and then click the **Populate Replica** button. Data will be placed in the replica.

12. Open **Staff111111114.mdb**, and verify that the table includes the correct rows.

13. Close all open forms and databases.

Once the partial replica is created, you can copy it to the instructor's laptop computer.

You have just created a fairly advanced VBA procedure. The creation of partial replicas, two-way synchronization, and transactions are commonly used techniques that can be used to satisfy an organization's needs. Of course, many other techniques exist. Although we cannot provide examples of all possible techniques here, understanding fundamental Access programming concepts, gaining greater experience, and exploring additional Access features on your own will help you to develop new types of database solutions.

CHAPTER SUMMARY

❐ Many database applications function in complex environments. The environments may or may not include a network, but it is very likely that multiple users will have access to the system. In addition, errors will occur during the life of an application. Features such as transactions, locking, and replication help Access developers prepare an application to function in complex environments.

❑ One side effect of allowing multiple users to access a database is that those users may access the same record simultaneously. If this situation occurs, one user's changes may destroy those of another user. The notion of a transaction helps control how such concurrent access occurs. A transaction is a logical grouping of database operations that define a unit of work.

❑ One way that transactions control database processing is by defining when changes affected by the transaction may actually be applied to the database. If a transaction completes all of its database operations successfully, then its effects can be committed to the database. If a problem occurs, these effects are rolled back. The CommitTrans and RollbackTrans connection methods handle these processes in Access. The BeginTrans method indicates the start of a transaction.

❑ In Access, to control problems caused by the actions of multiple users, transactions use a locking scheme. A user can lock a record, page, table, or database. Page and record locking can be pessimistic or optimistic. Pessimistic locking locks a record as soon as the record is edited. Optimistic locking locks a record when it is about to be updated. Locks are released when a transaction is either committed or rolled back. The application programmer must write the code necessary to handle the errors that occur with locked resources.

❑ Replication is used when more than one site needs access to an application, but network access is not available or desired. A replica is a copy of an application; it may include the entire application or just a few of the application's objects. A partial replica filters a table, so that the records in the replica are a subset of the original table's records. After a period of time, replicas must be synchronized—that is, updates made in one replica must be propagated to other replicas.

❑ Replication difficulties occur when two replicas modify the same column and record. In such a case, a conflict occurs. A conflict resolution function is used to determine whether the correct value was placed in the database. The Access default conflict function asks the user to pick the correct record.

❑ Ideally, few conflicts should occur in a replica set. When many conflicts are expected, replication should not be used. Instead, the developer should plan a new type of interaction between database applications.

REVIEW QUESTIONS

1. A database transaction consists of one or more database operations that must be completed in their entirety. True or False?

2. When does the lost update problem occur?

   a. When a system crash occurs in the middle of a transaction

   b. When one transaction overwrites the changes made by another transaction

   c. When one transaction attempts to lock a record that is already locked by another transaction

   d. When a user reads data that has been rolled back

3. What is the difference between a committed transaction and a rolled back transaction?

4. Which three Connection object methods are used to define transaction processing in Access?

5. Name four locking granularities supported by Access.

6. If a procedure contains BeginTrans, CommitTrans, and Rollback methods and pessimistic locking is in place, which method or statement signals the beginning of a record lock?

7. If a procedure contains BeginTrans, CommitTrans, and Rollback methods and optimistic locking is in place, which method or statement signals the beginning of a record lock?

8. If a procedure contains BeginTrans, CommitTrans, and Rollback methods and pessimistic locking is in place, which method(s) unlocks a record?

9. _____ locking locks a page or record when the Update method is encountered in VBA and releases the lock after the record is written.

10. Encountering a locked record triggers an error. Identify at least two other types of errors that VBA code should anticipate in a multiuser environment.

11. A(n) _____ occurs when one user reads a record from a transaction that is subsequently rolled back.

12. The Number of Update Retries is the number of times that Access will attempt to obtain a record before an error is generated. True or False?

13. Which objects and properties can be used to determine the type of concurrency error that occurred?

    a. The SQLState property of the Error object

    b. The Status property of a recordset object

    c. The Number property of the Error object

    d. All of the above

14. What is database replication?

15. The Design Master is the only database that can make changes to a Form object that will be propagated to other members of the replica set. True or False?

16. What is partial replication?

17. What is database synchronization?

18. Under what circumstances does a synchronization conflict occur?

    a. When two replicas update a record in the same table

    b. When two replicas update the same field in the same record

    c. When two transactions attempt to lock the same record

    d. When one transaction overwrites the changes provided in another transaction

19. Which is the difference between a replicable object and a local object?

20. Which methods are used in VBA to create a partial replication?

HANDS-ON PROJECTS

Project 10-1

Natural Parent International. Most groups that use the NPI system will not have a LAN that supports multiple simultaneous users. Nevertheless, some groups in large cities may have such a system. In addition, most NPI groups have more than one leader, and perhaps a librarian. Procedures should therefore be modified to support multiple simultaneous users. In addition, replicas of the system should be developed to support the smaller NPI groups.

Complete these steps:

1. Open **NPI.mdb**. Add code to the Compress procedure that is located in cmoAttendance and that starts a transaction prior to executing the delete query. If an error does not occur, the updates should be committed. Locked records should trigger an error procedure. The error handler must roll back the transaction, display the error-handling message, and ask the user whether he or she would like to try executing the query again.

2. Create a new database called **NPICopy.mdb** and use the **Import** feature found on the **Get External Data** menu of the **File** menu to import the NPI tables. Close all databases other than **NPICopy.mdb**.

3. If it is not open, open **NPICopy.mdb**. Create a Design Master and a replica from this database. Add and modify data in both replicas using table datasheets, and then synchronize the database.

4. Save your work.

Project 10-2

Metropolitan Performing Arts Company. More than one ticket agent may use the system that you are developing for the MPAC. Consequently, you must augment your code and update the MPCA forms to prevent ticket agents from selling the same seat to two different customers. In addition, the ReturnTicketProcedure created earlier needs to include code that tests for records that have been locked or updated by another user.

Complete these steps:

1. Open **MPA.mdb** and refresh the table links, if necessary.

2. Change the RecordLocks property of frmPerformanceDateSeats to **Edited Record**. Pessimistic locking must be used, because changes in the cboStatus combo box update values in frmSales.

3. Change the RecordLocks property of qrySeatsForPerformance to **Edited Record** (this value is found in the property sheet for the query). This query will be used to test error handling in procedures to be modified later.

4. Create a new query called **qryReturnTest** that includes all of the fields of tblReturn. The RecordLocks property should be set to **Edited Record**. This query will also be used for testing.

5. Modify the **cboStatus_DblClick** procedure found in **frmSeatsAvailableSubform** so that an error-handling routine is invoked when someone else has locked the row and seat. The error handler does not have to test for a particular error. The routine should display the Err.Number and Err.Description in a message box and then end the sub procedure. Test the procedure by changing a record in qrySeatForPerformance (without saving the record) and then changing the same record through the frmPerformanceDateSeats form. The error message should be displayed.

6. Create a Sub procedure **Pause** inside a new module called **Utilities**. The sub procedure should cause the system to wait for a few seconds.

7. Modify the **ReturnTicket** function that is located in **frmPerformanceDateSeats** so that it detects locked and updated records. The SQLState error codes corresponding to a locked record are 3008, 3009, 3188, 3189, 3211, 3212, and 3198. The SQLState error code corresponding to a changed record by another user is 3197. Errors caused by a locked record should invoke the Pause Sub procedure and then attempt to resume the Update (locked records were detected by the Update method). Errors caused by a changed record should cancel the previous update (with the CancelUpdate method), requery the recordset, and then repeat the code that adds a new record or updates an existing record. To test the code, change a record in qryReturnTest (noting the performance and section) while simultaneously returning a ticket to the same performance and section through frmPerformanceDateSeats.

8. Save your work.

Project 10-3

Foreign Language Institute System. As the FLI system expands, you can expect more nodes to be added to support the company's information processing. One can foresee additional terminals being accessed by sales staff, customer service staff, production workers, and management. The processing across the LAN will be more efficient if the database is replicated.

Complete these steps:

1. Open **FLI.mdb**. Make a copy of the source database. (Use the copy to make replicas. You will use the unreplicated version of the database in future chapters.) Create a copy of the entire application. Create a Design Master and a replica from the copied database. Add data to both replicas and synchronize the database.

2. Develop VBA code that synchronizes a database that is located in a Replica directory. The Replica directory is always contained within the directory of the application. Assume that all replicas will have the same name. The code should be triggered from an item on the switchboard form. Users of the system will place a replica in the Replica folder and then click the Replica command button. In turn, the replica and Design Master will be synchronized.

3. Save your work.

Project 10-4

King William Hotel. As the King William Hotel system expands, you can expect more nodes to be added to support the hotel's information processing. One can foresee terminals on each floor being accessed by housekeeping staff, additional terminals in the management offices, and terminals in use by parking and bellhop staff. The processing across the LAN will be more efficient if the database is replicated.

Complete these steps:

1. Open **KWH.mdb**. Make a copy of the source database. (Use the copy to make replicas. You will use the unreplicated version of the database in future chapters.) Create a copy of the entire application. Create a Design Master and a replica from the copied database. Add data to both replicas and synchronize the database. This problem is designed to help you understand the replication and synchronization process.

2. Develop VBA code that synchronizes a database that is located in a Replica directory. The Replica directory is always contained within the directory of the application. Assume that all replicas will have the same name. The code should be triggered from an item on the switchboard form. Users of the system will place a replica in the Replica folder and then click the Replica command button. In turn, the replica and Design Master will be synchronized.

3. Save your work.

Project 10-5

Workers' Compensation Commission. Because the WCC system is used across the state in a networked environment, replicas of the database system should be developed to support efficient processing in the smaller clinics.

Complete these steps:

1. Open **WCC.mdb**. Make a copy of the source database. (Use the copy to make replicas. You will use the unreplicated version of the database in future chapters.) Create a copy of the entire application. Create a Design Master and a replica from the copied database. Add data to both replicas and synchronize the database. This problem is designed to help you understand the replication and synchronization process.

2. Develop VBA code that synchronizes a database that is located in a Replica directory. The Replica directory is always contained within the directory of the application. Assume that all replicas will have the same name. The code should be triggered from an item on the switchboard form. Users of the system will place a replica in the Replica folder and then click the Replica command button. In turn, the replica and Design Master will be synchronized.

3. Save your work.

CHAPTER

11

DEVELOPING CUSTOM HELP

In this chapter you will:

- ◆ Use HTML to create customized Help topics for an application
- ◆ Use the HTML Help Workshop to create the Help Index and Contents tabs
- ◆ Create a compiled Help file with the HTML Help Workshop
- ◆ Link a Help file to an Access application
- ◆ Learn the process of creating a customized Help system

The online Help that comes with Microsoft Access describes how to use the general features of any Access application, but it cannot adequately describe the features of a customized application. It is your responsibility as the developer to include customized Help and/or a tutorial that illustrates the use of your application's features.

Customized Help is contained in one or more Help files that are delivered along with the Access application. You create these Help files through the use of a Help file compiler such **HTML Help Workshop** or **WinHelp**.

Of the two, HTML Help Workshop is the newer. This tool is based on **Hypertext Markup Language (HTML)**, the language used to construct World Wide Web (WWW) pages. WinHelp, on the other hand, uses **Rich Text Format (RTF)** files to develop the components of Help. RTF is a common file format that can be specified in most word processors.

You can download HTML Help Workshop and WinHelp, free of charge, from the Microsoft Developers Network (MSDN) Web site. (As of March 27, 2000, the URL for this site was http://msdn.microsoft.com/workshop/author/htmlhelp/download.asp.) In addition, HTML Help Workshop is supplied with the Microsoft 2000 Developers edition.

In this chapter, you will learn the features of customized Help and the process of creating customized Help. You will also develop a Help file through HTML Help Workshop and then link this file to an Access application. While this process may seem like a lot of work, creating this customized Help system will reduce the number of phone calls that you receive after the application is delivered. That alone makes the endeavor worthwhile.

THE FEATURES, COMPONENTS, AND PROCESS OF CREATING CUSTOMIZED HELP

The features and components of customized Help are similar to the features and components of the generic Help that comes with Microsoft Access, as shown in Figure 11-1. The Help window contains several tabs and subwindows, including a **Topic window** and the **Index**, **Contents**, and **Answer Wizard** tabs.

The Topic window displays Help for a particular task. The Index tab alphabetically lists keywords that assist a user in finding a particular topic. When the user clicks the keyword, the appropriate topic is displayed. The Contents tab organizes topics according to an outline. Closely associated topics are grouped within a common category. The Answer Wizard tab allows the user to type in a question; Help then attempts to answer the question by finding relevant Help topics.

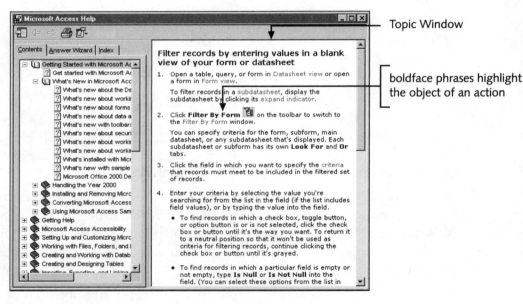

Figure 11-1   Components of customized Help

A Help developer must create the following:

- **Topic files** that are based on HTML. These files end with an **htm** extension (for example, Tutorial.htm) and are displayed in the Topic window. Usually, many topic files are created for a particular Help file.

- An **index file** that uses an **hhk** file extension (for example, MyIndex.hhk). This file is also based on HTML, but it can be generated automatically through HTML Help Workshop. The contents of the index file are placed in the Index tab.

- A **contents file** that uses an **hhc** file extension (for example, Contents.hhc). This file corresponds to the Contents tab. Like the other files, it is based on HTML. The contents file can be created automatically in the HTML Help Workshop.

- A **project file** that uses an **hhp** file extension. This file identifies the topic, index, and contents files that will be compiled together to form the Help file. It also specifies other options, such as the size and type of Help windows. Compiling a project generates a **compiled Help file** that ends with a **chm** extension. The compiled Help file is given to the user of the Access application.

- The files for the Answer Wizard tab. These files are developed through the use of the **Answer Wizard Builder**, a separate program. This program will not be discussed in this text. For more information on it, see the MSDN Web site.

Once a Help developer compiles (creates) the Help file, the file must be linked to the application. The way that a programmer sets up the links is influenced by the ways in which users activate Help. Typically, Help is activated through the Help menu. Users, however, also expect context-sensitive Help. **Context-sensitive Help** displays different Help topics depending upon the location of the user's cursor. For example, in the MU-DSci application, a Help topic corresponding to new prospects should be displayed when frmProspects is the active form, and Help about leveling courses should be offered when a student's leveling courses are displayed.

Context-sensitive Help is typically activated when a user presses the F1 key, selects the What's This button from the Help menu, or clicks Help inside a message box. You can create linkages between a Help file and an Access application through the use of the HelpFile and HelpContextID properties of forms and controls, and through the use of Help File and HelpContextID arguments in the MsgBox function. In addition, programmers can use the HTMLHelp API function to trigger the appropriate Help. These properties and functions will be discussed in detail later in this chapter.

To develop quality customized Help, first you must determine the Help requirements. Both the system's features and the expertise of the users will influence these requirements. Second, you must design the Help topics. Help topics should have a common format. HTML templates can be created to enforce this common format. Third, you should design the Index and Contents tabs so that a consistent standard is used. Fourth, you must create the topics, index, contents, and projects files. Fifth, you must compile the Help files through the use of a Help file compiler. Finally, you must link the files to the application.

Like the database application itself, Help must be tested continually. Testing requires the development of a test plan and the creation of standards for documenting bugs. Tests should include spell checking and grammar checking. In addition, they should ensure that the appropriate context-sensitive Help is displayed. Users should also be consulted over time to determine whether Help topics, indexes, and contents should be modified or added.

You should not infer from these steps that developing Help is a separate activity from developing the application. In fact, you should determine the Help requirements at the same time that you determine the system's requirements, and the design of Help should be integrated into the design of the system as a whole. You will learn more about these steps as you learn to create the various Help files later in this chapter.

CREATING HELP TOPICS

Help topics frequently list the steps necessary to accomplish a desired database action. As you saw in Figure 11-1, these steps may include boldface phrases that catch the attention of the user. They may also contain links to other relevant Help topics, links to pop-up windows that define a term, and pictures that graphically illustrate a concept.

Developers use HTML to create topic files. Unlike Microsoft Word documents, HTML files are text files that do not contain special formatting. In this way, they are similar to the text files produced by Microsoft Notepad. You can also create text files in word processors by saving the file as Text Only.

HTML uses tags that surround letters, words, or phrases to specify the desired format. The Web browser or the Help viewer then reads these tags and formats the text accordingly. For example, the <B> tags in the following statement cause the word "Find ID" to appear in boldface type:

```
Click <B>Find ID</B> to open a form that prompts for
student IDs.
```

Table 11-1 lists many of the tags used in HTML. Tags that appear in almost every HTML document are <H#> and <P>. The series of <H#> tags create headings similar to the chapter headings that appear in a book. The <H1> tag creates the largest heading; <H2> headings are not as large and are considered a subheading within the heading created with the previous <H1> tag. The <P> tag identifies a new paragraph. Figure 11-2 illustrates a sample Help file that contains tags. Figure 11-3 displays the user's view of Help.

Table 11-1 Commonly used HTML tags

Tag	Example	Description
<! >	<!—Create an object –>	Documentation tag; contents of the tag are not displayed
<H#>	<H1>Welcome</H1> <H2>Brief Description</H2>	Header tag that surrounds text that describes the following section; the # ranges from 1 to 6, where <H1> is a major header, <H2> is a subsection in an <H1> header, and so forth
<P>	<P>To use the system, click the Start key and …</P>	Starts a new paragraph; <P align=center> centers the paragraph
 	 Second, identify the report.	Causes a line break that is single-spaced; <BR clear=left> forces the system to start a new line after the image on the left
<B>	Click <B>Start</B>	Boldface; <strong> tag is similar
<I>	The title is <I>Database Management</I>	Italic; <emphasize> tag is similar
<ul>	<ul> <li>Reports <li>Forms </ul>	Unordered list (that is, bullets)
<ol>	<ol> <li>Open the form <li>Click report <li>Click print report </ol>	Ordered list
<li>	See examples above	Identifies an item in a list
<img>	<img src="image.gif">	Inserts an image into a file
<a href>	<a href="local.htm">Local</a>	Create a hyperlink that causes the system to jump to local.htm
<table> <th> <td> <tr>	<table> <tr><th>Action<th>Result <tr><td>Click Start<td> Open Start window <tr><td>Click Close<td> Closes the form</table>	Creates a table; <th> specifies a column header, <td> specifies table data, and <tr> indicates the start of a row

11

```
<HTML>
<HEAD>
<meta name="GENERATOR" content="Microsoft&reg; HTML Help Workshop
4.1">
<Title>Prospect Help</Title>
</HEAD>
<BODY><Object type="application/x-oleobject"
classid="clsid:1e2a7bd0-dab9-11d0-b93a-00c04fc99f9e">
     <param name="Keyword" value="Applicants">
     <param name="Keyword" value="Prospects">
</OBJECT>
<H1>Prospect Help</H1>
This Prospects form is used to enter information about applicants to
the program.
Admitted prospects become current students and are displayed in the <A
HREF="CurrentStudentsHelp.htm">Current Student form</A>.
<H2>What do you want to do?</H2>
<ul>
<li><A HREF="#Find">Find a prospect</A>
<li><A HREF="#Add">Add a new prospect</A>
<li><A HREF="Admit.htm">Admit a prospect</A>
</ul>
<H3><A NAME="Find">Find a Prospect</A></H3>
To find a prospect, click the <B>Student ID List</B> combo box and
type the Student ID. Alternatively, click the <B>Name List</B> and
type the name.
<H3><A NAME="#Add">Add a Prospect</A></H3>
To add a new prospect, click New Record <IMG SRC="newrec.gif"> and
type the values.
</BODY>
</HTML>
[END CODE]
```

header tag

header tag

Figure 11-2   HTML tags used in a Help file

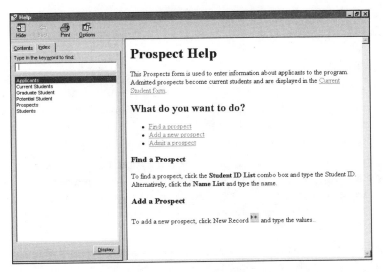

Figure 11-3   Displayed Help file corresponding to Figure 11-2

All HTML files follow the same basic structure, as shown here:

```
<HTML>
<HEAD>
<TITLE>Place the title here</TITLE>
</HEAD>
<BODY>
Place the text and tags that appear in the Topic window
here
</BODY>
</HTML>
```

The <HTML></HTML> tags indicate the beginning and end of an HTML document. The <HEAD></HEAD> tags surround text that provides overhead information to the browser. The <TITLE></TITLE> tags appear inside the <HEAD> tags. The phrase inside the <TITLE> tags is placed in the title bar of a document if it is displayed in a browser. In addition, these titles appear in the Contents tab of the Help window when the Contents tab is generated automatically in the HTML Help Workshop. Finally, the <BODY></BODY> tags surround the text that will be displayed in the Topic window.

The Help developer can use different tools to create HTML files. Microsoft FrontPage—software that is specialized for developing Web pages—is one example. Microsoft Word, which can save documents in HTML format, is another example. In Word, saving files in HTML format converts the formatting used in a Word document into HTML tags; consequently, Word can be used to create topic files. An HTML template that comes with Microsoft Word provides additional support. As another option, the developer can use the limited HTML editor that comes with HTML Help Workshop; this editor is adequate for developing simple Help files. As a final choice, the developer can use Notepad to create HTML files. In this case, the Help developer must type in the tags manually.

Many books have been written about the HTML language and HTML editors. If you are not familiar with HTML, you should obtain an HTML book or access additional HTML Help through the Web.

Help Templates

As you begin the process of developing Help topics, you should concentrate on classifying those topics into general types. Possible types include term definitions, multistep instructions, single-step instructions, and actions that can be performed with a form.

To display a consistent Help screen, you should develop a topic template for each topic type. A **topic template** is simply an HTML file that contains the headings, tags, fonts, and colors (fonts and colors are specified with tags) used for topics of a particular type. This template may also contain text that describes where certain types of instructions are placed in the topic file.

Figures 11-4, 11-5, and 11-6 display the code for three topic templates that are suggested in the HTML Help Workshop. Besides topic templates, **cascading style sheets** may be used to control the fonts, colors, and backgrounds of the topic files. To learn more about cascading style sheets, consult an HTML textbook.

```
[BEG CODE]

<html>
<head>
<title>Example overview topic</title>
</head>
<body>
<h1>Enter heading for overview topic here</h1>
<p>Enter first paragraph of overview text here </p>
<h2>What do you want to do?</h2>
<ul>
<li>First item of bulleted list with a <a href="example.htm">link</a> in
it.
<li>Second item in bulleted list.
<li>Third item in bulleted list.
</ul>
<p>Sometimes another paragraph follows the list. </p>
</body>
</html>
[END CODE]
```

Figure 11-4　Overview topic template

```
[BEG CODE]

<html>

<head>

<title>Example one-step procedure topic</title>

</head>

<body>

<h1>Enter heading for one-step procedure here</h1>

<ul>

<li>To do this procedure, click the <b>Menu name</b> menu, and then
click <b>command</b>.

</li>

</ul>

<h3>Note</h3>

<ul>

<li>Note text goes here. </li>

</ul>

</body>

</html>

[END CODE]
```

Figure 11-5   Single-step procedure topic template

11

```
<html>

<head>

<title>Example procedure topic</title>

</head>

<body>

<h1>Enter heading for multistep procedure here</h1>

<ol>

<li>Do the first task.

<li>Do the next task, which may have a <a href="example.htm">link</a> in it.

<li>Do the last task.

</li>

</ol>

<h3>Note</h3>

<ul>

<li>Note text goes here.

</li>

</ul>

</body>

</html>

[END CODE]
```

Figure 11-6   Multistep procedure topic template

In addition to using templates to support consistency, sentences should be written in a standard style. In general, the following rules should be followed:

- Use verb phrases consistently to indicate a user action. For example, use "Click" to refer to a mouse button, click and "Press" to refer to a keystroke. It is not a good idea to write "Press the F1 key" in one sentence and "Push the Tab key" in another sentence.

- Boldface the object that is the subject of the action. For example, write "Press the **F1 key**" and "Display the **Prospect form**."

- Use terminology consistently. Do not call something a form in one sentence and a window in another sentence (for example, Prospects form versus Prospects window).

The default Help provided with Microsoft Access represents a good guide for learning the intricacies and nuances of creating useful Help files. When you are in doubt about a term (for example, "combo box" versus "list box"), analyze the Help topics in Access to determine how it uses the terminology.

Creating a Help Record Payment Topic for the Swim Lessons Application

You developed the Swim Lessons application so as to allow for flexible data entry. For example, users can record payment information before registration information, or vice versa. Although this flexibility is desirable, customized Help is necessary to explain how to complete some fundamental tasks.

In creating relevant Help files for the Swim Lessons application, you will begin by developing the HTML topic file that is specified in Figure 11-7. Although you can use any HTML editor to create the file, the following steps work with the HTML Help Workshop.

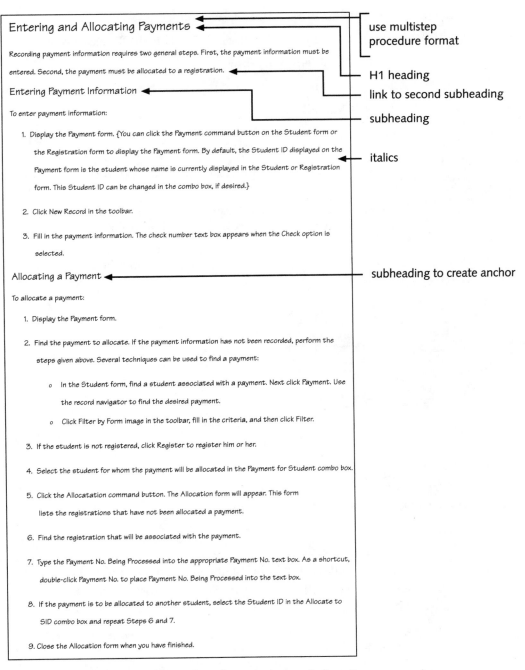

Entering and Allocating Payments

Recording payment information requires two general steps. First, the payment information must be entered. Second, the payment must be allocated to a registration.

Entering Payment Information

To enter payment information:

1. Display the Payment form. {You can click the Payment command button on the Student form or the Registration form to display the Payment form. By default, the Student ID displayed on the Payment form is the student whose name is currently displayed in the Student or Registration form. This Student ID can be changed in the combo box, if desired.}

2. Click New Record in the toolbar.

3. Fill in the payment information. The check number text box appears when the Check option is selected.

Allocating a Payment

To allocate a payment:

1. Display the Payment form.

2. Find the payment to allocate. If the payment information has not been recorded, perform the steps given above. Several techniques can be used to find a payment:

   o In the Student form, find a student associated with a payment. Next click Payment. Use the record navigator to find the desired payment.

   o Click Filter by Form image in the toolbar, fill in the criteria, and then click Filter.

3. If the student is not registered, click Register to register him or her.

4. Select the student for whom the payment will be allocated in the Payment for Student combo box.

5. Click the Allocatation command button. The Allocation form will appear. This form lists the registrations that have not been allocated a payment.

6. Find the registration that will be associated with the payment.

7. Type the Payment No. Being Processed into the appropriate Payment No. text box. As a shortcut, double-click Payment No. to place Payment No. Being Processed into the text box.

8. If the payment is to be allocated to another student, select the Student ID in the Allocate to SID combo box and repeat Steps 6 and 7.

9. Close the Allocation form when you have finished.

use multistep procedure format

H1 heading

link to second subheading

subheading

italics

subheading to create anchor

11

Figure 11-7   Help topic file markup for entering and allocating payments

To create a topic file using HTML Help Workshop:

1. If it is not already installed, install **HTML Help Workshop** on your computer.

2. Start **HTML Help Workshop**.

3. Click **File** on the menu bar, and then click **New**. The New dialog box will open.

4. Click **HTML File** in the New dialog box, and then click **OK**.

5. Enter **How to Enter and Allocate a Payment** in the HTML Title dialog box, and then click **OK**.

   A window is displayed that contains the HEAD, BODY, and TITLE tags. The title has been created for you.

6. Make sure that the cursor is located under the <BODY> tag. Click **Tags** on the menu bar, and then click **Heading**. The Head dialog box will appear.

7. Make sure that the Head level is **1**. Type **Entering and Allocating Payments** in the Text text box, as shown in Figure 11-8, and then click **OK**. An H1 heading is created.

Figure 11-8   Creating a heading

8. Type the following text and tags in the window (boldface indicates the tags and text that have not already been entered through the earlier steps). You can type the tags manually or use the tag menu (in some cases) to help enter a tag.

```
<!DOCTYPE HTML PUBLIC "-//IETF//DTD HTML//EN">
<HTML>
<HEAD>
<meta name="GENERATOR" content="Microsoft&reg; HTML Help
Workshop 4.1">
<Title>How to Enter and Allocate a Payment</Title>
</HEAD>
<BODY>
<H1>Entering and Allocating Payments</H1>
```

Recording payment information requires two general steps.
First, the payment information must be entered. Second, the
payment must be allocated to a registration.
<H4>Entering Payment Information</H4>
To enter payment information:
<! --Create a numbered list-->
<ol>
<li>Display the <B>Payment form</B>. <i>You can click the
<B>Payment command button</B> on the Student form or the
Registration form to display the Payment form. By default,
the Student ID displayed on the Payment form is the
student whose name is currently displayed in the Student or
Registration form. This Student ID can be changed in the
combo box,if desired.</i></li>
<li>Click <B>New Record</B> in the toolbar.</li>
<li>Fill in the payment information. The check number text
box appears when the Check option is selected. </li>
</ol>
<H4>Allocating a Payment</H4>
To allocate a payment:
<ol>
<li>Display the <B>Payment form</B>.</li>
<li>Find the payment to allocate. If the payment
information has not been recorded, perform the steps given
above. Several techniques can be used to find a payment:
<!— Create a list within a list —>
<ul>
<li>In the <B>Student form</B>, find a student associated
with a payment. Next, click <B>Payment</B>. Use the record
navigator to find the desired payment.</li>
<li>Click <B>Filter By Form</B> in the toolbar, fill in the
 criteria, and then click <B>Apply Filter</B>.</li>
</ul>
<li>If the student is not registered, click <B>Register</B>
 to register him or her.</li>
<li>Select the student for whom the payment will be
allocated in the <B>Payment for Student</B> combo box.</li>
<li>Click the <B>Allocatation</B> command button. The
Allocation form will appear. This form lists the
registrations that have not been allocated a payment.</li>
<li>Find the registration that will be associated with the
payment.</li>
<li>Type the <B>Payment No. Being Processed</B> into the
appropriate <B>Payment No.</B> text box. As a shortcut,
double-click Payment No. to place Payment No. Being
Processed into the text box.</li>
<li>If the payment is to be allocated to another student,
select the Student ID in the <B>Allocate to SID</B> combo
box and repeat Steps 6 and 7.

```
<li>Close the Allocation form when you have finished.</li>
</ol>
</BODY>
</HTML>
```

9. Click the **Save** button in the toolbar, type **payment.htm** as the file name, browse to the folder where the Swim Lessons application files are located, and then click **Save**.

10. Click **View** on the menu bar, and then click **In Browser** to display the formatted version of the topic (see Figure 11-9).

11. Close the formatted version of the topic.

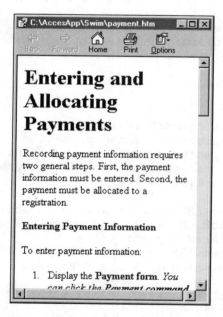

Figure 11-9   Payment Help topic as displayed through the Help viewer

Congratulations! You have created the first topic file.

Including Images in Topic Files

While concise and accurate text is invaluable in a Help file, images also have their place. Images of toolbar buttons, for example, help the user identify which button to click. In addition, images of forms may help establish a context that can augment the text.

Incorporating pictures into Help topic files requires two general steps. First, the image must be prepared with imaging software. Second, the developer must use an HTML tag to insert the image into the file.

Several image-editing programs exist. One such program, the HTML Help Image Editor, is included with the HTML Help Workshop. This software enables you to capture an image from the screen and then edit (for example, crop and color) that image. The HTML Help Image Editor allows you to use a mouse, timer, or keyboard to capture the image; it can save that image only in .gif, .jpeg, or .bmp format.

You specify how you want to capture the image by choosing an option from the Capture menu, as shown in Figure 11-10. When you select the keyboard option, the mouse is used to highlight a window or menu; the user then presses F11 to initiate the capture. When you select the mouse option, the first item clicked with the mouse is captured. When you select the timer, the screen is captured after a specified number of seconds.

Figure 11-10   Capture options in the HTML Help Image Editor

Once you capture an image, you may have to edit it to reduce its size or crop it so that only the relevant portion is included in the topic file. These editing features are available from both the toolbar and the edit menu. In addition to using the HTML Help Image Editor to alter the image, you can use Microsoft Paint to annotate bitmap files and Microsoft Photo Edit to modify image files. Paint and Microsoft Photo Edit are found on many systems.

Help developers use the <IMG> HTML tag to insert an image into an HTML file. The syntax for the IMG tag is as follows:

Syntax

<IMG SRC=*"filename"*, **border**=*integer*, **align**=[**middle**| **left**| **right**| **top**| **bottom**], **height**=*string*, **width**=*string*>

Syntax Dissection

- **SRC** is a parameter that identifies the file. The *filename* is the path to the file.

- The *border* argument identifies the thickness of the border. A border equal to 0 means that a border is not placed around the image.

- The *align* argument indicates the position of the image relative to the text and the page.

- The *height* argument allows you to adjust the height of the image on the screen. The string consists of the size in pixels or a percentage.

- The *width* argument allows you to adjust the width of the image. The string consists of the size of the image in pixels or a percentage (for example, width=10%).

Code Example

In code, an <IMG> tag is used as follows:

```
<img src= "Prospects.gif" border = 0>
```

Many other parameters can be associated with the IMG tag. If you need additional information, consult an HTML textbook.

Including a Filter Toolbar Image in a Help File

The **payment.htm** Help topic file created earlier referenced the Filter by Form and Filter toolbar buttons. Many users are unfamiliar with these buttons; consequently, images of them are desirable additions to the Help file.

To place toolbar buttons in the Help file:

1. Click **Tools**, and then click **HTML Help Image Editor** in the HTML Help Workshop. The HTML Help Image Editor will be displayed. (If you are familiar with other software for capturing screens, you can use it instead.)

2. Open **SwimReg.mdb** in Access, refresh the links, if necessary, and then open **frmPayment** in Form view.

3. Activate the **Microsoft HTML Help Image Editor** (that is, click the application in the taskbar).

4. Click **Capture**, and then click **Using the Mouse**. Microsoft Access will appear.

5. Click the **Filter By Form** toolbar button. Clicking this button causes the toolbar to be captured.

6. In the HTML Help Image Editor, use the mouse to trace a square around the Filter By Form toolbar button.

7. Click the **Clip** button in the HTML Help Image Editor toolbar. The image of the Filter By Form toolbar button should appear. If you make a mistake, click Edit and then click Undo Clip.

8. Click **File**, and then click **Save As**. Browse to the directory that contains your Swim Lessons files. Change the file type to **gif** and the file name to **FilterByForm.gif**, and then click **Save**. Click **OK** in response to any dialog boxes that appear.

9. Repeat Steps 4 through 8 to create an image for the Apply Filter button, naming the image **Filter.gif**. Note that you may need to close and reopen the form to get a good image of the Apply Filter button.

10. In HTML Help Workshop, open **payment.htm** and modify the code as follows (boldface indicates new text):

```
. . .
<li>Click <B>Filter by Form </B> <img src="FilterByForm.gif
" border =0> in the toolbar, fill in the criteria, and then
 click <B>ApplyFilter</B> <img src="Filter.gif"
border=0>.</li>
```

11. Save your changes, click **View**, and then click **In Browser** to display the Help file. The images should appear.

12. Close the formatted view of the file, and then close payment.htm. Close all other open windows.

Now that you know how to create a single Help file, you are ready to learn how to link multiple Help files together.

Linking to Other Topic Files and Creating Pop-up Windows

A hyperlink from one Help topic to another allows the user to quickly find related information. Hyperlinks may take the user to a different file or to a different location within the same file. Frequently, the related information is displayed in the Topic window. When the information is brief (for example, a definition), however, it can be displayed in a pop-up window.

The following tag supports hyperlinks:

Syntax

<A HREF=*Location>Text or Image to Click*</A>

Syntax Dissection

- **A HREF** tells the browser to jump to the specified *Location*.

- *Location* is a string that specifies the file name (or path) and/or the location of the information to display. A # (pound sign) in the location indicates that the browser should jump to the anchor point identified by name following the #.

- *Text or Image to Click* is a string or <IMG> tag that can be clicked to trigger the hyperlink.

An example of a hyperlink tag follows:

```
An admitted prospect becomes a <A HREF="student.htm">Current
Student</A>.
```

When "Current Student" is clicked, the Help viewer will display the topic represented in the file student.htm.

To jump to a particular location within a file, the location must be named. The following syntax names a location:

Syntax

<A Name=*name>Target*</A>

Syntax Dissection

- **A Name** establishes a name for a target phrase.

- The *name* is a string that uniquely identifies the *Target* within the document. Hyperlinks refer to the *name* to cause the system to jump to the *Target*.

- *Target* is a word or phrase in the HTML topic file.

11

The following is an example of the <A Name> tag:

```
For more information, see the <A href="#Comments">comments b
elow</A>.
. . .
<H4><A Name="Comments">Final Comments</A></H4>
```

A hyperlink that displays information in a pop-up window requires the use of JavaScript. **JavaScript** is a programming language that can be embedded in an HTML file. Like VBA, the JavaScript language uses objects and methods. A special object called the **HTML Help ActiveX control** is associated with many methods and parameters (similar to properties) that can be used in a Help file.

The text and font of the pop-up window are specified as follows:

Syntax

<SCRIPT Language=JavaScript>
  font_variable =“*FaceName*[, *point size*[, *charset*[, PLAIN BOLD ITALIC UNDERLINE]]]”
  text_variable = “*Text for pop-up window*”
  text_variable2 = “*Text for another pop-up window*”
</SCRIPT>

Syntax Dissection

- *font_variable* gives a name to the font specification. The *point size* is an integer that refers to the size of the font. The *charset* refers to the desired character set (this argument is normally omitted). The default for the font item is Helvetica, 12, PLAIN.

- *text_variable* contains the text that will be displayed in the pop-up window.

- *text_variable2* contains the text that will be displayed in another pop-up window. You can include as many text variables as desired.

- The font and text variables can be placed within a text file whose name ends with a .js extension (hereafter called a “js file”). Alternatively, the syntax can be placed within the BODY tags of an HTML file. The Help files are easier to maintain when all pop-up window text and fonts are located in the same js text file.

After a js file is created, you need to be able to reference it. To do so, you use the following syntax in the HTML file that will trigger the pop-up window:

Syntax

<SCRIPT Language=JavaScript
SRC = “*filename.js*”>

Syntax Dissection

- *filename.js* refers to the file that contains the text and font variables.

- This code is typically placed between the HEAD tags in the HTML file that contains the hyperlink.

In addition to the reference information, the Help developer must insert the HTML Help ActiveX control into the HTML file that contains the hyperlink to the pop-up window. The following syntax is used to insert the object:

Syntax

```
<OBJECT
    id=popup
    type="application/x-oleobject"
    classid="clsid:adb88-a6-d8ff-11cf-9377-00aa003b7a11"
>
</OBJECT>
```

Syntax Dissection

- *popup* is the ID for the object. Although any unique name can be specified for the ID, *popup* is commonly used for pop-up windows.

- The classID must be specified as indicated. It identifies the HTML Help ActiveX control.

- In HTML Help Workshop, clicking Tags and then clicking the HTML Help control starts a wizard that will insert the HTML Help ActiveX control object into the HTML file. Because this wizard does not contain a pop-up window option, you should pick some other option (for example, Close Window) and then delete the portion of the object that does not match the above syntax.

- This syntax is placed between the HEAD tags.

11

Finally, the developer writes code that activates the pop-up window with a hyperlink reference that is similar to the A HREF tag described earlier. The syntax for the tag is as follows:

Syntax

<A   HREF="JavaScript:<i>popup.</i>**TextPopup**(*text_variable, font_variable, hmargin, vmargin, ColorText, ColorBackground*) **">**<i>Click Here text</i>**</A>**

Syntax Dissection

- *popup* is the ID of the HTML Help ActiveX control.

- *text_variable* is the variable containing the text to display.

- *font_variable* is the variable containing the font information.

- *hmargin* is an integer specifying the side margin (in pixels) of the pop-up window. The integer 9 is commonly used.

- *vmargin* is an integer that specifies the vertical margin (in pixels) of the pop-up widow. The integer 9 is commonly used.

- *ColorText* specifies the color of the text in the pop-up window. This color is specified in RRGGBB format (R is the amount of red, G is the amount of green, and B is the amount of blue). To specify the default text color of black, type −1.

- *ColorBackground* specifies the background color of the pop-up window in RRGGBB format. Type −1 to specify the default of pale yellow.

- *Click Here text* is the text that will be clicked to activate the pop-up window.

An example of a pop-up window appears in the following section.

Creating Hyperlinks and Pop-up Windows in the Swim Lessons Application Help

The Swim Lessons application will contain many Help topic files. One Help topic file will correspond to the frmStudent form. This Help topic file will discuss, in general, the various operations that can be performed. It will also contain hyperlinks to Help on registration, payment, and payment allocation issues.

You will create the registration Help file first. This Help file refers to a wait list. "Wait list" will be defined through a pop-up window. The wait list definition will be contained in a file called **terms.js**. This file will also contain the definitions of other terms used in the Help system.

To create a file that contains the terms that appear in pop-up windows:

1. Open **HTML Help Workshop**, if necessary. Alternatively, you can open Notepad or Word. The advantage of Word is that spelling and grammar check can be used. If you use Word, save the file as Text Only.

2. Click **File**, and then click **New**. Click **Text** in the New dialog box, and then click **OK**. A window that supports the entry of text will appear.

3. Type the following in the window:

```
PopFont="Helvetica, 10,, PLAIN";

WaitList="A wait list is an ordered list of students who
are waiting to get into the class. When a student drops the
class, the first student on the wait list is added to the
class roster.";
```

4. Click **File**, and then click **Save File As**. Place the file in the same directory as your other Help file. Name the file **terms.js** and then save it.

Next, you will link the **terms.js** file to **register.htm**. The variables defined in **terms.js** are arguments in the TextPopup method.

To create the **register.htm** Help topic file and display the definition of a wait list in a pop-up window:

1. Click **File**, click **New**, and then click **HTML File** in the New dialog box. Click **OK**.

2. When prompted, type **How to Register a Student** in the HTML Title dialog box, and then click **OK**. Next, enter the boldface text to complete the file:

```
<!DOCTYPE HTML PUBLIC "-//IETF//DTD HTML//EN">

<HTML>
<HEAD>
<meta name="GENERATOR" content="Microsoft&reg; HTML Help Wo
rkshop 4.1">
<Title>How to Register a Student</Title>

<!-- Include the HTML Help ActiveX Control. -->
<OBJECT id=popup type="application/x-oleobject"
        classid="clsid:adb880a6-d8ff-11cf-9377-
        00aa003b7a11"
>
</OBJECT>

<!-The following script links this file to terms.js->
<SCRIPT Language=JavaScript
SRC="terms.js">
</SCRIPT>
</HEAD>
<BODY>
<H1>Registering a Student</H1>
To register a student for a class:
<ol>
<li>Find the student to register in the Student Data form.
</li>
<li>Click <B>Register</B>. The Registration form will
appear.</li>
<li>Select the desired <B>semester</B> and <B>level</B> in
the combo boxes.</li>
<li>Move the cursor to a <B>new record</B> in the class enr
olled subform.</li>
<li>Select the desired time in the <B>Index</B> combo box.
</li>
<li>Click <B>Save</B> to save the record. If the class is
full, you will be prompted to enter the student on the <A H
REF = "JavaScript:popup.TextPopup(WaitList, PopFont, 9, 9,
-1, -1)">wait list</A> and the class will disappear from
the screen.</li>
</ol>
</BODY>
</HTML>
```

3. Click **File**, and then click **Save File As**. Name the file register.htm, and then click **Save**.

4. Open the file in your browser, and then click the **wait list** hyperlink. A pop-up window will appear, as shown in Figure 11-11. Close the file in your browser.

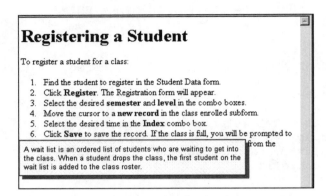

Figure 11-11   Pop-up window inside the Register window

Next, the payment.htm file requires the use of an <A Name> tag so that hyperlinks can reference the Allocation portion of the file.

To create a target phrase in **payment.htm**:

1. Open **payment.htm** in HTML Help Workshop (or another HTML editor).

2. Place the **<A Name=>** tag around the Allocation header line as follows:

   ```
   <H4><A Name="allocation">Allocating a Payment</A></H4>
   ```

3. Place the <A HREF= > tag around a phrase in the first paragraph of **payment.htm** as follows:

   ```
   Recording payment information requires two general steps.
   First, the payment information must be entered. Second, the
   payment must be <A HREF="#allocation">allocated to a
   registration</A>.
   ```

4. Save the file, click **View** on the menu bar, and then click **In Browser**. The Help will be displayed.

5. Click **allocated to a registration**. The browser will jump to the **Allocating a Payment** heading.

6. Close the window.

Your last step is to create the student Help file. This file will contain A HREF tags that reference **register.htm**, **payment.htm**, and the allocation target in **payment.htm**.

To create a student Help file that contains hyperlinks to other files:

1. Create a new HTML file with the following text and the name **student.htm**:

   ```
   <HTML>
   <HEAD>
   ```

```
<meta name="GENERATOR" content="Microsoft&reg; HTML Help Wo
rkshop 4.1">
<Title>The Student Form</Title>
</HEAD>
<BODY>
<H1>Using the Student Data Form</H1>
The Student Data form supports the insertion, deletion, and
entry of student information.  You can use Filter By Form
to locate information about a particular student. Once a
student is located, several operations can be performed.
<H3>What do you want to do?</H3>
<ul>
<li><A HREF="register.htm">Register a student for a class
</A></li>
<li><A HREF="payment.htm">Record payment information</A>
</li>
<li><A HREF="payment.htm#allocation">Allocate a payment to
a registration</A></li>
</ul>
</BODY>
</HTML>
```

2. Save the file.

3. Click the **Display in Browser** button on the toolbar. Figure 11-12 shows the results.

11

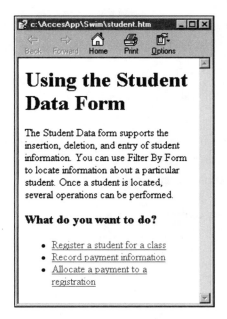

Figure 11-12   Student Help window

4. Click the hyperlinks to verify that the correct Help appears.

5. Close all open files.

The final version of the Swim Lessons application will require the development of additional hyperlinks and Help topics. The Help topics created in this section, however, are adequate for building the Help files.

CREATING THE PROJECT, CONTENTS, AND INDEX HELP FILES

Although the project, contents, and index files can be built in a variety of sequences, it is best to start with the project file, build the contents and index files, and then finish the project file. This sequence is preferable because the project file contains a number of options that influence the features of the contents and index files. In addition, some of the wizards that build the contents and index files are easier to use after the project has already been started.

Starting a Project File

Similar to the process used with other Help files, clicking File, clicking New, and then clicking Project in the HTML Help Workshop menu starts a project file. Next, a wizard appears that leads you through the steps for creating the project file. Upon completion of the wizard, the window in Figure 11-13 is displayed. Table 11-2 summarizes the Project window toolbar buttons.

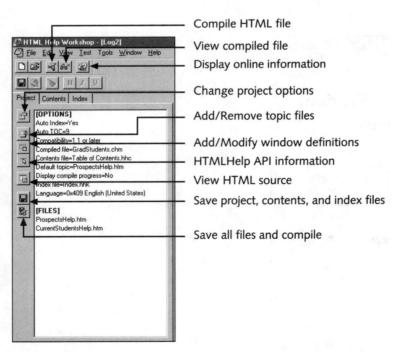

Figure 11-13   Project tab toolbar buttons

Table 11-2   Project tab toolbar buttons

Toolbar Button	Description
Change project options	Displays an options window that allows you to: • Specify a title for the compiled Help file (General tab) • Declare a default topic file (General tab) • Define the path and name of the compiled Help file (Files tab) • Specify the path to the contents, index, and full text search files (Files tab) • Indicate that the contents file should be created automatically (Files tab) • Indicate that keywords should be added to the index file based on a keyword list that is declared in the topic file (Files tab) • Declare compiler options (Compiler tab) • Specify that multiple compiled Help files (chm extension) should be merged (Merge tab)
Add/Remove topic files	Opens a window that allows you to browse for additional topic files; topic files can also be deleted
Add/Modify window definitions	Opens a window that supports the creation of additional Help file windows; used when the contents, index, and topic windows are not adequate for your Help system; features such as the toolbar buttons, size, and location can be specified
HTMLHelp API information	Displays a window that allows you to create mapping and alias information; the information is used by Help API functions that can be called inside of VBA; the Text Pop-ups tab allows you to identify text files that contain information used in pop-up windows that are called through an API function
View HTML source	Displays the HTML topic file for the htm file that is highlighted in the [Files] section
Save project, contents, and index files	Saves the files that are associated with the project
Save all files and compile	Saves the files that are associated with the project and creates a compiled chm file
Compile HTML file	Creates a compiled chm file for the project
View compiled file	Displays the compiled Help file in the Help viewer
Display online information	Displays Help that is related to a Help project

11

The toolbar buttons and the Preference window allow the Help developer to specify many Help features, including whether a single or double click should display a Help topic from an index keyword (Preference window), whether a contents file should be created automatically (Options toolbar button), and whether a Full Text Search tab should be included in the Help window (Options toolbar button).

When you are starting a new project file, you must add all of the topic files to the project by using the New Project Wizard or the Add/Remove topic files button. You should also add any text files that are used by the topic files. These files may have a js extension (JavaScript files); the files can be added through the Add/Remove topic files window. The file names must be manually typed in the File Name text box, however, because the Open window supports finding only files with an htm extension.

Starting the Swim Lessons Application Help Project File

As discussed in the previous section, you will create your project file before creating the contents and index files. Then, you will add the topic files and the terms.js file to the project file.

To initiate a project Help file:

1. Open **HTML Help Workshop**, if it is not already open.

2. Click **File**, and then click **New**. Click **Project**, and then click **OK** in the New dialog box. The New Project Wizard will appear.

3. Click the **Next** button (a WinHelp file is not to be converted). Click the **Browse** button to specify the path and file name of the project. Name the project file **swim.hhp**. Place the file in the same folder as your htm topic files. Click the **Open** button, and then click the **Next** button.

4. Click the **HTML files (.htm)** check box, and then click **Next**. A window appears that allows you to specify the location of your HTML files. The HTML topic files were created previously; you will now add these files to your project. If desired, more topic files can be added later.

5. Click **Add**. The Open dialog box will appear.

6. Click **payment.htm**, and then click **Open**. The file is added to the HTML File window.

7. Repeat Steps 5 and 6 to add the **register.htm** and **student.htm** files. Click **Next** when you are finished.

8. Click **Finish**. The wizard creates the project file.

9. Click the **Add/Remove topic files** button. The Topic Files window will appear.

10. Click **Add**. The Open window will appear.

11. Type **terms.js** in the File name text box. Click **Open**. The terms.js file will be added to the Topic Files window. Click **OK**. The window in Figure 11-14 will be displayed.

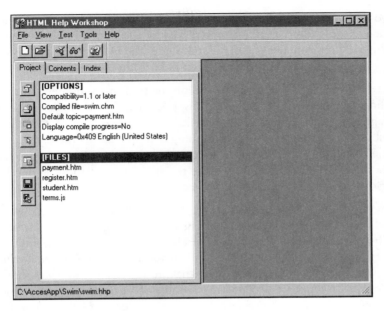

Figure 11-14   Project tab

Creating the Contents File

11

The Help contents file is simply an HTML file that includes a list of words or phrases that are linked to the topic files. HTML Help Workshop contains an editor that supports the process of creating the contents file. The editor is invoked through the New menu in HTML Help Workshop or by clicking the Contents tab within the Project window. The contents tab's toolbar appears in Figure 11-15.

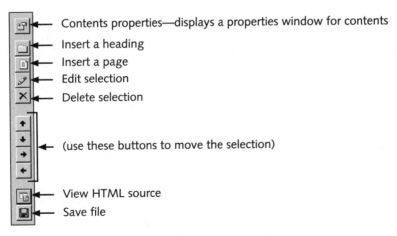

Figure 11-15   Contents tab toolbar buttons

You can add two types of items to the contents files: pages and headings. A page is a title that points to a particular topic file. A heading, represented by a folder or book icon when Help is displayed to the end user, contains pages. An end user of the Help system displays the pages associated with a heading by clicking the plus sign next to the heading icon.

Help developers click the Insert a heading button on the toolbar to add new headings to the contents file. Clicking the Insert a page button displays a window that allows the programmer to add a page. After the Help developer clicks one of these buttons, the Heading and Page window asks for the title of the page or heading and then allows the user to specify the HTML topic file that is associated with the heading or page. Headings do not have to be associated with a topic file. The developer can use the arrow keys to move and indent headings and pages (for example, a page can be promoted to a heading).

Besides declaring the structure of the contents file, HTML Help Workshop allows the developer to tag items in the contents file with a particular information type. An **information type** is associated with a particular group of users. After Help is delivered with the application, the end user of the Help file identifies the desired information type; the Contents window and the Index window then display only those topics that are associated with the specified information type. Information types are declared in the Table of Contents property window. This window also allows the developer to specify different icons for representing contents items, the Help window that should be used for displaying the contents, the background color, and the foreground color. For more information, consult Help in HTML Help Workshop.

Creating a Contents File for the Swim Lessons Application

At this point, you are ready to create a contents file for the Swim Lessons application. Because only three topic files have been created, the single contents file generated here will be sufficient for the basic structure. If desired, you could add more contents page icons later as you create more HTML topic files. The steps that you execute will create the contents file shown in Figure 11-16.

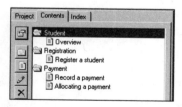

Figure 11-16   File headings and pages in the Contents tab

To create a contents file for the Swim Lessons application:

1. Click the **Contents** tab. A Table of Contents Not Specified dialog box will appear.

2. Make sure that the **Create a new contents file** option button is selected, and then click **OK**. The Save As dialog box opens.

3. Save the file in the same directory as your htm files and name it **Contents.hhc**. Click **Save**. The Contents tab will appear.

4. Click the **Insert a heading** button. The Table of Contents Entry dialog box will open.

5. Type **Student** in the Entry Title text box. Click **OK**. The Student folder is displayed within the Contents tab.

6. Click the **Insert a page** button. If prompted, click **No** in response to the "Do you want to insert this entry at the beginning of the table of contents?" question, because this entry will be inserted into the Student folder. The Table of Contents Entry dialog box will open.

7. Type **Overview** as the Entry Title. Click **Add**. The Path or URL dialog box opens.

8. Click **The Student Form** in the HTML Titles window. The student.htm file will appear in the File or URL text box. (See Figure 11-17.) Click **OK**. Click **OK** in the Table of Contents Entry Dialog box.

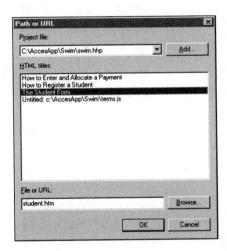

Figure 11-17   Identifying an associated topic file

9. Create a heading for **Registration**. If necessary, click the **Move selection left** arrow key to align Registration with the left margin.

10. Create a page with the title **Register a student**. The page should point to **register.htm**.

11. Create a heading for **Payment**, using the toolbar buttons as necessary.

12. Create a page with the title **Record a payment**. The page should point to **payment.htm**.

13. Create a page with the title **Allocating a payment**. Click **Add**. Click **How to Enter and Allocate a Payment** in the HTML Titles window. Next, type **payment.htm#allocation** into the File or URL text box. Click **OK** until you see the Contents tab.

14. Compare your Contents tab with Figure 11–16 and make any necessary adjustments using the arrow buttons.

15. Click the **Save file** button (you may need to make your window larger to see the button).

Creating an Index File

Creating an index file though the Index tab is similar to creating a contents file. The exception is that headings are not used and the index toolbar contains a button to sort the file. You can also specify index keywords in the HTML topic files.

Creating an Index File for the Swim Lessons Application

You will create indexes for the Swim Lessons application by inserting keywords into the HTML topic files. These keywords will be merged with additional keywords that are specified in the hhk index file.

To create an index for the Swim Lessons application:

1. Click **student.htm** within the Project tab.

2. Click the **View HTML source** button, if necessary, to display the HTML source for student.htm.

3. Click somewhere after the **</TITLE>** tag and before the **</HEAD>** tag so that the cursor is within the HEAD section of the HTML file.

4. Click **Edit**, and then click **Compiler information**. The Compiler Information dialog box will appear.

5. Click **Add**, and then type **student; overview** in the Add keyword dialog box (multiple keywords are separated with semicolons). Click **OK**, and then click **OK** again. An object with keyword parameters will be placed in the HTML file.

6. Repeat Steps 1through 5 for register.htm and payment.htm. The keywords for register.htm are **registration; add class**. The keywords for payment.htm are **payment; allocate payment**.

7. Click the **Index** tab. The Index Not Specified dialog box will open. Make sure that the **Create a new index file** option button is selected, and then click **OK**. Save the file as **Index.hhk** in the same folder as your other Help files. The Index tab will appear.

8. Click the **Insert a keyword** button. Type **Payment** as the title, click **Add**, and then click **How to Enter and Allocate a Payment**. Click **OK**, and then click **OK** again.

9. Add keywords for **allocate** and **class, add**. The *allocate* keyword should refer to **payment.htm** (similar to the contents file created earlier). The *class, add* title should refer to **register.htm**. Indent **allocate** so that it appears within payment (Figure 11-18 shows the correct indentation).

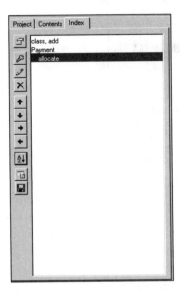

Figure 11-18   Initial Index tab

10. Click the **Project** tab.

11. Click the **Change project options** button. Click the **Files** tab in the Options window. Check the **Include keywords from HTML files** check box. Click **OK**.

12. Click the **Save all files and compile** button. The file swim.chm will be generated.

13. Click the **View compiled file** toolbar button. If necessary, click **Browse** in the View compiled file dialog box and open **swim.chm**. Next, click **View**. The Help file will be displayed.

14. Click the **Index** tab and double-click **student**. The Help viewer should appear as shown in Figure 11-19.

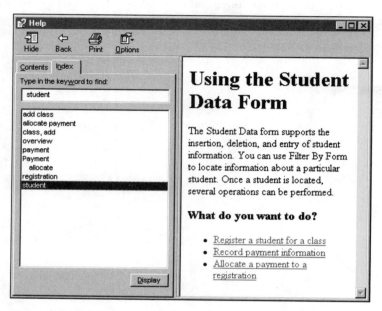

Figure 11-19   Help viewer for the Swim Lessons application

15. Close all open files.

Preparing the Project File for Access

Before a Help file can be linked to an Access application, an alias and map section must be created within the project file. The **alias** and **map** sections associate a topic HTML file with a numerical ID. A numerical ID is the value placed in the Help Context Id property of a form. The Help Context Id property must have a value other than zero for customized Help to be activated. The numerical ID is also used as an argument in MsgBox and other functions that refer to Help. Figure 11-20 summarizes the relationships among the various files used to link Help with an Access application. The contents of these files are discussed below.

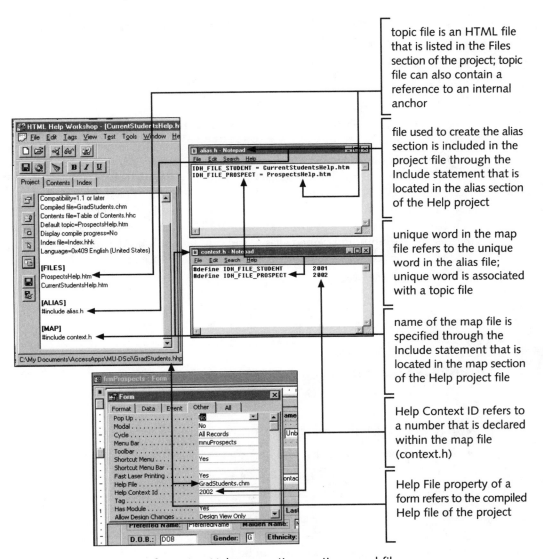

Figure 11-20   Cross-referencing Help properties, sections, and files

The syntax for an entry in the alias section is as follows:

Syntax

IDH_FILE_*UniqueWord* = *Topicfile*.**htm**

Syntax Dissection

- **IDH_FILE_***UniqueWord* is a constant used to refer to the topic file. The IDH_FILE prefix is customary when the constant refers to a file. The IDH portion of the prefix causes the HTML Help Workshop to verify the consistency between the map and alias section upon compilation.

- *Topicfile*.**htm** is a Help topic file.

Examples of alias entries are as follows:

```
IDH_FILE_STUDENT = CurrentStudentsHelp.htm
IDH_FILE_PROSPECT = ProspectsHelp.htm
```

You can place the alias entries under an [ALIAS] section of the project file. You should use Microsoft Notepad to edit the project file (due to a known bug in HTML Help Workshop version 1.2, Microsoft recommends that you do not use HTML Help Workshop to create the alias section). Alternatively, the alias entries can be placed in a separate text file that ends with an .h extension; a file that ends with an .h extension is called a **header file**. The alias header file is commonly named alias.h. You can include a header file within the alias section by placing the following statement under the [ALIAS] section:

```
#include Alias.h
```

In this statement, Alias.h refers to the alias header file.

The syntax for a map section entry is as follows:

Syntax

#define IDH_FILE_*UniqueWord*   *NumberID*

Syntax Dissection

- **IDH_FILE_***UniqueWord* refers to a constant created in the alias section.
- *NumberID* is a number that will be associated with the constant.

Examples of a map entry are as follows:

```
#define IDH_FILE_STUDENT        2001
#define IDH_FILE_PROSPECT       2002
```

Similar to alias entries, map entries can be placed under the [MAP] section of the project or within a separate header file (a file that ends with an .h extension). If the map entries are contained in a header file, the following statement, within the map section of the project file, includes the file within the map section:

```
#include context.h
```

In this statement, context.h is the name of the file that contains the map information. The Include statement is inserted when the developer clicks API Help Information, clicks the Map tab, and then clicks Header file. The developer must then locate the map file.

Creating Map and Alias Sections for the Swim Lessons Application

Now it's time to put your knowledge to work. In this section, you will integrate the Help file created earlier into the Swim Lessons application. For this process to be successful, you must create map and alias sections.

To create map and alias sections:

1. Use Microsoft Notepad or some other text editor to create a text file with the following alias entries. Name the alias file **alias.h**, and save it in the same location as your other files.

```
IDH_FILE_STUDENT = student.htm
IDH_FILE_PAYMENT = payment.htm
IDH_FILE_REGISTER = register.htm
```

2. Use Microsoft Notepad or some other text editor to create a text file with the following map entries. Name the file **context.h**, and save it in the same location as your other files.

```
#define IDH_FILE_STUDENT     1001
#define IDH_FILE_PAYMENT     1002
#define IDH_FILE_REGISTER    1003
```

3. Open the **swim.hhp** project file in HTML Help Workshop (if it is not already open).

4. Click the **HTMLHelp API information** button. The HTMLHelp API information dialog box will open.

5. Click the **Alias** tab and then click the **Include** button. The Include File dialog box will open. Click **Browse**, and locate and select the **alias.h** file. Click **Open**, and then click **OK**. The #include alias.h statement will appear within the Alias Strings to HTML Files window.

6. Click the **Map** tab, and then click the **Header file** button. The Include File dialog box will open. Click **Browse**, locate and select **context.h**, and then click **Open**. Click **OK** until the Project window appears. The #include context.h statement will appear within the [MAP] section and the #include alias.h statement will appear in the [ALIAS] section.

7. Click the **Save all files and compile** button. The compiled Help file will be created.

The numerical IDs created within the map section and then cross-referenced to the topic files in the alias section will be used to create the context-sensitive Help in the Swim Lessons application.

11

INTEGRATING HELP WITH AN ACCESS APPLICATION

Once the map and alias sections are created in the project file and compiled, linking context-sensitive Help to an application is relatively easy. The customized Help can be activated through properties of a form and control, functions that contain Help arguments, and API procedure calls. An **API procedure** is a function or sub procedure that is created outside the scope of an Access application. Microsoft supplies many API procedures that are written in the C++ language.

The simplest way to trigger context-sensitive Help is to set the HelpFile property of a form or report to the name of the compiled Help file (that is, a file name ending with chm). In addition, the HelpFile property, the HelpContextID property must be set to one of the numerical Ids that were created in the map section of the project file.

The HelpContextID can be set in a form, a control on a form, or a report's property sheet. If the value of a control's HelpContextID is zero, the HelpContextID of the form is used to display context-sensitive Help. If the control's and the form's HelpContextIDs are both zero, Access's standard Help is displayed. Clicking F1 while a form is open activates context-sensitive Help. In contrast, clicking Help in the menu and then clicking Microsoft Access Help displays the standard Help.

The MsgBox and InputBox functions contain Helpfile and context arguments. Unlike the HelpFile property of a form or report, the **Helpfile** argument must contain the complete path to the compiled Help file. The **context** argument is a numerical expression that specifies a numerical ID that is listed in the map section of the project file.

After specifying the Helpfile and context arguments, you place a Help button in the message box or input box. The intrinsic constant for a Help button is **vbMsgBoxHelpButton**. It is placed in the buttons argument. Following is an example of a MsgBox that specifies a Help file:

```
Dim plngContext As Long
plngContext = 1003
MsgBox "Incorrect Data Was Entered", _
    vbOKOnly + vbMsgBoxHelpButton, "Error", _
    "C:\AccesApp\MU-DSci\Student.chm", plngContext
```

Finally, context-sensitive Help can be invoked through an API function call. The API function that invokes Help is **HtmlHelp**. Before an API function can be used in Access, it must be declared in the Declarations section of a module. The declaration for HtmlHelp is as follows:

```
Public Declare Function HtmlHelp Lib "HHCtrl.ocx" _
Alias "HtmlHelpA" (ByVal hwndCaller As Long, _
ByVal pszFile As String, ByVal uCommand As Long, _
dwData As Any) As Long
```

In the preceding code, **HHCtrol.ocx** is the name of the library outside Access that contains the function. The **hwndCaller** argument is the Hwnd property of the form or control that will be associated with the Help viewer. The **Hwnd** property uniquely identifies an open window (that is, a form) across all Windows applications. When the form or control is closed, the Help viewer disappears. If hwndCaller has a value of 0, the Help viewer is associated with the application (as is normally the case).

The **pszFile** argument specifies the complete path to the Help file. The **uCommand** argument influences the operation of the HtmlHelp function. Finally, the **dwData** argument is the numerical ID of the context-sensitive Help when the value of uCommand is the hexadecimal number represented by &HF. This string indicates the topic file when the value of uCommand is the hexadecimal number &H0 (note that the last digit is a zero, not an O).

The symbol &H is a prefix to a hexadecimal number (a base-16 number). Such numbers are commonly used in API calls. For easier maintenance, most programmers use symbolic constants to represent them. The constant names that are frequently used in the uCommand argument are HH_HELP_CONTEXT and HH_DISPLAY_TOPIC. You should place the following statements in the Declarations section next to the declaration of the HTMLHelp function:

```
Public Const HH_DISPLAY_TOPIC = &H0
Public Const HH_HELP_CONTEXT = &HF
```

Once the function and the constants are declared, both the function and the constant can be used inside a procedure. The following code uses the HTMLHelp function:

```
Dim plngReturn As Long
Display Help for Prospects
plngReturn = HtmlHelp(Screen.ActiveForm.Hwnd, _
"C:\AccesApp\MU-DSci\Student.chm", HH_DISPLAY_TOPIC, _
ByVal "ProspectsHelp.htm")
```

The requirement of a complete path for the Helpfile argument can create difficulties when the user places an application in a folder other than the one anticipated. To counteract this problem, the Path property of the CurrentProject object specifies the path to the running application. For example, if the Help file appears in the same directory as the Access application, the following code specifies the path to Student.htm:

```
pstrHelpPath = Application.CurrentProject.Path & _
    "Student.chm"
```

You can use the pstrHelpPath argument in the MsgBox, InputBox, and HtmlHelp functions to replace of the file arguments.

Unfortunately, Help does not work perfectly with Access. For example, all of the techniques described earlier, except the API function, will display Help through the Access Help viewer. Although the Topics and Contents windows display correctly, the Index tab does not. Instead, the Index tab displays the index for the generic Access Help. This quirk may not be a problem if your user is unlikely to need the index after pressing F1. If the user requires the index, however, the API function call must activate the HTML Help viewer. The HTML Help viewer then displays all components of Help correctly. This problem is likely to be corrected in future versions of Access.

11

Connecting Help to the Swim Lessons Application

Once again, it is time to apply what you know. The Swim Lessons application should support context-sensitive Help. Users should be able to trigger that context-sensitive Help by using the F1 key and by using menu and toolbar commands. First, you will specify the compiled Help file that a form should use in the Help File property and the context ID for the form in the Help Context ID property. Then, you will write a procedure that invokes an API function that references these properties to display context-sensitive Help correctly.

To activate context-sensitive Help:

1. Open Access and open SwimReg. Display **frmPayment** in Design view.

2. Display the property sheet for the form, if it is not already displayed.

3. Click the **Other** tab, and type **swim.chm** in the Help File property. This file is the compiled Help file.

4. Type **1002** in the Help Context ID property, as shown in Figure 11-21.

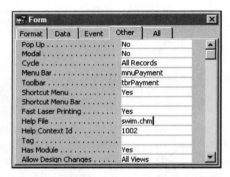

Figure 11-21   Entering the Help File and Help Context Id properties

5. Save **frmPayment**.

6. Display **frmPayment** in Form view.

7. Press the **F1** key. Context-sensitive Help should be displayed. Close the Help window and the form.

8. Repeat Steps 1 through 7 for **frmStudent** (Help Context Id is **1001**) and **frmRegistration** (Help Context ID is **1003**).

Although the F1 key works fairly well, users may not always remember that the F1 key is a shortcut. In addition, the Index tab does not work correctly with this approach. Consequently, you will create a GetHelp function that is triggered from a menu and toolbar command.

To create a function that triggers Help:

1. Open the **basUtilities** module in Code view.

2. Type the following code into the Declarations section:

```
Public Declare Function HtmlHelp Lib "HHCtrl.ocx" _
    Alias "HtmlHelpA" (ByVal hwndCaller As Long, _
    ByVal pszFile As String, ByVal uCommand As Long, _
    dwData As Any) As Long
Public Const HH_HELP_CONTEXT = &HF
```

3. Create the following function in basUtilities:

```
Public Function CallHelp()
'This function can be invoked from any form that has
'declared a Help file and Help Context Id.
    Dim plngReturn As Long
    Dim pstrPath As String
    Dim plngContext As Long
    Dim pobjForm As Form
    'Set pobjForm to the active form
    Set pobjForm = Screen.ActiveForm
    'Create the path to the file
    pstrPath = Application.CurrentProject.Path & "\" & _
        pobjForm.HelpFile
    'Determine the context Id
    If pobjForm.ActiveControl.HelpContextId <> 0 Then
        plngContext = pobjForm.ActiveControl.HelpContextId
    Else
        plngContext = pobjForm.HelpContextId
    End If
    'Invoke the API function
    plngReturn = HtmlHelp(pobjForm.Hwnd, pstrPath, _
     HH_HELP_CONTEXT, ByVal plngContext)
End Function
```

4. Save your code, and then close the Visual Basic window.

The next step is to create the menu and toolbar item.

To create menu and toolbar items for frmPayment:

1. Click **View**, point to **Toolbars**, and then click **Customize**. The Customize window will appear.

2. In the Toolbars tab, click the **mnuPayment** check box. The mnuPayment command bar will appear.

3. Click and drag **Help** off the mnuPayment command bar. You need to remove the Help menu and create a new Help menu from scratch. The Help menu is being rebuilt because, earlier in the book you dragged the entire Help menu to mnuPayment. Changes to the Help menu in mnuPayment will change the

11

default Help menu. Reconstructing the Help menu in the fashion described below will prevent such a change from occurring.

4. Click the **Commands** tab, and then click **New Menu** in the Categories list box.

5. Drag **New Menu** from the Commands list box to the end of **mnuPayment** (where the Help menu originally appeared). New Menu will appear in the command bar.

6. Right-click **New Menu**, and enter **&Help** as the Name in the pop-up window. Press **Enter**.

7. Move the mnuPayment toolbar so that you can drag commands from the Help menu of the database toolbar to the new Help menu in mnuPayment.

8. Hold down the **Ctrl** key and drag **Microsoft Access Help**, **Show the Office Assistant**, and **What's This** to the new Help menu on mnuPayment.

9. Right-click **What's This** on the new Help menu in mnuPayment, and then click **Begin a Group** on the pop-up window. This action creates a line above What's This.

10. Click the **Commands** tab in the Customize window, and then click **File** in the Categories list box. Drag **Custom** from the Commands list box to the bottom of Help in the mnuPayment command bar.

11. Right-click **Custom**, and type **&Context Help** in the Name text box.

12. Right-click **Context Help** (if the pop-up window is not present), and click **Properties**.

13. Click the **On Action** combo box and type **=CallHelp()** (see Figure 11-22). When Context Help is clicked, CallHelp will be invoked.

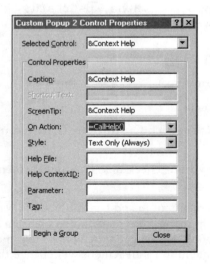

Figure 11-22   Invoking a function from a command bar

14. Type **Activate context-sensitive Help** in the ScreenTip text box. Click **Close**.

15. Right-click **Context Help**, and point to **Change Button Image**. Click the **question mark**. A question mark icon will be associated with command bar.

16. If necessary, drag the **mnuPayment** command bar toward the top of the screen to dock it.

17. Click the **Toolbars** tab in the Customize window, and then check the **tbrPayment** check box. The toolbar will appear.

18. Hold the **Ctrl** key, and drag **Context Help** from mnuPayment to tbrPayment. The command will appear in the toolbar.

19. Right-click **Context Help** in the toolbar, and then click **Default Style**. Only the question mark will appear.

20. Click the check boxes of **mnuPayment** and **tbrPayment** in the Toolbars tab. These command bars will be removed from the screen.

21. Close the Customize window.

22. Open frmPayment in Form view. When you click **Help** on the menu bar, the menu and toolbar (if docked) will appear, as shown in Figure 11-23.

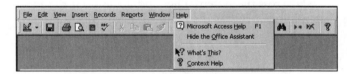

Figure 11-23   Final version of mnuPayment and tbrpayment

23. Click the **Context Help** menu or toolbar command. The appropriate Help will be displayed. Exit Access.

A similar procedure could be performed for the other forms in the Swim Lessons application.

DELIVERING HELP WITH THE APPLICATION

Users of an application view customized Help that is created with the HTML Help Workshop through the HTML Help viewer. To view customized Help, the user must have the compiled Help file, the HTML Help Installation and Update package (Hhupd.exe), and Microsoft Internet Explorer (version 3.02 or later). The HTML Help Workshop\redist directory contains the Hhupd.exe file. The Microsoft Office Developers edition contains tools that allow you to zip and install all of the necessary files on a user's computer.

CHAPTER SUMMARY

❑ A well-designed application is a failure when users cannot perform the basic functions that the system supports. Customized Help is a vital tool that tells users how to perform both basic and advanced functions. The HTML Help Workshop supports the creation of customized Help.

❑ Customized Help consists of various sections and files. The Topic window displays an HTML topic file. Topic files define a term or display the steps necessary to perform a function. The Index tab contains an alphabetic list of keywords. Double-clicking a keyword displays the appropriate topic file. The Contents tab contains an outline of Help topics. You create a Help file by compiling files associated with topics, contents, and indexes. The project file identifies the files to be compiled.

❑ You can connect the compiled Help file to the Access application by using the HelpFile and HelpContextID properties. The HelpFile property identifies the compiled Help file. The HelpContextID property identifies a number that is mapped to an HTML topic file through the use of map and alias sections. Help can also be connected to an Access application via MsgBox arguments and the HtmlHelp API function.

❑ Like the development of a high-quality application, the development of a high-quality Help system requires care and attention to detail. Developers should use topic templates so as to promote consistency across the system. They should also test the Help system and make the appropriate improvements as the result of user feedback.

REVIEW QUESTIONS

1. What is a Help file compiler?
2. With context-sensitive Help, the Help topic displayed depends on the form or control that has focus. True or False?
3. Which tabs or windows are found inside a Help window?
4. How do the Help Index tab and the Contents tab differ?
   a. The Index tab displays alphabetically ordered keywords that point to Help topics; the Contents tab is used to type natural-language questions.
   b. The Contents tab displays alphabetically ordered keywords that point to Help topics that are displayed in the Index tab.
   c. The Index tab displays alphabetically ordered keywords that point to Help topics; the Contents tab organizes the topics into categories.
   d. The Index tab is used only when the Contents tab is not included in the Help files.
5. Which language is used to build a topic file in the HTML Help Workshop?
   a. HTML
   b. Rich Text Format
   c. VBA
   d. C++

6. What is the purpose of the project file in the HTML Help Workshop?

7. Which keyboard key triggers context-sensitive Help?

8. Describe the series of steps that you should follow during the process of creating customized Help.

9. What is the purpose of a Help topic template?

   a. To create a consistent format for your topic files

   b. To create an index to the topic files

   c. To compile your Help files

   d. To connect a Help file to an Access application

10. What words are typically boldface in a Help topic file?

11. What are the purpose and capabilities of the HTML Help Image Editor?

12. Write an HTML tag that inserts the Move.gif file into a topic file.

13. Write an HTML tag that creates a hyperlink to modify.htm. The hyperlink should consist of the phrase "change the student data."

14. Which two HTML tags cause an HTML file to jump to a different position in the same file?

   a. <A HREF> and <IMG SRC>

   b. <SRC> and <IMG SRC>

   c. <ol> and <ul>

   d. <A HREF> and <A NAME>

15. What is the HTML Help ActiveX control?

16. What is the purpose of the map and alias sections?

17. What is the relationship between the map section and the HelpContextID property?

18. What is an API procedure?

19. Which API procedure is used to invoke Help?

20. What is the purpose of the HelpFile property?

11

HANDS-ON PROJECTS

Project 11-1

Natural Parent International. Users of the NPI system will benefit from customized Help. Among other topics, the Help system should explain shortcuts for performing certain operations. For example, double-clicking date controls should automatically add the current date to the control. The Help system should also explain the features of each form. Finally, clicking NPI Help in the Help menu should trigger customized Help.

Complete these steps:

1. Open **NPI.mdb**. Create a customized Help file. The customized file should have Contents and Index tabs. At least four HTML pages should be created. At least one screen picture should be included on a page.

2. Create a procedure that activates context-sensitive Help. The procedure should be invoked from the Help menu.

3. Save your work.

Project 11-2

Metropolitan Performing Arts Company. Users of the MPAC system will benefit from customized Help. Among other topics, the Help system should explain shortcuts for performing certain operations. For example, double-clicking the status combo box in frmPerformanceDateSeats should cause Access to set the status to unavailable. The Help system should also explain the features of each form. Clicking MPA Help in the Help menu should trigger customized Help.

Complete these steps:

1. Open **MPA.mdb** and refresh the links. Create a customized Help file. The customized file should have Contents and Index tabs. At least four HTML pages should be created. At least one screen picture should be included on a page.

2. Create a procedure that activates context-sensitive Help. The procedure should be invoked from some source, such as the Help menu, toolbar buttons, or command buttons.

3. Save your work.

Project 11-3

Foreign Language Institute. Users of the FLI system will benefit from customized Help. Because this system is primarily concerned with data entry, the Help files should facilitate that action.

Complete these steps:

1. Open **FLI.mdb**. Create a customized Help file. The customized file should have Contents and Index tabs. Create Help entries for entering data related to Calls, Customers, Products, and Speakers.
2. Save your work.

Project 11-4

King William Hotel. Users of the King William Hotel system will benefit from customized Help. Because this system is primarily concerned with data entry, the Help files should facilitate that action.

Complete these steps:

1. Open **KWH.mdb**. Create a customized Help file. The customized file should have Contents and Index tabs. Create Help entries for entering a new customer, making a new reservation, checking in a customer, and checking out a customer.
2. Save your work.

11

Project 11-5

Workers' Compensation Commission. Users of the WCC system will benefit from customized Help. Because this system is primarily concerned with data entry, the Help files should facilitate that action.

Complete these steps:

1. Open **WCC.mdb**. Create a customized Help file. The customized file should have Contents and Index tabs. Create Help entries for entering a new patient and for entering data that will appear on one of the WCC forms. Create separate files for each of the three forms.
2. Save your work.

12

WORKING WITH ACCESS 2000 ON THE INTERNET

> **In this chapter you will:**
> - Review hyperlinks, HTML, and cascading style sheets
> - Learn about data access pages
> - Explorer server-side sorting and filtering
> - Learn about scripts and Active Server Pages

This chapter describes some of the ways you can integrate Access 2000 into an Internet environment. Two fundamental ways exist to link an Access 2000 database to a Web application. The first way is to use the Data Access Page (DAP) object that exists in Access 2000. DAPs are similar to forms and reports in many ways, but are also very different in some other ways. We'll discuss these issues in the first part of this chapter.

The second way to link Access 2000 to a Web application is through Active Server Pages (ASP) technology. ASP provides a mechanism for using either VBScript or JavaScript to create applications. SQL commands can be embedded in the script to access, manipulate, and update data in an Access database. In the latter part of this chapter, we will illustrate basic manipulation of data in an Access database using VBScript.

> **TIP** To develop and test Internet applications, you must have access to a computer that will act as the server for your application. If you do not have access to such a computer, you can develop an Internet application, but you will not be able to test it thoroughly.

ACCESSING AND FORMATTING WEB PAGES

A fundamental understanding of some basic Web-related concepts is useful prior to getting into the details of data access pages. We will briefly review hyperlinks, HTML, and cascading style sheets in this section to prepare you for learning the details of DAPs.

Hyperlinks

A **hyperlink field** contains the specification for a universal resource locator (URL). You can create hyperlink fields in a table simply by choosing the hyperlink data type as the field format for the attribute when you are designing the table. You can specify hyperlinks in tables, on forms and reports, and on buttons. They provide a mechanism for navigating in the Internet environment.

A hyperlink field has two properties that can be manipulated by programmers. The first—the **Hyperlink Address** property—specifies the URL. It may designate a specific file on a local area network or a local hard drive. The second property is the **Hyperlink SubAddress** property. If the Hyperlink Address property specifies an Access database, the Hyperlink SubAddress property may specify a specific form within that database.

HTML

Hypertext Markup Language (HTML) is not a programming language, but rather a formatting language. Access 2000 permits tables, forms, reports, and queries to be saved in an HTML format, which allows those elements to be accessed on the Internet.

An HTML file is a static file. Thus, when working with forms, only a form's Datasheet view can be saved as HTML. When you access a datasheet in HTML format, you are actually accessing a snapshot of the original data source. As a result, you won't see any changes made to the original data while you have the HTML version open. You must close and reopen the table to see those changes. Additionally, you cannot update the HTML version from within Access, because snapshots are not updateable.

Cascading Style Sheets

The HTML 4.0 standard formats Web pages using **cascading style sheets (CSS)**, which make it easier to change page formats. A CSS contains the definition of various format properties, such as margins, borders, and fonts. Web pages can contain a reference to a file containing a CSS. In fact, many Web pages can be formatted using the same CSS. In this manner, a programmer can ensure that all of the Web pages in a particular application share a common format. Such consistency is desirable, because it minimizes distractions caused by a frequently changing environment. The user can therefore focus more closely on the content of the Web pages. From a design viewpoint, if a change is made in the CSS, then all of the Web pages using it will reflect the change. This approach saves the developer a great deal of work.

 You can also use the Internet Database Connector/HTML extension (IDC/HTX) file format in dynamic Web publishing. When this format is selected, two files are actually created. One is an .HTX file that contains HTML code. The other is an .IDC file that contains an SQL statement and other information needed by the server to connect to a database. Microsoft supports the IDC/HTX approach only for backward compatibility, so we will not discuss it further in this book.

WORKING WITH DATA ACCESS PAGES

As noted earlier, data access pages are external files that provide a means to use Access 2000 on the Internet. They are not stored in the .mdb file, as are other Access objects. Instead, they are stored as separate HTML files, although shortcuts to them will appear in the listing of Data Access Pages objects in the Database window.

When you open a data access page in Access 2000, it appears in a separate window. To preview a page as it would appear in a browser, right-click the shortcut in the Database window and choose Web Page Preview. Because the pages are not stored in the database or project file, Access will not be able to locate them if they are moved. If the pages have been moved, you must specify the new location of the pages using the dialog window that Access will open automatically when it cannot find the pages.

If desired, you can change the appearance of a data access page. For instance, Access 2000 ships with a variety of predefined formats for data access pages. These formats, or **themes**, are simply formatting templates. You can also add text, labels, and controls to a data access page, just as you would to a form or report.

In Access 2000 tables, you can add a picture or other image file as data in an OLE Object field. You cannot, however, display the OLE Object data from a database. The only picture you can add is a static one. You can include such a picture by using the Image control and supplying the path to the file that contains the image. This path can consist of a relative path specification.

Associating a record source with a data access page involves a different process than associating a record source with a form or report. After opening the Field List window, you will see two expandable lists. One list contains tables; the other contains queries. To add all of the fields in a table or query, click and drag the table or query name to the data access page. To add a single field, expand the associated table or query, and then click and drag the field name to the page.

12

You need Internet Explorer 5 to display or edit data access pages.

DATA ACCESS PAGE PROPERTIES

You can display and change data access page property settings by working with the property sheet or by manipulating program code. The easiest way to view a data access page's properties is to click the title bar of the data access page after opening the Properties window. (In early releases of Office 2000, if the page is not maximized, this feature will not work.) Figure 12-1 shows the Properties window for a data access page.

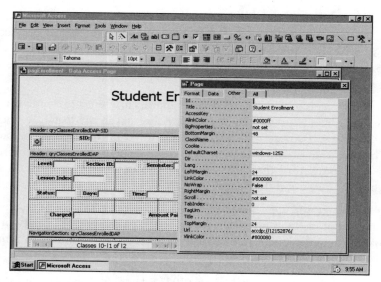

Figure 12-1 Property sheet for a data access page

Three properties of a data access page are worth noting, even though they do not appear in Figure 12-1.

The first, the DataEntry property, controls whether new records can be added to the underlying table. When it is set to True, records can be added. When it is set to False, new records cannot be added.

The second, the MaxRecords property, allows you to designate the number of records sent to a client computer from a server. The setting of this property is critical to the application's performance. If it is too large, performance may be degraded while large numbers of records are transferred from the server to the client. If it is too small, many requests to the server must be made when a user desires to see a large recordset. You should determine a value for this property that will balance these concerns.

The third, the RecordsetType property, determines whether a recordset is updatable. If the value of this property is dscUpdatableSnapshot, then the recordset may be modified. Otherwise, the value is dscSnapshot and the recordset is not updatable.

The Record Navigation Control

The record navigation control (see Figure 12-2) is unique to data access pages. By default, it provides the capability to perform many tasks involving record navigation, record creation and deletion, and record sorting. Access to these capabilities can be controlled by modifying the properties of the control. If you have record navigation controls displayed in more than one group (groups are discussed in the next section), their properties may be set differently.

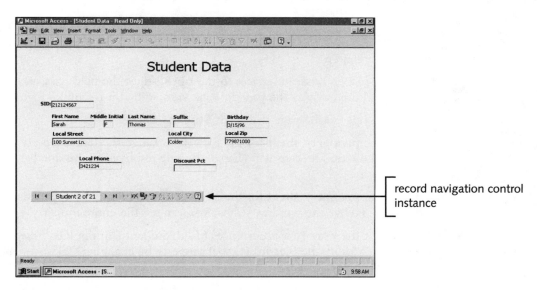

record navigation control instance

Figure 12-2   Record navigation control instance

The RecordSource property of this type of control designates the table or query that provides records to the page. ShowSortAscendingButton and ShowSortDescendingButton determine how sorts will occur. To use these buttons, a user first clicks in the field on which the sort will occur. Next, the user clicks the appropriate button. ShowToggleFilterButton works in a similar fashion. The user clicks in the field that will be used as a filter. The underlying recordset will be filtered based on the current value of the field.

Displaying Students in the Swim Lessons Database

We will now construct a simple, nongrouped data access page to display the students in the Swim Lessons application. It will allow a user to scroll through the student data, modify data, delete records, and add new records.

To create a nongrouped data access page:

1. Open **SwimReg**, and then refresh the links, if necessary. Click **Pages** in the Object Bar.

2. Double-click **Create data access page in Design View**. If this option is not available, make sure that the New Objects shortcuts check box is selected in the View tab of the Options dialog box.

3. Click **View** on the menu bar, and then click **Field List**, if necessary.

4. Expand the Tables folder by clicking the **plus sign** to the left of it.

5. Expand **tblStudents** by clicking the plus sign to the left of it.

6. Select each control, one at a time, and click the **Add to Page** button to add it to the page. Do this for all the fields in tblStudents.

7. Close the field list.

8. Make the labels bold, add spaces to the labels, adjust the field sizes, arrange the fields, and then display the page in Page view so that it resembles Figure 12-2.

9. Create a title on the page that reads **Student Data**.

10. Open the **property sheet** for the page and change the Title property to **Student Data**. This step will change the title displayed in the title bar when the page opens.

11. Open the **property sheet** for the navigation bar. Locate the **RecordsetLabel** property. Resize the window so that you can see the entire property.

12. Note that there are two occurrences of "tblStudents" in the RecordsetLabel property. Modify the RecordsetLabel property by changing "tblStudents" to **Student** in both places.

13. Save the page as **pagStudentData** in the folder that holds your other project files.

14. Close the page.

A user can now click the New Record button to add a new record or click in the Last Name field and sort the records based on the last name.

Grouping Data in Data Access Pages

The most common relationship embedded in a database is the one-to-many relationship. Data access pages display data related in this fashion by grouping the information.

Grouping data on a data access page is very similar to grouping data on a report with a sub-report. A data access page has an advantage over a report, however, in that the data displayed are dynamic and data access pages are interactive. This characteristic means, for instance, that a user can send a data access page in an e-mail attachment that, when opened, will display the most current data.

Although they are dynamic, data access pages that display grouped data are read–only. That is, grouped records are connected to the database and display current data, but a user cannot modify them. Also, new records cannot be added. When data are not grouped, a user may edit the data and add new records to underlying tables.

When you group data, you add several new objects to the data access page. You add a group header and footer, a group caption, and a navigation section. The header and footer display data and calculate totals. Any calculated field for grouped records must be a bound HTML control. The group caption appears above the group header and appears only when the next higher group is expanded. The navigation section displays the record navigation control for the group. The record source for the group appears on the group section bars.

When possible, you should try to group records based on tables rather than queries. This approach will bind the grouping to the table, which is a more efficient process. When grouping is based on a query, the query must be executed before displaying the data; this step consumes more resources and takes more time.

Two group properties deserve specific mention because of their influence on the manner in which the page is displayed. The first group property is the Expanded by Default property. When it is set to Yes, the data access page automatically displays the data within a grouping. Figure 12-3 shows the expand control instance, which controls the display of grouped data. The second group property is the Data Page Size property. Its setting determines the maximum number of records to display within a particular grouping level.

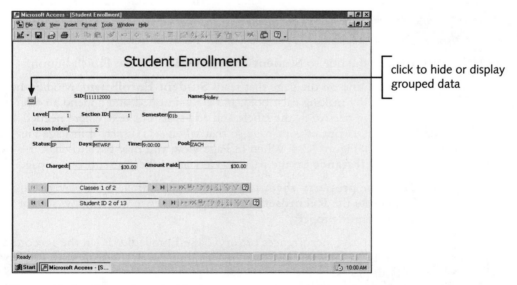

Figure 12-3   Expand control instance on a grouped data access page

Displaying a Student's Classes

To demonstrate a grouped data access page, we will create a page that displays the classes in which a student has enrolled. Remember that grouped DAPs are read-only, so we won't be able to modify any data.

To create a grouped data access page:

1. Click the **Queries** Object Type to display the queries in the database. Copy **qryClassesEnrolled**, and paste it with the new name **qryClassesEnrolledDAP**.

2. Open **qryClassesEnrolledDAP** in Design view.

3. Add **tblStudents** to the query by right-clicking in a blank area on the top pane, clicking **Show Table**, selecting **tblStudents** from the list, clicking Add, and then clicking Close.

4. Add the **LastName** field from tblStudents to the query. Adding this field allows you to avoid writing code to display the name.

5. Save and close the query.

6. Click the **Pages** Object Type, and then double-click **Create data access page by using wizard**.

7. Select **qryClassesEnrolledDAP** from the drop-down list.

8. Add all of the fields by clicking the **All Fields** button. Click the **Next** button once, and then click it again.

9. Do not specify any sorting. Click the **Next** button.

10. Change the title to **Student Enrollment**. Click the **Finish** button.

11. Create a title on the page that reads **Student Enrollment**. Modify the labels on the page by making each bold, and right-justified, and append a colon to each. Adjust the sizes to fit the labels, and add spaces or text where needed. Next, adjust the layout of your page so that when you display it in Page view, it resembles Figure 12-4. When in Page view, you may have to click the **expand control instance** on the page to view all of the contents of the page.

12. Open the **property sheet** for the qryClassesEnrolledDAPNavigation navigation bar. Locate the **RecordsetLabel** property. Resize the window so that you can see the entire property.

13. There are two occurrences of "qryClassesEnrolledDAP" in the RecordsetLabel property. Modify this property by changing "qryClassesEnrolledDAP" to **Classes** in both places.

14. Open the **property sheet** for the qryClassesEnrolledDAP-SIDNavigation navigation bar.

Figure 12-4   pagEnrollment

15. There are two occurrences of "qryClassesEnrolledDAP-SID" in the RecordsetLabel property. Modify this property by changing "qryClassesEnrolledDAP-SID" to **Student ID** in both places.

16. Close the property sheet.

17. Open the Sorting and Grouping window by clicking the **Sorting and Grouping** button on the Page Design toolbar.

18. Change the Expand By Default property for the qryClassesEnrolledDAP-SID entry to **Yes**.

19. Close the Sorting and Grouping window.

20. Save the data access page as **pagStudentEnrollment** and in the folder that contains your other project files.

You can now cycle through each student's enrollment records by opening the data access page. You can also display or hide enrollment records as needed.

SERVER-SIDE SORTING AND FILTERING

Although the record navigation control provides buttons for sorting and filtering records, you may also want to sort or filter records prior to displaying them for a user. Server-side sorting and filtering can save time when downloading data to the client.

You can establish a default server-side sort order by setting the Default Sort property in the Sorting and Grouping dialog box. If the control on which you want to sort is bound to an expression or a grouped control, make sure that you enter the name of the control correctly. For example, if you have an expression such as "FullName: [LastName] & ", " & [FirstName]", then enter "FullName" in the Default Sort property. If you sort on a grouped field, Access 2000 adds the prefix "GroupOf" to the name of the control automatically. You can refer to the ControlSource property of controls to determine the appropriate value to enter.

When Access publishes a page as an Active Server Page, a server filter can be applied to perform the filtering operation on the server. In this event, only the filtered data are downloaded. Server filters work quickly and can be specified in the URL of the page. For example, the following specification shows a server filter set to display only records in which the Semester field is set to "01a":

```
http://www.domainname.com/dap.asp?serverfilter=
"Semester='01a'"
```

Active Server Page technology and scripting provide other functionality as well. We discuss them next.

SCRIPTS AND ACCESS 2000

You can associate Visual Basic for Applications (VBA) program code with events to customize an application in an Internet environment. For instance, you can add scripts by using VBScript. VBScript is a variation of VBA that works seamlessly with Internet Explorer 5. (Netscape Navigator doesn't currently support VBScript.) You must write your scripts in VBScript (or JavaScript) because Internet Explorer does not recognize VBA.

Although you will find some similarities between the two languages, VBScript differs from VBA in several ways. All variables in VBScript are variants. Arguments passed to procedures and functions cannot be typed. Many of the functions found in VBA are not available in VBScript. Error-handling capabilities are not as sophisticated in VBScript. In addition, symbolic constants such as vbYes are not predefined. If you want to use them, you must create a file and include it yourself.

Despite these differences, once you are familiar with VBA, you will find that VBScript is relatively easy to learn. If you are already familiar with JavaScript, however, you may choose to continue programming in it. However, certain data access page events are not recognized when coded in JavaScript and that script elements are case-sensitive in JavaScript, unlike in VBScript.

You can add scripts by choosing Tools, Macro, and then Microsoft Script Editor from the menu bar. This selection will display the Microsoft Development Environment window, as shown in Figure 12-5. The default setting for adding scripts, which is specified in the defaultClientScript property, is to use VBScript.

To enter VBScript code, move the cursor to the end of the </STYLE> tag and above the </HEAD> tag in the code window. Next, choose HTML, Script Block, and then Client from the menu bar. The following lines will be inserted into your code:

```
<script language=vbscript>
<!--
-->
</script>
```

The <!-- entry is an opening HTML comment tag. It causes the VBScript code to be ignored by browsers that do not recognize it. The closing --> entry marks the end of the "comment."

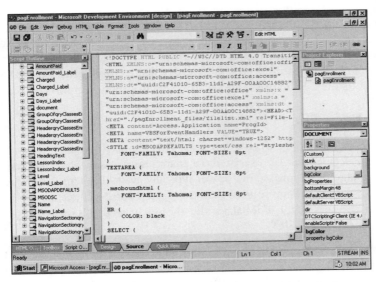

Figure 12-5 Microsoft Development Environment window

When you connect an Active Server Page to an Access 2000 database, you'll want to include a file that contains predefined symbolic constants to facilitate establishing the database connection. This file is named adovbs.inc. You include it by using the following code:

```
<!--#INCLUDE FILE="adovbs.inc"-->
```

ACTIVE SERVER PAGES AND ACCESS 2000

Active Server Pages (ASP) are implemented as an Internet Server application programming interface (ISAPI) filter running under Microsoft's Internet Information Server (IIS). Whenever a Web client sends an HTTP request to a Web server, the Active Server ISAPI filter has a chance to intercept and interpret the request. If the request involves an ASP file, the filter parses the entire file and returns HTML output to IIS. IIS then returns these data to the client.

To implement ASP, you must have a Web server configured to support the technology. Maintaining a Web server can be a complicated and expensive proposition. Your server must run Microsoft's IIS software. If you are using Windows NT, Service Pack 3.0 or higher must be installed, and the Windows NT 4.0 Option Pack must be installed on top of Service Pack 3.0.

A critical aspect of accessing Access databases using ASP is that the database must be established as a system data source on the server. A **system data source** is a data source that is accessible to all users. The ODBC 32 control panel on the server is used to establish an Access database such as a system data source. Using this control panel does not affect the database in any way. It simply makes known to IIS the location of the database and the type (that is, Microsoft Access) of data source it is.

Because server operation is complex and often critical in almost all environments, you will not likely have access to the server to configure it for ASP, although your server administrators can do so for you. Consequently, this chapter does not include activities in which you construct an ASP application. It does provide two detailed examples that you can study and use to prototype your own ASP applications if your environment supports ASP technology.

Using the Global.asa File

Active Server Pages utilize a file named Global.asa. This file performs two functions. First, it indicates where the scripts will be executed. In many cases, execution takes place on the server to take advantage of the processing power typically available there. Also, when data are manipulated on the server, the amount of data transferred to the client can be minimized. To run scripts on the server, the Global.asa file should have the RunAt property in the <SCRIPT> tag set to "SERVER".

Second, the Global.asa file implements scripts associated with four specific events. These events occur for the Application and Session objects. The Application object is created when the application runs; it can respond to an OnStart event and an OnEnd event. A separate Session object is created for each user of the application; it also responds to its own OnStart and OnEnd events. Scripts can be written for the OnStart and OnEnd events for each object. If the application does not need to respond to these events, then the Global.asa file can be empty.

Variables and the OnStart Event

Programmers use the OnStart event of the Application object to initialize or update variables used by the application. These variables might include the number of users of the application or the number of users who have visited the Web site since the application started. The OnStart event for the Session object can similarly initialize variables for a particular user's session.

Another variable that might be altered in the OnStart event of a Session object is the Timeout variable. This variable indicates how long a session is allowed to be idle before it is automatically terminated by the server. For example, if the Timeout variable is set to 15, then the server will terminate the session after 15 minutes of idle processing. At that time, the OnEnd event for the session will occur.

Session Variables in ASP

The Timeout variable is a special instance of a Session variable. One very flexible feature of ASP technology is that you can declare any number of Session variables simply by using them. The following line of code declares a Session variable named LoginTime and assigns the current time to it:

```
<% Session("LoginTime") = Now %>
```

Once created, a Session variable is available to all ASP files that execute during the session. In a sense, it acts like a global variable in other programming languages.

All variable and database item references in ASP code have the following syntax. When a variable or database item is used as an argument to some object or function reference, you must always enclose the variable or database item in quotes.

Syntax

Object("*dataitem*")

Syntax Dissection

- **Object** is a Recordset reference when *dataitem* is a database item returned in an SQL query, the word "Request" when *dataitem* is a variable on a form that has been posted, or the word "Session" when *dataitem* is a Session variable.

- *dataitem* is a database item, a form variable, or a Session variable name.

12

The OnEnd Event

The OnEnd event for the Application object occurs when the application ends. Similarly, the OnEnd event for the Session object occurs when the session ends. For both objects, programmers can use the OnEnd event to update persistent data (that is, data that will be stored even when the application is not running) relevant to the application. Such data could include many things, such as the name of the user and the date and time that the user last ran the application.

An ASP Application to Retrieve a Student's Data

We will now examine a small ASP application designed to retrieve data. We are presenting this application as an illustration, rather than asking you to construct it, because of the many issues related to configuring a server to support ASP applications. The ASP application connects to the MU-DSci database and allows prospective students to check on their application status. The flow of the application occurs as follows: A prospective student logs into a Web site using his or her student ID number. The student ID number is verified against the MU-DSci database. If the ID number is validated, then the application accesses the student' data in the tblProspects table in the database and creates a Web page presenting the application status.

This application consists of three files. The first file, named Login.asp, contains the following code:

```
<%@ LANGUAGE="VBSCRIPT" %>
<HTML>
<HEAD><TITLE>Student Display Login</TITLE></HEAD>
<BODY>
<%
Session.Abandon
%>
<P><FONT SIZE=5>Welcome to the MU-DSCI Web site.</FONT></P>
<P><FONT SIZE=4>Current day and time is: <% =Now%></P>
<HR>
<P>To check your status, enter your Student ID number and
then click the Login button.</P>
<FORM ACTION=Validate.asp METHOD=POST>
<P>Student ID:
<INPUT TYPE="TEXT" SIZE=9 NAME="txtUserID">
<INPUT TYPE="SUBMIT" VALUE="LOGIN" NAME="btnLogin"></P>
</FORM>
</BODY>
</HTML>
```

This code begins with a statement establishing VBScript as the language to be interpreted in the script. It uses standard HTML code to create a title in the title bar (Student Display Login). The Session.Abandon statement terminates any existing session, so that the subsequent code does not conflict with any prior ASP applications that may have been in progress. This statement is often executed early in an ASP application. The code then creates a simple HTML form that executes the second file, named Validate.asp, when the user clicks the Login button. Notice that the form contains a text box control named txtUserID. This control is referenced in Validate.asp. The code in Validate.asp is as follows:

```
<%@ LANGUAGE="VBSCRIPT" %>
<%
'Grab variable from the login form
UserID = Request("txtUserID")
```

```
'Connection to check the user ID
'Create Connection object
Set Conn = Server.CreateObject("ADODB.Connection")
     Conn.ConnectionTimeout = Session("15")
     Conn.CommandTimeout = Session("5")

'Open connection
Set Conn = Server.CreateObject("ADODB.Connection")
     Conn.Open ("ctiMUDSci")

'Prepare and open result set
strSQL = _
"SELECT [StudentID] FROM tblProspects WHERE
[StudentID]='" _
     & UserID & "';"
Set RS = Conn.Execute(strSQL)

If RS.EOF then
     'user was not found so send them back to the login
     screen
     RS.Close
     Conn.Close
     Response.redirect "Login.asp"

Else
     'Load session variable and execute next file
     Session("UserID") = RS("StudentID")
     Response.Redirect "Status.asp"
End If

RS.Close
Conn.Close
%>
```

The first line in Validate.asp establishes VBScript as the language being used. The next executable line of code uses the Request object to obtain the value in the txtUserID control that appears on the login form. The next two sections of Validate.asp establish an ADO database connection to the server and open the system data source named ctiMUDSci.

An SQL statement is then constructed to retrieve student identification numbers from the database. The SQL statement is set up to retrieve the student ID that matches the one input by the user on the login form. This value is stored in the variable UserID. The results of the SQL statement will be stored in the RS variable; RS is a recordset. When the statement executes, either the StudentID will be found and stored in RS, or the StudentID will not be found and an end-of-file condition will occur. When the end-of-file condition occurs, the EOF property of the RS recordset will be set to the value True and the next section of the script will test the conditions.

If the student ID does not exist in the database, then the EOF property will be True and statements to close the RS recordset variable and the database connection will execute. Control also returns to the log in screen. If a record exists for this student, then a session variable to store the StudentID from the database is created to make this value available to the next ASP file that will be executed: Status.asp. Control passes to Status.asp, which accesses the database and creates a Web page to display the status.

Status.asp contains the following code:

```
<%@ LANGUAGE="VBSCRIPT" %>
<HTML>
<HEAD><TITLE>Status Display</TITLE></HEAD>
<BODY>
<%
'This page is activated only after the user ID has been
validated.
UserID = Session("UserID")

'Open connection to database
Set Conn = Server.CreateObject("ADODB.Connection")
Conn.Open ("ctiMUDSci")

'Execute SQL statement to retrieve data
strSQL = "SELECT * FROM tblProspects WHERE [StudentID]='" _
    & UserID & "';"
Set RS = Conn.Execute(strSQL)

'Should always have at least one row returned, but check EOF
anyway
If Not RS.EOF Then
    Response.Write ("<FONT SIZE=4>")
    strOutLine = "<P>Status posted as of " & <%=Now%> & "
    </P>"
    Response.Write (strOutLine)

'Output confirmatory information
    strOutLine = "For Student ID " & RS("StudentID") & ": "
    strOutLine = strOutLine & RS("FirstName") & " " &
        RS("LastName")
    Response.Write (strOutLine)
    strOutLine = "Date of Birth: " & RS("DOB")
    Response.Write (strOutLine)

'Determine status
    strOutLine = "Current Status: "
    intStatusFlag = RS("AdmittedDenied")
    If intStatusFlag = 0 Then
        strOutLine = strOutLine & "Decision still
        pending."
    ElseIf intStatusFlag = 1 Then
```

```
        strOutLine = strOutLine & "Admitted to program."
    ElseIf intStatusFlag = 2 Then
        strOutLine = strOutLine & "Admission denied."
    Else
        strOutLine = strOutLine & "Status unknown."
    End If

'output status
    Response.Write (strOutLine)
    Response.Write ("</FONT>")
End If

RS.Close
Conn.Close
%>
</BODY>
</HTML>
```

Status.asp begins with a statement establishing VBScript as the scripting language to be used. It uses standard HTML code to create a title in the title bar (Status Display). The next line of script moves the value in the session variable UserID into a local variable for more efficient access. The next section again establishes a connection to the server to access the ctiMUDSci system data source. The SQL statement created this time, however, retrieves all of the data for the student with the student ID number specified in the UserID variable.

Because the ID number was validated by Validate.asp, we fully expect to have data for the student. Status.asp tests for the end-of-file condition anyway, because some other situation could cause the SQL statement to fail. For example, a corrupted database could cause a retrieval problem. Testing the EOF property provides some insurance against all adverse events that could happen, however unlikely they may be.

If data are returned to the RS recordset by the SQL statement, then the EOF property will be False and the condition Not RS.EOF will be True. When it is True, Status.asp executes a series of statements that output the data retrieved from the database. The Write method of the Response object outputs HTML code and values stored in the local variable strOutLine. strOutLine is used to construct strings that will appear as text in the page being constructed. For example, the statement

```
    strOutLine = "For Student ID " & RS("StudentID") & ": "
```

constructs a string that concatenates the student's ID number onto the literal string "For Student ID" and then concatenates a colon. For example, if the student ID number is 123456789, then strOutLine will contain the following value:

```
    For Student ID 123456789:
```

Notice that the attribute StudentID, which exists in the recordset returned by the SQL statement, is accessed from the RS recordset variable by placing the attribute name in quotes and parentheses following the RS variable reference. The rest of the output is constructed by accessing the AdmittedDenied attribute in the RS recordset, creating an appropriate line of text to be displayed on the page, and outputting that text. The script ends by closing the RS recordset and the database connection.

As you can see, writing Active Server Pages for data retrieval from Access databases does not require very much in the way of sophisticated programming. Writing Active Server Pages for updates to an Access database is a little more involved, however.

An ASP Application to Update a Student's Record

The following code demonstrates how to update an Access database using ASP and VBScript. This application allows users to input biographical information directly into the MU-DSci database. To deter unauthorized access to someone's biographical data, the application implements a simple password system that allows the user to change his or her password at any time. It also allows the user to update the information as needed.

This ASP application contains four files. The first, named BioLogin.asp, presents a login screen and an opportunity to change the password.

```
<%@ LANGUAGE="VBSCRIPT" %>

<HTML>
<HEAD><TITLE>Biographical Data Login</TITLE></HEAD>
<BODY>
<%
Session.Abandon
%>

<P><FONT SIZE=5>
Welcome to the MU-
DSci biographical data collection Web site.
</FONT></P>
<P><FONT SIZE=4>Current day and time is: <% =Now%></P>
<HR>

Enter your student ID and password, then click the Login
button.<BR>
To change your password, enter it twice BEFORE clicking the
Login button.<BR>
<FORM ACTION=BioValidate.asp METHOD=POST>
Student ID:
<INPUT TYPE="TEXT" SIZE=9 NAME="txtUserID">
Password:
<INPUT TYPE="PASSWORD" SIZE=10 NAME="txtPassword" >
<INPUT TYPE="SUBMIT" VALUE="LOGIN" NAME="btnLogin">
<BR><BR>
Change Password:
<INPUT TYPE="PASSWORD" SIZE=10 NAME="txtNewPwd1">
Verification:
<INPUT TYPE="PASSWORD" SIZE=10 NAME="txtNewPwd2">
</FORM>
</BODY>
</HTML>
```

This code begins with a statement establishing VBScript as the language to be interpreted in the script. It uses standard HTML code to create a title in the title bar (Biographical Data Login). The Session.Abandon statement terminates any existing session, so that the subsequent code does not conflict with any prior ASP applications that may have been in progress. Next, the VBScript function named Now is used to access the current day and time, which is displayed.

The code then creates a simple HTML form that executes the second file, named BioValidate.asp, when the user clicks the Login button. Notice that the form contains a text box control named txtUserID, one named txtPassword, and two text boxes named txtNewPwd1 and txtNewPwd2. These controls are referenced in BioValidate.asp. If the user just wants to log in, then a valid user ID and password must be entered. The user may, however, choose to change his or her password as well. In this case, the new password must be entered twice (once for verification of the first entry) before the user clicks the Login button. The code in BioValidate.asp checks all of these text boxes and performs the required actions (that is, checking the user ID and password and changing the password if requested). The contents of BioValidate.asp are as follows:

```
<%@ LANGUAGE="VBSCRIPT" %>
<!--#INCLUDE FILE="adovbs.inc"-->

<%
'Grab variables from the login form
strSID = Request("txtUserID")
Password = Request("txtPassword")
NewPwd1 = Request("txtNewPwd1")
NewPwd2 = Request("txtNewPwd2")

'Connection to check the user ID
'Create Connection object and open it
Set Conn = Server.CreateObject("ADODB.Connection")
    Conn.ConnectionTimeout = Session("15")
    Conn.CommandTimeout = Session("5")
    Conn.Open ("ctiMUDsci")

'Prepare and open recordset
strSQL =
    "SELECT * FROM tblProspects WHERE [StudentID]='"
        & strSID & "';"
Set RS = Conn.Execute(strSQL)

If RS.EOF then
    'user was not found so send them back to the login
    screen
    RS.Close
    Conn.Close
    Response.Redirect "BioLogin.asp"
End IF
```

12

```
If Not IsNull(RS("Password")) and Password <> RS("Password") _
then
     'User found but password incorrect; send back to login
     'screen
     RS.Close
     Conn.Close
     Response.Redirect "BioLogin.asp"
End If


'If get to here, everything OK -- load local variable
'used later
strSID = RS("StudentID")

'Change password, if applicable
If Len(NewPwd1) <> 0 then
     If NewPwd1 <> NewPwd2 then
          Session("PwdMsg") =
               "Password unchanged. Verification failed."
          RS.Close
     Else
          'Prepare to update table with new password
          RS.Close
'Position to proper row in table
'Need to open recordset with dynamic characteristics and
'optimistic locking.
          Set cmdTemp = Server.CreateObject("ADODB.Command")
          Set ResultTable = Server.CreateObject _
          ("ADODB.Recordset")
          cmdTemp.CommandText = _
          "SELECT [Password] FROM tblProspects " _
          "WHERE [StudentID]= '" & strSID & "';"
          cmdTemp.CommandType = 1
          Set cmdTemp.ActiveConnection = Conn
          ResultTable.CacheSize = 10
          ResultTable.Open cmdTemp, , adOpenDynamic,
               adLockOptimistic
'Update row
          ResultTable("Password") = NewPwd1
          ResultTable.Update
          ResultTable.Close
          Session("PwdMsg") = "Password modified."
     End If
Else
'No change in password
     Session("PwdMsg") = Null
End If
Conn.Close
Response.Redirect "BioCollect.asp"
%>
```

The first line in BioValidate.asp establishes VBScript as the language being used. The second line includes a file of symbolic constants, named adovbs.inc, in the script. This file contains constants that are used in specifying connection parameters. These parameters will be discussed shortly when we explain the part of the script that updates the password. The next executable section of code uses the Request object to obtain the values in the txtUserID, txtPassword, txtNewPwd1, and txtNewPwd2 controls that appear on the login form. The next two sections of BioValidate.asp establish an ADO database connection to the server and open the system data source named ctiMUDSci.

An SQL statement is then constructed to retrieve student ID numbers from the database. The SQL statement is set up to retrieve the student ID that matches the one input by the user on the login form. This value is stored in variable strSID. The results of the SQL statement will be stored in the RS recordset variable. When the statements executes, either the StudentID will be found and stored in RS, or the StudentID will not be found and an end-of-file condition will occur. When the end-of-file condition occurs, the EOF property of the RS recordset will be set to the value True. The next section of the script tests these conditions.

If the student ID does not exist in the database, then the EOF property will be True and statements to close the RS recordset variable and the database connection will execute. Control also returns to the login screen. If a record exists for this student, then the password is compared with the password stored in the database. If a password exists in the database that is not matched by the one entered by the user, then the RS recordset variable and the database connections are closed and control returns to the BioLogin.asp file. If the password is validated, however, a local variable to store the StudentID from the database is created to make this value available later in the ASP file. Before control can go to the next file, however, the script checks whether the user is changing the password.

In determining whether the password will be changed, the BioValidate.asp file first checks whether the length of the value stored in NewPwd1 is nonzero. If it is zero, then no attempt is made to change the password. In this case, control flows to the Else part of the If statement, where a variable used to construct messages related to updating the password is set to null and the RS recordset is closed. Control then flows naturally to the end of the If statement, where the database connection is closed and the BioCollect.asp file is executed.

If the length of NewPwd1 is nonzero, then the user entered a value that must be checked against the verification value stored in NewPwd2. If these values are not the same, then a message informing the user that the verification failed is constructed, the RS recordset is closed, and control flows naturally to the end of the If statement, where the database connection is closed and the BioCollect.asp file is executed.

If the verification process is successful (that is, if NewPwd1 is equal to NewPwd2), then the process of changing the password begins. The existing RS recordset is no longer needed, so it is closed. The next section of the script establishes a new connection to the database with different characteristics than have been described thus far. When a database is being updated, the database connection must be created with parameters that explicitly indicate how to create the recordset and how to handle locking issues. This point is where the adovbs.inc file, included earlier, comes into play.

12

The first statements in this section create a Command object and a Recordset object. The Command object will contain the SQL statement used to position the table to the proper row to be updated. This time, the SQL statement will assign values to a Recordset object named ResultTable. The Recordset object will be used to manipulate the data. Notice particularly the statement that reads

```
ResultTable.Open cmdTemp, , adOpenDynamic, adLockOptimistic
```

The adOpenDynamic and adLockOptimistic parameters are symbolic constants contained in the adovbs.inc file. They indicate that the Recordset object must be a dynamic recordset cursor (and therefore updateable) and that optimistic locking will be used.

The next section of the script actually performs the update. The value in NewPwd1 is assigned to the Password attribute, and the Update method is executed. Notice again the use of the quotes around the Password attribute name in the ResultTable recordset reference. The ResultTable recordset is closed, and an appropriate message is constructed to be output later. Control flows naturally to the end of the If statement, the database connection is closed, and the BioCollect.asp file executes.

Once the user is validated and any processing related a password change is complete, control flows to BioCollect.asp. This file presents a form for collecting the biographical data. Its code is listed below:

```
<%@ LANGUAGE="VBSCRIPT" %>
<HTML>
<HEAD><TITLE>Biographical Data Questions</TITLE></HEAD>
<BODY>
<H2>Biographical Data Questions</H2><BR>
<FORM NAME="frmReview" ACTION="BioUpdate.asp" METHOD=POST>
<% Response.Write("<B>Gender:</B> ") %>
<% Response.Write("M ") %>
<INPUT NAME="Gender" TYPE="radio" VALUE="M">
<% Response.Write("F ") %>
<INPUT NAME="Gender" TYPE="radio" VALUE="F">
<BR>
<% Response.Write("<B>US Citizen?</B> ") %>
<% Response.Write("Yes") %>
<INPUT NAME="USCitizen" TYPE="radio" VALUE="Yes">
<% Response.Write("No") %>
<INPUT NAME="USCitizen" TYPE="radio" VALUE="No">
<BR><BR>
<BR>
<% Response.Write("<B>Ethnicity:</B> ") %>
<% Response.Write("American Indian / Alaskan Native") %>
<INPUT NAME="Ethnicity" TYPE="radio" VALUE="1">
<% Response.Write("Asian / Pacific Islander") %>
<INPUT NAME="Ethnicity" TYPE="radio" VALUE="2">
<% Response.Write("Black, Non-Hispanic") %>
<INPUT NAME="Ethnicity" TYPE="radio" VALUE="3">
<% Response.Write("Hispanic") %>
<INPUT NAME="Ethnicity" TYPE="radio" VALUE="4">
```

```
<% Response.Write("White, Non-Hispanic") %>
<INPUT NAME="Ethnicity" TYPE="radio" VALUE="5">
<% Response.Write("Other") %>
<INPUT NAME="Ethnicity" TYPE="radio" VALUE="6">
<BR><BR><BR>
<% Response.Write
("What kind of job would you like upon graduation? ") %>
<BR>
<INPUT TYPE="text" NAME="Job" SIZE=100>
<BR><HR><BR>
<INPUT TYPE="SUBMIT" NAME="btnSubmit" VALUE="SUBMIT">
</BODY>
</HTML>
```

As with the other files in this application, this code begins with a statement establishing VBScript as the language to be interpreted in the script. It uses standard HTML code to create a title in the title bar (Biographical Data Questions). Next, the code creates an HTML form that executes the fourth file, named BioUpdate.asp, when the user clicks the Submit button.

The form contains three sets of radio buttons and a text box for collecting data. The first set of radio buttons captures the user's gender. The second set captures his or her citizenship. The third set allows the user to specify his or her ethnicity. The text box provides a place for the user to enter a brief description of the type of job the student hopes to obtain upon graduation. The Submit button is located at the bottom of the form.

When the user submits this information by clicking the Submit button, the BioUpdate.asp file executes. This file actually updates the database and presents confirmatory information to the user. The code for BioUpdate.asp is as follows:

```
<%@ LANGUAGE="VBSCRIPT" %>
<!--#INCLUDE FILE="adovbs.inc"-->

<%
'Connection to check the user ID
'Create Connection object and open it
Set Conn = Server.CreateObject("ADODB.Connection")
     Conn.ConnectionTimeout = Session("15")
     Conn.CommandTimeout = Session("5")
     Conn.Open ("ctiMUDsci")
%>

<HTML>
<HEAD><TITLE>Biographical Data Update</TITLE></HEAD>
<BODY>
<H2>Biographical Data Update</H2><BR>

<%
'Output any message related to changing the password
strOutLine = Session("PwdMsg") & "<BR><BR>"
```

```
Response.Write (strOutLine)
'Output confirmatory information
strOutLine = "Your answers will be placed in the database."
strOutLine = strOutLine & "You may update anytime later."
strOutLine = strOutLine & "<BR>"
Response.Write (strOutLine)
strOutLine = "Future updates only change affected fields."
strOutLine = strOutLine & "<BR>"
Response.Write (strOutLine)
strOutLine = "Thank you for providing this information.<BR>"
Response.Write (strOutLine)
%>

<%
'Prepare to update table of results
'Open connection
UserID = Session("SID")
strOut = "UserID: " & UserID

'Position to proper row in table
Set cmdTemp = Server.CreateObject("ADODB.Command")
Set ResultTable = Server.CreateObject("ADODB.Recordset")
cmdTemp.CommandText = "SELECT * FROM tblProspects WHERE " & _
"[StudentID] = '" & UserID & "';"
cmdTemp.CommandType = 1
Set cmdTemp.ActiveConnection = Conn
ResultTable.CacheSize = 10
ResultTable.Open cmdTemp, , adOpenDynamic, adLockOptimistic

cnsEMPTYSTRING = ""
strOutLine = "<BR><BR><B>Confirmation:</B><BR>"
Response.Write (strOutLine)
If ResultTable.EOF then

        'User was not found, so send user back to the login
        screen
        RS.Close
        Conn.Close
        Response.Redirect "BioLogin.asp"

Else
        'Update database
        If Request("Gender") <> cnsEMPTYSTRING then
            ResultTable("Gender") = Request("Gender")
            strOutLine = "Gender = " & Request("Gender") _
            & "<BR>"
        Else
            strOutLine = "No change in gender, still: " & _
                ResultTable("Gender") & ".<BR>"
        End If
        Response.Write (strOutLine)
```

```
    If Request("USCitizen") <> cnsEMPTYSTRING then
        ResultTable("USCitizen") =
            CBool(Request("USCitizen") = "Yes")
        If ResultTable("USCitizen") Then
            strOutLine = "USCitizen: Yes.<BR>"
        Else
            strOutLine = "US citizen: No.<BR>"
        End If
    Else
        If ResultTable("USCitizen") then
            strOutLine =
            "No change in US citizenship, still:
                Yes.<BR>"
        Else
            strOutLine =
            "No change in US citizenship, still:
                No.<BR>"
        End If
    End If
    Response.Write (strOutLine)

    If Request("Job") <> cnsEMPTYSTRING then
        ResultTable("Job") = Left(Request("Job"), 200)
        strOutLine = "Job objective: " & Request("Job") _
        & "<BR>"
    Else
        strOutLine = "No change in job objective: " & _
            ResultTable("Job") & ".<BR>"
    End If
    Response.Write (strOutLine)


    ResultTable.Update
End If

%>
</BODY>
</HTML>
```

This file incorporates many of the same techniques illustrated in the process to modify passwords discussed earlier. Like the other files, it establishes VBScript as the scripting language first. Like the BioValidate.asp file, which may also update the database, it includes the adovbs.inc file so that the connection parameters required when updating the database become available to the script. This ASP file uses the Response object to write lines that are constructed in a variable named strOutLine, as in earlier files. Notice that the message related to any attempt to change the password (created in BioValidate.asp) is output in this file. Because this message is stored in a Session variable, it is now available to be processed. And, although we would fully expect to locate the user in the database because of the prior validation processing, the file nevertheless checks for an end-of-file condition before processing the update, just to provide some protection against a failure that could occur, however unlikely.

Notice again where the update occurs. In this section of the file, each small If statement checks whether data have been input. If no data are input, the database is not updated. In other words, the database is updated only when the user provides data. This approach allows a user to change selected fields at a later date.

Notice also the section of the code that updates the USCitizen attribute. This attribute is a Yes/No field in the Access database. All data in an ASP application are captured as strings, however. To store the "Yes" value correctly, the value must be converted to a Boolean value. The CBool function performs that conversion. In a similar manner, any numeric data stored in an Access database by an ASP application must be converted, as must any dates and times.

The four files described here employ typical database access and updating techniques when using an Access database with Active Server Pages. The prior code examples illustrate general scripting approaches. Adding a script for a specific event associated with a specific object is a little different from this general scripting approach. It is also slightly different from the event procedure programming you've learned throughout this book. We'll take a look at the specifics in the next section.

Adding a Button to pagClassLocation to Display a Pool's Location

We will now add a button to the data access page named pagClassLocation to illustrate the process of writing VBScript code for such a page. The button will perform a simple task because VBScript, when utilized without Active Server Pages technology, provides limited capabilities. This button will display more information about the location of the pool where the lesson will be given. This information is stored in the Location attribute of tblPool.

To add a button to pagClassLocation to display information about the pool location:

1. Click the **Pages** Object Type, if necessary, and then double-click **Edit Web page that already exists**. Select **pagClassLocation**, and then click **Open**. Close the Field List dialog.

2. When the Data Link Properties dialog box opens, navigate to the location of your project's database. Select **SwimReg.mdb**, click **Open**, and then click **OK**. Click **OK** in response to the dialog box that states that the data link could not be established.

3. Click the **Command Button** tool in the toolbox, and place a command button instance on the page. Close the wizard, if it starts, and then open the **property sheet** for the command button.

4. Set the Id property to **cmdLocation**. The Id property is analogous to the Name property of a control on a form.

5. Set the InnerText property to **Status**. The InnerText property is analogous to the Caption property of a command button on a form.

6. Right-click the **command button**, and select **Microsoft Script Editor** from the pop-up menu. If you are prompted to install Web Scripting, do so.

7. If necessary, open the **Script Outline** window by clicking the **Script Outline** tab in the lower-left corner of the screen.

8. Locate **cmdLocation** in the Script Outline window.

9. Expand the entry for cmdLocation by clicking the **plus sign** to the left of it.

10. Double-click the **onclick** entry.

11. Enter the following code in the Script window:

```
Dim MessageText
If txtPool.Value = "CITY" Then
    MessageText = "City Pool: 2 blocks North of Muroff " _
    & "Municipal Building."
Elseif txtPool.Value = "ZACH" Then
    MessageText = "Zachary Pool: 1 mile West of " _
    & "Batistick Gardens"
Elseif txtPool.Value = "NAUT" Then
    MessageText = "Natatorium: 1 block George P. " _
    & "Burdell Arena"
Else
    Messagetext = "Pool location currently unavailable."
End If
MsgBox MessageText,,"Pool Location"
```

12. Click the **Quick View** tab at the bottom of the Script window to test your button.

13. Use the navigation control to select records with different pool locations and click the cmdLocation button.

14. Close each message box as it opens after you've had a chance to read its contents.

15. Save your work, exit all windows, and then exit Access.

Although this exercise involves a simple example of writing code for a button on a data access page, you can see that the process is very different than that used when writing ASP scripts. As the Internet and Microsoft's strategy for integrating Access into it continue to evolve, future releases of Access 2000 will likely contain more sophisticated (and easier-to-use) means for publishing database information on the Web.

12

CHAPTER SUMMARY

❏ Access 2000 provides several ways to create Web-enabled database applications. Older versions of Access supported the hyperlink data type, which is a fundamental Web-enabling object. Hyperlinks allowed the user only to reach a Web page that had been created in another development environment. In contrast, Access 2000 adds new capability within the Access development environment for developing Web-enabled applications.

❏ You learned about the data access pages in this chapter. Unlike previous Access objects, DAP objects are not totally contained in the .mdb file associated with an Access application. Instead, the data access page is a Web page that must be accessible by a server. Consequently, the Web page must be saved as an HTML file outside the .mdb file.

❏ Data access pages can be created in much the same manner as forms or reports. Although the same toolbox is used for their creation, this toolbox contains additional, Web-specific tools for operations such as creating a bound HTML control.

❏ Concurrent with the evolution of Access 2000 to include Web-enabling features has been the development of VBScript and Active Server Pages (ASP) technology. VBScript is a variation of Visual Basic for Applications (VBA) that is used to program Web applications. Learning VBA in Access 2000 is good preparation for adding VBScript to your skills. ASP technology provides an environment in which VBScript and embedded SQL commands can be used to access data in Access databases and to create Web pages dynamically.

❏ Future implementations of Access, VBScript, and ASP will undoubtedly bring these features closer together into a tightly integrated Web development environment.

REVIEW QUESTIONS

1. What is a hyperlink field type?
2. What is a URL?
3. How is the Hyperlink SubAddress property in Access used?
4. What are cascading style sheets, and why are they used?
5. An HTML file is a dynamic file. True or False?
6. What is a dynamic Web page?
7. Where and how are data access pages stored?
8. If a Hyperlink Address property specifies an Access database, the _____ property may specify a specific form within that database.
9. How do data access pages display OLE objects stored in a database?
10. What is the purpose of the MaxRecords property of a data access page?
11. How does the setting of the MaxRecords property affect performance?
12. Are data access pages that display grouped data read-only?

13. How can you set a data access page to automatically display the detail records in a grouped data access page?

14. The Session variable is a special instance of the Timeout variable. True or False?

15. Are Active Server Pages limited to using VBScript?

16. What are the ASP Application object events? How are they used?

17. What is the Global.asa file? How is it used?

18. What is a Session variable?

19. In Access, you can display OLE Object data from a database. True or False?

20. The _____ file, which is used by ASP, indicates where scripts will be executed.

    a. Server.asa

    b. Application.asa

    c. Script.asa

    d. Global.asa

HANDS-ON PROJECTS

Project 12-1

Natural Parent International. NPI would like to display some of its information on the Web. In particular, the books in the organization's library and the date and location of the next meeting should be made visible to users. The data and location should be available only when the correct password is entered, however. You should note that this project is designed to help you construct simple VBScript code. Someone familiar with VBScript could compromise the security.

12

Complete these steps:

1. Open **NPI.mdb**. Use the Data Access Page Wizard to create a data access page that is based on qryBooksByCategory. Select all the fields. Group the data on the Description field, and sort the records on the Title. Name the data access page **pagBooksByCategory**.

2. Create a new table called **tblWWWPassword**. The table should contain one field named **NPIPassword**. It should also contain a single record that holds the value of the password.

3. Create a query called **qryLocationForWeb**. This query requires two tables: **tblProgram** and **tblWWWPassword**. A join line will not be placed between the tables, although this omission does not matter because tblWWWPassword contains only one record. The query should display three fields: **NPIPassword**, **CompleteAddress** (the concatenation of street, city, and state), and **Date**. The Date row should contain the following criterion: **>=Date() And <=DateAdd("d",31,Date())**. This criterion will find programs that are within one month of the current date. Sort the records by Date in ascending order. To test the query, you will need to add or modify a record in tblProgram so that one record has a date that is within a month of the current date.

4. Use the wizard to create a data access page that is based on qryLocationForWeb. Select all the fields. Name the data access page **pagLocation**. No sorting or grouping is necessary.

5. Use the property sheets to change the Id properties of Date and CompleteAddress to **objDate** and **objCompleteAddress**, respectively ("date" is a reserved word in VBScript). In addition, use the property sheets to change the Display property of NPIPassword to **None** (when displayed in Internet Explorer, NPIPassword will not take up space and will not be displayed on the screen). Change the Visibility properties of both objCompleteAddress and objDate to **Hidden**. Visibility is similar to Display, except that space is reserved on the form for the values.

6. Use the Sorting and Grouping Window to remove the Record Navigation Section.

7. Use the toolbox to add a **text box** to the data access page; the ID of the text box is **txtPassword**. Use the toolbox to add a command button to the data access page; the ID of the command button is **cmdSubmit**. The InnerText property is **Submit**.

8. Use the script editor to create code for the Click event of cmdSubmit. The code should compare the value of txtPassword with NPIPassword. If the values are equal, the code should set the Visibility property of objCompleteAddress and objDate to **visible**. The format for the visibility property is object.Style.Visibility = "visible".

9. Test your code.

10. Save your work.

Project 12-2

Metropolitan Performing Arts Company. The managers and directors at MPAC would like to monitor sales figures from their home computers. The sales figures should not be available to the general public, however. You are to create data access pages that support a simple password mechanism.

To create this system, perform the following steps:

1. Open **MPA.mdb**. Create a table called **tblWebPassword**. The table should contain a single field called **WebPassword**. Using Datasheet view, type a value for the password.

2. Create a data access page, called **pagSales**, that uses qryTotalPerPerformance as its data source. Select all fields. Create a group field based on the PerformanceName. Change the **InnerText** properties of any labels to create a user-friendly display.

3. Use the property sheet of the total textbox to set the Visibility property to **hidden**. In the VBScript code, you will set this property to "visible" when the user enters the correct password.

4. Create a command button with the ID **cmdPassword** and an InnerText property equal to **"Make Visible"**.

5. Create a **script** for the OnClick event of cmdPassword. This procedure will open another window that will prompt the user for the password. After the window is opened, a value is returned that is used to determine whether the Visibility property should be set to visible. You can use the following code:

```
bln = window.showModalDialog("pagpassword.htm")
If bln = True Then
     Total.style.visibility = "visible"
End If
```

6. Create a data access page named **pagPassword**. The tblWebPassword table should be used as the data source. Set the Display property of WebPassword to **None** (this property is similar to the Visibility property except the box does not take up space on the page). Using the toolbox, add a **text box** to pagPassword, and name the text box **txtPassword**. Using the Sorting and Grouping window, remove the Record Navigation Section.

7. Add a command button to **pagPassword**. Name the command button **cmdSubmit** and change the InnerText property to **submit**.

8. Write a VBScript procedure for the OnClick event of **cmdSubmit**. This procedure should compare WebPassword with txtPassword. If the passwords are equal, the following code should be executed:

```
window.returnvalue = True
window.close()
```

If the values are not equal, returnvalue should be set equal to False, a message box should be displayed that indicates the submission of an incorrect password, and the window should be closed. Note that the returnvalue property is not listed in the list box that appears when you type "window" in the script editor. You should also note that the code created for pagPassword will work only when pagPassword is opened with cmdPassword in pagSales.

9. Save your work.

12

Project 12-3

Foreign Language Institute. Salespersons for FLI would like to access basic product information through the Web. You will create a data access page that displays product information.

Complete these steps:

1. Open **FLI.mdb**.
2. Create a data access page. To include the product's target language without writing a script, make sure that you base the page on a query that joins tblProducts and tblLanguage.
3. Save your work.

Project 12-4

King William Hotel System. Customers would like to access their reservation information through the Web. You will create a data access page that displays reservation information.

Complete these steps:

1. Open **KWH.mdb**.
2. Create a data access page. To include the customer's name without writing a script, make sure that you base the page on a query that joins tblCustomer and tblReservation.
3. Save your work.

Project 12-5

Workers' Compensation Commission. The staff at the WCC offices would like to access basic patient information through the Web. You will create a data access page that displays patient information.

Complete these steps:

1. Open **WCC.mdb**.
2. Create a data access page. Remember that you can complete the requirements without writing a script by making sure that you base the page on an appropriate query.
3. Save your work.

13

SECURING AN ACCESS APPLICATION

Planning Security for the Swim Lessons Application

In this chapter you will:

♦ Learn about the elements of security

♦ Explore application-level security

♦ Use user-level security

In this book, you have reviewed the basics of Access and the fundamentals of VBA, macros, and the command bars. After conquering those concepts, you moved on to object-based programming, the intricacies of applications, developing customized Help, and working with Access 2000 on the Internet. It's fitting, then, that your journey through Access ends with a discussion on security; without security, all of your work could be for naught.

In this chapter, you will review the elements of security and then explore the intricacies of application-level and user-level security. It is likely that your network administrator will not permit you to execute some of the step sequences given in this chapter. These particular step sequences are nevertheless included for your reference; someday, you may be in the position to use the information.

THE ELEMENTS OF SECURITY

Making an application and its data secure from unauthorized modification is a critical aspect of delivering an application to users. In the process of securing the application and data, you should follow several guidelines. First, only authorized personnel should be able to access an Access application. Second, legitimate users should be restricted to only those portions of the system that they actually need. Third, no user other than members of the development team should be authorized to change an application's code.

Security and authorization mistakes are time-consuming to correct and may lead to an unsecured application. (**Security** refers to the protection of an application from unauthorized use; **authorization** specifies who can access and update different objects in the application.) To counteract this possibility, Access supports comprehensive security and authorization mechanisms.

As an example of these mechanisms, databases can be given passwords so that unauthorized users cannot even launch the application. This **application-level security** makes it difficult for unauthorized users to view the contents of the application. Application-level security, however, does not distinguish among users. Once users have permission to access the system, their privileges are not necessarily restricted.

To account for this situation, users (and groups of users) can be given authorization to different components of the application, thus preventing unauthorized processing. Such **user-level security** gives different users different permissions for various objects that comprise an application. (A **permission** is the ability to perform an action on an object, such as reading records, updating data, and changing the design of a form.)

To further enhance security, data can be encrypted, providing a layer of protection against hackers, and applications can be compiled, preventing modification to the source code that underlies an application.

Now that you understand the basics of security, it is time to go into specifics. We will start the discussion with application-level security and then move to user-level security.

APPLICATION-LEVEL SECURITY

Application-level security is applied equally to all users of a particular Access application (which may involve one or more .mdb or .mde files). Three types of security can be applied to these files: the source code in an .mdb file can be stripped from the file, creating an .mde file; an .mdb file can be encrypted so that other applications cannot easily read its contents; and a database password can be assigned to the file.

Stripping Source Code

Saving an .mdb file as an .mde file compiles modules, removes source code, and compacts the application. The resulting .**mde** file is a compiled database file that cannot be modified, even though it is smaller and runs more quickly. It will run, but modules, forms, and reports can no longer be viewed in Design view. Likewise, they cannot be modified or created.

From a security standpoint, the advantage of an .mde file is that the application can be distributed, but users cannot view or change the application's objects. This approach prevents users from changing the functionality in their copies of the application. If each user modified his or her copy of an application in different ways, long-run maintenance of the application would be impossible. Additionally, distributing an .mde file protects a developer's investment in the application.

 An .mde file cannot be converted back into an .mdb file. The developer must maintain a copy of the .mdb file to enhance the application with additional features or correct errors in the application.

Creating a .mde File

To create a .mde file of the Swim Lessons application:

1. Outside of Access, select the **SwimReg.mdb** file and create a copy of it for backup. Open Access, click **Tools** on the menu bar, point to **Database Utilities**, and then click **Make MDE File**.

2. Navigate to and select the copy of **SwimReg.mdb**.

3. Type **SwimMDE** as the name and place the file in the same folder as your other project files, and then click the **Make MDE** button. If necessary, re-enter the filename.

4. Click the **Save** button.

Because .mde files do not transform data, encrypting private data should be considered. This step is discussed next.

13

Data Encryption and Decryption

Encryption is the conversion of data from one representation into another. The new representation is coded so that it cannot be easily understood. **Decryption** reverses the process of encryption.

The security measures supplied by Access apply only to Access. That is, measures will not prevent someone from accessing the data in an Access database by using another application (for example, a file editor). Encryption won't prevent this type of access either, but it will make the data more difficult to read.

For people to read an encrypted file, they must possess processes and the decoding key necessary to decrypt the file. Access automatically decrypts data when the user requests the data from within Access. Use of an encrypted database therefore slows Access operations by 10% to 15%. Unlike when working with .mde files, Access can change a database file back to its nonencrypted state through an Access menu command.

Encrypting and Decrypting a Database File

To encrypt the **SwimData.mdb** database:

1. Close **SwimReg**, if it is open.

2. Click **Tools** on the menu bar, point to **Security**, and then click **Encrypt/Decrypt Database**.

3. Select **SwimData.mdb** and then click **OK**. If the selected database is not encrypted, Access assumes that you want to encrypt the database. If the selected database is encrypted, Access assumes that you want to decrypt the database.

4. Type SwimDateE for the new database and then click **Save**. You can use the same name, but you'll need to confirm that the system should overwrite the existing database. If you use a different name, you'll need to use the Linked Tables Manager to refresh the links to the tables in **SwimReg** before that application can access the encrypted data.

Even though a database is encrypted, data values are available to anyone who has access to the application. Using database passwords prevents unauthorized use of the application.

Creating a Database Password

A database password is the simplest way to prevent unauthorized access to an Access application. This password can be set in the Set Database Password dialog box. Once it is set, the database will prompt the user for the password when the database is open.

If the application is on a network, ask all users to close the database before you try to set a password. You can ensure that others cannot open the database at the same time you have it open by clicking the Exclusive check box in the Open Database dialog box. All passwords are case-sensitive. Every time you set a password, you will be asked for verification (that is, to type the password again).

TIP Database passwords should not be defined for databases that will be replicated. Replicated databases can't be synchronized if database passwords are defined.

You can't set a database password if user-level security has been defined for your database and you don't have Administer permission for the database. If user-level security has been defined, any restrictions based on user-level security permissions remain in effect. If a table from a password-protected database is linked, the password must be provided to establish the link.

Protecting a Database by Adding a Database Password

To protect **SwimReg** by adding a database password:

1. Close **SwimReg**, if it is open.

2. Outside of Access, make a copy of the database and store it in a secure place, preferably on a disk other than your hard drive.

3. Inside Access, click **File** on the menu bar, click **Open**, select **SwimReg**, and then select **Open Exclusive** from the Open drop-down list, as show in Figure 13-1.

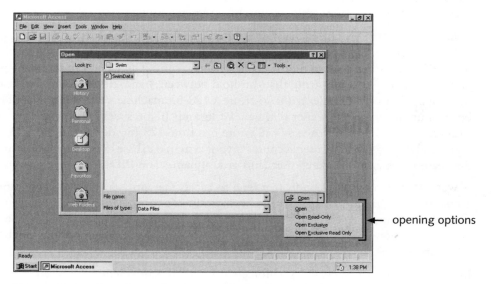

                  ◄— opening options

Figure 13-1 Opening a database with the Open Exclusive option

4. Click **Tools** on the menu bar, point to **Security**, and then click **Set Database Password**.

5. In the Password text box, type a password. Remember that passwords are case-sensitive.

6. In the Verify text box, type the password again, and then click the **OK** button.

7. Close **SwimReg**, and then reopen it in Exclusive mode. You will be required to use the password to open the database until you remove the password.

8. To remove the password, click **Tools** on the menu bar, point to **Security**, click **Unset Database Password**, enter the correct password, and then click **OK**.

When an application in an .mdb file is successfully opened within the full version of Access, the user can read and modify all aspects of the application, including program code. If all users should not have this capability, a different type of security mechanism must be used.

13

USER-LEVEL SECURITY

Greater control over an individual's access to the components of an application is possible through the establishment of user-level security. The key to understanding how this mechanism operates is to become familiar with the five concepts that define user-level security: user accounts, workgroups, owners, groups, and permissions.

A **user account** is an object that represents a user (or developer) of an Access application. When you create a new account, Access prompts you for a user name and a personal identifier (PID). Access identifies a user account by these items. The **PID** is not the user's password; rather it is a case-sensitive string that can hold between 4 and 20 characters and that is used in combination with the user name to create a 128-bit machine-readable number. This number will uniquely identify a user within a workgroup. If you specify the same user name and PID on a second occasion, Access will create the same 128-bit identifier. This approach gives you the ability to re-create user accounts if your system database ever becomes corrupted. For this reason, it is critical to keep user (and group) names and PIDs in a safe place.

A **workgroup** is a set of accounts that tend to access the same set of Access applications. The accounts in a workgroup share the same **workgroup information file**. These files have the .mdw extension. Microsoft Access reads the workgroup information file when it starts. The file contains information—users' account names, their passwords, and the groups of which they are members—about the users in a workgroup.

In Access, user-level security is enforced through the interaction between a workgroup information file and the Access application. The workgroup information file is used to prompt for a user name and password. Once a user types a correct user name and password, the Access application determines the capabilities of the user based upon the permissions stored as part of the application's objects.

A workgroup has a workgroup identifier (WID) that uniquely identifies that workgroup. The **WID** is a case-sensitive string that can hold between 4 and 20 characters. Two workgroups stored in different locations are considered equivalent when they share the same WID. Access remembers the WID of the active workgroup that was used to create the application.

Some accounts in the workgroup that were active when the application was created will likely be able to modify objects in the application, as these users will have owner privileges on the objects. An **owner** of an object is a special user, identified by the user name and PID (regardless of the workgroup), who always has full (that is, all) permissions on the object. By default, the owner of the object is the user who created the object.

User accounts may belong to one or more groups. A **group** is a named collection of user accounts that share the same set of permissions on an application's objects. Similar to a user account, a group has a name and a PID. A particular user can view or update an object of the application when that **permission** (that is, privilege) has been granted to the user account or to a user group of which the user account is a member. A user account is a member of a group when the account is contained within the group's users collection.

Be careful not to confuse groups and workgroups. Groups are collections of users that share some type of characteristics. By forming groups of users, permissions on objects (for example, read-only or update) may be assigned to each member of the group by assigning the permission to the group. In contrast, workgroups are collections of accounts. These accounts may be user accounts or group accounts. An Access application is associated with a workgroup to specify which accounts have access to the application.

Creating and Joining Workgroups

Workgroups are created and managed through the Microsoft Access Workgroup Administrator. The Workgroup Administrator is an application separate from Access. Search for it on your computer; its file name is **Wrkgadm.exe**.

To create a new workgroup:

1. If you are in Access, exit Access and open the Workgroup Administrator.

2. Click the **Create** button.

3. Enter your name, organization, and a WID into the dialog box. Write this information down; you'll need it later. Click **OK**.

4. Click the **Browse** button, name the file **SwimReg.mdw**, and place it in the same folder as your other project files. Click **Open**, and then click **OK**.

5. When the final confirmation window indicates that the new workgroup information file was successfully created, click **OK**, and then click **OK** again.

6. Click **Exit**. This process automatically joins you to the workgroup you just created.

Although many workgroup files may reside on a particular personal computer, only one workgroup information file is active at any given time. A different workgroup information file can be made active by **joining** the workgroup through the Workgroup Administrator. When a new workgroup is joined, the old workgroup is no longer considered active. The active workgroup information file is consulted, by default, whenever an Access application is opened. Consequently, users must be careful to join the appropriate workgroup prior to starting an Access application, so as to ensure that the user name they intend to employ will be recognized by the application. Alternatively, an Access application can specify the workgroup file to use when the application starts. The application does so by including the /wrkgrp *PathToWorkgroup* option on the command line used to start the application.

Joining a Workgroup

To join a workgroup:

1. Create a copy of **SwimReg.mdw**, and then place it in the same folder as your other project files.

2. Start the Workgroup Administrator again, and then click the **Join** button.

3. Make a note of the name and location of the workgroup information file to which you are currently joined. You may want to rejoin it later to return to your original operating environment.

4. Click the **Browse** button, and then navigate to and select the copy of the workgroup information file you created previously. Click **Open**, and then click **OK**.

5. Access will respond with a message indicating that a new workgroup has been joined. Click **OK**, and then click **Exit**.

6. To rejoin the original (default) workgroup later, repeat Steps 2–5, but select the workgroup information file you noted in Step 3.

When Access is installed, a default workgroup, named System.mdw, is created. Each System.mdw file has the same WID. Consequently, applications that are created within the default System.mdw file consider all other default workgroups to be equivalent to the one that was used to create it.

It is important to remember that a distributed Access application should not use the default workgroup when it is created. If an application was created within the confines of the default WID, you can create a new workgroup to be used with the application so as to add the security that you need.

Once you have joined a workgroup, you can modify the user accounts, as described next.

User Accounts and Passwords

Although the workgroup information file stores information about accounts, the Workgroup Administrator is not used to create the accounts. Instead, user accounts are created and deleted in Access through the Users tab in the User and Group Accounts dialog box. Users created with this dialog box are stored in the active workgroup information file. Therefore, any Access application that uses the same workgroup information file can reference this user account, regardless of the application used to create it.

Access automatically creates a default user account with a user name of Admin when a new workgroup is created. The default workgroup, System.mdw, also contains an Admin user. The Admin user belongs to the Admins group and the Users group. The **Admins** group is the group account that retains full permissions on all databases created when the workgroup was active. The Setup program that installs Access and the "create workgroup" procedure automatically adds the default Admin user account to the Admins group. Access requires that at least one user be in the Admins group at all times.

The **Users** group is the group account that contains all user accounts. Microsoft Access automatically adds user accounts to the Users group when you create them. By default, this account has full permissions on all objects created after the account is created. Part of the process of creating a secure database involves revoking selected permissions for members of the Users group.

Access will not prompt for a user name or password until the Admin account has been assigned a password. Until that point, all users of an application enter the application as the

Admin user. That is, until a password is assigned to the Admin account, all users enter an application with full permission on all of the application's objects! After a password is assigned to the Admin account, Access will prompt for a user name and password (a password does not need to be entered for user names that do not have passwords). When Access uses a workgroup that prompts for a user name and password, this workgroup is called a **secure workgroup**. A user must enter a valid user name and password to open any Access application as long as a secure workgroup is active.

Access does not provide a way to recover a forgotten Admin password or workgroup ID. If the passwords are forgotten, or if the workgroup associated with the database becomes corrupt and the workgroup ID is forgotten, the Access application cannot be opened. Consequently, backup copies of the application and the default workgroup file, System.mdw, should be created prior to setting the Admin password. The backup copy should be kept in a secure, offline location (for example, on a removable disk). As a final recovery measure, the original versions of the Access application (those that existed prior to setting the security features) and the System.mdw file can be used to return to an unsecured environment.

Creating a New Account Password

Because Access will not prompt you to log in until the Admin account has been assigned a password, you must first set a password on the Admin account.

To create a password for the Admin account:

1. Open the **SwimReg** database, if necessary.

2. Click **Tools** on the menu bar, point to **Security**, and then click **User and Group Accounts**.

3. Click the **Change Logon Password** tab.

4. Verify that the User Name is **Admin**.

5. Do not enter anything in the Old Password text box. Type **adminpass** into both the New Password and Verify text boxes.

6. Click **OK**. Your actions have created a secure workgroup.

TIP Although the Admin account possesses full permissions on Access objects, the User and Group Accounts dialog box does not allow the Admin user to set a password for another user. Members of the Admins group, however, can clear a user's password. This feature is commonly used when a user forgets his or her password.

Once a password is set on the Admin account, passwords may be set on other accounts as well. We will set up one next.

Creating a New User Account

To create a new user account in **SwimReg**:

1. Open the **User and Group Accounts** dialog box.

2. Click the **Users** tab, and then click the **New** button.

3. Type **John Public** as the name and **jpublic** as the personal ID, as shown in Figure 13-2. Click **OK**, and then click **OK** again.

Figure 13-2   Entering a user

With the exception of the Admin user, users with the same user name and PID receive the same permissions for a particular application, even when the user information is stored in different workgroups. An Access application uses the user name and PID to determine the identity of the current user.

New user accounts do not have a password. Users can assign themselves a password when a database is open by using the Change Logon Password tab of the User and Group Accounts dialog box, as shown in Figure 13-3. The characters you type in the Password text boxes will not appear on your screen. Instead, Access will display an asterisk for each character. When the information is entered correctly and the user clicks the OK button, the password will change.

Figure 13-3   Change Logon Password tab

Next, we will create a new account password for John Public.

To create a new account password for the John Public account:

1. Exit Access.

2. Restart Access and open **SwimReg**. Type **John Public** as the name, but do not enter anything for the password.

3. Click **OK**, and then open the **User and Group Accounts** dialog box.

4. Click the **Change Logon Password** tab.

5. Type **access2k** into the New Password and Verify text boxes, and then click **OK**.

6. To remove an account password, repeat these steps but enter the old password in Step 5 and click **OK**.

Workgroup Dynamics

Workgroups do not share information. That is, a user name and password created when one workgroup is active will not be recognized when a different workgroup is active. Thus, a user account and password must be created for each workgroup that a particular user must use. If, for some reason, a user needs to access the same application through different workgroups, the user should be assigned the same user name and PID for each workgroup, so that the user needs to remember only one user name to log in, regardless of which workgroup is active.

You can also modify passwords and create new users within VBA. For example, procedures can be developed to allow Admin users to change passwords. Procedures that create user accounts are desired when many accounts need to be created and the list of users is in electronic form (for example, a class roll and records in the tblStaff table in the Swim Lessons application). You can change passwords in VBA by using the following syntax:

Syntax

Catalog.**Users**(*UserIndex*).**ChangePassword** *OldPassword, NewPassword*

Syntax Dissection

- *Catalog* is any object variable that represents the catalog containing the user object whose Password property you want to set or change.

- **Users** refers to the Users collection.

- *UserIndex* designates the specific user in the collection to modify. It may be an ordinal index (that is, 0, 1, 2, . . .) or a string value. If it is a string constant, it must be enclosed in quotes.

- The **ChangePassword** method takes two arguments: *OldPassword* and *NewPassword*. *OldPassword* is a string that is the current setting of the Password property of the User object. *NewPassword* is a string that is the new setting of the Password property of the User object. If the user does not have a password, *OldPassword* is a zero-length string ("").

13

- If input boxes are used to obtain a password, then the **ChangePassword** method is generally included in a loop to verify that the user knows the new password entered. The loop should not exit until the new password and the verified passwords are equal.

- The **ChangePassword** method will generate an error when an invalid user object is identified or the user provides an incorrect **OldPassword**. An error handler should be established that catches this error.

A sample procedure that changes a password follows:

```
Function ChangePassword(pstrUserName As String) As Boolean
Dim pstrMsg As String
Dim pstrTitle As String
Dim pstrDefValue As String
Dim pstrOldPW As String
Dim pstrNewPW As String
Dim pstrVerifyPW As String
Dim cat as New ADOX.Catalog
On Error GoTo NewPWError
pstrTitle = "Password Modification"     'Set title
pstrMsg = "Enter old password."
pstrDefValue = ""
'Get old password
pstrOldPW = InputBox$(pstrMsg, pstrTitle, pstrDefValue)
'Make sure NewPW and pstrVerifyPW are not equal before loop
pstrNewPW = "A"
pstrVerifyPW = "Z"
'Loop until the new and verified passwords are equal
Do While pstrNewPW <> pstrVerifyPW
    pstrMsg = "Enter new password."
    'Get new password
    pstrNewPW = InputBox$(pstrMsg,pstrTitle,pstrDefValue)
    pstrMsg = "Re-enter new password to verify change."
    'Verify new password
    pstrVerifyPW = InputBox$(pstrMsg,pstrTitle,pstrDefValue)
    If pstrNewPW <> pstrVerifyPW Then
        MsgBox "Password not verified."
    End If
Loop
'Change the password
cat.ActiveConnection = CurrentProject.Connection
cat.Users(pstrUserName).ChangePassword pstrOldPW, pstrNewPW
Exit Function
NewPWError:
ChangePassword = False
MsgBox "Error in password change."
End Function
```

To fully understand the VBA code that creates new user accounts, you must understand the relationship between Users and Groups. This relationship is discussed next.

Users and Their Groups

An Access application associates permissions with a group (as identified by a group name and PID). Groups with the same group name and PID, regardless of the workgroup, receive the same permissions on a particular application. When an application supports a large number of users, permissions should be managed through groups. After all, it is easier to assign permissions to a few groups than it is to assign permissions to each user individually.

You can create or delete groups in the Groups tab of the User and Group Accounts dialog box. When you click the New button in the Groups tab, the New User/Group dialog box shown in Figure 13-4 appears. Figure 13-4 shows the creation of a group named Development with a personal identifier of devgroup.

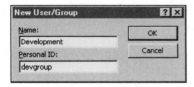

Figure 13-4   Entering a new group

Creating a New Group

To create a new group in the **SwimReg** file:

1. Login to **SwimReg** using the Admin account. Remember, only accounts that are members of the Admins group can create new groups.

2. Open the **User and Group Accounts** dialog box, and then click the **Groups** tab. Click the **New** button.

3. Enter **DBClass** for the name and **DBClassPID** as the personal ID, and then click **OK** twice.

Once a group is created, user accounts can be assigned to that group. You assign an account to a group through the Users tab of the User and Group Accounts dialog box. Figure 13-5 displays this tab.

13

Figure 13-5 Users tab

Adding and Removing Users to and from Groups

To modify a user's participation in a group:

1. Open the **User and Group Accounts** dialog box, and then click the **Users** tab.

2. Use the Name combo box to select the **John Public** user account. It will be assigned (or removed) from a group.

3. To add the **John Public** user to the Admins group, click the **Admins** group in the Available Groups list box, and then click **Add**.

4. Click **OK**.

Creating users and groups is less cumbersome under the ADO model than it is under the DAO model. Programmers simply append the new user to the Users collection or the new group to the Groups collection. To add a user to a group, the programmer simply appends the name of the group to the user's Groups collection.

Figure 13-6 highlights the relationship between the objects used by Access security. A User object's Groups collection contains objects that have the same user names as objects in the workspace's Groups collection. A Group object's Users collection contains objects that have the same user names as objects in the workspace's Users collection. A reciprocal relationship exists between the objects in a user's Groups collection and the objects in the group's Users collection. For example, if a Group object named G1 is placed in user A's Groups collection, a User object named A is automatically placed in G1's Users collection. In this manner, Access always maintains the relationship between a user and any group to which the user belongs, regardless of how the user was added to the group.

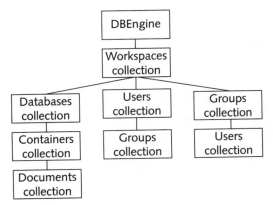

Figure 13-6   Relationship between security-related objects in collections

The following code creates a new user and assigns the user to the Users group:

```
Function NewUser (pstrNewUserName As String, _
    pstrNewUserPW As String) As Boolean
    Dim cat As New ADOX.Catalog
    On Error GoTo NewUserError
    NewUser = True
    Cat.ActiveConnection = CurrentProject.Connection
    'Save user account definition by appending it to
    'Users collection.
    cat.Users.Append pstrNewUserName, pstrNewUserPW
    'Add user to predefined Users group
    cat.Users(pstrNewUserName).Groups.Append "Users"
    Exit Function
NewUserError:
    pobjNewUser = False
End Function
```

Permissions of groups and objects are stored in the Documents collection. We discuss those permissions next.

Using and Assigning Permissions

Permissions can be assigned to all database objects as well as to the database itself. You can assign permissions to a user individually, or you can assign permissions to the group to which a user belongs. When you assign permissions to a group, all members of the group have the same permissions.

Permissions can be assigned through the User and Group Permissions dialog box, shown in Figure 13-7. The permission assigned applies to object(s) selected in the Object Name box, and to the user or group selected in the User/Group Name box. Some permissions imply (or require) other permissions. For example, if you assign Modify Design permission, Access will automatically select the Read Design, Read Data, Update Data, and Delete Data permissions. If you select the Administer permission, Access grants all other permissions automatically.

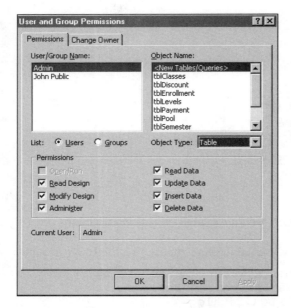

Figure 13-7 User and Group Permissions dialog box

Note that all newly defined groups have all permissions on all objects, except Administer. The Users group also has Administer permissions. Normally, you should change these permissions to properly secure the application. Unless these permissions are desired, change them before distributing the application.

Assigning Permissions Through the User and Group Permissions Dialog Box

You may not be allowed to assign permissions on your system if Access has been installed on a network so as to provide many students access to this program. Changing the permissions on objects could create a situation where certain objects cannot be manipulated by other students, because they do not know the user accounts and passwords you have used when modifying the database. If you are allowed to assign permissions, here are the steps to follow.

To assign permissions:

1. Open the Access application for which permissions will be assigned.

2. Open the **User and Group Permissions** dialog box.

3. If permissions will be assigned to a user, click the **Users** option button. If permissions will be assigned to a group, click the **Groups** option button.

4. On the **Permissions** tab, click the user or group that will be assigned the permissions.

5. Select an object type from the Object Type combo box. The Object Name box displays objects of the selected type.

6. Click objects in the Object Name box.

7. Under Permissions, select the permission you want to assign, or clear the permissions you want to remove for the identified user on the identified object. Selecting or removing one permission may cause Access to automatically select or remove other permissions.

8. Click **OK** to implement the permissions.

9. Continue setting permissions on other database objects as needed.

One facet of permission merits an additional note. Normally, to use a query, a user must have Read Data permission on all tables that the query references. If the query updates a table, the user also requires Update Data permission. One problem with the security mechanism of Access is that a table's Update Data permission requires the user to possess Read Design permission. Many times a developer would like the user to update data in a table, but does not want the user to view the details of the table's design. The remedy for this problem involves the use of the **With OwnerAccess Option** declaration. When a query possesses the With OwnerAccess Option declaration, a user can run the query as long as the owner of the query has the appropriate permissions.

Using With OwnerAccess Option to Hide the Design of a Table

You may not be allowed to hide the design of a table on your system if Access has been installed on a network so as to provide many students access to this program. Hiding the table design could create a situation where exercises cannot be completed by other students, because they cannot access the table to modify it. If you are allowed to hide the design of a table, here are the steps to follow.

To hide the design of a table:

1. Create a **select query** that displays all fields in the table. In the Design view of the select query, display the **property sheet**.

2. Select **Owner's** as the value for the Run Permission property of the query.

3. For users other than the owner of the query, clear the **Update Data** and **Read Design** permissions for the table on the User and Group Permissions dialog box.

4. Change the permissions on the query so that the user or group has **Read Data** and **Update Data** permissions on the query.

5. Change the **record source** of forms that used the table to become the name of the query by opening the Properties window for the form and changing the Record Source property.

Setting and Using Permissions in VBA

Access stores information related to Permissions in properties of the Container and Document objects. The Containers collection is located inside a database object. A container exists for every type of object used in an Access application, including databases, tables,

13

relations, forms, modules, reports, and scripts (that is, macros). Each container, in turn, contains a Documents collection. A document exists for each object in the application (for example, frmCurrentStudents and tblCourses).

The SetPermissions method sets a value that establishes the permissions for the user or group identified by the Group or User object. Its syntax is as follows:

Syntax

Object.**SetPermissions** *Name, ObjectType, Action, Rights*

Syntax Dissection

- *Object* is an object variable that refers to a User or Group object.

- *Name* is a string value that specifies the name of the object for which you want to set permissions. For example, if you are setting the permissions on a particular table, the table name would be specified here.

- *ObjectType* is a long integer intrinsic constant that specifies the type of object for which you want to set the permissions. For example, if you are setting the permissions on a particular table, the constant adPermObjTable would be specified here.

- *Action* is a long integer intrinsic constant that specifies the type of action to perform when setting permissions. The constants used here refer to the actions of granting, setting, revoking, and denying permissions, among others.

- *Rights* is a long integer intrinsic constants that contains a bitmask indicating which rights to set. The constants used here refer to rights such as reading, updating, and deleting, among others.

Each possible value of an object's permission rights (for example, Modify Design, Insert Data) is represented within Access by a long integer intrinsic constant that is a bitmask indicating the rights to set. Because a user may have multiple permissions on an object, rights can be created by using a logical OR to combine the bitmasks.

Once permissions have been set, they may be retrieved using the GetPermissions method. This method has the following syntax:

Syntax

ReturnValue = *Object*.**GetPermissions** (*Name, ObjectType*)

Syntax Dissection

- *ReturnValue* is a long integer bitmask containing the permissions that the group or user has on the object.

- *Object* is an object variable that refers to a user or group object.

- *Name* is a string value that specifies the name of the object for which you want to set permissions. For example, if you are setting the permissions on a particular table, the table name would be specified here.

- *ObjectType* is a long integer intrinsic constant that specifies the type of object for which you want to set the permissions. For example, if you are setting the permissions on a particular table, the constant adPermObjTable would be specified here.

The following code fragment illustrates how to set the permissions on the tblCourses table to Insert Data, Update Data, and Delete Data for a user account named John Public:

```
Dim cat As New ADOX.Catalog
Cat.ActiveConnection = CurrentProject.Connection
Cat.Users("John Public").SetPermissions "tblCourses", _
    adPermObjTable, _
    AdRightInsert Or adRightUpdate Or adRightDelete
```

The use of bitmasks in VBA necessitates using bitwise arithmetic to determine the permissions settings. **Bitwise arithmetic** involves a bit-by-bit comparison of identically positioned bits in two numeric expressions. Bitwise arithmetic using the OR operator was used in the preceding code to modify permissions. The following code fragment illustrates how to determine whether the John Public user account has Read permission on a table named tblCourses:

```
Dim plngPermissions As Long
Dim cat As New ADOX.Catalog
cat.ActiveConnection = CurrentProject.Connection
plngPermissions = cat.Users("John Public").GetPermissions _
    ("tblCourses", adPermObjTable)
If (plngPermissions And adRightRead) = adRightRead Then
'If condition is true, Read permission exists
...
```

The AND operator tells Access to look for the intersection of the bits set in the plngPermissions variable and the bits set in the adRightRead value. If this intersection equals the value of adRightRead, then John Public must have Read permission.

Owner and Admins Group Security Problems

User-level security is not complete until you have considered the special capabilities of Admins group members and owners. Owners of an object such as a database, form, or table always have the ability to assign themselves full permissions on the object. If an application is created in an unsecured environment, the Admin account is the owner of all objects. If an individual enters an application as the owner of an object, even under a different workgroup, that individual can obtain full permissions on the object. Consequently, when the Admin account is the owner of an object, even in a secured environment, users entering the application as Admin through an unsecured workgroup have full permissions on the object. In addition, members of the Admins group of the workgroup that was active when the application was created can modify permissions on any object within the application. Table 13-1 summarizes some of these relationships.

Table 13-1 Permissions granted to users

Type of User	When the Active Workgroup Has the Same WID as the One Used to Create the Application, User Has:	When the Active Workgroup Does Not Have the Same WID as the One Used to Create the Application, User Has:
Owner	Full permissions	Full permissions
Members of Admins	Full permissions	Permissions defined by the application
Users who are not members of Admins	Permissions defined by the application	Permissions defined by the application

These relationships have two important implications. First, the Admin account should not own any object in a secure application. Second, the workgroup used to create an application should not be distributed as part of the application. Normally, when an application is distributed, at least one user needs to be a member of the Admins group so as to create new user accounts. Nevertheless, the system developer may not want this person to modify the design of the system. To enforce this limitation, the developer must restrict the permissions of the Admin account and Admins group. If the original workgroup is distributed with the application, Admins members can change their own permissions, thereby leading to compromised security. Changing the ownership of objects can remedy these problems.

Changing Object Ownership and Creating a Secure Application

In Access, the user who creates an Access object is the owner of the object. An object owner always has full permissions applicable to an object—that is, he or she always has **Administer** permission for the object. This permission exists regardless of whether the user is a member of the Admins group and regardless of whether an account in the Admins group attempts to change the owner's permissions.

Because job roles change over time and people may come and go, Access provides a mechanism for changing the ownership of an object. The same mechanism can also be used to switch the ownership of an object to someone other than the Admin object. If the object is not a database, the object's ownership may be changed through the Change Owner tab on the User and Group Permissions dialog box, as shown in Figure 13-8.

Figure 13-8   Change Owner tab

Changing Object Ownership

You may not be allowed to change the ownership of an object on your system if Access has been installed on a network so as to provide many students access to the program. Changing an object's owner could create a situation where exercises cannot be completed by other students, because they might not be able to access the object to modify it. If you are allowed to change an object's ownership, here are the steps to follow.

To change an object's ownership:

1. Open the application that contains the desired objects, and then open the **User and Group Permissions** dialog box. Click the **Change Owner** tab, and then select the desired object type in the Object Type combo box.

2. Select the desired object or objects in the Object/Current Owner list box.

3. Click the **Users or Groups** option button to display the corresponding accounts in the New Owner combo box. Select the desired owner from the New Owner combo box.

4. Click the **Change Owner** button.

Owners of a database always have the right to open the database. The only way to change the ownership of an entire database is to import the database into Access while you are logged on using the account of the new owner, as shown in Figure 13-9.

13

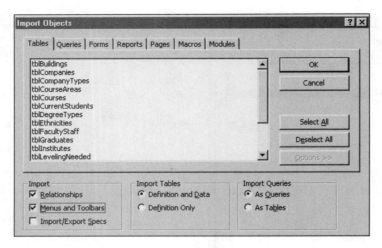

Figure 13-9   Import Objects dialog box

Changing Database Ownership and Securing an Application

As with the process of changing an object's ownership, you may not be allowed to change the ownership of the database in your environment. Changing the ownership of the database could create a situation where exercises cannot be completed by other students, because they cannot access the database. If you are allowed to change database ownership, here are the steps to follow

To change a database's ownership:

1. Join a secure workgroup, and then open **Microsoft Access** as the user who will receive the database ownership and create a new database.

2. If you want to limit the permissions of the Admin user, make sure that the current user is a member of the Admins group and then remove the **Admin** user from the Admins group.

3. Click **File** on the menu bar, point to **Get External Data**, and then click **Import**

4. In the Import dialog box, find and select the database whose ownership is to be changed, and then click **Import**.

5. Click the **Options** button to select the necessary import options.

6. Using the various tabs, select the objects that are to be imported. Click the **Select All** button to select all of the objects. Click the **OK** button to begin the import process.

7. If desired, after the database has been imported successfully, you can delete the original database.

The import database technique is one way to secure an unsecured application. The ownership of all objects, including the database, can be transferred from an unsecured database (with Admin as the owner) using this technique. Access also provides a User-Level Security Wizard to support securing a database.

The User-Level Security Wizard

The User-Level Security Wizard will create a new database, import all the objects from the old database, remove all permissions from the Users group, and encrypt the new database. Remember, however, that the application's performance will be degraded slightly because it now uses an encrypted database.

The last security issue we will address arises when you prepare a workgroup for distribution.

Preparing a Workgroup for Distribution

Each computer that runs an Access application must have access to the application files (that is, the ones ending in .mdb or .mde) and a workgroup information file. In some cases, the Access default workgroup information file is used to run an application. In other cases, the application developer will distribute a workgroup information file. You can use either of two processes to prepare the workgroup information file so that the appropriate level of security is maintained.

The First Process: Restricting Access to an Application Without Prompting for a User Name and Password

Many times an organization does not require user-level security. In some cases, all users other than the developer should have the same permissions. As a result, the Access application does not need to prompt for a user name and password. To accommodate this situation, the application must be created in a secure workgroup and the Admin account must be given limited permissions.

You may not be allowed to execute the following steps on your system if Access has been installed on a network so as to provide many students access to this program. These steps restrict access to an application, which can make it inaccessible to other students. If you are allowed to restrict access to an application, here are the steps to follow.

To restrict access to an application:

1. Prepare a secure application using a workgroup other than Access's default workgroup. If the application was not originally created in a secure workgroup, use the Import database feature or the User-Level Security Wizard to create the secure application. The Admin user should not be the owner of any object in the application, including the Database object.

2. Remove all permissions associated with the Admins group and the Admin user. Make sure that at least one user (for example, the owner of the database) other than the Admin user maintains Administer permission.

3. Adjust the permissions in the Users group to apply the appropriate security. Usually, permissions such as Read and Modify Design are avoided. The Admin user should be a member of the Users group.

4. Make sure that each computer that accesses the application can also access a workgroup information file that does not contain a password for the Admin user. (This goal can be achieved by specifying the workgroup file using the /wrkgrp parameter or by modifying the Windows Registry. See Access Help for more information on these items.) You will want to take this step because all users can

13

enter the application as the Admin user through this workgroup. The previous steps limit the Admin user's permissions to those identified in the Users group.

The Second Process: Preparing a Secure Workgroup for Distribution

When an organization requires different permissions for different users, a secure workgroup should be distributed with the application. This workgroup should contain group account that correspond to different types of users.

You may not be allowed to execute the following steps on your system if Access has been installed on a network so as to provide many students access to this program. These step restrict access to an application, which can make it inaccessible to other students. If you are allowed to prepare a secure workgroup for distribution, here are the steps to follow.

To prepare a secure workgroup for distribution:

1. Prepare a secure application using a workgroup other than the Access default workgroup. If the application was not originally created in a secure workgroup, use the Import database feature or the User-Level Security Wizard to create the secure application. The Admin user should not be the owner of any object in the application, including the Database object.

2. Remove all the permissions associated with the Admins group and the Admin user. Make sure that at least one user, called **TempAdmin** for convenience, other than the Admin user maintains Administer permissions. Write down the personal ID of TempAdmin; you will use it later.

3. Remove all permissions related to the Users group. Create a new workgroup. Create a new user in the new workgroup that has the same user name and personal ID as TempAdmin.

4. Assign a password to the Admin user in the new workgroup, creating a secure workgroup.

5. Exit and reenter Access as **TempAdmin**. Open the Access application that you plan to distribute.

6. Create the necessary group accounts.

7. Assign permissions to each group account.

8. Exit and reenter Access as the **Admin** user. Delete **TempAdmin**. Now, the distributed workgroup does not possess any user that has full permissions to the application.

9. Distribute the application and the newly created workgroup information file.

User-level security used in combination with .mde files and encryption can create a secure application.

CHAPTER SUMMARY

- Access offers extensive security mechanisms for a desktop-level database management system. Security can be provided at both the application and the user levels. Application-level security has the same effect on all users of a particular Access database file. For example, an Access database file can be converted to an .mde file that does not provide a Design view of any of its objects. The database file can also be encrypted and assigned a password.

- User-level security provides different types of security for different users. The key to understanding how user-level security is implemented is to understand the relationships between workgroups, groups, users, owners, and permissions. User accounts and group accounts are identified by a PID and user name. Frequently, a password is also assigned to a user account. When the Admin account is assigned a password, the workgroup is called a secured workgroup. A secured workgroup prompts a user for a user name and password before it allows Access or an Access application to be opened. Groups define collections of users. They are established so that users with similar access characteristics can be treated as single entities. The access characteristics, which specify whether a user can modify an Access object, are collectively called permissions. A workgroup defines the groups and users recognized by Access. Workgroups are created and joined through the Microsoft Access Workgroup Administrator.

- The choice of members of the Admins group and owners of objects must be carefully planned. Admins members can always modify their own permissions when the workgroup that created an Access application is active. Owners can modify their own permissions no matter which workgroup is active.

- Security features can be implemented through Access menus and VBA. In VBA, security features are accessed and updated through properties and methods associated with objects.

13

REVIEW QUESTIONS

1. Define and describe application-level security.
2. What is a permission?
3. How does user-level security differ from application-level security?
4. What is an .mde file? What happens to an .mdb file when it is converted to an .mde file?
5. Can an .mde file be converted to an .mdb file?
6. What advantage exists in distributing .mde files?
7. A workgroup information file can be made active by _____ the workgroup.
8. Define encryption and decryption.
9. What is a database password?
10. Can database passwords be used in replicated databases?

11. What is a user account? What is a PID?

12. What is a workgroup? What is a workgroup information file? What is a WID?

13. What is the default user when the Access security mechanism has not been turned on? How do you turn on Access security in the default workgroup?

14. What is a group? How are groups used?

15. Are object permissions interrelated? If so, give an example.

16. Can permissions for any user be changed in VBA?

17. What problems exist regarding Admins group users and secure applications?

18. A database can have permissions assigned to it. True or False?

19. Except for _____, all newly defined groups have all permissions on all objects.

20. In Access, each Documents collection has a container. True or False?

HANDS-ON PROJECTS

Project 13-1

Natural Parent International. Some NPI groups appoint a librarian to manage their books. This librarian should have read and write access to frmLibrary, frmAuthors, frmCategory, frmLentBooks, and frmCheckout. He or she should be able to read frmMembers, but not update or delete member or attendance information. The librarian does not have access to frmProgram.

Complete these steps:

1. Open **NPI.mdb**. Create a copy of the databases.

2. Create a secure NPI application. That is, users need to type a user ID and password to access the application.

3. Develop a **Librarians** group and a **Leaders** group. Assign the appropriate privileges to each group. (*Hint:* You will need to assign permissions to the appropriate tables, queries, reports, and forms.)

4. Create a **librarian** and **leader** user, and assign them to the Librarians and Leaders groups, respectively.

5. Modify the NPI application so that the menus and switchboard display only forms that a particular user (Librarians or Leaders) is allowed to access. If you used the Switchboard Manager to create a switchboard, consider creating another switchboard for librarians. Use the Autoexec macro to trigger VBA code that determines which switchboard to display. If you have not already done so, update the Forms menu in the various command bars so that a menu item opens frmProgram. This menu item is disabled when the user does not have permission to open frmProgram. (*Hint:* You can use the CurrentUser method to determine the user ID of the person who logged into

the application. You can determine whether a user is a member of a group by setting an object variable equal to a member of a user's Group collections. If an error is triggered, the user is not a member of the group.)

6. Save your work.

Project 13-2

Metropolitan Performing Arts Company. The MPAC system supports two types of users: managers have read and write privileges for all forms in the database, whereas ticket agents can update data only through frmSales, frmReturns, frmPerformanceDateSeats, and frmSeatsAvailableSubform. Ticket agents cannot enter new performances or generate seats for a scheduled performance. When a manager opens the application, frmPerformance should appear automatically. When a ticket agent opens the application, frmSales should appear.

Complete the following steps:

1. Open **MPA.mdb**. Create a copy of the databases.
2. Create a menu bar for frmPerformance. This menu bar should be similar to the other menus that you have created for the application. A Forms menu should contain menu items that open forms that are of interest to the manager. A Reports menu should contain a link to the report that you created for the application.
3. Create a secure MPAC application. That is, users need to type a user ID and password to access the application (including MPA.mdb and MPAData.mdb).
4. Develop the **Managers** and **Ticket Agents** groups. Assign the appropriate privileges to each group.
5. Create a **manager** and a **ticket agent** user, and assign them to the Managers and Ticket Agents groups, respectively.
6. Create the appropriate permissions. You may need to update permissions for forms, tables, and queries. In addition, consider using the Owner Access option for some queries.
7. Create a function that opens either frmPerformance or frmSales, depending on which person is logged into the system. This function should be triggered through a macro called AUTOEXEC.
8. Modify the MPAC application so that the cmdGenerate command button that appears on frmPerformance is enabled only when the user has permission to insert new records into tblSeatsAvailable.
9. Save your work.

13

Project 13-3

Foreign Language Institute. Secure the FLI application by performing the followin tasks. For some of these tasks, you will need access to the Workgroup Administrator.

Complete these steps:

1. Open **FLI.mdb**. Create a new workgroup information file named **fli.mdw**. Add a user account named **John Public**. Set the PID to **jpublic**.
2. Join the fli.mdw workgroup.
3. Set the Admin user account password to **access2k**.
4. Convert the **FLI.mdb** database to an .mde file.
5. Save your work.

Project 13-4

King William Hotel. Secure the King William Hotel application by performing the fol lowing tasks. For some of these tasks, you will need access to the Workgroup Administrato

Complete these steps:

1. Open **KWH.mdb**. Create a new workgroup information file named **kwh.mdw**. Add a user account named **John Public**. Set the PID to **jpublic**.
2. Join the kwh.mdw workgroup.
3. Set the Admin user account password to **access2k**.
4. Convert the **KWH.mdb** database to an .mde file.
5. Save your work.

Project 13-5

Workers' Compensation Commission. Secure the WCC application by performing th following tasks. For some of these tasks, you will need access to the Workgroup Administrato

Complete these steps:

1. Open **WCC.mdb**. Create a new workgroup information file named **wcc.mdw**. Add user account named **John Public**. Set the PID to **jpublic**.
2. Join the wcc.mdw workgroup.
3. Set the Admin user account password to **access2k**.
4. Convert the **WCC.mdb** database to an .mde file.
5. Save your work.

THE REDDICK VBA NAMING CONVENTIONS

Naming conventions provide a guideline for naming objects and variables in Visual Basic for Applications (VBA). The name of an object or variable should convey information about the object or variable. Modifying VBA code is easier when the name itself indicates how the object or variable can be used.

With few exceptions, this book has followed the Reddick VBA (RVBA) naming conventions (named after their author, Greg Reddick). The Reddick naming conventions are widely used and are listed on several Web sites. At the time of this writing, you can find complete information about the current conventions at *http://www.xoc.net/ standards/index.html.* In this appendix, however, we limit our discussion to those topics that were mentioned in the text.

An Introduction to the Syntax

Names in the RVBA convention have four parts: prefixes, a tag, a BaseName, and suffixes. The syntax of the RVBA convention is as follows:

Syntax

[prefixes]tag[BaseName[Suffixes]]

Syntax Dissection

- The optional *prefixes* portion of the name modifies the tag to indicate additional information, such as the scope and life of a variable. Prefixes are all lowercase.

- A *tag* is a short set of characters, usually mnemonic, that indicates the type of the object or data type of a variable. It is all lowercase.

- The optional *BaseName* is one or more words that indicate what the object represents. The first letter of each word in the *BaseName* is capitalized.

- The optional *Suffixes* provide additional information about the meaning of the *BaseName.* The first letter of each word in the suffix is capitalized. Suffixes are usually picked from a standardized list. We do not use suffixes in this text, so no further information on them will be provided.

In Access, objects are given names at a variety of times and locations. For example, form: reports, and tables are given names when you initially save them. On the other hand, con trols are named through the Name property located on the control's property sheet. Finall variables are given names through a dimension statement in a VBA module.

Regardless of the location, the same technique is employed for determining the name:

1. Determine the tag. The tag depends upon the data type of the variable or the object type of the object. The tables provided in this appendix display the standard tags. For example, all forms use the frm tag and all text boxes use the txt tag.

2. Determine the BaseName that describes the unique aspect of the object. For example, a form may contain information about current students, so the BaseName of the form is CurrentStudents and the entire name is frmCurrentStudents. Because VBA operates best when spaces are not included ir the name, the RVBA convention does not allow spaces in the BaseName. Instead, the first letter of each word in the BaseName is capitalized. You should also note that the BaseName is not required. If a particular procedure uses only one recordset, for example, you can name the recordset rst (the tag for record-sets). Normally, however, BaseNames are used.

3. Add a prefix, if necessary. A prefix further qualifies the name to supply additional information. For example, prefixes should be added to specify the scope and life of a variable.

Naming Microsoft Access Application Objects

Microsoft Access application objects appear in the Database window or within a form report, or data access page. When a tag is used, VBA programmers can more easily recogniz the properties and methods that apply to the object. Table A-1 lists tags for Microsoft Acces application objects. The tags for menus and toolbars are also given (although these are tech nically part of the Microsoft Office library).

Table A-1   Access and Microsoft Office object variable tags

Tag	Object Type
app	Application
chk	CheckBox
cls (we use cmo in the book)	Class Module
cbo	ComboBox
cmd	CommandButton
ctl	Control
ctls	Controls
ocx	CustomControl
dap (we use pag in this book)	DataAccessPage
frm	Form

Table A-1   Access and Microsoft Office object variable tags (continued)

Tag	Object Type
frms	Forms
grl	GroupLevel
img	Image
lbl	Label
lin	Line
lst	ListBox
mcr	Macro
bas	Module
mnu	Menu
ole	ObjectFrame
opt	OptionButton
fra	OptionGroup (frame)
brk	PageBreak
pal	PaletteButton
prps	Properties
shp	Rectangle
rpt	Report
rpts	Reports
scr	Screen
sec	Section
sfr	SubForm
srp	SubReport
tab	Tab Control
txt	TextBox
tgl	ToggleButton
tbr	Toolbar

Examples of the usage of the tags include the following:

```
txtName
frmProspects
rptInvoice
lblInput
```

These tags are used when you save an object or through the use of a control's name property.

Naming ADO and DAO Objects

DAO and ADO are the programmatic interfaces to a database engine. Their tags are used to name objects that appear in the Database window; they may also be used to name object variables inside of VBA code. Table A-2 displays the tags for ADO and DAO objects.

Table A-2   ADO and DAO object tags

Tag	Object Type
cat	Catalog
clm	Column
clms	Columns
cmn or cmd	Command
cnn or cnx	Connection
cnt	Container
cnts	Containers
db	Database
dbs	Databases
dbe	DBEngine
doc	Document
docs	Documents
err	Error
errs	Errors
fld	Field
flds	Fields
flt	Filter
grp	Group
grps	Groups
idx	Index
idxs	Indexes
key	Key
prm (we use par in the book)	Parameter
prms	Parameters
pdbe	PrivDBEngine
prp	Property
prps	Properties
qry	QueryDef
qrys	QueryDefs
rst	Recordset
rsts	Recordsets
rel	Relation
rels	Relations
rpl	Replica
tbl	TableDef
tbls	TableDefs
usr	User

Table A-2   ADO and DAO object tags (continued)

Tag	Object Type
usrs	Users
vw	View
vws	Views
wrk	Workspace
wrks	Workspaces

Some examples follow:

```
rstCustomers
idxPrimaryKey
qryQuarterlySales
```

A debate continues over whether fields in a table should have tags. We do not use tags for field objects in this text.

Naming Variables in a VBA Module

Variables are named through a dimension statement. Table A-3 lists the tags for standard variables. Object variables, such as recordset or form object variables, use a tag that corresponds to their object type. These tags were specified in Tables A-1 and A-2. When the exact object type cannot be specified, the obj tag is used.

Table A-3   Tags for VBA variables

Tag	Object Type
bool	Boolean
byte	Byte
cur	Currency
date	Date
dec	Decimal
dbl	Double
int	Integer
lng	Long
obj	Object
sng	Single
str	String
stf	String (fixed length)
var or vnt	Variant

Here are several examples:

```
Dim intTotal As Integer
Dim varField As Variant
Dim strName As String
Dim frmCurrentStudents As Form
```

Prefixes for Scope and Lifetime

In addition to tags, variables frequently contain prefixes. The most common prefix identifie the scope and life of the variable. Three levels of scope exist: Public, Private, and Local. A variable may also be declared as Static to extend its life. Use the prefixes in Table A-4 to indi cate scope and lifetime.

Table A-4   Prefixes for scope and lifetime

Prefix	Object Type
(none) or p	Local variable, procedure-level lifetime, declared with "Dim"
s	Local variable, object lifetime, declared with "Static"
m	Private (module) variable, object lifetime, declared with "Private"
g	Public (global) variable, object lifetime, declared with "Public"

Examples of the use of prefixes follow:

```
Dim intTotal As Integer
Private mlngLastTotal As Long
Public gintLastRecord As Integer
```

The preceding Private and Public dimension statements would be contained in th Declarations section of a module.

Prefix for Arrays

In addition to prefixes for scope and life, arrays of an object type use the prefix "a". Fo example,

```
Dim aintFontSizes(10) As Integer
Dim astrNames(20) As String
```

Naming Constants

Constants are indicated by appending the letter c to the end of a data type tag. For example

```
Const intcVisa As Integer = 2
```

If you are more concerned about identifying the item as a constant, you can use the generi tag *con* instead. For example,

```
Const conVisa As Integer = 2
```

Other Names

Many other tags, prefixes, and suffixes exist. In addition to object and variable naming con ventions, Reddick has established conventions for procedure names and other programmin; conventions. These naming conventions are available through the Web. If the Web site men tioned in the introduction to this document is no longer available, search for "Reddick VBA naming conventions." You should check these naming conventions periodically to ensur that you write code that is consistent with other applications being developed in the field.